KINGSHIP and SACRIFICE

KINGSHIP and SACRIFICE

RITUAL and SOCIETY in ANCIENT HAWAII

Valerio Valeri

Translated by Paula Wissing

The University of Chicago Press   Chicago and London

The University of Chicago Press, Chicago 60637
The University of Chicago Press, Ltd., London
© 1985 by The University of Chicago
All rights reserved. Published 1985
Printed in the United States of America
94 93 92 91 90 89 88 87   5432

Library of Congress Cataloging in Publication Data

Valeri, Valerio.
  Kingship and sacrifice.

  Translated from the French.
  Bibliography: p.
  Includes index.
  1. Hawaii—Religion. 2. Hawaii—Kings and rulers—
Religious aspects. 3. Sacrifice. 4. Hawaii—Social
life and customs. 5. Rites and ceremonies—Hawaii.
I. Title.
BL2620.H3V35   1985   299'.92   84-23991
ISBN 0-226-84559-1
ISBN 0-226-84560-5 (pbk.)

PARENTIBUS OPTIMIS

CONTENTS

PREFACE

Nous avons pu, à cette occasion, concevoir certains traits fondamentaux du style de la religion et de la poësie polynésiennes en général: passage constant, même dans les mots et les noms, du naturel et de l'universel au personnel et à l'humain.

Mauss 1968–69, 2:191

This book is a study of Hawaiian sacrificial rituals in their social and cosmological context. But since sacrifices accompany every important social act and reproduce mental and social structures, it is also, by necessity, a study of Hawaiian culture and society in general.

The book is divided into three parts. In the first I attempt to give a systematic account of Hawaiian religious notions, the most important of which is *akua*, "deity." A deity is the personified and naturalized concept of a human subject defined by his predicates, the most important of which is the aptitude to perform certain actions in certain social contexts. Thus a deity includes the interrelated concepts of a subject, his actions, and their social contexts. A concept is a general idea; but this idea is personified, given a concrete (albeit imaginary) form; therefore it becomes a type. Indeed, the latter is defined as an "être *concret*, réel ou imaginaire, qui est représentatif d'une classe d'êtres" because it is "ce qui en présente la forme la plus charactéristique ou la plus parfaite" (Lalande 1960, 1155–56). Since as types the deities personify classes of moral, social beings, I consider them as moral, social species as well. In sum, "concept," "type," and "species" can all be used, depending on the context, to designate what the deities stand for.

While a human type is embodied more directly by the anthropomorphic body of a deity, it is also symbolized by his natural bodies, that is, natural species or other phenomena associated with him. By "working" with both natural and anthropomorphic bodies of the deities, sacrificial rituals reproduce the corresponding ideas. The latter transform the sacrificer and his actions by confronting him with socially sanctioned criteria of evaluation and models for acting. Sacrifice is efficacious insofar as ideas order or even constitute praxis.

In part 2 the hierarchical implications of sacrifice are treated. The deities, that is, types or groupings of types, form a hierarchy. Hence sacrifices hierarchize concrete subjects, actions, and social contexts by relating them to different gods.

Part 3 attempts to analyze the highest level of the ritual practice, the one performed under the direction of the king. Because this ritual reproduces the global system reconstructed in parts 1 and 2, it displays it in a single concrete action. Therefore the analysis of this ritual makes it possible to prove the validity of the reconstruction of the system and to further develop it.

In the Conclusion, the interplay of conventional and nonconventional, communicative and inferential, conceptual and experiential aspects of ritual, as well as the relation between ritual and material processes, is assessed at a somewhat more abstract level of discourse.

Let me stress that parts 1 and 2 do not attempt to be complete accounts of their subject matter but merely form an extended introduction to the ritual system described in part 3. Only the latter attempts to be complete.

I also wish to point out that the book has two complementary purposes: giving a coherent interpretation of Hawaiian religious ideas (the first one, to my knowledge) and working out a number of theoretical principles for the interpretation of ritual, especially in its interrelation with social practice.

Writing the book, I have felt that the more I understood the logic of Hawaiian thought, the clearer certain crucial anthropological problems became to me. Conversely, the more I reflected on these problems, the more I understood the Hawaiian facts. This dialectical relationship between theory and interpretation may seem trivial, but I must stress that it has become believable to me through this interpretive experience. I hope I will be excused for saying this at the outset of a book claiming that ritual teaches people to *believe* in cultural principles by creating experiences in which they can be apprehended.

This is not the place to relate my approach to Hawaiian religion to the theoretical debate on religion in general. I simply wish to point out that I take as my starting point the Hegelian idea that religion is "objective spirit," that is, the objectified system of ideas of a community. This view is essentially the same that is found not only in Hegel's pupils—such as Feuerbach and Marx—but also in anthropology's forefathers such as Robertson Smith and Durkheim.

Of course Durkheim differs from his predecessors in narrowing the view, that is, in postulating that the exclusive content of religious representations is society. This is due to a conceptual confusion: the fact that all religious concepts *presuppose* society and therefore—at the very least—*index* it becomes the idea that they "represent" it (cf. Valeri 1981b).

Hawaiian religious notions, for one example, do not lend themselves to this sociomorphic reductionism. They do not seem to be principally representations of social units or even of the social totality; rather, they are—as I have just mentioned—representations of ideal types of subjects acting in certain types of social contexts or in certain concrete groups.

Hawaiian religion is essentially anthropomorphic. All gods have in common what all subjects have in common: the fact of belonging to one single species, the human species. Because I insist on this fact, my argument has a certain Feuerbachian ring. But I must stress that when I speak of "human species" I am referring not to an abstract and universal notion, but to a presupposed concept of Hawaiian culture, which makes different forms of action commensurable and complementary.

Moreover, I insist that the types of subjectivity personified by the gods presuppose social relations not only because they are created by them, but also because—as I have just indicated—they index them and are conceived as interrelated with them. Thus society is present in the concept of the species both as cause and as signified.

A "Feuerbachian" perspective is therefore not incompatible with a "Marxian" or "Durkheimian" one: in fact, they must be combined to make Hawaiian religious ideas intelligible.

It seems to me that Durkheim's most important and original contribution is his explanation of the efficacy of ritual as due to the power of collective consciousness on concrete social agents and relations. This view of ritual efficacy has been refined in the modern "performative" theories of ritual, both the "Austinian" ones (which stress the conventional relationship between performance and effect) and the "Turnerian" ones (which emphasize the nonconventional and psychological effects of performance).

I have drawn on both types of theory and in fact attempted to reconcile them, at least programmatically. But it will be apparent that the major influence on my thought has been Hegel's *Phenomenology*, for I have attempted to view Hawaiian ritual as a manifestation of the dialectics of consciousness, as consciousness's "relating of itself to itself as object" (Hegel 1952, 481).

Throughout this book I have emphasized that, by collectively ordering the subject's consciousness, ritual produces social order by producing conceptual order—sense. But sense is produced by creating contrasts in the continuum of experience. This implies suppressing certain elements of experience in order to give relevance to others (cf. Valeri 1970). Thus the creation of conceptual order is also, constitutively, the suppression of aspects of reality.

From this point of view the ordering virtue of ritual is not due simply to enlightening, but also to blinding. Indeed, we shall see that Hawaiians come very close to experiencing this necessary interdependence—where authority can nest itself—at the culmination of their greatest ritual. For the observer this interdependence is clear in every rite. Most give sense and efficacy to the subject's actions by stressing that they are part of a harmonious hierarchical whole. But this also implies suppressing in the subject's experience all that points to the conflictual character of social relations and to the exploitative nature of the nobility's rule.

Analogously, in the *luakini* temple ritual described in part 3, the ordering power of the king is put in the foreground to give sense to all social relations; but this also implies not giving relevance to the fact that the very necessity for the king to constantly perform the ritual that establishes his power denies his claim to promote order (cf. Valeri 1982b, 31–32).

In sum, I believe that the traditional conflict between the view that power is founded on sense and the view that it is founded on mystification has no reason to exist. Both views are true, because creating sense necessarily implies mystifying, and mystifying is impossible without the creation of sense. There is no place in culture for the illusion of transparence.

While I recognize this dialectics of sense and mystification, I have concentrated on sense, because I believe that its deciphering is the first analytic task. But a full analysis of the *efficacy* of Hawaiian religious representations and the attached ritual practices would have to include what it is they mystify, and the contribution of this mystification to social order.

I have worked intermittently at this book since 1969. Much of the present version (particularly chapters 1, 4, 6, 7, and 8) was written in 1979. At that time I planned to publish the book in French, but when that proved impossible I gladly accepted the University of Chicago Press's offer to translate it into English. Following the suggestions of one reader's report and of several friends, I reorganized the manuscript in its present shape (in 1981). The translation was prepared from this reorganized version. In checking the translation, I have liberally made changes: yet the substance of the argument has not changed since 1981. Moreover—with few exceptions—I have not been able to take into account more recent work done on Hawaii and on the theoretical subjects discussed in the book.

At the end of my effort, my mind goes back to two illustrious predecessors whose images have haunted me throughout these years—Robert Hertz and Marcel Mauss, who both worked on the Hawaiian rituals that are my subject. Unfortunately Hertz never wrote up his research on this topic. After Hertz's death Mauss attempted to make a book out of his friend's notes and in the process recognized the need for further research. A very short record of Mauss's conclusions is contained in the *résumés de cours* at the Collège de France for the years 1933 to 1940. These have been republished in his *Oeuvres* (Mauss 1968–69, 2:190–91; 266–67; 3:515–16). Unfortunately Mauss did not reach the stage of publication or write down the text of his lectures. The published summaries were too brief to be helpful; at the same time, their existence was sufficient to intimidate me with the thought that two great scholars had been at work on the same problems and facts I was struggling with. Where Hertz and Mauss had failed to come to a satisfactory conclusion, how could I hope to succeed? Today when my book seems, strangely enough, finished, I still do not dare to consider myself "terzo tra cotanto senno."

Readers should be aware of certain conventions I have adopted in transcribing Hawaiian words, names, and texts. All Hawaiian texts given in quotation marks or as block quotations are as in the original source. I have myself written Hawaiian words as they appear in Pukui and Elbert's *Hawaiian Dictionary*, 1971 edition (cited throughout as PE). I give place names as they appear in Pukui, Elbert, and Mookini (1974), but I use the spelling Hawaii to refer to the Hawaiian archipelago and Hawai'i to refer to the island. To further lessen ambiguity, I used the expression "island of Hawai'i" where necessary.

Personal names are a more complex matter. Names of gods or heroes that appear in Pukui and Elbert's dictionary have been given according to their transcriptions. I have also used the rendering of several names of kings and high-ranking nobles found in the genealogies published in Freycinet (1978) and in other recent works. In other cases I have had to follow my own guesses.

Names of Hawaiian authors are given as they appear in their writings whenever they are followed by the date of publication or by "MS." In other contexts, however, they are spelled as they should be except when the author, though aware of the new spelling system, has deliberately chosen to preserve the traditional spelling of his name. For instance, I use both the spellings Ii 1963 and 'Ī'ī, but Pukui 1942 and Pukui.

The manuscript of *Ka Mooolelo Hawaii* by David Malo is usually cited as "Malo MS" followed by a page number. When I wish to cite a specific verse, however, I use Malo's name and two numbers; for instance, Malo 26.32. The first number is the chapter, the second is the verse.

Lunar dates are reconstructed (with some approximation) from the dates of the Gregorian or Julian calendar by using the simple method and tables given in every good encyclopaedia (for instance the *Britannica* 11th edition). I have been able, however, to check my reconstructions against a computer printout of the correlations between lunar and civil dates from 1778 onward prepared by Jocelyn Linnekin and her husband. I am grateful to them for providing me with a copy of this work.

ACKNOWLEDGMENTS

Researching and writing this book in many different parts of the world has meant incurring many debts, which cannot all be mentioned here. I wish most of all to thank my first and best teacher, my father, who has been the invisible hand guiding my pen throughout this book. The influence of my former esteemed teachers in Paris, Claude Lévi-Strauss and Louis Dumont, is evident: I am most grateful to them. I owe an even greater debt to another former teacher and now colleague: Marshall Sahlins. His work has been an inspiration to me, and I learned enormously from our numerous conversations on Hawaiian and non-Hawaiian subjects. Moreover, he has provided me with copies of important unpublished documents.

Many students at the University of Chicago have listened to this book over the years and helped me to better it by their comments, suggestions, and reactions. During my visit to Hawaii in 1980, John Charlot gave me detailed written comments on the French manuscript of this book. Although we seldom agreed, I warmly thank him for his help. I am also extremely grateful to Dorothy Barrère, who read the book in its English translation and motivated last-minute corrections.

Of course none of the persons mentioned above should be held responsible for the views expressed in this book and for the errors it probably contains.

My work at several libraries has been greatly facilitated by their staffs, whom I thank with pleasure. I wish to single out particularly the following: the Library of the Bishop Museum in Honolulu, the Hamilton Library of the University of Hawaii, the Newberry Library of Chicago, and the Regenstein Library of the University of Chicago.

The Lichtstern Fund and the Division of the Social Sciences of the University of Chicago have made possible part of my research in Hawaii. Their help is gratefully acknowledged. Didi Kaspin helped to compile the bibliographical references, and Webb Keane prepared the index.

Last but not least I wish to thank my wife Renée and my son Tancredi, whose patience has been so often put to the test by my writing this book. Renée also typed several versions of the manuscript.

INTRODUCTION: THE SOURCES

Remontant aux sources ethnographiques, aux origines des mythologies
dont il comparait et démêlait les sanglantes enigmes. . . . il restait à ja-
mais douloureux, hanté par les symboles des perversités et des amours
surhumaines, des stupres divins consommés sans abandons et sans
espoirs.

    Huysmans 1961, 90–91

Many are the strange things to be learned about Hawaii. However dili-
gently the foreigner seeks he cannot find out all. He gets a fragment here
and there and goes home.

    Kepelino 1932, 142

Perhaps some people did it differently. Not all learning comes from the
same school.

    Kauea in *Ka Nupepa Kuokoa*, 5 January 1867
    (trans. M. K. Pukui in Handy 1972, 197)

The literature on Hawaii extends over a period of two centuries. Thus
these documents cannot all be treated in the same manner, without taking
into account when they were written. It also goes without saying that not
all are of equal value.

    For this reason a discussion of sources is necessary, especially for this
book, which concerns a system of ritual practices that was modified and
began to weaken even before its abolition in 1819 and the arrival of the
first Christian missionaries in 1820. I will restrict myself at this point to a
general discussion that will permit readers to orient themselves each time,
throughout the analysis, that I need to evaluate the documentary value of
this material with respect to specific points.

    Three main groups of sources can be distinguished: the accounts of Eu-
ropean voyagers who, from the time of Cook (1778), visited the Hawaiian
archipelago; the writings of missionaries (from 1820); and the traditions

or eyewitness accounts recorded by the Hawaiians in their own language. The last group began to be produced only in the 1830s. Thus the oldest sources are European, and it is with these that we must begin our discussion.

Voyage Accounts

From the time Cook discovered it (18 January 1778) the Hawaiian archipelago was visited by a great number of ships. Aside from some expeditions having scientific or political purposes, this intense maritime activity was first stimulated by the fur trade (fur was obtained in Alaska or on the Northwest Coast of America and sold in Canton), then by the exploitation of Hawaiian sandalwood (from 1810 to 1826) (Kuykendall, 1938, 85–86) and whaling (from 1820—Kuykendall 1938, 305; Bradley 1942, 79). The ships landed in the islands to obtain provisions. This foreign influence contributed to changing Hawaiian society and favored the unification of the archipelago under King Kamehameha and his son and successor Liholiho.

Bernice Judd (1974 [1929]) counted approximately two hundred publications resulting from voyages to Hawaii from 1788 to 1860. To this a considerable number of unpublished journals must be added, some of which have appeared since 1974. Most are the work of American or English voyagers, but there are also important works in German, French, Russian, Spanish, Dutch, and the Scandinavian languages. For the problems that are the subject of this book the most important documents are those containing observations on the period 1788 to 1825. I have systematically examined the printed works and those unpublished journals to which I had access.[1] This material is extremely uneven in value, especially concerning ritual practices, and must be used with discernment.

The journals from Cook's third voyage (1778–79) and Vancouver's voyage (1792–94) are the most important. The officers and naturalists of these scientific expeditions display a talent and penetration that many modern ethnographers would envy. Of course the value of their testimony is limited by their ignorance of the Hawaiian tongue (although they could understand it somewhat because of their knowledge of Tahitian words or, in Vancouver's case, could avail themselves of European interpreters) and by their relatively short stay in the islands. Yet these sailors witnessed events and customs that the nineteenth-century Hawaiian historians themselves knew only by tradition, which more than compensates for these shortcomings.

In addition to the official account of the Cook voyage (Cook and King 1784), seven other books were published by as many members of the expedition (Rickman 1966; Zimmerman 1781; Ellis 1782; Bayly 1782;

Ledyard 1963; Samwell 1786; Burney 1819). Today we have the superb edition of Cook's original journals by Beaglehole (1967), complete with generous excerpts from the journals of King, Clerke, Burney, Williamson, Edgar, and Samwell. This publication is our principal source concerning the state of Hawaiian society in 1788–89.[2] Among the books published by Cook's companions, the best is by Ellis, and the worst are those of Rickman and Ledyard (see Beaglehole 1967, cxcviii–ccx). The iconographic documentation by John Webber and, to a lesser extent, by W. Ellis is of great value (cf. Beaglehole 1967, ccxi–xvii).

The most brilliant of the journals published by Beaglehole are those of Samwell, King, and Cook. In the work of Samwell, a surgeon but also a poet, we find the first recording of literary works in Hawaiian and Maori. Indeed, he transcribed two Hawaiian chants (Samwell 1967, 1234) and several Maori chants (ibid., 1295–1300), which gives some idea of his ethnographic sensitivity. His observations have all the more value because he is extremely aware of the difficulty of understanding a culture without sufficient knowledge of its language. He states, in fact, "There is not much dependence to be placed upon these Constructions that we put upon Signs and Words which we understand but very little of, & at best can only give a probable Guess at their Meaning" (ibid., 1223). Moreover, as he himself emphasizes, the expedition spent only three and a half months in Hawaii, and only a fifth of that time was spent ashore—a good part of the communication taking place on shipboard, most often with commoners who brought provisions by canoe (ibid., 603, 604).

King's seriousness is indicated by his genealogical research on the royal families of the archipelago. His findings are generally confirmed by Hawaiian genealogical traditions. An excellent observer himself, Cook was also the protagonist in important ritual events, but because of his death at Kealakekua on 14 February 1779 his journal remains incomplete. After Cook no vessel landed in the islands until 1786 (Kuykendall 1938, 20).

The most important journals concerning the period from 1786 until 1792 (the date of Vancouver's first visit) follow.

1786–87   Dixon (1789); Portlock (1789); Nicol (1822). Both Dixon and Portlock had been members of Cook's expedition.
1786   Lapérouse (1970 [1798])
1787–88   Meares (1790, 1916)
1786–88   Colnett (1798, 101, 157, and n.d. [manuscript journal, 16 October 1786–7 November 1788])
1788–89   Douglas (Meares 1790)
1789   Mortimer (1791)
1791   Quimper (1822 [1937]); Marchand (Fleurieu 1801); Ingraham (1918, n.d.); Colnett, manuscript journal (29 March 1791–18 April 1791)

The expedition led by Vancouver, who had been a member of Cook's crew, visited Hawaii three times between 1792 and 1794, and in all spent about four months in the archipelago. Vancouver's account (1801 [1798]) and journals by Menzies (1920), Manby (1929), and Bell (1929–30) have been published. Vancouver and his men had a major advantage over their predecessors in that they were able to use European interpreters, particularly the Englishmen John Young and John Davis,[3] who had settled in Hawaii in 1790 (Fornander 1878–80, 1:231, 235, 322) and had become the friends and advisers of King Kamehameha. Henceforth they would become the informants and interpreters of many voyagers.[4] Another interpreter was the Spaniard Don Francisco de Paula Marin, who settled in Hawaii in 1793 or 1794 (Gast 1973, 4) and remained there until his death in 1837 (Anonymous 1837). Unfortunately, no voyager was able to exploit his knowledge fully. According to von Chamisso (in Kotzebue 1821a, 3:244–45), Marin had recorded a great number of Hawaiian traditions, but the manuscript, if it really existed, has not been preserved. There remain only some excerpts from his journal, covering the period 1809–26, whose importance can easily be imagined (Conrad 1973; on Marin see also Paulding 1831, 227).

The most important published journals or voyage accounts concerning the period from 1792 to 1819 follow:[5]

1792	Boit (1920); Howay (1941, 363–431)
1795	Meyers (1817)
1796	Broughton (1804)
1796	Péron (1824)
1798	Townsend (1888; 1921 [1888])
1799	Cleveland (1843; cf. Cleveland 1886)
1800	Meyers (1817)
1801	Delano (1817)
1802	Extracts (1804); Turnbull (1813 [1805]); Meyers (1817)
1803	Cleveland (1843)
1804	Krusenstern (1813); Langsdorff (1908 [1817]); Lisiansky (1814) (cf. Tumarkin 1979)
1805	Shaler (1808, 1935)
1805–7	Patterson (1817)
1806	Delano (1817); Martin (1817)
1807	Iselin (n.d.)
1809–10	Campbell (1816, 1967; Campbell, an intelligent sailor who spent more than a year on O'ahu, is an important source); Little (1843)
1811	Franchère (1820); Ross (1849, 1904)
1811–13	Reynolds (Howay 1938)
1812	Cox (1831)

Although this last expedition spent only six weeks on Hawaii, it was a remarkable one. Never had so much talent been gathered on one ship. In addition to Kotzebue, the son of a famous playwright and himself a clear and penetrating writer (Kotzebue 1821a,b), were Louis (or Ludovik) Choris, an artist who left some of the most charming views of Hawaii and its chiefs, as well as an account of his observations (1822, 1826; Charlot 1958), and the writer and naturalist Adelbert von Chamisso de Boncourt, the author of a journal and an essay on the Hawaiian language (1821, 1837, 1864).[6] Von Chamisso had the idea for a veritable fieldwork project in Hawaii to study and transcribe rites, prayers, and myths, whose disappearance he feared. Unfortunately for us, Kotzebue did not permit him to leave the expedition. Marin was the interpreter and one of the informants for these travelers.

In 1819 two French expeditions landed at the archipelago. One of them, a commercial voyage, is recorded by Roquefeuil (1843), whose book is interesting because of the information he gives on the Hawaiian political situation shortly before Kamehameha's death. The other was an official expedition commanded by Freycinet, which stopped in the islands after the Hawaiian king's death. This expedition had scientific and political ends. The official account of the voyage published by Freycinet (1825–39) is interesting but has the disadvantage that the author mixed information he obtained directly with what he had read.

Two other authors described this voyage: Madame de Freycinet (1927; Bassett 1962), whose journal holds little interest, and Jacques Arago, the ship's artist. Arago is a particularly frustrating case. The first version of his Hawaiian journal (1822) is a mixture of extremely interesting information and pure invention, generally motivated by his passionate anticlericalism. In his hands Hawaiian priests are French clergy thinly disguised. These defects are nothing compared with what one finds in his later reminiscences (1844), in which he rewrote and embellished his journal. Although the journal, used with care, is overall an important source, the *Souvenirs* must be set aside or used only for details.[7]

The key informants and interpreters for the French expedition were Marin and also Jean Rives, an adventurer from Bordeaux who became

Liholiho's secretary (Alexander 1896, 19; Conrad 1973, 116–17). Today we have an English edition of the Hawaiian segment of Freycinet's voyage, enriched with abundant and important notes by Marion Kelly (Freycinet 1978).

The year 1819 marks a turning point in Hawaiian history. Kamehameha died and the taboo system (the body of ritual practices sanctioned by the priesthood and royalty) was abolished.[8] From this point on the literature left by sailors and other voyagers loses its interest for us. Of the rites and traditional practices constituting the object of this study, little remained—or too little for the hurried visitor to observe. Nevertheless, let us note the last of the great official English voyages, led by Lord Byron, who was entrusted with returning the remains of Liholiho and his queen, who had both died during their journey to London. In addition to the official account edited by Martha Graham (Byron 1826), which contains errors and useless embellishments, we possess accounts by the ship's artist (Dampier 1971), botanist (Macrae 1922), naturalist (A. Bloxam 1925) and chaplain (R. Bloxam 1924).

A very interesting account has been left by Mathison (1825), who made a two-month visit to Oʻahu in 1822. In 1824–25 there was another voyage led by Kotzebue (1830a), which lacks the interest of the first one. The Dutch expedition that landed in the archipelago in 1828 provided good observations, especially concerning temple ruins (Boelen 1835–36). The same can be said of the Prussian expedition of 1831 (Meyen 1834). In 1840 an American scientific expedition commanded by Wilkes undertook a visit of almost three months; in addition to direct observations (of the temples, for example), this expedition was able to take advantage of information acquired by missionaries, particularly William Richards (cf. Richards 1973). The official account of the voyage contains the translation of a Hawaiian text describing the inauguration ritual of a temple of the *luakini* type. This is the first complete published description of such a ritual, and it retains its full value despite slight errors in transcription (Wilkes 1845, 4:506–8).

Missionary Accounts

Among the many accounts by missionaries, which begin in 1820, are the journals published in the *Missionary Herald* (referred to in the text as MH). Some of the unpublished missionary journals were later published;[9] most were written by women (Holman 1931; Judd 1880; Ruggles 1924; Thurston 1882).[10] Although the books published by their husbands or colleagues do not have the same freshness, they contain more systematic information on Hawaiian religion and politics. The most important of these are by Dibble (1839, 1843, 1909), Stewart (1830, 1831, 1839), and Bingham (1848).

Dibble's *History* contains errors but has the merit of being based on data obtained by Hawaiian students from the Lahainaluna School (see below) and the Royal Hawaiian Historical Society, founded in 1841 in the same town (Leib and Day 1979, 8). Stewart gives important data, especially in his first book (1830 and 1839), but his tendency to embellish (which becomes overtly unhealthy in his book of 1831) sometimes diminishes the value of his writings.

The formula Bingham used to sum up traditional Hawaiian culture, "The whole policy of Satan here, seemed to be, *to make that to be sin which is no sin, and that to be no sin which is sin*" (1848, 21, italics in original), gives one an idea of the documentary value of his work, at least in matters of religion. It is thus of little interest here.

A different judgment must be formed of the English missionaries sent by the London Missionary Society, who visited the Hawaiian archipelago in 1822 and 1823–24. Daniel Tyerman and George Bennett certainly indulged in the biblical sport of breaking pagan idols with their stout workmen's hands, but these theatrical gestures (perhaps for the benefit of a public that wanted its money's worth) did not prevent them from recording interesting material (Tyerman and Bennett 1831).

It is William Ellis (not to be confused with the surgeon on the Cook expedition) who has left us the most precious information, however. His extensive knowledge of the Tahitian language enabled him to learn Hawaiian rapidly, and he attracted the goodwill and interest of many Hawaiians (Ellis 1842, 43). His two-month tour of the island of Hawai'i, made in the company of three American missionaries, enabled him to make important ethnographic observations and to gather texts in the Hawaiian language (see, for example, Ellis 1842, 297). His principal informants on ritual and mythology were Kelou Kamakau, a chief of Kona whom I will mention again (Ellis 1842, 427, 150–62, and Hewahewa, King Kamehameha's last high priest (ibid., 158).

Sources in Hawaiian

The missionaries' most important work toward preserving Hawaiian traditions was done in the framework of the school they opened at Lahainaluna (Maui) in 1831. Several members of the Hawaiian aristocracy studied there, including David Malo, who was then thirty-six years old (Emory 1971, xix). Encouraged by Richards and Dibble, Malo and his comrades inquired among the old Hawaiians, delved into their own memories, and wrote (in 1836–37) documents that Sheldon Dibble "corrected" by adding dates and his reflections (Tinker 1839, 59). The work was published in 1838 with the title *Ka Mooolelo Hawaii*, "History of Hawaii." We possess a rather bad English translation of this work by Reuben Tinker (1839–42) and a better French one, which gives the Hawaiian text on the facing page, by Jules Remy (1862). In the bibliographies the first *Mooolelo* is generally attributed to Malo, owing to his important part in its composition (cf. Leib and Day 1979, 8).

Malo is the only author of another *Mooolelo Hawaii*, which he wrote about 1840 for Lorrin Andrews (Alexander, in Malo 1951, xviii), the missionary who compiled the first dictionary of the Hawaiian language (Andrews 1865). The original Hawaiian text, kept in the Library of the Bishop Museum in Honolulu, has never been published, but a translation by Nathaniel B. Emerson was published in 1903. Emerson added copious notes. W. D. Alexander also added his part. As Eloise Christian remarks in her preface to the second edition (Malo 1951), "It is not clear just how much Alexander did. For that matter, it is hard to tell where Malo leaves off and Emerson takes over, or how much of the parenthetical material in the actual text is Emerson's" (in Malo 1951, xxi).

There is only one way to be sure, and that is to consult Malo's own manuscript. The comparison between the original and the translation reveals that Emerson often took liberties with a text that he sometimes poorly understood. Above all, in any translation, no matter how well done, precious information is lost. As for Emerson's notes, I am convinced that they are a mixture of data of great value and unfounded or misunderstood information. It is thus necessary to consider Malo's Hawaiian text and Emerson's notes as two completely different sources and to establish in each case to what degree the second completes the first.

Malo's work is the most important source on ancient Hawaiian culture, written by a man of great intelligence, well versed in the traditions and events of the time of Kamehameha and Liholiho. Malo's father had been connected with Kamehameha's court and army. Malo was born at Keauhou, in the northern part of the Kona district (island of Hawai'i), in 1795 (Emory 1971, xix). In his youth he was part of the entourage of Kuakini, brother of Queen Ka'ahumanu. Himself an able poet, Malo was the pupil of 'Auwae, Kamehameha's bard, genealogist, and ritual expert (Emerson in Malo 1951, viii). His work is not without some traces of his conversion to Christianity, however, especially in his judgments on Hawaiian culture,[11] but unlike some of his successors, Malo never mixed ancient traditions with biblical stories.[12]

In 1858 the Reverend J. F. Pogue published a new edition of the *Mooolelo* of 1838, incorporating excerpts from Malo's book and other materials (Pogue 1858). A questionable translation of it has recently been published by Charles W. Kenn (1978).

Directly through their students or indirectly because of the diffusion of the *Mooolelo Hawaii*, Richards and Dibble stimulated the formation of a Hawaiian-language historiography that continued the tradition of the court bards but was also influenced by Western models and criteria.

The most important of these writers are Samuel Manaiākalani Kamakau, John Papa 'Ī'ī, and S. N. Hale'ole (d. 1866). The last of these displayed the talents of both a historian (he is the author of an important description of some cults, written in 1862—in Fornander 1916–20, 6:56–159), and a novelist (in 1863 he published a literary masterpiece, the story of Laieikawai—Beckwith 1919). As for S. M. Kamakau (1815–1876; see Thrum 1918), his abundant writings, which appeared between 1865 and 1871, were conceived as an amplification of Malo's *Mooolelo* and in part follow his model (Barrère in Kamakau 1976, v). On several points they are our only source today.

Unlike Malo and the contributors to the first *Mooolelo Hawaii*, S. M. Kamakau was not an eyewitness of Kamehameha's time; but he was able to gather traditions still fresh in the memory of many old people (particularly his grandfather, Kuikealaikauaokalani—see Barrère in Kamakau 1976, 146, n. 13). Moreover, he carefully distinguished between what belonged to the past and what belonged to his own time (this unfortunately does not come through in the translations of his texts—see Barrère in Kamakau 1976, vi).

Until recently and with very few exceptions (see, for example, Kamakau 1891, 1911), this imposing mass of documents was inaccessible to the reader who did not know Hawaiian. In 1931 the Bishop Museum undertook their translation, overseen by Mary Kawena Pukui and annotated by Martha W. Beckwith. Some ethnologists and historians were able to consult them, but this material did not become truly accessible until after its publication in 1961, 1964, and 1976 (a fourth volume remains unpublished).

John Papa 'Ī'ī (1800–1870) published his articles in the newspaper *Ka Nupepa Kuokoa* between 1866 and 1870. Because of his recollections we possess details concerning daily life at the courts of Kamehameha and Liholiho, where 'Ī'ī was one of the intimates. Malo and S. M. Kamakau explicate the principles of Hawaiian culture; 'Ī'ī gives us its flavor by telling us how things actually happened, even the feelings of those who had to live with rules and events that we have a tendency to consider in the abstract, like signs on paper, having no consequence in the lives of real people.

In the same years that 'Ī'ī and S. M. Kamakau published their accounts, Kepelino (his Hawaiian name was Kahoaliikumaieiwakamoku) composed his *Mooolelo Hawaii* (in 1868, according to Yzendoorn 1909, 17), which remained unpublished until 1932 (Beckwith 1932). Unlike other Hawaiian historians, Kepelino (?1830–?1878) was not a pupil of the Lahainaluna School; indeed, he was part of a Catholic family. His father Namiki, a descendant of the Priest Pāʻao, was the "old savage" whose narratives were collected by Jules Remy (Remy 1859); his mother was a daughter of Kamehameha (Beckwith 1932, 4). As a result of his family heritage, then, Kepelino was well versed in the traditions of the priests and chiefs. Among the works published during his lifetime is a series in four fascicles that appeared from 1858 to 1860, called *Hooiliili Hawaii*, "Hawaiian Collection." The first of these fascicles (republished and translated by Kirtley and Mookini 1977) is an important source for knowledge of Hawaiian religion.

Kepelino's *Mooolelo* is constructed according to a scheme that only partly recalls that of those that preceded it. It contains precious data, but especially in the creation stories Kepelino mixes Christian and Hawaiian traditions. He also tends to follow a European model in representing the traditional political system as a form of despotism; thus it is not surprising to note that Wittfogel uses Kepelino's text above all to support his thesis that Hawaii was a characteristic case of "oriental despotism" (Wittfogel 1981).

S. M. Kamakau, ʻĪʻī, and Kepelino are only the most remarkable representatives of a vast literature, for the most part unpublished or published only in Hawaiian-language journals.[13] The most interesting documents have been transcribed and edited by Mary Kawena Pukui, who devoted her entire life to this gigantic effort. Several thousand typed pages have been deposited in the Library of the Bishop Museum in Honolulu, under the heading Hawaiian Ethnographical Notes (cited in the text as HEN). This material is divided into three parts: the first, bearing the title "Kahuna Wisdom, Lore," comprises above all materials on traditional religion and kingship. The second is entitled "Legends, Stories, and Historical Tales" and consists of a vast collection of myths. The third is devoted to the *mele*—traditional chants. Let us hope that this collection of materials, indispensable for any research on Hawaii, will one day be published.

I have left a special case for last: Kēlou Kamakau, who with Malo is the most important source on the traditional ritual system. His manuscript was probably written at the same time as Malo's. Much later it was acquired by Alexander (Thrum, in Fornander 1916–20, 6:1). It was published with an English translation by John Wise, in 1919–20, in a volume of Fornander's collection of *Hawaiian Antiquities* (1916–20, 6:2–45). K. Kamakau was a lesser aliʻi, chief of Kaʻawaloa in Kona (on the island of Hawaiʻi) (Kamakau 1961, 306; Ellis 1842, 62). Thus he lived close to Hikiau, the most important *luakini* temple of the district.

In 1823, when Ellis met him and used his services as an informant, K. Kamakau was about fifty years old (Ellis 1842, 68). Consequently he must have been born about 1773, even before Cook's arrival. Thus he had a much more direct and profound knowledge of the rites than Malo (who was born in 1795) or 'I'ī (born in 1800), to say nothing of S. M. Kamakau (born in 1815). Ellis found him "more intelligent and enterprising than the people around him" (1842, 64). In 1823 he had taught himself to read and write without waiting for the establishment of schools in his district (Ellis 1842, 64, cf. also 67–68, 139–40). His text bears witness to his intelligence and his knowledge of minute details.

The Contribution of the Ethnologists

If the literature just discussed is the result of Hawaiian initiative (though inspired at the outset by foreigners who were interested in traditional culture), another literature exists that can be termed ethnological, for it is the Westerners who ask the questions and elaborate the model for organizing and interpreting the data. In the nineteenth century the only part of this literature that interests us is that based on or inspired by Hawaiian texts.

The little book by Jules Remy (1859), based on information given by Namiki, is perhaps the oldest example of this literature. Adolf Bastian (1881) was the first to draw attention to the *Kumulipo*, the genealogical chant of the Hawaiian chiefs, which had been written down at an unknown date and communicated to him by King Kalākaua (his sister, Queen Lili'uokalani, published a complete translation of this chant in 1897—cf. Davis 1979, 224–26). But the ethnologist to whom we owe the most is the Swede Abraham Fornander, who compiled the largest and most important published collection of mythological, historical, and ritual texts in the Hawaiian language. This collection was made largely during three years, with the help of Hawaiians, including "S. N. Hakuole" (probably a misprint for Hale'ole), S. M. Kamakau, and Kepelino (Fornander 1878–80, 1:v–vi). This collection, along with other texts, was published in nine volumes in 1916–20. The Hawaiian texts are accompanied by translations of uneven value (mostly due to John Wise and Emma Metcalf Nakuina [Davis 1979, 276]) and notes, sometimes incorrect, provided by the editor, T. G. Thrum. Fornander used the materials he had collected as well as Malo's manuscript (Fornander 1878–80, 1:v–vi) and articles from Hawaiian journals (particularly by S. M. Kamakau—see Barrère 1969, 2) to write a book in which he reconstructed the history of the Hawaiian people, whose Aryan origin he claimed to prove and who, according to him, had been influenced by "Cushitic," "Chaldeo-Arabic," and Dravidian civilizations during migrations as numerous as they are improbable (Fornander 1878–80). Fornander believed he had found confirmation for these theories in some myths furnished to him by Kepelino and S. M. Kamakau, but these two, influenced by Fornander's opinions and their own reading of the Bible, had invented them (using traditional materials, however—cf. Barrère 1969 and Davis 1979, 244–45).

If the first volume of Fornander's history is an inextricable mixture of facts and absurd interpretation, the second retains its value as a summary of the traditional history of Hawaii up to the unification of the archipelago under Kamehameha.

At the end of the nineteenth century and the beginning of the twentieth, other Westerners collected or translated texts and made ethnographic or archaeological observations. Their works are somewhat heterogeneous, for it is often impossible to sort out what is "traditional" from what was part of Hawaiian culture as it had been reelaborated in the second half of the nineteenth century. The work done by modern scholars is based either on the sources just described, or on archaeological surveys, or on the culture of twentieth-century Hawaiians. The most important modern works are those of Mary Kawena Pukui, Martha W. Beckwith, E. S. C. Handy, Te Rangi Hiroa (Peter Buck), and K. Emory.

This panorama of the sources may seem long, but it is necessary for readers to be able to date the information used throughout this work and follow the more specific evaluations I will be led to make during the exposition and analysis of the data; and it is necessary to show at the outset that the documents at our disposal cannot be treated like the *Ersatz* of a nonexistent ethnography.

Although influenced by our culture, the Hawaiian authors constructed their texts according to their own principles. By neglecting them one unconsciously attributes to these writings our own principles of organization and criteria of intelligibility, thus running the risk of misunderstandings. As for the European accounts, they come from people who changed, sometimes by their very presence, what they were describing. This is particularly true of the accounts of Cook and Vancouver. In all cases the interests and presuppositions of each author—foreign or Hawaiian—condition his account; one cannot ignore them.

PART 1
SACRIFICE AND THE GODS

1
SUMMARY OF HAWAIIAN THEOLOGY

C'est là que conviendrait éminemment la célèbre formule de Bossuet: *Tout était dieu excepté Dieu même,* pourvu qu'on l'appliquât à un point de départ, et non pas à une chimérique dégénération.
    Comte 1877, 5:31

La loi d'analogie, qui régit toutes les choses divines.
    de Maistre 1884, 5:174

Der Mensch ist *nichts ohne Gegenstand.* . . . An dem Gegenstande wird daher der Mensch *seiner selbst* bewusst: das Bewusstsein des Gegenstands ist das *Selbstbewusstsein* des Menschen.
    Feuerbach 1956, 1:39, 40

The fundamental notions of Hawaiian culture, particularly concerning the deities (*akua*) and their powers (*mana*), are very complex. A full understanding of them is possible only after a long and minute analysis of the contexts in which they operate. It is just such an analysis that I will undertake in this book.

It is, however, necessary to begin somewhere, to give a global frame of reference even though it is still approximate. This is all the more necessary because the sources at our disposal are often fragmentary, contradictory, or obscure, and available interpretations are insufficient if not hasty. After much hesitation I decided that the best course was to begin at the beginning, with a brief look at the genesis of the cosmos according to Hawaiian mythology. I will then go on to describe the Hawaiian pantheon by classifying the different categories of deities as a function of their attributes and the hierarchical levels on which they are situated.

Cosmogony

The most important account of the origin of the cosmos is found in the chant, the *Kumulipo*.[1] The notice preceding the oldest extant manuscript of this chant calls it a "prayer for the consecration of the ali'i" (*"he pule ho'ola'a ali'i"*) and affirms that it was chanted in a temple shortly after the birth of Kalaninui'iamamao, son and heir of King Keawe, at the time his umbilical cord was cut and taboos were placed upon him (Liliuokalani 1978, introduction). This information indicates that the *Kumulipo* is, among other things, a *mele inoa*, that is, a "name" or "celebrating" chant, which is supposed to reflect the personality and rank of the ali'i to whom it pertains (Beckwith 1951, 36). Nevertheless, the *Kumulipo* is both older and more recent than the notice claims. Older, for it incorporates an entire cosmogony that was not invented by one poet alone and that corresponds to other Polynesian cosmogonies; more recent, for, at least in the genealogical section, changes continued to be made until the time of King Kalākaua (second half of the nineteenth century).

The translation and interpretation of the *Kumulipo* are especially difficult. Native exegesis reads it at once as the description of the origins of the cosmos, of the life of an ali'i from infancy to maturity, and of the formation of a new dynasty (Beckwith 1951, 40–41). These interpretations are not mutually exclusive, for the conception, birth, and development of an ali'i or dynasty reproduce the cosmogonic process and thereby aid in reproducing natural and social distinctions. This is precisely the reason the *Kumulipo* or similar compositions are chanted at the birth of an ali'i[2] and during other rites of passage (Liliuokalani 1978, introduction).

The cosmogonic process described in the *Kumulipo* is divided into two major periods, "Night" (Pō) and "Light" (Ao). In the first period, "the god [or the divine] enters, man cannot enter" (*"o ke Akua ke komo, 'a'oe komo kanaka,"* line 39; in the second, men multiply (lines 598–600; p. 97). The Pō period is thus entirely divine;[3] Ao is compatible with man.

In the beginning the cosmos is encompassed by Pō "night, obscurity" (also "the unseen," Handy and Pukui 1972, 131, and "realm of the gods," PE, 307). The heavens warm the earth by rubbing against it (lines 1–2). This is the Hawaiian equivalent of the marriage of heaven and earth. Then Pō divides in two forms, one male the other female. The male form is called Kumulipo ("beginning [in] deep obscurity" according to Beckwith 1951, 37; "origin of life" according to PE, 168); the female form is called Pō'ele ("black," "darkness"—PE, 308). From their union are born the most primitive species, which include corals and mollusks. Thus the Kumulipo-Pō'ele couple represents a whole class of animal species and the "evolutionary" stage corresponding to it. The genesis of these species is described in the first section of the chant. The first child born of the couple is the coral, which seems to indicate that the poet believes the islands were produced by the accumulation of corals, out of which were born the first forms of marine life. At least this is the interpretation of one Hawaiian commentator, Poepoe, whom Beckwith summarizes in the following re-mark: "The Prologue for the first section, if read literally, seems to picture the rising of the land out of the fathomless depths of Ocean. Along its shores the lower forms of life begin to gather, and these are arranged as births from parent to child" (1951, 55).

The second section of the chant describes the fruits of the pairing of two other manifestations of the generative principle Pō: Pōuliuli ("Deep-profound-darkness"), who is male, and Pōwehiwehi ("Darkness-streaked-with-glimmers-of-light"), who is female (p. 61). They engender fish. In the third section, Pōʻeleʻele ("Dark night") and Pōhāhā ("Night-just-breaking-into-dawn") engender "winged creatures": first insects, then birds (p. 68). In the fourth section of the chant, Pōpanopano and Pōlalo-wehi engender amphibians.

The first four sections, which describe the first four epochs of the Pō period, have an identical structure. After the generating pair is introduced, the species issuing from it are enumerated. This part is followed by another in which the poetic device of assonance is used to couple marine with land species.

Except for the third section, in which land birds are coupled with sea-birds, the land species paired with marine species are plants. As I have said, these pairings are essentially verbal. Consequently, the engendering of plants is not justified in "evolutionary" terms, as is the case for animals. Each section groups plants that share no taxonomic features. For example, in the first section can be found ferns, land grass, taro, sugarcane, and so on; in the second are found yams, several trees, ʻawa (kava; *Piper methysti-cum*), and so on. The only pertinent opposition is between marine and ter-restrial habitats.

We may ask why the *Kumulipo* takes into account animal genera but not those of the plant world. The principal reason for this appears to be that animal species more easily lend themselves to the construction of a scale going without interruption from the least complex and differentiated forms of life to the most complex and differentiated form, man. The latter can thus be presented as the culmination, or end, of the cosmogonic pro-cess. In this way it is shown that all lives are produced in order to produce the life of man. They constitute it because they are practically and intellec-tually appropriated by him. Beckwith has justly said that the cosmogonic process is "actuated by desire, which is represented by the duality of sex-generation" (1919, 300); but since this innate desire in nature culminates with man and is satisfied only in him, it is clear that it is the projection of human desire to make nature serve man and be his reflection.

But let us follow the "evolutionary" process by which animal species are engendered. Beginning with the fifth section, the *Kumulipo* describes the appearance of the four terrestrial mammals existing on Hawaii: the pig (fifth section), the rat (sixth section), the dog (seventh section), and man (eighth section). Man's appearance marks the passage from the Pō to the Ao period. The process of differentiation among biological species ends with man; at this point begins differentiation within the human species, which is described in the specifically genealogical section of the chant. In an "ontogenetic" reading of the process, contained in the chant itself, this moment of transition is assimilated to the stage at which the fetus is well formed ("well-formed is the child, well-formed now," line 595) and thus ready to be born. We have, then, a series of equivalences; cosmogenesis is equated with anthropogenesis and the latter with the ontogenesis of an individual human. In sum, the human species recapitulates all natural species, and the human individual recapitulates the process that has brought about his own species.

Like the preceding periods, the "period of living men called 'Day' or Ao" (Beckwith 1951, 94) is engendered by a pair of manifestations of Pō: Pōkinikini and Pōhe'enalumamao (lines 596–97). Humans and two of the principal personal gods issue from this couple, who also produce light (cf. Beckwith 1951, 94–95).

Born was La'ila'i a woman
Born was Ki'i a man
Born was Kane a god
Born was Kanaloa the hot-striking octopus
It was day.
[lines 612–15, trans. Beckwith 1951, 97–98]

The contemporaneous birth of man and two personal gods closely associated in the pantheon (see below) deserves commentary. It indicates that the existence of men and that of the personal gods are correlated. This notion is reinforced by a curious detail. The god Kāne bears the name of his worshiper, the human male (*kāne*); the man is called Ki'i ("image"), the generic name attributed to the anthropomorphic images of the gods used in worship. The complementarity of gods and man could not be better represented, nor could the relationship of equivalence that exists between man as species (the first man) and the major personal gods—an equivalence to which I shall return. Between a man named as god and a god named as man, the status of the woman (La'ila'i) is ambivalent, perhaps structurally so. Both man and god need the woman to reproduce themselves. But at this crucial moment it is the man—not the god—who secures her first. As a consequence, the human lineage issuing from La'ila'i and Ki'i becomes the elder in relation to the divine lineage issued from La'ila'i and Kāne:

Kane was angry and jealous because he slept last with her [La'ila'i]
His descendants would hence belong to the younger line
The children of the older would be lord,
First through La'ila'i, first through Ki'i.
    [lines 702–5, trans. Beckwith 1951, 106]

This episode from the *Kumulipo* thus makes explicit what seems implicit in all Hawaiian religious ideology: man's dependence on the gods in fact conceals the gods' dependence on men. If on the manifest level gods are superior to men, on the latent level men are superior to gods because men control them in ritual or because—as in this example—men are their "seniors." The open expression of this superiority is nevertheless exceptional. In reality, the relationship between men and gods is constitutionally ambivalent. In vain does the myth of Ki'i proclaim that men are superior to the gods; its very existence proves at the same time that men cannot do without them. In fact, we shall be led to recognize that man's "superiority" over the gods is limited to the following: that man can control divine power by manipulating it and transforming it by means of symbols. From this standpoint it is highly significant that the first man is called Ki'i, "image." Since Ki'i has equivalents in succeeding generations in characters such as Wākea[4] and Kauakāhi, who manage to seduce various goddesses by carving divine images (Malo 1951, 86–87; Beckwith 1951, 123, 127; Valeri 1981a), it is likely that he owes his name to the fact that he represents man's ability to control the divine by means of images.

Man's appearance as the creator of divine anthropomorphic images (*ki'i*) marks, then, a transformation of the divine. Before that it comprised only natural species, which, as we shall see, are considered "bodies" of the gods, but excluded the human species, as indicated by the refrain that characterizes the age of Pō: "the god enters, man cannot enter" (repeated thirteen times in the first section of the chant, fifteen in the second, six in the third, and nine in the fourth).

By producing the first man, however, the divine brings about its own transformation. From now on it will be constituted by personal, anthropomorphic gods such as Kāne and Kanaloa. Moreover, as I shall demonstrate, these personal gods regroup the natural species on the basis of a human, "moral" logic that takes the place of or modifies the "natural" classificatory logic that the *Kumulipo* identifies with the state of the divine until man appears on the scene.

It is immediately clear, then, that the personal gods, represented by images man carves in his own image, do not exist independent from him and from the symbolic power that, as his very name demonstrates, characterizes him.

Among the metaphors designating the divine origins, the *Kumulipo*'s Pō, "Night," is the most encompassing and the most powerful but also the most undifferentiated. More concrete metaphors exist, with primarily spatial connotations. The most important of these is Kahiki,[5] the distant place (invisible from Hawaii—see below) out of which come the gods, ancestors, regalia, edible plants, and ritual institutions—the life of the Hawaiians and the means to reproduce it. Let us consider a few facts that demonstrate the connection of Kahiki with all the above entities.

That the god Lono inhabits Kahiki is demonstrated by the fact that the New Year's festival celebrates his arrival from Kahiki and ends with his return there. This association between Lono and Kahiki is confirmed, moreover, by many texts (see, for example, Malo 1951, 146; Thrum 1923, 108–16; Beckwith 1940, 33–36; Handy 1972, 329–88). As for the gods Kū and Hina, according to one tradition they are the first to arrive in Hawaii from Kahiki (Beckwith 1940, 11). In one prayer Kū is called "*e Ku, e lana i Kahiki*" "O Kū who is moored at Kahiki" (Malo 1951, 181, translation mine). The gods Kāne and Kanaloa, who in the *Kumulipo* originate in Pō, are said in other texts to come from Kahiki: for example, in the lines from a prayer, "*No Ku, no Kane / No Kanaloa, ka pukoa ku i Kahiki*," "for Ku, Kane, and Kanaloa were the supreme in Kahiki" (Fornander 1916–20, 6:506, lines 51–52).

I mention only the four major gods here, since as we shall see they encompass most of the others, but it should be remembered that the deities of Pele's family, associated with volcanism, sorcery, and the dance, have direct ties to Kahiki (Emerson 1915, x–xi). Furthermore, we need only glance through Hawaiian mythology to note that heroes go to Kahiki to approach the gods and acquire powers. At least one prayer exists in which Kahiki is addressed as a synonym for the totality of the gods (Fornander 1916–20, 6:54–55).

Mythology also demonstrates that Kahiki is the origin of the royal dynasties and of the priesthood of Kū, as well as of the principal rituals and regalia (Emerson 1893, 5–28; Beckwith 1940, 238–75, 352–86). As for edible plants, there are myths that connect the coconut palm and other life-giving plants with Kahiki (Fornander 1916–20, 5:590–95).

Kahiki is primarily a place, but as the place of origins it also has a temporal connotation. Hence it refers to all that is distant in time (NK, 2:31) not only in space ("abroad," Andrews 1865, 244; PE, 104). The name Kahiki also refers to various zones of the celestial dome which are, like Kahiki as land, distant and connected with the gods as origins of things. Indeed, the meanings "foreign land" and "sky areas" form one single grouping in PE, 104. In Makemson's (1938, 378–80) interpretation, the four celestial Kahiki are parallels of declination that coincide with the daily east-west trajectory of certain stars (*na alanui o na hōkū hoʻokele,* "the great star routes for navigation"). A fifth Kahiki (Kahiki moe) is defined by Malo as "the circle or zone of the earth's surface, whether sea or land, which the eye traverses in looking to the horizon" (1951, 10) and by Kamakau as "the circle seen as the eye traverses land and sea to the firmament where it meets the sea (*ka huina aouli*) . . . and all the lands 'below' (*malalo;* within) this circle are called *ʻaina o Kahiki-moe,* lands of Kahiki-moe (1976, 5).

Makemson's interpretation corresponds well with Malo's account of the various Kahiki. As for Kamakau, his system coincides with Malo's in the case of Kahiki moe and Kahiki kū, which make up the lowest zone of the sky over the horizon, but it differs on the other Kahiki. In fact, according to Kamakau these Kahiki are situated on the horizon beyond Kahiki kū, which defines the limits of the visible from the Hawaiian archipelago. As for the zones of the sky, according to him they are called not Kahiki, but *lani* ("sky") (1976, 5–6, cf. p. 8). In Kamakau's system, then, Kahiki defines the horizon and beyond it the lands invisible from Hawaii. On the contrary, for Malo Kahiki designates the different zones of the celestial sphere, again at the limits of the visible and beyond.

The Pantheon
The Theory of the Multiple Bodies

We have seen that, correlative to man, the divine takes on a personal form. It is as personal beings that the deities are the objects of man's worship and appear in ritual. We must therefore turn our attention to the personal deities that constitute the Hawaiian pantheon.

Each deity is defined by his manifestations, which reveal his attributes, or predicates. As elsewhere in Polynesia (cf. Firth 1930–31), these manifestations can take three main forms: natural phenomena, particularly biological species; living human forms; and artificial human forms, or anthropomorphic images. Although there are meaningful differences among the various human representations, living or artificial, they all instantiate the same human form. This last statement may seem to contradict a passage of Malo (1951, 83–84) claiming that images can be patterned after natural objects or species. The fact is that all surviving images are anthropomorphic, though sometimes nonanthropomorphic components are included, for reasons to be given later. Malo was probably carried away by his Christian zeal in denouncing "brute-worship" in traditional religion.

Since all human representations of the gods instantiate the same human form, they make evident that the unity of the divine is provided by the human species. In contrast, the nonhuman manifestations of the deities are bewilderingly varied and, some overlappings notwithstanding, different for each deity. In our attempt to distinguish and classify the deities we must therefore begin with their natural manifestations.

Each deity is characterized by a number of natural manifestations, mostly species, which are said to be his *kino lau*, "myriad bodies" (literally, "four hundred bodies"), or "interchangeable body forms" (Kamakau 1964, 82), or "multiple forms" (Handy and Pukui 1972, 123). Although our knowledge of Hawaiian botanical and zoological classifications is limited, it is evident that the personal gods, unlike the various animal forms of Pō,[6] do not correspond to any known genus. An example will make this quite clear. Let us consider the principal species constituting the "bodies" of Kamapua'a. This deity, a particularization of the god Lono (Handy 1968, 46), is half man, half pig. Consequently the pig is the natural species with which he is primarily associated; he is linked with other species only through the metonymic and above all metaphoric associations such species have with the pig.

These metonymic relations essentially involve plants associated with the pig because they are his food: '*ama'u* (*Sadleria*), which is also called *pua'a 'ehu'ehu*, "ruddy pig" (PE, 21, 317); *hāpu'u* (*Cibotium splendens*) (cf. Handy 1940, 214); young taro leaves (*lau kalo*) and *kukui* (*Aleurites moluccana*), the nut of which is eaten by the pig (Handy 1968, 47). At least two of these species also have analogical relationships with this animal. In the case of *hāpu'u*, "the analogy lies in the fact that the stalks of the tree-fern are hairy, or bristly like the legs of a hog" (Handy 1968, 46). As for the *kukui*, its leaves "suggest in outline the snout and ears of a pig" (ibid.).

The metaphoric relationships between natural species and Kamapua'a (i.e., the pig) are more numerous and important than the metonymic ones. Thus the sweet potato ('*uala*) is a "body" of Kamapua'a because one of the forms of its leaves resembles the *kukui* leaf, which in turn recalls the form of the pig, as we have seen. Moreover, these tubers are eaten by wild pigs (ibid.). The seaweed *limu līpu'upu'u* is considered another "body" because it recalls the pig's excrement (ibid., 48); the banana variety *hinu-pua'a*, "hog's grease," "has a dark shiny stem that looks greasy" (ibid.). Round dark clouds laden with rain are also his "bodies" (ibid.) because they evoke the black pigs in which the god prefers to be incarnated (Kahiolo 1978, 95). The last detail also explains why taro of the *hiwa*, "black," variety is considered his "body" (ibid.).

The *humuhumu* fish (Balistidae) is considered a "sea pig" because of its odor and because it grunts "like a pig" when it is taken out of the water (Titcomb and Pukui 1972, 81). One variety of this fish is called *humu-*

humu nukunuku-a-puaʻa, "humuhumu with a snout like a pig" (PE, 85; cf. Handy 1972, 449); its anatomy leads it to be connected with the pig. Other species are associated with the pig—and therefore with Kamapuaʻa—because of less direct metaphorical relationships. Thus the *olomea* species (*Perrottetia sandvicensis*) is considered a "vegetable pig," probably because, like Kamapuaʻa, it connotes masculine sexuality. In fact the "male" stick used to make fire by rubbing it on "female" wood is made from this plant (Neal 1965, 464). This operation is reserved for men and is a metaphor for sexual intercourse (cf. Hiroa 1957, 17).

The *kūmū, moano* (goatfish), *ʻamaʻama* (*Mugil cephalus*) and *āholehole* (immature stage of the *Kuhlia sandvicensis*) fish are considered "sea pigs" and therefore bodies of Kamapuaʻa for unknown reasons (Titcomb 1972, 60, 66, 92), although the *ʻamaʻama* and the *āholehole* are similar to the pig in that like it they are raised.[7] One of Handy's informants even claimed that the *āholehole* might be "raised like pet pigs" in fishponds and fed with taro (Handy 1972, 262; cf. Kamakau 1976, 49–50).

Other associations among Kamapuaʻa's "bodies" are determined by resemblances among the words designating them (see for example Handy 1972, 116).[8]

It is clear that all these species are grouped together not because they share taxonomic features (which would make them members of the same genus), but because for different reasons they are all associated with the pig. Consequently a particular species takes the place that in a true classificatory system belongs to the genus. But, in turn this species is focalizing and totalizing because it represents better than all others the human properties that are the true signifieds of the god. It is easy to see this in the case of Kamapuaʻa himself. This deity, who is a human pig or a "pig-man" (the very meaning of his name), represents human properties evoked by certain of the pig's qualities: virility, activity, bellicosity,[9] and so on.

The example of Kamapuaʻa illustrates the following principle: *the "genus" of all species included in one god belongs not to the natural world but to the human, social world.* Thus the *kino lau* of gods are constituted by the projection of human predicates and their subjects (individual or collective) on the species and other phenomena of the natural world that evoke them.

Let us illustrate the same principle by referring to one of the major gods, Kū. His fundamental human signified is the class constituted by activities pertaining to and performed by human male. These are war, fishing, and all related activities: the construction of canoes, images, and temples and the fabrication of ritual objects and so forth. It is easy to demonstrate that all natural manifestations of Kū are either symbols of these activities or objects appropriated thereby or, finally, their spatial and temporal frameworks. Thus, for example, the dog, the hawk, and the game fish are "bodies" of Kū because they evoke the warrior and his different attributes. Birds with precious plumage are the "bodies" of Kū because their feathers adorn the images carried onto the battlefield and decorate the helmets and capes of the warriors. All the plant species considered the "bodies" of Kū are used in ritual or technical activities related to fishing and warfare. Some, for example, are used to build canoes. Many of Kū's "bodies" evoke virility because they are "straight," "erect." Moreover, these are signifieds of the word *kū*. More generally, everything that is straight, vertical, high, or deep in nature tends to be associated with Kū, that is, with human virility. The color red belongs to him as well, perhaps because it evokes blood spilled during warfare and fishing. Last, Kū is associated with the period of the month in which his rituals are performed and the time of year when his temples are open and war is waged.

Besides representing the unity of the human, social reality in the multiplicity of its objective, natural correlatives, the theory of the *kino lau* accounts for the transformative power of the deity and of the rites it makes possible. By transforming himself into different but interchangeable bodies, by his power of metamorphosis, the deity accomplishes wondrous "miracles" (*hana mana*), produces transformations at the mythic or ritual level (cf. Kamakau 1964, 88).

For example, Kamapua'a, whose transformative exploits are abundantly documented in mythology, can accomplish them because he alternately takes on porcine, human, and fishlike forms (Kahiolo 1978, 44, 28–30) or even because he mobilizes a great number of individuals of one species connected with him (Kahiolo 1978, 40, 42, 48, 68, 70, 84, etc.; Fornander 1916–20, 5:343, 332).

The Major Gods and Their Particularizations

Having established the general principles that govern the grouping of different phenomena under one god, let us consider the main classes of the deities and their manifestations.

The structure of the pantheon—like that of the *Kumulipo*—reflects the primacy of the sexual principle. The duality of the sexes is in effect divinized in the couple, Kū (male)/Hina (female). At least in certain representations, this "Kū-and-Hina godhead" (NK, 2:122, cf. 147) encompasses all the deities: "Ku is said to preside over all male spirits (gods), Hina over the females" (Beckwith 1940, 13). In fact, in this context Kū encompasses all the properties of the masculine gods, Hina (whose name means "prostrated," "horizontal," "woman"), all feminine attributes. As many myths demonstrate, this divine couple is purely and simply the essence, or type, of the human couple and manifests itself in everything in nature associated with men and women, respectively, as well as with their activities (pp. 12–13).

But Kū is not only the god that encompasses all the other masculine gods or, what amounts to the same thing, the whole of divinized masculine attributes. He also exists on a lower level, as a member of the tetrad of "major gods" to which Lono, Kāne, and Kanaloa also belong. On this level his attributes are more limited in number. Thus Kū operates on two different classificatory levels, and his properties differ somewhat accordingly. This illustrates a fundamental principle. It is impossible to define Hawaiian gods in and for themselves; it can be done only with respect to the context in which they are situated at a given moment. Nevertheless, Kū's two classificatory positions interconnect, since Kū, as the god encompassing all the others, occupies the first place in the tetrad formed by the major gods.

The four "major gods" are called po'o ki'eki'e, "high heads" (Kepelino 1932, 19) or, collectively, ke kōko'oha o ke akua, "the association of four gods" (Fornander 1916–20, 4:605). These gods, who directly or indirectly encompass the majority of the others, are probably four in number because four, as the basis of the principal numerical system (Fornander 1878–80, 1:145, 157–58; HEN, 1:191),[10] connotes totality and, above all, the possibility of comprehending it—in both senses of the word—and dominating it through enumeration: "Four is assumed as the lowest class or collection of numbers, and the classes proceed in a regular scale upwards, from four to four hundred thousand, increasing by ten; as four, forty, four hundred, four thousand, forty thousand, four hundred thousand" (Dibble 1909, 89). It should be noted that the totality of deities is defined by the expression—often placed at the beginning of prayers (cf. Beckwith 1940, 82)—"i kini o ke akua, ka lehu o ke akua, ka mano o ke akua," "the 40,000 deities, the 400,000 deities, the 4,000 deities" (Emerson 1965, 21).

One or more attributes of each major god are connected with each of his particularizations.[11] Hence the names of these "particularized gods" take a binominal form: the first part of the name is that of the major god; the second is an expression referring to one attribute or a group of attributes of this major god. Each major god can thus be considered as a class of particularized gods. For example, the class of Kū gods includes Kūnuiākea, "Kū of the vast expanse," representing the encompassing and sovereign aspect of Kū; Kūkā'ilimoku, "Kū island-snatcher," the conquering and warriorlike aspect; Kū'ula, "Kū the red one," the aspect concerning fish and fishing; Kūka'ie'ie, the manifestation of Kū as the plant Freycinetia arborea ('ie'ie); and so forth. Long lists of the particularizations of Kū, Kāne, and Lono may be found in Kamakau (1964, 57–59).

The particularized forms of the major gods have different values and thus are hierarchized. The principle of this hierarchy is not only that of inclusion, for each god corresponds to activities or domains that are differently evaluated in relation to human interest. In addition, certain gods may index social groups or individuals.[12] As a result, two gods may be differentiated not only, or not at all, according to their attributes, but because different social groups worship them.[13]

The relationship between major and minor gods is presented in a somewhat confused and contradictory manner in the literature (Emerson 1892, 5–24; Handy and Pukui 1972, 117–31; NK, 1 : 35–43; Kamakau 1961, 200). According to one Hawaiian author this relationship is identical to that of the eldest brother and his younger brothers; the first reigns over the group, and the younger ones rule over special domains assigned to them (*kuleana*) (Anonymous 1927, 76).[14] For Kamakau, on the contrary, subordinate gods are produced by a "segmentation" (*mahae'ana*) of the major gods. The first he calls *akua 'aumakua* (1964, 58–59, 28). In this he is incorrect, since, as we shall see, the *akua 'aumakua* are a special category among these subordinate gods.

As I have said, the attributes of the gods, connected either with the four unmarked forms or the binominal forms, consist of aspects of reality that signify human activities and their frameworks (cf. Handy and Pukui 1972, 117–19). The domains belonging to each god are called *kuleana* ("areas of responsibility," according to NK, 1 : 23). Here I will limit myself to giving a simplified and schematic table listing the principal attributes of the four major gods (see table 1). Its only purpose is to orient readers in the more detailed discussions that will be encountered in the course of this study.

I should add that each god is said to be associated with a smell, a cloud or rainbow formation, the sign of a storm, the song of certain birds, certain stars (see Johnson and Mahelona 1975, ix), or even a particular number (Beckwith 1940, 4).[15] Available sources contain no details on these associations, however.[16] Some domains belong to several gods at once (NK, 1 : 23). In many cases the ensuing confusion of attributes is only apparent, since different gods may represent different aspects of the same domain or the same domain in different contexts. For instance, as the god of wealth and growth in general (NK, 2 : 121, 122), Lono is at the same time the supreme god of medicine. The Kū-Hina pair is also associated with medicine, but for a different reason. This couple symbolizes the equilibrium of opposed principles on which all good health depends (NK, 2 : 147, 155–56). Another example is found in the connection the major gods have with agriculture. Lono presides particularly over nonirrigated agriculture, because he is the god of rain. Kāne, who presides over springs, is usually associated with irrigated agriculture. Kanaloa has to some extent the same value. Kū is associated with the digging stick, because he is the god of all that is "straight" and of all masculine penetration, both literal and figurative.

Therefore we see that different hierarchies, associations, and oppositions exist among the gods depending on the context. Ultimately, all gods

TABLE 1   Principal Attributes of the Four Major Gods

	Kū	Kāne	Kanaloa	Lono
Colors	Red[1]	Red, black, white (yellow)[9]	Red, black[17]	Black[25]
Directions	High, east, right[2]	Right, east, north[10]	Left, west, south[18]	High, leeward (kona), (left?)[26]
Days of month, periods of day	1st to 3d days of lunar month, dawn[3]	27th to 28th days of lunar month, dawn[11]	23d to 24th days of lunar month, sunset[19]	28th day of-lunar month[27]
Natural and inorganic phenomena	High mountains, high sea, sky[4]	Emerged world, light, lightning, spring water (wai)[12]	Subterranean world, sea bottom, seawater (kai), tides[20]	Clouds bearing rain, thunder, noise[28]
Plants	Forest trees (lehua, koa, etc.), coconut tree, breadfruit ('ulu), 'ie'ie[5]	Banana, sugarcane, bamboo, 'awa[13]	Banana, bamboo, 'awa[21]	Gourd, sweet potato, kukui (Aleurites moluccana)[29]
Animals	Dog, 'io (hawk), fish (esp. game fish), 'ō'ō bird[6]	'ama'ama and āholehole fish (rooster), (pig)[14]	Octopus (or squid), ('ama'ama, āholehole), (rooster), (pig)[22]	Pig's attributes represented by deity Kamapua'a[30]
Seasons	Season of kapu pule (temple ritual)[7]	Sun's northern limit on ellipse, summer[15]	Winter[23]	Makahiki season (winter), rise of Pleiades, rainy season[31]
Functions	Fishing, war, canoe building, sorcery[8]	Male power of procreation, irrigated agriculture, fishponds, sorcery[16]	Death[24]	Nonirrigated agriculture, fertility, birth, medicine[32]

[1] Beckwith, 1940, 19.

[2] Beckwith 1940, 12–14; PE, 389. On Kū's association with the right hand, cf. PE, 389; NK, 2:13, 30.

[3] Malo 1951, 32.

[4] Beckwith 1940, 13–20, 30; Handy and Pukui 1972, 32–33. In the Kumulipo we find a form of Kū called Kūkahakualani ("Kū lord of heaven," line 1761, Beckwith 1951, 114).

[5] Handy 1972, 23, 169, 241; Beckwith 1940, 13, 15. When he materializes in the 'ie'ie (Freycinetia arborea), Kū takes the name Kūka'ie'ie ("Kū the 'ie'ie"—Malo 1951, 127).

[6] On Kū's association with the 'io bird, see PE, 389; on his association with ocean fish, see Kaawa 1865a; Malo 1951, 264. Kū's association with the 'ō'ō bird is attested in Fornander (1916–20, 5:150–51). This bird gives yellow feathers that decorate the gods and the ali'i. We can suppose that all birds bearing precious plumage belong to Kū's domain. In any case, this is suggested by the ritual of the bird snarers, which is addressed to Kūhulumanu ("Kū bird feathers") ("Bird-catching" prayer in HEN, 1:418).

[7] Malo 1951, 159–76.

[8] Beckwith 1940, 15–16. According to Kawena Pukui (NK, 2:19), when Kū is asso-

(continued)

(*Notes to table 1 continued*)
ciated with Hina, he is considered the god of human fertility. On the contrary, Lono would be the god of "fertility in general."

[9] Fornander 1878–80, 1:42–43, 127; Beckwith 1940, 62; Johnson and Mahelona 1975, 80–81. Kāne and Kanaloa make up the two axes that define the entire universe. On the north/south axis (associated with the color black), Kāne occupies the north, Kanaloa the south. On the east/west axis (associated with the color red), Kāne occupies the east, Kanaloa the west. When facing north, east is to the right, west to the left; thus Kāne is connected to the right, Kanaloa to the left. Kāne keeps his water of life in the place where the sun rises (Fornander 1916–20, 4:82), which is associated with the appearance of light, with the beginning, with the right. Kanaloa, on the contrary, represents death, which is associated with the left, with sunset (or the setting of the moon—cf. Ii 1963, 33), with darkness and the end. See below, notes 10, 16, 17, and 24.

[10] Beckwith 1940, 52, 62, 48.

[11] Malo 1951, 33.

[12] Kāne is responsible for the origin of many springs (Beckwith 1940, 63–64), and Kanaloa is the one who induces him to make them gush forth, in order to be able to prepare 'awa (Green and Pukui 1929, 113). Kāneikawaiola, "Kane in the water of life," is the form of Kāne representing life-giving spring water (Handy 1940, 35) and sperm (Handy and Pukui 1972, 33–34; Beckwith 1951, 56, 60; Titcomb 1948, 155; Emerson 1965, 257–59).

[13] Handy 1972, 23; Beckwith 1940, 63. According to Beckwith, Kāne introduced cultivated plants to Hawaii: "The heiau of Ka-mau-ai (the heap of vegetable food) at Keauhou, Kona, dedicated to Kane, is said to be the site of the introduction of cultivated food plants. Pigs, coconuts, breadfruit, awa and the wauke plant from which bark cloth is made are sacred to Kane" (1940, 62). Kāne was, however, principally associated with poi, the taro puree that forms a daily food (Handy and Pukui 1972, 34) and is "the Hawaiian staff of life" (PE, 310). On Kāne's association with bamboo, see Malo 1951, 94; Handy and Pukui 1972, 95; Liliuokalani 1978, 75; on his association with 'awa, see Liliuokalani 1978, 75; on Kāne's and Kanaloa's association with bananas, see Kamakau 1976, 38.

[14] Beckwith 1940, 62–63. On Kāne as rooster, see Titcomb 1948, 152. The 'ama-'ama and āholehole fish have a status midway between land and sea; this might explain their association with both Kāne and Kanaloa, who represent the land and sea, respectively. These fish are also considered as the marine equivalents of the pig, in which Kāne is embodied (cf. Beckwith 1940, 62–63). "The white albatross of Kane" appears in a myth made up by Kamakau on the basis of traditional elements (Beckwith 1940, 61; cf. Westervelt 1915b, 70).

[15] Johnson and Mahelona 1975, 80–81.

[16] Cf. note 12.

[17] Beckwith 1940, 60–66.

[18] See note 9.

[19] Malo 1951, 32–33.

[20] Seawater belongs to Kanaloa, who is also the god of the tides (NK, 1:24); however, when seawater is used ritually for purification, it belongs to Kāne (Beckwith 1940, 61; Fornander 1916–20, 6:273). Kanaloa seems to be associated with negative aspects of water (cf. NK, 2:146).

[21] Handy 1972, 23, 156; see Kāne (note 13); "Kanaloa the 'awa drinker" (prayer cited by Beckwith 1940, 62, 63; Liliuokalani 1978, 75). Kanaloa plants banana trees (text in Handy 1972, 157; cf. Liliuokalani 1978, 75; Handy and Pukui 1972, 177). He is called "the banana brother of Pele" (Kahiolo 1978, 72), which indicates that the banana tree is one of his "bodies."

[22] Beckwith 1940, 60–63. On Kanaloa's connection with the rooster, see Titcomb 1948, 152. In the *Kumulipo* (line 615; Liliuokalani 1978), Kanaloa is called Kahe'ehaunawela, "the stinking squid" (Beckwith 1940, 60), which some read as Kahe'ehāunawela, "the hot-striking octopus" (Beckwith 1951, 95). *He'e* means either "octopus" or "squid" (PE, 59). Cf. the prayer given by Emerson: "O Kanaloa, god of the squid," "*E Kanaloa, ke akua o ka hee*" (Malo 1951, 111). Kanaloa is also associated with the pig (Beckwith 1940, 61).

[23] Johnson and Mahelona 1975, 80–81.

[24] On Kanaloa's association with death, cf. Beckwith 1940, 61. Although this associa-

tion took a form that reveals the influence of biblical myths, I believe it to be traditional. The relationship between Kanaloa and the subterranean world, the left, sunset, and stench, as well as his relationship of opposition and complementarity with Kāne, confirms this hypothesis. Besides, Kanaloa is the god of the ocean, which is a symbol of death (see NK, 2:180). On this god's association with sacrificial drums, called *pahu Kanaloa*, which connote death, see HEN, 1:528; PE, 277.

[25] Lono is associated with the black color of clouds that bring rain (Handy 1972, 339).

[26] Lono is associated with the "winds of Kona" [leeward winds] (Handy 1972, 220).

[27] Malo 1951, 153. The twenty-eighth day of the lunar month is consecrated to Lono. It is part of the two-day period called *kapu Kāne*. Note that while Kū opens the month, Lono brings it to a close (cf. part 3, Introduction).

[28] Handy 1972, 342–43; Handy and Pukui 1972, 31–32; Beckwith 1940, 31–32. One form of Lono is called Lononuinohoikawai, "Great Lono who lives in the water" (Beckwith 1940, 31–32), or Lonokawai, "Lono the water" (Malo 1951, 6, 8). On Lono in the form of rain, see Fornander 1916–20, 6:364, 366–67, 507–9, 510; 4:95; Emerson 1915, 150; Malo 1951, 88–89, 178. Rain clouds are called *puapua'a* (reduplication of "pig"—cf. Handy 1972, 145) and assimilated with black pigs, themselves the incarnation of Lono (Handy 1972, 339). On Lono in the form of thunder and noise, see Handy 1972, 339; Beckwith 1940, 350.

[29] Handy 1972, 23; Beckwith 1940, 32. On Lono's connection with the gourd, see Handy 1972, 220; Beckwith 1940, 32–33; on his connection with the sweet potato, see Handy 1972, 137–38; his connection with *kukui* is illustrated in Handy 1972, 229, 340.

[30] See Handy 1972, 340. One of Lono's incarnations is the mythical pig Kamapua'a (Fornander 1916–20, 5:317; Beckwith 1940, 210–11; Handy and Pukui 1972, 31). In one chant, Kamapua'a defines his relation to Lono in this way: "Lono is the eye [the most important part], I am the body [as a pig]" (Kahiolo 1978, 66). But various aspects of the pig seem to be associated with all the major gods. Handy (1972) exaggerates the importance of the pig's relation to Lono. If Lono is associated with this animal, it is above all because the rain-bearing clouds are metaphorically assimilated to pigs (see note 28), and perhaps also because pigs are aware of approaching rain before men are (J. Charlot, personal communication).

[31] Malo 1951, 141–52.

[32] Malo 1951, 159; NK, 2:121–22, 147.

---

can be implicated in all activities, for each activity can be analyzed in aspects that may each be reducible to one of the four gods. In every prayer, moreover, the four major gods can be generically invoked. Their collective invocation is prescribed in the ritual of consecration of the royal temples (see part 3).

That certain attributes belong to several gods at a time indicates that the quadripartite classification of the gods coexists with other classificatory forms, which most often remain implicit. For example, in table 1 we see that the god Kanaloa is barely distinguished from Kāne by his attributes. As Beckwith notes, "about Kanaloa as a god apart from Kane there is very little information" (1940, 60; cf. Emerson 1892, 16; Frazer 1922, 2: 394– 95). Actually, Kāne and Kanaloa are said to be twin brothers (*Kumulipo*, line 1714; cf. Bastian 1881, 131–32; Liliuokalani 1978, 23, 65; Marcuse 1894, 97). It seems that Kanaloa represents the negative or "sinister" aspect of Kāne and that together these gods form a whole, in which they polarize some features (e.g., dawn/dusk, birth/death, beginning/end) but not others (colors, perhaps, certain plants, and so forth). But if Kāne and Kanaloa can be considered two aspects of the same category, one positive and the other negative, we must conclude that the quadripartition of the gods is a superficial phenomenon that conceals a tripartition on a deeper level. (It is true that in some cases the trinitary organization of the gods is due to Christian influence; see Kepelino 1932, 8–11).

The gods or their properties may also be organized on a binary principle. On the most general level this principle manifests itself in the "double nature"—positive and negative (NK, 2:122, 146)—that is attributed to all gods.

The ambivalence of the gods is, however, a subject that will have to be addressed elsewhere.[17] It interests us here only because it accounts for a tendency to pair the major gods in couples, with one god representing the positive element, the other the negative one. The Kāne-Kanaloa pair is a good example of this tendency. In some contexts the pairing of Kū and Lono appears analogous to that of Kanaloa and Kāne. The most fundamental pair, however, is constituted by Kū and Hina, who, as we have seen, polarize all conceivable attributes (cf. NK, 2:122, cf. 147).

Goddesses, *Akua Wahine*

Just as Kū is the prototype of the gods, Hina (or her equivalents Haumea and Papa)[18] is the prototype of the goddesses. This implies that she represents the attributes of women and their natural counterparts.

Among these typically feminine attributes can be found everything that is associated with the begetting of children, beginning with seduction (thus beauty, dance, chants, and adornments are the attributes of goddesses such as Laka—Emerson 1965, 25; NK, 2:122, 87–or the four Maile sisters) and ending with childbirth (over which Haumea presides—Beckwith 1940, 283–85, 289).

Along with these positive attributes, women—and therefore goddesses—have negative ones, springing from the fact that they are considered impure (see part 2). Beckwith even believed she had established a relation between the name Haumea and the word *haumia*, which means "impure" and refers, among other things, to the state of women during menstruation (1940, 289). Female impurity explains women's close connection with sorcery. Even male sorcerers "seem to work through a female companion" (ibid., 114). In the origin myth of sorcery reported by Kamakau (1964, 131–32) women play a preponderant role because they constitute the majority of "sorcery" deities and because the cult of these deities becomes truly destructive only as the result of the intervention of a priestess (1964, 132).

Another destructive phenomenon associated almost exclusively with goddesses (particularly with Pele, the daughter of Haumea—cf. Emerson 1965, 47, ix; Beckwith 1940, 169–71) is volcanism (Ellis 1842, 248–49;

Kalakaua 1888, 49; Westervelt 1916, 69–71). It even seems that eruptions are identified with Pele's menstruation, since it is said that the goddess "went into the sea for her *kapu kai* [women's purification in the sea after their periods—V. V.] after erupting" (NK, 1:123).

Pele and her sisters are also fearsome sorceresses (Beckwith 1940, 113). The most terrible of Pele's sisters is Kapo (Kamakau 1964, 129), whose murderous vagina can become detached to trap its victims (Beckwith 1940, 113, 186–87). This is why she is called Kapokohelele ("Kapo of the traveling vagina").

Nevertheless these goddesses also have positive aspects or are linked with goddesses having a positive value. Thus Kapo is paired with Laka, who, as we have seen, is associated with the beauties and pleasures of the dance (Emerson 1965, 25; NK, 2:122).[19] Pele takes contrasting forms; sometimes that of a very lovely and young person, sometimes that of an old sorceress (Emerson 1892, 7).

In the same way, other sorcery goddesses (for example, Walinu'u, Walimānoanoa, Kalamainu'u, Kihawahine, Kāmeha'ikana) appear either in the form of seductive women or in the monstrous form of *mo'o* ("dragons," "water deities"—cf. Kamakau 1964, 82ff.), in which they try to devour their human husbands (Beckwith 1940, 194–95; Ii 1869g,i).

A comparison of the myths dealing with these sorcery goddesses reveals that they are all forms of Haumea (Kamakau 1964, 28; cf. Beckwith 1940, 281–83). I will return to these myths and the meaning of the goddesses when I analyze their role in ritual. Here it is sufficient to say that goddesses are few and have a marginal position in the Hawaiian pantheon. This corresponds to the marginal position of women in the ritual system. Moreover, while all deities are more or less ambivalent, the utmost ambivalence of the goddesses reflects—as I shall demonstrate in due time—the ambiguous position of the female principle in the hierarchical and ritual systems.

The *Akua 'Aumakua*

The deities considered so far are the most encompassing both conceptually and socially. As generic, almost abstract (NK, 1:23, 24) expressions of a variety of predicates common to most or even all men, these gods, especially in their monomial form (Kū, Kāne, Kanaloa, Lono) may be invoked by every male in all situations that fall into their *kuleana*. Yet, as we shall see, these apparently unmediated relationships of individual men with the gods presuppose hierarchically mediated ones, which are periodically reestablished in the great collective rituals or in those performed by the king and the aristocracy. Such at least seems to be the ideology imposed by the aristocracy.

But whether or not this hierarchical mediation is presupposed in every case, it is a fact that the invocation of the great gods presupposes the social totality, precisely because everybody may invoke them. These gods, then, make all Hawaiians commensurable, so to speak, and correspond to the consciousness that they all have something in common, that they belong to the same species.

For this reason the great gods are in sharp contrast with another class of deities, the *akua ʻaumakua*, who are related to kinship groups or to professional, mostly hereditary, groups (Emerson 1892, 17; cf. Fornander 1916–20, 6:120). Many *ʻaumakua* are individually acquired but, since they are usually transmitted to the descendants of the original acquirer, they become associated with a group of kinsmen. Thus Kamakau defines the "*ʻaumakua* gods" as "the personal gods, *akua pili kino*, of the chiefs and people" (1964, 55) and as the "ancestral deities of the family" (ibid., 28; cf. Emerson 1892, 16; NK, 1:36).

The contrast of great deities and *ʻaumakua* is reflected by a number of contrasts among their natural manifestations. Thus, as we shall see, the *ʻaumakua* tend to be mostly associated with dangerous, anomalous, or simply mediating species. Moreover, whenever possible they are associated with marked individuals of natural species rather than with the species as a whole, as happens with the great deities (cf. Kamakau 1964, 74; NK, 1:41; Emerson 1892, 8). In this way individual differences are used to differentiate kinship groups or individuals that have something in common, since they all relate to the same species.

The *ʻaumakua* are not simply *worshiped* by kinship groups; they are *related* to them by kinship bonds; they are, in other words, ancestors, personifications of the kinship principles reproducing the groups to which they are attached. It is therefore not surprising that the *ʻaumakua* ideology reflects the highly flexible and optional nature of Hawaiian kinship.

Precisely because the kinship system is bilateral but coexists with an elaborate hierarchy, it encourages weighting relationships and emphasizing some at the expense of others. This probably explains why the kinsmen of a dead person may wish to incorporate him or her—by means of rites called *kākūʻai*—into a natural species of their choice. The choice may be dictated by the desire to emphasize a relationship with another group, whose dead manifest themselves in the same species. This is just a hypothesis, however.

A reason explicitly given for performing the *kākūʻai* rite is the desire to neutralize dangerous species or phenomena by incorporating one's kinsmen into them (cf. Kamakau 1964, 78, 81, 82, 64–65, and below).

The establishment of relationships with *ʻaumakua* may also be motivated by the dreaming of a certain species, or by the chance resemblance of an aborted fetus to a certain animal. It is believed that the fetus results from the union (in dream, for instance) of its mother with that animal. Consequently, the fetus is ritually transformed into an *ʻaumakua* that manifests itself in an individual of that animal species. The great deities themselves can become '*aumakua* for certain (presumably high-ranking) groups by marrying humans and thus obtaining descendants who worship them as ancestors (NK, 1:36; Kamakau 1964, 68–69; cf. Kepelino 1977, 56). As all other deities, the '*aumakua* can appear in human form or manifest themselves in living humans (for instance in *haka*, "mediums") or in anthropomorphic images. Sometimes they even manifest themselves in stones with remarkable shapes—phallic, for instance (Kamakau 1964, 79–80; Kihe in HEN, 1:572; cf. Handy and Pukui 1972, 138–39).

In sum, even in these deities the human form is the most generic component, while their natural forms differentiate them. Moreover, since these natural forms are taboo to those who consider them the "bodies" of their '*aumakua*, they help to differentiate the worshipers as well (NK, 1:38; Kamakau 1964, 87).

Let us consider in more detail, then, the species in which the '*aumakua* tend to manifest. themselves. Because their symbolic values are better known, I shall begin with the species most commonly associated with '*aumakua*: shark, owl,[20] lizard, sea turtle, caterpillar, '*alae* bird (mud hen, *Gallinula chloropus sandvicensis*), and field mouse (NK, 2:123; Handy and Pukui 1972, 35–38; Malo 1951, 38, 39; Kamakau 1964, 87). These animals can be divided into the following groups.

1. *Predators*. This group contains the two animals that correspond to the two most important '*aumakua*, the shark and the owl. Two properties of the shark are relevant in this context: it is a man-eater (Malo 1951, 47), and it is man's rival in fishing. The two aspects are frequently associated, since fatal encounters with man-eating sharks often take place in the fishing grounds (cf. Kamakau 1964, 78). The owl is also predatory. It devours mice and birds, but it also feeds on human corpses that have been abandoned on the battlefield; it particularly relishes human eyes (Fornander 1878–80, 2:265–66). Like the shark, the owl is associated with death,[21] but it is less terrible.

2. *Agricultural pests: caterpillar and field mouse*. One species of caterpillar (*pe‘elua*, *Cirphis unipuncta*) destroys sugarcane (Fullaway and Krauss 1945, 128–29); another ('*enuhe* or *nuhe* or '*anuhe*, *Herse cingulata* Fabr.) eats the shoots of the sweet potato (Fullaway and Krauss 1945, 98). As for the mouse, it should be noted that not the domestic variety, but the one that lives in the fields and destroys the crops is a manifestation of an '*aumakua*. Significantly, this variety of '*aumakua* is worshiped by farmers (Kihe in HEN, 1:569).

3. *Animals straddling different genera: sea turtle, lizard (mo‘o), 'alae*. Like the fish, the turtle is a creature of the sea. Unlike the fish, it breathes. It can swim but can also walk on land. Furthermore, although it lives in water, it is born on land, where it lays its eggs (cf. Beckwith 1940, 22). Finally, unlike other breathing quadrupeds, it is not vivaparous and mam-

miferous but is oviparous like birds, reptiles, and fish. Therefore one can surmise that it is viewed as an "irregular" animal, straddling different genera and families, although there is no definite proof for this hypothesis.

The '*aumakua mo'o* are imaginary animals, living in rivers, ponds, and fishponds (Emerson 1892, 6). They are reputed to be huge and black (Kamakau 1964, 83) and are considered the usually feminine equivalents[22] of shark '*aumakua*: "The *Akooah Mo-o*, or the Reptile God, which resembles a large shark, devours men" (MH, July 1822, 208; Kamakau 1964, 83).[23] The name *mo'o* also refers to lizards of the Gekkonidae and Scincidae (Stejneger 1899, 783; Cochran and Goin 1970, 230–31, 178–79), and these reptiles furnish the model from which the '*aumakua mo'o* are imagined (Kamakau 1964, 83) and are therefore the object of the same taboos (cf. Emerson 1892, 6–7; Snyder 1919, 19).[24]

It seems that one important reason lizards are connected with ancestral deities is that they evoke the idea of ancestrality. Thus their prominent backbone—made of equal segments extending from head to tail—is an image of the genealogy that connects ancestors to descendants. For this reason the word *mo'o* also means "succession, series, especially a genealogical one" (PE, 234).

Another reason lizards are connected with '*aumakua* concerns the Gekkonidae alone. Geckos seem to have a symbolically intermediary position between "otherness" and "sameness" that is analogous to that of the ancestral deities. Indeed, they live in the house[25] like kinsmen, display human traits such as gregariousness (Snyder 1919, 21), and even have five-toed feet that resemble human hands. Yet they are animals also, and as such "other."

Another feature common to both the Scincidae and the Gekkonidae has a symbolic value that links them both to the '*aumakua mo'o*. The skin of all lizards evokes the diseases that these deities are supposed to produce and therefore to cure: pox, leprosy, ulcers, scrofula. Moreover, it evokes gooseflesh associated with the chills preceding the onset of fever (Emerson 1892, 6–7).[26] Most of these diseases are of European origin; this is why the *mo'o* that produce them took on increasing importance at the end of the eighteenth century (cf. Kamakau 1964, 20).

The '*alae* is an ominous bird. It appears in the origin myth of fire, doubtless because its appearance evokes the red of flames and the black or bluish color of smoke (cf. Munro 1960, 52; Northwood 1940, 21). In any case, the myth explicitly attributes the origin of the red beak and crest of the '*alae* to a burn inflicted by the hero Maui when he stole the secret of fire from it. For at the beginning it was the '*alae* and not man who knew how to make fire and cook (Westervelt 1910, 61–67; articles in *Ka Nupepa Kuokoa*, 27 June, 4 July, 1863; Dickey 1917, 17–18; Bastian 1888, 278ff.; Fornander 1916–20, 5:560–64; Beckwith 1940, 229–33). Thus a human trait (eating cooked food) passed from bird to man, and an animal trait (eating raw food) passed from man to bird. From this perspective the 'alae, like the gecko, is in an intermediary position between humanity and animality, between society and nature.

Thus a natural property that suggests fire made the 'alae man's antagonist in the myth of the origin of fire. Having assumed this mythological role, the bird came to occupy a place midway between humanity and animality. In like manner, the hostility this bird is supposed to bear toward man is best explained by the fact that it was dispossessed to man's advantage. And its feminine nature is perhaps explained by its parallelism with women, who are also deprived by men of the use of the cooking fire, at least in the most important contexts (cf. Malo 1951, 27, and below).

The information above can be summarized as follows: (1) The two most important manifestations of 'aumakua are animals dangerous to man and predatory (shark, owl). (2) A second class includes agricultural pests (field mouse, caterpillar) that take part of man's food away and thereby threaten his life. The same can be said of the shark, which is man's rival in fishing and whose presence frightens the fish away. (3) The lizard and the 'alae occupy a position similar to that of human ancestors and thus become metaphors for them. But they also evoke illness. The meaning of the turtle is less clear, but this animal is perhaps the mediator par excellence, because it is situated at the intersection of several classes of animals and, above all, at the intersection of two domains, ocean and shore. The former connotes death (NK, 2:180) and the latter, probably, human life, since men generally live near the shore. The turtle can thereby function as a metaphor for the relation between the dead and the living—a relation that makes it an appropriate manifestation of the 'aumakua.

What conclusions can we draw from these facts? It seems that we are witnessing the convergence of two phenomena. On the one hand, there are animals that are believed dangerous to man, and consequently there is a desire to neutralize this danger. This is why it is thought possible to transform some individuals of these dangerous species into protectors that can provide a defense against the danger present in the species as a whole. Consider, for example, the shark, the most important of the 'aumakua (Emerson 1892, 8). Kamakau clearly affirms: "This is the main reason why the people of Maui worshipped sharks—in order to be saved from being eaten by a shark when they went fishing" (1964, 78). The worship of some sharks makes it possible to reverse their value. Instead of devouring those who worship them, they protect them against ordinary sharks. Instead of stealing fish from such men, "the akua mano [shark gods] would lead fishes right to them" (Kamakau 1964, 82).

On the other hand, there are the dead, who incarnate the moral principles of kinship that they taught when alive as well as the protection and solidarity that any relative owes another. By alienating the dead, by integrating them into the feared animal species, the two properties of the dead are transferred to the animal. As a protector, it will neutralize danger; as the representative of moral law, it will explain all misfortune in moral terms. In other words, if sharks do not kill, it is because the 'aumakua protect their living relatives; if they do kill, it is because these same 'aumakua are punishing a transgression (see Kamakau 1964, 81; NK, 2:123; HEN, 1:705). Thus, no matter what happens, the social universe encompasses the natural universe. If misfortune cannot be neutralized, it can at least be rationalized. One can say to oneself that if one follows the rules one has nothing to fear from sharks.

The same explanation is valid for caterpillars and mice. If they do not destroy crops, it is because of the 'aumakua; if they do destroy them, again it is the 'aumakua who are responsible. As for the owl, its negative qualities are neutralized when an 'aumakua is incarnated in it. Then it is capable of preventing death (cf. Kamakau 1961, 169–70; Ii 1963, 8; Remy 1859, 51–52; Fornander 1916–20, 4:600; Kihe in HEN, 1:571–72).

Although with animals like the shark, caterpillar, field mouse, and owl it is the negative and destructive aspect that is the principal motivation for the association with ancestors, in the case of the 'alae and lizard it is perhaps this identification with ancestors or sorcerers that basically motivates the menacing aspect. These animals present much more complicated cases than the others, however. For example, one aspect of their negativity is explained by the homology between their position and that of women, as well as by other analogical relations. As for the turtle, we do not know if it is seen as threatening. It is unlikely that it is. Rather, it seems that only its intermediate character, halfway between human and animal, is retained and that this animal simply represents ideas of ancestrality and divinity.

In short, the few cases considered here show that animal symbolism has complex motivations. If it is foolish to ignore the idea that the value of an animal such as the turtle is due to factors that are first of all intellectual (such a case is explained rather well by the theory proposed by Leach [1964] and Douglas [1966, 1975]), it would be equally foolish to make the fear of sharks a phenomenon derived from some imagined anomaly. As we have seen, the shark is divinized because people are afraid of it (cf. Ellis 1842, 375); it is not feared because it has been divinized by its anomalous status. More exactly, its divinization, its transformation into a manifestation of the moral principle, transforms the animal fear of an animal into a truly human, social fear. By deanimalizing the animal that is the object of his fear, man deanimalizes himself.

The explanation I have proposed seems sufficient to account for the most important and frequently worshiped 'aumakua. Can it be extended to tell why other species or natural phenomena are considered 'aumakua manifestations? Establishing the legitimacy of such an extension is not easy, for the lists of manifestations of '*aumakua* are confusing; they were compiled very late, at a time when Hawaiian religion had long broken down. Above all, we are seldom sure of the symbolic value of the species listed, so that in the end we are reduced to simple hypotheses. Nevertheless an attempt must be made, at least in order to gain some sense of the likelihood or unlikelihood of my explanation.

In the papers of J. S. Emerson we find two lists of natural species considered manifestations of '*aumakua*.[27] One was taken from Lilinoe in 1915 (HEN, 1:728). The other was given by Isaac Kihe, doubtless before 1892 (HEN, 1:566–72), since it is at that date that Emerson published the essential part of it (1892). These lists are the longest I have encountered, but they are probably incomplete (cf. Emerson 1892, 13). It is useful to divide the items mentioned by Kihe and Lilinoe into three main groupings: marine species, birds, plants and other phenomena. I have omitted from their lists the principal animal '*aumakua* manifestations, since I have already discussed them.

Marine Species

All these species are called *i'a*, "fish," and may be classified in the following way:

1. Species that resemble the principal species in which '*aumakua* manifest themselves: Found on this list are the lizard fish '*ulae* (different species of Synodontidae), whose head recalls that of a lizard, and the freshwater fish '*ōkuhekuhe* (youthful form of the '*o'pu*, *Eleutheris fusca*), which Kaaie (1862) places in the same category as the '*aumakua mo'o*.

2. Species that are quite unlike true fish:

'*ōpae* (shrimp)
he'e (octopus or squid)
wana (sea urchin)
loli (*Holothuria*, "bêche-de-mer," sea slug)
leho (cowrie)
'*opihi* (limpet)
pūhi (eels)

3. Bizarre and dangerous species:

'*o'opu-hue* or '*o'opu-kawa* (*Arathron hispides*). This fish inflates like a balloon, which makes it "the subject of much curiosity" (Tinker 1978, 492). If eaten, it can cause death (Malo 1951, 45).

kōkala (porcupine fish, *Diodon hystrix*, *D. holocanthus*, *Cheilomicterus affinis*). This poisonous fish is covered with spines and can inflate like the preceding one (Tinker 1978, 499).

moa (a variety of *pahu*, trunkfish). These odd fish, which resemble boxes, exude a poison that is fatal to approaching fish (ibid., 486).

pūhi-ao or *pūhi-kauila*; *pūhi* '*ou*; *pūhi-paka* (morays) All of these are dangerous eels.

4. Merely bizarre species:

nūnū (trumpet fish, *Aulostomus chinensis*). These fish, which resemble trumpets, "are easily identified because of this unusual appearance" (ibid., 153).

lā'ī-pala (literally, "yellow ti leaf," *Zebrasoma flavescens*). According to Tinker, this fish is one of the most beautiful of all. It has a striking and unusual appearance because it resembles a leaf and is completely and uniformly yellow (ibid., 382).

pāo'o. This name refers to several varieties of the '*o'opu* species. These are fish whose form recalls that of the eel (Malo 1951, 45) and that have the strange habit of jumping from one tide pool to another. They occupy a very important place in mythology (Titcomb and Pukui 1972, 122–24). The '*o'opu* also have the peculiarity that some varieties live in fresh water, others in salt water; still other varieties alternate between the two (PE, 267). Thus this fish straddles the two principal domains that Hawaiian thought places in opposition, *wai* "fresh water" and *kai* "salt water." In addition to being an '*aumakua* for some people, the '*o'opu* is considered as a god by the collectivity and as such is given offerings so that it may multiply (Fornander 1916–20, 5:511).

5. Species whose presence on the list remains inexplicable:

'*ū'ū* (squirrel fish, *Mypristis*).

This classification of the fish species is in large part hypothetical. It does in any case confirm the theory advanced to explain the principal '*aumakua* species. In fact, most '*aumakua* fish are either hostile to man—poisonous, ferocious—or anomalous. Some of them are notable because of unique characteristics. Naturally other hostile or bizarre species are found in Hawaii, but the ones listed above (insofar as the list is complete) have the peculiarity of living near the coast or at the border between fresh and salt water—in a word, near human habitation. They are thus in a metonymic relation with man and at the same time opposed to him. Their position, intermediary between identity and difference, makes them good metaphors of the '*aumakua*, who are themselves intermediary between a distant divine and ego's nearer social circle (family, etc.).

Birds

1. The '*elepaio* bird (a flycatcher) is distinguished from all others because it approaches man without fear (Northwood, 1940, 43). Moreover, it has a special relationship with canoe builders because it is able to indicate the presence of rotten wood inside a log selected for digging a canoe (Munro, 1960, 81; Emerson 1892, 13; Fornander 1916–20, 6:144–45). It is also the first bird to announce the dawn (Emerson 1892, 13).

2. The *noio* bird (*Anous minutus melanogenys* Gray) is the only Hawaiian bird that always remains close to the coastline. It lives there seeking its food without ever moving into the interior or out to sea. It is thus the only bird to be exclusively associated with the border region between land and ocean. Sometimes small groups of *noio* follow canoes "to pick up small fish thrown on the water to attract large fish" (Munro 1960, 64). The *noio* thus also stands in metonymic relation to man.

3. Two birds are symbolically marked as migrators. One, *kōlea*, comes from Kahiki to Hawaii during the winter period, coinciding with the return of the god Lonomakua. The other, *nēnē*, joins by its migrations the highlands and the coast, where it stays during the winter. Malo writes that the *nēnē* "differs from all other birds" (1957, 37), without, however, explaining why.

4. The status of two other birds is not clear. The *'amakihi* seems to be distinguished by its very strong odor, which makes it unique among birds (Munro 1960, 103). All we know of the *'ua'u* is that "the young birds were considered a delicacy, *kapu* to the common people and reserved for the chiefs" (Munro 1960, 26). That they are eaten by ali'i implies that they are not their *'aumakua*, since it is forbidden to eat the animal in which one's own *'aumakua* manifests itself. Perhaps the inclusion of this bird in the list of manifestations of the *'aumakua* is due to a confusion. It is a taboo animal because it is reserved for the ali'i, not because it is an *'aumakua*.

The *noio* and *'elepaio* birds are connected with transitions: the *'elepaio* with a temporal one (from night to day), the *noio* with a spatial one (the coastline, which mediates land and ocean). The two migratory birds, *kōlea* and *nēnē*, are similar to the *noio* in that they mediate dynamically (in time) the two domains (land and ocean) that the *noio* mediates statically.

Therefore we can group all these birds with other species that have a mediating value. As such, they are capable of representing human ancestors. Their associations are primarily positive, as is shown by the facts that the *kōlea* bird is also a manifestation of Kāne in his role as god of medicine (Ii 1963, 84) and that the *kōlea* as well as the *nēnē* are visible during the New Year's festival, which has a positive connotation because it excludes war and violence.

As for the *'elepaio*, it is perhaps the friendliest of birds, since it spontaneously seeks out the company of men. Not all birds are seen as favorable, however, since two of the principal *'aumakua* are birds that are considered potentially dangerous (*'alae* and owl).

Plants and Other Phenomena

Plants make up the most puzzling part of the *'aumakua* list given by Kihe. Some of the species listed (*lama*, *'ōhi'a-lehua*, *koa*, *kauila*) provide the wood in which the anthropomorphic images of the *'aumakua* are carved.

Since the word 'aumakua also refers to the carved images of these deities, it is possible that when Kihe says these are 'aumakua trees, he means that they are appropriate for carving 'aumakua images.

Alternatively, it may be that they are believed to embody the ancestral deities of a professional group, the image carvers, whom they provide with the substance of their activity and also with a natural sign for it.

Analogously, it is likely that many plants renowned for their medicinal virtues (kākalaoia, 'āheahea, alani, pilo, ipu 'awa'awa; cf. Neal 1965, 433, 331, 368) incorporate the professional 'aumakua of healers (cf. Emerson 1892, 15).

Some plants included in Kihe's list (koa, manono, kōpilo, alani) are used in the construction of canoes. Perhaps, as natural correlatives of the canoe builders, they are conceived as manifestations of their 'aumakua.

In sum, most plants in the 'aumakua list may be manifestations of professional 'aumakua, that is, of ancestors who personify certain specialized activities for a given kin-based group.

Some fish and birds may also be professional 'aumakua. Thus the i'iwi, 'ō'ū, 'ā'ā (male of the 'ō'ō), and nēnē "Hawaiian goose" (Malo 1951, 37), which furnish precious feathers, seem to be the 'aumakua of the birdmen who despoil them of their plumage (cf. "bird-catching prayer"—HEN, 1:481; Emerson 1892, 17).

The aku, "bonito, skipjack" and 'ōpelu, "mackerel scad," are considered the 'aumakua of the descendants of the priest Pā'ao (see Titcomb and Pukui 1972, 36–37, 61; NK, 2:123). Insofar as these descendants are themselves priests who officiate in the annual rituals for fishing for these two species, the latter may be considered "professional" 'aumakua. Note also that the aku fish helped Pā'ao in his voyage from Kahiki to Hawaii: it may thus be considered a protective 'aumakua by his descendants (Kamakau 1866; Emerson 1892, 9).

Many other substances or natural phenomena that are considered 'aumakua by Kihe and Lilinoe may also be "professional." Thus feces and urine are the manifestations of the professional 'aumakua of those who use them to cure madness and chronic pain (Emerson 1892, 15; cf. NK, 1: 181–82).

Meteoric phenomena and celestial bodies found in the lists may be viewed as the 'aumakua of the diviners who read omens in them (cf. Emerson 1892, 15; Fornander 1916–20, 6:52–55, 84–87, 98–100, 106).

Volcanic phenomena and phenomena—such as thunder and lightning—that have analogic relationships with them are considered the embodiment of an important class of 'aumakua, presided over by the goddess Pele and the members of her family (Handy and Pukui 1972, 29–31; Kaaie 1862; Kihe, n.d.). By throwing the bones of one's dead into a crater

(Kamakau 1964, 64–65) one acquires '*aumakua* whose "bodies" are volcanic phenomena. In this way one hopes to neutralize their danger. At any rate, one can attribute the devastation provoked by eruptions to the anger of the ancestors: "When the spirits are angry, they appease their anger and chagrin (*lili*) by ruining the land and causing death to man" (ibid., 66).

Finally it must be mentioned that according to Kihe all domestic animals—chicken, dog, pig—can be considered manifestations of some '*aumakua* (for the chicken see Golovnin 1979, 179). The pig, together with the marine and plant species associated with it, is said by Kihe to be an '*aumakua* of farmers. The reason seems similar to that which makes the field mouse a favorite '*aumakua* of farmers: pigs are a constant threat to gardens (cf. Emerson 1892, 13).

Having thus considered all the known manifestations of the '*aumakua*, what can we conclude about our initial hypothesis concerning the relation between this class of deities and their natural manifestations?

The hypothesis, recall, stated that the '*aumakua* tended to be associated with species that are dangerous or mediating or both. In some species the mediating value took the form of taxonomic anomaly. The extended list of manifestations of the '*aumakua* seems to confirm this hypothesis. Most fish are both anomalous and dangerous; birds are mostly mediating and sometimes anomalous. Volcanic phenomena are dangerous, and domestic animals are mediating and sometimes dangerous (cf. the pig).

The list, however, also shows that some '*aumakua* manifest themselves in species or other natural phenomena that are neither dangerous nor mediating but instead are the objective correlatives of "professional" activities such as medicine, canoe building, bird catching, or priestcraft. These professional '*aumakua* embody the concept of the activity that they also make possible on the material plane. The activity is associated with the ancestors from whom it has been learned. Hence the professional '*aumakua* are ancestral deities like the nonprofessional ones. The only difference is that the species connected with the latter are not usually appropriated; those connected with the former are used, but they require firstfruit sacrifices and other propitiatory rituals (see chap. 2).

To conclude this analysis of the natural manifestations of '*aumakua*, two observations are in order. It is likely that since the cult of the '*aumakua* survived the abolition of the traditional, official religion, this notion was used increasingly to describe the deities of the past and their natural manifestations even when they did not traditionally belong to the '*aumakua* class. Thus the late compilations of '*aumakua* manifestations probably contain phenomena that were not traditionally associated with this class of deities. It is also likely that the list of '*aumakua* species cannot be exhaustively analyzed in structural terms, since the choice of a species might depend on random or highly contextual factors unknown to us. My analysis must therefore be considered conjectural, as I have warned several times.[28]

The *Akua 'Unihipili*

We have seen that the *'aumakua* are formed from the dead, that above all they are human ancestors. *'Aumakua* worship, however, differs from a classic ancestral cult in that these deities have lost their original human identity. The proper name given to an *'aumakua* is not that of the ancestor from which it is originally formed. In fact, it is not even a human name (NK, 1:41, 2:294).[29] This peculiarity and the links connecting various individual *'aumakua* to a single natural species effectively make these deities much less individualized than true ancestors. In contrast, the *akua 'unihipili* are dead who have preserved their names and individuality because they have been attached to some residue of their body (bone, hair, etc.) instead of being completely incorporated into an animal or a plant or some other natural phenomenon, and because they continue to be "fed" as if they were still alive and part of the family.[30]

The difference between the vessels of the two types of deities correlates with a difference in their moral status. Attached to natural phenomena extraneous to man, the *'aumakua* are more transcendent and less controllable than the *'unihipili*, which are attached to human remains preserved by the worshipers. While the *'aumakua*, overtly at least, do not depend on man for their existence (on the contrary, man depends on them), the existence of the *'unihipili* depends entirely on the men who "feed" them. The only way to control the *'aumakua* is to propitiate them by acting in agreement with the moral rules they personify and sanction; on the contrary, the *'unihipili*, being totally dependent on the individual who maintains them in existence and inseparable from him, are the reifications of his individual and even antisocial ends or those of his customers (cf. Emerson 1892, 4–5).[31]

The amoral, or even antimoral, character of the *'unihipili* explains why these deities are often formed from the corpses of newborn infants, who are not yet integrated into society, or of aborted fetuses, especially those that are monstrous. Natural monstrosity here becomes the metaphor for an irregular power used for ends that from a moral standpoint are themselves monstrous (Emerson 1892, 3).

In short, an *akua 'unihipili* exists as a function of the individual's desire, which feeds it metaphorically and literally. The moment this desire ceases to nourish it, the *'unihipili* leaves its material embodiment and dissolves into Pō, the undifferentiated divine world (NK, 1:196).

The Notion of *Akua*: Preliminary Conclusions

The facts given above are sufficient to draw some preliminary conclusions on the Hawaiian notion of *akua*, "divine," "deity." This notion is clearly characterized by two dualities. The divine manifests itself in both natural and human forms and is associated with both morally normal and morally anomalous actions. The significations of these dualities will become fully apparent only in the course of my study, but it is possible to anticipate here some of its main aspects, especially as they are revealed or illustrated by the facts considered so far.

Let us begin with the first duality. As we have seen, deities are characterized by two kinds of "bodies," that is, concrete manifestations: natural bodies and the human body. This opposition, then, is also the opposition of the many and the one: it signifies that the human species is the common element underlying all natural manifestations of the divine.

Thus all nature has a human dimension, which is manifested by the fact that all gods equally represent the human species. But each god is also particularized by his connection with specific natural phenomena or groups of phenomena. These signify only some predicate or predicates of the human species. Through a deity, then, a certain set of predicates of action, signified by natural species or phenomena, is inscribed in the general representation of the human species.

The relationship between the natural bodies of the god and the human predicates he typifies is a sign relationship. The natural objects signify those predicates because of metaphorical or metonymic connections with them. An example of metaphorical connection is the one between everything straight in nature and the properties of the human male typified by Kū. An example of metonymic connection is the one between the trees used for making canoes and the predicates of canoe making, typified by certain 'aumakua. Also metonymic is the connection between the bird species that give precious feathers and the predicates of bird snaring, that is to say, the type of the birdman as represented by certain 'aumakua or by a particularization of the god Kū.

In sum, the natural substance or analogue of a human activity—and therefore of certain types of subjects—evokes it. This is precisely why certain species come to be considered the natural manifestations of the deity that embodies the type of a human activity.

Being types, deities must stand to the concrete entities that instantiate them as types stand to their tokens (cf. Lyons 1977, 1 : 13). Traditionally, a type is defined as a "représentation schématique où s'exprime l'essence d'une chose" (Lalande 1960, 1155; cf. Foulquié and Saint-Jean 1969, 242–43). As scheme or form a type is also considered, ever since Plato, as a model (cf. Abbagnano 1961, 853) or "a perfect or universal example or ἰδέα, to which particular instances more or less fully approximate" (Baldwin 1940, 2:721). In other words, the deity is also a paragon (cf. Tyler 1978, 275–76) for empirical actions and subjects. Thus the apprehension of the concept embodied by the deity makes it possible to give value and signification to concrete subjects acting in certain ways in certain contexts. This constitutes them as social, cultural realities. In this sense the type is a model "for" simply by virtue of being a model "of"; it is productive because it is representative. It creates a subject acting in a social context because what it represents cannot exist without the act that represents it.

The experience of the social creativity of these concepts and of the power of the collective judgments and reactions based on them is the basis for the attribution of power to them—for the belief in the divine power.

Although the gods are conceived as entities and persons rather than as concepts, they retain a fundamental feature of the concept: nonempirical, transcendental reality. Thus, in principle, they cannot be confused with those among their instantiations (such as images, certain humans, or other living beings) that are supposed to *empirically* manifest the god's properties to the highest possible degree. In practice, however, Hawaiians could subscribe to this statement by a linguist: "It makes little difference whether we think of the type as an abstract concept having no concrete manifestations except in its tokens or whether we look at the type simply as an elevated concrete token" (Tyler 1978, 279).

Indeed I have shown that the terms *akua* and '*aumakua* are used to refer to both the conceptual and the material aspects of the god, to both the invisible type and its visible manifestations in images, human bodies, and natural bodies. The reason for this lack of a sharp differentiation between the conceptual type and its most elevated tokens is that religious thought is concrete and cannot conceive abstract being except in terms of concrete being.

Thus the gods have a somewhat contradictory status in that they are on the one hand concrete and on the other abstract; they exist in particulars and at the same time are distinguished from them.[32]

The ideas of deity and type seem to be explicitly connected in Hawaiian thought, since one of the most frequent predicates of deities is *kumu*, which means, among other things, "model, pattern." Because this model is recognized to be productive, *kumu* also means "reason, cause," "beginning, source, origin," as well as "base, foundation, basis" (PE, 167). Gods are said to be *kumupa'a* (from *kumu* and *pa'a*) "fixed origin," "fixed model," "fixed foundations" of the domains they typify (cf. HEN, 1:705). This explains why *kumupa'a* is often used as a synonym for '*aumakua* (PE, 168).

Kamakau seems to connect the gods' "guiding" function (which results from their typicality) with their life-giving function, as witnessed by this text: "The god was the guide to all things, the giver of boundless life; therefore every person who was learning the arts depended upon the god" (1964, 107). Indeed, the god produces life because as a type he constitutes and guides human action.

To recapitulate: All deities personify collectively recognized types of action and, as will appear more and more in the course of this book, the efficacy of the collective evaluations and reactions made possible by those types.

But human activity can be either morally positive or morally negative: accordingly, there are types of "normal" and types of "anomalous" action. This brings us to the second duality manifested by the divine.

Positive gods personify types of morally approved actions and the efficacy of the community's positive reactions to the concrete subjects who are their tokens.

In contrast, negative gods, such as sorcery gods, personify types of morally reprehensible actions to which the community lends efficacy by its reactions of revulsion and fear (cf. Durkheim 1912, 584–92). In other words, the community empowers the subject to act positively or negatively toward it, and insofar as it recognizes that his actions affect it, they do affect it.

The two classes of deities are hierarchically related, and this hierarchy is expressed by the identification of the morally inferior deities with the impure and the morally superior ones with the pure. As I shall show later (chap. 3), "purity" indicates "completeness," "impurity," "lack of completeness." Thus a god who is impure personifies an action that is incomplete from the moral point of view. In other words, an action that contrasts the subject to the community is polluting for him, because his action can be complete only in the community. Moreover, it also creates a lack in the community, which is precisely expressed by the impure person's power over the community. In sum, the subject's positive or negative efficacy on the community shows that he can never escape it, that he is destined to be pure with it or impure with it.

Being the types of morally anomalous and dangerous actions that produce death rather than life, the 'unihipili and similar sorcery gods are signified by anomalous and dangerous natural phenomena, such as aborted, especially monstrous, human fetuses, parts of any corpse, and so on.

However, anomalous and dangerous phenomena are by no means associated with sorcery gods alone. Indeed, I have shown that they are often the "bodies" of 'aumakua and have attempted to explain why. Some of the reasons given also explain why anomalous or simply dangerous phenomena are also associated with the great, "pure" gods. For instance, these phenomena may be a means of implementing, by means of fear and the interpretation of misfortune, the morally "normal" types personified by these gods. Moreover, the association of what is anomalous and dangerous in nature with the gods of "normal" action may be due to the hope of controlling those disquieting phenomena by acting morally.

Anomaly may also signify, for all deities, "transcendence," because an anomalous or simply bizarre thing is a "thing out of this world," is a kind of empirical equivalent of transcendence and therefore evokes it.

Another signification of anomaly is mediation. This signification derives from the fact that an anomalous phenomenon violates the boundary between classes or domains that are normally separate. Thus anomalous phenomena are often associated with deities in order to make possible the connection between deities and men. Indeed, as we shall see in chapters 2 and 4, many of the anomalous bodies of the deities are prescribed as offerings in the sacrifices consecrated to them.

Anomalous species may also index an intermediate position in the pantheon. This is perhaps one of the reasons so many of the 'aumakua—who are intermediate between great gods and men—manifest themselves in anomalous species or anomalous individuals.[33]

In sum, the divine manifests itself in both "regular" and "irregular" phenomena. Moreover, this duality corresponds in part to the duality of beneficent and maleficent. Hence the ambivalence of the divine, which is found at all levels of the pantheon. However, in the great gods the anomalous and maleficent manifestations are subordinated to the normal and beneficent ones: in fact the former are some of the means by which the latter are implemented. In the sorcery gods, in contrast, the anomalous and maleficent manifestations predominate or are the only ones.

We may well ask ourselves at this point why Hawaiians see the concepts of their species properties reflected in natural species—indeed, blended with them, since the semiotic relationship between natural and human properties is not recognized. The obvious reason is that the subject experiences his properties in the act by which he appropriates—intellectually and practically—the objects of nature. Therefore the properties of his subjectivity are experienced as part of the properties of the objects, at least to some extent. It is this spontaneous process of consciousness that humanizes nature, not, as in the "intellectualist" theory of religion, the analogic projection of a preexisting knowledge of the self onto nature in order to explain the latter by the former.[34] In fact, this analogic extension presupposes the process of consciousness I am referring to, since it presupposes that the world of nature and the world of man are comparable and therefore that nature is already humanized and man already naturalized. Moreover, it should be obvious since Hegel if not since Vico that the subject is not capable of knowing himself in a Cartesian way, that is, independent of his knowledge of objects and before it.

The intellectualist identification of religion with a primitive form of natural science is at any rate not applicable to the Hawaiian pantheon: indeed, I have shown that grouping natural species under each god actually violates the Hawaiian taxonomy of these species. This indicates that religious thought has properties and motivations other than the taxonomic knowledge of nature. Far from being based on an analogic transfer from the human to the nonhuman, taxonomic knowledge deemphasizes the human element spontaneously projected onto the individual species: in other words, it deemphasizes its sign function. In contrast, religious representations reinforce this sign function—make more evident the human content of the natural species. This is precisely why species having the same or related signifieds can be grouped together under one god.

As we shall see, the reinforcing of the sign function of natural species occurs mostly on ritual occasions, that is, in the course of events where the human signifieds of those species are emphasized in order to induce certain mental states in those who participate in the ritual.

It is thus clear that a purely intellectualistic approach to Hawaiian religion is insufficient, since this religion is no protoscience and no theology pure and simple either. Its representations are inseparable from the ritual praxis that reproduces them and makes them *believable* by providing contexts in which the concrete subjects can *experience* their truth. To fully understand the Hawaiian religious notions, it is therefore necessary to turn our attention to ritual.

But before we do this, we must dwell for a moment on a point repeatedly made in this chapter. The unity of the divine is the unity of the human species. This unity is represented not by a supreme god, but simply by the body that is common to all deities: the human body. In a sense, what is *Kwoth* for the Nuer is the divinized image of the human body for the Hawaiians.

However, I have already mentioned that Kū can function as the most encompassing male god. This is confirmed by the great *luakini* temple ritual, in which Kū comes close to personifying all the attributes of the human species. Another god, Lono, acquires the same signification during the New Year festival, as we shall see. But these gods are never alone: they represent unity precisely where multiplicity is most displayed. The closest approximation to a generalized notion of the divine is Pō, since it is ultimately defined as "the realm of the gods; pertaining to or of the gods" (PE, 307). As "night" or "darkness," Pō is also a metaphor of the divine as "unseen" (Handy and Pukui 1972, 131) and therefore as formless and transcendent from the point of view of empirical knowledge. But transcendence of perceived form also evokes the potentiality of any form and transformation and therefore divine creativity in its most generalized state. Thus ultimately in the Pō metaphor the generic and the genetic coincide: Pō is the origin of the cosmos and at the same time a metaphor of the divine in general. Moreover, since Pō has spatial correlates, space and time also become one in it. Indeed Pō is conceived as both the divine past of the world and the invisible world inhabited by the gods, synchronically coexisting with the world of humans (NK 1:35, 40, 136–37; Beckwith 1951, 48).

To conclude this chapter, let me stress that the highly systematic nature of the Hawaiian pantheon should not be surprising given the existence of a powerful class of priests, that is, of professional intellectuals. This systemic, priestly view of the pantheon is undoubtedly the most prominent in the available documents. But deities are also created spontaneously and unsystematically at the lower levels of the pantheon, where their proliferation is allowed by the very system I have delineated. Spontaneous creation and systemic ordering are thus two dialectical moments in the constitution of the divine in this hierarchical society.

2

THE ELEMENTS OF SACRIFICE

Ἔπειτα αἱ μὲν χωρὶς θυσιῶν εὐχαὶ λόγοι μόνον εἰσίν, αἱ δὲ μετὰ
θυσιῶν ἔμψυχοι λόγοι, τοῦ μὲν λόγου τὴν ζωὴν δυναμοῦντος τῆς δὲ
ζωῆς τὸν λόγον ψυχούσης.
Sallustius, Περὶ Θεῶν καὶ Κόσμου 16.1

L'animal meurt. Mais la mort de l'animal est le devenir de la conscience.
Hegel, quoted in Bataille 1955, 21

On choisissait dans l'espèce animale les victimes les plus *humaines*, s'il est
permis de s'exprimer ainsi.
de Maistre 1884a, 5 : 302

Unum pro multibus dabitur caput.
Virgil, *Aeneid* 5.815

Preliminary Definition

Having treated the deities and their manifestations, we may now examine
their role in ritual. The most important, most frequently used Hawaiian
ritual is sacrifice. By "sacrifice" I mean any ritual action that includes the
consecration of an "offering" to a deity. This offering is made up of one or
more individuals belonging to species having symbolic values exploited in
the course of the ritual. In addition to this principal component, always
made up of living and edible beings, the offering may consist of inanimate
objects such as bark cloths.

Every sacrifice implies a subject, individual or collective, who performs
it or on whose behalf it is performed. Following a usage introduced by
Hubert and Mauss (1899), I call this subject the "sacrifier." Sometimes the
sacrifier employs a ritual specialist to perform the sacrifice for him. Again
following Hubert and Mauss I call this specialist the "sacrificer" (the English word that comes closest to the French *sacrificateur*).

Usually the offering, after having been entirely consecrated to the deity, is divided in two parts: the first goes to the deity alone, the second goes to the sacrifier and the other participants, among whom it is shared according to the order of their rank.

In short, the term "sacrifice" designates a complex ritual action, during which an offering made up of animal, vegetable, or artificial components having symbolic values is consecrated to one or several deities, on certain occasions and with certain ends in view. Thus every sacrifice must be described as a function of the following features: (1) its end and the occasion on which it is made; (2) the deity or deities to whom it is addressed; (3) the content of the offering and its symbolic value; (4) the way the offering is treated and apportioned in the rite.

The ends and occasions of sacrifices, as well as the offerings' symbolic values and treatment, will receive particular emphasis as the features that best make it possible to discover the fundamental principles of sacrificial action.

Classification of Sacrifices according to Their End or the Occasion on Which They Are Made

Sacrifices are prescribed for certain occasions or are necessary to realize certain ends and may be classified accordingly. The following are the main classes resulting from the use of these two criteria.

Life Cycle

The principal stages of life marked by sacrificial rites are birth, especially of the first child (*'aha 'aina māwaewae*); a boy's entry into the men's house (*ua kā i ka mua*); incision of the penis (*kahe ule*); betrothal; marriage;[1] and death (Malo 1951, 87–95, 136–38; Kamakau 1964, 27, 33, 41, 34, 39; Kamakau 1961, 212; Kepelino 1932, 20–21; Green and Beckwith 1924; Handy and Pukui 1972, 80–86, 94–98, 105–12, 152–57; NK, 1:183, 136, 137, 175, 2:19 ff.; MH, October 1823, 317; Fornander 1916–20, 5:572; Tyerman and Bennett 1832, 2:16). Commemorative funeral sacrifices (Whitman 1979, 69; MH, May 1821, August 1824, 246; Handy and Pukui 1972, 157 ff.) and sacrifices to transform the dead into *'aumakua* deities (*kākū'ai* rites) (Kamakau 1964, 64, 66, 85–86; NK, 1:115–16, 36–37; Malo 1951, 106) can also be considered part of the "life cycle."

These rites of passage are performed for all individuals, but their complexity varies as a function of the sacrifier's rank (Malo 1951, 84, 94). Rites made for ali'i of very high rank and particularly for the crown prince take place in state temples (K. Kamakau 1919–20, 2–7). Rites involving people of less importance are performed in domestic temples or simply in the domestic compound.

Rites of passage appropriate only for ali'i also exist—rites of installation held when a noble takes on prerogatives or titles (kapu). The sacrifice consecrated by the high priest to purify the crown prince after the death of the king belongs in this category (Kamakau 1961, 212–13). This rite constitutes the first stage of the process of succession to kingly office.

Activities and Work

Every important activity demands sacrifices of commencement (ho'okua-kāhi—NK, 2:130) for the action about to begin and sacrifices of closure; the latter may also serve as inaugural sacrifices for the object made or for a professional career. Sacrifices may even mark intermediary stages. The following are the most important of the activities marked by sacrifices.

Apprenticeship

Instruction in dance (hula) begins and ends with sacrificial feasts. In addition, fresh offerings are placed on the altar of the dance deities during the entire training period (Pukui in Barrère, Pukui, and Kelly 1980, 70–93; Emerson 1965, 23). The final sacrifice, marking the completion of the pupils' initiation, is called 'ailolo, "to eat the brain," for the initiates eat a part of the sacrificial animal's brain (Emerson 1965, 34–35). This is done because the brain, as part of the head, connotes the beginning of the initiate's performing career.

Rites with a similar form although differing in content mark the stages of instruction in other arts (cf. PE, 10, 194), such as sorcery (Kamakau 1964, 120–21; Kepelino 1977, 54–55), wrestling, spear dodging (Ii 1963, 9–10), bone breaking (lua) (Kaula 1865, Kepelino 1977, 67 n.22), and so forth.

Manufacture and Inauguration of Artifacts

Each stage of house construction is accompanied by rites, some of which include sacrifices; the most important sacrifice occurs when the house is inaugurated (Malo 1951, 121; Kamakau 1976, 106–8; Handy and Pukui 1972, 113–15). Sacrificial rites play an even greater role in the construction of canoes. First, a sacrifice precedes the felling of the tree out of which the canoe will be dug. This is followed by sacrifices marking each important step of the construction. The inauguration of the canoe is accompanied by a sacrifice, once again called 'ailolo, although instead of the brain other parts of the victim's head may be eaten (PE, 194; Malo 1951, 127–29; Kamakau 1976, 119–22; HEN, 1:1621; Whitman 1979, 52; NK, 2:131–33; Pukui 1939).

Inaugural sacrifices are also performed for fishnets and lines (Fornander 1916–20, 6:120–21; Kamakau 1976, 61). Any important collective work, such as the construction of fishponds, irrigation ditches and dams, or irrigated taro fields, includes sacrificial feasts culminating in the inauguration (Handy and Pukui 1972, 103; Nakuina 1894, 84). The sacrifice to inaugurate an irrigation ditch also belongs to the '*ailolo* category (Nakuina 1894, 84).

Agricultural Work

The cultivation of the two basic food plants, taro and sweet potato, is punctuated by rites, most including sacrifices (Kamakau 1976, 34–37, 29–30).[2]

Fishing

Most sacrifices associated with fishing consist of offerings of the first catch. I will discuss these at the appropriate time. Seasonal rites for the '*ōpelu* fish and the *aku* fish also include inaugural sacrifices, which have a propitiatory value as well (see K. Kamakau 1919–20, 30–35).

War and Peace

Sacrificial rites connected with war are highly developed and possess multiple functions and meanings, which I will discuss later. Suffice it to say here that sacrificial rites take place in the state temple (*luakini*) before war, then on the battlefield, and finally once again in the state temple after the war or battle has been concluded (see Ellis 1842, 148, 161; Malo 38.14; Menzies 1920, 93; Valeri 1982a, 1984). There is also a sacrificial rite for restoring peace between two kings (Ellis 1842, 161–62).

Dance

Every performance of a dance requires a sacrifice identical to the one made on the occasion of the dancers' initiation (see Barrère, Pukui, and Kelly 1980, 64; MH, July 1822, 207).

Beginning and End of a Voyage

The beginning and end of a voyage are marked by sacrifices (PE, 194; Handy and Pukui 1972, 104–5). The sacrifice made at the beginning belongs to the '*ailolo* category (PE, 194).

Sacrifices of Expiation and Purification

In the words of Hubert and Mauss, "Il n'y a pas de sacrifice où n'intervienne quelque idée de rachat" (1899, 1:304; cf. Hertz 1922). In fact, expiation is an important dimension in almost every Hawaiian sacrificial rite (cf., for example, Kamakau 1976, 138–39). But there exist sacrifices whose specific end is the expiation of ritual faults, or the infraction of a vow, or the violation of kinship morality. These transgressions (*hewa*, *hala*)[3] produce a state of sin, represented metaphorically as a cord binding

The Elements of Sacrifice   41

the offender to the offended. In addition, "as others are inevitably drawn into the conflict, the cord of *hala* is visualized as a network of ever-spreading unpleasantness called *hihia*" (NK, 1:71; cf. NK, 2:229). *Hihia* thus indicates a state of "entanglement" or confusion in which the transgressor and his entire social network are embroiled. For this reason it is necessary to "untangle" (*kala, huikala*) them by rites of expiation (NK, 1:72, 74–75, 2:172). For convenience I translate *huikala* as "purification," but the metaphors the Hawaiians use would lead me instead to translate it as "disentangling" or better yet, as the French *dénouement*, where both senses of the Hawaiian word—a literal untying as well as the "unraveling" of an action—occur.

When sickness is attributed to divine sanction of a transgression, the *huikala* rite can also function as a healing rite, for purification is supposed to end the sickness (Kamakau 1964, 32, 95, 97; Handy and Pukui 1972, 142–43, 122; Malo 1951, 95–96, 108, 112–13). In no case is it sufficient for the individual merely to ask pardon from the one he has offended; a sacrifice to their common deity or deities is required (NK, 1: 186; cf. Handy and Pukui 1972, 49–50; Kamakau 1964, 85). With the deity's acceptance of the offering the disorder comes to an end (Kamakau 1961, 186; Kamakau 1964, 29, 30; Kauhane 1865). Yet, since this sacrificial rite is also a rite of communion among all members of the social network in which offender and offended alike participate, the deity's acceptance is inseparable from that of the community (see the texts of Malo, Kamakau, and Handy and Pukui cited above; see also Kamakau 1964, 114–15, 130, cf. 13; Handy and Pukui 1972, 50; NK, 2:230).

Propitiatory Sacrifices

While expiatory sacrifices are directed toward ending a present state of disorder attributed to an offense, propitiatory sacrifices are meant to avert potential disorder or favor the realization of a project or a desired state. Thus, propitiatory sacrifices "*e maliu mai ai ke 'kua*" (Fornander 1916–20, 5:598),[4] "to make the deity favorable," can have any of the following purposes: to assure the "life of the body" (Kamakau 1865), to secure the fertility of the fields (Kaawa 1865b; Kamakau 1976, 37), to avoid famine (Kepelino 1932, 18; cf. NK, 1:6; Kamakau 1976, 37), to obtain rain (Malo 38.18), to increase the number of fish and guarantee the success of fishing activities (*ho'oūlu i'a* rites) (Emerson in Malo 1951, 157–59; Kamakau 1976, 4–9, 82–83; Ii 1963, 26; Fornander 1916–20, 5:511; cf. article in *Ka Hae Hawaii* 1861, translated in HEN, 1:371), to prevent shark bites (Kamakau 1964, 74–75; HEN, 1:588), to prevent volcanic eruptions (Whitman 1979, 64; Jarves 1843, 29; Kamakau 1964, 66–67; Kamakau 1961, 184–86), to win a battle (Kaawa 1865b; Malo 1951, 197), to obtain children (Kamakau 1964, 99–100; Westervelt 1915a, 39), to cure a disease (Ii 1963, 46; Kamakau 1976, 43; NK, 2:156, etc.), and to make possible the appropriation of certain natural species that belong to a deity and in which the deity manifests himself (as in birds with precious plumage, for example—see HEN, 1:118). This list could be continued. It should be obvious, moreover, that many of the sacrifices I have examined under other headings may also be considered propitiatory.

Sacrifices in Rites of Sorcery

Sacrifices are included in sorcery rituals of both offensive (*'anā'anā*) and defensive types (*kuni*) (Malo 1951, 100–103; Whitman 1979, 25, 29, 30; Kamakau 1964, 132, 135–36, 125). Sacrifices in this class are similar in purpose to those of the two preceding classes, since like them they are intended to eliminate evil or produce good in the sacrifier. However, they differ from both expiatory and propitiatory sacrifices because the deities they engage personify amoral actions and aims.

Nevertheless, the contrast of sorcery rites and other sacrifices should not be exaggerated. For one thing, it is likely that when the sorcerer or his client has been in some way harmed by his intended victim, the latter's unconscious feelings of guilt contribute to making the rite effective.[5] From this point of view sorcery may have a moral function.

Note also that ali'i use sorcery (or the fear thereof) to check would-be rebels or transgressors (cf. Whitman 1979, 27; Corney 1896, 104; Kamakau 1961, 179; Malo 1951, 100; Ii 1963, 123).

Divinatory Sacrifices

Every sacrifice involves a divinatory component, since the participants believe they are observing signs of the outcome of the sacrifice in such phenomena as the victim's state, atmospheric conditions during the ritual, or the appearance of certain animals. For example, the sources contain details about signs that reveal the issue of the following sacrifices: *mōhai kala hewa*, "sacrifice for the pardoning of a sin" (NK, 2:246), *kakū'ai* sacrifice (cf. Kamakau 1964, 64), the sacrifice for obtaining the proprietary god's permission to fell a tree needed to build a canoe (Whitman 1979, 52), or the sacrifice made to the feather gods (Kamakau 1964, 12; cf. HEN, 1:749).

Sacrifices that are truly divinatory also exist, especially those made before war (Ellis 1842, 150–51; Kalakaua 1888, 294) or to establish the identity of the sorcerer responsible for disease or death (Malo 1951, 100).[6]

Firstfruits Sacrifices

Sacrifice of the firstfruits is extremely important: "The first fruits were sacred to the gods. The first-born children, animals, the first fruits of the land, the first fish caught, the first product of any labor was sacred to the gods. This was an old practice" (Kamakau 1961, 190–91; cf. Malo 1951, 190).

Let us examine the most important areas in which these sacrifices are made.

Agriculture

As Kamakau writes, "Always the first food of the harvest was offered to the gods" (1961, 237).[7] When the crops reach maturity, the farmer and his family prepare a celebration. The sacrificial fire is lit during the period of the month consecrated to the god worshiped by the farmer, either Kū, Lono, Kāne, or Kanaloa. After the firstfruits (*kāmauli hou*) are consecrated to the deity, each participant eats his share of the first oven of food. "After this ceremony of fire-lighting the man's farm was *noa* ['free'] and he might help himself to the food at any time without again kindling a fire. But every time the farmer cooked an oven of food, he offered to the deity a potato or a *taro* before eating of it, laying it on the altar or putting it on a tree" (Malo 1951, 207; cf. Kamakau 1976, 30–31, 36–37).[8] Thus, in addition to the firstfruits of the harvest the first portion of each meal is offered to the deity. This is the daily form of the cult (Handy and Pukui 1972, 96, 9). For each farmer the time of his harvest determines the time of the firstfruits sacrifice, but the community as a whole offers annual firstfruit sacrifices on the occasion of the New Year (kapu Makahiki). I shall return to these rites later. Another collective sacrifice of firstfruits also takes place anytime a new harvest brings an end to a period of famine (Ii 1963, 77; cf. Anonymous 1927, 77).

Fishing

Collective seasonal fishing sacrifices are a royal duty and will be examined further on. They involve *aku* and *'ōpelu* fishes in particular (Ellis 1842, 117; K. Kamakau 1919–20, 30–35; Malo 1951, 208–10; Whitman 1979, 75–76). The *'o'opu* (*Eleutheris fusca*—Fornander 1916–20, 5:510–14) and the *kala* (Acanthuridae—Kamakau 1976, 84–85) are also the objects of complex collective rituals, but these are not attached to the ritual calendar of the whole society.

Each fishing expedition is followed by the consecration of the first fish of the catch to the deities presiding over this activity, whose "bodies" are the fish caught. The most important fishing deities are Kū, in his particularization Kū'ula, and his wife Hinahele (Kamakau 1976, 61; Ellis 1842, 117; Ii 1963, 24, 26, 46; Fornander 1916–20, 4:490, 494). Only these sacrifices can legitimate human consumption of fish (Kamakau 1976, 78, 64, 73–74).

Sacrifice of the First Result of Generative Activities and Labor

The firstborn (*hiapo*) is consecrated to the deities at birth (Handy and Pukui 1972, 80). This is especially true among the nobility: "Chiefs gave (*ha'awi*) their children to the gods" (Kamakau 1964, 64).[9] This consecration can be assimilated to a sacrifice of the firstfruits of generative activity. This activity is made possible by the deities, and therefore its products belong to them. However, in this area as in the others, the consecration of the firstfruits "frees" the remaining ones. Thus, by consecrating the firstborn one "clears the way" (*māwaewae*) for the younger siblings (Handy and Pukui 1972, 80). Naturally the firstborn is not sacrificed to the deity in person, but only through a substitute, a pig. Perhaps this pig was called *mōhai pāna'i*, "substitute offering"—that is, an offering given instead of a human victim—in the *māwaewae* rite, as it was in the rite that incorporated the male child into the *hale mua* (the men's house; Malo 1951, 87).

Just as the firstborn is consecrated to the deities, so is the first artifact that has been manufactured. In fact, as the eldest child becomes the guarantor of the existence of his younger siblings, the first object produced is the guarantee of all those that follow it.[10]

Obviously the rites consecrating the first products of labor, like those for a firstborn at the moment of birth, are also rites of passage and inauguration.

First Victims of War

The consecration of the first three victims of a battle (Ellis 1842, 159) can be considered the sacrifice of the firstfruits of war (cf. Fornander 1878–80, 1:241; Kamakau 1961, 136; Handy 1972, 189).

Prestations to the Ali'i and the Gods

According to the sources, firstfruits are also given to the ali'i (Kamakau 1961, 314–15; Ellis 1842, 417; Whitman 1979, 76).[11] These payments, called *ho'okupu*, traditionally did not differ from seasonal oblations (called *ho'okupu* as well) made to the deities. In reality, as we shall see, one gives to the ali'i so that they in turn may give in sacrifice to the supreme gods.[12] Thus, *ho'okupu* eventually become *mōhai*, "sacrifices," and in fact Kepelino includes the former category in the latter (1932, 151). Moreover, as we shall see, the ali'i themselves can be considered deities and as such prestations made to them can be viewed as sacrificial oblations. But in principle the ali'i cannot appropriate any part of the offering if they do not consecrate some of it to their gods (see below). However, toward the end of the Old Regime the aristocracy gave an increasingly secular turn to *ho'okupu* payments, until finally this term came to designate embryonic forms of a tax or revenue (cf. Whitman 1979, 79; Golovnin 1979, 205; Ruggles 1821; see also Menzies 1920, 83).

The Symbolism of the Offering
The Offering as Symbol of the Deity

It seems that the offering consecrated to a deity must include species considered its "bodies." This rule is mentioned by N. Emerson, who had a profound knowledge of Hawaiian beliefs, while speaking of the offerings consecrated to the goddess Laka: "A spirit of fitness . . . limited choice among these to certain species that were deemed acceptable to the goddess because they were reckoned as among her favorite forms of metamorphosis [*kino lau*]. To go outside this ordained and traditional range would have been an offense, a sacrilege" (1965, 19, cf. 20).[13]

Some other examples of offerings constituted by the "bodies" of the deity are as follows. The principal components of the sacrifice consecrated to the god Lono on the occasion of the birth of a first child are the "bodies" of this god: the pig, the '*ama'ama*, and the *āholehole* fish (Handy and Pukui 1972, 80–82). Sacrifices made to Kū usually include some of his bodies, such as coconuts and an *ulua* fish (see the *kapu luakini* ritual, part 3).[14] Kāne and Kanaloa, as well as deities such as the so-called Kālaipāhoa, which are particularizations of Kāne or deities associated with him (see Valeri 1982b), receive offerings of bananas, considered to be their manifestations (Handy and Pukui 1972, 177; Kamakau 1964, 135; Beckwith 1940, 26; Handy 1972, 196–98, 164, 165, and below).[15] In addition, Kanaloa may receive sacrifices of octopus or squid (*he'e*), which are his bodies (Malo 1951, 111).

The *kākū'ai* rites that make it possible to transform a dead person into an '*aumakua* require offerings that are manifestations of the deity into which one wishes to incorporate the dead. Thus, if one desires to incorporate the dead person into the thunder deities, it is necessary to sacrifice everything that is *la'a* [sacred] to them (Kamakau 1964, 71). If, on the contrary, one wishes to incorporate the dead person into the *mo'o* deities, offerings that correspond to them are used, such as dogs whose fur recalls the colors and patterns of lizards' skin (Kamakau 1964, 85–86; Handy and Pukui 1972, 151; cf. Titcomb 1969, 18–19).[16]

However, in most cases a deity is related to some aspects of a species rather than to the species in its totality. This is why the same species—especially important ones such as the pig—can be offered to a plurality of gods.[17] Offerings consecrated to a certain deity often have a common quality that justifies their association with this deity. Often this quality is a color. Thus black offerings are sacrificed to thunder deities, and offerings that are yellow or wrapped in yellow bark cloths are consecrated to the *mo'o* deities (Kamakau 1964, 71, 85–86; NK, 1:117). Theoretically, a given combination of colors, decorations, and other "symbols" (*hō'ailona*) corresponds to each deity.[18] For example, one gives a black pig, rooster, and loincloth to a shark 'aumakua (HEN, 1:704–7). Pele receives black and red bark cloths, or black and white or striped ones (Kamakau 1964, 64). Sometimes the deity is offered a species whose name evokes either this deity in particular or properties that belong to the divine realm in general.[19]

The sex of the principal sacrificial animals is also pertinent. In the main temples, where only masculine deities are worshiped, only male animals may be offered in sacrifice. Even the vegetable offerings, such as coconuts or bananas, and the fish sacrificed in these temples have a masculine connotation.[20] Likewise, it seems that goddesses and female sorcery deities receive female animals, especially sows.[21] However, it is possible that male victims are preferred but not prescribed in sacrifices made to minor male deities.

In short, while theoretically the offering must correspond—at least in part—to the deity and is even considered the deity's body, the application of this principle is ambiguous and imprecise because of the multiple relationships between species and deities—relationships, moreover, that are only imperfectly known to us.

The Offering as Symbol of the Sacrifier

We have seen that a deity is nothing but a reified representation of certain human properties. It follows from this that the offerings that symbolize the deity also symbolize human traits and therefore traits that characterize the sacrifier. This human content is particularly emphasized by the main natural offerings: banana, coconut, pig, dog, chicken.

Both the banana tree and its fruit are considered metaphors of man. The trunk of the banana tree is used ritually as a substitute for the human body (Auwai in Barrère 1975, 69; NK, 1:147); the fruit of the banana is conceived of as a phallic symbol. Likewise, the coconut tree is a metaphor for man: "The coconut tree was a man, said the ancients, whose head was buried in the ground with his penis and testicles above" (Kamakau 1961, 120). As a matter of fact, the primordial coconut tree had only two coconuts (Handy 1972, 168–69; cf. Neal 1929, 51–52), which goes to show that coconuts are considered analogous to testicles.

Domestic animals not only evoke the men with whom they live and eat, they are also the objects of psychological identification on the part of their owners. The Hawaiian feels about his pigs somewhat as Westerners feel about cats and dogs.[22] They are household favorites (Ellis 1842, 41, 218; Gough 1973, 134; Beckwith 1951, 81; Mathison 1825, 365, 373). People express their affection for pigs as if they were human beings (Ellis 1842, 302)[23] and at times even eat with them (Stewart 1839, 105). Moreover, pigs feed on some species, such as tubers, that are staples for men and eat the leftovers from human meals (Handy 1972, 253). Thus they are close to man because of their feeding habits. Sometimes the identification between man and pig is so strong that the animal is killed when his master dies.[24]

In many respects the dog is closely associated with the pig. Both are scavengers (cf. Leach 1964, 50), and they herd together (Cook and King 1784, 3 : 118). Like pigs, dogs can become favorites, and in such cases the animal may be killed when its master dies or be given funeral honors if it dies before him (cf. MH, January 1826, 15–16). Macrae reports noticing

a young woman walking along the street, and at the same time suckling several puppies that were wrapped up in a piece of tapa cloth hanging round her shoulders and breasts. This custom of suckling dogs and pigs is common to the natives of the Sandwich Islands. These animals are held by them in great estimation, little inferior to their own offspring, and my journeys to the woods in search of plants often afforded me an opportunity of being an eyewitness to this habit. I often saw them feeding the young pigs and dogs with the poi made from taro roots, in the same way a mother would her child. [1922, 42]

Portlock mentions that a member of his crew encountered a Hawaiian woman who "had two puppies, one at each breast" and showed them great affection (1789, 188). Tyerman and Bennett note that Hawaiians are "singularly tender and kind" to their dogs. "In traveling, they frequently take up their dogs, and carry them over dirty or rugged parts of the road, lest they should soil their skins or hurt their feet; and it is said a man would sooner resent an injury to his dog than to his child" (1832, 2 : 57).

Such behavior indicates that pigs and dogs are often treated like human beings. The existence of a strong identification between men and these animals is also attested by numerous myths where pigs and dogs appear in human form (for dogs, see Fornander 1916–20, 5 : 332; for pigs, see the myth of Kamapua'a in Kahiolo 1978; Fornander 1916–20, 5 : 314–63; Rice 1923, 51–53; Kalakaua 1888, 139–54; Westervelt 1915b, 246–77).

The third domestic and sacrificial animal, the chicken, has a great deal in common with the pig and the dog (cf. Handy 1972, 254–56). Like the other two, the chicken appears in human form in various myths and may alternate between its animal and human forms. Some heroes, such as Kepakailiua, are born from a chicken's egg (Fornander 1916–20, 5 : 384).[25]

But the sacrificial species are also different from man, even to the point of displaying traits that are the contrary of human. Let us consider some of the differences and the function of this combination of human and non-human traits in the offerings.

The differences between banana and coconut trees, on the one hand, and man on the other are too obvious to require explaining. Instead, let us concentrate on the pig, the most important sacrificial animal. The strong conceptual and even emotional identification between man and pig coexists with the perception of a radical difference. After all, the pig is an animal. Indeed, its human traits serve all the better to bring out its animal qualities. It is significant that in mythology the pig represents a distortion, even a perversion, of human behavior (cf. Emerson 1892, 14). Man cannot fully identify with its actions. The comic nature of the god Kamapua'a and the fascination he provokes in the public are rooted in the mixture of identification and distance that this mythological character elicits in the listener.

Yet it is precisely because of the pig's capacity to represent the perversion of the truly human, because it is *falsely* human, that this creature may function as a sacrificial animal in many contexts. For instance, the pig may represent the sacrifier as transgressor, as well as the very idea of transgression. In expiatory sacrifices, its death thus represents the destruction of what is falsely human in the sacrifier because it is connected with his transgression of the norms that make him human. As in Bataille's interpretation of the Hegelian theory of sacrifice, by killing the animal the sacrifier kills his own animality and thereby becomes truly human (1955, 31). Thus, for the sacrifice to be efficacious, it is necessary for the victim to be at once identified with and distinct from the sacrifier. Man can thus, through the victim, both relate to his own essence and separate from the negative aspect of himself that contradicts his essence. This is true not only of sacrifices of expiation and purification, as we shall see.

Naturally, every domestic animal can be said to exhibit a combination of human and nonhuman traits. Yet that this combination is particularly evident in the pig helps explain why this animal is much more important as a victim than the dog and the chicken.

Having shown that sacrifice exploits the global relationship between certain natural species and the human species, I must add that in many cases it becomes necessary to create a relationship between the *individual* victim and the *individual* sacrifier. Thus, for example, the pig sacrificed during the rite for the birth of a firstborn child takes on a strong connection with the child, because the animal is set aside and fattened from the moment the child's mother knows she is pregnant (Handy and Pukui 1972, 80). Thus an analogic relationship is established between a pig's growth and the development of a fetus.

Although sacrifice always presupposes objective symbolic paradigms, it is also a subjective act, since it is always made for the benefit of the sacrifier, whether an individual or a collectivity. Thus it has a subjective value, with both quantitative and qualitative aspects that interfere with the values determined by the paradigmatic symbolic classification.

In a quantitative appraisal of the offering, two variables are relevant: the aims of the sacrifier and his rank. It is obvious that a serious illness requires a larger offering than a mild complaint (cf. Kamakau 1964, 97). But the quantitative importance of the offering can be measured only against the sacrifier's wealth, which is theoretically proportionate to his rank. The richer an individual, the more he must give: "The offerings to the god, and the fees to the priest [the sacrificer], are regulated according to the wealth or rank of the individual" (Ellis 1842, 293; cf. Kamakau 1964, 96, 97). So, for example, a commoner must provide forty dogs and eighty chickens for a *kuni* sacrifice, but an ali'i must sacrifice four hundred dogs and an enormous number of chickens (Malo 1951, 100–103).

Let us now turn to the qualitative determination of the offering's value to the sacrifier. This value changes as a function of the degree to which the victim is equivalent to the sacrifier. It follows that even if their different economic value is ignored, an '*ama'ama* fish cannot be considered perfectly equivalent to a pig although paradigmatically it is (the '*ama'ama* being a "sea pig"). The pig has greater value because it is more "human" than the fish. Moreover, if it has a close relationship with the man for whom it is sacrificed, if it is a favorite, its value is even greater. By sacrificing it, the sacrifier is consenting to the loss of a part of himself.

Thus it is possible to rank offerings in terms of their value to the sacrifier; this value ultimately depends on the offering's capacity to symbolize the sacrifier, to replace him adequately in the sacrifice.[26] The resulting hierarchy includes the sacrifier's own body. And, in fact, if the offering is the symbol of the sacrifier, nothing is a more appropriate symbol for him than parts of his own body: hair, teeth, eyes, and so on.[27]

Far more effective than these metonymic symbols of the sacrifier is his supreme metaphoric symbol, the human victim. Closer to the sacrifier than all other offerings, the human offering is endowed with the greatest value and efficacy. Beyond human sacrifice remains only the sacrifier's own death. In fact, this death is the logical limit of the sacrificial system and gives it its full meaning. For it is precisely the sacrifier's death that the sacrifice aims to avoid by representing it.[28]

Thus we are led to consider human sacrifice not as a separate category but rather as the ultimate form that every sacrifice may take—or the essence common to all sacrifices. This explains why several of the rites we have considered may be performed with human victims. However, sacrifices carried out in this manner require the king or a sacred ali'i serving as his representative to consecrate the offerings. Consecration of human sacrifices is in fact the principal prerogative of royalty (cf. Ii 1963, 4–6, 158–59; Kamakau 1961, 108–9, 129, 185, 120, 121; Fornander 1878–80, 2:308–9, 218, 202). Now, as we shall see, the king incarnates society as a whole. Thus his monopoly of human sacrifice means that this sacrifice, which encompasses all the others, can be made only for the benefit of the collectivity. This statement may seem surprising at first. It could be objected that human sacrifices are also made on the occasion of rites of passage for the king and high-ranking ali'i,[29] or to heal them,[30] or to mark the stages of the construction of their possessions, such as canoes,[31] houses,[32] temples,[33] or for any other activities they undertake, especially war.[34] The fact is that in these rites society is not distinguished from the person of the king who symbolizes it.[35] As a result, whatever has value for the king has value for society, and, inversely, whatever has value for society has value for the king. Thus, in sacrifices performed by the king it is difficult to distinguish between what pertains to him and what pertains to society. At any rate, most of the royal sacrifices are explicitly performed for reasons of a collective interest: to avert public calamities or epidemics,[36] to avoid the misfortunes announced by bad omens such as eclipses (Marin 1973, 205; Arago 1822, 2 : 134, 178), to put an end to volcanic eruptions (Whitman 1979, 64; cf. Kamakau 1961, 185; 1964, 66), or to increase the fertility of the population and that of the various species on which it depends (Malo 36.78, 37.10; 1951, 189, 152). As for war, whether offensive or defensive, it is not an activity that concerns the king only, since the entire society is affected.[37] It should also be mentioned that victims of human sacrifices are usually transgressors or rebels. By sacrificing them, the king purifies society from the pollution brought on by their sins and the disorders they have provoked.[38] In other instances—if, for example, his personal taboos have been violated[39]—the king purifies himself with a human sacrifice. However, since the king's person embodies the whole community, this purification is not a private but a public concern.

The Offering as Symbol of the Outcome of the Sacrifice

The offering, or some of its components, must evoke not only the deity and the sacrifier, but also the results sought by the sacrifier. This evocative power may reside in the name of the species chosen to function as the offering, in its physical properties, or in a combination of the two.

The following are some offerings chosen because of their names. Once more let us refer to the sacrifice made at the birth of the first child. In addition to species that evoke Lono and the sacrifier, or their relationship, species evoking the state that the rite is intended to produce are consecrated in this sacrifice. As Handy and Pukui write,

There must be shrimp, one name for which is *mahiki*, a word meaning to peel off like removing fish scales (or the skin of the shrimp). There must be *kala* seaweed: *kala* means "to loosen," "set free." There must be *'a'ama* crab: *'a'ama* means to loose a hold or grip. These three foods helped to free the child from malicious influences, thus preventing bad behavior and ill luck due to mischievous psychic effects. Another sea food that must be eaten was a chiton of the species *kuapa'a* (*Acanthochiton viridis*), a bilaterally symmetrical mollusc with a shell consisting of eight transverse plates, found on the under surface of stones in shallow water to which it "holds fast," *pa'a*. This was the only occasion on which this shellfish was eaten: *pa'a* means to fix, hold fast, hence the implication that the *kuapa'a* would be instrumental in securing firmly through the mother and others who ate of it the goodness induced in the hearts of all present and especially the child.

There may have been a special implication also in the offering of the *'ama-'ama*, or mullet, and the *'a'ama* crab for the first born, in the fact that the word *'ama* means a first fruit offering. [1972, 81–82; cf. Pukui 1942, 367–68]

As the text makes clear, offerings symbolize the states sought through sacrifice. However, I do not think that the specific interpretations Handy and Pukui give the meanings of the various offerings are the correct or important ones. They appear rather to be rationalizations; it is not clear whether they are produced by the informants or by the authors.

To understand the meanings of these offerings correctly, it is necessary to take into account their occurrence in other sacrifices as well. For instance, the 'a'ama crab, the limu-kala seaweed, or the kala fish are used in numerous sacrifices of purification or desacralization (see NK, 2:156, 1:2; Kamakau 1964, 97; cf. Fornander 1916–20, 4:289). This seems to indicate that the rite for the firstborn can also be considered a desacralization or purification sacrifice and that it is in this light that the offering it includes must be interpreted. Moreover, as Handy and Pukui themselves remark, the use of the 'ama'ama and 'a'ama seems to connect this sacrifice with a firstfruit sacrifice. I believe it is indeed so. The firstborn, like every other "firstfruit," must be consecrated to the god. Taken literally, this prescription should imply the actual sacrifice of the firstborn. What actually is sacrificed are his substitutes (pig, 'ama'ama) and concrete symbols of the effects of this substitution: the "freeing" of the child (kala, 'a'ama) and its firm establishment (pa'a, symbolized by the kuapa'a) in the human—as opposed to the divine—world, and so forth.

"Verbal magic" abounds in sacrificial rites. Bananas of the maoli variety are offered (Ii 1963, 56) in luakini temples, doubtless to influence the transformation of images into akua maoli, "true gods" (cf. Malo 1951, 106, 171, 184). A well-known myth tells that the cannibalism of Kamapua'a is neutralized by the sacrifice of species whose names all contain the morpheme lau (Fornander 1916–20, 5:323). In my view this is because of its double meaning, "numerous" and "seine" (PE, 179). Lau is a trick word indeed, for "numerous" offerings entice Kamapua'a and paralyze him in a "seine."

The consecration of hīnālea fish, whose name contains the word lea, "clear," and that of the weke fish, whose name means, among other things, "opening or removal," are appropriate in sacrifices of expiation, desacralization, and so on (see Kamakau 1964, 97; Malo 1951, 112–13; NK, 1:26–27). The resemblance between the name of the kūmū fish and the word kumu, which means "foundation," "base," "beginning," "origin," "model," "source," "cause," "master," and so on, probably is one of the motivations for the sacrificial use of this fish (see, for example, Kamakau 1964, 96 and above, note 17). Through this fish the sacrifier is connected with the deities as "models" and "sources" of certain actions and certain knowledge so that he can "base" his existence and activities on a solid "foundation." Moreover, that kumu also means "beginning" probably explains why the kūmū fish appears among the offerings consecrated on the occasion of any beginning, such as the launching of a canoe, a birth, or an initiation. Another meaning of *kumu* is "master": this seems to explain why the *kūmū* fish "was offered by those who had been through a course of teaching and were now 'master' of an art" (Titcomb and Pukui 1972, 92).

One of the offerings used in fertility rites (*ho'oūluūlu*) is a variety of taro called *mana* (Emerson in Malo 1951, 158), probably because *mana* also means "divine power."[40]

The choice of other offerings is due to the evocative power of their physical properties. Thus, in rites of purification (*huikala*) one may use any plant that is considered "slippery," since it evokes "freeing" (NK, 1:75).

On a more abstract level, the color of the offerings can motivate their selection. For example, in a *huikala* rite described by Malo we find a group of offerings (a dog, a chicken, ten bark cloths) that all share the color white, which is evocative of the "purity" that is sought (1951, 112–13).

The rite for inaugurating a canoe (*lolo ka wa'a*) consists of the sacrifice of a pig and a dog, because "the pig symbolized the 'rooting' (*'eku*) of the canoe in the open sea, and the dog the 'tearing apart' (*hae aku*) [of] the billows of the ocean" (Kamakau 1976, 121). In this case specific traits are isolated in very common sacrificial species to furnish an index of the precise goal of this sacrifice.

In other cases, evocations provoked by physical properties combine with those called forth by the name of the species. For example, the octopus or squid (*he'e*) is used in *huikala* rites because the movements of these creatures' tentacles symbolize the transition from a "bound" to an "unbound" state[41] and also because *he'e* means "to melt" (PE, 59).

The properties of a species contribute to the successful outcome of the sacrifice only if the individual that functions as victim perfectly represents the species to which it belongs. This is one of the reasons behind the need to sacrifice perfect victims (Whitman 1979, 23; Emerson 1965, 32). Moreover, a perfect victim may evoke a perfect deity[42] and perfect ritual results (cf. Kamakau 1964, 121; Emerson 1965, 33–34).

The Role of Prayer

We have seen that the offering is constituted by objects having the status of ambiguous signs. For the sacrifice to achieve a precise result it is necessary to translate these imprecise signs into precise ones, that is, to organize them into a discourse. In other words, it is necessary for the offering to be associated with a prayer, since "les nécessités du langage font que la prière précise souvent elle-même les circonstances, les motifs de son énonciation" (Mauss 1909, 1:359).

It is not my purpose to discuss in detail here the multiform aspects of Hawaiian prayer, which merit a study of their own. I will limit myself to some observations that are essential to understanding the mechanism of sacrifice.

The most typical scheme underlying a sacrificial prayer is as follows: (1) invocation of the deities; (2) description of the offerings; (3) statement of the request; (4) statement to the effect that the kapu in force during the consecration is lifted.

This scheme is simplified or complicated depending on the context or degree of elaboration of the prayer. Some leave out the introductory statement of the names of the deities,[43] doubtless because the extralinguistic context clearly indicates which ones are being invoked. The description of the offerings also varies. Usually the prayer lists the components of the offering in detail,[44] but at times it simply refers to it as a whole with expressions such as "here is the food,"[45] or "here is the offering."[46] Some prayers develop the third and fourth parts of the scheme more fully (see Kamakau 1976, 27, 28, 29; Pogue 1858, 10–11, 12–13). The most beautiful poetic effects are often found in these developments (see, for example, Kamakau 1976, 31).

The following prayer perfectly corresponds to the ideal type:

Na aumakua o ka po,
For the '*aumakua* of the night,

Na aumakua o ke ao,
For the '*aumakua* of the day,

Na aumakua o ke ahi me ka kuahiwi,
For the '*aumakua* of the fire and the mountain,

Na aumakua o ke kai
For the '*aumakua* of the sea

Na aumakua o ka wai,
For the '*aumakua* of the fresh water,

Ka paa iluna, ka paa ilalo,
The foundation of above, the foundation of below,

Ka hookui, ka halawai,
The zenith, the horizon.

Eia ka puaa,
Here is the pig

Eia ka awa,
Here is the '*awa*

Eia ka moa,
Here is the chicken

Eia ka ia,
Here is the fish,

Eia ka ai,
Here is the vegetable food,

He mohai na Puhi.
A sacrifice offered by Puhi [name of the sacrifier].

He uku no kana mau hewa a pau i hana ai.
A compensation for all the sins he has committed.

E kala mai.
Deliver.

Hoopau i ka pilikia o ka oukou pulapula.
Put an end to all the misfortunes of your descendant.

E lawe aku i na pilikia a pau mai kona kino ae.
Take away the diseases of his body.

Eia kana uku ia oukou,
Here is his compensation offered to you,

Na aumakua kane,
Na aumakua wahine,
Na aumakua keiki,
E hele mai e ai a e ike ia Puhi,
Ka mea nana keia mohai.
Amama, ua noa.

[Emerson 1892, 22; translation mine]

To the male 'aumakua,
To the female 'aumakua.
To the child 'aumakua.
Come eat and recognize Puhi,
Who is making this sacrifice.
It is effected ['amama], it is already
free [noa].

The first three parts of the prayer are almost perfectly balanced. The text concludes with a brief summary of all that precedes it ("Come and eat and recognize Puhi / who is making this sacrifice") and by the final formula, which announces the passage from the *kapu* (taboo) to the *noa* (free) state.

Another prayer, pronounced at the sacrifice of the firstfruits of a field of sweet potatoes, provides an example in which the first and third parts are expanded:

E ke akua; e Kukulia,
E Kukeaoloa, e Kukeaopoko,

E Kukeaolewa, e Kukeaoho'o-
mihamihaikalani,

E Kupulupulu, e Kumokuhali'i, e
Kuka'ohi'alaka;

Ou mau kino, e Kama i ka lani,

E Kanepua'a,
Eia ka 'ai, eia ka i'a.
Eia ka 'ai, e ke akua,
E Kahela, e ka wahine e moe ana iluna
ka alo,
O Moe a Hanuna, O Milika'a-a-
kalepoahulu,
O Pahukini, O Pahulau, O Kulana-a-
ka-pahu,
O 'Olekahua,
O Kapapaialaka, O Kapaepaenuialei-
moku e,
E ala!
E ala e ka ua, e ka la, e ka po,
'Ohu kolo mai i uka, 'ohu kolo mai i
kai,

O gods; O Ku-[of]-the-striver,
O Ku-of-the-long-cloud, O Ku-of-the-
short-cloud,
O Ku-of-the-hanging-cloud, O Ku-of-
the-intensely-dark-clouds-of-
heaven,
O Ku-of-the-thickets, O Ku-who-
spreads-greenery, O Ku-of-
the-'ohi'a-tree;
Your many forms, O Kama of the
heavens,
O Kanepua'a,
Here is "food," here is "fish."
Here is food, O gods,
O Kahela, woman who lies supine,

O Moe-a-Hanuna, Milika'a-a-ka-lepo-
ahulu,
Pahukini, Pahulau, Kulana-a-ka-pahu,

O 'Olekahua,
O Ka-papa-ia-laka, Ka-papa[sic]-nui-a-
lei-moku,
Awake!
Awake O rain, O sun, O darkness,
O mists creeping upland, mists
creeping seaward,

Kai kane, kai wahine, kai ulala,
Kai hehena, kai piliaiku, e.
Ua puni na moku i ke kai;
O huʻahuʻa nui ke kai
A ka ʻale iki, a ka ʻale moe,
A ka ʻale hakoʻikoʻi i ka lana a Kahiki.

E ola, e ola i ka Mo-ʻi,
E ola i naʻliʻi,
E ola i ka hu, i ka makaʻainana,

E ola iaʻu, i ka mahiʻai nui,
E ola i koʻu ʻohana,
E ola i koʻu ʻohua,
E ola i ka ʻaiʻai aʻu a ka mahiʻai nui;

ʻEliʻeli i ola ka honua.
ʻAmama, ua noa; lele wale aku la.

E ʻai, e ʻai.
     [Kamakau 1976, 30–31]

O violent sea, mild sea, mad sea,
Delirious, numbing sea.
The islands are surrounded by the sea;
The sea foams
With small billows, low-lying billows,
Turbulent billows that float from
     Kahiki.
Grant life, grant life to the king,
Grant life to the chiefs,
Grant life to the masses, to the
     commoners,
Grant life to me, the mighty farmer,
Grant life to my family,
Grant life to my household
Grant life to the dependents of the
     mighty farmer;
From the depths grant life to the earth.
ʻAmama, the kapu is freed; the prayer
     has flown.
Eat, eat.

The prayer begins with a list of the deities responsible for the efficacy of this particular agricultural rite. This list is interrupted by a brief mention of the offering. The third part of the prayer uses sublime metaphors to create a verbal replica of the transfer of forces that is the condition of the success of the rite. The most important of these refer to the ocean, which like the gods surrounds the islands and is immensely powerful. Like the waves coming from over the horizon to break on the Hawaiian shores, the gods come from Kahiki to bring life. Here we find an example of the use of the power of speech in rites. According to the Hawaiians, the word itself is a "force" (NK, 2:124), it bears a "fruit" (*huaʻōlelo*—NK, 1:85). "Hawaiian tradition holds that a spoken word becomes an actual entity, an operative agent that can bring about events" (NK, 1:86, 94, cf. 98; Emerson 1892, 27). More precisely, between thought and its object lies a whole series of intermediate states that are accorded different degrees of reality. While it is true that the spoken word is closer than thought to the reality it represents,[47] symbolic species are even closer. Still, for these species to function fully as signs within the ritual context, it is necessary that they be named in prayers and that their symbolic values be put into words.

In summary, prayer works to translate the offering into signs that are articulated in a discourse; reciprocally, the offering works to translate this discourse into reality, with which it has a greater affinity than does speech.

The Offering as Food

Not only are sacrificial victims signs, they are also usually food and as such contribute to making the sacrificial process possible. We will consider evidence that proves the god is supposed to be fed by offerings; that of these offerings he eats either the "essence" or the "first portion" or both; that the greater part of the offering is generally consumed by the sacrifiers; and that in this manner they are supposed to absorb divine mana.

Innumerable data document the belief that the god eats the offering, which is often called *'ai*, "food."[48] Prayers and myths describe the deities as eating victims[49] or "smacking their lips" when they see them.[50] A warrior can threaten his adversary by telling him, "Tomorrow my god shall devour you" (i.e., "Tomorrow I shall sacrifice you to my god"; Kamakau 1961, 81; cf. Fornander 1916–20, 4:520). Sacrificial offerings or parts of them can be placed in the mouth of a divine image (Arago 1822, 2:113; 1844, 2:62–63; article in *Ka Hoku o Hawaii*, 14 March 1912). The mouth of an image is generally open, with the tongue flexed backward as if the god were swallowing (Cox and Davenport 1974, 42–45, 106).[51] "*He ai na ke akua*," "to eat like a god," means to eat enormous quantities, like a god during the sacrifice (Fornander 1916–20, 4:457). Inversely, gods to whom no victims are sacrificed are regarded as famished and even dying of hunger.[52]

To interpret these statements we must recognize the metaphoric value of the act of eating. To eat is to encompass, to possess, to transform. Thus it is said that a god or king "eats" an island when he has conquered or encompassed it (cf. Kamakau 1964, 85). "To eat" also means "to destroy" or kill in punishment (cf. Kamakau 1961, 108); NK, 1:6–7)—actions that manifest divine power and its connection with moral rules. Eating and destroying are also metaphors of transformation.

Canonically, the entire offering is consecrated to the god and from this standpoint is completely eaten by him. However, this all-inclusive absorption takes place only on an invisible plane. The "whole" that goes to the god is either the "essence" of the offering (cf. PE, 11)[53] or its first portion. In the first case, the sacrifier and his associates eat the material counterpart in its entirety.[54] In the second they eat only what is left of the offering after certain victims or parts of them are placed (*kau*) on the god's altar, where they are left to rot.[55] The equivalence postulated between part and whole, between "essence" and "matter," makes it possible to reconcile two apparently contradictory needs. The offering must be completely consumed, that is, encompassed and transformed, by the god to whom it is given; but at the same time it is necessary for the sacrifier to eat the offering so that he may absorb the power, or divine mana, that has been incorporated into it as a consequence of the god's having encompassed it.

Thus a true understanding of the mechanism of Hawaiian sacrifice is impossible if one conceives of the god's and sacrifier's shares as rigidly separated.[56] The offering is both one and two. The prescription to cook both the god's and sacrifier's portions with the same fire, which is especially prepared for each sacrifice and is radically distinct from profane fire (Whitman 1979:23; cf. Kamakau 1964, 86, 83, and passim; Portlock 1789, 61; Bingham [1824] in HEN, 1:647; K. Kamakau 1919–20, 25; Malo 1951, 207), suffices to indicate that god's and man's share of the offering together form a whole.[57] It also implies that the sacrifiers are in communion with the gods even if they do not directly consume the part that is placed on the altar.[58] As a matter of fact, the indirectness of this communion of god and sacrifier reflects the hierarchical nature of sacrificial commensality: hierarchy involves distinction as much as connection.

It is for these reasons that I have called the entire amount of food consecrated in sacrificial rites "the offering" and have termed the "god's share" what interpreters have usually called "the offering"—that is, what is left on the altar. An analysis of the great rituals that take place in the *luakini* temples will enable me to demonstrate more fully that this choice is well justified (see part 3).

For the time being, let me quote in support of my thesis two texts that, by stating that the sacrifiers eat offerings, and particularly temple offerings, imply that *all* the food consecrated in the temple—not only what is put on the altar—is considered an offering. Speaking of a high-ranking female ali'i of old, 'Ī'ī writes, "Though a woman, Keakealaniwahine was permitted to enter the heiaus to give her offerings and sacrifices. However, she was not allowed to eat any of the offerings and gifts with the priests and the men, who ate by themselves" (1963, 160). Kepelino writes quite openly that the priests eat "*na mea i mohaia na ke Akua*," "the things sacrificed [= the offering] to the gods" (1932, 23). Since the offering put on the altar could not be eaten, in these texts the term "offering" must include the sacrifier's share, otherwise they would not state that priests and ali'i eat "the things sacrificed."

The relationship between man and god in sacrifice is also qualified by the way their respective shares are cooked. Moreover, the choice of cooking styles may also indicate the relative importance of the sacrificial rite itself. Despite uncertainties and contradictions in the various accounts, the following hierarchy of cooking types emerges.

The most valorized of these types seems to be "cremation" (*puhi*).[59] The missionary Bingham claims to have seen in Pu'ukoholā temple "the ashes and burnt bones of many *human victims* sacrificed to demons" (MH, April 1821, 115; cf. Thrum 1909, 52–53). This suggests that the holocaust of human victims is practiced in the *luakini* temple rites. It is true that the supreme sacrificial prerogative of royalty is called *kapu puhi ka-*

naka, "the privilege to burn men" (Kamakau 1964, 9–10), but nothing in the accounts of *luakini* temple rituals leads us to confirm the existence of the holocaust. On the contrary, 'Ī'ī, who was an eyewitness, states that only the victim's *skin* is burned on the sacrificial fire: "*puhipuhia na ili o lakou i ke ahi*" (1869d).[60] At any rate, whether the victims are completely burned or burned only on the surface and left raw inside, they are not fit for human consumption. Therefore they can only be the god's share. Only in exceptional cases, in the rite of Kahōāli'i, for example, does a man eat part of the god's share. But this happens because he is impersonating the god.

Broiling (*pūlehu*) is second in value, after the burned/raw combination. Broiled victims are shared between men and gods in the most sacred rites. Of course, broiling lends itself to symbolizing the differentiation between the "essence"—the odorous smoke arising into the open sky from the victims as they cook—which goes to the god, and the "flesh," which is edible for man. In addition to smoke from all the victims, the gods generally receive the "first portion" of the offering, in the form of either a certain part of the victim's body or certain whole individual victims that are put on the altar. There is thus a double relationship of equivalence between the god's share and the whole offering; it is metaphoric in the case of smoke and metonymic in the case of the "first portion."

Kelou Kamakau (1919–20, 21) establishes a radical opposition between broiled (*pūlehu*) victims and those roasted in the oven (*kālua*). When the latter make up man's share of the sacrifice, the former are attributed to the gods.[61] This combination connotes a more profound separation between men and gods than where broiled victims are shared by both. Note also that in the latter case the sacrifiers are made closer to the gods. But when even the god's share is cooked in the oven (*kālua*), the gods are made closer to men, since this method is habitually used in everyday cooking. This implies that the sacrifice is less important than that in which the victims are broiled or cremated.[62] These three types of cooking are used in alternation or in conjunction in the *luakini* temple rites, as we shall see.

In the preceding discussion I have shown that the sacrifiers consume food encompassed by the gods and therefore endowed with their power, their mana. It must follow that through these offerings divine mana is transferred to the sacrifier. This deduction is confirmed by the effects linked to the consumption of sacrificial offerings. For example, in certain sacrifices the sacrifier will be cured by eating the eye of a sacrificed fish (HEN, 1:704). By eating the eyes of sacrificed fish or human victims, Kahōāli'i, the "royal companion," is supposed to acquire divine qualities for himself and probably for the king as well (see part 3). Dancers who eat offerings consecrated to the goddess Laka ("eat to the Laka"), who presides over the *hula*, obtain "good knowledge and expertness to dance well," while those who "refuse to do this, will not become accomplished in the art" (MH, July 1822, 207). By eating part of the offering consecrated to Lono, the mother of a firstborn child obtains the mana of this god (that is, the principle of growth that he embodies) for herself and the child she feeds:

The pig was cooked in the imu [Polynesian oven], and all the other foods were wrapped in ti leaves and steamed with it. A cup of *'awa* was prepared and when the food was ready to serve, the kahuna [the priest] cut off the tip of the snout of the pig, the tips of the ears, and the end of the tail, a piece from each of the four feet, and a piece from the liver, spleen and lungs and placed them in a dish for the mother. A bundle of taro tops and sea foods was also set apart for her. Then the kahuna offered a long prayer offering the essence of the food to the gods and making their blessing for the first-born and subsequent brothers and sisters. After the prayer, the mother ate the food set apart for her, and relatives and family friends ate the remaining food. [Pukui 1942, 368]

As Handy and Pukui write, by eating a bit of each part of the pig, the mother symbolically "eats" the whole thing (1972, 82). She also eats a piece of each of the pig's vegetable and marine forms, also sacrificed on this occasion. In other words, she eats the god's mana by eating the very forms in which the god manifests himself. Since women could not eat pork (see below, p. 115), it is not clear whether Pukui's account refers to a practice that developed after the abolition of the taboos (1819) or if, as is more probable, it was exceptionally permitted to a woman to eat pork on behalf of her newborn first child.

In the same vein, by eating bananas consecrated to Kāne and coconuts consecrated to Kū, men ingest the constitutive principles of virility incorporated in these gods. By drinking *'awa* (*Piper methysticum*) offered to a deity in a sacrificial context, the deity's knowledge and power of vision are thought to be acquired (see for example the prayers given by Emerson 1965, 44–45, 46, etc.). Such examples could be multiplied. They illustrate a mechanism that operates in most sacrifices, albeit in different forms.

Remarks concerning the Vocabulary of Sacrifice

To understand some aspects, however superficial, of the Hawaiian conceptualization of sacrifice, it is helpful to make a few observations about the terms used to designate this institution and its different forms. First, let us note that the words referring to sacrificial practices, particularly to the offering, belong to the class that takes the possessive prepositions *a*- and *ka-*. According to Elbert and Pukui, "The possessive indicates the *nature of the relationship* of the possessed and the possessor. The *a*- forms . . . show that the possessor ('his' or 'her') *caused* the ownership" (1979, 137–38). Moreover, the use of this form indicates that the thing possessed is subordinated to the possessor. From this standpoint, the sacrifier's relation to the offering is the inverse of his relation to the deity. Possession of the latter is marked by the form *o-*, which indicates that the possessor is not the cause of what he possesses and that he is subordinate to it (ibid.). The two relations are nevertheless complementary. Because of the offering he encompasses, the sacrifier enters into a relationship with a deity that in turn encompasses him. The offering then returns to the sacrifier endowed with divine mana, which he may himself encompass. Here language reflects a polarity that must be understood as part of a continuous ritual process.

Among the words that mean "sacrifice," *mōhai* has the broadest extension. It derives from the word *hai*, which has the same extension but is used especially as a verb ("to sacrifice"), and it denotes human as well as animal and vegetable sacrifices (Kepelino 1932, 19, 21, 22–23).[63] It is possible to say, for example, *hai kanaka*, "to offer human sacrifice" (PE, 44), *hai 'ai*, "to sacrifice agricultural food" (Malo 38.7), and so forth.

The word *haina*, "offering" or "victim," also is derived from *hai*. It refers to either flesh or vegetable offerings, as witnessed by the expressions "*ka haina kanaka*," "human offering, human victim" (*Kumulipo*, line 2098) and "*ka haina 'awa*," "'*awa* offering" (PE, 45).

The word *'ālana* is defined by Pukui and Elbert as "offering, especially a free-will offering, contrasting with a *mōhai* that was prescribed by a priest" (PE, 17). However, several texts indicate that no opposition exists between *mōhai* and *'ālana*. For example, we find the following expressions: "*na mohai* [*mōhai*] *i alanaia* [*'ālana 'ia*]," "the sacrifices that had been offered" (Kepelino 1932, 59); "*eia ka 'alana, ka mohai*," "here is the *'alana*, the *mohai*" (Kamakau 1976, 143; cf. Kamakau 1964, 98). Other texts show that the expression *'alana* designates prescribed sacrifices (see, for example, Malo 1951, 180), notably human sacrifices that take place in the *luakini* temple (Fornander 1916–20, 6: 377). It is likely that *'ālana* connotes the oblative aspect of the sacrifice. At least this is suggested by some of the examples given above, as well as by the fact that *'ālana* is sometimes the object of the verb *hā'awi*, "to give." At times, *'ālana* seems to connote a sacrifice of expiation, as in the following text:

"*He 'ālana ka mea e hā'awi aku ai e kala 'ia mai ai ka hala o ka mea lawehala*," "an *'ālana* is the thing given so that the sin of a transgressor will be pardoned" (PE, 17).

Sacrifices may be called gifts (*makana*) as, for instance, in the expression "*he makana na ke akua*," "a gift for the gods" (Fornander 1916–20, 4: 155; Kamakau 1976, 28). It is also said that one "gives" (*hā'awi*) the gods offerings or persons (Remy 1862, 28; Kepelino 1932, 18, 19, 57; Ii 1963, 26; Kahiolo 1978, 175).[64] However, *makana* and *hā'awi* are used less often than the technical terms to designate sacrifice, and I take this as an indication that sacrifice is considered something more than a gift or at least that the sacrificial gift differs from the gift exchanged between men. Moreover, from the fact that, materially speaking, an offering is always *given*, one cannot infer that it always has gift status, or that the efficacy of sacrifice rests exclusively on the mechanism of the gift. (See below, the discussion of the firstfruits sacrifice.)

The literal meanings of other terms of the sacrificial vocabulary may refer to material acts or gestures in the ritual action. Thus, for example, *mōlia* literally means "to set apart [the offering—V. V.] for the gods" (PE, 233) and connotes the initial act of separating the sacrificial object from the profane world. The first lines of two prayers furnish two examples: "*E molia e alana ia oe*," "set apart is an offering to you" (Kamakau 1976, 27); and "*he molia he mohai, he makana, / he 'alana ia 'oe, e ke Akua*," "set apart is a sacrifice, a gift, / an offering to you, O god" (Kamakau 1976, 28; cf. Handy 1972, 140–41). However, metonymically, this initial "separation" can mean the sacrifice as a whole.

In the same vein, '*āmama*, "finished," refers first of all to the ritual stage that coincides with the end of the prayer of consecration, when the attribution of the offering to the god takes place, but it can also refer to the entire sacrificial action (Fornander 1916–20, 6:340; PE, 21).

Kau, which literally means "to place," "to hang up," "to suspend" (PE, 124), refers to the action of placing the offering on the altar or hanging it on sacrificial poles, but it may also refer to the sacrifice as a whole. Thus "*ke kau ana o ke kanaka i ka lele*" literally means "the placing of the human victim on the altar" and, by extension, "the making of a human sacrifice" (Fornander 1916–20, 5:325; cf. 323; cf. as well Fornander 1916–20, 4:147, 149; J. S. Emerson in HEN, 1:525 line 10).

Hau or *hahau*, meaning "to place before" and, by extension, "to consecrate a sacrifice," is a case analogous to *kau* (PE, 50, s.v. *hahau*).

When it occurs without a determinant, *kaumaha* can refer to any type of sacrifice but especially, it appears, to the consecration of the god's share in a sacrificial meal or in any meal (Fornander 1916–20, 5:15; cf. Koskinen 1967, 74–79). This more specific meaning is sometimes indicated by the expression *kaumaha 'ai* (cf. Kamakau 1964, 77; Kahiolo 1978, 39, 171; Ellis 1842, 236; Fornander 1916–20, 5:329). The *pule kaumaha 'ai* is the prayer recited before beginning a meal; its recitation entails consecrating the first part of the meal, or its essence, to the deities invoked. *Kaumaha* can also refer to the sacrifice of human victims (*po'e heana*— Fornander 1916–20, 4:219, cf. 221; Kamakau 1976, 14), since in some sacrifices they are the god's share par excellence. In conclusion, it seems that using the term *kaumaha* emphasizes the alimentary aspect of the sacrifice in contexts where this aspect is highlighted (cf. Elbert 1956–57, 70:270).

In the analysis of royal rituals, we will have the opportunity to mention more specialized or less important sacrificial terms. Those discussed here suffice to show that in Hawaiian no rigidly separated categories exist to designate different forms of sacrifice. Moreover, the distinction, arbitrarily introduced by some lexicographers on the basis of biblical reminiscences (cf. Smith 1892, 21:132, 1894, 243, 217) between "offering" (used as a synonym for "vegetable offering" or "offering of an inanimate object") and "sacrifice" (in the sense of "bloody sacrifice") has no equivalent in the Hawaiian language.

Although sometimes they emphasize different aspects of the sacrificial action (oblative, alimentary, separative, etc.), most terms in the sacrificial vocabulary can mean "sacrifice" in the generic sense. It is obvious that this rite is conceived of as one, and thus we are justified in studying it as such.

Theories of Sacrifice

Before putting forward a theory explaining the practices I have just outlined, it is necessary to review very briefly the principal theories of sacrifice. This is not, of course, the place for a complete discussion. The task at hand requires only that I place my theoretical stand against the background of existing theories.

Most theories of sacrifice are based on one of the following theses or on some combination of them:

1. Sacrifice is a gift to the gods and is part of a process of exchange between gods and humans.

2. Sacrifice is a communion between man and god through a meal.

3. Sacrifice is an efficacious representation.

4. Sacrifice is a cathartic act.

In one form or another, these theses are as old in Western thought as the religious and philosophical speculations of both classical and biblical antiquity (cf. Tautain 1921; Lods 1935, 332–36).

Certainly the most common theory of sacrifice since Plato (*Eutyphro* 14e–15a) is the gift theory. It was reformulated in the nineteenth century by Tylor, for whom "sacrifice is a gift made to a deity as if he were a man" (1889, 2:375). By classifying sacrifices "according to the manner in which the offering is given by the worshipper and received by the deity" (ibid.), Tylor attempts to demonstrate that the direction of religious evolution proceeds "from practical reality to formal ceremony" (ibid., 376). Thus the "gift theory" proper is followed by the "homage theory," which is followed in turn by the "abnegation theory." This sequence corresponds to a progressive "spiritualization" of sacrifice; at first it is believed that the efficacy of the offering is based on its real transmission (in a more or less material form) to the god. In the homage stage, the offering is thought to be efficacious through knowledge; the god does not need or receive the offering, but the knowledge that it is given prompts him to use his power on behalf of the giver. As for the abnegation theory, it is a purely anthropocentric notion of sacrifice; no benefit for the god, only loss for man determines the value and efficacy of the sacrifice. Thus the efficacy attributed to sacrifice by the sacrifier is purely "moral."

Throughout this evolution there is one constant: the value of the offering always coincides with its utility. Even when sacrifice is a "loss," it is the loss of a commodity and is conceived of as meritorious because it is a loss (cf. Hume 1826, 4:477).

Tylor thus fails to recognize the fundamental fact that—as the Hawaiian evidence also shows—the object given symbolizes the sacrifier, and often the god and the aim of the sacrifice as well. Accordingly, he reduces sacrifice to a *do ut des*—to a misplaced application of the sound principle of utilitarian exchange. Moreover, he artificially separates the sacrificial oblation from the total symbolic process of which it is only a part. Thus, his asymbolic view of the offering creates a double distortion: it reduces the gift to a commodity and reduces the ritual action to mere gift giving. Moreover, Tylor does not see that, *as a gift*, sacrifice is effective because it is a token of the relationship between god and man—because it creates that relationship by instantiating it. In other words, by being presented as a token, the sacrificial gift evokes the presence of the type (the relation) that it presupposes.[65] In Marett's simpler words, sacrifice presupposes communion (a reciprocal relationship) rather than a "one-sided mode of propitiation" (1936, 156–57).

It was left for Robertson Smith to recognize the connection between sacrifice and communion. For him the central fact of religion is the relation of the god and his worshipers. But this relationship is identical to that binding the members of the community. Thus, in a society based on kinship, the relationship with the god is conceived as the relationship with a kinsman (1894, 99, 36, 60). Sacrifice, in reestablishing the relationship ("communion") with the god, reestablishes the relationship between the members of the community. The two relationships coincide; the god is the personification of the society, of the principle that makes it possible. This is the basis of the efficacy of sacrifice. Since the true signifieds of religious representations and of ritual action coexist with conscious beliefs that misconstrue them, Robertson Smith is bound to give more importance to the "unspoken ideas embodied in the traditional form of ritual praxis" (1894, 26), than to the conscious ideas and purposes of ritual—in other words, belief. Thus, Robertson Smith's perspective reverses Tylor's, for whom the reconstruction of "plain original purpose" (Tylor 1889, 2:397) and conscious belief is the basis of explanation. Against him, Robertson Smith—probably influenced by the Kantianism of the liberal Protestant theologians—emphasizes that religious representations and ritual contain a truth; but this truth has to be measured with the yardstick of morality (sociologically conceived), not of science, as for Tylor (cf. Valeri 1981b, 212–14).

Unfortunately, the true import of Robertson Smith's theory was obscured by the form it took. He restricted the idea of communion to its most literal and material expression: a communion of substance brought about by sharing the same food. Hence, he failed to recognize that the gift contained an element of communion in a more abstract sense than the meal. This resulted in his displacing Tylor's gift theory to a later stage of evolution, not in a revolution of the idea of the gift. Consequently, many felt that Smith's communion theory was an arbitrary attempt to destroy the unity of sacrifice and endeavored to defend the thesis of the universal validity of the gift theory against the Scot and his followers (Wilken 1891; Marillier 1897–98; Frazer in Black and Chrystal 1912, 517–19). Nevertheless, Smith's influence is clearly felt in the reformulation of the gift theory of sacrifice that followed the publication of his book. The shift toward such a reformulation is already apparent in Hubert and Mauss (1899), although their classic essay contains a number of ambiguities and conflicting tendencies.

Perhaps more than any other work on sacrifice, that of Hubert and Mauss reflects a traditional priestly perspective. The Brahmanas (Lévi 1898) and the so-called Priestly Code of the Bible (Lods 1935, 332–33) not only are Hubert and Mauss's basic texts, they also influence their outlook in at least two related respects. In the first place, Hubert and Mauss seem more interested in the "technology" of sacrifice than in its "nature and function" (cf. Girard 1972, 31). In the second place, they tend to construct an "essential sacrifice"—"Sacrifice" with a capital S—and to isolate it from its concrete social and cultural contexts (cf. Biardeau and Malamoud 1976, 7–8). Thus they have an unfortunate tendency to pass from form to generic function without taking precise meanings into account. On the positive side, the adoption of a "technical," "ritualistic" perspective encourages Hubert and Mauss to develop a "syntactic" study of sacrifice (cf. Evans-Pritchard 1965, 71) and therefore to view it as a global ritual process, which is not exhausted by the simple act of giving.

There is, however, a certain tension in the "Essai" between two definitions of sacrifice. On the one hand, Hubert and Mauss agree with Tylor in characterizing sacrifice as an oblation, while adding the qualification that an oblation must be destroyed to be called a sacrifice. On the other hand, they define sacrifice as a technique for connecting sacred and profane through a victim that functions as a mediator (Mauss 1968–69, 1:302). The two definitions overlap but do not fully coincide—as every careful reader of the "Essai" knows.

In the first place, the victim does not have to be a gift to function as a mediator: this is obviously demonstrated by Hubert and Mauss's interpretation of the sacrifice of the firstfruits.[66] In the second place, the idea of sacrifice as gift must correlate with the belief in personal, anthropomorphic spiritual beings than can be conceived as recipients of "gifts." But as good Durkheimians, Hubert and Mauss believe there can be "sacredness" without "spiritual beings." Thus the notion of sacrifice as the mediation between sacred and profane must be wider than the notion of sacrifice as gift. This explains a certain oscillation in Hubert and Mauss's view of sacrifice. On the one hand, they make it a phenomenon of greater generality than the oblation; on the other hand, by defining it as oblation, they have to limit it to a stage of religious evolution in which spiritual beings are worshiped. Eventually, in the preface to the 1906 reprint of the "Essai," they adopt the second position[67] (cf. Hubert and Mauss 1929). But in the "Essai" the tension remains unresolved. Its effect, however, is to leave undeveloped the new notion of the sacrificial gift that the "Essai" implicitly contains. This new notion follows from the idea that the oblation is a "buffer" between sacred and profane; as such, it must also be a substitute for the sacrifier. Thus the gift ceases to be a commodity, a mere utilitarian object; *it is the subject in an objective form.* But this shift from the "utilitarian theory" to the "objectivation theory" of the gift, and its implications for the theory of sacrifice, are not made fully explicit by Hubert and Mauss.

Lagrange (1905, 247 ff.) was one of the first to perceive the new notion of oblation implicit in the "Essai" and to use it against both Tylor and Robertson Smith. He notices that the gift theory and the communion theory appear irreconcilable because of the utilitarian conception of the gift common to both Tylor and Smith. Instead, the gift has to be conceived as a symbol of the relationship between man and god. Only when it is seen as such, according to Lagrange, can it be viewed as the common feature of all sacrifices.

Basically, then, the gift can be said to be the common element of all sacrifices because it incorporates the idea of communion in a form more abstract than Robertson Smith's. This synthesis of communion and gift in a wider formula (the reciprocal but hierarchical relation of sacred and profane) was lucidly expounded by Durkheim (1912, 486–500), who is also notable for giving a more systematic and coherent form to Robertson Smith's and Hubert and Mauss's idea that sacrifice is the objectified metaphor of a moral reality: the mutual dependence of individual and society.

A problem left unsolved by Hubert and Mauss as well as by Durkheim concerns the connection between reciprocity and inequality in the sacrificial oblation. To put it crudely, the sacrifier gives little in exchange for much. How can this be explained? Some theorists view this as the consequence of a "magical" (or is it bourgeois?) belief in the productive power of exchange (cf. van der Leeuw 1920–21, 252; 1938, 354; cf. also Bertholet 1942; Stanner 1963, 3). There is in fact an array of "power working theories of sacrifice," as Thompson (1963, 6) calls them, that are better left alone (cf. especially Will 1925, 1:84; Griaule 1940).[68]

More fruitful is the tantalizingly brief suggestion of Mauss in the "Essai sur le don": "ces dieux qui donnent et rendent sont là pour donner une grande chose à la place d'une petite" (1978b, 169). This means the gods must establish their superiority by giving more than they receive from man; reciprocity is not based on the equivalence of the things given per se, but the value of the thing given is inversely proportional to that of the giver. In other words, for a god, giving much is giving little; for man, giving little is giving much. Hence man's small gift to the god is as valuable as god's big gift to man, but at the same time this equivalence of the gifts signifies and establishes the nonequivalence of the givers, of god and man. It is in this way that reciprocity can coexist with hierarchy and that the sacrificial exchange can represent the gods' superiority over men.

Van Baal (1975a,b) has recently attempted to build on Mauss's insight,[69] but by denying, quite unrealistically it seems, that the sacrifier has any expectation of reciprocity from the gods, he shows his misunderstanding of the hierarchical relationship. The latter implies *both* gift and countergift; it is a reciprocal relationship and not simply subordination. Van Baal goes so far as to refuse to take at face value the requests contained in the sacrificial prayers. According to him these requests are made by the sacrifier only to humiliate himself, not to obtain what he says he wants (1975b, 170). Van Baal forgets that not all religions make man a hypocrite.

More interesting than this Calvinistic reading of the gift theory (which has the consequence of leaving out of the field of sacrifice all that does not fit the theory—cf. van Baal 1975b, 177), is Gusdorf's attempt to characterize "religious" (as opposed to "magical") sacrifice as the expression of an ideology of *debt*.[70]

According to the *do ut des* theory, the sacrifier gives in order to receive. The purpose precedes the god, who is only the condition of its satisfaction. In contrast, in the perspective developed by Gusdorf, the sacrificial gift is motivated by a preexisting debt. Man is forever in debt to the gods that sustain his existence. He must give to them without ever being able to repay (Gusdorf 1948, 72; cf. also Lacan 1973, 247). Such a notion of sacrifice as debt is, of course, frequent in Brahmanic literature (cf. Lévi 1898, 131–33); it emphasizes man's utter dependence on the gods.

But in Hawaii, at least, the god does not give only spontaneously: he must often be forced by man to give; reciprocally, man does not give only out of a sense of debt, but because he wants something. As we have seen, Hawaiian sacrifice usually has an aim—although we might add now that the public sacrifices offered four times a month in the temples (cf. part 3) do not necessarily have any aim other than maintaining the proper relationship between human and divine. The important fact is, however, that this relationship is conceived as reciprocal—in a sense, as one of mutual indebtedness.

Let us now turn to the theories that emphasize that sacrifice is an efficacious representation. We have seen that Hubert and Mauss already tended to focus on the sacrificial rite *as a whole* rather than on the simple giving of the offering. Alfred Loisy (1920) makes a further and fundamental step in this direction by considering sacrifice as a particular form of a phenomenon that is the only legitimate object of analysis, ritual as *efficacious representation*. Anticipating Hocart (1927, 1970) he views ritual representation as a mimesis—an icon—of what the sacrifier wants to obtain and of the conditions for its realization. Among these conditions, the principal one is the establishment of a relationship with the gods, who are conceived as means to an end. Sacrifices are distinguished from other rituals in that they involve the destruction of a living thing. The latter may or may not be conceived as a gift; the crucial fact is that it is an icon. Sacrifice, then, requires less a theory of the gift than a theory of representation. Why is a representation made in the ritual context considered effective? Why is it not simply considered fictitious?

As the Hawaiian data abundantly show, the offering always represents much more than a simple equivalent in exchange; it represents the deities, the sacrifier, their relationship, and the results required—in other words, the entire relationship, its partners, and the process that brings about the result. Finally, in the matter of symbols, every sacrificial rite involves much more than the offering. I therefore find that Loisy's approach makes perfect sense, both because it accounts for sacrifice as a global ritual that cannot be reduced to the symbolism of gift or communion and because it reduces the problem of its explanation to the fundamental problem of the efficacy of symbolic action. His answer to the problem matters less here than the fact that he has correctly formulated it. Loisy's theory is clearly one of the best examples of that class of theories that constitute the self-reflecting, anthropological stage of the traditional religious view, according to which sacrifice works *ex opere operato*,[71] thus by "magic" (cf. Lods 1921, 505). Hocart, whose formulations are very similar to Loisy's in many respects,[72] belongs to the same class. It is unnecessary here to discuss other examples (such as Lienhardt 1961, to which I shall return).

The final class of theories I wish to consider is the one that focuses on the violent nature of sacrifice and sees in this violence a collective "purifying" device. I shall briefly discuss only two recent and slightly different formulations of this theory.

The first is Girard's, which is fundamentally an extension of the scapegoat mechanism—whose importance Frazer had already recognized[73]—to all forms of sacrifice. In Girard's view, the sacrificial victim is always an outlet for the violence inherent in human relationships; by concentrating the diffuse and reciprocal violence that exists among individuals onto one single individual, the victim, sacrifice makes violence "unanimous." This "unanimous violence" at the expense of a victim drains society of its internal violence and therefore becomes the foundation for the positive forms of unanimity of which society consists. Moreover, Girard believes in an original event in which the mechanical "play of violence" found, quite by chance, its outlet in an "innocent" ("arbitrary") victim; thus the latter became the first symbol, in the sense that it became for every individual the substitute for the original object of his violence. From this first symbol developed all the others. Sacrifice as a ritual institution repeats this original event, which constituted society and symbolism and therefore reproduces them.

Thus the gods, together with the other religious representations and the entire culture, are rationalizations of a mechanical psychological process by which violence is produced and then expelled. The gods are, quite literally, collective violence encapsulated, masked—transformed into its contrary— since they are *violence transcended*. This is why they are conceived of as the basis of society's existence.

In Girard's theory, it makes no sense at all to speak of sacrifice as a "gift" or as a "representational action," and so forth. All these views are just rationalizations, secondary formations based on a very simple, unchanging reality: the mechanism of violence formation and expulsion. These secondary formations must exist in order to obfuscate the mechanism of violence, to keep it separate from consciousness and therefore to maintain it in its externalized, reified state. Violence expelled is also violence unrecognized, claims Girard. Hence, in the sacrificial ritual violence must be both present and unknown.

It is immediately clear from this summary that violence is the crucial concept on which Girard's theory rests. Why do human relations produce violence? Why can this violence not be repressed—as most other theorists believe—but must be expelled cathartically? A proper criticism of Girard's theory of sacrifice would have to start from a criticism of his theory of violence as a correlate of desire. But there is no place here for such an extended discussion. Nor is it necessary for my purpose, since a briefer and simpler criticism will do.

Girard believes it is possible to isolate a psychological process in its pure state, independent of the cultural order. He believes, therefore, that the cultural order is just a rationalization, a cover-up, of this very simple eternal process. I object that it is impossible to postulate a "pure" psychic dynamics that would be considered the "cause" of culture. Psychic processes take place in culture and presuppose it. From this it follows that cultural motivations—that is, meaningful motivations—cannot be simply treated as false motivations or rationalizations. They must be recognized as real and constitutive in their own way. Sacrifice, then, presupposes the cultural order; the gods cannot be conceived of as the mechanical *result* of the sacrificial catharsis, since they are its presupposition. Even violence does not exist prior to the values and concepts incorporated in the gods, since there is no violence, or judgment of an act as violent, without values that make it possible to define it as such. In this connection, let me point out that the victims of human sacrifice in Hawaii must be *guilty*. Violence can be exerted against them because they have threatened the values that constitute society. Their sacrifice "purifies" and reproduces society because it reestablishes its values against those who have threatened the social order with their violence. Hence both the violence of the transgressor who becomes victim and that of the sacrifier presuppose the constitutive values of society—their violence is effective because it is significant, not because it is prior to signification. Doubtless Girard would view the fact that the victims must be guilty as a cover-up, a way of keeping the mechanism of violence separate from consciousness and therefore guaranteeing catharsis. But anything can be proved with an argument that posits a priori that the truth is always beyond consciousness. Unfortunately, this argument does not explain why the truth resides only in Girard's consciousness. Naturally my criticism of Girard does not imply that an explanation based on unconscious processes underlying conscious ones must be ruled out. Quite the contrary. But the unconscious cannot be separated from the cultural system it presupposes. Nor can one leave out of the explanation the concrete operations by which unconscious processes become conscious beliefs. This requires a theory of concept formation, not a theory of unthinking violence.

To conclude this discussion let me point out that the excessive emphasis Girard puts on violence obfuscates the symbolic, figurative value of the victim's death or destruction. Sacrificial death and destruction are also images; they represent the passage from the visible to the invisible and thereby make it possible to conceive the transformations the sacrifice is supposed to produce. This figurative element of death or destruction is common both to blood sacrifice and to the sacrifice of vegetable offerings—which, of course, is not in the least accounted for by Girard's theory. In fact, the vegetable offerings that are simply abandoned on the altar rot and disappear exactly like the animals that are put to death. Decomposition, which marks the separation from the human and visible world, seems thus a more general and perhaps more important element than the violent act of killing, which is present only in animal and human sacrifices.

Finally, a psychological aspect of sacrificial violence itself should not be forgotten. It creates a strong impression and therefore a *memory*. It associ-

ates the moral laws that are reproduced in sacrifice with fear and pain and
therefore helps perpetuate them. This aspect of sacrifice was well understood by Nietzsche, who wrote,

Es ging niemals ohne Blut, Martern, Opfer ab, wenn der Mensch es nötig hielt,
sich ein Gedächtnis zu machen; die schauerlichsten Opfer und Pfänder (wohin
die Erstlingsopfer gehören), die widerlichsten Verstümmelungen (zum Beispiel
die Kastrationen), die grausamsten Ritualformen aller religiösen Kulte (und alle
Religionen sind auf dem untersten Grunde Systeme von Grausamkeiten)—alles
das hat in jenem Instinkte seinen Ursprung, welcher im Schmerz das mächtigste
Hilfsmittel der Mnemonik erriet. [1968, 4:60–61]

But this indicates that sacrificial violence itself has a symbolic value and
cultural aim and therefore cannot be defined without taking these into
account.

Girard's theory is remarkably similar to that of Burkert, whose book
Homo necans was published in the same year (1972) as Girard's *La violence
et le sacré*. Like Girard, Burkert postulates that the sacred is violence transcended and that sacrifice is a violent act making this transcendence possible. However, while Girard explains violence with a murky metaphysics
of desire, Burkert founds it on genetic platitudes. According to him, the
biological program acquired by the human species at the hunting stage involved the development of a strong intraspecific violence that originally
found its outlet in the violence exerted on game. Therefore the latter was
conceived as a quasi-human adversary, a substitute for the human enemy.
Later, in conditions of settled agriculture, when the big game disappeared
or was domesticated, the sacrifice of domestic animals took the place of
hunting as an outlet for intrahuman violence. Sacrifice is thus a "ritualized" equivalent of hunting and has the same power to perpetuate the
social bond. Society has a negative foundation, as in Girard: it is the positive result of the catharsis of a negative impulse. Burkert's genetic reductionism is no better than Girard's psychological reductionism and can be
subjected to a similar (and stronger) criticism. I spare readers its reformulation, since it is obvious.

A Model of Hawaiian Sacrifice

Of all the theories of sacrifice just discussed, the one that views it as a complex ritual process, as a "symbolic action" that cannot be reduced to any of
the elements ("gift," "communion," "catharsis," etc.) recognized in it by
native consciousness or by the interpreter seems the most adequate to me.
Thus I believe that Hawaiian sacrificial ritual should be viewed as a "symbolic action" that effects transformations of the relationships of sacrifier,

god, and group by representing them in public. This symbolic action consists of three main stages.

It begins with what motivates it: a perceived lack. Thus if a man has transgressed, he is in a state of lack because he is not "in communion" with his group and the god thereof, but is marked off from them by a taboo. Moreover, the transgressor's lack also implies a lack in the god (as we shall see) and in the group, which have lost their integrity because of the transgression.

To take another example: the sacrifice by which a young boy is incorporated into the men's house of his homestead is motivated by his lack: he is not yet considered an adult. But his lack is also a lack of his group, which does not yet have him as a full male member, and of the god, who does not yet receive his cult. A similar state of lack is the starting point of the sacrifices that empower the sacrifier to perform certain technical activities together with a given group of people or on their behalf.

Whether it is due to transgression or to being unable to perform certain acts, the initial state of lack is perceived as an imperfection that must be overcome. This imperfection or even disorder is represented by an aspect of the offering that is emphasized at this stage. Thus, as I have noted, that the pig is a kind of disordered equivalent of a human (cf. Emerson 1892, 14) may be relevant at this moment. That the offering is a double of the sacrifier opens the possibility of transforming him, both by destroying (and eventually punishing) his present person and by making him a new person. This transformation is represented—in the second main stage of the symbolic action—by the god's devouring the offering.

This devouring is an incorporation of the offering (and therefore of the sacrifier) in the god. It signifies that the sacrifier is now encompassed by the god, is part of his *kuleana*, "domain." This means, concretely, that the sacrifier now corresponds to the concept for which the god stands and that he instantiates it. In other words, the sacrifier views himself and is viewed by the audience as a token of which the god is the type.

In the third stage of the sacrificial action the offering incorporated into the god is divided in two parts: one stays permanently with the god, the other returns to the sacrifier and is partaken of by him and by those who participate in the ritual.

Each part of the offering, which is a double of the sacrifier, signifies a different state of his. The part that remains with the god signifies the state of the sacrifier when he is intensely conscious of what the god stands for: the concept of the sacrifier's subject. This level of consciousness was in the foreground when the sacrifier's attention was entirely focused on the god and the offering entirely consecrated to him.

The part that is detached from the god signifies the state of the sacrifier's consciousness when his attention is redirected toward the concrete world. Eating this part creates a transition from the previous state of consciousness to the ordinary one and at the same time subordinates the latter to the former, since the two parts are metonymically related. The eating also marks the effects of this subordination: the reproduction of the sacrifier's relationship with his group and of his ability to act in it.

This model of sacrifice presupposes that the rite is the objective form of a process of consciousness that it stimulates. The structure of this process is the triadic one isolated by Hubert and Mauss: the sacrifier moves from state A to state C by passing through state B, which implies being in contact with the god.

But I shall now show that this view of sacrifice is incomplete and that—rather than describing the real process—it focuses on its marked moments only. Moreover, it treats sacrifice as a bilateral relationship between sacrifier and god and fails to stress that the collective judgment of the audience always mediates that relationship. It seems to me that a more adequate description of Hawaiian sacrifice is one that recognizes the constant coexistence and interrelation of four parallel processes, concerning as many terms: the sacrifier; the god; the group (represented by the audience); and the signifiers (principally offerings and images).

Let me redescribe the sacrificial process by taking into consideration all four components. In the initial stage, sacrifier, god, and group are in the same state of lack or disorder. This state is represented by signifiers borne by the offering. In addition, the offering as a whole consists for the most part of natural species, which have indexical or incompletely iconic relationships with the predicates personified by the god involved in the sacrifice. Because they are indexical or partially iconic, these signifiers evoke the corresponding predicates less clearly and completely than does a purely iconic signifier such as the anthropomorphic image of the god. Being fully iconic, the image directly represents what it stands for and therefore produces a clearer consciousness of the human type personified by the god.

The first stage of the sacrificial rite, then, is characterized by the following chain of implications: focus on the indexical or partially iconic signifiers of the god ⊃ lesser consciousness of their signifieds ⊃ lesser order in the sacrifier, who realizes less the divine type or is in contrast with it ⊃ lesser order in the group because of the disorder of the sacrifier.

The common feature of all terms at this stage is disorder, imperfect realization of humanness; this feature may be signified by emphasizing the animal or disordered dimension in the offering. In the case of human sacrifice, it is emphasized by the choice of a transgressor as victim.

In the second stage, the natural signifiers are brought into contact (by consecration) with the anthropomorphic signifier (the image). This results in a transformation of the consciousness of what the god stands for: the human type he personifies becomes more evident. Correlatively, the sacrifier is allegedly transformed: he is made perfectly ordered by the presence of the concept in his consciousness. And of course this state of the sacrifier corresponds to a heightened state of order and attention in the audience, that is, the group to which he belongs.

In the next stage, attention and orderliness are lessened by somewhat removing the divine concept from consciousness and—as we shall see—by reducing the bodily and speech control required during the consecration (see chap. 8). This removal is effected by focusing again on the natural offering, that is, on the signifier that evokes the god less clearly. But the share of the offering eaten by sacrifier and group retains an indexical relationship with the god in his most evident human form: therefore, by eating it the sacrifier and his commensals both remove to the background and preserve in a superordinate position their previous state of consciousness. It is in this position that it can influence their actions and make them compatible.

If the four terms of the rite coexist and vary together at every stage, how is it that sacrifice can be described—in the fashion of Hubert and Mauss—as a movement from sacrifier in state A to god and then to sacrifier in state B? The reason is that this description connects the terms that are marked, and therefore most evident, in each of the three stages of the process. But we are not allowed to forget that the unmarked terms are *always* present and *always* presupposed by the process. Thus it would be wrong to view—as Hubert and Mauss do—the god as always identical to what he is when he is a marked term, that is, in the second stage. He is himself transformed in the process, as I shall show in detail in the next chapter and in part 3. Moreover, the state of the group can never be separated from that of the other terms, since it is the collective judgment of the audience that lends the process much (sometimes most) of its efficacy.

I have used the terms "much" and "most" on purpose. Indeed, having analyzed Hawaiian sacrifice as an objectified process of consciousness, I have implied that its efficacy depends at least to some extent on its ability to induce what it represents in the sacrifier's consciousness.

But this claim may be questioned. Isn't sacrifice efficacious in a purely conventional way? Doesn't its efficacy depend only on the collective recognition that it has been correctly performed? And even if we wish to take the sacrifier's consciousness into account, should we not suppose that the effect of the rite on consciousness (an effect that may be called "understanding") is taken for granted whenever the rite has been correctly performed, so that the relation between rite and effect must be viewed as purely conventional in this case as well?

My answer to these questions is that the effects of sacrifice are related to the correct performance of the rite both conventionally and nonconventionally. In other words, to borrow Austin's (1975) terminology, the rite is performative because of illocutionary (conventionally produced) and perlocutionary (nonconventionally produced) effects at the same time. More-over, I am prepared to maintain that there is an implicit belief that the results of sacrifice, whatever they are, depend on a previous effect, conventionally produced or not, on the sacrifier's understanding. In other words, the understanding and consequent introjection of what the god stands for is assumed or recognized in every collective judgment as to the efficacy of the rite with regard to its stated aims, which usually are not understanding itself. I maintain this precisely because I claim that the god is essentially a concept of human action: thus a rite that consists in empowering a subject to act in a certain way by reference to the concept of that action must be based on the presupposition that the subject understands that concept (albeit in reified form). Therefore, when a rite of passage is declared successful, and as a result the sacrifier is incorporated into a new group (for instance the group of adult males), it is conventionally supposed that he has "understood," and therefore taken as a guide for his new actions as an adult, the concept of that action as personified by the god. Analogously, in a sacrifice of purification, the sacrifier is effectively reincorporated in his group because the latter assumes that, as a result of the correct performance of the rite, he has understood the rule of the actions of the members of that group relative to one another.

In the two examples I have just given, the effect of the rite is illocutionary. The correct performance of the rite makes it successful because the audience supposes that the sacrifier has "understood," simply by performing the rite, and therefore it accepts him into its fold. But in other cases the effect (both the understanding and its consequences) cannot be considered purely illocutionary. Take, for instance, the numerous sacrifices connected with ergological activities, curing, war, propitiation, and so on. In these cases the efficacy of the rite depends on events that may occur or not occur *after* it has been performed: health recovered, a victory, a good harvest.

It is the occurrence of favorable events, therefore, that makes it possible retrospectively to assess the effectiveness of sacrifice (see Valeri 1982b, 35, n. 20). The audience's evaluation of the rite at the end of its performance, therefore, is not sufficient to create the event whose attainment the rite represents (in certain offerings) or mentions (in the prayers). In other words, the event is not purely conventional, as a purification or the passage from one status to another (see Valeri 1981b, 234–37). The audience's assessment of the success of the rite must therefore be viewed as conditional and as a constative rather than a performative statement.

All the audience can say at the end of the performance is that it seems to have had a certain effect on the status of the sacrifier, that it has transformed him, and therefore that his actions should be successful.

It goes without saying that no sacrifice can be viewed as having only illocutionary or only perlocutionary effects, whatever the nature of its effects. Given that every sacrificial rite is multipurpose and multivalent, it has a variety of effects through a variety of mechanisms that are incompletely codified. Thus the empowering of a king may seem a purely illocutionary effect of a rite; but since, as we shall see, this empowering takes place in a rite that has multiple purposes, one of them being, very often, success in war, it is vulnerable to the rite's perlocutionary effects with regard to these purposes. In other words, if the king wins the war that follows the rite, it is retrospectively declared that he has really been made a king by the rite; if he does not win, the judgment that he has been made king may be revised. It is therefore difficult to decide if the collective judgment at the time of the performance must be considered performative or constative. In a sense, it is partly performative and partly constative only, because the establishment of the king's legitimacy does not simply depend on formal criteria.

Firstfruits Sacrifice

As we have seen, firstfruits sacrifices are consecrated to deities who are believed to produce the species appropriated by man. Indeed, the whole of nature is produced by the gods and therefore consists of their bodies.[74] For this reason one cannot freely appropriate it but must ask forgiveness or return a part of what is appropriated.[75] This divinization of nature is of course the consequence of the circumstance that every natural species or phenomenon has a symbolic content, that it evokes human properties and activities that are collectively sanctioned and therefore made sacred. The species that have this evocative power to the highest degree cannot in fact be desacralized at all but are employed only semiotically, that is, in a ritual context; the other species are made available for material use after they have been freed of their symbolic content by firstfruits rites.

Although the symbolic content of most if not all aspects of nature suffices to account for the necessity of desacralizing nature by firstfruits sacrifices, the most important and frequent of such sacrifices are consecrated to the gods who personify the human activity that makes it possible to acquire the species whose first part is sacrificed. Thus, as we have seen, the firstfruits of fishing are consecrated to Kū'ulakai, who is a form of Kū as fisherman. Indeed, as I shall show shortly, he is the god who—through his son—teaches men to fish. Analogously, the firstfruits of farming are consecrated primarily to Lono as a personification of the farmer, and also to any of the other major gods worshiped in their "farmer" aspect (Malo 1951, 206–7; cf. chap. 7).

By offering the god who personifies his activity the firstfruits thereof, then, the sacrifier recognizes his dependence on the collectively sanctioned type of what he does. The sacrificial homage is therefore an homage to the real source of the productivity of his work, of what makes fish or taro exist for him. Hence the idea that the god who personifies fishing is also the producer of fish, the personification of fish as species.

The critical point, however, is that the sacrifice of the firstfruits frees the rest of the harvest or of the catch from the divine content that is initially recognized in it and therefore makes this rest *noa*, available for material consumption. A sign of this desacralization is, as we shall see, that the food becomes available even to women (see chap. 4). I interpret this effect of firstfruits sacrifices in the following way. As a product of the human activity that has made it possible to acquire it, the catch or the harvest evokes this activity and therefore appears as a manifestation of its divine type.

This human signified of the fish or taro cannot be ignored: on the contrary, it must be reaffirmed, for the reason just mentioned. At the same time, the fish must be eaten; it must lose its human subjective dimension to become a purely natural object. A firstfruits sacrifice both reaffirms the human content of a natural species and negates it by a metonymic device: by making the firstfruits signify the whole of the species' human content. In other words, the firstfruits become the only signifiers of what was initially signified by all fish caught, all taro farmed. The consecration of the firstfruits to the god of fishing or to the god of farming, then, is the transfer into transcendence, outside the empirical world, of the human, subjective content recognized in the product of man's work.[76] This interpretation is confirmed by the origin myth of the firstfruits of fishing. Three versions of this myth are extant (Fornander 1916–20, 6:172–75; Manu 1901, reprinted in Thrum 1907a, 215–49; Wahiako [1930] in Beckwith 1940, 20–22).[77] Manu's version bears the marks of modern reworkings yet contains important details. Fornander's version is unadulterated but very brief. All things considered, the best version appears to be that provided by Martha Beckwith, who recorded it from Thomas Wahiako in 1930. It can be used as a sort of backdrop to be filled in with details taken from other versions, which are all very close to it.

The story takes place in Hāna (Maui). The king of this district is called Kamohoaliʻi (Kahōāliʻi, in Fornander's account). Near the coast lives the god Kūʻulakai ("Kū the red one [sacred one] of the sea"), who is the chief fisherman. In the back country lives his brother Kūʻulauka ("Kū the red one of the inland"; his younger brother—cf. Thrum 1907a, 215), who is the chief farmer. Together they provide the two components of Hawaiian food: *ʻai* (agricultural products) and *iʻa* (seafood). The two brothers are two particularizations of the god Kū. They marry two sisters. Hinapukuiʻa ("Hina gathering seafood"), associated with the shore, becomes the wife of Kūʻulakai and gives him a son, called ʻAiʻai ("eats food").[78] Hinauluʻōhiʻa ("Hina of the growth of the ʻōhiʻa tree"), associated with the mountain, becomes the wife of Kūʻulauka. They are sisters of the gods of canoe builders, whose activity connects the sea and the uplands, where the trees grow that furnish the wood for canoes. The story concerns only Kū'ulakai, however, who builds an enormous fishpond, ever teeming with fish. These fish are in fact the "bodies" of the god (cf. Fornander 1916–20, 6:175), who gives them to men very sparingly. One day, an ali'i changes himself into a giant eel, gets into the fishpond, and eats so many fish that to escape he has to destroy part of it. Fleeing the vengeance of Kū'ulakai, he hides in a hole. But Kū'ulakai ('Ai'ai, according to Manu) succeeds in catching the "eel" with his hook Manaiākalani and kills it. The dead ali'i's favorite decides to take revenge. He enters the service of Kamohoali'i (or Kahōāli'i) and becomes his messenger. One day the king sends him to ask Kū'ulakai for some fish. The god gives him a fish and asks him to communicate his instructions to the king. These vary in each version. In those of Manu and Wahiako, the king is ordered to cut off the fish head, cook it in the oven, and eat it, but he must salt the body, dry it in the sun, and keep it. In Fornander's version Kū'ulakai orders Kahōāli'i to eat only the bones of the fish, "for it is a time of famine."

But the messenger throws away the fish and comes back reporting the god's words as if they referred to the king's own body. It is the king's head that must be cut off and cooked in the oven, his flesh that must be dried and preserved. Furious at being treated by Kū'ulakai as if he were fish, the king orders the fisherman and his family put to death. Because he is a god, Kū'ulakai is aware of the king's order, and he decides to leave his human form to return to the sea as a fish. But he leaves his son 'Ai'ai among men and, according to Manu, gives him one of his manifestations, a stone, also called Kū'ula, that is the "ancestor," or generative principle, of all fish (cf. Thrum 1907a, 222). He also entrusts him with the fishhook Manaiākalani and other fishing implements and teaches him how to invoke his parents to obtain fish.

When the king's men set fire to the god's house, Kū'ulakai and his wife disappear, taking with them all the fish and seafood. 'Ai'ai is sheltered by a man to whom he gratefully teaches the secret of fishing. He puts the stone Kū'ulakai next to the fishpond and informs his host that, in order to be able to continue fishing, from then on he will have to offer the first two fish of every catch to Kū'ulakai and Hina upon this stone. After the institution of the sacrifice of the firstfruits of fishing, the fish return and can be caught.[79] Some fish are sent to the king. Since he does not know that he must consecrate a share to the god, the god makes him choke on the first one and thus die.

The myth demonstrates that the fish is divinized because it is conceived of as human; Kū'ulakai, the god of fish, is both the fish in human form and man in the form of a fish, that is, man who objectifies himself in fish. He thus personifies an aspect of the human species in the fish species. In addition, he represents the implication of this identification; man cannot freely appropriate fish, since it is made sacred by its human signified. Only the god can take the initiative of giving man some fish, but this happens only rarely. In sum, the initial situation represented in myth is identical to the situation that precedes the firstfruits sacrifice. The divine is immanent in the totality of individuals of the natural species in which it manifests itself.

Consequently, each individual fish is equivalent to each individual human, and a relationship of reciprocity exists between them, similar to the one existing among humans. This reciprocity is revealed by an event at the beginning of the myth. Having decided to eat fish freely, a man experiences the revenge of Kū'ulakai, who kills him. That this reciprocity involves the equivalence of man and fish is emphasized by the fact that the man takes the shape of an eel (which is an *i'a*, "fish," in Hawaiian), while the fish (Kū'ulakai or his son) takes the shape of a man and fishes for him.

The same point is made by the dead man's favorite when he falsely reports Kū'ulakai's message to the king and substitutes the latter's name for that of a fish.

To put an end to this dangerous reciprocity, it is necessary to dehumanize the fish and therefore dedivinize it. Accordingly, the king orders the fish-god killed. But, having become totally dehumanized, nature becomes totally distant from man; the fish disappear. This demonstrates that the humanization of nature is the necessary correlate of its appropriation by man. From a Hawaiian point of view, a totally dehumanized nature is by definition a nature unappropriated by man.

Thus the reversal of the original situation has the same effect, if indeed the result is not even more serious: the famine becomes worse. In short, it seems that man cannot live without a humanized nature, nor can he live with it. The institution of the firstfruits sacrifice (the efficacy of which is guaranteed by the god himself) puts an end to the contradiction or, rather, creates a compromise. The humanization of nature—that is, the correlate of its appropriation by man—is preserved, but only in transcendence. As a consequence, the god of fish (who is also the god of fishing, of man's appropriation of fish, which transforms the fish into an objectification of the properties of man the fisherman) becomes separate from the empirical fish.

Thus the myth recapitulates the transformation at the basis of every firstfruits sacrifice and shows that at the root of this practice is the fact that it is impossible for man not to relate to his own species when appropriating a natural species.

The final episode of the myth confirms the necessity of sacrifice *a contrario*. Kahōāli'i, or Kamohoali'i, the king who has ordered the god killed—who therefore refuses to acknowledge and respect the human element in nature—chokes on a fish and is killed. He thus symbolizes the wrongful appropriation of nature: that which refuses to subordinate man's relationship with nature to his relationship with the concept of his own species. Significantly, Kahōāliʻi, who refuses to apperceive his species in nature, also evokes the refusal to apperceive and respect a common species in a fellow human being, since, as we shall see, he is a cannibal (man is not sacred to him).

Another version of the myth transposes it into more human terms, because the god's place is taken by a priest (Luahoʻomoe),[80] who is the god's representative (Anonymous 1924, 133). This version holds a particular interest, for it associates the origin of the sacrifice of the firstfruits of fishing with the origin of the sacrifice of the firstfruits of the harvest. This association enables us to put forth the following hypothesis: the origin myth of the sacrifice of the firstfruits of fishing was part of a larger mythological ensemble, now partially lost, in which the origin of the sacrifice of the firstfruits of the harvest was explained like that of the firstfruits of fishing. That in the main version of the myth Kūʻulakai is introduced by mentioning his agricultural counterpart, Kūʻulauka, and indicating both their parallelism and their affinal relationship strengthens this hypothesis.

The myth of Kūʻulakai seems to be related in some way to the annual rite for the desacralization of the *aku* fish, since in that rite the main officiant bears the title Kahōāliʻi. This rite confirms that a human element is recognized in the fish, since besides the restitution of the firstfruits of fishing to the god it includes a human sacrifice. The latter is a sacrifice of expiation: it is the giving of a man for a man or, rather, for what is human in the fish (Malo MS, 159; cf. Marin 1973, 199; Menzies 1920, 72–73; Bell 1929–30, 1:62).

The second most important annual rite of fishing, that for the *ʻōpelu* fish, expresses the same idea but only by threatening to sacrifice the man who brings to the temple the fruits of the first fishing of the year. As this man goes to the temple bearing the fish all kneel, probably as a sign of respect for the still divine fish. The instant the king has received the first portion of the catch, the bearer flees at top speed, apparently to avoid being sacrificed himself. Deprived of a human victim, the king limits himself to consecrating the first part of the catch to the god (K. Kamakau 1919–20, 32–35), that is, to giving it back as a token of the divine component of all the fish that will be caught during the season. By analogy with the Roman *regifugium*, this rite could be called *piscatorifugium*.[81]

The sacrifice of firstfruits of fishing concerns animals, sensitive beings like man. Since these are among the most elaborate firstfruits rites and contain an element of expiation, one may ask if my explanation does not leave out an element that is instead emphasized by another theory of firstfruits sacrifice, the one put forward by Karl Meuli (1975, 978, 250–51; cf. Burkert 1979, 55, 56).

According to Meuli, the ritual appropriation of animals is motivated by man's identification with them. This identification would explain why he pities them and feels guilty when he kills them. The guilt would be relieved by ritual, which consists in denying the death of the animal or in putting the responsibility on someone else (cf. Jensen 1963, 186; Frazer 1963, 682–98). Meuli's theory is inspired by Schopenhauer's famous definition of the *Mitlied* (*Über die Grundlage der Morale* 16) as the feeling in which ego and nonego are identified. This definition recalls in turn Rousseau's *pitié* (1782, 1:43–45). It turns out, then, that Meuli puts at the basis of sacrifice the same notion that Lévi-Strauss (1962a, 291, 1962b, 149) puts at the basis of totemism—an unexpected avatar of the old relation between totemism and sacrifice!

I do not deny that compassion is one motivation of firstfruits sacrifices in certain cases. Indeed, I have recognized that the firstfruits sacrifices of fishing contain an element of expiation that seems absent from the firstfruits rites connected with farming. Moreover, all animals that are most sensitive and with which man feels the greatest affinity—pig, dog, tortoise, and even chicken, perhaps—can be killed only ritually.

However, Meuli's theory is not satisfactory in that it makes the identification a purely emotional phenomenon. Thus, not only does he fail to recognize that man also identifies with animals because they are perceived as signifiers of social predicates, he is also unable to explain why identification with plants, which is clearly not based on "compassion," might take place at all.

To give an example of how this identification with plants may be explained, let us consider the most important cultivated plant, taro. Its identification with man is partly due to awareness that it is a product of human labor. As such, it must reflect the predicates of the species-laborer. This is why myth places man himself at the origin of the taro plant; it derives it from the transformation of an aborted human child, the first issue of the marriage between Wākea and Papa, progenitors of all Hawaiians (Malo 1951, 244; NK, 1:167). At the same time, taro is identified with man because, as his staple food, it is human life in a potential state. This idea is perfectly expressed in a prayer recited at one stage of the plant's cultivation: "That a man may be hidden / amongst our taro, O Ku" (Kamakau 1976, 35). In truth, there is a "hidden man," a potential man, in the taro plant, since it is by eating taro that man is able to exist.

The relationship between man and taro is thus symmetrical. Man produces taro, and taro produces man. Their lives are marked by solidarity that involves a certain degree of identification. Thus the name of the ancestor of all taro, Hāloa, is the same as that of the ancestor of all men, Hāloa. Moreover, there is an absolute parallelism between the two "lineages of Hāloa," the one formed by taro and the one formed by man, since the reproduction of taro provides many metaphors that designate aspects of kinship: for example, the word '*ohana*, "family," "kindred," is made to derive (in what perhaps is a folk etymology) from the word '*ohā*, "taro growing from the older root" (PE, 254; Handy and Pukui 1972, 197–98). In sum, man sees his species properties in taro because it is his "congealed" labor and because it is a conceptual and material correlate of his existence.

As this example shows, man identifies with a natural species, animal or vegetable, because he finds in it some properties of his own species in an objective, external form. But these properties, contrary to what Meuli believes, are not only those of his physical and feeling being, but also, and more important, those of his social, cultural being.

Conclusion

It is now possible to relate the classification of the deities to the classification of sacrifices. My discussion has indicated that most deities personify socially recognized or accepted types of action in certain social contexts. Three main kinds of types personified by deities can be distinguished:

1. Types of moral actions that perpetuate a given type of group (kinship group, political group of a certain order, age group, functional group, etc.) or social category (kinship category, hierarchical category, etc.).

2. Types of technical actions that produce artifacts.

3. Types of actions that make certain species available for use, that "produce" them.

Each of these kinds of types corresponds to a different kind of "body" or natural manifestation of the deity. A deity or an aspect of a deity that refers to moral actions and their subjects (groups, hierarchical categories, etc.) tends to be especially associated with natural phenomena that symbolize those actions, the subjects of the latter, or the operations necessary to their realization. The natural correlates of a deity or an aspect of a deity that refer to "technical" actions are phenomena symbolizing the process of work or constituting its substance and results. As for the types that make certain species available, they are symbolized by these species.

To each of these classes of divine types corresponds a class of sacrificial rituals or aspects thereof. The sacrifices that relate to the first class of types include all that concern the relations of the subject with the social group or category in which he is classified or reclassified by the rite. It also includes the sacrifices concerned with the reproduction of a group or category as such. I call all these sacrifices *nomocentric*.

The sacrifices that relate to the second class of divine types include all that concern technical work. Therefore it is appropriate to call them *ergocentric*.

The sacrifices that relate to the third class of divine types are of course firstfruits sacrifices. Since they are directly concerned with natural species as reflections of the human species, I propose to call them *genocentric*.

Classes of sacrifices can also be generated by distinguishing the different kinds of type/token relationships involved in nomocentric and ergocentric sacrifices. Two main kinds of relationships can be distinguished: (1) the sacrifier moves from the status of an inferior token of the deity to the status of superior token of the same deity; (2) the sacrifier moves from the status of token of the deity x to the status of token of the deity y, the two deities being sequentially linked as stages of a process of transformation. Alternatively, x and y can be viewed as two aspects or particularizations of the same deity.

The distinction between (1) and (2) is only relative, since the passage from inferior to superior status can be represented both by the passage from one token to another and by the passage from one type to another. The case in which the sacrifier passes from the status in which he has no relationship with a deity to the status in which he has a relationship with it does not deserve separate treatment, since it is usually a particular moment of (2) or an extreme case of (1).

One can immediately see that sacrifices of purification, expiation, propitiation, and in fact all sacrifices connected with rites of passage can be classified on the basis of these two kinds of relationship. For instance, "purification" is nothing else than the reestablishment of the token/type relationship between sacrifier and god. (This, in turn, makes it possible for the sacrifier to be reintegrated into his group.) It can also be seen in relative terms, as a passage from the status of an inferior token to the status of a token that fully displays the properties of the type (see part 2). Analogously, "expiation" is the destruction of the sacrifier's old self when it is in contrast with the type it should incarnate, and its transformation into a token of this type. A sacrifice of propitiation reinforces the sacrifier's status as a token of the god type, in order to avoid future negative consequences inherent in an inappropriate instantiation.

Thus, on the basis of an abstract system of relations derived from our model of sacrifice, it is possible to deduce the concrete types of sacrifice enumerated at the beginning of this chapter.

Note also that ergocentric and nomocentric sacrifices, on the one hand, and firstfruits sacrifices, on the other, are both different and complementary. They are different because, as indicated, the first two reinforce the semiotic aspect of all the individuals of the natural species they employ, while the third reinforce it only in certain individuals—the firstfruits—in order to suppress it in all others.

This contrast is made evident by the fact that while firstfruits sacrifices exclude eating the offering (the divine part that must be separated from the empirical whole) but make it lawful to eat the species outside the sacrificial context, the other sacrifices require eating some of the offering but forbid eating the species used as offering outside the sacrificial context.

But it is evident that these contrasts derive from a fundamental complementarity. For firstfruits sacrifices dedivinize nature in order to make it "free," available for material appropriation; the other sacrifices divinize man and his implements in order to make him able to effect the material appropriation of nature.

Thus the desacralization of nature implies the sacralization of man. Perhaps, then, it is possible to follow Kojève when he reformulates Hegel's interpretation of sacrifice by writing that in this rite "il faut . . . supprimer une partie du divin pour sanctifier l'homme" (1947, 247).

3

Gods and Humans

Eclaircissons, s'il se peut, cette matière: étudions l'esprit humain dans une de ses plus étranges productions: c'est là bien souvent qu'il se donne le mieux à connaître.
Fontenelle 1932, 11

Dans ces actions et réactions, il n'entre pas d'autres forces que du *mana*. Elles se produisent comme dans un cercle fermé où tout est *mana* et qui, lui-même, doit être le *mana*, si nous pouvons nous exprimer ainsi.
Hubert and Mauss 1978, 105

In the previous chapter I described sacrifice as a process consisting in a passage from incompleteness to completeness. Because the four terms of this process—sacrifier, audience, offering, and god—vary together, I implied that the movement from incompleteness to completeness applies to the god as much as to the other terms.

This chapter is dedicated to confirming this implication and developing its consequences. In doing so, I shall be able to explicate some fundamental notions governing the relations between human and divine: pure and impure, *kapu* and *noa*, mana.

Pure and Impure

Although our information is often scanty on this point, it appears that Hawaiians classify a variety of states as "pure" and "impure." Basically, purity denotes a state of integrity, that is, of close realization of a normative type. Impurity denotes, of course, the opposite state. The two states depend, then, on the relation of a being to its type. But as we shall see, this relation, and therefore the state of the being, may depend in turn on his relationship with other beings.

The equivalence of lack of integrity and impurity and, by implication, of integrity and purity is clearest in the evaluation of bodily phenomena.

The most impure bodily process is menstruation. The term used for menstrual blood, *peʻa*, is synonymous with impurity in general (PE, 297). Along with menstrual blood, all shed blood is impure to different degrees. This is indicated, for instance, by the statement that the gods "despised (*hoʻo pailua*) all bloody things" (Kamakau 1961, 3). Thus all who lose blood or come in contact with shed blood are impure: not only women menstruating or in labor, but also wounded people,[1] virgins being deflowered,[2] and so on (Kamakau 1961, 121; Fornander 1878–80, 2:310; Fornander 1916–20, 4:159, 5:512; NK, 1:114, 167; NK, 2:79).

Loss of grease (which is apparently believed to embody life) also produces pollution (Kamakau 1964, 37). Therefore those who are "greasy" are polluted. Indeed, the word *kūhinu*, "greasy," is a metaphor for impurity (Kepelino 1932, 33).

Also impure is anything organic that putrefies, such as corpses or excrement—and everybody who comes in contact with these things[3] or even worships them (Malo 1951, 96–97, 105; Remy 1862, 135; NK, 1:107; Kamakau 1961, 212–13, 264, 11; Fornander 1916–20, 4:504; cf. Emerson 1892, 15). Finally, aborted fetuses, deformed individuals, dwarfs, and cretins are also impure and polluting (Stewart 1838, 191; cf. Ii 1963, 101).

All these are impure because they manifest a loss of integrity, of life (examples: loss of blood or of grease, corruption) or the nonachievement of a normal form, of a perfectly functioning life (examples: aborted fetuses, monsters). These phenomena do not simply imply a contrast with the divine type that they should instantiate; they also involve a contrast with the group constituted by the people who correctly instantiate that type. Any lack of bodily integrity therefore entails a lack of social integrity, a state of disorder in the relationship between afflicted person and group. Thus a dead person or a menstruating woman produces a disorder, a weakness, in the group that must be resolved by purification.

Given this correlation of bodily and social integrity, bodily states can function as signifiers of social states and relations. A transgressor, for instance, is usually symbolized by a bodily state of impurity. Thus the *kauwā*, who are the transgressors par excellence, are called "corpses" (Kepelino 1832, 144).[4] Rank is also signified by bodily states of purity or impurity (see part 2) or by parts of the body that are viewed as relatively pure or impure (Malo 1951, 187–88).[5]

Note that the basic metaphors of purity and impurity are taken from the human body; nevertheless, aspects of the external world may be used, particularly if they are viewed as extensions of the human body. Although our information is not clear on this point, it seems that many anomalous or monstrous things in the environment, said to be *ʻeʻepa*, "peculiar," are treated as impure and studiously avoided.

That purity is the normal state while impurity is the anomalous one explains why there is a great abundance of statements about impurity and prescriptions for warding it off, in contrast to the relative paucity of statements concerning purity. Moreover, there are more terms and metaphors signifying impurity than purity. The two most common terms for impurity are *haumia* and *pela* (cf. Malo 1951, 97, 105), and their commonest metaphors are, as mentioned, "bloody" and "greasy" ("muddy" also seems to be frequent; cf. Malo 1951, 56). Purity is often referred to as *ma'ema'e*, which means "clean, pure, attractive, chaste; cleanliness, purity" (PE, 201). "To cleanse, to purify" is *ho'oma'ema'e* (Malo 1951, 138). Light, shine, clarity, and whiteness are common metaphors of purity, as we shall see (especially in part 3).

Given that impurity is a state of incompleteness while purity is a state of completeness, we must deduce that at the beginning of the sacrificial process sacrifier, group, offering, *and* god are all impure, though in different degrees. In other words, we must suppose that sacrifice makes complete and therefore pure (or purer) not only its human actors, but also its divine ones, while transgression, or any other state of lack that motivates sacrifice, implicitly make the god less pure.

Is this inference confirmed by the evidence? Should we not suppose instead that, as in other cultures, the state of the god is always neutral with regard to purity and impurity and that these qualities pertain only to the humans, who are pure when in a proper relation to the gods, impure when in an improper relation to them?

In fact, the data already given show clearly that Hawaiians view certain gods and their manifestations as impure and others as pure. For instance, corpses, which are impure, are also called *akua*, "divine" (NK, 1:23), and may become the manifestations of certain categories of gods, such as the *'unihipili*. Also divine are monstrous beings or aborted fetuses, which, as I have just said, are considered impure. We have also seen that some consider human waste a manifestation of their *'aumakua* (Emerson 1892, 15). Given that Hawaiians do not strongly distinguish between the god and his manifestations, it seems difficult to deny that gods embodied in excrement, abortions, or more generally corpses are themselves impure.

In contrast, the gods who personify to the highest degree the accepted types of human action are clearly viewed as pure. I have just reported that they "despise" all bloody things, which are impure. I may add that they desire "only those who [are] clean and pure" (Kamakau 1964, 64). This seems to indicate that they fear being polluted by impurity. This is precisely why women, who are "unclean and defiled by blood" (ibid.), are rigorously excluded from the worship of these gods, both as sacrifiers and as victims. In contrast, they are often indispensable (chaps. 1, 4) in the worship of the sorcery gods, a fact that confirms that these gods are viewed as impure.[6]

Another indication that there are pure gods is that perfect offerings and perfect children (who are considered pure precisely because of their perfection) are consecrated to them (cf. chaps. 1 and 2). We may conclude, then, that the divine has a "demonic" aspect—which is signified by incomplete or monstrous or decayed things—together with a pure aspect that is signified by integrity and perfection.

But the question that interests me most is the one that arises from the analysis of sacrifice: Are the pure gods themselves relatively impure, or less pure, in certain contexts?

I believe there is enough evidence to answer this question in the affirmative. First a piece of circumstantial evidence. In chapter 2 I reported that both the offender and the offended and in the end their entire social network are "entangled" in the offense. This entanglement paralyzes and diminishes them: thus it makes them impure. Now the gods are always conceived as part of the system of social relationships over which they preside. It seems reasonable to suppose, then, that they are themselves entangled and polluted by a disorder in those relationships. Indeed, this is the reason for their wrath against the transgressor.

But there is more direct proof. It is provided by the most developed Hawaiian ritual: the consecration of the *luakini* temple. As we shall see in part 3, this ritual clearly represents the transformation of the god Kū from a lesser state, which is indexed by disorder and pollution, to a higher, more complete state associated with order and purity. This ritual also confirms that there is a very close correspondence between the state of relative purity of the god at each stage of its performance and the states of the main sacrifier (the king), of the other participants, and of the victims.

Thus the initial stage, when the god is still incomplete and impure, is characterized by violence, the shedding of blood, and the lack of bodily and verbal control in the participants. In the following stages, the participants become more restrained, until absolute bodily discipline and spatial ordering according to rank are realized in the temple. The relative purity of the human victims offered at each stage also varies: the initial human sacrifice involves beheading and therefore shedding of much blood, which as we know produces impurity. But in the next human sacrifice the victim is dispatched in a way that avoids shedding his blood. Later, the supreme human sacrifice correlated with the final purification of the god (who accedes to the status of a perfect adult male) requires that the victim be killed outside the temple, that his body remain intact, be washed to remove any trace of blood, and finally be purified by the priests (chap. 8).

It seems to me that this ritual clearly displays a progression that occurs in every sacrifice and in which there exists the same parallelism of the state of god, victim, and participants. Thus, as I have shown, at the beginning of the rite the disordered, incompletely human aspects of the offering are emphasized. These signify the state of lack that exists both in the sacrifier and in the god, whose value as guiding principle is diminished by the sacrifier's failure to follow and realize it. But once the sacrifier, through the offering, has been incorporated in the god, the latter reacquires his lost integrity or increases it: his status as recognized type, his force in his worshiper's consciousness, has been reproduced. Thus he is indeed made pure or purer, together with the sacrifier and his group. Their correlative purification is signified by that of the offering after its consecration. This is again demonstrated in the clearest way by the *luakini* temple ritual. There the human victims are transgressors and rebels, that is, extremely impure persons. But once they have been incorporated in the god they become so pure that their bones are religiously preserved by the ali'i and priests (see chap. 8).

Further evidence that pure gods have impure manifestations correlated with a state of disorder in humans is offered by several particularizations of Kū and Kāne used by the king or high nobles in sorcery, which is an impure activity.[7] These gods are "sent" to punish and devour transgressors and rebels (Beckwith 1940, 110; Kamakau 1964, 129; Ellis 1842, 93; Ii 1963, 123, 45; Malo 1951, 113; Valeri 1982b, 26, 28).

It is clear, then, that when the pure gods are diminished by men's rebellion against the gods' human representative the king, or by other forms of transgression, their impure forms (the sorcery forms) are activated.[8] These forms are neutralized by their very success in "devouring," that is, encompassing, the transgressors, which makes Kū and Kāne complete and pure again. This shows that the god's desire to "devour" men is a desire to be made complete by them.

In sum, the evidence suggests that, at least to some extent, man's actions, which reflect the degree of his recognition of the god, influence the god's completeness and therefore purity. This implies that the god's purity depends in part on men—which seems paradoxical in view of certain representations of the divine found in the literature.

Thus Andrews writes: "It would seem that the ancient idea of an *Akua* embraced something incomprehensible, powerful and yet complete, full orbed" (1865, 44; cf. J. S. Emerson, "Gods," in HEN, 1:605). This definition suggests that the completeness, and therefore purity, of the gods is absolute and depends on no one but the gods themselves. Indeed a number of things considered *akua* evoke total autonomy and independence. For example, automatic instruments (the watch, the compass, the clock) owned by Cook and the members of his crew were considered *akua* (Andrews 1865, 44), for they were capable of autonomous movements independent of any external force. Moreover, these movements were mostly circular, as were the instruments. For the Hawaiians the circle evokes a being closed in on itself because it is complete and self-sufficient. Accordingly, circular things and things capable of circular movement are often considered divine, especially if they are powerful and distant, such as the stars or the moon. For instance, the full moon is called *akua*; "the name ('god') indicates a great moon, beautiful and well-rounded" (Kepelino 1932, 108). Even an arc of a circle, such as the rainbow, evokes the divine perfection (EH, 65, 124).

The idea of the circle is also associated with incestuous marriages, which are seen as a folding on oneself, as manifestations of self-sufficiency. Thus the marriage between true siblings is called *pi'o*, "arch, arc; bent, arched, curved; to arch, of a rainbow" (PE, 305; Malo 1951, 54; Kamakau 1964, 4); the child born of the union of half-siblings is called *nī'aupi'o*, "coconut frond arched back upon itself" (Handy and Pukui 1972, 108). These marriages are an attribute of the gods, both the invisible ones[9] and the (relatively) visible ones—the ali'i of royal blood that are their human counterparts.

These facts suggest that the gods are absolutely transcendent, that their perfection does not depend on man. However, a different notion of the divine perfection is suggested by the *Kumulipo*, where the entire cosmogonic process is explained as the result of a lack in the divine, of a desire (signified by the sexual production of the cosmos) that is finally satisfied by the engendering of man, with whom the cosmogonic process comes to an end. Moreover, the same text suggests that personal gods are correlatives of man and in fact depend on him (see chap. 1).

This indicates that for the *Kumulipo* the divine is not complete until it has created man and has brought about its own transformation by this act of creation. By implication, the divine is not pure until man is produced. What happens in the present, then, reproduces what happened in the past: the god's perfection consists in producing concrete human tokens of himself, on being a modeling type, a rule, for as many men as pertain to him. But this productivity does not depend on the god alone, because human recognition and acceptance of the god are necessary to the god's realization in human action. The latter is thus viewed as the true criterion of the god's perfection.

In sum, two notions of divine perfection or purity seem to coexist. One stresses the transcendent character of the divine precisely because it stresses that it perfectly personifies the concept of a human subject; the other stresses that the god is perfect only when he is recognized by men, that is, when they all accept him as the normative concept of their activity. Reciprocally, man is pure only when he recognizes and follows the god. Thus this second conception stresses the reciprocal dependence of man and god. In this respect the Hawaiian ideology of the pure and impure is in sharp contrast with the Indian one as described by Dumont:

Purity and impurity are restricted to the human sphere; they cannot be equated with sacredness, positive or negative, which belongs to a wider sphere. Purity and impurity appear as human correspondents of these, or perhaps human modalities of them: I have to become pure to approach the gods, and even if I come in contact with them, this does not mean that their nature is purity, but only that purity is a condition for the contact with them to be beneficial to me (or other men or human things). We are told about purity, i.e. about the *means* of contact, not about the nature of the *object* of contact, the sacred. (1959, 31) [10]

This Indian ideology can be described by the following scheme:

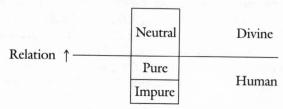

This scheme can be contrasted with another one, which describes the Hawaiian ideology:

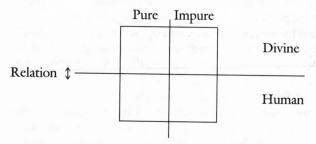

The schemes make clear that the contrast of the two ideologies ultimately rests on the contrast between a conception that views the relationship between divine and human as nonreciprocal, and a conception that views it as both reciprocal and hierarchical. [11]

Kapu and Noa

Kapu may be translated as "marked" and indexes the need to pay attention, while "unmarked" may be translated *noa*, which indicates that there is no need to pay attention (cf. Steiner 1967, 31–32; Johansen 1954, 186). The divine, pure or impure, is *kapu* to persons or things that are not divine. This means that the latter have to pay attention and relate to the former in a prescribed way. Inversely, things or persons that are not divine are *noa*, because the divine beings are not supposed to be careful with them. Moreover, persons or things that are closer to the divine are *kapu* to those that are less close to it. Vice versa, the latter are *noa* to the former.

Kapu and *noa* are purely relative notions. They are therefore not substances or states but marks of relations between substances or states. A being cannot be absolutely *kapu* or absolutely *noa*, but is *kapu* relative to certain beings and *noa* relative to others. On the other hand, at least some part of the divine must always remain *kapu* for the human sphere, otherwise the whole system would lose its fixed foundation.

In certain respects, then, the notion of *kapu* can be compared to the notion of holiness as understood by Robertson Smith: "The idea of holiness comes into prominence whenever the gods come into touch with men; it is not so much a thing that characterizes the gods and divine things in themselves, as the most general notions that govern their relations with humanity" (1894, 141–42).

As indicated, superiors—that is, those who are closer to the divine—are *kapu* to inferiors, who are *noa* to them. For instance ali'i are *kapu* to commoners and commoners are *noa* to ali'i (Kepelino 1932, 124). That inferiors are not *kapu* to superiors may seem strange if one adopts the perspective of other social systems based on the opposition of the pure and the impure. For instance, in the Indian caste system, the superior must guard himself from the inferior, who is polluting to him. Therefore we may be tempted to conclude that the Hawaiian system is the reverse of the Indian one, and that inferiors do not pollute superiors but superiors pollute inferiors.

The facts, however, show that this view would be misleading, because impure inferiors do pollute their pure superiors in Hawaii. For instance, Malo reports that a man is put to death if his shadow falls upon the back (a most sacred part) of the king or upon his clothes, or upon anything that belongs to him (Malo 1951, 56). Obviously the man would not be punished if his shadow did not pollute the king. Other cases indicate more clearly that a person in a state of impurity pollutes a pure superior: "If a man entered the *alii*'s house without changing his wet malo, or with his head smeared with mud, he was put to death" (ibid.). Note also that the eating place and food of a king or high-ranking noble are *kapu* to inferiors, who may pollute them (Kamakau 1961, 212). Sexual intercourse with inferiors is also polluting to superiors (Kamakau 1961, 128; Malo 1951, 70–71).[12]

In sum, inferiors may pollute superiors, exactly as in India. Yet, contrary to the situation in India, superiors may also pollute inferiors. Thus if a low-status person—who is forbidden to enter the royal residence—does enter, he is automatically made *la'a*, "cursed, defiled" (PE, 173; Fornander 1916–20, 4:185).

Note, however, that the superior pollutes the inferior more than the inferior pollutes the superior. Therefore hierarchy is not expressed simply by relative purity and impurity, but also by the relative power to pollute. In other words, the purer a person, the greater his power of pollution on inferiors.

This seems paradoxical, but I think that the paradox arises only when we view the Hawaiian system from an "Indian" perspective, that is, from a perspective in which purity and power are disjoined. If taken to its extreme consequences (as by Dumont), this view seems to imply a definition of purity as *absence* of impurity rather than as the expression of an intrinsic potency.

But this is not the Hawaiian view. In Hawaii, purity is first and foremost a positive quality: it is the mark of a close instantiation of the divine, and therefore of full development, of integrity. Impurity, in contrast, is lesser purity—a lesser instantiation of the divine model. In fact, superior purity implies superior mana: superior potency or efficacy (see next section).

Different degrees of purity, of mana, must be associated in a way that preserves their hierarchical distinction, that is, in a way that requires the inferior's respect for the superior. This is why the superior is marked by a *kapu* for the inferior. If this *kapu* is not respected, the hierarchical difference is negated: the inferior implicitly equates the superior to himself, that is, lowers him, makes him less pure.

But on the other hand, if the superior indeed has the mana he claims to have, he is able to retaliate by polluting the inferior. This pollution may be due simply to supernatural means, or to more material ones. In the first case, the pollution of the inferior is, as in ancient Greece, "the effect of a supernatural power on one whose religious standing is inadequate to receive it" (Vernant 1980, 126)—that is, on one who is too weak for it. In the second case, pollution is due to death, since the transgressor is killed by the man who has the superior mana (Malo 1951, 56–57, 188–89; cf. chap. 5).

In fact, both "supernatural" and "natural," or rather invisible and visible, modes of operation often combine in the superior's action on the inferior (cf. Kamakau 1961, 220–21).

In sum, the Hawaiian system is not simply the reverse of the Indian one; it is rather a system that makes potency and purity congruent and that, by the same token, gives the inferior a certain power of pollution on the superior. It is also a system in which the relative purity of a person depends both on his relationship with the divine and on his relationship with other humans. Indeed, the two relationships are interdependent because a man's claim to instantiate the divine in a certain degree is invalid if it is not recognized by other men—that is, if he is "polluted" by them.

This should explain why the superior is marked by a *kapu* for the inferior but not vice versa. This asymmetry arises because it is the inferior, not the superior, who stands to lose most in any wrong hierarchical encounter and because the superior, as a closer instantiation of the divine, must have a greater value for the inferior than the inferior has for the superior.

Since *noa*, the absence of marking, indicates that a person is not a prescribed object of attention, it can refer not only to inferiors, but also to equals. Thus if two individuals have the same rank, that is, are in the same relation with the divine, they are *noa* to one another. Indeed, Kamakau writes that between two ali'i of the *pi'o* rank, "No divine law (*kanawai akua*) would arise" (1964, 4). And he describes the relations between two ali'i of the *nī'aupio'o* rank thus: "Neither need remove his kapa in deference to the royal kapu of the other, and they would be equally warm in their regard for each other" (ibid.).

Taking all the facts into consideration, I venture to say that the opposition *kapu/noa* reflects various aspects of the opposition between syntagmatic and paradigmatic relations, without, however, being coextensive with it. In effect, in one of its two dimensions *noa* refers to paradigmatic relations—to the relations between terms that are mutually substitutable in the same point of the syntagmatic (that is, hierarchical) chain. Thus two ali'i of the same rank, their regalia, and whatever they put "under the shadow" of their *kapu*, that is assimilate to their persons, are *noa* to one another because they have the same position in the social syntagm, because they are equivalent.

Kapu refers exclusively to syntagmatic relations. But it refers to them as the reciprocal of *noa* in its second dimension. Indeed, as we have seen, that one term is *noa* relative to another that is *kapu* to it does not simply indicate that they are not equivalent: it also indicates that the first term is inferior to the second. Thus the *kapu/noa* opposition brings out the hierarchical nature of syntagmatic relations, that is to say, of relations of combinations between social categories (cf. Valeri 1982a).

In sum, when *noa* is the reciprocal of *noa*, it indicates a paradigmatic relation; when *noa* is the reciprocal of *kapu*, it indicates the syntagmatic relation of inferior to superior. Thus *kapu* indexes separation only as counterpart of metonymic, syntagmatic combination in the social hierarchy.[13]

We saw above that *la'a* means "accursed, polluted." But it may also mean "holy"—that is, sacred in a positive sense (PE, 173). This is because *la'a* refers to the presence of a divine quality in something or somebody as a result of its contact with a god or a close human representative of a god. This contact results in pollution or purification, depending on whether it is right or wrong. In any event, the state of *la'a* is dangerous and is therefore marked by a *kapu*. Thus in a sense *la'a* is a substantial counterpart of *kapu*.[14]

Perhaps, then, the relation between *kapu* and *la'a* may be compared to the relation that, according to Benveniste, exists between *sacer* and *sanctus* in Latin and between *hierós* and *hágios* in Greek: "*Sacer* and *hierós*, "sacré" ou "divin," se disent de la personne ou de la chose consacrée aux dieux, tandis que *hágios* comme *sanctus* indiquent que l'objet est défendu contre toute violation, concept négatif, et non, positivement, qu'il est chargé de la présence divine, ce qui est le sens spécifique de *hierós*" (Benveniste 1969, 2:204–5).

Long before Benveniste, de Maistre had written: "*Sacré* signifie, dans les langues anciennes, ce qui est *livré à la Divinité* à n'importe quel titre, et qui se trouve *lié*" (de Maistre 1884, 5:308). In sum, the fact of being "bound" follows from the fact of being surrendered, devoted to the divine. To use Benveniste's words once again: "Rendre *sacer* consiste en une espèce de retranchement, de mise hors du domaine humain par une affectation au divin" (1969, 2:197–98).

These formulations correspond rather well to the Hawaiian ones. Thus de Maistre uses the same metaphor, "tied," that the Hawaiians often use to refer to *kapu*, and that Steiner (1967) thinks is the best translation of *tapu*, its Maori equivalent. As for *la'a*, it is clearly the state of being that is produced by an "affectation au divin," which may be voluntary or not. For instance, as we have seen, an inferior who comes in contact with something royal becomes imbued with its divine substance, and therefore *la'a* (Fornander 1916–20, 4:185). But the same happens to a boy who voluntarily enters the divine sphere in order to become a priest: "A boy so consecrated to the gods was placed under restrictions (*ho'okapu 'ia* [lit. 'he was made taboo'—V. V.]). His food, his food calabash, his water gourd, his clothing (*mea 'a'ahu*), his loincloth (*mea hume*), his mat, and his house were *la'a*, hallowed. His body was *la'a*, and not to be defiled with women. His hair was *la'a*, and could not be cut or trimmed; it grew tangled and snarled (*a wilika'eka*) and the beard hung down (*a kau i kokiki*)" (Kamakau 1964, 27).

As this passage shows, the *kapu* is the arbitrary sign that makes socially known the status of *la'a* that is produced not by an arbitrary decision, but by contact with the divine. The different outcome of the two cases—pollution in one, purification in the other—is explained, as I have said, by the fact that in one case the association with the divine is made improperly, while in the other it is made properly, with due respect. Still, the state of *la'a* is rather ambivalent, because the contact with the divine is always dangerous.

It remains to be said that the term *ho'okapu* ("to make *kapu*") refers to a passage from the *noa* state to the *kapu* state, while the terms *ho'onoa* ("to make *noa*") and, more frequently, *huikala*, refer to the reverse passage. Although *huikala* often refers to a purification, it is wrong to translate it as such in every case, as is usually done, because the state of *kapu* it brings to an end may be due to extreme purity, not to impurity. Perhaps the best translation of *huikala* is a literal one: "to untie" (cf. Handy and Pukui 1972, 184–85). *Huikala* unties the "tangles" that the consecration and its sign, the *kapu*, have tied around someone or something (see in the text by Kamakau above the reference to the initiate's "tangled and snarled" hair, which symbolizes his *kapu* state).

Mana

In the previous discussion I introduced the notion of mana, which must now be explicated in detail. Because this notion has been much discussed, it is useful to begin by recapitulating a few interpretations that are relevant to the Hawaiian case.[15]

Codrington was responsible for introducing the notion of mana into the anthropological debate. Most of the points subsequently made by other scholars are already contained in his account of the concept. Thus he writes that mana "is what works to effect everything which is beyond the ordinary power of men, outside the common processes of nature" (1891, 118–19). Echoes of this view can be found in Mauss, Hocart, and Firth. Although Codrington claims that this power is impersonal, he also stresses that it "is always connected with some person who directs it" (ibid.).

He recognizes that mana is used as a verb, but he also points out that it can be used as such only when predicated of objects and spirits, not humans: "No man . . . has this power of his own; all that he does is done by the aid of personal beings, ghosts or spirits; he cannot be said, as spirits can, to be *mana* himself, using the word to express a quality; he can be said to have *mana*, it may be said to be with him, the word being used as a substantive" (p. 191).

That humans allegedly can have mana but cannot be mana probably prompted Codrington to think of mana as an invisible substance that could be transmitted. His successors—Hubert and Mauss and Durkheim among others—went even further in this direction. But recent inquiries have established that, at least in Melanesia and perhaps in western Polynesia, mana need not be conveyed by spirits or be conceived as an invisible substance. Keesing (n.d.) has even claimed that the influence of Codrington's view has blinded anthropologists: "We have not understood that *mana*-ness represented a common *quality* of efficacy or success, retrospectively interpreted, but not a universal *medium* of it."[16]

According to Keesing, Melanesians and many Polynesians have a purely "pragmatic world view" and no metaphysical notions about mana. Mana, when used as a noun, means "success" or "luck." It should never be glossed as "power" but rather as "potency." Moreover, it should be recognized that mana is mostly used as a stative verb. Fundamentally, it is a notion that accounts for the difference between something that works and something that does not work, when the material effort put in the two things is the same.

Keesing's generalizations about mana appear close to those of some older ethnographers who knew Polynesian or Melanesian cultures first-hand. For instance, according to Hogbin (1935–36, 245, 265), mana means "success," "good luck" in Guadalcanal and Malaita. Hocart stressed that two meanings, "efficacious" and "true," combine to form the fundamental idea that is at the core of the concept of mana in Fiji and elsewhere: "to come true" (1914, 100; 1952, 219). For Fijians and other Oceanic peoples, the truth is found in the realization, which amounts to saying that "the proof of the pudding is in the eating" (Hocart 1922, 139). Nevertheless, this truth deals only with the "supernatural"; mana would consequently refer to efficacy postulated in the absence of a perceived physical cause.

Similar views are expressed by Firth in his study of the Tikopian notions of *mana* and *manu*, which he believes to be related and translates as "success" or "to be successful"; "efficacy," "to be efficacious" (1967, 191).[17] Like Hocart, Firth insists that this success has its origins in "the world of spirits" (p. 189): "For the Tikopia success is not merely a matter of human effort. It is essentially success in certain spheres, those which affect human interests most vitally—food, health, and weather-control, but in ways with which ordinary techniques cannot cope" (1967, 191). Thus Firth gives a thoroughly Malinowskian foundation (but also Humean, cf. Canguilhem 1968, 86–96; Valeri 1979b) to his interpretation of mana. Firth also observes that the success granted by spirits can occur through intermediate human agents—the chiefs—to whom they grant mana.

The most innovative aspect of Firth's essay lies not in its conclusions about mana, but in its method. Again following Malinowskian precepts, Firth studies the various meanings of mana as they occur in all texts he recorded.

As a starting point, this method is of course a must. Yet few have followed Firth's footsteps on this path. One exception is Johansen, who has attempted to understand the Maori concept of mana by studying its various textual occurrences. He concludes that the notion of mana is closely related to that of *tupu*, which signifies "to enfold one's nature" (1954, 40), to grow. The social value of a being is directly proportional to his growth. Thus *tupu* involves "honor" or "fame" (pp. 43–44).[18]

Johansen notes that both *tupu* and mana "denote unfolding, activity and life; but whereas *tupu* is an expression of the nature of things and human beings as unfolded from within, mana expresses something participated, an active fellowship which according to its nature is never inextricably bound up with any single thing or any single human being. . . . Mana is a kind of fellowship" (p. 85).

In short, Johansen interprets mana as a *tupu* that, so to speak, outgrows a single being, as "the aspect of life which from the point of view of the individual turns outwards, 'influence' we might say in this connection" (p. 87) and is therefore what creates a group of relations, a "fellowship."

It is clear that in the Maori notion of mana as reconstructed by Johansen the idea of efficacy is prominent, particularly as it applies to social relations. But contrary to what happens in Melanesia according to Keesing, this efficacy is grounded in a philosophy of life based on the idea of growth—that is to say, a concept much more encompassing than "luck." Moreover, the hierarchical and relational dimensions of mana are emphasized: although from the point of view of an individual mana is life turning outward, influencing less vital beings, it is also and more importantly a relation linking all of them and therefore not located in that individual only. Mana is, in a sense, the efficacy of a system of relations personified by an individual (for instance a chief): it is the notion that that system "works." This notion of mana perhaps confirms Hubert and Mauss's intuition that mana identifies more with the "circle" connecting the terms said to be mana than with the terms as such (Hubert and Mauss 1978, 105, cf. 114).

In conclusion, the meanings most often attributed to the word mana in the literature are "efficacy," "to be efficacious," "potency," "to be potent," "success," "to be successful," "to be true." These meanings obviously imply each other, since success is the necessary consequence of efficacy and efficacy implies potency. As for the meaning "to be true," which is rarer (cf. Keesing, n.d.), it connotes the actuality of a claim to efficacy.

Moreover, mana involves what most authors call a "supernatural" or "nonordinary" component of efficacy that is the necessary condition for the "natural" or "ordinary" components to take effect in certain areas of action. Finally, Keesing in particular insists that canonically mana is a stative verb, not a noun, although it is also used as a transitive verb, as a causative verb, or a verbal noun. He recognizes, however, that in eastern Polynesia mana is substantivized and therefore closer to the "Codringtonian" definition of mana. He attributes this development to the existence of a class of theologians.

To what extent do these propositions apply to the Hawaiian notion of mana? To answer this question we must apply Firth's and Johansen's method: we must study the textual occurrences of mana in their contexts.

One result of the study deserves to be mentioned first: the word mana does not frequently occur in the texts. For instance, in Malo's and K. Kamakau's descriptions of the *luakini* temple ritual—which is the most important occasion for the transmission of mana from the divine to the human realm—the most frequent occurrence of the word refers to a sacred house of the temple. This house is called *hale mana* ("house that is mana") or simply *mana*.

In its second most frequent occurrence in the same descriptions mana is in the form of a causative verb: *hoʻomana*, "to cause to be mana," "to empower." Mana occurs only once as a transitive verb (K. Kamakau 1919–20, 29), twice as a noun not referring to the sacred house (K. Kamakau 1919–20, 33, 19), and once as a stative (Malo 37.87).

However, it would be wrong to make much of the rare occurrence of mana in these descriptions. For one thing, Malo and Kelou Kamakau give only very few of the prayers that were uttered in the ritual, in which the word mana must have been included rather often. I infer this from the fact that all occurrences of mana as noun and as (noncausative) verb found in K. Kamakau's text come from prayers. Moreover, mana is often found in the prayers Emerson appends to his translation of Malo's account of the temple ritual, which he says were uttered during its performance. It is true that the origin and date of these prayers are unknown, and several seem to have little relation to the ritual described by Malo.

Another reason for not considering the rare occurrence of mana excessively relevant is that the rituals described by these two sources clearly involve the transmission of mana. The fact that the word itself is not mentioned frequently therefore is not very significant. To think otherwise would be to confuse the texts with complete accounts of what happens in ritual and especially of what is presupposed throughout it and therefore does not have to be explicitly stated. Indeed, if there is a criticism that can be raised against Firth's treatment of mana in Tikopia it is that he uses as sources of information only verbal statements about mana. Presumably a ritual that involves mana can tell us a lot about this notion even if the corresponding word is never pronounced during the performance.

Thus we know from the *Mooolelo Hawaii* (1838, 76) that the sacrifices of the temple ritual make the image of the god mana ("potent"),[19] although Malo and K. Kamakau do not explicitly say so. Since Malo was the principal author of the *Mooolelo Hawaii* of 1838, it seems legitimate to assume that in his other description he implies that making the image mana is the purpose of the *luakini* temple ritual, although he does not explicitly say so there. This example shows, I believe, the dangers of a blind literalism and of the assumption that only verbal statements are informative.

But let us turn to the more substantive conclusions of my inquiry. The glosses "potency, to be potent," "efficacy, to be efficacious," "success, to be successful" all apply to the Hawaiian word mana. In this respect there is no difference between the Hawaiian notion and its counterparts in other areas of Polynesia.

The Hawaiian case also confirms that mana is a quality of divine origin (NK, 1 : 150). It is therefore predicated most often of the gods [20] and of the persons or things that are closest to them: aliʻi,[21] priests,[22] prayers,[23] temples

(Fornander 1916–20, 5:151), sacred houses within the temples (the *hale mana*), images of the gods (which are referred to as *akua*, like the gods themselves),[24] ritual objects,[25] and omens (*hōʻailona*; cf. Fornander 1916–20, 6:163).[26]

Humans become mana by descent (ultimately humans descend from the gods) or by ritual means (Malo, 38.24) or by both at once. One óf the modes of mana's transmission among humans clearly indicates that mana is conceived as a substance. Indeed a man is able to transmit his mana to another by spitting in his mouth or by breathing on his *manawa*, "anterior fontanel" (NK, 1:44, 2:31; HEN, 1:1379). This mode of transmission also gives clues to what kind of "substance" mana is: it seems to be connected with speech, with which spit, breath, and mouth are obviously associated. Moreover, breath is connected with life (Beckwith 1919, 300): thus we may deduce that mana is a sort of life in speech and life-giving power in speech. That this power may be transmitted through the anterior fontanel is interesting in view of the identification of that part of the head with an aspect of the "soul" having to do with feelings, affections, sympathy, and dispositions (Handy and Pukui 1972, 87; PE, 219; cf. Fischer 1965, 215–16). This seems to imply that a man's speech having mana can become another man's speech having mana by affecting the seat of his feelings, sympathies, and dispositions.

Putting all these clues together, I feel inclined to hypothesize that mana depends on feelings and dispositions (such as sympathy) that are eminently connected with "fellowship"—to use Johansen's definition. This hypothesis is confirmed by the temple ritual, in which the constitution of mana in both gods and humans is explicitly related to the constitution of mutual feelings of love and sympathy (*aloha*) (see chap. 8, p. 307). It is also confirmed by the fact that the most frequently used form of the word mana is a verb that implies a reciprocal relationship, as I shall show in a moment.

Although mana is the efficacy of a working "fellowship," it is substantialized, probably because it is viewed as a quality that circulates, that can be moved from one term of the fellowship to another. Thus mana is conceived as an invisible substance that manifests itself in a variety of visible signifiers. But it is interesting that it has a closer affinity with a signifier, breath, that is itself invisible. Indeed breath, as the seat of speech, is the nearest equivalent of mana as an invisible force that circulates in the society and animates it, orders it, makes it successful in its actions on itself and nature.

That in Hawaii the use of the word *mana* as a noun is as common as is its use as a stative verb, and that the two usages appear to be interchangeable,[27] can perhaps be viewed as a reflex of the tendency to conceive mana in substantialist terms. This tendency is clearly illustrated by the temple

100   Sacrifice and the Gods

ritual analyzed in part 3. Here I will only mention some texts in which mana is referred to as a thing that can be increased and transferred as a result of speech acts or of other ritual acts.

For instance, during the annual rite in which the first *'ōpelu* fish is caught (*kapu 'ōpelu*), the ritual fisherman prays: "*I nui ko mana ia'u i keia la*," "increase my mana today" (K. Kamakau 1919–20, 33; my translation).

In another prayer, it is the gods who are asked to increase their own mana: "*E i nui ka mana oukou e na akua*," "increase your mana, O gods" (K. Kamakau 1919–20, 19, my translation). Let me also quote two lines from a prayer to which I shall return (chap. 8):

'O 'oloa hulihihia ka mana
The *'oloa* [barkcloth] [by which] the mana is entangled
He mana pūkī no ka 'aha 'oloa
A mana is curbed because of the *'oloa* cord.
     (Given by Emerson in Malo 1951, 184)

These lines refer to a rite in which mana is treated as a substance that is bound and conveyed into a temple house to make it mana.

Mana is clearly used as a substantive when it means "authority"—a meaning derived from "having efficacy with regard to something." Thus one speaks of "*o ka mana o na ali'i maluna o ka 'aina*," "the authority of the ali'i over the land" (Kamakau 1961, 229; cf. Kepelino 1932, 159; PE, 217) and of *mana makua*, "parental authority" (PE, 217).

Note also that in Hawaiian usage mana may mean a formally recognized and transmitted aptitude to perform efficaciously a certain task, a certain activity. Thus the mana of the canoe builder is his divinely originated and ancestrally transmitted ability to build canoes with success (NK, 1:43–44). Of course this efficacy presupposes a "fellowship" both with a coordinated group of people in which the building takes place and with a departmental god with a specific area of competence. Thus the primary meaning of mana as "fellowship" is presupposed by its meaning "aptitude to perform a certain task efficaciously."

But in certain contexts the word mana seems to be banalized, to lose its connection with both god and community, as in the following text: "Those who understood the 'properties' (*mana*) of baits would come to shore with a good catch" (Kamakau 1976, 79).

All in all, it is clear that the meaning "luck" retreats from the mana notion in Hawaii. Mana is a much more stable and predictable quality than luck: it is acquired and transmitted in predictable ways in ritual and therefore becomes to a large extent "routinized." Thus mana ceases to be simply related to the imponderabilia of life—as in Tikopia according to Firth. It is a much more encompassing concept that accounts for the efficacious performance of any kind of social task; it reflects an ideology of divinity as the collectively shared and sanctioned concept of human action, whatever its content and aim.

This explains why, contrary to what happens in Tikopia, mana does not always have a positive, auspicious connotation (Firth 1967, 193), does not always cover "a category of socially approved phenomena" (p. 185). As a Hawaiian prayer puts it, there is "death mana" and "life mana" (Kepelino 1977, 54). Thus mana may be used in parallel with *ola*, "life," as in these two examples: "*Kane ke akua ola / ke akua mana*," "Kāne god of life / god of mana (or god who is mana)" (Malo 1951, 180, cf. 182); "*He wai e mana, he wai e ola*," "It is a water that gives mana, a water that gives life" (Emerson 1965, 258).

But mana can also parallel death, as when it is associated with sorcery (Kamakau 1961, 179, 151; Kamakau 1964, 130, 135; Ii 1963, 124; Beckwith 1940, 112; PE, 14; Kepelino 1977, 54–55; Fornander 1916–20, 6:397, 463, 407, lines 703, 705, 706).

Thus the duality of mana parallels the duality of the divine itself and is its logical consequence (cf. chap. 1). Note, however, that in both its positive and its negative applications mana presupposes the "fellowship" it reproduces or threatens, and it cannot be effective without it, for reasons I indicated when discussing sorcery (cf. chap. 2).

Note also that, as demonstrated in the previous section, the wrong association of two unequal degrees of mana produces pollution: thus mana may be again related to negative and inauspicious events.

In sum, because of its great scope, its substantialization, and the fact that it is the counterpart of a system of gods that encompasses every human activity and is coextensive with a system of social groups and categories in which those activities take place, I find that the Hawaiian notion of mana is closer to Hubert and Mauss's and Johansen's descriptions of the concept than to Firth's (or Keesing's) description. This is not to say, of course, that all aspects of Hubert and Mauss's account apply to Hawaii or that their view of the substantial aspect of mana is adequate.

We must now turn our attention to two further uses of the word mana that are of particular interest, since they concern the relationship between gods and men in the constitution of mana. The first type of use is intransitive and more specifically imperative: "*E mana hoi makou imua ou*," "let us be mana before thee" (said to a goddess by her worshipers; K. Kamakau 1919–20, 29). "*E mana i ke akua*," "let it be mana by the god" (Emerson in Malo in 1951, 184). These two texts show that the mana must come from a god, but also that its transfer to man is effected by the potency of speech and of the accompanying ritual actions (which are usually sacrificial). Thus, by an apparent paradox the acquisition of mana from the god already requires a certain mana: in other words, it presupposes the relationship of man and god.

The paradox appears even greater in the most common usage of mana, which is the causative form *ho'omana*. This form always has a human subject.[28] Andrews defines *ho'omana* in the following manner: "to ascribe divine honors; to worship; to cause one to have regal authority" (1865, 198); "to reverence or worship, as a superior being, i.e., of superhuman power; *a hoomana aku la i ua alii la e like me ka hoomana akua*, they worshiped that chief as if [more literally: "like"—V. V.] they worshiped a god" (p. 382). Pukui and Elbert gives a series of analogous definitions: "1) to place in a position of authority, install in power, authorize; 2) to worship, religion, sect" (PE, 217).

The frequentative form *ho'omanamana* is defined as "to impart mana, as to idols or objects; superstitious" (PE, 218). J. S. Emerson translates it "the causing one to have mana" and observes that in this form "the *imparting* of supernatural power seems to be the prominent idea, rather than the ascription of a power already possessed by the object worshiped." He adds: "Naturally *ho'omana* is the word used for the worship of Jehovah, while *hoomanamana* is only used of heathen worship" (1892, 4). But I wonder if this sharp opposition of *ho'omana* and *ho'omanamana* has been projected on the past as a result of Christianization. After all *ho'omana* literally means "to cause one to be mana," and it is worth asking oneself if its other meanings—"to worship," "to ascribe divine honors"—do not presuppose the literal one or are not in some way derived from it.

Judging from the texts, particularly the descriptions of the *luakini* temple ritual by Kelou Kamakau and Malo, the verb *ho'omana* often occurs in contexts where worshiping presupposes the presence of a divine image that is *made* mana by means of sacrifices and prayers (K. Kamakau 1919– 20, 29, 17, 21, 29; Malo 1951, 103, 127; Ii 1963, 124). As Alexander remarked long ago, "the Hawaiians usually worshiped their gods by means of idols, believing that by the performance of certain rites power, *mana*, was imparted to the idols, so that they became a means of communication with unseen divinities. They imagined that a spirit resided in or conveyed influence through the image representing it" (1891, 41; cf. Handy 1972, 192).

Paradigmatically, then, an act of worship presupposes making mana an image of the god worshiped. In fact, we have seen that without this the worshiping is not complete, because ritual is fully efficacious only when the god is present in an anthropomorphic, controllable form. In this sense the meaning "to worship" presupposes the meaning "to make something mana." I think that this connection was lost when Hawaiians converted to Christianity. The two meanings are all the more difficult to separate in that *akua*, which is the object of *ho'omana*, may refer either to the god or to his image.

Note also that textual material shows that, contrary to what the lexicographers and Emerson suggest, *ho'omanamana* does not always mean "to impart mana by magic." It may simply mean, like *ho'omana*, "to make something mana" by transferring the god or the god's mana to it. Consider the following example: "*ua hoomanamanaia kela koa i mua o ke akua*," "that fishing ground was made *mana* before the god" (Fornander 1916–20, 4 : 297). The formula "before the god" signifies, here as elsewhere, that the mana comes from him: the *ho'omana* or *ho'omanamana* simply consists in a transfer. The text also shows that this transfer of mana from god to object is effected by bringing the god in contact with the object, which is thereby made *la'a*. Indeed, the sentence above is put in parallel with another, which is its equivalent: "*ua hoolaaia keia koa i ke akua*," "this fishing ground was consecrated (*ho'ola'a*) to the god" (Fornander 1916–20, 4 : 295).

Recognizing a paradigmatic relationship between worshiping the gods and making their images mana does not mean, however, claiming that *ho'omana* always presupposes making images mana. There are cases, in the texts of Malo and Kelou Kamakau, where *ho'omana* does not or does not necessarily involve images (cf. K. Kamakau 1919–20, 33, 31; Malo MS, 146, 159, 117). And when—in a myth—a priest "*kukuli aku la me ka hoomana i ke 'kua*," "worships the god on his knees" (Fornander 1916–20, 5 : 324–25), in order to be saved by him, he is simply making an invocation.

That worshiping may simply imply "ascribing mana," "recognizing mana" is also indicated by the following text: "*ua hoomana no o Kalaniopuu ia ia*," "Kalani 'ōpu'u worshiped him" (Remy 1862, 30). This refers to the worship of Cook as a manifestation of the god Lono.

Let me also quote once again a text from the *Mooolelo Hawaii* already given in Andrews's definition of *ho'omana*: "*a hoomana aku la i ua alii la e like me ka hoomana akua*," "they worshiped that ali'i like they worshiped a god" (Remy 1862, 154–55).

But note that even in these two cases *ho'omana* means more than "ascribing mana" because, by virtue of this ascription, something more is added to the mana ascribed to the god or man-god: authority (itself called mana) over the ascribers. In other words, the act of recognition is also an act of creation. Mana is presupposed, but also made by the act of recognition. More precisely, recognition (expressed by its signs: prayers, sacrifices, etc.) fully realizes in the god an efficacy that cannot exist without his relationship with humans.

The reason for this is precisely that the god is a concept, a type, a rule for human action and therefore cannot be efficacious without human action, which in turn implies human recognition of the god's status. In this sense the god's mana, and indeed his very existence, depends on man's *ho'omana*—whether or not this involves transferring the god to an image that is thereby made mana.

An awareness of the gods' dependence on man's recognition, on man's empowering of them, is indicated by several statements found in the texts. Thus a king, as supreme sacrifier, is addressed in a chant by saying "*ola ia kini akua iā 'oe*," "you give life to a multitude of gods" (Pukui and Korn 1973, 10).

Another text says that gods who no longer receive human recognition in the form of sacrifices and prayers die (Kahiolo 1978, 82).

Even more striking are the texts in which sacrifice is said to increase the mana of a god, *not* of his image. For instance, in the chant *Haui i ka lani* we find, in line 669, that *'awa* (kava) is consecrated (*kaumaha*)[29] "in order to increase the mana of the god" (*"i nui ka mana o ke akua,"* Fornander 1916–20, 6:405). Here, as in other contexts, the god is clearly treated as a commensal who eats with his worshipers and is fed by them as they are fed by him.

In sum, the act of human recognition is itself part of what the mana of the god is. Ultimately, then, the real locus of mana is in the reciprocal but hierarchical relation between the gods whose actions demonstrate efficacy and the men who, by recognizing that efficacy, increase and fully actualize it.

That mana ultimately depends on the relationship of man and god rather than on the god alone agrees with the fact that the possessive form *o*- must be used even when one refers to the possession of mana by the gods.[30]

Pukui and Elbert observe that "the possessive indicates the *nature of the relationship* of the possessed and the possessor. The *a*- forms . . . show that the possessor . . . caused the ownership. The *o*- forms show that the possessor . . . had nothing to do with the cause" (1979, 137–39). Were we to apply this rule to the case of mana, we would have to conclude that neither gods nor men cause their ownership of mana. This would be exaggerated because it would imply the equality of men and gods relative to the causing of mana. Yet in a more limited sense the statement is true, because for both man and god having mana depends on their relationship. It is their relationship, therefore, that truly causes their ownership of mana.

Conclusion

In this chapter I have attempted to show that the relationship between men and gods is constitutive of the state in which both are found at a given moment. Thus, if their relationship is wrong, both are polluted (although not to the same extent); if their relationship is right, both are pure (again, not equally).

The relationship between men and gods is right when men recognize and respect the status of the gods and therefore give the gods power to act on them. The gods' power to act on men is the power that the acknowledgment of a prescribed concept of action has on human consciousness, and therefore on concrete acts insofar as they depend on that consciousness. The gods' purity and efficacy (mana) thus depend on the degree to which humans recognize them as the personifications of normative concepts of their actions. The relative purity and efficacy of humans also depend on the degree of this recognition, which makes their action socially efficacious.

Thus the states of relative purity and efficacy of gods and humans are interconnected.

PART 2
SACRIFICE AND HIERARCHY

4
THE HIERARCHY OF SACRIFICES

Gli eroi non celebravano banchetti che non fussero sagrifizi, dov'essi dovevano esser i sacerdoti.
Vico 1959, 702

Essen heisst Opfern, und Opfern heisst Selbstessen.
Hegel 1974, 2,1:170

The Hierarchy of the Gods and the Hierarchy of Men

Treating the logic of sacrifice in general, I have not paid attention to a fundamental fact on which I must now focus: the gods are hierarchized, so that by performing a sacrifice—that is, by instantiating a given god—one puts oneself in a given hierarchical category. Of course the choice of the gods to instantiate is not free: one can sacrifice only to the gods that correspond to one's hierarchical position in society.

Thus, sacrifice ensures that the hierarchy of the gods is translated into a social hierarchy and reproduces it (cf. Beckwith 1919, 299–300). While this principle is clear, the way it is implemented is not known in a completely satisfactory way. But on the basis of a variety of facts and arguments that will be discussed or developed in this part of the book and in the next part, I feel it is possible to say what follows.

There is no doubt that Kū, Lono, Kāne, and Kanaloa are the highest gods. Moreover, at least in Hawai'i, they seem to be ranked in the order in which I have enumerated them (see chap. 6). As we have seen (chap. 1) together the gods represent all the predicates of the human species as conceived by the Hawaiians.

Lower-level deities are either particularizations of these gods or personifications of some of their predicates. The former deities have binomial names the first part of which is the name of one of the four major gods; the latter deities have a variety of individual names.

The major gods are gods of the entire society; in fact, of all Hawaiians. The lower gods belong to more restricted social groups, or sometimes to individuals or lines who rule over them. For this reason lower gods are not simply personifications of predicates that are ultimately included in the major gods: they also embody these predicates as they relate to different hierarchical levels or groups of the society. For instance, the particular forms of Kū that are gods of fishing are connected either with all the fishermen of the society or with the fishermen of certain districts; but each fishing 'aumakua relates the divinized predicates of the fisherman to a family group or even to an individual.

All in all, I think that most inferior gods that are not antistructural (cf. pp. 30, 42, 138, 351 n. 31, 370 n. 32) are encompassed by the major gods at least in the dumontian sense that they *presuppose* them logically and ritually. This implies that for a worshiper instantiating a given inferior god correlates with, and sometimes is equivalent to, instantiating one or more major gods to a certain degree. This degree varies with the number of the god's predicates instantiated and with the extent to which each predicate is instantiated.[1]

In other words, worshiping Kū in—say—hierarchical position three is logically and sociologically correlated with worshiping an inferior god or group of gods corresponding to that hierarchical position. The system can therefore be represented as in table 2.

This system implies that a man belonging to a certain basic hierarchical level may oscillate in time from a somewhat superior to a somewhat inferior state by sacrificing to different major gods. As we shall see, these oscillations are instantiated by the king himself (cf. Valeri 1982b).

Let me emphasize that the scheme I have presented is a simplified model; nevertheless I believe it is not an arbitrary construction. On the contrary, it will be confirmed by the analysis of the temple system (chap. 6) and by that of the ritual cycle of the society (part 3).

I acknowledge that the reality is more complex than this model, but it must also be recognized that a tendency to unify the pantheon and the entire cult under the major gods is quite evident. One sign of this is the hierarchization of the cults, their performers, and the gods on the basis of one single criterion: purity.

In this chapter I shall attempt to show that sacrifices and sacrifiers are indeed ranked as relatively pure or impure. In particular, I shall be concerned with two dimensions of the sacrificial system. In the first place, since men are purer than women, men's sacrifices are superior to women's. Actually, as I shall show, women have only a marginal relation to the sacrificial system; hence male sacrifice makes the absence, or the limited extent, of female sacrifice possible. In the second place, since men of superior rank are purer than men of inferior rank, their sacrifices are correspondingly purer. But again, the purer is the condition of possibility of the less pure. Through their metonymic relationship with their superiors, inferiors can benefit from a complete relationship with the divine without having to realize it themselves.

TABLE 2   Model of Hierarchical Positions of Worshipers

Hierarchical Levels of Inferior Gods	Major Gods			
	Kū →	Lono →	Kāne →	Kanaloa
1 ↓				
2 ↓				
3 ↓				
n ↓				

Note: Direction of arrows indicates the relation superior → inferior; cells indicate possible hierarchical positions of men as worshipers.

Sacrifice and the Hierarchy of the Sexes

First let us consider the question of women's sacrifice. According to Kepelino, "Women . . . were not allowed to offer sacrifice in the hand, only men. They were called by a name which denotes unclean and presumptuous—*kahinu* [in reality the Hawaiian text has *kuhinu*, which means the same]. Only if the woman herself was a prophet, or kahuna, was it permitted" (1932, 22; cf. Shaler 1935, 92; Pogue 1858, 22). Strictly speaking, Kepelino's statement must refer to women as *sacrificers* (ritual specialists who perform the sacrifice), not *sacrifiers* (those on whose behalf the rite is performed and who benefit from it—cf. Hubert and Mauss 1899), because the existence of some rituals in which they play the latter role is attested. These rituals involve goddesses. Just as the gods are the types of men and masculine actions, goddesses are the types of women and their activities (cf. Malo 1951, 81, 82–83). It is therefore logical that women establish a relationship with the goddesses through sacrifices. Thus dancing is an activity in which women have a predominant role; consequently, they are among the sacrifiers in the sacrifices offered to the female deities of the *hula* even though the sacrifices are apparently consecrated by a man (the *po'o pua'a*) (Emerson 1965, 26, 29). The goddess Haumea presides over that preeminently feminine function procreation, especially childbirth. Thus it is not surprising to note that noble women sacrifice to this goddess in order to have children. The sacrificer, however, is a man (K. Kamakau 1919–20, 29; Malo 1951, 175; Ii 1963, 44–45). Moreover, since this rite is performed at the end of the masculine rites of the *kapu luakini*, it shows more clearly than all others that feminine sacrifices presuppose masculine ones.

Another case where the women's sacrifice is only a complement to the men's is a medical rite in which men sacrifice and eat the victim (a dog) with the sick person and the god of medicine, and the women, on their side, eat another dog with the goddess of medicine (Malo 1951, 108). We must suppose that in this case as well the sacrificer of the women's dog is a man, since, as we shall see, men are always in charge of the oven in which the food (in this case, the dog) eaten by the women is cooked.

In sum, by acting as sacrificers, men make women's sacrifices possible; moreover, the sacrifices men offer to their own gods precede—logically and often even temporally—those that women offer to their goddesses.

In one realm only can women play the role of sacrificer for themselves and for men: sorcery. In fact, women have a privileged relationship with the female deities of sorcery (cf. Malo 1951, 82–83). Thus, the relationship with Pele and other goddesses of her family is often established through priestesses (cf. Ellis 1842, 310–12, 275; Stewart 1831, 2:109). Most often, these priestesses are *kāula*, "prophetesses" (NK, 2:110–11), or even *haka*, "mediums" (NK, 1:46). Their mediating role thus takes on a typically feminine form: they are possessed, penetrated by the deity who speaks through them. These priestesses seem to have a great importance in the marginal zones of Hawaiian society: for example, on the small island of Ni'ihau. A member of Cook's expedition writes in his journal: "There are at Neehow many priests and, what we have not seen at any other of these Islands, priestesses, who all act as if they were inspired by some supernatural power, performing numberless Mad and strange pranks" (Burney in Beaglehole 1967, 620, n. 2).

Samwell observes that these priestesses could consecrate sacrifices: "An old woman named Waratoi whom we supposed to be mad lived with our people all the time they were on shore; she performed daily some religious Ceremonies as we supposed them to be & offered Up some small pigs as Sacrifices for some purpose, and used many Extravagant Gestures like the Thracian Priestesses of old as if possessed with some fury" (1967, 1085). Priestesses most often are women past menopause or consecrated women who do not marry. However, some of these *kāula* are the daughters or wives of high priests, who utilize them in rites of divination (cf., for example, Kamakau 1961, 121; Fornander 1878–80, 2:309).

Although the evidence is too fragmentary to be conclusive, it seems to me that one general principle can be discerned: the sex of the sacrificer depends less on that of the deity invoked than on his or her relative purity or impurity. Thus pure goddesses often require male sacrificers as mediators between them and women, while impure gods may in certain cases by approached by men through female mediators. This happens because purity is an essentially masculine property, while impurity is essentially feminine. Thus, certain goddesses have a relatively "masculine" character in that they are relatively purer than actual women, while certain gods (especially sorcery gods or god aspects) have a relatively "feminine" character in that they are impure.

But on the other hand, certain women find themselves relatively purer than men because they happen to be the only representatives of the highest social rank. In this case they may play a role, either as sacrifier or sacrificer, in rites involving male deities. Thus Hawaiian chronicles mention that the chiefess Keakealaniwahine, having the supreme rank on the island of Hawai'i, had the right to enter state temples—normally taboo to women—to consecrate human sacrifices to the gods. But her rank compensated for her sex only up to a certain point; she could be the sacrificer but could not fully be the sacrifier, since it was still forbidden for her to eat a portion of the offering: "She was not allowed to eat any of the offerings and gifts with the priests and the men, who ate by themselves. She participated only in the ceremonies, for men and women continued to eat apart. . . . Thus Keakealaniwahine ate in her house of the food permitted to women" (Ii 1963, 160; cf. Ii 1869b,c).[2] High-ranking women seem to sacrifice to a male god in another case as well—when they give a pig to Lono in order to obtain children from this god of fertility (Ii 1963, 75). On closer inspection, however, it appears that this is not properly a sacrifice, because the pig is not killed and cooked, nor is any part of it eaten by the chiefess.

On the whole, the evidence indicates that women play a marginal role in the sacrificial system. The exceptional nature of women's sacrifice is underscored by Malo, who writes, "The majority of women . . . had no deity and just worshipped nothing" (1951, 82). This is confirmed by the fact that goddesses are few in comparison with the gods and are not as hierarchized as the latter.

As Kepelino makes clear in the text quoted at the beginning of this chapter, the exclusion of women from most sacrifices is explained by the belief in female impurity (cf. also Kamakau 1964, 64; NK, 1:114; Fornander 1916–20, 5:512; Kepelino 1932, 22).

The global inferiority of women relative to men in the sacrificial system contrasts sharply with their equality to men in the genealogically determined hierarchy. Are we then to suppose that the genealogical system determines a "profane" hierarchy, while the sacrificial system is associated with a "sacred" hierarchy? Clearly there is no evidence in Hawaii to support such a distinction. All hierarchical positions are determined by their degree of proximity to a divine reference point, which is the same for both men and women. But the relationship with this defining divine is obtained by two different means: the sacrificial means, in which men dominate, and the genealogical means, which is equally accessible to men and women and is therefore unmarked. As the *Kumulipo* demonstrates, all humans, irrespective of sex, descend from the gods, to whom they are more or less close (as tokens are to type) depending on their closeness to the senior descent line, that is, to the royal line.

Men's superiority to women, then, expresses only the superiority of a sacrificial relationship with the gods over a purely genealogical relationship with them. It is necessary, therefore, to explain why sacrifice is superior to genealogy.

In brief, both genealogy and sacrifice make it possible to create human replicas of the divine, but they create these replicas in different yet complementary ways. The genealogical connection with the gods allows a couple to produce a child who is a replica of the god as ancestor. This, however, only establishes a generic potentiality for action, which must be actualized in specific activities by sacrifice. It is this ability to bring to fulfillment and actuality a given potentiality that makes sacrifice superior to genealogy. Moreover, sacrifice implies a *direct* relationship with the gods, in contrast to the indirect relationship involved in genealogy. In sum, the superiority of sacrificial links over genealogical ones is the superiority of action over passivity, of direct relations over indirect ones, and, ultimately, of political relations over kinship.

Action is conceived as a masculine quality in contrast to feminine passivity. Hence only men are allowed to effect a sacrificial—that is, a direct and fully accomplished—realization of the divine types. Women are relegated to the unmarked, "passive" category and therefore are its representatives par excellence. This is only natural, for genealogical links are created by sexual reproduction, in which women play the main role as childbearers. Moreover, women's role in reproduction involves the shedding of blood and therefore impurity, which also disqualifies them from a direct relationship with the gods.

In the end, it appears that women's exclusion from sacrificial reproduction is symmetrical to men's exclusion from childbearing. It expresses the idea that the two activities are complementary and, in a way, equivalent. The ultimate reconciliation of genealogy and sacrifice lies precisely in the metonymic relation between the sexes. Thanks to the association of men and women of the same rank, sacrificially produced replicas are translated into "genealogical" ones and vice versa. Consequently it is possible to represent childbearing as woman's sacrifice and sacrifice as man's childbearing. As we shall see at length, only the second metaphor is strongly emphasized. This indicates that sacrifice is the truly encompassing and totalizing element, since it contains its conversion into "biological," "genealogical" reproduction and at the same time actualizes it as social, political reproduction (see part 3).

Because every meal taken by men implies eating with the gods (that is, it implies a relationship with the human predicates, and ultimately the human species, embodied in what is eaten), it is a sacrifice. Consequently women may never eat with men. As Kamakau explains the taboo, "It was made kapu for men and women to eat together. This was to separate from the worship of the god those who were unclean and defiled by blood" (1964, 64). A fortiori, women were barred from eating the species that could *only* be consumed during sacrificial rites (pig, coconut, etc.). Let us first consider the case of the species forbidden to women.

Species Taboo to Women

Not all sources agree on the species that are forbidden to women. Table 3 makes it possible to compare their lists at a glance. (I have left out pork, which is universally considered taboo to women.)

A comparison of these lists reveals some interesting facts. The oldest but also the shortest list is from the *Mooolelo Hawaii* of 1838. The list that follows it chronologically, given by Malo, is the most complete. Malo also mentions the existence of other taboo species but does not name them (1951, 29). The *Mooolelo* of 1858, edited by Pogue, reproduces the 1838 list and adds a second one, in a text visibly taken from Malo—except that Pogue has omitted the part that mentions the species *honu*, '*ea*, and *nai'a*, probably because *honu* and '*ea* are already mentioned in the first list and *nai'a* must have seemed to Pogue to be a simple duplication of *nu'ao* (both mean porpoise, according to the dictionaries).

Another problem involves the *moano* fish, which is mentioned only in the *Mooolelo* of 1838. A comparison of the 1838 text (p. 39) with that of 1858 (p. 24) reveals that Pogue substituted *manō*, "shark," for *moano*. He therefore judged that *moano* was a printer's error. It is possible that Pogue is right; nonetheless, the inclusion of *moano* in the list is not illogical, since this fish is closely related to the *kūmū* fish (Titcomb and Pukui 1972, 109–10, 91–92; PE, 229, 167), which is found on the list. If Pogue is wrong and the "*moano*" in the 1838 text is not a printer's error, Malo was the first Hawaiian author to mention the taboo on shark meat, which, however, is mentioned by earlier European observers.

The sources also differ on the variety of coconuts that is forbidden to women. According to the 1838 *Mooolelo* and Kepelino (1932), it is the yellow variety (*niu-lelo*) that is taboo; according to Pukui and Elbert it is the "black" variety (*niu-hiwa*) (p. 247). The latter opinion fits in with the fact that *hiwa* is a metaphor for *kapu*, but it is contradicted by older sources. The question is difficult to resolve.

There are also conflicting statements on dog meat. Lucy Thurston, who arrived in Hawaii several months after the abolition of the taboo system, learned that dog meat had been forbidden to women "in the days of idolatry" (1882, 40; cf. Luomala 1960, 229). Kawena Pukui shares this opinion and affirms that only after the abolition of the taboos did dog meat slowly become a preeminent woman's food (in Handy 1972, 245; Handy and Pukui 1972, 113).

These statements are contradicted by earlier accounts, however. Patterson declares that in 1805 women "eat dogs instead of pork, raised and fatted for them" (1817, 68). In 1809 "dogs' flesh and fish were the only kinds

TABLE 3   Species Taboo to Women

Species	Mooolelo 1838, 39	Malo 1951, 29, 47 (11.13, 15.19)	Mooolelo 1858, 24 (list a)	Mooolelo 1858 (list b)	Other Sources
Mai'a (banana)	All varieties but pōpō-'ulu, iho-lena, niu-hiwa	+	Same as Mooolelo 1838	+	Laanui 1930, 93; Manby 1929, 22; Choris 1822, 11; Kamakau 1964, 63–64; Kamakau 1976, 38; Whitman 1979, 22
Niu (coconut)	Forbidden variety niu-lelo (yellow)	+		+	Laanui 1930, 93; Kepelino 1932, 65 (niu-lelo); Choris 1822, 11; Kamakau 1964, 63–64 (niu-lelo); Whitman 1979, 22; Fornander 1916–20, 5:598
Honu (turtle)	+	+	+		King 1967, 624; Bell 1929–30, 2:19
'ea (turtle)	+	+	+		
Koholā (or palaoa) (whale)		+		+	Kepelino 1932, 64
Nai'a (dolphin, porpoise)		+			
Nu'ao (porpoise)		+		+	Kepelino 1932, 65

(continued)

of animal food lawful for them to eat" (Campbell 1816, 187–88). Another author states that the dog "is the only flesh the women are allowed to eat" (Hussey 1958, 35). But according to Freycinet women can eat only the meat of reddish dogs (1978, 73), and other accounts suggest that only women of high rank may eat dog flesh (Cox 1831, 37; Kotzebue 1821a, 2:202, 249–50; Golovnin 1979, 208; Kamakau 1961, 225). It is sure at any rate that women eat this meat only in some ritual contexts: the women's sacrifices mentioned above (Malo 1951, 138–39; Ii 1963, 44; K. Kamakau, 1919–20, 29) and at the meal that takes place during the celebration of the New Year (Fornander 1916–20, 6:41). Moreover, the

Species	Mooolelo 1838, 39	Malo 1951, 29, 47 (11.13, 15.19)	Mooolelo 1858, 24 (list a)	Mooolelo 1858 (list b)	Other Sources
Pahu (Ostracion, etc.)		+		+	
Manō (shark)		Manō-niuhi (man-eating shark)	+	Manō-niuhi	Campbell 1967, 136 (manō-niuhi); Kepelino 1932, 65; Kamakau 1964, 63–64
Hīhīmanu (Dasyatidae and Myliobatidae)		+		+	Fornander 1878–80, 1:72; 1916–20, 4:528
Hāhālua (Manta alfredi)		+		+	Kepelino 1932, 65 ("spotted stingray")
Hailepo (Variety of ray)		+		+	Kepelino 1932, 65 ("kailepo")
Ulua (Carangidae)		+	+	+	Kepelino 1932, 65; Kamakau 1964, 63–64
Kūmū (Upeneus porphyreus)	+	+	+	+	Kepelino 1932, 65; Kamakau 1964, 63–64
Moano (Parupeneus multifasciatus)	+				

Note: Plus sign indicates that the species is listed as taboo in the source at the head of the column.

queen drinks broth made from dog after giving birth to her husband's heir (Malo 1951, 138–39).

Yet it is possible that the data concerning women's consumption of dog meat are contradictory in appearance only, either because the interdiction on this meat was relaxed even before the end of the taboo system or, as is more probable, because it concerned only some varieties of dogs.

According to Ellis, "The flesh of hogs, fowls, turtle, and several other kinds of fish, cocoa-nuts and almost every thing offered in sacrifice, were tabu to the use of gods and men; hence the women were, except in cases of particular indulgence, restricted from using them" (1842, 387). Kepelino confirms this statement (1932, 65).[3] In short, it is the sacrificial species, or rather the species offered in sacrifice to the male deities, that are forbidden to women. Nevertheless the lists contain a few species that are not prescribed, apparently, in any nomo- or ergocentric sacrifice: cetaceans, sharks, mantas and rays, *pahu*, perhaps even the turtle. Can we then state that all these species are forbidden to women because they are sacrificed to the gods? Strictly speaking yes, for the Hawaiian notion of sacrifice includes that of "restitution" or "returning" to the divine that which belongs to it. Thus Malo uses the word *hai* to designate the consecration of these animals to the gods each time they wash up on shore or in some way enter into men's possession (38.13, 15.19). These sacrifices are accounted for by the ideology of the firstfruits sacrifice but differ from ordinary sacrifices of this kind in that they involve the return of the animals in their entirety, or nearly so. This happens because the animals involved are much more sacred than all the others, and because this sacredness is believed to be eminently dangerous. Therefore the consecration of these animals is a privilege/duty that belongs exclusively to the king; this explains why some parts of their bodies (whale teeth and bones, for example) (see Kamakau 1961, 129; Titcomb and Pukui 1972, 90, 139) become regalia.[4] Leaving aside the shark for the moment, it is possible to divide these sacred species into two groups:

1. *Mantas and rays*: *hīhīmanu, hāhālua, hailepo* (which may be identical to the *hīhīmanu*—see PE, 45). All of these fish are "winged" (Malo 15.20); moreover, the name *hīhīmanu* probably means "birdlike" (Titcomb and Pukui 1972, 73). This ray is also called *lupe*, "kite" (ibid.). Mantas and rays are distinguished from other "winged" fish, which are not included on this list, because they are large and poisonous and consequently dangerous.

2. *Animals "that breathe on the surface of the sea"* (Malo 1951, 19): turtles (*honu, 'ea*), whales, porpoises (*nu'ao, nai'a*). Malo also places the *pahu* fish in this class. This is surprising, for the fish in question is not a breathing animal; apparently this is the Hawaiian belief, however.

All these animals seem to be anomalous and to straddle normally distinct, even opposing categories: mantas and rays are "birdfish"; marine mammals and turtles are animals that breathe like land animals but live in the sea like fish. However, species of the first group mix two categories that are equally alien to man (birds and fish), while those of the second group mix sea animal, a category alien to man, with breathing animal, a category to which man belongs. From this standpoint, cetaceans and turtles are closer to the pig and dog than to mantas and rays, but unlike the pig and dog they are not domesticated and therefore not controlled by man. On the contrary, these animals live in the depths of the ocean or, in the case of turtles, on small islands that are difficult to reach (cf. Rickman 1966, 310).

They are generally powerful and, in the case of the whale, impossible to hunt.[5] It is thus possible to organize species taboo to women into three groups of increasing proximity to humanity.

1. Mantas and rays confuse two opposing terms, both equally distant from man. These "monsters" represent a commingling in the purely "other"; moreover, they constitute a real threat to man. They are not caught like fish, but if they wash up on the beach or are taken in nets they are reintegrated into the divine realm. The latter has a purely negative connotation in this context; in fact, mantas and rays are considered the "bodies" of Kanaloa, the most "sinister" of the major Hawaiian gods (Handy and Pukui 1972, 177).[6]

2. Cetaceans and turtles confuse a class opposed to man and one to which man belongs. These marine animals thus can represent a relating of the human and the divine; nonetheless, this is a relating that is due to and controlled by divine initiative, since neither cetaceans nor turtles are controlled by man. Thus, like everything that is uncontrollable, they have a negative connotation,[7] which explains why they too are associated with Kanaloa (Handy and Pukui 1972, 177).

3. Species such as the pig and the dog, which are employed in nomo- and ergocentric sacrifices, also constitute a point where opposite terms, one human and the other nonhuman, blend. They can then function as mediators between men and the deities, but this mediation, unlike the preceding one, is controlled by man, for it is made possible by species that man controls.

As for the man-eating shark, in some ways it has the same value as the species of the second group, but its man-eating quality associates it with the species of the first. In the last analysis it is a special case, which signifies the encompassing of the human by the divine in its destructive, punitive aspect.

The alimentary status of these groups of species is parallel to their conceptual status.

1. According to Kawena Pukui, the *hīhīmanu* was not eaten by Hawaiians of old, either male or female (Titcomb and Pukui, 1972, 74). Its inclusion on the list of species taboo to women therefore seems pleonastic. The inclusion of the man-eating shark seems equally pleonastic, since it is not eaten by men either (ibid., 108).

2. Species of the second group have an ambiguous status. Turtles are eaten by male ali'i. According to some, porpoises can be eaten by men; according to others, they cannot (ibid., 112–13). Whale meat is eaten by no one; but since the appropriation of this animal's bones and teeth is reserved for the king, the animal is considered taboo to commoners (ibid., 90). Here again the inclusion of the whale in the list of species that cannot be eaten by women seems strange. Is it necessary to interpret this inclusion

as the sign of a distinction between a "taboo" (a formal proscription that would be limited to women) and "avoidance" (men are not forbidden to eat whale meat but are averse to it because of its symbolic connotation)? Perhaps this distinction would also explain the inclusion of rays, mantas, porpoises, and such, on the list of species forbidden to women—men do not eat them either but are not positively forbidden to do so. Nonetheless, the avoidance is explained in the same overall fashion as the taboo. If some animals arouse a certain distaste, it is because from a symbolic standpoint they have negative connotations. They are bad to eat because they lead one to think about bad things.

3. Unlike the preceding species, species used in male nomo- and ergo-centric sacrifices are "sacred" in a sense that is mainly positive. They thus are men's food par excellence but are strictly forbidden to women because of women's impurity.

In conclusion, the list of species said to be taboo to women can be broken down into subclasses. Species of the first and second subclasses, as uncontrollable and dangerous manifestations of the divine, have a negative value. These species are taboo to women not because men eat them (except rarely, when they want to incorporate negative aspects of the divine), but because men, particularly those of high rank, reserve for themselves the task of neutralizing them and freeing society of them. Taboo species of the third subclass instead are eaten exclusively by men because they make it possible to establish a relationship with primarily positive, "pure" deities or to transform the negative aspects of these deities into positive ones.

Species Permitted to Women

All other species are available to women after men have performed certain ritual operations. These operations aim to separate the species into two parts: one is sacred and reserved for men; the other, which is profane, goes to the women. The existence of the profane part is made possible by the ritual concentration of the sacral character of the entire species in the gods' part, which itself is inseparable from the part belonging to the men. Men thus assume the servitudes of the taboo, "sacrificing themselves" in making the sacrifice, in order to secure "freedom" (*noa*) for the women. It must not be forgotten, in fact, that although these species are less sacred than those mentioned above, they are still considered manifestations of the deities, their "bodies." As we have seen, their appropriation presupposes a symbolic preservation; it is the men who have this responsibility. Since they represent the principle of integrity in their social group, since they are "pure," men can approach pure species without polluting them and make their real appropriation possible by practicing its symbolic negation.

In the end a complementarity exists between the role of women and men in the process of appropriating nature. Men deny the appropriation, women affirm it. Pure men enact the fiction of feeding that preserves the integrity and life of that which is appropriated; impure women are there to assume the burden of the irreducible reality of pollution, of the destruction of divine nature. In this sense women enable men to eat just as much as men permit women to do so. Men are the support for the symbolic construction justifying the human appropriation of nature; women are the support for the acceptance of the empirical reality of this appropriation.

The male task of mediating between the pure divine and the human is not limited to the meal but also concerns the process of appropriating food before the meal. In fact, not only fishing but also the cultivation and cooking of the principal food plants are traditionally exclusively male duties. As Handy writes, "The production and preparation of food devolved upon men (as did likewise the offerings to the family gods in the *mua*) not upon women as later came to be the custom after the formal overthrow of the old religious system" (1972, 301).[8] In particular, "every aspect of taro economy and culture was man's work; the making and tending of fields and irrigated terraces and irrigation ditches, planting, cultivating and harvesting taro, steaming it in a ground oven, peeling it, and pounding the steamed corms to make *poi* for the womenfolk as well as for men and boys" (ibid.).[9]

Malo describes the preparation and cooking of taro in the domestic group:

The husband was burdened and wearied with the preparation of two ovens of food, one for himself and a separate one for his wife. The man first started an oven of food for his wife, and, when that was done, he went to the house [called] *mua* [the men's house, as well as the domestic temple—V. V.] and started an oven of food for himself. Then he would return to the house and open his wife's oven, peel the *taro*, pound it into *poi*, knead it and put it into the calabash. This ended the food-cooking for his wife. Then he must return to *mua*, open his own oven, peel the *taro*, pound and knead it into *poi*, put the mass into a (separate) calabash for himself and remove the lumps. Thus did he prepare his food (*ai*, vegetable food); and thus was he ever compelled to do so long as he and his wife lived. [1951, 27; cf. Pogue 1858, 22]

The form taken by the appropriation of taro confirms some of the notions summarized above. Taro cultivation is necessarily a male task, since it entails the relationship with a sacred, divine species. In fact, taro is the natural body of Hāloa, the elder brother of the ancestor of all Hawaiians. His integrity and purity must be respected, for upon these qualities depend the integrity and purity—in a word, the life—of his "younger brother," man. Cooking puts an end to that integrity and constitutes the killing of the taro, its passage from the state of supersubject (man's older brother, the transcendental condition of his existence) to the state of infraobject (food, an amorphous substance constituting man on the material plane). When taro is in its first state, man identifies it with his own subjectivity and considers it a priori human; in the second, taro is identified with man only a posteriori because its material appropriation transforms it into a human substance. This radical reversal of the status accorded to taro seems to take place following contact with the feminine, destructive, polluting pole. According to Malo, in fact, the women's taro is cooked first. But if the destructive cooking gives the first place to women, the restorative consumption gives precedence to men.[10] In other words, the masculine meal, which entails commensality with the gods representing the pole of integrity and purity, must counterbalance the feminine destructive work,[11] a residue whose inevitability is recognized in the very act that denies it.

The similarities and differences existing between these Hawaiian practices and Maori ones are remarkable. Both use the principle that "cooked food is the very antithesis of *tapu*" (Best 1924, 1:260; cf. Smith 1974, 32–33) as a means of desacralization; however, if I am not mistaken, the Hawaiians accept it only on the condition that it be encapsulated, as it were, within its negation. This encapsulation is made possible by associating the principle of desacralization with women and the principle of its negation with men.

It is obvious that the reproduction of the species' integrity in relation to the group always entails the reproduction of the group as well. These two reproductions can be combined in the sacrificial meal, or each can be associated with a different stage of the ritual action, as happens when fish are appropriated. Fish become accessible only after a sacrifice of the first catch, which takes place on an altar or in a temple, called *koʻa*, where Kūʻula and his wife are worshiped (Ii 1963, 24; Titcomb and Pukui 1972, 44; Kamakau 1976, 74) together with the familial deities (*ʻaumakua*) of fishing. Here is what occurs, for example, after catching the *uhu* (parrot) fish:

By the time the fisherman turned homeward and beached the canoe at the landing his *ʻie* basket would be full of fish jostling each other. His wife, children, and family all rejoiced. Fish were given to the family members and kinfolk who carried the canoe ashore, then the fisherman went home. He bathed, girded on his *malo*, put on his *kapa* covering and then removed the restrictions of the god on the fish and made his offering. Then the fish for the *mua*, the men's house, was cut up for the men, and the fish for the *hale ʻaina*, the women's eating house, was cut up for the women and the little boys who had not yet been consecrated to the gods. The bigger boys, who had been consecrated, lived in the *mua* with the men; they no longer ate free from tabu, *ʻainoa*, with their mothers in the women's house. [Kamakau 1964, 66]

Similar rites are performed for the catching of other fish (see Kamakau 1976, 64, 73–74). Their common scheme seems to imply a reduplication of the sacrificial rite. First, the firstfruits of the catch are consecrated *raw* to the fish deities present on the altar serving the fisherman. This consecration of the raw firstfruits represents the restitutory aspect of the sacrifice and reconstitutes the integrity of the species when it seems threatened by human appropriation. But we must suppose that after the fish has been cooked, the first share, like that of any other food on any occasion, is consecrated to the familial deities sheltered in the men's house. These deities have no relation to fishing, but rather are connected with the household as such. Consequently, the consecration of cooked fish in the *mua* constitutes the more properly nomocentric aspect of the sacrifice—the reproduction of the social unit in conjunction with its deities.

It does not seem that the disjunction between the raw offering and the cooked offering exists in the everyday appropriation of taro (cf. Kamakau 1976, 36–37); however, it exists during the celebration of the New Year and on other occasions when cultivators place their offerings of raw taro on the altar of their district. After these offerings (as well as other products of the land) are appropriated by the god Lono, who presides over agriculture, it becomes possible for the farmers to appropriate the cooked taro for themselves and to offer the first portion of it to their own family deities (see below p. 210).

What holds for the appropriation of taro and fish also holds for the appropriation of other important food. Women are excluded from the production and cooking of these foods, even though at times they may play an indirect role, as we have seen. At most, they are given the task of appropriating some secondary foods—which in a way are "residual," like the women themselves: shellfish, mollusks, seaweed, small crustaceans, and so on. Sometimes they are able to grow sweet potatoes (*'uala*), a little-prized tuber reserved for marginal land, which has the dubious honor of being associated with the excrement of the pig Kamapua'a (Kamakau 1976, 23–31; Handy 1972, 137–42).

What work do women do, then? Samwell describes their activities in this fashion: "As to their Employments they seem to lead a very easy Life, beating the Cloth is the most laborious . . . : the rest of their business is confined to nursing their Children and other domestic Cares, the Young women spend most of their time in singing and dancing of which they are very fond" (1967, 1181). Townsend (n.d., 15) observes, "The young women never work out-door but the old ones do," which is confirmed by Holman (1931, 28): "Women in Owwhyhee never work until they get to be old and despised." Essentially, then, the occupation of a young woman is to procreate, which in Hawaiian culture implies all that relates to seduction, in which it is said that women play a more active role than men (cf. Thurston 1882, 64). This explains why properly feminine activities are making ornaments (Stewart 1839, 116–17) and clothing, chanting, dancing, and other activities that promote eroticism. It is the women who often compose and chant the *mele inoa*, "name chants," with their deliberately erotic content, and even the *mele ma'i* "chant [praising] the genitals" of the members of their families or their chiefs (Handy 1972, 305–6; Malo 1951, 67; Pukui 1949, 255–56).

These facts confirm the existence of the previously mentioned opposition between sexual reproduction, which is primarily associated with the feminine pole, and the sacrificial reproduction of social units with their natural correlatives, which is primarily associated with the masculine pole. In the first form of reproduction the sexes are conjoined. Consequently, the distinction between pure and impure is lost, and man, finding himself in an impure situation, cannot approach pure food. In the second form of reproduction, on the contrary, he can approach it; being separated from women, he is pure:

| *Sexual reproduction* | $\neq$ | *Social reproduction* |
| Sexes conjoined = impure | | Sexes disjoined = pure |

The opposition between the two forms of reproduction[12] and the different relations existing between the sexes in each are reflected by the subdivision of the unit of habitation (*kauhale*, "homestead") into three types of functional units: men's houses, women's houses, and houses where men and women can live together.[13]

Properly masculine activities take place in the *hale mua*. There men sacrifice to their family gods and take their meals (Handy 1972, 316). The *hale ʻaina* ("eating house") is reserved for the meals of women and of boys who have not yet been admitted into the *hale mua* (Handy and Pukui 1972, 9; Ii 1963, 46).[14] The *hale ʻaina* is forbidden to men, just as the *hale mua* is forbidden to women (cf. Pogue 1858, 24; Bell 1929–30, 1:78; Townsend 1921, 15–16; Shaler 1935, 94; Ross 1904, 63; Choris 1822, 11; Kamakau 1961, 225).[15] Women use two other houses, the *hale kua* or *kuku* (Malo 1951, 29), where they prepare bark cloth (*kapa*) and gather to gossip (Handy 1972, 299, 306), and the *hale peʻa*, or menstrual hut (Handy and Pukui 1972, 10–11).[16]

Men and women sleep together in the *hale noa* ("free house") or *hale moe* ("sleeping house"—Malo 1951, 29), in which the interior is apportioned into spaces reserved for different categories of persons (Handy 1972, 291–93). Cooking and eating there are forbidden (Handy 1972, 294–95; Handy and Pukui 1972, 10), since food is radically separated from sexual activity.

In a noble's *kauhale*, each of his wives has her own group of houses. Thus, in the residence of Kamehameha in Honolulu each of his three main wives had three houses at her disposal (Ross 1904, 63).

Sacrifice and Rank

In eating, not only is one separated from persons of the opposite sex but equal genealogical rank, one is also separated from persons of the same sex but unequal rank. Only people of the same rank and sex are proper commensals. The rule of separation extends to the fires over which the food is cooked.[17]

It is also obvious that commensality is forbidden with those who do not respect these rules of separation, in particular the rules separating the sexes for eating. These people in effect become like their inferiors or the women with whom they eat. This is why the Hawaiian nobles refused to eat with Europeans,[18] who ate with women, or had to purify themselves after doing so.[19]

Europeans who entered the service of an aliʻi and became his commensals had to respect his alimentary taboos.[20] The higher the rank the more severe the separation (cf. Malo 1951, 190),[21] not only with respect to inferior ranks, but also in relation to women. Thus, whereas before their initiation into the men's house ordinary male children can eat food cooked in the women's ovens, the sons of priests or high-ranking aliʻi cannot do this at all; the only food permitted to them at this stage is their mothers' milk or that of a nurse (Malo 1951, 94). This implies that even before initiation these children cannot appropriate nature in an impure, "nonmasculine" manner. Further, if by accident an aliʻi eats of *noa*, unconsecrated, "feminine" food, he must be purified in a special sacrifice (sometimes a human sacrifice), failing which he is punished by the gods and becomes sick (Malo 1951, 189).[22]

Whether it takes place in a temple or his *mua* house, the meal of an aliʻi is a religious act, a sacrifice; the gods, who receive the first portion of his meal, are always present. To be convinced of this, one only need read one of many descriptions of these meals:

Amongst their religious ceremonies, may be reckoned the prayers and offerings made by the priests before their meals. Whilst the *ava* is chewing, of which they always drink before they begin their repast, the person of the highest rank takes the lead in a sort of hymn, in which he is presently joined by one, two, or more of the company; the rest moving their bodies, and striking their hands gently together in concert with the singers. When the *ava* is ready, cups of it are handed about to those who do not join in the song, which they keep in their hands until it is ended; when, uniting in one loud response, they drink of their cup. The performers of the hymn are then served with *ava*, who drink it after a repetition of the same ceremony; and, if there be present one of a very superior rank, a cup is, last of all, presented to him, which, after chanting some time alone, and being answered by the rest, and pouring a little out on the ground, he drinks off. A piece of the flesh that is dressed, is next cut off, without any selection of the part of the animal; which, together with some of the vegetables, being deposited at the foot of the image of the *Eatooa* [*akua*], and a hymn chanted, their meal commences. A ceremony of much the same kind is also performed by the Chiefs, whenever they drink *ava* between their meals. [Cook and King 1784, 3:161; cf. King 1967, 620]

Cf. Ellis 1782, 2:166–67; Samwell 1967, 1160–61, 1169; Whitman 1979, 34–35; cf. Titcomb 1948, 106–16, 118; Handy 1972, 193–94.)[23]

Here in addition is the description of a meal of a high-ranking ali'i Kaumuali'i (1792):

No one dared to touch anything but the youngster [Kaumuali'i]: he tore everything to pieces with his hands, making his distributions to all around him, only reserving the most delicious morsels for himself. . . . Whenever the son of royalty drank a priest spoke two or three sentences; everybody then squatted close down, holding up both their hands remaining in the state until the Cocoa nut or calabash was taken from his lips: none of his attendants could drink Cocoa Nuts under the same roof with him. [Manby 1929, 23–24][24]

Malo confirms these observations, "When a tabu chief ate, the people in his presence must kneel, and if anyone raised his knee from the ground, he was put to death" (1951, 57; cf. Ii 1963, 58–59; Menzies 1920, 78).

The meal of a high-ranking man never has anything ordinary about it, since it is the prolonging of sacrificial actions that regularly take place four times a month during eight months of the year in the temples.[25] In fact, a high-ranking ali'i can eat only food consecrated in the temples, which is part of the offering as I have defined it.[26] Even a European, if he has been raised to the dignity of an ali'i, "was allowed to make use of nothing [i.e., no food] but what had been consecrated at the marae [*heiau*, temple]" (Menzies 1920, 78). The one with whom Menzies and his friends made an excursion "could not even chew a sugar cane as we were coming up the path because it had not been properly consecrated" (1920, 78). The obligation to eat food consecrated in the temples concerns first of all pork: "The pork must first be consecrated in the morai [temple] before it is touched by them" (Kotzebue 1821a, 1 : 310; Menzies 1920, 59; Townsend 1921, 15; Mortimer 1791, 52; Campbell 1816, 131; 1967, 93; von Chamisso 1864, 4 : 138; Malo 1951, 138; Kamakau 1961, 200, 206). This is the reason von Chamisso wittily observes that Hawaiians eat pork only if it is "kosher" (1864, 4 : 138).

I must insist that, contrary to what one of Malo's passages may seem to imply (a passage, moreover, that is poorly translated by N. Emerson— 1951, 138),[27] the ali'i are not the only ones to eat pork ritually.

The consumption of this meat is never strictly profane but is ritualized to different degrees.[28] Moreover, there is a complementarity between these degrees. In other words, it is precisely the extreme ritualization of the consumption of pork (as well as all other foods) by the ali'i that makes possible the lesser ritualization of its consumption by those of inferior rank. Thus the meals of people of different rank form an ideal series: closer to the gods, an ali'i of high rank takes the first step in the process of approaching them, and this step makes all the others possible, whether they are directly associated (but in a subordinate position) with the ali'i's meal or are separate from it.

The scheme that applies to the relations between men of different rank is not structurally different from the one governing the relations between the sexes. In this connection it is necessary to remark that the position of inferior men approaches that of women, in that the most sacred species (pork, coconuts, etc.) are only rarely consumed by them,[29] being eaten most often by high-ranking men [30] in temples to which male commoners are not admitted any more than women.[31]

It can be said in any case that what is daily food for the ali'i is, at best, holiday food for men of inferior rank. This difference is logically connected to the fact that the ali'i are continually or almost continually in relation with the gods, while commoners are in relation with them only occasionally (during holidays, precisely) and always by means of a more or less direct mediation on the part of the ali'i.

An ali'i's daily meal, which often involves the consumption of meat consecrated in the temple sacrifices, is the continuation of the latter on a reduced and less sacred scale.

On the purity of the king's eating place, then, depends the life of the entire society, which metonymically participates in his appropriation of the food's meaning. As Kamakau writes concerning the king's eating place, "defilement must be avoided lest the whole race perish in consequence" (1961, 212).[32]

While the sources describe only the male eating classes, it seems likely that women too were divided into eating classes. However, the logic of the system implies that the female eating classes were not ideally linked in a hierarchical chain as were the male classes. The reason is that women's connection with food (and through it, the deities) is always mediated by their menfolk. Therefore women eat only the food desacralized for them by men of their own rank. The food eaten by their female superiors does not have the same justificative function for them as the food of male superiors has for their male inferiors. Nor does it give them the same indirect access to the divine. If women depended only on other women, they could dispense with the mediating function of their men.

Thus only male eating classes must have formed a hierarchical chain; it is probable that female eating classes were logically attached only to the corresponding male classes that desacralized food for each of them.

In conclusion, this system of "regulated eating" ('ai kapu) is based on a hierarchy of principles. Its first requisite is the noncommensality of the sexes, which makes it possible to separate the pure from the impure, or rather, to create within society a special category—males—that mediates between the pure deities and impure empirical reality.

Once this first distinction is established, it is possible to create further distinctions among men; these are also predicated on the opposition of pure and impure, that is, on the creation of mediators. More precisely, in the hierarchical chain each class mediates between the classes superior to it and the ones inferior to it. The mediator, thus, is always established relatively; consequently, every mediation presupposes the entire system.

In this sense the whole system is based on the opposition of the pure and the impure, and is summarized by the follow proportion: pure : impure :: male : female :: male superior : male inferior.

Since the hierarchy of males has as its precondition the hierarchy of sex, and since the latter manifests itself in the food taboos imposed on women ('ai kapu), it is perfectly understandable that the Hawaiians see in the alimentary separation of the sexes the epitome and the basis of their hierarchical system.

Thus Kamakau affirms that it was the 'ai kapu "that gave the chiefs their high station" (1961, 223). This connection between rank and the 'ai kapu explains why, in 1819, King Liholiho could symbolically abolish the traditional hierarchy and the system of religious practices to which it was related by eating in the company of women; as a consequence, "the people saw clearly that the royal kapu and the food kapu had just been abolished," correlatively (Remy 1862, 141).[33]

Henceforth the hierarchy survived only in its genealogical form and consequently in its female-centered mode of reproduction. It is no accident, then, that female, not male, chiefs played the most important political roles after the abolition of the Old Regime (cf. Kuykendall 1938).

Conclusions

Because the most sacred species cannot be completely desacralized, they are consumed only in spatial or temporal contexts where only men can be present. This is in accord with the fact that men are purer than women and with the masculine connotation of the most sacred species. The other species, on the contrary, are eaten in ordinary contexts and as a result women may take part in their consumption, albeit while separated from men.

Exceptional contexts, reserved for men, where the most sacred species are eaten, are those that concern the household as a whole (see, for example, initiation) and, more often still, the entire community (temple rituals). In these rites of collective interest a relationship is established with the most important deities by means of mediating species rich in meaning that consequently assume a markedly sacred character.

On the contrary, in daily rites, with which women are indirectly associated, the emphasis is placed on the desacralization of species that have a lesser symbolic value.

In sum, in important ordinary and extraordinary rites men eat certain species to enter into contact with the gods; in daily rites, they eat with the gods to make certain species available. To a certain extent, this opposition also corresponds to an opposition between rites where the nomo- or ergo-centric aspect of the sacrifice is dominant and rites where the genocentric aspect is in the foreground.

Last, I have shown that since marked species tend to be eaten above all in sacrifices of collective interest, and most especially in those relating to the social totality, they are eaten most often by those who, among men, have most to do with the totality, that is, the ali'i.

5

SACRIFICE AND KINGSHIP

Posto che le nazioni tutte cominciarono da un culto di una qualche
divinità, i padri nello stato delle famiglie dovetter esser i sappienti in
divinità d'auspici, i sacerdoti che sagrificavano per procurargli o sian ben
intendergli, e gli re che portavano le divine leggi alle loro famiglie.
Vico 1959, 356–57

Der Mensch ist das 'Εν καὶ πᾶν [Ein und alles] des Staats. Der Staat ist
die realisierte, ausgebildete, explizierte Totalität des menschlichen Wesens.
Im Staate werden die wesentlichen Qualitäten oder Tätigkeiten des
Menschen in besondern Ständen verwirklicht, aber in der Person
des Staatsoberhaupts wieder zur Identität zurückgeführt. Das Staatsoberhaupts hat alle Stände ohne Unterscheid zu vertreten; vor ihm sind
sie alle gleich notwendig, gleich berechtigt. Das Staatsoberhaupt ist der
Repräsentant des universalen Menschen.
Feuerbach 1970, 2:262–63

The "Sacrificer": Kahuna and Ali'i

Up to this point we have mainly considered three terms of the sacrifice: the
sacrifier, the god and the victim. Now it is time to consider a fourth term,
the sacrificer, and his relations with the others.

The *sacrificer* is the ritual specialist who performs the sacrifice, as opposed to the *sacrifier*, who pays for it and benefits from it (cf. Hubert and
Mauss 1899). Obviously, the more complex the sacrifice, the more it demands a technical expertise beyond the reach of the average man. Consequently, it often happens that a sacrifier employs one or more "experts," or
"priests" (kahuna),[1] to officiate in his sacrificial rite (see, for example, Malo
1951, 103, and descriptions of the *luakini* temple rites in part 3). But the
sacrificer's presence along with that of the sacrifier is not due only to
the need for specialized knowledge.[2] What characterizes the sacrificer, in
fact, is that he is permanently in contact with the god (cf. Fornander
1916–20, 6:70)[3] and that, participating in this way in the god's nature

130

and mana,[4] even being his manifestation in a human form,[5] he can function as a mediator between the sacrifier and the god. In the person of the sacrificer human actions are translated into divine actions, divine actions into human ones. Visible symbols are transformed into invisible realities and invisible realities into visible symbols. The sacrificer can function, then, not only as a specialist who lends his knowledge to the sacrifier, but as a substitute for the latter with respect to the god to whom he is connected. Reciprocally, he can function as a manifestation and spokesperson for the god within the context of the rite.[6] Thus he is in a position completely analogous to that of the victim. But the victim has a passive role, the sacrificer an active one (cf. Loisy 1920, 78). The victim constitutes the mediation between the sacrifier and the god in a usually naturalized form, while the sacrificer always constitutes it in a human one. This relates to the fact that the victim is silent and symbolizes on a nonverbal level, while the sacrificer is the master of the word; he is the one who prays, who actualizes in speech the meanings of the victim and the sacrifier's intentions.

Let us then consider some facts that prove that (1) the sacrificer participates in the nature of the god on whom his actions are efficacious and is often seen as a human manifestation of this god; and (2) the sacrificer is closely related to the victim, to such a degree that he may become a victim himself or be seen as the transformation of a victim.

1. The sacrifice made on the occasion of a boy's entry into the *hale mua* provides an excellent illustration of the postulate that identifies the sacrificer with the god. Functioning as the sacrificer, the boy's father impersonates the god, for he drinks '*awa* and eats the honorable portion of the sacrifice (the head) in his stead (Malo 1951, 89). Even more striking examples of the identity between priests and gods can be found. One of Pele's priestesses states, "I am Pele; I shall never die" (Ellis 1842, 310, cf. 312). Another priestess of the same deity, having been invited by the noble woman Kāpi'olani to share her meal, refuses with the words, "I am a god; I will not eat" (Bingham 1848, 255).

Certainly the identification between priests and deity is particularly strong, when—as in the case of the priestesses above—the deity is supposed to inhabit their bodies and use their voices (Malo 1951, 117; Ellis 1842, 65),[7] but it also exists when true possession is absent (cf. Kepelino 1977, 60).[8] Thus, whether he is "possessed" or not, the man Kahōāli'i is said to incarnate the god of the same name (Kamakau 1964, 14, 54; 1961, 180; Beckwith 1940, 129, 130). That a priest cannot be put to death with impunity (cf. for example Kamakau 1961, 132; N. Emerson in Malo 1951, 80; Franchère 1820, 57) must also be viewed as an indication of the presence of divine mana in his person. This presence is due, in most cases, to either or both of two reasons: the priest issues from the god or has consecrated himself to him. In all cases he differs from the sacrifier in that he is incorporated into the god in a permanent way, while the sacrifier, as we have seen, is incorporated only temporarily.

We can conclude from this that the brief consecration of the sacrifier presupposes the sacrificer's permanent consecration. The sacrificer can function as such because he is a sacrifier who has not returned to a profane state or, rather, who has returned to it only partially, just enough to allow him to be sacrificer.

2. The close kinship existing between the victim and the sacrificer is illustrated by the origin myths of some cults or lineages of priests. Thus, according to one tradition, the cult of the thunder god (Kānehekili or Kahekili) spread on the island of Maui in the following manner:

The temple of Pakanaloa, has a tradition of claiming origin in the worship of the thunder to the effect that his kahu, Kanehekili, died within its walls, and when his brother-in-law realized the fact he cut off the head and took it to Lanai. The people of Hamakualoa, wondering at his disappearance, searched till they found his body in the temple at Keanae, and when it was made known that the guardian of the god was dead, the people came out and cut his body into small pieces and distributed it. As each place all over Maui received a portion of his body it became their duty to worship the thunder. Those who had the head, they worshipped it; and also his eyes, or his mouth; they were called the eye of the god, or mouth of the god, and so on. [Thrum 1909, 48–49]

According to this myth, worship of the god is made possible by the victimization of his priest, who is obviously identified with him (he even bears his name). Thus each piece of the priest's body makes a relation to the god possible. Here sacrificer coincides with god and victim. Moreover, he coincides with the sacrifiers as well, since they are named after the parts of his body that they have appropriated (ibid.). The myth thus illustrates the pivotal role of the sacrificer and underlines his functional homology with the victim by transforming it into an identity. The extreme situation in which sacrificer coincides with victim can, moreover, occur at any moment; we are told that when human victims were lacking "some of the priests were offered up" (Thrum 1908b, 52).[9]

According to a myth collected by Stokes, the lineage of the priest-guardians of the royal mausoleum Hale o Keawe descends from a victim. At the time of the inauguration of this mausoleum, a seer reveals to King Keawe that he must sacrifice his priestly iwikuamoʻo ("near and trusted relative of a chief who attended to his personal needs and possessions, and executed private orders"—PE, 98), who is called "Keawe-ai," "in order to give mana to the house." The bones of the victim are buried in the temple, of which his son becomes the priest-guardian. His descendants succeed him in this office (Stokes, n.d., GR box 2, n. 1, 26 May 1919).

This myth emphasizes several equations implicit in any sacrifice. In it the priest becomes the victim, and the victim, through his son and lineage, becomes the priest. Moreover, the priest is identified with the sacrifier (the king), whose name (Keawe) he bears and whose companion and relative he is. Thus the myth brings the symbolic equations down to their literal value, in which lie their origin and foundation. Hence the myth implies that the symbolic can be the efficacious equivalent of the real because it derives from it genetically. The symbolic sacrifice is thereby permanently inscribed in the literal sacrifice.

In other cases the priest is presented as a victim who has *survived* his sacrifice. At any rate, this would be the way one is tempted to define the priestess of Pele, since the edges of her garment are burned by the fire of the goddess (Ellis 1842, 275).

Whether the sacrificer obtains his close relationship with the god through sacrificial victims in the present, or through an ancestor who was a victim in the past, or by both means,[10] it is necessary for him to preserve his relative state of separation with respect to the profane world. Therefore priests and ali'i of high rank, who are, as we will see, the supreme sacrificers of society, must not leave certain sacred places, such as temples (Kaawa 1865a). They must eat "pure" food, that is, food consecrated in the temples of the gods with whom they have a commensal, and therefore a consubstantial, relationship (Malo 35.18). They must not come into contact with impure beings or things: menstruating women (Malo 18.7) and sometimes women altogether (Kamakau 1961, 235; 1964, 120–21), corpses (Kamakau 1961, 212–13; Remy 1862, 135),[11] excrement (Kamakau 1961, 264), and people of inferior rank, who are considered impure relative to them (Menzies 1920, 112; NK, 1:188 and passim; Laanui 1930).

Other rules aim to perpetuate the integrity of these sacred persons, since this integrity is a positive sign of their participation in the divine mana. Thus they cannot cut their hair and beards[12] (King 1967, 612; Ellis 1782, 2:150; Rickman 1966, 227; Kamakau 1961, 108, 235; Fornander 1916–20, 4:264; Fornander 1878–80, 2:115, 202; NK, 2:269) or lose their vital substance by having, at least during certain times, sexual relations (Kamakau 1976, 139).[13]

In sum, priests do not belong to themselves, they belong to the deities to whom they are consecrated (Kamakau 1964, 120). Thus, if a priest of Pele cuts his hair he cannot dispose of it freely, but must reintegrate it into the goddess to whom it belongs by throwing it into a volcanic pit (NK, 2:269).

Prescriptions concerning children initiated into the priesthood reveal the need for the concentration, separation, and preservation of integrity that are the basis for the rules of purity to which priests are bound: "The boy's body must be kept pure. He must not cut his hair, his clothing was tabu, his loin cloth, his sleeping mats, his house, everything he had to eat and drink must not be touched by others. This was also true of the boys who were to take up some branch of learning; they were guarded from defilement" [Kamakau 1961, 235].[14]

Naturally this need for purity is related to the pure deities, who "despise" (*hoʻokae*) impure beings and "only desire those who [are] clean and pure" (Kamakau 1964, 64; Fornander 1916–20, 5:513). But it is precisely these life-dispensing deities that one normally wishes to reach. Even if the production of life inevitably requires contact with impurity and death, any socially approved ritual aims at a pure goal. Moreover, whether he comes into contact with pure or impure deities, the sacrificer must follow the same rules of separation with regard to the profane world (cf. Kamakau 1964, 120–21).

The sacrificer's function is thus essential to ritual. But on a concrete level this function is realized in two ways. On the one hand, it is realized in the priest who participates in the rite and makes it efficacious through his knowledge and because he incarnates the relationship between god and man in a permanent fashion. On the other hand, it is realized in the sacrifier's hierarchical superiors who, as we have seen, make his sacrifice possible and efficacious without directly taking part in it. The relationship between sacrifier and sacrificer is not established only in the rite, then, but also by means of the hierarchy that connects the different sacrifiers and their rites. Participation in the hierarchical chain is in fact the fundamental criterion for the efficacy of any sacrifice. This proves that the hierarchy is itself a ritual context of which different sacrifiers and sacrifices are the parts.

To simplify, then, we will say that the function of the sacrificer in Hawaii is carried out by two persons, the kahuna and the aliʻi. The first is always an "employee" of the sacrifier and does not have a higher rank. The second is the one upon whom the sacrifier depends and who relates him to the upper echelons of the hierarchy, that is, in the last analysis, to the king at its summit, whose person and rites are the ultimate condition of the efficacy of any rite.

The kahuna permits the mediation between a man and the gods corresponding to his rank and activities; the aliʻi permits this mediation to be encompassed within a mediation of a higher order. The kahuna is defined above all by his knowledge, by his expertise, by his connection with a particular deity; the aliʻi is defined by his belonging to a superior state of being, embodied by a whole group of gods or level of the divine. Through the kahuna the sacrificing subject is particularized by coming into contact with a specific god and activity. Through his superior, the aliʻi, the sacrifier is universalized; he takes part in the totality.

Participation in the totality is thus always made possible by a properly social relationship. Access to the major gods is available only through one's hierarchical superiors or at least through the effect of their rituals. On the other hand, everyone has direct access to his own gods. If priests are used it is because this access presupposes a knowledge and a permanent relationship with the deities that are not practically realizable for everyone who has a right to them.

Let us consider these two categories, kahuna and ali'i, in greater detail. Since every ali'i refers in the end to the supreme ali'i, the king, the properties of the latter will be sufficient to define those realized in a more imperfect fashion in an ali'i of a lower order. In contrast, it is necessary to distinguish between different categories of priests, since these are defined by their specialized functions and their relationship with the social categories they serve. Let us begin, then, by briefly examining the subdivisions of the priesthood.

The Priesthood

Before taking up the classification of priests, it is necessary to try to understand the relation between the term *kahu akua* and the term *kahuna*.[15] Literally, *kahu* means "keeper," "guardian," "one who tends an oven, a cook" (PE, 105). The expression *kahu akua*, "keeper of a god," usually refers to a priest who has been delegated by the proprietor of a god to "feed" him by making daily sacrifices to him (Emerson in Malo 1951, 76; cf. Kamakau 1964, 86, 135);[16] to take care of his temple and image; to carry the latter in processions, if it is mobile, and so forth. Like any priest, the *kahu* is identified with the god he cares for (N. Emerson in Malo 1951, 80); he even appears as his flesh-and-blood double, since he receives the god's share in the great sacrifices in the *luakini* temple and since, at least on some occasions, he is fed in order to feed the god whose image he carries (Ii 1963, 73–75). In short, he is a kind of living image of the god.

Strictly speaking, then, *kahu akua* refers to a function of the priesthood and consequently also to the priests in whom it predominates. In a more general sense, however, the word *kahu akua* can designate any person who "takes care" of a god, who worships him by "feeding" him—any of the "faithful" (cf. for example Kamakau 1964, 82). Thus an ali'i is said to be the *kahu* of a god if he supervises his cult and provides the material means for his support (cf. for example N. Emerson in Malo 1951, 257; Kamakau 1961, 9, 11, 109; Fornander 1916–20, 4:185).

Whether or not they are considered a god's *kahu*, the kahuna are divided among many classes, which can be grouped into three fundamental categories:

Kahuna Pule

The priests officiating in temples controlled by the *ali'i* are called *kahuna pule*. They themselves are ali'i[17] and, according to Kamakau, many belong more specifically to the *papa* rank, which is given to children born of a mother having one of the three highest ranks (*nī'aupi'o, pi'o, naha*) and a father who is a *kaukauali'i*, "lesser chief" (1964, 7, 5).[18] Essentially, these priests are ali'i of somewhat lower rank,[19] delegated by higher-ranking ali'i to maintain a constant relationship with the gods that belong to them or belong collectively to the nobility.[20]

In addition to officiating in the rites of the temples of the ali'i, the *kahuna pule* officiate in rites for inaugurating houses (Malo 1951, 97, 121). All rites where *kahuna pule* officiate are called *kapu pule*.

Many kinds of *kahuna pule* exist, several of which will be considered in the description of the rites of the *luakini* temple. But the most important *kahuna pule* belong to two orders, that of Kū and that of Lono, the two principal gods. The order of Kū (*mo'o Kū*) is also called the order of Kanalu, after the name of the ancestor of these priests (Malo 1951, 159). According to some sources, however, this order was founded by the priest Pā'ao (Kamakau 1964, 7). Kū's priests are above all others. The order of Lono (*mo'o Lono*) is also called the order of Paliku (Malo 1951, 159).[21] It seems in principle that membership in these orders is hereditary (Kamakau 1961, 187; Malo 1951, 190; Shaler 1935, 92); it is known, however, that many members were co-opted by hereditary priests or chosen by the king from among the children of secondary unions of high-ranking ali'i (Malo 1951, 190; Kamakau 1961, 235; 1964, 7). Sometimes the orders were endowed with lands in perpetuity (Kamakau 1961, 231), but it seems that most often priests received land rights on an individual basis in return for their services. Their rights endured as long as the services were appreciated (cf. Malo 1951, 190, 172).[22]

The most important priest of the order of Kū is also the royal chaplain, who is called *kahuna nui*, "high priest."[23] He is responsible for most of the king's religious duties as well as his temples and main gods (Malo 1951, 188; Kepelino 1932, 132; Haleole in Fornander 1916–20, 6:150, 156–59). In particular, he controls two main classes of rituals: those of the *luakini* (Kū's temple, where rites for war, as well as certain apotropeic or propitiatory rites are performed), and the agricultural and festive rites of the New Year (Malo 1951, 188). Since the latter rites are associated with Lono we must conclude that the high priest also controls Lono's priests on his lord's account.[24] He also controls a great number of specialized priests and keeps watch over the respect for basic taboos (Malo 1951, 188–89; Kepelino 1932, 24–25). The recognition of the king's legitimacy depends largely upon him, since he has an essential role in rituals where this legitimacy is established or reestablished.[25] Nevertheless, the balance of power between the king and the chaplain is such that a denial of the king's legitimacy on the part of the chaplain is rare unless the latter has secretly attached himself to a would-be usurper. Moreover, it must not be forgotten that the king is the true head of the cult and takes the principal role in rituals.[26] The recognition of this primacy depends in part on the high priest, but it is a primacy nonetheless.

"Professional" Kahuna

This heterogeneous category includes specialists in different ritualized activities on the one hand and medical priests (*kahuna lapa'au*) on the other. Among the first can be mentioned the *papa hulihonua* (experts on the properties of sites), *papa kuhikuhipu'uone* ("a class of priests who advised concerning building and locating of temples, homes, fish ponds, hence a professional architect"—PE, 160; cf. Malo 1951, 161, 177),[27] *papa kilokilo lani* ("those who could read the signs, or omens, in the sky"—Kamakau 1964, 8), *kilo hōkū* (astrologers), *kilo 'ōpua* ("those who studied and read omens in the clouds"—Kamakau 1964, 8), *kilo honua* ("those who read the signs in the earth"—ibid.), *nānā uli* (meteorologists—Haleole in Fornander 1916–20, 6:59, 85),[28] *papa ku'i-a-lua* ("experts in *lua* fighting"—ibid.), *papa lono-maka-ihe* (expert in spear throwing—PE, 195), *kahuna kālai wa'a* (expert in the construction of canoes—Malo 1951, 126–30; Haleole in Fornander 1916–20, 6:143–47), and so on.

In the extreme, any artisan or possessor of a specialized knowledge is a kahuna (Kamakau 1961, 176–77); moreover, no productive activity exists that does not include ritual knowledge and a relationship with the deities. As Malo writes, "Each man worshipped the *akua* that presided over the occupation or the profession he followed, because it was generally believed that the *akua* could prosper any man in his calling" (1951, 81). Every man, then, is forced to be his own kahuna or to seek the kahuna of the activity he is undertaking.

According to S. M. Kamakau, the category of *kahuna lapa'au* ("curing expert"—PE, 106) includes eight classes:

CLASS 1—*Kahuna ho'ohapai keiki* and *ho'ohanau keiki* [who induced pregnancy and delivered babies];

CLASS 2—*Kahuna pa'ao'ao* and *kahuna'ea* [who diagnosed and treated childhood ailments of] puniness and fretfulness (*'omali 'alalehe*);

CLASS 3—*Kahuna 'o'o*, who "held back" [kept closed] the fontanel (*ho'opa'a manawa*) [and practiced lancing];

CLASS 4—*Kahuna haha*, who used a "table of pebbles" (*papa 'ili'ili*) and the ends of their fingers (*welau lima*) [that is, who diagnosed by "feel" (*haha*), or palpation];

CLASS 5—*Kahuna a ka 'alawa maka* and *'ike lihilihi*, who could "see at a glance" (*'alawa*) or "through the eyelashes" (*'ike lihilihi*), dislocations (*uwai*) and sprains (*anu'u*) [and who diagnosed by insight (*'alawa maka*) or critical observation (*'ike lihilihi*)];

CLASS 6—*Kahuna 'ana'ana* and *kahuna kuni*, who used *'ana'ana* and *kuni* magic in treatment (*ma ka lapa'au*);

CLASS 7—*Kahuna hoʻopiʻopiʻo*, who used [counteracting] sorcery (*hoʻopiʻopiʻo*) in their treatment (*ma ka lapaʻau*);
CLASS 8—*Kahuna makani*, who "treated" (*ma ka lapaʻau*) the spirits of illness. [1964, 98][29]

As can be seen, sorcerers (*kahuna ʻanāʻanā, kahuna kuni*, and *kahuna hoʻopiʻopiʻo*)[30] are grouped with the *kahuna lapaʻau* when they use their arts for medical purposes. Nevertheless, they fall outside this category when they use their arts for other ends, especially destructive ones. Kamakau emphasizes, in fact, that sorcerers know two arts; "that of killing, and that of saving (*o ka make a me ke ola*)" (1964, 98).

Sorcerers are in clear opposition to the priests of the "central" cult (the *kahuna pule*). Broadly speaking, this opposition corresponds to that of the pure and the impure; this is indicated, for instance, by the fact that sorcerers are excluded from rites of purification, for which it is necessary to call on the *kahuna pule heiau* (Malo 1951, 97). The role the latter have in rites of purification confirms that these rites consist in establishing a relation of conformity with the idea of human essence that the priests of the "central" cult represent. On the contrary, the impurity of the *kahuna ʻanāʻanā* (Kamakau 1964, 120; 1961, 215) is the sign of their nonconformity to this idea, a fact that makes them marginal and residual.[31] It is also the sign of their antisocial individualism or that of their clients, and of the fact that they have "repressed," unsatisfied and socially unsatisfiable, desires.[32] Their antagonism to the representatives of order often found expression on the political level: *kahuna ʻanāʻanā* "spoke openly, without fear of a kapu chief, even if he was a ruler" (Kamakau 1964, 122). This rebellious spirit contrasts with the politically neutral position held by professional kahuna. The latter are outside the hierarchical cult system and do not seem to be recruited from among the aliʻi (except perhaps those that the important aliʻi attach to their courts). Nevertheless, their functions are not antagonistic to those of the *kahuna pule*; moreover, the kings seem to have tried to control and regiment them (at least this is true in the case of Kamehameha—see Kamakau 1961, 176).

Kāula "Prophets"

With respect to official worship, the position of the *kāula* "prophets" is as marginal as that of the sorcerers. The two categories seem, moreover, to take their recruits especially from the humble and the solitary. Malo writes that the *kāula* "were a very eccentric class of people. They lived apart in desert places, and did not associate with people or fraternize with any one" (1951, 114).

But the *kāula*'s marginality has a very different meaning from that of the sorcerer. The latter is in contradiction to society because he is believed to pursue individual desires that are irreducible to social norms; the *kāula*, on the other hand, transcends society because he is free from all desire, or rather, because his desire has only the deity as its object: "Their thoughts were very much taken up with the deity" (Malo 1951, 114). While for the sorcerers the deities are simply a means, for the *kāula* they are ends. The *kāula* isolate themselves from society to reach the gods without passing through the social mediation of the human hierarchy or of the specialists. Having reached the deity, they become consubstantial with him; he speaks through their mouth, for he possesses them permanently. This is why the *kāula* are attributed a mana that is superior to that of the other kahuna and above all the capacity to prophesy the destiny of the social totality and that of its representatives:

> They foretold an overthrow of the government, the death of a ruler, the times when good or evil chiefs would rise up in the kingdom, when there would be an increase of the race, and the sources of the blessings which would be obtained. The prophets were independent people, and were inspired by the spirit of a god (*he poʻe i uluhia i ka ʻuhane o ke akua*). They spoke (*hoʻoko*, literally, "fulfilled") the words of the god without fear before chiefs and men. Even though they might die, they spoke out fearlessly. [Kamakau 1964, 7; cf. Andrews 1875, 35]

A difficult relationship seems to have existed between king and *kāula*, sometimes of complementarity, but more often of opposition (see, for example, Kamakau 1961, 112, 188, 223, 225, 263; Laanui 1930, 92).[33] This arises from the fact that each represents the totality in an opposing and competing form: the *kāula* represents a totality directly accessible to the individual and thus in opposition to the social hierarchy; the king represents a totality consubstantial with the social hierarchy. The *kāula* transcends society almost completely to coincide with the god. The king, on the other hand, coincides with the god only to the extent that he coincides with society, that he reproduces its hierarchical order. This difference is the correlate of another. The *kāula* really has no need to sacrifice; having a direct relationship with the god, he needs no mediating term. On the contrary, the king is the sacrifier par excellence. This difference in the modality of the relationship with the god implies a difference in the respective relationships of *kāula* and king to society. Sacrifice always entails a relationship with a human community; it is usually public and involves commensality with kin, neighbors, and so on. The relationship of the sacrifier with the god is thus inseparable from his relationship with the social unit of which he is a part in a given context. In contrast, the *kāula*—somewhat like the sorcerer—realizes a relationship with the god that does not depend on the social unit. Confronted with his god the prophet is alone, while the sacrifier is always surrounded by a group of commensals and his relationship with the god contains a relationship with men.

The dimensions of the social unit implied in any sacrifice vary with its importance and that of the sacrifier. The king's sacrifice implicates society as a whole; his relation to the major gods contains the hierarchy of his relations with all other members of society. The king's sacrifice reproduces, then, the relation of all of society to the major gods. In the king, society as a whole is transformed into a sacrifier. Thus we can say that, as a sacrifier, the king is also the sacrificer for society. Let us then turn our attention to his sacrifice and the conditions he must fulfill in order to accomplish it.

Kingship
The King and the Supreme Sacrifice

Our sources are explicit; the king is the supreme mediator between men and gods. Direct contact with the most important gods of the society is possible only for the king and his chaplains: "The gods were tapu objects to the common people; only the kahunas, the keepers of the gods, and the attendants at the god houses were allowed to see them. The chief [the king—V. V.] also might look upon them whenever he wished to go with the keepers to worship in the heiau and the god houses. . . . These places were so tabu that not even the favorites of the chief might enter, only the chief himself" (Kamakau 1961, 181). As we have seen and this text confirms, the king can delegate certain aspects of his mediating function to priests or even to other members of the nobility. Nevertheless, in cases where all of society is threatened or simply involved, no delegation is possible; the king himself must approach the gods and consecrate sacrifices to them.

This principle emerges clearly from an episode narrated by Kamakau. At the time of a volcanic eruption, King Kamehameha sent for a priest of Pele to seek his advice on what he should do. "'You must offer the proper sacrifices,' said the seer. 'Take and offer them,' replied the chief. 'Not so! Troubles and afflictions which befall the nation require that the ruling chief himself offer the propitiatory sacrifice, not a seer or a kahuna.' 'But I am afraid lest Pele kill me.' 'You will not be killed,' the seer promised" (1961, 185).

This story also shows that by sacrificing to the gods the king always runs the risk of being their victim. His privilege is in fact a fearsome duty.

The king is king, therefore, because he is the head of the cult, the supreme sacrifier, the man closest to the divine.[34] This explains the words that Kekuhaupi'o addresses to Kamehameha: "Become a worshipper of the god; stand at the head of the island" (Kamakau 1961, 117). A "pious" king is a victorious king (Fornander 1916–20, 4:228; Kamakau 1961, 167, 9, 141);[35] an "impious" king loses his legitimacy and ends up being overthrown (Remy 1862, 85; Thrum 1908b:54). This idea is illustrated by a speech that the high priest of the island of Oʻahu makes to King Kahahana when the latter indicates his intention to make a tour of the island to reconsecrate the most important temples:

Ka-hahana said to Ka-ʻopulupulu [the high priest], "I wish to go around the island and restore the houses dedicated to the gods." Ka-ʻopulupulu answered, "It is a good wish, O chief! for the gods are the pillars of the dominion, and the chief who serves the gods as did your ancestor Kualiʻi, will rule long, grow old, blear-eyed like a rat, well-nigh bloodless, withered as a dry pandanus leaf, tottering with age, and in the end reach the world of light. The gods give such life to a religious person, and none shall rebel against his rule. If the land becomes poor or suffers from famine or is scorched by the sun or lacks fish or servitors, the gods can be found in Kahikimelemele. There are two roads for the chief to take about the island, one which will support the dominion and make it fast so that it shall remain fixed and immovable, a second which will give the dominion to others. [Kamakau 1961, 133–34]

Having the role of supreme sacrifier, the king must consecrate the supreme sacrifice, human sacrifice. It is this privilege/duty, rather than a special title,[36] that sets him apart from the rest of the nobility (Malo 1951, 53; Kamakau 1961, 129, 120, 121; Fornander 1878–80, 2:308, 309, 218), as the following story makes clear.

According to ʻIʻi, this privilege to consecrate human sacrifices was transmitted to Kamehameha by King Alapaʻi. But, advised by his mother, Kamehameha ceded it temporarily to his uncle Kalaniʻopuʻu. The story is dubious and is probably a fabrication intended as an a posteriori justification for Kamehameha's usurpation of this power, but it clearly shows the paradigmatic equivalence between royalty and the practice of human sacrifice.

After the sun had set, Kamehameha followed his mother's command, keeping in mind all she had told him. He went into the presence of Kalaniopuu, who sat him upon his lap and wailed over him. When Kalaniopuu had finished, he asked, "What purpose brings my lord (kuʻu haku) down here at night?"

Kamehameha replied, "I have brought this message to you: 'Above and below, inland and sea; that is my purpose in coming here,'"—figuratively saying that the kingdom was to be Kalaniopuu's and, with it, the privilege of offering human sacrifice.

Kalaniopuu asked, "Has your mother heard of this?" After Kamehameha replied that she had, Kalaniopuu turned and said to all of the chiefs, "This is a valuable guest."

"What is his value?" asked the chiefs.

"He is telling me to beat the drum and offer the human sacrifice."

"Then he is valuable indeed," replied the chiefs.

Thus we see how Kamehameha left (waiho ana) the kingdom he had received from Alapai, who favored him, to his uncle Kalaniopuu. [Ii 1963, 4–6]

The Divine King

That the king consecrates the supreme form of sacrifice to the supreme gods implies that he is the closest instantiation of what these gods stand for: the human species in all its aspects. It is precisely this that gives him authority over men, since it makes his actions more perfect and efficacious than theirs. Moreover, because this divinely originated authority makes it possible for the king to metonymically reproduce the inferior instantiations of the divine that make up the social hierarchy (cf. chap. 6), he also signifies the intangibility of that hierarchy. He is, in sum, the point of connection between the social whole and the concept that justifies it.

The idea that the king is the closest instantiation of the major gods implies that he is the most divine of men. Before giving the facts that prove that the king is indeed "divine" in this sense, let me stress that he instantiates different major gods or groups of their particularizations according to a precise ritual calendar (see chap. 6 and part 3) and also according to the political vicissitudes of his reign. Thus if he goes to war he stresses his connection with Kū, particularly in his warrior forms; but if he is at peace he stresses his connection with Lono or perhaps with Kāne, as is shown by the fact that he consecrates temples to them.

His connection with Kū, however, is preeminent because it is the necessary presupposition of his connection with the other gods (cf. Valeri 1981b, 1982b, 1984).

Turning now to the testimonies of the king's "divinity" (that is, of the fact that he is closer to the divine than any other human, and therefore *akua* relative to others), I must emphasize that since the divine quality of the king is transmitted first of all by filiation, it is common to all members of the royal lineage. Its intensity varies, however, with the distance from the "core" of the lineage.

That divinity qualifies the entire dynasty explains why the king can associate other high-ranking aliʻi with himself when he consecrates human sacrifices and on some occasions can even delegate this task to them (cf. Laanui 1930). Thus, "sometimes Kalaniopuu would ask Kamehameha [his nephew] to offer a [sacrificial] prayer, but when it came time for the ʻamama, or concluding portion, he would join in, and they would say it together" (Ii 1963, 9). As this text proves, by pronouncing the ʻamama the king manifests his ultimate right of consecration even when he associates with other aliʻi in the performance of the ritual (cf. Kamakau 1961, 109). In some cases it seems likely that a certain ambiguity concerning the respective rights of the officiants is deliberately maintained. In fact, the royal function may be appropriated by an aliʻi of lower rank than his rivals; in this case, either he kills his rivals or he is obliged to share his prerogatives with them. This can even result in a diarchic or triarchic solution, in which different aspects of the royal function are apportioned among different individuals of royal blood (cf. Valeri 1982b).

The texts that mention the divine features of the king or of the royal lineage can be classed as follows:

1. Ancient texts, mostly chants, in which certain ali'i are explicitly called *akua*. One story says of King Kūali'i that he "sometimes took on the nature of a true god" ("*a he akua maoli no o Kualii ma kekahi ano i kekahi manawa*"—Fornander 1916–20, 4:365) or even, simply, that "he was a god" ("*he akua o Kualii*"—Fornander 1916–20, 4:389). In the chant attached to his story, Kuali'i is called *akua* because, like the gods, he comes from Kahiki (ibid., 395, lines 594–96; cf. 375, lines 149–59).

In the name chant *(mele inoa)* of King Kākuhihewa, the latter is called "*he akua olelo*," "a god of speech" (in Malo 1951, 200), while in the famous chant composed by the bard Keāulumoku, the ali'i of the district of Hilo are ironically referred to as *akua* whose eyes have been blinded with salt, which indicates that these aristocrats claimed divine status (Fornander 1916–20, 6:408, 5:734). Something similar is implied by another ancient chant, in which the ali'i of the Kona district (island of Hawai'i) are collectively called *akua* ("*he akua na 'lii o Kona*"—Kahiolo 1978, 61). The same line is found in still another chant (Dickey 1928, 149).[37] Finally, in a traditional story recorded by Kamakau, King Peleiōhōlani is addressed as "god" by his councillor (Kamakau 1961, 71).

2. Another group of texts calls the victorious king *akua* in opposition to his vanquished enemies, who are called *kanaka* ("men"). Thus we read in the *Mooolelo Hawaii* (1838) that when an ali'i "était vainqueur, le peuple le craignait et adorait [*ho'omana*] ce dit chef comme on adore un dieu" (Remy 1862, 157). Kamakau confirms that if an ali'i was victorious "some worshipped him like a god" ("*ua hoomana aku kekahi poe iaia me he akua la*"—Kamakau 1867c).

In a traditional narrative, a priest is reported as saying to Kamalalawalu, king of Maui, that he cannot hope to defeat Lonoikamakahiki, king of Hawai'i, for "you are a man, he is a god" ("*he kanaka oe, a he akua kela*"—Fornander 1916–20, 4:339).

Generally speaking, the opposition *akua/kanaka*, "god"/"man," seems to be relative when applied to ali'i; thus the same Kamehameha who is referred to by Keāulumoku as "the king of divine blood" ("*ka lani waiakua*," ibid., 6:388) treated his descendants of higher rank than himself as his gods: "Those of his children whom Kamehameha considered in the line of succession he always treated as though they were his gods" (Kamakau 1961, 208). For instance, he addressed his son Liholiho as *ko akua*, "my god" (Kamakau 1967b).

3. In other texts, all more recent, the generalization is put forward that the nobles with the three upper ranks—*pi'o*, *nī'aupi'o*, and *wohi*—are,

"*ali'i akua*," "divine *ali'i*" (Kamakau 1961, 4). Alternatively, only the *nī'aupi'o* are said to be *akua* (Malo 1951, 54; cf. also Lilikalani in Beckwith 1932, 195). Kamakau also states that "the kapus of the *ni'aupi'o* and *pi'o* chiefs were equal to the gods'" (1964, 10).

These statements are sometimes tempered by postulating an *analogic* relationship between the ali'i and the gods or their respective kapu. Thus Kamakau also says that the *pi'o*, *nī'aupi'o*, and *wohi ali'i* are *equal* to the gods rather than being gods (Kamakau 1961, 223). King Kahekili, for instance, is said by him to be just "equal to a god" (1961, 4). But it is clear that somebody equal to a god must also be a god in some sense. Thus when Kamakau writes that Keōpūolani and her ancestors of the islands of Hawai'i and Maui were all "tabu chiefs of divine rank" (1961, 259) he implies, at the very least, that they are the bearer of a divine quality.

4. Other texts confine themselves to stating that the ali'i *descend* from the gods, and particularly from marriages between gods and men (Ii 1963, 15;[38] cf. Freycinet 1978, 66; NK, 2:286, 1:36; Stokes 1932, 18–19; Beckwith 1940, 7). Thus it is said of one king that he has an "*aoao* ['*ao'ao*] *akua*," a "divine side" in his genealogy (Fornander 1916–20, 5:275) and that Queen Pi'ikea's maternal grandmothers were divine (Kamakau 1961, 20; Fornander 1916–20, 4:230).

These texts clearly establish that the highest-ranking ali'i have qualities considered divine even before they are totally divinized after their death (cf. Malo 1951, 106, for the funeral rituals of ali'i as rites of deification). Moreover, they prove that some kings, at least, are called *akua*, "gods." This is because no sharp distinction is made between the gods and their closest manifestations among humans. Indeed, it seems that the opposition *akua/kanaka* is a relative one and that certain men may be called the gods of others.

Probably because he does not take this relativity into account, John Charlot (n.d.) has recently maintained that Hawaiian ali'i were not traditionally called *akua*. He claims that all the chants in which they are called so—except the chant of Kūali'i—date from the period between the abolition of the traditional royal religion (1819) and the beginning of the missionary influence; furthermore, he claims that the usage of calling high-ranking ali'i *akua* was started by Kamehameha when he began addressing Liholiho and other children of his who were in the line of succession as "gods."

While it is true that the chants to which Charlot refers date from the early missionary period,[39] it is not true that the only traditional chant referring to ali'i as *akua* is the chant of Kūali'i. I have mentioned above two other cases: the chant composed by Keāulumoku and the *mele inoa* of Kakuhihewa. Moreover, I see no reason to ignore the line "*he akua na 'lii o Kona*," which, as we have seen, appears in two sources, on the pretext that *akua* in this context would mean "ghosts" (cf. note 37). But above all, why limit oneself to the common noun *akua* when aliʻi are often called by their god's *proper name?* Thus, in the chant for Kūaliʻi (a name that means "Kū the king") this king is often called Kū (see for example Fornander 1916–20, 4:373, line 81). Kamehameha takes the names of his gods: Kūkaʻilimoku, Kūnuiākea, Kūmakakaiakaʻa, or simply Kū (Kauhane 1865; Kamakau 1961, 79; NK, 1:22; Fornander 1916–20, 6:370, line 37, 372, line 154). His son Kauikeaouli is also called Kū in his birth chant (Pukui and Korn 1973, 19, 25). In fact, judging from the chant *Haui ka lani*, in many cases the name Kū is automatically given to the king (see for example Fornander 1916–20, 6:395, line 429 and passim). Further, a king of Molokaʻi is called Keoloʻewa, which is the name of one form of Kū (Kūkeoloʻewa—Beckwith 1940, 32; PE, 390). King Kahekili of Maui bears the name and insignia of the thunder god to whom he is consecrated (Beckwith 1940, 48). In my opinion the custom of naming kings after their gods attests to the belief that the king is a manifestation of his gods and is therefore himself a god relative to all other men.

Charlot's argument that Kamehameha was the first to divinize the aliʻi in the line of succession to kingship is based on the text by Kamakau I have quoted above: "Those of his children whom Kamehameha considered in the line of succession he always treated as though they were his gods." But this text does not imply that Kamehameha's treatment of those among his children who ranked higher than he was an innovation. It is also hard to see how Kamehameha could have imposed the belief in Liholiho's divinity precisely when traditional religious concepts were undergoing a crisis (cf. Choris 1822, 123; von Chamisso 1864, 4:133–40) and the aliʻi were losing their sanctity in the eyes of the people. Moreover, Charlot attributes no motivation to this supposed innovation and no cause for its alleged success in the protomissionary period. Like others (see, for example, Kelly 1967), Charlot ends up treating Kamehameha as a culture hero who possesses quasi-supernatural powers of transformation and innovation. This is in line with Hawaiian ideology—which, precisely, considers kings to be gods—but I doubt that it falls within the line of historical truth.

Whatever the case, the essential is that, contrary to Charlot's opinion, one cannot hope to solve the question of the "divinity" of the aliʻi by considering some texts independently of the global ideology that has produced them. Notions are not expressed only in words. And even if the ancient texts in which the word *akua* refers to aliʻi are few, it can be safely assumed that this usage really existed because it follows necessarily from the attribution to aliʻi of the fundamental properties of the divine. Let us turn our attention, then, to the properties common to both gods and royalty.

First it must be noted that kingship, like divinity, is identified with totality. This totality is the totality of human predicates as reflected in nature; it is the totality of nature as it reflects man's activity and thought. Thus, kingship is metaphorically referred to as "above and below, inland and sea" (Ii 1963, 4). These are the two pairs of opposites that together encompass all that exists. The king's relation to the totality explains why his birth has cosmic effects: "a great storm swept over the land; the thunder roared, the earth was shaken by a great earthquake, the lightning flashed, the rivers and streams were overflowed, the wind blew and the rain came down in torrents" (Fornander 1916–20, 5 : 192). The marriage of two divine ali'i has similar effects: "At their union, the thunder was heard, the lightning flashed; eight rainbows arched the leaves; the pools of Kahoolana on Kahua were flooded; red rain passed in procession on the ocean; the hills were covered with fog; and a thick mist covered the land for ten days. These were the signs [of recognition]" (ibid., 4 : 538–39). With the appearance of another legendary ali'i, "the woods rejoiced, the wind, the earth, the rocks; rainbows appeared; colored rain-clouds moved, dry thunder pealed, lightnings flashed" (ibid., 4 : 552; cf. 4 : 168, 170). That all of nature resonates from the ali'i's presence enables us to understand better the belief that they, just like the gods, act through natural species. Of course this is particularly true of mythical ali'i, who are readily placed at the origin of certain species, especially foods (cf. ibid., 5 : 266, 270, 272, 279). As for living ali'i, they are often associated, in more than metaphoric ways, with powerful and sometimes terrible animals (see below p. 151).[40]

The formation of the fetus of an ali'i and his birth and development are supposed to reproduce the formation of the cosmos (see Pukui and Korn 1973, 14–25). As we have seen, native exegesis reads the *Kumulipo* simultaneously as a description of the origin of the cosmos, of the life of an ali'i, and of the development of a royal dynasty (Beckwith 1951, 40–41). In reality all these processes are equivalent; each king produces the cosmos in his person and secures the correspondence between the human and the natural order. Since the king is identified with the cosmos, a fortiori he is identified with his kingdom, that is, with the land[41] and its inhabitants. In fact, he personifies them;[42] his kingdom is assimilated with his body or, what amounts to the same thing, is considered his child (Fornander 1916–20, 6 : 404–5, lines 645–48; 1878–80, 2 : 11–12). By appropriating the king's body, it is thus possible to appropriate his realm.[43]

Kings also share with the gods their association with emblems of transcendence and perfection. They are thus connected with celestial entities (rainbow,[44] stars[45]), which, like transcendent realities, are unapproachable and whose circular form and movements connote perfection.[46] The sky itself, which is above all and encompasses everything, is identified with the king, who is addressed by the title *kalani* ("heaven") or *kalaninui* ("great heaven") (Fornander 1916–20, 4:394, 6:383, line 232; Kamakau 1961, 86, 90, 102–3).[47]

Conceived of as autonomous, from one point of view the ali'i are also thought to be free of desire, precisely like the gods. This is why they are characterized by immobility and inactivity, not only on the mythical level (see for example Kahiolo 1978, 128; Elbert 1956–57, 69:353, 354), but on the real level as well: "The highest point of etiquette among illustrious Hawaiians was, *not to move*" (Thurston 1882, 44). Laziness for a high-ranking ali'i is a duty, not a vice;[48] it is a manifestation of his absolute plentitude, of the absence of any lack, and, moreover, of perfect self-control. The prescription of immobility helps explain why divine ali'i do not walk but are carried; moreover, this custom reveals that the ali'i belong to the realm of above (heaven) as opposed to the realm of below, represented by the ground (Ellis 1782, 1:143–44; Dixon 1789, 120; Quimper 1937, 7; Manby 1929, 24; Fornander 1916–20, 4:388, 364, 5:142–44; Manu 1928, 87).

Like the gods, the high-ranking ali'i manifest their autonomy, their capacity to be self-sufficient, by practicing incestuous marriage. This marriage not only helps preserve a divinity hereditary by rule of bilateral filiation (Kamakau 1961, 207–8; Ellis 1842, 435–36; Fornander 1916–20, 4:178–79), it *re-creates* it because it is itself a divine behavior, a positive sign of divinity. Incestuous marriage is forbidden to lower-ranking ali'i (Kamakau 1961, 208) precisely because it has a creative and not solely a preservative value.

High-ranking ali'i share with the deities another sign of transcendence: invisibility. "Such tabu chiefs were of old a mere legend; it was only in later times that anyone was allowed to see them" (Kamakau 1961, 209, cf. 8; Kamakau 1964, 10). They could go out only at night when darkness made them invisible (Ii 1963, 51–52; Malo 1951, 54, 57; cf. Kotzebue 1821a, 1:308; von Chamisso in Kotzebue 1821a, 3:247; Byron 1826, 30). Thus, in the first part of her life, Keōpūolani "never walked abroad except at evening, and all who met her at that time, prostrated themselves to the earth" (Gough 1973, 195).

The prostration taboo (*kapu moe*), a prerogative shared by gods and the highest-ranking ali'i,[49] is a means of making these sacred beings invisible by acting not on their persons, but on their beholders. Naturally, prostration also connotes the impotence and helplessness of ordinary beings relative to the potency of divine beings (cf. Beaglehole 1967, 269, 504, n. 5, 513, 518, n. 1, 572, 584, 586, 596, 1083, 1159, 1162; Kamakau 1961, 88, 140; Ii 1963, 51–52, 58; Malo 1951, 54, 55; Kepelino 1932, 12; Dampier 1971, 35; Bishop 1916, 47; Thurston 1882, 50).

The relative invisibility and inaccessibility of high-ranking ali'i are additionally marked by the fact that, like the images of the gods, they are wrapped in cloths, feather cloaks, and such, while lower-ranking people must emphasize their visibility and vulnerability by stripping to the waist in the presence of gods and royal personages[50] (Vancouver 1801, 5:73; Quimper 1937, 4; Lisiansky 1814, 105; Campbell 1967, 93–95; Laanui 1930, 92; Ii 1963, 58; Kamakau 1961, 208–9).

The autonomy and transcendence of the divine ali'i are manifest on a communicative level as well. Because he is supposed to be self-sufficient, without desire or sadness, always in control of himself, a divine ali'i cannot openly display his emotions; this is why he expresses them metaphorically, poetically.[51] This requirement of sublimation explains that the practice of poetry and chant occupies a good deal of his time (see Ii 1963, 108). Several sources mention the existence of a "language of the ali'i" that would be understandable only to them and would thereby manifest their transcendence with respect to the common people (Bennett 1840, 1:225; Kamakau 1961, 245; Choris 1822, 18; von Chamisso in Kotzebue 1821a, 2:393–94). It is probable that this "secret language" is a poetic and highly metaphorical use of ordinary language. Be that as it may, an asymmetry exists in communication between ali'i and common people. Commoners must keep silent in the presence of the nobility (cf. Kahiolo 1978, 103), whom they cannot address directly (Kamakau 1961, 88). Alternatively, they are required to speak to them using words and titles similar to those they use in praying to the gods.

Each man, being an imperfect and incomplete realization of the ideal human species, needs other men; he must associate with them in order to attain the integrity of the species at the level of exchange. In contrast, the king is ideally a perfect realization of the species in the individual. Hence, in theory, he is completely self-sufficient, completely integral, and therefore "pure." He is indeed the species pure and simple. Most of the taboos surrounding his sacred person[52] are intended to maintain this purity, this integrity that makes him divine. Not only is it forbidden to touch or soil the ali'i (Kamakau 1961, 264), to approach him in a state of impurity (Remy 1862, 159; Malo 1951, 56–57), or to give him impure things to eat (Malo 38.12), it is even taboo to use foul language in his presence (as well, moreover, as in the presence of the priests—Ii 1869c). It is not fitting for the king and divine ali'i to come into contact with the impurity of death (Kamakau 1961, 212; Remy 1862, 135). If any violence is exercised against these persons, or even worse, if their integrity and corporeal perfection are attacked, they lose their status (cf. Fornander 1916–20, 4:272–74; Kamakau 1961, 62). Hence their enemies try to pollute[53] or kill them. When King Kahekili suppressed the revolt of the traditional nobility of O'ahu, "a number of chiefesses of the highest rank—'Kapumoe'—were killed, mutilated, or otherwise severely afflicted" (Fornander 1878–80, 2:227; cf. Kamakau 1961, 138–40). 'Ī'ī observes, "the descendants of the ancient chiefs of Maui, from Kamalalawalu down, became as nothing when they were taken captive at the battles of Iao and Keoneula. So it was with those of Oahu who were taken captive by Kahekili" (1963, 100).

The purity of sacred ali'i is preserved not only by the behavior of their inferiors or rivals, but also by their own comportment. For example, divine ali'i are forbidden to have sexual relations with women of lower rank, and they are obliged—men and women—to remain virgin until marriage (NK, 2:88–89; Malo 1951, 54–55, 135–36; Fornander 1916–20, 4: 540; 5:194). Tradition stigmatizes the ali'i Kahahana, who degraded himself by making love to women of lower rank: "When he became a man he caused a breach in the tabu by making love to the lesser chiefesses and so lost the tabu of fire (*Ahi*), heat (*Wela*) and extraordinary heat (*Hahana*), which had been his, and he was called Walia (*wale 'ia*) [an elision, meaning 'is degraded']" (Kamakau 1961, 128).

In short, the ali'i is divine as long as he acts like a god, as long as he manifests his perfection by not desiring or needing other human beings. He is allowed to desire only a replica of himself: his sister or a woman of the same rank. If on the other hand he desires his inferiors, he betrays a lack, an imperfection, and at the same time he disperses his seed and the rank it is capable of transmitting.

However, it is clear that the king, just like the god, is caught up in an insurmountable contradiction. The plenitude of his being must be preserved, precisely because it is necessary to use it socially, because the king's being is the foundation of any social thing.[54] The king thus must maintain his transcendence, be separated from all men, but at the same time he must enter into contact with them to demonstrate his power. Hence it is necessary for him to lose his absolute transcendence, to desire the Other—without which he would not be able to create anything that is not himself.

Created by society through a myriad of rules of separation, the king's divinity incurs a debt in relation to society that it must pay sooner or later. It follows from this that all properties of royalty connoting transcendence come to be associated with their opposites, which connote the realization of the royal power in immanence—as concrete humanness that can exist only in society. For example, we have seen that the king's perfection and autonomy are manifested by his immobility, his "laziness." But, in mythology as in reality (cf. Beckwith 1940, 412–13, Elbert 1956–57, 69:353), a time comes when passivity turns into an explosion of activity and the king reveals himself to be king precisely because he produces and acts. In reality, it is enough for the passive king to show himself for his passivity to become action almost in spite of itself. Thus, an ali'i having the *kapu moe* can always end a battle by becoming visible and thus forcing everyone to throw down his weapons and fall prostrate (Ii 1963:52). Here is a famous example:

As Kiwala'o advanced, splendidly arrayed, endowed with the tabu of a god and covered with the colors of the rainbow, down fell the fighting men of both sides prostrate to the ground because of his divine rank as a *niʻaupiʻo* and the severe tabu which demanded prostration to avoid facing the sacred back of a chief. The soldiers of Maui wished to ignore the tabu, regretting the cessation of the fighting, but Kiwalaʻo continued on to Wailuku. [Kamakau 1961, 88]

Kiwalaʻō's case proves that an aliʻi normally remains invisible but must show himself from time to time for his divine power to be recognized. In some myths these two contradictory needs—to be invisible and to be visible—are reconciled by the "radiance" of the divine aliʻi. Thus a girl of royal rank is shut up in a house she may never leave, so that she stays out of the view of common mortals, but her beauty "could be seen on the outside of the house, like a bright light" (Fornander 1916–20, 4:602). The radiation emanating from Kila makes that hero, although wrapped up and packaged, visible nonetheless (Fornander 1916–20, 4:164).

The king's sexuality manifests a similar contradiction. We have seen that the king must preserve his generative power and that consequently he cannot fecundate women of lower rank. The same taboo operates for women of royal blood; in theory, they cannot have children by inferior men. Thus royalty would reproduce only itself; it would be characterized by a lineal narcissism, so to speak. But the king is also regarded as the life source for all his people (Pukui and Korn 1973, 11), as their father, and this not only in a metaphorical sense, for he is supposed to become their father[55] literally, by fertilizing as high a number of women as possible.[56] Thus, according to tradition, King ʻUmi "had many wives, among whom were daughters of the common people, so that he became an ancestor both of the chiefs and the common people. There is not a commoner of Hawaii who would say that Umi-a-Liloa was not an ancestor of his" (Fornander 1916–20, 4:228; cf. Kamakau 1961, 19; Vancouver 1801, 5:40—on the subject of King Kamahameha; Beckwith 1951, 30—on the subject of King Keawe). The contradiction between these two views of the king's sexuality seems flagrant, though it is partially resolved by recourse to the temporal dimension. From birth up to the incest that produces a successor of appropriate rank, absolute continence and purity are prescribed to the royal husband and wife; after the child's conception they both may unite freely with as many partners as they wish (Malo 1951, 135–36, 55; cf. Beckwith 1951, 30).

Like the power of the gods, the power of the king does not manifest itself only in positive terms; it can also have destructive aspects. The king can kill, just as he can give life. He kills, however, those who do not recognize the ideal human essence for which he stands or who do not recognize him as its personification. Thus he destroys transgressors and, more generally, those who, by resisting his rule, make him imperfect and less than all-encompassing.

This is the reason the king is often represented as a devourer: the devourer of transgressors and the devourer of land (with its inhabitants), which he must encompass in order to be complete and therefore perfect, divine.[57] Thus, like many a god in his "terrible" aspect, the king is often equated with a shark: "a shark was sometimes called chief, and a chief called a shark" (NK, 2:6; cf. Kamakau 1964, 84; Fornander 1916–20, 5:294, 136). It is by mystically controlling sharks that the king often punishes transgressors and rebels (see, for instance, Kamakau 1961, 106–7). Inversely, his presence keeps a man-eating shark from doing harm to his faithful subjects (Kamakau 1964, 73).

Here is a typical example of chants in which the king is compared to a shark:

A shark going inland is my chief,
A very strong shark able to devour all on land;
A shark of very red gills is the chief,
He has a throat to swallow the island without choking.
    [Fornander 1916–20, 6:393–94, lines 388–91]

One of course appreciates the ambiguity of these statements. They can be used to represent the king as rapacious and destructive even toward the just.

The shark's connection with this aspect of kingly divine power explains why this fish is placed at the origin of some royal lineages,[58] and why certain kings, particularly the conquering ones, have a special relationship with it. Thus Kamehameha was supposed to have a close affinity with the *niuhi* shark (tiger shark, *Galeocerdo cuvieri*). It is said that as a fetus he made his mother want to eat the eyes of this fish. In this manner he absorbed its qualities (the eye, as we have seen, is a substitute for the entire body). The priests then prophesied that the child would be an ali'i "whose anger would flash through his eyes like that of the ferocious shark and whose power might be likened to that of a *niuhi*" (Handy, Pukui, and Livermore 1934, 8–9). It is said that this prophecy prompted the ali'i of Hawai'i to make an attempt on the child's life.

This example indicates that natural phenomena with which the divine ali'i are associated are not thought of as simple metaphors. Like the gods, the ali'i have a true affinity with the things they are associated with. Thus, the king is not only compared to the shark: he can act through this animal, he has a substantial relation to it, he is its descendant. The same goes for all other natural phenomena associated with the ali'i.

Not only the ali'i are represented as gods, the gods are represented as ali'i: "Gods are represented in Hawaiian story as chiefs dwelling in far lands or in the heavens and coming as visitors or immigrants to some special locality in the group [Hawaiian archipelago—V. V.] sacred to their worship"(Beckwith 1940, 3). This is a further sign that gods and ali'i are closely related.

Another such sign is that the insignia and prerogatives of the gods and sacred ali'i are identical. We have already seen that the major gods and ali'i of supreme rank share the prostration taboo (*kapu moe*); in other words, men prostrate themselves in front of the divine ali'i as they prostrate themselves in front of the other gods. Moreover, the ali'i and gods of the second rank share the *kapu noho*, that is, the obligation imposed on their inferiors to sit in their presence or in the presence of the objects most directly associated with their persons. Gods and ali'i of the supreme rank also share the following insignia: *pūlo'ulo'u*, *'aha kapu* "sacred cords," cloaks and helmets covered with red and yellow feathers. Probably they share the feather standards (*kāhili*) as well.

Let us briefly examine these objects and their significations. The *pūlo'ulo'u* is a "tapa-covered ball on a stick (*pahu*)" (PE, 326). It precedes the gods and divine ali'i on their way and protects their houses or temples (Fornander 1878–80, 2:63; Brigham 1911, 100; PE, 326; Fornander 1916–20, 4:146, n. 1). The symbolism of these insignia is not certain. We know, however, that stars are compared to balls covered with tapa (Liliuokalani 1978, 70; Beckwith 1951, 120–21, 125). Perhaps, then, the *pūlo'ulo'u* represent the *akua* as stars, and thus in their transcendent dimension, as "spherical" or autonomous. It is also possible that the balls, being wrapped with tapa, evoke the invisibility of the divine.

The *kāhili* symbolizes divine power in its active, destructive, and terrible form. It is a "feather standard" made with one of the "long bones" of a sacrificed enemy king (Ellis 1782, 2:156; Bishop 1916, 30), at the top of which are tied precious plumage and feathers from birds of prey.[59] The *kāhili* always surround the ali'i and are supposed to protect him (Fornander 1916–20, 4:182–83; Bishop 1916, 13; Malo 1951, 77). Each *kāhili* has a proper name (Fornander 1878–80, 2:115; Kamakau 1961, 207) and can function as a substitute for its owner's person (cf. Fornander 1916–20, 4:270). Since it incorporates the bones of a conquered ali'i, it probably represents the conqueror's link to the conquered land.[60] We have seen in fact that the body of an ali'i is ritually interchangeable with his land. The violent connotation of the *kāhili* is confirmed by its use in sorcery (Ii 1963, 124–25); it is also used to gouge out the eyes of human victims (Fornander 1916–20, 4:583).

The *'aha ula* "red [= sacred] cord" or *'aha kapu* (Fornander 1916–20, 4:552; Fornander 1878–80, 2:63–64; Stokes 1932, 19) symbolizes the active divine power in its productive and essentially benevolent form. I will return to these cords in detail, for they play a major role in the ritual of the *luakini* temple. Here it is enough to say that they represent the divine power that binds the members of society by functioning as both a unifying and a separating force. The sacred cord is separating because it is supposed to separate friends from enemies (see Ii 1869a,b); it is unifying because it represents the king's genealogy (Stokes 1932, 19) and thus the means by which he connects the groups of nobles that support him. In the last analysis, as we shall see, the 'aha kapu represents the social bond in general, which is reproduced by reproducing the king's (and therefore the society's) connection with the god.

Note also that feather cloaks and helmets are identical for male ali'i and for the images of their gods (Rickman 1966, 303–4; King 1967, 512; Samwell 1967, 1228; Ellis 1842, 89, 157; Ellis 1782, 2:91, 155; Golovnin 1979, 221). These objects divinize what they envelop and give it a splendid aspect, similar to that of the rainbow (Kamakau 1961, 88). In fact, the form of these cloaks and helmets might be said to evoke the rainbow. The dimensions of the cloaks worn by the ali'i and their gods measure the extent of their power and influence, for they are made with an incalculable number of feathers furnished by their worshipers and subjects.[61] Hence these cloaks convey the idea that the king's divinity, his mana, is made by his subjects. His divine splendor exists only as a function of their work and their acceptance of him. But reciprocally, this splendor increases their acceptance, hence their work and their prosperity. Thus the king can be experienced as really giving life (see Valeri 1982b, 18–19).

The facts I have discussed leave little doubt that the predicates of the king are identical to the predicates of the divine. Moreover, as I have mentioned and shall have occasion to demonstrate in the course of my analysis of the royal rituals, the king assumes the properties of different gods at different moments. Having all the generic properties of the divine, he can take up the specific properties of each god as the occasion demands. The king, therefore, can do everything and be everything because each god constitutes the possibility of a different action or form of being. He unifies the divine in relation to the human; he is the perfect human because he instantiates all the properties of the divine.

Kingship and Society

I have said that the king is recognized as divine by virtue of the successful performance of certain sacrificial rituals. But the ability to perform them successfully depends in turn on "pragmatic," "political" actions. I must therefore say something of these actions and their relation to ritual actions.

Conceptually, "pragmatic" and "ritual" actions are not related to separate domains, each with its own autonomous values and content. Rather, they differ in the degree to which they realize the same values, instantiate certain ideal types of action. As such, they can be opposed in terms of relative order: ritual is more ordered than is pragmatic, empirical action because it represents a closer instantiation of a divine model; pragmatic action is less ordered because it is less close to this model and sometimes so distant that it is in contrast to it and actually becomes disordered.

Precisely because the distinction between pragmatic and ritual action is conceived as one of relative order and not of content (the aims of ritual are always very mundane!), practically every important pragmatic action is associated with and regulated by a ritual counterpart. Ritual is thus the stage in which action represents itself, becomes conscious of itself in relation to its ideal type, its paragon, and thus orients itself toward it. In addition to this "prospective" or "anticipatory" relationship between ritual action and pragmatic action, there can be a "retrospective" or "confirmatory" one (cf. Valeri 1982b). In the latter case, the performance of the ritual marks the process of attainment of an aim by reiterating its signification and making it the object of a socially shared judgment.

Although this book deals with only the ritual, that is the *evaluative* stage of a global social process, let us briefly consider its political and pragmatic stages.

Hawaiian society is characterized by a system of unequal relationships to land, that is, to the divine source of life. Each right to a piece of land is contained in a higher, more encompassing right. The ultimate right is vested in the king, who is therefore the source of all land rights. At the time of his accession to the throne, the king divides the lands of the kingdom in the following way.

First he sets aside certain lands for himself. These are administered for him by his *konohiki* (stewards, caretakers). Then he divides what is left among the high-ranking nobles who are his main supporters. The recipients, in turn, put aside certain lands for their use and distribute the rest of what they have received from the king among their own main supporters. Each of the latter does the same with his own portion, and so on.[62]

The system is characterized as follows by Richards:

all those who had received portions were considered as owing fealty to the lord of their fee; and these feuds were the links of that chain by which the victorious king always expected to bind to himself and his interests the whole body of the landlords. These landlords were the persons on whom the king relied to fight his battles, support him in all difficulties and aid him in all his plans. They of course had every inducement to support his authority, for just so far as his power was weakened their landed property became unsafe.

I speak of each of these persons who received lands as landlords because each of these again divided out his particular fief into smaller portions, the tenants or possessors of which owed the same fealty, and performed the same duties, as a chief of the first rank did to the king.

These last divisions were divided and subdivided again, and thus carried on in many instances to the sixth or seventh degree. [1973, 22]

Richards goes too far when he uses feudal juridical terminology, but his account shows that there is indeed some similarity between the feudal system and the Hawaiian system.[63] Be that as it may, in Hawaii every land right rests upon a relationship of subordination that entails mutual duties for superior and inferior. If the inferior does not carry out his duties to his superior, he may lose his land right (Malo 1951, 61), but, reciprocally, if the superior does not act as he should toward his inferior, he may lose the latter's support.

Since the relationship to a piece of land depends on a relationship to a superior that is contractual in nature, no right to land is permanent or hereditary *in principle*. On a man's death his land goes back to his overlord, who can give it to whomever he pleases.[64] On the overlord's death or disgrace, his dependents automatically lose their rights and must renegotiate them with his successor. Since labor is scarce,[65] however, it is in the interest of the nonlaboring right-holders (the nobility) not to despoil the commoners of their rights unless they are lazy or rebel (Richards 1973, 22, 24). At the same time, the threat of taking away the commoners' land rights is an important means of commanding their continuing support. As one chief said to Richards, "If we cannot take away their lands, what will they care for us? They will be as rich as we" (ibid., 23).

The following are the basic units of land segmentation below the *moku*, "kingdom" (literally, "island" or "region of an island"): *'okana*, "district" ("probably a contraction of *'oki'ana*, 'cutting'"—PE 258); *ahupua'a* (unit corresponding to an autarkic community); *'ili 'āina*. The last is divided into parcels and subparcels, the names of which vary according to the level of segmentation, type of tenure, and other criteria (cf. Malo 1951, 16, 192; Richards 1973, 22; Chinen 1958:1–8; Principles 1925, preface).[66]

Economically, sociologically, and ritually the most important land unit is the *ahupua'a*, the best description of which is given by Lyons:

Its name is derived from the *ahu* or altar (literally, pile, kuahu being the specific term for altar) which was erected at the point where the boundary of the land was intersected by the main road, *alaloa*, which circumferented each of the islands. Upon this altar at the annual progress of the akua makahiki (year god) was deposited the tax paid by the land whose boundary it marked, and also an image of a hog, *puaa*, carved out of kukui wood and stained with red ochre. How long this was left on the altar, I do not know, but from this came the name, *ahupuaa*, of the pile of stones, which title was also given to the division of land marked thereby.

The *ahupuaa* ran from the sea to the mountain, theoretically. That is to say the central idea of the Hawaiian division of land was emphatically central, or rather radial. Hawaiian life vibrated from *uka*, mountain, whence came wood, kapa, for clothing, *olona*, for fish-line, ti-leaf for wrapping paper, *ie* for rattan lashing, wild birds for food, to the *kai*, sea, whence came *ia*, fish, and all connected therewith. Mauka and makai are thereof fundamental ideas to the native of an island. Land . . . was divided accordingly. [1875a, 1:103–4]

The dimensions of the *ahupua'a* are extremely variable (cf. Lydgate 1925, 60); some are not subdivided while others include up to thirty or forty '*ili* '*āina* (Lyons 1875a, 3:118).

The most important requirement for legitimizing one's land rights consists in giving prestations (*ho'okupu*) of its produce and, more important, of its firstfruits to one's overlord. The chain of land rights, then, corresponds to a chain of firstfruits prestations.[67]

This form of validation of rights springs from the idea that the entire land, indeed all of nature used by man, is produced by the gods and hence ultimately belongs to them. As we have seen, the divinity inherent in nature must be removed by firstfruits sacrifices. Ordinarily it is sufficient to offer these sacrifices to the deities connected with a particular piece of land, or to one's particular deities, to be able to appropriate its products. These ordinary sacrifices, however, presuppose annual sacrifices in which the relationship that exists between the particular appropriation and the collective one, through the global hierarchical system, is made apparent.

On these occasions, each holder of a land title gives the firstfruits of his land to the individual from whom he holds his title. These prestations follow the hierarchical route until they reach the king, who consecrates them to the major gods. At each point in the chain the human recipient of the firstfruits of a land segment is only the representative, through his own overlords, of the major gods. The higher one is in the hierarchy, the more closely one represents these gods. The king is thus their closest representative. Hence he is the sacrifier who encompasses all other sacrifiers; his high sacrifice makes their low sacrifices possible.

The system of land tenure I have just outlined reflects the operation of one single principle underlying the hierarchy at every level. From this point of view, the bond existing between the lowest commoner and his immediate superior on whom he depends is no different in nature from the bond existing between a "grandee" and his king.

The continuity of the hierarchical chain is, however, partly belied by two major discontinuities. The most important one is that which exists between nobles (ali'i) and commoners. A less important discontinuity concerns the commoners, who are divided among "those who attend the land" (*maka'āinana*) and the landless ones who attach themselves to a noble lord (*haku*) as clients or servants (*kanaka*).[68]

Clients who reside at court often seem to have a higher status than those who cultivate their lord's land; they constitute the backbone of his faction (see below).

The distinction between nobles and commoners is based on a simple principle: a noble is an individual who is able to trace a genealogical relationship to the reigning king. This relationship, however, must be traced through an ancestor (on the maternal or paternal side) lying within the tenth ascending generation. Beyond that it seems that the status of noble is lost. (At least this is what is implied by Malo 1951, 192).[69] A nobleman must therefore carefully preserve his genealogies. In contrast, commoners do not preserve them and are even forbidden to do so, at least officially. Hence they do not usually remember (or are not supposed to remember) their ancestors as individuals beyond the generation of their grandparents (Kamakau, cited by Earle 1978, 14).

Ideally, relationships of subordination among nobles depend on genealogical distance. The closer one is genealogically to the senior line, the higher one is and the more land one receives. Thus, in theory, one cannot obtain more wealth and power than accrues by virtue of rank as determined by birth. In practice, however, it is genealogical rank that follows wealth and power, however acquired, rather than the other way around. This is made possible by the very principles on which the system of rank is based.

In the first place, rank is inherited bilaterally. More precisely, an individual's rank depends on the combination of the rank of his father and the rank of his mother. Each combination of ranks gives a determined rank as a result. It is obvious that this rule allows a genealogically inferior "strong man" to marry a very high ranking woman in order to produce a high-ranking son (Valeri 1972, 1976). Hence, in the space of a generation or two the de facto might of a line will become genealogical right.

In the second place, the genealogical relationships that establish an individual's rank and ultimately his right to belong to the nobility must be recognized by the king to be valid in his realm. This, of course, allows for the genealogical claims of a strong supporter of the king to be "recognized" by him. In this case, might is immediately transformed into right by the fabrication of a genealogy, without the need for passing through a hypogamous alliance with a royal woman. Conversely, the right of a collateral who happens to be an enemy of the king might be denied by him.

Hence, the *actual* relationships of subordination and political alliance tend to be more important, in the long run at least, than the genealogical relationships. The ideological dominance of the genealogical principle is demonstrated, however, by the necessity of transforming power into rank. As in sacrifice, the actual must be reduced to the ideal, which is its regulating principle.

The king's control over all genealogical claims is manifested by a ceremony that takes place immediately after his accession to power. The ceremony is described by Malo as follows:

A *hale naua* was then built for the king, and when this was accomplished an investigation was entered into as to what persons were related to the king. The doings at the house were conducted in the following manner. When the king had entered the house and taken his seat, in the midst of a large assembly of people including many skilled genealogists, two guards were posted outside at the gate of the *pa*. (The guards were called *kaikuono*.)

When any one presented himself for admission to the *hale naua*, or king's house, the guards called out "here comes So-and-so about to enter." Thereupon the company called out, "From whom are you descended, Mr. So-and-so *naua*? Who was your father, *naua*? Who was your father, *naua*?" To this the man made answer, "I am descended from So-and-so; such and such a one is my father."

The question was then put to the man, "Who was your father's father, *naua*?" and the man answered, "Such an one was my father's father, he was my grandfather." "Who was the father of your grandfather, *naua*?" The man answered, "Such an one was my grandfather's father." Thus they continued to question him until they reached in their inquiry the man's tenth ancestor.

If the genealogists who were sitting with the king recognized a suitable relationship to exist between the ancestry of the candidate and that of the king he was approved of.

When another candidate arrived the outside guards again called out, "Here enters such an one." Thereupon those sitting with the king made their inquiries as to the ancestry on the mother's side in a loud tone. "Who was your mother, *naua*?" And the man answered, "I am descended from such an one; So-and-so was my mother." Again the question was put to him, "Who was the mother of your mother, *naua*?" Whereupon he answered, "Such a person was my grandmother."

The questions were kept up in this manner until they had come to the tenth ancestor in their inquiry. When the genealogists had satisfied themselves as to the closeness of the man's pedigree to that of the king, special inquiries having been made as to his grandfather and grandmother, the candidate was approved of.

On the satisfactory conclusion of this investigation the commoner,[70] or chief, was admitted as a member of the *hale naua*, another name for which was *ualo malie*.

In this way they learned who were closely related to the king, who also were in his direct line, as well as the relative rank of the *ali'i* to each other and to the king. [1951, 191–92]

Thus the king, who theoretically is the highest-ranking man, establishes both the rank of everyone relative to him and the boundaries of the ramage that encompasses the nobles of his realm. Moreover, by establishing the proper hierarchy between nobles, he indirectly affects the order of the commoners who are under each noble. Hence he is the veritable creator of society as a coherent whole. By creating society, the king's actions are the conditions of possibility of all other actions and therefore they ideally contain them. It is this factor that makes him a visible personification of the human species, that is, of what contains all predicates of human action.

The meeting of the *hale naua* is only the final and official stage of the process whereby the king creates society; I must still describe what comes before it—how he becomes king.

Only a high-ranking noble may become king, although some of the most famous kings (such as 'Umi) were of low rank. There are no clear or automatic rules of succession; in addition, the system of transmission of rank is such that it creates a number of pretenders with equal or near-equal claims. This is the consequence of several facts: genealogical relationships among ali'i are incredibly tangled; kinship is ambilateral or even overtly bilateral; consanguineal unions (with a half-sister or niece, etc.) are extremely frequent; each ali'i, man or woman, contracts a high number of unions; polyandry and polygyny (*punalua* unions) coexist, and so forth.

In this situation even the order of birth loses much of its meaning, and this is so for at least two reasons. First, this order is calculated with respect to each parent. In other words, a child can be the eldest with respect to his mother but the youngest with respect to his father (and their respective groups), or vice versa. Second, rank and order of birth with respect to a given parent do not necessarily correspond, since rank is calculated by taking both parents into consideration (Handy and Pukui 1972, 58). Thus it is conceivable that a father's firstborn is outranked by a child born after him if the mother of the second child holds a higher rank than the mother of the first.

Ultimately it becomes impossible to distinguish clearly between elder and cadet lines within this entanglement of relationships (cf. Goody 1966, 33). Thus the crucial factor in establishing succession is the amount of support a pretender is able to obtain. This was clearly perceived by foreign observers. Townsend (1921), for instance, states that "At the demise of a king there are always several candidates whose claims are nearly equal; although hereditary, not closely defined but these are possible claims. The most popular gets it." More bluntly, Shaler writes that "the monarchy is not acknowledged to be hereditary, but, after the death of the reigning prince, is generally usurped by the chief of the most talents and powers" (1935, 97).

How is support obtained, then? By constituting a large faction of people who believe that their interests coincide with those of their leader. The process of formation of this faction is complicated and imperfectly known. It can be said to begin at the very birth of a noble, when his parents create a separate household for him comprising a number of clients and servants (the two are not clearly distinguished) under the supervision of a *kahu*, "guardian," "who directs the affairs of the child until he is old enough to exercise a will of his own" (Stewart 1839, 108). The number of these clients and servants may vary from thirty to one hundred; they "always live and move" with their master "and share in the provisions of his house" (ibid., 107). Some of these people are the offspring of secondary unions or occasional liaisons of their leader or of his parents (Kamakau 1961, 207, 8); others are adopted children of low status (Remy 1862, 157), but most seem to be adventurers who pass from one lord (*haku*) to another, often moving from district to district and even from island to island, in the hope of improving their situation.[71] In fact, "the search for a superior and the finding of a chief [to become one's lord (*'imi haku*)] was a custom considered high and honorable in old days and one which might carry the seeker from one end of the group to the other. On the other hand, chiefs of rank sought trustworthy followers" (Kamakau 1961, 207; cf. 229, 178, 111–12; Ii 1963, 147; Fornander 1916–20, 4:365, 189, 190, 364–65).

Thus, "Les gens s'attachaient en foule à la suite des chefs pour demeurer avec eux, par gourmandise et dans le but de s'assurer leur nourriture. Les chefs, de leur côté, nourrissaient un grand nombre d'hommes dans le but de se procurer des soldats pour défendre leurs terres" (Remy 1862, 155; cf. Fornander 1878–80, 2:29)—or, one may add, in order to acquire new ones (cf. Kamakau 1961, 229; Richards 1973, 22).

This policy of attracting clients was followed by all high-ranking ali'i and by the king in the first place.

It was well for the king to gather many people about him and for him and his queen to deal out food and meat, as well as *tapa* and *malo* with a liberal hand. Thus he would dispose the men to be as a shield to him in the day of battle. . . . The chiefs below the king also should gather men about them, the same as the king himself. And these men should be constantly practiced in the arts of war. [Malo 1951, 194]

Thus the clients form a kind of standing army on which their *haku*, "lord," can rely to further his ambitions. Basically, his aim is to have the highest possible role in a confederation of ali'i in order to obtain as much land as possible. Each main pretender to the throne is the leader of one such confederation or faction. Some of the competitors might reach an agreement and divide the lands of the realm accordingly, but most often they fight each other militarily, and the leader who defeats all the others becomes the king[72] (Ii 1963, 13–15; Kamakau 1961, 117–24; Beckwith 1919, 309; Fornander 1878–80, 2:302–10; Bloxam 1924, 66, cf. 78).

Thus, the kingdom is always *conquered* by its king, who, moreover, must constantly defend it from the "rebels," that is, from his rivals. Alliances shift constantly, and therefore the hierarchical chain must constantly be renewed. Temple rituals are the main occasions in which the chain is collectively recognized and thereby renewed or, on the contrary, challenged, modified, or destroyed.

I do not wish to go into detail here. But the system I have outlined is amply illustrated by Hawaiian chronicles, which also describe at length its consequences: the rise and fall of kings, the instability of relationships of allegiance, the state of war that almost invariably follows the death of a king,[73] the king's attempt to maintain his faction by employing it in continuous wars of conquest, and the revolts that occur at each redistribution of lands, which inevitably involves the displacement of previous landholders and the frustration of several of the king's supporters, who think they have not been sufficiently rewarded.

I want to insist only on one point. The victory that transforms one of the high-ranking pretenders into a divine king (recall that according to the *Mooolelo Hawaii* of 1838 the victorious ali'i was adored as a god) implies the elimination of the other pretenders or those who destroy the cohesion of the group that the king has formed and that is the origin of his victory.

But these rivals are not simply killed; they are sacrificed, hence incorporated into the god, reduced to him. Moreover, they are not only enemies, but also close relatives of the victor. Hence they are his doubles. Thus, by sacrificing them the victor is indirectly incorporated into the god, given a divine status. In sum, he becomes a divine king.

It seems, then, that the fact that the sacrificed rivals are the consanguines of the victor is not simply a structural consequence of the system but also is one of its fundamental symbolic conditions. We must therefore analyze it in more detail.

Royal Sacrifice and Royal Incest

The fratricidal nature of the king's sacrifice is amply borne out by the chronicles of the Hawaiian kings. A detailed study of succession in the dynasty of the kings of the island of Hawai'i, for example, would reveal that each generation is marked by a violent confrontation among closely related pretenders. He who succeeds in sacrificing all the others becomes the only king.

Let us confine ourselves to an examination of the major outline of the history of succession from Kalani'ōpu'u down to Liholiho. According to Kamakau, Kalani'ōpu'u, in agreement with all his nobles, decides to leave the "land" to his son Kiwala'ō, who has the highest rank, and to leave the god Kūkā'ilimoku to Kamehameha.[74] This implies that Kiwala'ō has the right to consecrate the state temples (*luakini heiau*) and that "whatever ivory [of whale or walrus tusks] came ashore should belong to him" (1961, 107). Kamehameha, on the contrary, controls the warlike side of kingship through Kūkā'ilimoku (Valeri 1982a).

These decisions are proclaimed by Kiwala'ō in the Hale o Keawe mausoleum after he has placed Kalani'ōpu'u's remains there. The end of this rite actually coincides with the moment that the succession officially takes place (Kamakau 1961, 118–19).

162   Sacrifice and Hierarchy

Thus, according to custom Kiwala'ō begins to redistribute all the lands among his followers. The ali'i who lose their lands or who do not receive enough, particularly Keōua, force the latent conflict to erupt, and it quickly polarizes around the two key rivals, Kiwala'ō and Kamehameha. The two are quite conscious of the ineluctable nature of their confrontation. During their final meeting, Kiwala'ō addresses these tragic words to his cousin: "Where are you? Perhaps we two are to die, for our uncle [Keaweamauhili] is urging us to war. Perhaps just we two will be put to death" (Kamakau 1961, 118; cf. Pogue 1858, 42; Fornander 1878–80, 2:305; Bingham 1848, 36).

It is Kiwala'ō who soon ends up on the altar. After his death, Kamehameha must deal with Keaweamauhili, the ruler of Hilo in the eastern part of the island, and Keōua, the ruler of Ka'ū and Puna in the south. The three adversaries fight bitterly. Keaweamauhili is sacrificed by Keōua in 1790, leaving two rivals, Keōua and Kamehameha, who each deny the other's legitimacy (cf. Kamakau 1961, 153) and who, being perfectly identical, cannot coexist. One must sacrifice the other; the god will decide which one. This is what the priest Kapoukāhi foretells: "War shall cease on Hawaii when one shall come and shall be laid above on the altar (*lele*) of Pu'u-kohola, the house of the god" (Kamakau 1961, 157). Having learned of this prophecy, Kamehameha begins to build the temple in question.

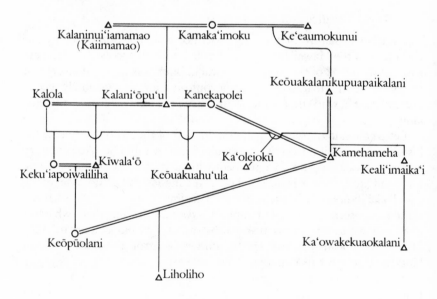

Fig. 1.   Main genealogical connections of ali'i involved in the succession from Kalani'ōpu'u to Liholiho.

When Pu'ukoholā is finished (1792), it must be consecrated by the sacrifice of the rival. Then something strange occurs; Keōua accepts to be sacrificed there. He makes a pretense, like everyone, of believing he is going to meet his rival to discuss the possibility of making peace. In fact he knows perfectly well that he will be sacrificed, and he prepares himself for death.[75]

When he disembarks on the beach below the sinister Pu'ukoholā temple, he is attacked with spears. Theoretically this is a mock attack, the *kāli 'i* rite (cf. Kamakau 1961, 157 and below, chap. 7), and thus a tribute made to his rank. But the fiction becomes a reality, for Keōua is massacred along with all his followers.[76] Their bodies are offered up on the altars; after nine years of bitter conflict with his rival, Kamehameha becomes the sole king of the island of Hawai'i, and he makes ready to conquer the entire archipelago (Kamakau 1961, 155–58; Fornander 1878–80, 2:331–34, 245, 236; Ii 1963, 14–15; Kalakaua 1888, 396, 358; Bingham 1848, 38–41; Ellis 1842, 210–12).

The tragic nature of this conflict can be recognized in at least three features: (1) it is inevitable, and only the death of one of the adversaries can bring it to an end; (2) it is an expression of the contradictory nature of consanguineal relationships among ali'i; consanguinity implies identity, which in turn requires solidarity on the "kinship" level but entails conflict on a "political" level; (3) the relationship between the rivals is ambivalent; their hatred coexists with their love for one another—this at least is declared by Kamakau, according to whom Kamehameha "loved Keoua" (1961, 157). Above all, the outcome of the conflict is made possible by a kind of *amor fati*—itself deeply tragic—that gives Keōua's heroic devotion its barbaric grandeur and a pitiable quality vividly felt by the people, who followed his drama with compassion. At each stage of his voyage to Pu'ukoholā, the inhabitants "crowded around him, brought him presents of food, hogs, tapa, and fruits, and by every means in their power, demonstrated their attachment to him. Many of them wept, some on account of the joy they felt at seeing him again; others, from a foreboding fear of the result of his surrender to Tamehameha" (Ellis 1842, 211).

The tragedy of succession is repeated with Kamehameha's death in 1819. Following the traditional model, the old king in effect leaves the right to consecrate the *luakini heiau* (and thus to make human sacrifices) to Liholiho, and the god Kūkā'ilimoku to his nephew Kekuaokalani (Ellis 1842, 126, 128).[77] There is already a certain enmity between the two ali'i (Ii 1963, 140),[78] which erupts into open conflict when Liholiho abolishes the taboo system. Kekuaokalani, who rises up in arms to defend it, is beaten and killed with his men. But he is not sacrificed, since Liholiho had put an end to the sacrificial system and therefore to the king's divinity.

Although the most highly valorized victims of the human sacrifice are enemy brothers,[79] ordinarily the king sacrifices those who have broken either his taboos or taboos basic to the whole of society, which is identified with him. Transgressors and enemy brothers are homologous, however. On the one hand, enemy brothers are identified with transgressors since, like them, they violate or deny the king's prerogatives ("taboos"). On the other hand, the most likely transgressors of the royal taboos are indeed his close rivals. Moreover, the transgression of royal taboos is enough to create a close relationship between the transgressor and the king. Consequently, transgressors, like enemy brothers, can act as substitutes for the king, who sacrifices them.

The close association created between transgressor and king is attested by several facts. For example, it is believed that the transgressor of a royal taboo, by entering the domain imbued with the king's divine mana, is contaminated by it and therefore made la'a, sacred. Thus the guards of King Lïloa's residence exclaim as they see 'Umi scale the wall, "ua laa keiki," "the child is consecrated [has become la'a, sacred]" (Fornander 1916–20, 4:185; cf. Malo MS, 67.44). This is a way of conceptualizing the relationship that arises between transgressor and transgressed.

Another indication of this association is constituted by the close relationships between ali'i and kauwā. The latter are apparently enemies that have been taken prisoner or transgressors[80] who have not been sacrificed immediately but spared to serve as future sacrificial victims (Kamakau 1961, 109n.; Ellis 1842, 161).[81] Now these kauwā, whom all avoid because they are polluted by their transgressions (Kepelino 1932, 144; Kamakau 1964, 8; Malo 1951, 70; Handy 1972, 324; Remy 1859, 19), have a close relationship with the ali'i; kauwā can have access to their houses, which commoners may not enter (Malo 1951, 70). Moreover, ali'i consider the kauwā their 'aumakua (ibid.). Kauwā and ali'i are both endogamous (ibid., 69), and both are called akua (ibid., 70).

Why does a transgression create such a bond between king and transgressor? The explanation is that transgression consists of a negation of the difference between two hierarchical positions. The transgressor of royal taboos or of taboos on which all of society is based does not recognize them because he does not respect them (it matters little whether this is intentional); consequently he does not recognize the hierarchical difference between himself and the king (as representative of the society) and thus the latter's legitimacy.[82] From this standpoint he is in a position similar to that of the enemy. By abolishing the foundation of the hierarchy, he endangers the entire social order as it has been constituted by the king. The pollution inherent in his act is anticipated death, the sign of the disaggregating effects of undifferentiation. This risk of death, of a loss of identity, strikes transgressor and violated alike, for a disturbance of the hierarchical relationship threatens them equally.[83] The one who has been violated can purify himself only by destroying the person who, by identifying with him, has struck down the difference between superior and inferior, pure and impure. The transgressor must be put to death, then, in person or through a substitute. But this execution must take a form that permits the reaffirmation of the existing relationship between the social hierarchy and the gods that are its principal foundation. As a result, the transgressor will be consecrated to the gods, and his sacrifice will at once reconstitute these gods and the social hierarchy that rests upon them.

Of course, precisely because he is identified with the king whose taboos he has transgressed, the transgressor can become his substitute in any sacrifice that requires this substitution. Hence the sacrifice of a transgressor does not simply purify the king by reproducing the distinction between his status and that of the transgressor; it also makes it possible for him to realize a given end by establishing contact with the divine—by becoming indirectly incorporated in it, in fact.

In sum, the king's human sacrifice is always a fratricide: either a literal one—because his most likely rivals are his brothers—or a metaphorical one—since every transgressor implicitly identifies with him and therefore becomes his "double." The king, then, must reproduce his kingship by neutralizing his negative, destructive equivalents or "doubles." However, this sacrificial destruction of destructive *male* doubles (remember that females are never sacrificed) is logically connected with a matrimonial appropriation of productive *female* doubles. In fact, as we shall see, the transition from the former to the latter, that is, from the destructive to the reproductive aspect of the king's divine power, is built into the royal ritual of legitimation itself.

Here I would like to point out that the connection between kingship as the prize of the pretenders and marriage with the highest-ranking women, who are most often the sisters,[84] real or classificatory, of the pretenders to the throne, makes sense both strategically and symbolically.

Strategically, a king attempts to establish a line that is superior in rank to all others; hence, rank being transmitted bilaterally, he must monopolize all the high-ranking women of the kingdom.[85] This implies royal incest (which is the ideal case) or, if the king is an upstart, forced hypogamy. To pave the way for this latter marriage or to exclude his rivals from sharing the high-ranking women (his sisters) with him, the king must destroy them—unless, of course, they resign themselves to being excluded. Hence the sacrifice of the rivals (the brothers) is the logical correlate, at least in extreme cases, of marriage with high-ranking sisters.

Kingship must be productive, creative of life. The hierogamy of the king and his sisters constitutes the archetype of this generative process. It is therefore the fitting end (in both senses of the term) of a process of constitution of kingship that necessarily begins with destruction. In other words, what begins as fratricide must end as incest; the destruction of a brother must, through marriage with a sister, become the production of an heir. The negative double of the king is thus turned into a positive one. Appropriately, this transformation is mediated by a god who, as we shall see (part 3), is first put to death, then reborn as a child.

Incest manifests the king's divine power in another sense; it demonstrates the autonomy, the self-sufficiency, and therefore the transcendent status of the king. Thus the king's divinity is established by his complementary relationship to two "doubles": a male double who is destructive and elicits the king's destructive power; a female double who is productive and elicits the king's productive power. The former double is an object of jealousy and hate, the latter an object of love.

To demonstrate this, let us begin with love that, alas, lies for the most part in the realm of myth. A famous myth tells us of two siblings of opposite sex who, unaware of their relationship because they had been raised separately, are irresistibly attracted to each other, *since each sees in the other the image of himself* (Fornander 1916–20, 4 : 540–42). In another myth, a father commands his son and daughter to marry, not so much because they are brother and sister, but because they are perfectly identical and equally beautiful (Fornander 1916–20, 4 : 602; cf. as well 5 : 192). Indeed, it seems that brother/sister marriage is only a particular case of the marriage of two similar people of opposite sex.

Thus when the brothers of the queen of the island of Kahiki (hence, a goddess) notice that the hero 'Aukelenuiaiku resembles their sister, they ask her to marry him, saying, "He is just like you. We therefore made up our mind that it would be proper that you take him as your husband" (Fornander 1916–20, 4 : 58).[86]

In the same vein, a mother encourages her son to ask for the hand of a maiden with these words: "Yes, she shall be your wife, for you two are alike in looks and behavior, therefore you go and ask her" (Fornander 1916–20, 5 : 156). These statements seem to imply that the most perfect union is that of twins, but I know of no explicit mention of such marriages.[87]

Mythology, but especially history, also documents that, in contrast to relationships between brothers and sisters,[88] the relationship between brothers is dominated by hate. In Kamakau's words, "The chiefs of old were very jealous of each other" (1961, 165). Let us consider as examples some historical events in which the rivalry among male pretenders to the throne explicitly takes the form of a rivalry for the hand of a high-ranking "sister."

One such event, or rather series of events, comes to us both through Hawaiian sources and through travelers' accounts. It involves the royal dynasty of Kaua'i. At the end of the eighteenth century, the female ali'i Ka-

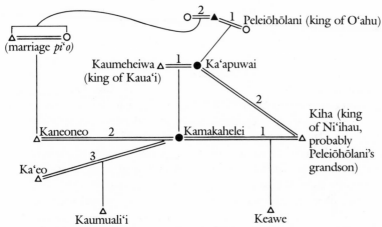

Fig. 2. Main genealogical connections of ali'i involved in the succession on Kaua'i. The numbers refer to the order in which the marriages were contracted by the individuals symbolized by solid triangles or circles.

makahelei takes a discriminative role with respect to her classificatory brothers. Kinsmen who successively manage to obtain her favors control the government. After her marriage to Kiha (who from a generational standpoint is her cousin but is considered her "father" for having married her mother—cf. Samwell 1967, 1224), she marries her cousin Kaneoneo, who, issuing from a brother-sister union (*pi'o*), is of a higher rank than she is. But in 1779 Kaneoneo is supplanted by Ka'eo, the half-brother of Kahekili, the king of Maui (cf. Ii 1963, 15), and loses to him on the battlefield (Clerke 1967, 576–77). After Kaneoneo's defeat, Kiha's son Keawe is first installed on the throne of Kaua'i (King 1967, 585) but it is finally Kaumuali'i, the son of the victor Ka'eo, who, despite his initial defeat (cf. Broughton 1804, 73), becomes king of Kaua'i (Clerke 1967, 576–77; King 1967, 579, 585, 590; Samwell 1967, 1224, 1227; Beaglehole 1967, 589, n. 2, 1224, n. 3, cf. 1226, n. 3; Portlock 1789, 86; Menzies 1920, 27; Bishop 1967, 145–46; Turnbull 1813, 213; Fornander 1878–80, 2:227; Kuykendall 1938, 48).[89]

This is a case of "enemy brothers" who fight to conquer a "sister" and, through her, the land. Moreover, the sons of the various unions of this "sister" inherit the rivalries of their fathers.

Another case in which two identical rivals (who moreover have the same name, Keawe) clash over a woman who holds the key to the land involves Keaweaheulu and Keaweamauhili. At first Keaweaheulu controls the land of Hilo because of his marriage with Ululani; but then this woman prefers Keaweamauhili to him. Out of this comes a conflict that will flow into the wider conflict between Kiwala'ō and Kamehameha (cf. Fornander 1878.–80, 2:309).

In the two cases just mentioned, the conflict between "brothers" be-comes more intense because their "sister" is senior and in a position to control the land. Nevertheless, these cases reflect a much more general ten-dency. As Richards's text quoted in note 85 implies, a man's control over the land is threatened by a rival's conquest of his sister/wife. The story of Kaholanuimāhu is evidence of this. This king of the island of Hawai'i goes off to Maui, and during his absence his wife (who is also probably his sister or half-sister) takes another husband, who becomes king of the island (Fornander 1878–80, 2:70–71). Kaholanuimāhu then comes back home, kills his adversary, and sacrifices him. In the same man-ner Kamehameha sacrifices his "son" Kanihonui when he discovers that he has become the lover of his wife Ka'ahumanu; he fears in effect that be-cause of this relationship Kanihonui will take his place at the head of the kingdom.[90] Here, incest provokes a "filiocide" intended to avoid a par-ricide (cf. Kamakau 1961, 194; Ii 1963, 50–51; Laanui 1930, 87).[91]

To conclude, I shall mention a famous example of the tendency for the sacrifice of a rival "brother" to be followed by his sacrificer's marriage with his high-ranking female relatives. After Kamehameha sacrificed his cousin Kiwala'ō,[92] he hastened to capture the dead man's mother (Kalola) and daughter (Keōpūolani) in order to marry the latter. Keōpūolani gave him his successor, Liholiho (Kamakau 1961, 149; Fornander 1878–80, 2:238; Kuykendall 1938, 35).

In sum, whether or not they are sisters (or even mothers), women, who cannot be sacrificed and therefore transcend the conflict among their male consanguineal kin, are often the stakes that provoke one brother's sacrifice by another, or the son's sacrifice by the father, or the father's sacrifice by the son.

This occurrence correlates with the idea that the relationship of similar beings is positive if their similarity is accompanied by a difference (sex) that makes them complementary and productive (they have children); it is negative if it involves no difference, since this makes them incompatible and therefore mutually destructive.

Similarity is in fact always threatening for a hierarchical system predi-cated on the ultimate dissimilarity, and therefore complementarity, of everybody. But the similarity of people of opposite sex can be neutralized by marriage, since it makes a single entity out of two. On the contrary, the similarity of people of the same sex can be neutralized only if one of them renounces his status or is destroyed.

Marriage with the female double and sacrifice of the male double are therefore complementary means of reestablishing differentiation in a hier-archical system that, paradoxically, produces a certain coefficient of un-differentiation because of the overlap of different principles.

The Myth of Wākea and Papa

All genealogies of Hawaiian aliʻi go back to the original couple, Wākea (the husband) and Papa (the wife). These ancestors are the protagonists of a myth that recounts the institution of the sacrificial system and demonstrates that it is consubstantial with kingship and royal incest.

The myth is given in several texts, which all seem to derive from the *Mooolelo* of 1838 (pp. 37–40, 64; Malo 1951, 28, 240; Pogue 1858, 23–24; Dibble 1909, 12; Bingham 1848, 20; Beckwith 1932, 192–93; Fornander 1916–20, 6:319; Anonymous, in *Ka Nupepa Kuokoa*, 25 November 1865). It can be summarized as follows.

The first child of Wākea and Papa is born prematurely (he is a *keiki* ʻaluʻalu*), and his parents bury him at the end of their house in the refuse heap (*lepo*).[93] But a stem grows up out of the body and it changes into the first taro. Wākea names it Hāloa ("waving stem") (Hāloanaka, "long waving stem," according to Malo 1951, 244).[94] After him is born a daughter, Hoʻohokukalani or Hoʻohokuikalani (cf. PE, 384), whom Wākea marries, and by whom he has a second son, also named Hāloa (Remy 1862, 64), who is human and becomes the ancestor of the aliʻi (the king is figuratively called "lineage of Hāloa"—cf. Ii 1963, 19) and in fact, the ancestor of all men (Malo 1951, 244).[95] Wākea's incest is the crucial event, narrated in detail.

When Hoʻohokuikalani grows up and becomes very beautiful, Wākea desires to sleep with her, but he finds no way to escape Papa's sight. So the priest advises him to establish the sacrificial system (with its correlate the temple system), which involves the separation of the pure and the impure, hence of the sexes. Henceforth women will be separated from men when they eat and when they menstruate or give birth.

During a taboo night when he must stay apart from Papa, Wākea goes to visit his daughter, first having asked the priest to awaken him before dawn with a prayer. But when the prayer is recited Wākea does not wake up, and as a result he is seen by Papa who, furious, will not listen to him; Wākea then spits in her face, thereby divorcing her.

Later on Papa assumes the aspect of Hinamanouluaʻe and marries her grandson Hāloa. Then, incarnated in other women she marries her descendants through five successive generations (*Mooolelo* 1838, 41; Remy 1862, 84–85).[96]

The story of Wākea and Papa can be considered the Hawaiian transformation of the Polynesian myth that recounts the separation of heaven and earth. Wākea—also named Ākea ("vast expanse," PE 352, 12) or Awakea ("Noon," PE, 31)— corresponds to Atea, who in central Polynesia is a symbol of clarity and light and as such is a double for Kāne, whom he sometimes replaces, as in the Marquesas (Tregear 1891, 28–29; Williamson 1933, 1:22, 26). As for Papa, she is the earth mother, wife of Rangi the sky for the Maori, of Vatea ("daylight") in Mangaia, and so on (Tregear 1891, 315).

These characters and their actions have been humanized in the Hawaiian version, however, where the origin of the separation of heaven and earth has been transformed into the origin of the separation of the sexes and, correlatively, of the separation of the sacred ali'i from other men. Moreover, the Hawaiian variant takes place in a particular genealogical context, which can be reconstructed on the basis of information contained in the *Kumulipo*. This context is relevant for the interpretation of the myth and is therefore given in figure 3:

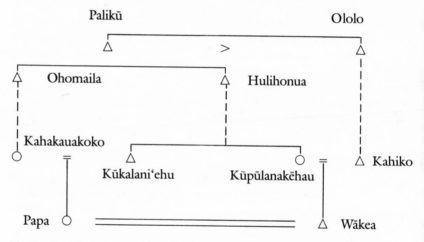

Fig. 3.   Genealogical connections of Wākea and Papa, according to the *Kumulipo*.

The myth explains the genesis of kingship—that is, of Hāloa II, the first ali'i having the divine rank of *nī'aupi'o* (Kepelino 1932, 61)—as the result of a process. The first stage is the production of taro, the most important material basis of cultural life. The second stage consists in the institution of the sacrificial system, which implies the separation of the sexes.

As the myth shows, the existence of the sacrificial system is what makes it possible for Wākea to realize his desire for incest, which produces the first divine king, Hāloa II. Incest is presented as the negation of a previous marriage practice, which is exemplified in Wākea's alliance with Papa. A glance at the genealogical diagram above will show that Papa is Wākea's matrilateral cross-cousin. Her marriage with Wākea, then, suggests the existence of a system of generalized exchange. Such a system allows for a hierarchical relationship between wife givers and wife takers (in effect, Papa's rank is superior to Wākea's), but insofar as it implies cycling it has the effect of equalizing everyone's rank from the point of view of the entire society. Thus hierarchy is encompassed by equality.

Wākea's refusal to give his daughter in marriage to another line and his decision to keep her for himself, then, interrupts this system of equalizing reciprocity and therefore effectively separates the king from his kinsmen. It also manifests his transcendence of society in a positive and a negative form. Negatively, he is the only man who violates the fundamental rule of society as a system of reciprocity (exogamy). But this is only the negative aspect of a positive feature: the king's incest demonstrates that he can do without reciprocity because he alone among men is perfect and does not need to exchange with other members of his species to exist. He is in fact the species itself made concrete and therefore the unity of society incarnated in an individual.

It should be added that the myth demonstrates not only that kingship, incest, and the sacrificial system (the condition of which is the separation of the pure and the impure and therefore the exclusion of women) are mutually entailing, but also that they are in a sequential relationship identical to the one we found in the political process and shall find again in its ritual recapitulation and model. In effect the myth shows that sacrifice is the means to realize incest, which itself produces the divine heir (Hāloa II).

6

THE HIERARCHY OF TEMPLES

[Opfer wird so zu] Arbeit. Monumente errichten, Tempelbauen ist schon
Beziehung auf das absolute Sein.
Hegel 1974, 1, 2:75

Introduction

The hierarchy of sacrifices, the chain of sacrifices that constitutes Hawaiian
society, has a correlate in the hierarchy of places in which these cultic acts
occur. Moreover, just as the sacrificer is necessary to the sacrifice because
he is in contact with the god in a permanent manner, so temples and other
sacred places are a condition of the efficacy of sacrifice because the gods are
permanently present in them. Let us turn our attention, then, to the Hawaiian temples.

A relatively rich literature exists on this subject. In addition to the accounts of the voyagers and the canonical sources (*Mooolelo Hawaii*, Malo,
S. M. Kamakau, K. Kamakau, Kepelino, 'Ī'ī, etc.), we can utilize archaeological evidence.

Writing at the beginning of the century, T. G. Thrum was the first to
attempt a complete survey of the temples in the Hawaiian archipelago, to
draw their plans and collect the extant traditions concerning each one. His
pioneering work is contained in a series of articles. He was followed by
professional archaeologists: Stokes,[1] Emory (1924), and above all, Bennett (1930, 1931) and McAllister (1933). These writers still had the opportunity to combine archaeological research with the collection of oral
traditions.

After World War II, excavations and restorations became more numerous. A comprehensive evaluation of these data has yet to be made. In an
unpublished thesis in 1930 Bennett tried to establish a complete typology
of Hawaiian temples and places of worship. But this attempt is flawed because the types utilized are constituted on the basis of primarily formal criteria without a sufficient questioning of the meanings that the Hawaiians
attributed to the elements so classified.

Taking these archaeological findings into account, I will briefly attempt to put some order into the confusion regarding a properly Hawaiian classi-fication of sacred places.

The Concept of "Heiau"

The word *heiau* or *haiau* designates any place of worship and thus the places where sacrifices are offered. The second form, *haiau*, shows more clearly than the first that they both derive from the word *hai*, "a sacrifice," "to sacrifice" (PE, 44; Pukui, Elbert, and Mookini 1975, 25, 20).[2] The temple is the place of the sacrifice, in short. It is therefore defined by its function, not its material aspect.

This is why the term *heiau* can sometimes refer to a simple natural object or to an element in a landscape where the god manifests himself and where sacrifices are offered to him. Thus, for example, the place known as 'Elekuna, on Kaua'i, "is termed a heiau by the natives of the district, and is without doubt a place of marked distinction as it was visited on various occasions by royalty; nothing of a structural character was found; simply a mound of outcropping sandstone at the base of which were placed the offerings of devotees" (Thrum 1907b, 39). Still on Kaua'i, a highly sacred stone on which sacrifices are made is called a *heiau* (Thrum 1907b, 40). On the island of Hawai'i, an immense flat stretch is called a *heiau* (Thrum 1908b, 63). This term is applied to a cave on the island of O'ahu (McAllister 1933, 8), a fact that leads McAllister to comment: "The term 'heiau' is now used loosely by the Hawaiians; in extreme cases it may designate anything sacred" (ibid.). This "looseness" may be more traditional than McAllister believes.

Functional Types, Architectural Types
Temples Not Reserved for the King
Hale Mua

The term *hale mua*, or simply *mua*, refers, strictly speaking, to the domestic temple, that is, the "men's house" of a *kauhale* (group of habitations occupied by a family group) or a group of *kauhale* (Kirch 1975, 178; Campbell 1967, 131). Since the *hale mua* is essentially a temple, it can be called *heiau*, "temple" (see Malo 1951, 28, 126; cf. N. Emerson in Malo 1951, 126, n. 8, and 132–33). According to Emerson the reverse is also true; a *heiau* can be called *hale mua* (cf. Malo 1951, 126, 210; Kepelino 1932, 60).[3] At any rate, the term *hale mua* can designate the most sacred house of the king's temple (*luakini*): the *hale mana*, "mana house," where priests and ali'i eat sacrificial meals (Fornander 1916–20, 4:127, 430; Kamakau 1976, 131; cf. McAllister 1933, 14). It can also refer to the temple's *hale umu*, "oven house" (Kamakau 1976, 138).

If the most sacred house in the king's temple, like the most sacred house of the *kauhale*, is called *hale mua*, it is because the two are defined by the same relationship, that which exists between the "front" and the "back." In fact, *mua* means "before; front; first; foremost; previously, beforehand; oldest, older brother or sister; senior branch of a family; leader, senior; more than" (PE, 235) and also "beginning" (Andrews 1865, 402).

At the level of the household, the *hale mua* is both the main house and the first to be built (Malo 1951, 28; Kamakau in Thrum 1910, 57; cf. Andrews 1922, 98). As the "front part" of the group, the *hale mua* is also the place where guests are received and business is transacted (Judd 1975, 21, 24; Kamakau 1961, 212). Here one also enters into relation with another aspect of the "outside," of the world that transcends the household: the gods. Their images are put above an altar (*kuahu*) (Malo 1951, 87), where daily offerings are set, especially at the beginning of each meal. Like any temple, the ʻmua is strictly forbidden to women (cf. Handy 1972, 316).

At the level of the society at large, the king's temple has the same position and function that the *hale mua* has with respect to the household; it is the *hale mua* of all *hale mua*, the "first house" of all "first houses," just as the king is the *mua* ("eldest") of all eldests. In one sense the use of the term *mua* to indicate the king's temple (or rather, the house within this temple that metonymically represents it) underscores the homogeneity of the hierarchy of sacrificial places and sacrifiers in Hawaiian society.

The *hale mua* can be completed by an enclosure, generally of an oval or horseshoe form, in which images of the gods and additional altars are erected (Kukāhi in McAllister 1933, 16; Quimper 1937, 5). In this case the whole complex is called *heiau* (Malo 1951, 29; Pogue 1858, 22; Andrews 1865, 143).

This extension of the *hale mua* appears to be obligatory for a noble's house (cf. Ii 1963, 117–21; Barrère 1975, 4–6; Manby 1929, 40) and can even result in duplication; the domestic *heiau*, with its *hale mua*, is doubled on a higher level by an "official" *heiau*. This duplication reflects the double role of the aliʻi: as head of the household, he sacrifices and eats (the two acts are always related, as we have seen) in his domestic temple; as head of a social segment, he sacrifices and eats in the company of his nobles and clients in his "official" temple.

Pōhaku o Kāne

The *pōhaku o Kāne* ("stone of Kāne") is not a temple sensu stricto (cf. Kamakau 1964, 32) but a shrine that is often associated with a domestic temple or even with fishing temples (cf. McAllister 1933, 184–85). It is formed of an erect stone and a *kuahu* altar around which are planted cordylines and other plants. Expiatory rites are made here. The place where the stone can be found is revealed by a god in a dream (Kamakau 1964, 32–33; Kamakau 1961, 201; Kamakau 1976, 130). The stone may be left there or may be transported to a temple (cf. Kamakau 1964, 33, 1976, 130; cf. as well Kamakau 1961, 201).

Pōhaku o Kāne are often found on points of transition: boundaries, passes, cliffs (McAllister 1933, 20).[4] Offerings wrapped in bark cloths and twigs are placed on them each time one passes by (Tyerman and Bennett 1831, 1:458; Ellis 1842, 15). Sometimes these stones are phallic in form or are considered phalli. This, moreover, is what their name—Kāne, "male"—indicates.

Koʻa

A koʻa ("coral") or koʻa Kūʻula (cf. Kamakau 1976, 129) is a fishing heiau, as is indicated by its association with Kūʻula, the god of fishing (Kamakau 1976, 130; 1964, 33; 1961, 201).[5] Most often a koʻa is a simple altar of coral, but it can be a true temple with platforms or small courtyards (McAllister 1933, 15–16; Kamakau 1976, 133).[6] Koʻa can be devoted to one or several species of fish (McAllister 1933, 68, 156, 163–64). They are usually built close to the sea, but may be along the banks of rivers, taro ponds, and so forth, if they are consecrated to the ʻoʻopu fish (Eleotridae or Gobiidae), which live in these places. Moreover, since these fish are considered to be "farmed" rather than "fished," their koʻa shrines are under the tutelage of Kānekoʻa,[7] a form of Kāne, a god of farming, rather than that of Kū.

Some koʻa have functions not directly connected with fishing. Thus Kamakau mentions the custom of erecting a koʻa heiau before leaving on a long voyage (1976, 144; cf. McAllister 1933, 15). Such expeditions are related to fishing both symbolically and practically, however. Koʻa are also built on little islands inhabited by seabirds, which are used by bird catchers (Kamakau 1976, 133), and also in the forest, to catch or multiply forest birds (D. Barrère, personal communication). Koʻa may even be consecrated to the ʻaumakua of the moʻo category, which live in fresh water. Perhaps this indicates that they are connected with fishing in streams and ponds (Kamakau 1964, 86).[8]

Unu and Waihau

According to one of McAllister's informants the heiau called koʻa and unu are functionally equivalent but differ in their construction: "The koʻa is built up of stones piled one on top the other into platform-like structures, whereas the unu is built of a single line of stones standing on end forming an oval.—'Resembling an open mouth,' was Hookala's [the informant's—V. V.] expression. Some sites were known as unu" (1933, 15).

S. M. Kamakau mentions the unu temple several times but is confused about its nature. In a text he speaks of the category of temples known as unuunu hoʻoūlu ʻai (unuunu being a reduplication of unu); these are temples "to increase food crops" ("*ho'oūlu 'ai*") (1964, 33), where the firstfruits of the land are offered (PE, 341). But in another text he states that the *heiau unu* belongs, together with the *heiau luakini* and *waihau*, to the *po'okanaka* category—temples for war and for human sacrifice (1976, 134). This statement is contested by Barrère (in Kamakau 1976, 145–46, n. 7), who apparently wants to restrict the *unu* type to the agricultural variety (*ho'oūlu 'ai*) without, however, clearly deciding the issue. At any rate, she proposes that those passages where Kamakau makes the *unu* a temple for human sacrifice are erroneous.

Her thesis is unconvincing, however, since there is no reason to suppose that the *unu* is a functional instead of an architectural category. Above all, Kamakau is not the only writer to associate the *unu* with human sacrifice. In fact, the *Mooolelo Hawaii*, which is an older, surer source than S. M. Kamakau, states that the *unu* is the part of the temple for human sacrifice where the king's *lele* altar is found (Pogue 1858, 21).[9] This altar is precisely the one where human victims are offered.

Before trying to propose a solution to account for these conflicting statements, it is necessary to review other sources on the subject of the *unu* type, as well as the *waihau*, which raises similar problems. Malo speaks of an *unu o Lono* temple consecrated to the god Lono (1951, 160, 176, 189). According to N. Emerson, the *unu kupukupu* is "a hummock or natural rock-pile such as would be selected by fishermen, with the addition, perhaps, of a few stones, as an altar on which to lay their offerings" (1915, 202). Brigham states, "The *unu* class should be applied to the pyramidal class of piled up stones, never to those walled about" (n.d., 161). In a forest on Kaua'i Thrum found a little temple that he depicted as follows: "It was only an 'unu' or shrine, for the shifting population of the forest belt" (1907c, 64).

Unfortunately, these statements do not clarify matters, and the information concerning the *waihau* type is no less confusing. In the text mentioned previously, Kamakau makes the *waihau* a variety of the *po'okanaka* type, along with the *luakini* and the *unu*. But in another text he speaks of "*luakini waihau*" that had been constructed "as war heiaus or heiaus for purifying the land" (1961, 291). Elsewhere he mentions the "*waihau-ipu-o-Lono*" (1976, 129), which he distinguishes from the "*hale ipu-o-Lono*" and the "*waihau hale-o-Papa*" (the latter are temples annexed to the *luakini* where human sacrifices are made; cf. as well Kamakau 1961, 201; 1964, 59, 83, 86, 96).[10] Brigham (n.d., 161) suggests that *waihau* is "the distinctive name of the round temples"; in fact, *waihau* means "a round heap," and "a small, tight bundle."[11] Thrum also thinks that *waihau* and *unu* are architectural rather than functional types, but he gives a different interpretation to their meaning (1910, 54, n. 1). Since the name *waihau* is given to several terraced temples on O'ahu and Kaua'i, he supposes that this term refers to the terraced temples, while *unu* refers to temples constructed in the form of a courtyard.

I think it is the view of Thrum and Brigham that must be accepted. *Unu* and *waihau* are not functional categories, since the term *unu* can be found in the literature associated with temples for fishing or agricultural rites and with temples or temple sections where human sacrifices are made (cf, also Fornander 1916–20, 6:403, line 609, 401, line 564), while the term *waihau* refers at once to agricultural temples, to temples of the *luakini* and *poʻokanaka* types (cf. Fornander 1916–20, 6:401, line 565), and to the *hale o Papa*.

Yet what architectural or material particularity is meant by the terms *unu* and *waihau*? The information is too scanty to permit a true answer to this question. Concerning the *unu* type, nevertheless, we have two details that could agree: first is the statement from Hoʻokala, according to whom the shape of the *unu* is an oval, or rather a horseshoe, since it resembles an open mouth formed by a line of stones; second is the statement from the *Mooolelo Hawaii*, in which *unu* refers to the part of the temple where the king's altar is found. In many *luakini* temples, where human sacrifices are made, the *lele* altar is placed in the area of the temple circumscribed by a platform that has the shape of a horsehoe or "open mouth." Thus we can suppose that *unu* refers to temples, whatever their function, that have this form, or to the sacrificial area that has this shape, and perhaps even to the temples that have a sacrificial area thus shaped.

Finally, it is noteworthy that the *waihau* type seems to be limited to the islands of Kauaʻi and Oʻahu. Malo, a native of the island of Hawaiʻi, does not mention it. Stokes puts forth the hypothesis that on Kauaʻi and Oʻahu *waihau* designates the same type of temple designated in Hawaiʻi by the term *māpele*, namely, an agricultural temple (n.d., GR 2, box 2.5). This hypothesis is contradicted, however, by some of Kamakau's statements mentioned above, as they refer to conditions in Kauaʻi and Oʻahu.

Hale o Lono and Similar Temples

The *hale o Lono*, "house of Lono," also called *waihau-ipu-o-Lono* ("*waihau* of Lono's gourd") (Kamakau 1976, 129) or *unu o Lono* (Malo 1951, 160, 189),[12] is a temple that secures abundant harvests (*heiau hoʻoūluulu ʻai*, "*heiau* for the increase of food crops"—PE, 60) or rain (*heiau hoʻoūluulu ua*, "*heiau* where offerings were made to insure rain"—PE, 60)[13] or both at once (Stokes 1919). In other words, this temple is built "so that the land might live" ("*no ke ola o ka ʻaina*"; Kamakau 1976, 129; cf. Thrum 1910, 56–57; Kamakau 1961, 201). In fact, Lono is preeminently the god of growth, of horticulture, of rain (he is associated with the clouds) and presides over the life of the people in general. As such he is a nourishing god. He is offered the firstfruits of the land, particularly taro, which he helps to produce. The offerings of '*awa* that are intended for him are placed in a gourd (*ipu*) hung about the neck of his image (cf. Malo 1951, 88–89, 207), since this plant is one of his bodies (Handy 1972, 219)—the one that perhaps better than all others condenses all the different manifestations of this god. In fact, the fruit of the gourd evokes the roundness of that which is developed, full, or pregnant, as well as the form of rain-bearing clouds. In addition, the two mainstays of life, poi (taro puree) and water, are ordinarily kept in gourds (Handy 1940, 209; Dodge 1978). In short, the gourd evokes life, its reproduction, and its sources. This is why Lono's temple can be called *waihau-ipu-o-Lono*, *hale-ipu-o-Lono* (Kamakau 1976, 129), or even *heiau-ipu-o-Lono* (Kamakau 1976, 133), that is, "temple [or house] of the gourd of Lono."

According to Kamakau the *hale o Lono* "was erected on the site of the altar in an old heiau" (1961, 200). It is difficult to understand what he means by this—perhaps that the *heiau* in question was an abandoned *luakini*. 'Ī'ī mentions a *hale o Lono* whose entrance faces the mountainside (*mauka*) (1963, 110; cf. Whitman 1979, 50), but we do not know if this orientation is the rule. The temple is built with *lama* wood (Ii 1963, 59–60; Malo 1951, 160) and the thatch on the roof is made of cordyline.

Samwell describes as follows the *hale o Lono* at Ke'ei (at Kealakekua Bay, island of Hawai'i), which was inhabited by the priest Ka'imiki'i:

the house of Kaimekee was inclosed in all with a kind of Pallisades, & before it was a Court; at one end of this was a curious sort of building which they told us was dedicated to Orono [Lono]; it has something the appearance of a triumphal arch, it is about six yards high, two in length, and ab' half a yard broad, being not wide enough to admit a Man in between the front & back of it; it is inclosed in with the bunches of the Cocoa nut tree and shreds of Cloth, and on the top are several pieces fluttering like ragged pendants; before it on a pole stuck in the ground hung a small dead pig, & round the pole a heap of Cocoa nuts and Plantains as an offering to the God Orono, who they told us lived in the Skies; on making a further enquiry after him they brought us out a small rude image of him which they kept in the House. He was tyed to a small round Cup made of the Cocoanut tree with a Cover to it, in which they kept some provisions for him [it is clearly an *ipu-o-Lono* and not a coconut, as Samwell believes]. [1967, 1163–64]

The "triumphal arch" described by Samwell is in reality a tower like the one that, as we will see, is erected in the *luakini* temple. It is not a necessary component of the *hale o Lono* since, for example, the temple of this type that in 1779 was adjacent to the *luakini* Hikiau did not have one but was formed of a simple house surrounded by a palisade. Two images of Lono were placed at the entrance (see Webber's drawing in Cook and King 1784, atlas; and one by Ellis reproduced in Ii 1963, 60).

In some cases the "house of Lono" is part of a more extensive complex that also includes the houses of other gods and one or two towers (see for example Ii 1963, 56; Valeri 1982b).

The *hale o Lono* is the king's and the highest-ranking nobles' "ordinary temple" (Malo 1951, 160); it is here that the pigs they eat are most often consecrated (Kamakau 1961, 200). But temples having the same function, if not the same aspect, can be built by lower-ranking nobles and commoners (Kamakau 1976, 120).

Malo distinguishes the *unu o Lono* from the *māpele*. The rites of the former as he describes them (1951, 160) correspond to those held monthly from the evening of the twenty-seventh to dawn of the twenty-ninth day,[14] which do not necessarily have an agricultural purpose (cf. Ii 1963, 59–61; 1841).[15] The *māpele*[16] is also dedicated to the cult of Lono, and Malo describes it as "a heiau covered with thatch (*pili*) in which agricultural food is increased" (*"ke heiau pili ka mapele i ka hoouluulu ai"*—Malo MS, 161; cf. 1951, 160).[17]

Other Temples

Since every activity is associated with a cult, naturally there are a great number of types of temples, only a few of which are known to us.

For example, there are temples dedicated to the deities of the *hula* dance (Emerson 1965, 14–22; Emory in Barrère, Pukui, and Kelly 1980, 141–48; Kelly in ibid., 95–115), temples for Pele and other volcanic deities, temples in which one prays for an easy delivery, temples built to obtain success in love (*heiau hana aloha*), temples for surfing, and so on (Stokes MS Report 1919).

Some temples consecrated to the deities of medicine are especially worth mentioning: for example, those which shelter the gods Lonopuhā ("Lono abscess") and Kāneikōleamoku, as well as other forms of the gods Kāne and Lono connected with healing (Malo 1951, 109; Ii 1963, 45–46). Kamakau also cites the "'*alaneo* house where men go to pray for healing" (1961, 181). The term '*alaneo* also refers to a group of twelve hermaphrodite gods (*māhū*) endowed with curative powers (PE, 17).

Temples Reserved Exclusively for the King
Luakini

The main temple reserved for the king is the *luakini*, that is, the temple where human sacrifices, which only the king and his delegates may consecrate, are made. It is therefore in the *luakini* that the principal royal rituals take place.

We will consider the architectural varieties of the *luakini* later on; here I will treat its principal functional varieties. It will also be necessary to mention the different names given to these varieties or even to the *luakini* type per se.

Two main types of *luakini* are distinguished by the materials used to construct the sacred houses within the enclosure of the temple:

The special form of worship was evident from the kind of house built for the god. If a house of '*ohi'a* wood was erected on the grounds of the heiau it was a *haku* '*ohi'a*, a *malu* '*ohi'a*, an '*ohi'a-ko*. Such a god house was one in which to pray to end rebellion, conspiracy, and war. . . . Some houses were built of *loulu* palms, or they might be mere shelters. Such a god house was for [the purpose of prayer for] the fertility of soil that had become infertile; at the death of chiefs and commoners, or at a time of trouble of any kind, such as pestilence, barrenness in women or animals, famine; hence such a god house was set up in the place where the trouble occurred. [Kamakau 1961, 200, cf. 221]

Malo calls temples whose structures are made of '*ohi'a-lehua* wood (*Metrosideros macropus, M. collina*) *luakini kaua*, "war *luakini*" (1951, 152, 160–61); he gives the name *heiau loulu* to the temples whose houses are thatched with *loulu* (ibid., 152). These are *luakini* nonetheless, as 'Ī'ī attests (1963, 33).[18]

The rites performed in the *heiau loulu* are called *kapu loulu* (ibid.). Like Kamakau, 'Ī'ī states that these rites "brought peace for the duration of the reign of the King" (1963, 45). Moreover, the *kapu loulu* he describes was performed, pecisely, to remedy a malady that struck King Kamehameha and his principal queen (ibid., 33).

Thus there seems to be a clear opposition between the temple for war and its ritual on the one hand, and the temple for peace on the other, the ritual of which has fertilizing, purifying, and apotropeic effects (cf. Kauhane 1865; Kupahu 1865; Kaawa 1865b).[19]

In fact, this opposition is only relative. First of all, there is no major difference between the *kapu loulu* that 'Ī'ī describes and the war ritual described by Malo, K. Kamakau, and the anonymous author of a text published by Wilkes (1845, 4:506–8). Second, the opposition does not necessarily concern the temple as a fixed structure (platforms, terraces, stone enclosures), but relates to the mobile and perishable superstructures (houses, wooden statues, etc.). The same *luakini* temple can thus be considered as a *heiau kaua* or a *heiau loulu*, depending on the occasion,[20] and the same ritual can be used for works of war or works of peace, depending on the context (see Valeri 1982b). More exactly, as we shall see, war and peace, destruction and fertilization, life and death are two moments, two phases that are necessarily present in any performance of the royal ritual. Only the emphasis on the two components varies. These variations are manifested above all in the use of different woods, for their colors evoke different situations. The wood of the '*ohi'a* is red and thus is associated with blood, violence, and destruction, to such an extent that it is believed that constructing a temple with '*ohi'a-lehua* will bring famine (Malo 1951, 189). In contrast, the wood of the *loulu* palm is whitish green, a color obviously associated with states of life and purity.

However, we should not insist too much on this opposition, for on the one hand the associations with the *loulu* palm are not entirely of a peaceful nature (for example, its wood can be used to make spears—Malo 1951, 21); on the other hand, according to some sources *loulu* and '*ōhi'a-lehua* are used together in the construction of the same temple. Thus Malo writes that the frame of sacred houses can be made with '*ōhi'a-lehua* wood and the thatch with '*uki*, "sedges," but also with leaves of the *loulu* palm (Malo 1951, 159).

Moreover, the text published by Wilkes describing a war ritual says that the houses built on this occasion are covered with "palm leaves" (1845, 4:506); most likely this is a reference to the *loulu* palm. It could even be that in this context the term *kapu loulu* refers to a segment of the ritual (the one concerning the thatching of roofs) rather than to a separate type of ritual performance. This interpretation, adopted by Thrum (1910, 54), could be supported by a text of Haleole's in which the '*aha hulahula* rite, during which the houses of the *luakini* temple are thatched, is identified with a rite he called '*aha loulu* (i.e., *kapu loulu*; Haleole in Fornander 1916–20, 6:158–59).[21]

Thus I am tempted to conclude that the ritual involves the use of houses made of both *loulu* and '*ōhi'a-lehua*, but that the place given to each wood varies according to the circumstances and the purpose of the performance.

To end this discussion of the *luakini* temple some facts must be mentioned. The term *heiau po'okanaka* ("temple of the human head," "of the skull"—PE, 315) is equivalent to the term *luakini* (Malo 1951, 53). The name *po'okanaka* probably derives from the custom of placing the skulls of human victims on top of poles erected around the temple (Samwell 1967, 1221; Clerke 1967, 1597; Ellis 1782, 2:18; Lisiansky 1814, 121–22; Fornander 1916–20, 4:219). According to Stokes, however, the name *heiau po'okanaka* has a different meaning: "temple of the leader [= head—V. V.] of the people" (n.d., GR 1, box 8.33). The two meanings are not incompatible.

Malo also mentions a category of *luakini* that he calls *luakini maoli* (MS 36.78). N. Emerson translates this term by the expression "ordinary *luakini*" (in Malo 1951, 152). Neither he nor Malo explains precisely which temple he is discussing. The most probable hypothesis is that the expression *luakini maoli* refers to a *luakini* that has no special purpose but is undifferentiated or multifunctional. Moreover, *luakini maoli* also means "true *luakini*"; a true *luakini* should, precisely, encompass all the functions that are otherwise separated among specialized *luakini* temples.

Other Temples

Among the temples reserved exclusively for the king, Malo (36.78) also mentions the *heiau ma'o*. According to Emerson this is "a temporary structure of small size for the use of the *alii* only; and when its purpose was over, it was taken down. It was a slight structure covered with *tapa* cloth stained with *mao*, of a reddish color" (in Malo 1951, 158).

However, according to Pukui and Elbert's dictionary, *ma'o* means "green" (p. 221). Andrews is more vague, for he writes that the *ma'o* is "a kind of shrub used in dyeing *kapa*" (1865, 361; cf. Neal 1929, 204). He adds that this name also indicates "a great heiau."

The definition of *heiau ma'o* given by Emerson recalls an event observed on O'ahu in December 1786 by the English captains Portlock and Dixon. The latter writes in his journal:

On the 14th, we perceived the natives very busily employed on the hill, at the South East extreme of the island; and by noon on the 15th, their work was so far advanced, that we could plainly discern they were erecting a house, though the distance from us was very considerable. [1789, 103]

Portlock writes on 12 December:

I had observed the natives building this house a day or two before the priest pointed it out to me, and had seen people constantly going up towards it loaded, probably with offerings to their different deities. Towards noon I could see, with the help of a glass, that the house was nearly finished, and the natives were covering it with red cloth [n.b.]. [1789, 162]

At that time a taboo begins. The entire population gathers around the house on the mountain, and no canoes appear in the bay. On 17 December Portlock "observed the natives uncovering and pulling to pieces their new-built house on the hill; and about eight o'clock several large houses were on fire along shore near the bay" (ibid., 166).

Dixon explains the meaning of these events:

Teereteere [Kahekili, king of Maui and O'ahu—V. V.] had caused the house I have mentioned at the top of the hill, to be built as a kind of repository, or store house, for such articles as the natives might obtain in the course of their traffic with our vessels: when this was compleated, he caused the bay to be tabooed, and convened a general assembly of the inhabitants at the top of this mountain, directing them at the same time, to bring whatever trade they had got, that it might be deposited in his new-erected edifice. This being effected, he found means, on some pretext or other, to appropriate one-half of these stores for his own use. [1789, 106]

Thus it is likely that the *heiau ma'o* is a temporary temple built for the king each time he wishes to receive a *ho'okupu*, that is, gifts offered by his subordinates as a sign of homage and allegiance.

'I'ī recounts an event similar to that witnessed by Dixon and Portlock. In 1817 two ships bearing Argentine mutineers arrive in Hawaii, where the crews spend a considerable sum.

While the ship and those who had stolen her were at Napoopoo [district of Kona, island of Hawai'i—V. V.], the king, realizing that hundreds of dollars were

being poured into the area, built two houses thatched with green ti leaves for
the money that the natives of the place were expected to give him. He received a
heap of money in that gift-giving, which was a customary thing. He was clever
in getting money by such planning and through his hospitality to strangers.
[1963, 129]

'Ī'ī does not say that the house in question is a temple, but he indicates that
building it is an ancient custom. Ellis, with quite a few other Europeans,
confirms that the construction of this house by the king and the very high
ranking nobles is a privilege that survived the abolition of the traditional
religious system (cf. Ellis 1842, 418–19; cf. Stewart 1839, 104).

Another class of temples belonging to the king is constituted by the *hale
hui 'ili mai' a*, or simply *hale 'ili mai' a*, which lodge the sorcery deities belonging to the king (Kālaipāhoa, Kihawahine, etc.). These deities, which
enable him to defend himself against sorcerers and secretly strike transgressors and rebels, are often forms of Kāne or at any rate are associated
with this god (cf. Valeri 1982b). They acquire a growing importance in
Kamehameha's time, especially during his stays in Honolulu (1809–12)
and Kailua (1813–19), since they progressively replace the war gods as a
means of political control (Valeri 1982b; Ii 1963, 58, 91; Kamakau 1964,
135; 1961, 179–80).

Finally, I must mention two other royal temples: the *hale poki* and the
kūkoa'e. The first is the royal mausoleum (of which Hale o Keawe is an
example), where the bones of the kings are housed (Malo 1951, 106; Ii
1963, 13); the second is the most important of the temples or huts where
the king purifies himself (Malo 1951, 151–52; see below, p. 227).[22]

The Temple System

From a functional point of view, most of the temples considered above can
be divided into two major classes: the first contains the temples predominantly associated with war (*heiau kaua*), and the second contains temples
where rites to "produce growth" (*ho'oūluulu* or *ho'oūlu*) are performed.
This second class in turn comprises three subclasses: temples for "producing the growth" of agricultural food (*heiau ho'oūluulu 'ai*), temples for
"producing the growth of rain" (*heiau ho'oūluulu ua*), and temples for
"producing the growth of fish" (*heiau ho'oūluulu i'a*).

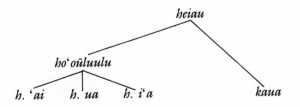

Each class is primarily associated with one or more of the major gods. Thus temples for war and fishing are associated with Kū, while those connected with agriculture are primarily associated with Lono and Kāne.

We have seen, however, that Kū and his temples are not associated exclusively with war and that they also function to ensure the prosperity and fertility of the kingdom. In reality, war—for reasons I noted while studying the political system—is the necessary condition for all other activities. Consequently Kū, precisely because of his privileged relationship to war, contains *in potentia* all peaceful activities that are made possible by conquest and victory. Thus he can be invoked to ensure the fertility of women and the land, to "stabilize" the kingdom and give it peace, to ward off disease, and so forth.

The correlation between war and the creative results that emerge from victory explains why Kū appears in two main forms, Kūkāʻilimoku (or the equivalents, Kūhoʻoneʻenuʻu, Kūkeoloʻewa, etc.) and Kūnuiākea. The first form is more properly associated with war, the second with its transcendence following victory (see below, part 3). Correlatively, there are temples associated primarily with Kūkāʻilimoku (*hale o Kāʻili*) and those predominantly associated with Kūnuiākea (see the demonstration of this thesis in Valeri 1982b).

For example, the temple of Puʻukoholā is a specimen of a *hale o Kāʻili* (Wilkes 1845, 4:506; cf. Stokes, n.d., GR 1, box 9.48), while Hikiau temple at Kealakekua, the most important temple in the Kona district and at times on the entire island of Hawaiʻi, is an example of a temple primarily associated with Kūnuiākea (cf. King 1967, 621, cf. 516, 506). I have shown elsewhere (Valeri 1982b) that this second type of temple is also associated with Lono, since it is precisely the activities connected with this god (agriculture, reproduction, etc.) that are made possible by the victory and transcendence of war that Kūnuiākea symbolizes. (I will return to these points; they are mentioned here only to explain the existence of two classes of *luakini* associated with Kū.)

It seems that on the whole the hierarchy of temple types corresponds to that of the major gods.

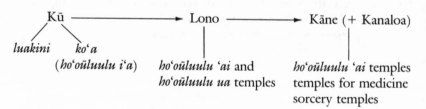

I should note that this system of correspondences between gods and temple types is valid mostly for the island of Hawaiʻi. With Kamehameha's conquest of the archipelago it became generalized throughout the group.

However, some traces of a different system exist, especially on the island of Kaua'i. If we can believe the list of temples on that island compiled by Thrum (1907b), in fact, the *luakini po'okanaka* there were usually consecrated to Kāne[23] and sometimes to Kanaloa[24]—not to Kū, as on Hawai'i. Thrum's list includes only one *po'okanaka* temple explicitly consecrated to Kū. Even Maui, as culturally close as it was to Hawai'i, had temples for human sacrifice whose main god was Kāne (HEN, 1:197; cf. 199–201; Fornander 1916–20, 4:287). Thus, on Kaua'i at least, Kāne and Kanaloa seem to have been the dominant gods. In any case, we are obliged in this study to analyze the only system that is truly known, that is, the one that became generalized from the island of Hawai'i.

Since, as I have shown, temple types are hierarchized, the hierarchical position of an individual temple depends in the first place on the type to which it belongs. A second criterion for establishing its hierarchical position is the rank of its owner. However, one type—the *luakini*—belongs exclusively to the king and his closest associates (Malo 1951, 160–61; Kamakau 1976, 129). This is because, by controlling the *luakini* rituals, which make possible inferior rituals by which inferior hierarchical positions are reproduced, the king can effectively encompass the entire hierarchy.

The *hale o Lono* (cf. Malo 1951, 176; Kamakau 1976, 129) and *ko'a* types can belong to the rest of the nobility and—especially the latter—to some commoners. However, the king owns the most important temples of these types in each district (cf. Malo 1951, 189; Kamakau 1976, 129–30). Only *mua* shrines are permitted to everyone, and thus this unmarked temple is the only one that all commoners may build.

On the basis of the above, it is possible to propose the model of the temple hierarchy in table 4. It must be emphasized that this model is too simple and conceals some ambiguities. For example, the *ko'a* are doubtless associated with Kū, who is the hierarchically superior god, but the rank of the principal *ko'a*, which apparently belongs to the king (cf. Kamakau 1976, 130; K. Kamakau, 1919–20, 35; Malo 1951, 152), is not clear relative to the other royal temples. Nevertheless, since fishing rites (notably those involving the '*ōpelu* fish, at least in the version given by K. Kamakau) are similar to the *luakini* temple rites, and since fishing and war are closely associated (cf. Handy 1972, 15–16), it is legitimate to suppose that the royal *ko'a* is close to the *luakini* in rank. Moreover, the yearly rituals for the *aku* fish are performed in the main *luakini* temples (Manby 1929, 39; Bell 1929–30, 1:62; Menzies 1920, 72–73), which therefore function at that time as *ko'a*.

The rank of Kāne's temples is also uncertain. If, however, it is permitted to generalize from the arrangement of the royal temples in Honolulu and Kailua during the period 1809–19, we can suppose that they occupy the third place in the hierarchy, at least insofar as they are connected with sorcery and medicine. In fact the temples that in Honolulu and Kailua are

TABLE 4   Model of the Temple Hierarchy

	Gods Principally Attached to Each Temple Type			
	Kū		Lono	Kāne (Kanaloa)
Principal types of temples	Luakini[1]	Koʻa	Hale o Lono Other hoʻouluulu ʻai temples	Medical temples Sorcery temples Agricultural temples
Rank of types of temples	Ia	Ib	II	III
Proprietor's rank (also expressed by his rank of his ʻaumakua and of his mua) — 1 (king) 2 3 4 n				

Note: Shaded areas indicate royal temples.

[1] The *luakini* are hierarchized, as is indicated, for instance, by the fact that each of the districts into which an island is divided is represented by its principal *luakini*. On the island of Hawaiʻi, these *luakini* are Hikiau in Kona, Punaluʻu in Kaʻū, Wahaʻula in Puna, Kānoa in Hilo, Honuaʻula in Hāmākua, and Moʻokini in Kohala (Ii 1963, 160).

called *hale hui*, or *hale hui ʻili maiʻa*, contained deities connected with Kāne (for example, the Kālaipāhoa).[25] Now, it is clear that in these localities these temples occupied the third place, following the *luakini* and the *hale o Lono*. The same can be said of the temples for medicine where forms of Kāne (for example, Kāneikōleamoku)[26] were worshiped (cf. Valeri 1982b).

It should also be recalled that the same function can be connected with different gods. For example, medical temples connected with Lono (Lonopuhā) or Kū (coupled with Hina) exist. In the same vein, Kāne and even Kū can be relevant to agriculture. Conversely, several functions may be linked to the same god. But a hierarchy of attributes exists for each god, and in my model I have considered only the principal functions of the major gods.

I must also mention that the lists of temples compiled by Thrum, Stokes, Bennett (concerning Kauaʻi), and McAllister (concerning Oʻahu) give the impression that another complicating factor is involved in the temple system. Some temples or altars are linked both with a territorial segment and with the aliʻi or priest who controls it.[27] Control of an area thus seems to be exercised through control of the temple connected with it. This would, moreover, represent an extension to lower levels of the prin-

ciple operative at the top of society, since, as we have seen, the king controls a district of an island by controlling its principal *luakini*.
    But many temples are simply chapels associated with their proprietors
and their courts. Thus the nine temples situated in Ka'awaloa (Kona district, Hawai'i) at the beginning of the nineteenth century were associated
not with territories, but simply with the habitations of the most important
ali'i of King Kamehameha's court (Lisiansky 1814, 109).
    The details I have just enumerated are so many limits on the validity of
the model in table 4. Nevertheless, I believe this model offers a valid pre-
sentation of the ideal background justifying the concrete temple hierarchy.
At any rate, on this point as on many others we are reduced to speculation,
for the actual relations between individual temples are very poorly known
to us.
    But two facts essential to my argument are certain. On the one hand,
the temples of type Ia belong exclusively to the king and the heads of the
principal districts who are the delegates of royal authority (Kamakau
1976, 129); on the other hand, the highest-ranking temples of the other
types also belong to the king (Kamakau 1976, 129–30; Malo 1951, 189).
Thus it is clear that kingship encompasses and guides all activities and
makes them possible in two ways: by its association with the main temple
in each type and by its association with the entire principal type (*luakini*),
which makes all the other types possible. By being at the head of the
temple hierarchy, and therefore of the hierarchy of sacrifices, the king reproduces society as a consistent system, as a totality.
    Since this totality is the result of a process, it has a temporal dimension
that can be apprehended on the level of ritual performance. The royal ritual
is in fact a process that makes each type of temple—and therefore each activity—possible on the basis of the god type presupposed by it.
    Each year, at the beginning of the eight-month period in which sacri-
fices are made and temples thus are open, the process begins at the main
luakini temple, which corresponds to Kū and to the human realities he
typifies. If the consecration of this temple is successful, the king is able to
consecrate the main agricultural temple connected with Lono and the corresponding activities. Following the royal reproduction of the hierarchy of
divine types (or at least of the core of this hierarchy), the concrete temple
hierarchy, corresponding to more or less adequate, more or less "pure" social realizations of these types, is reproduced. One after the other, according to rank, the king's subordinates build their temples (Malo 1951, 176;
Kamakau 1976, 129) and thereby reproduce themselves as social beings.
    An analogous process seems to occur in the fishing rites; the ritual of
the main *ko'a*, which belongs to the king, makes possible the reconsecration of subordinate *ko'a* and, consequently, fishing activities.[28]
    This process of reproduction of the social hierarchy through the temple

TABLE 5   *Heiau* Whose Existence Is Documented by Archaeology or Tradition

Island	Number of Heiau	Sources
Hawai'i	177	Bennett 1930, 153–54
Maui	221	Bennett 1930, 154–56
Kaho'olawe	2	Bennett 1930, 160
Lāna'i	21	Emory 1924, 61–69
Moloka'i	107	Bennett 1930, 159
O'ahu	165	McAllister 1933, 8; Thrum counted 108 of them (1916, 91)
Kaua'i	122	Bennett 1931, 61–69
Ni'ihau	1	Bennett 1930, 157
Total	816	

Note: These numbers do not include *ko'a* and *pōhaku* altars and, especially for Hawai'i and Ni'ihau, are probably lower than in reality.

hierarchy is repeated in each district if the king decides to tour his kingdom. After consecrating the main temples of the district where he resides, he moves from one to another, reconsecrating the *luakini* in each one and, very likely, the entire temple hierarchy that depends on it (cf. Malo 1951, 189; Ii 1963, 137; see table 5). It is to this ritual process by which the king reproduces society that we must now turn our attention.

PART 3
THE SACRIFICE OF THE
HAWAIIAN KING

En bref, c'est tout un raccourci parfaitement coordonné d'un nombre considérable de rituels dont ailleurs nous ne retrouvons pas ni d'exemple aussi typique, ni pareilles et aussi naturelles organisations.
Mauss 1968–69, 2:191

INTRODUCTION

Der liebe Gott steckt im Detail.
A. Warburg, quoted by Gombrich 1970, 13

Remarks on Method

In the preceding two parts I have attempted to give a coherent picture of the Hawaiian ideological system by considering all available information. In this third part I shall use the knowledge thus gained to analyze intensively a group of texts that describe the ritual cycle that conceptually encompasses and makes possible all other ritual acts. I hope in this way to confirm the accuracy of my reconstruction of the ideological system and at the same time to account for its most important means of reproduction.

The method used in this part of the book is dictated by the nature of the evidence. This is in the form of texts in the Hawaiian language by David Malo, Kēlou Kamakau, John Papa ʻĪʻī, and S. M. Kamakau. In addition, there is an anonymous text that exists only in translation (in Wilkes 1845, 4:506–8). There are also occasional references to parts of the ritual cycle in other texts, particularly legends and historical narratives.

Apart from the one published by Wilkes, all the texts exist both in the Hawaiian original and in translation. It is impossible, however, to rely on the existing translations of Malo's and K. Kamakau's accounts, since they are often inaccurate and misleading—particularly N. Emerson's translation of Malo. ʻĪʻī's and S. M. Kamakau's texts were excellently translated by M. K. Pukui and edited by D. Barrère, but this does not absolve us from using the originals whenever necessary.

The most important sources are the accounts of Malo and K. Kamakau, since they are the oldest (having been written between 1835 and 1840) and the most detailed; moreover, they are the work of witnesses. ʻĪʻī was also a witness, at least up to a certain point; however, he wrote fifty years after the last rites he observed had taken place, so he is not as accurate and detailed on all points.

On first inspection these basic sources often seem to be at odds. It is therefore impossible to construct a coherent account of the ritual without first establishing the significance of these differences. This implies that each of the principal texts must be considered separately and the elementary rules of source criticism be applied. In sum, it is evident from the above that the method to be followed is (1) to rely on the original Hawaiian texts instead of translations, except when the translation proves accurate; (2) to give a privileged status to the oldest accounts: that is, those of Malo and K. Kamakau; (3) to carefully evaluate the differences between the sources and to resist the temptation to arbitrarily construct a single account of the rites patched together from different sources.

Only by following these three rules does it become possible to establish the facts and therefore proceed to their analysis. However, it would be cumbersome always to give an account of the process by which I have gone from the texts to a coherent description and interpretation of the ritual action described by them. Therefore, I have decided to present the process in full only for the most important ritual of the cycle, that is, the *luakini* temple ritual. This choice is justified not only by the intrinsic importance of the ritual, but also because the texts seem to agree less on it than on other rituals.

Thus, each segment of the ritual is treated in the following way:

1. First, I give its description by the two main sources, Malo and K. Kamakau. In addition, I give Wilkes's text, because it usually complements the first two and is often very close to K. Kamakau's, which it therefore confirms. For some rites I add 'Ī'ī's account because it is particularly enlightening and trustworthy. Normally, however, 'Ī'ī's account, along with those provided by S. M. Kamakau and other writers, is considered only in the interpretive part of my text.

Malo's and K. Kamakau's accounts are summarized in great detail and sometimes paraphrased. Except when otherwise indicated, I give the texts of prayers and speeches in full in my own translation.

2. After what the basic sources actually say has been established as far as possible, I interpret their content. The interpretation usually involves two steps: first, I evaluate the differences between sources, then I attempt to establish whether they share a common logic and therefore whether there is a "grammar" underlying all versions of the ritual. This often brings me to discuss certain fundamental symbols or clusters of symbols used in ritual, relying on all the evidence available, other rituals, or even extraritual facts.

To those who object to this analytic method, finding it too cumbersome, I answer only that there is unfortunately no other way to establish the facts and that some of the most rewarding results are obtained when recalcitrant details and differences between the sources are seriously taken into consideration instead of being conveniently swept under the carpet.

Unlike the *luakini* temple ritual, the Makahiki festival—the other major component of the cycle—is not treated with this step-by-step procedure. This is because, as I have already noted, my analysis is less focused on it, but especially because the sources are in greater agreement about it than about the *kapu luakini*. Nevertheless, the distinction between the reconstruction of the facts—or, more exactly, of what the sources say—and their analysis is preserved in this part of the book as well.

As for the analysis itself, the reader will have surmised by now that it is of the structural kind, tempered, however, by as much skepticism and good sense as I am capable of. I believe that this form of analysis is the best possible one for the data at our disposal and that in fact it is dictated by them and is a natural extension of the methodological rules outlined above.

Indeed, in the absence of detailed information on the pragmatic and referential dimensions of the ritual and in the presence of texts that are mostly ideal representations of its different possible realizations, the only sensible analytical choice seems to be to reconstruct recurrent patterns that establish relations of substitution and combination between the elements of ritual. In other words, it seems possible to isolate certain paradigmatic and syntagmatic relations underlying our texts. I am well aware, of course, that in ritual, in contrast to what happens in discursive language, those two kinds of relations can be distinguished only to a limited extent (cf. Valeri 1981b). Nevertheless, I believe that a difference of *degree* between discursive language and ritual should not be confused with an *absolute* difference. One of the virtues of the Hawaiian ritual texts is that they show that the idea, advanced by such authors as Bloch (1974) and Rappaport (1979, 173–221), that ritual implies no choice and therefore has no semantic meaning is false. From my point of view such a position implies that ritual has no paradigmatic structure at all. It implies, further, a purely quantitative theory of meaning, based on the notion of information as the inverse of probability of occurrence. It therefore justifies an analysis of ritual that is purely pragmatic, indexical, and ultimately done in terms of "political power." In this view the performers seem to relate to ritual as to an unanalyzed and unanalyzable whole, without the intervening mediation of the understanding.

Such a view is wrong in principle because it fails to recognize that meaning is also "pattern recognition," that is, perception of relations of equivalence and of combination in context (cf. Tambiah 1979, 132). But it is also patently wrong when measured against the Hawaiian ritual texts I analyze here. Indeed, precisely because I have seriously considered the differences between all texts and the logic of each one, I am able to show that they reflect choices made on the basis of a system of paradigmatic and syntagmatic relations they all share. Moreover, these alternatives are not equivalent and determine, at least to some extent, variations in meaning.

In sum, I have attempted to approach ritual as structuralists have approached myth: the principle of analysis is that there is not one "true" version and that all versions must be considered insofar as they document that ritual presupposes a system of possibilities, each of which can be "transformed" into all the others.

The Calendar

In order to understand the annual and monthly ritual cycles, a familiarity with the calendar on which they are based is indispensable. According to Zepelinokalokuokamaile, P. Buck's and K. Emory's informant, *lā*, "day," includes the period from dawn to evening (*ao*) as well as the following night (*po*). *Lā* thus begins at dawn but takes its name from the following night (Emory, n.d.), since it is the phases of the moon that allow one to distinguish one day from another. This theory seems generally to be confirmed by the description of rituals given by David Malo and K. Kamakau.

The "month" (*mahina* or *malama*, "moon") is divided into three principal lunar phases (*ano*—cf. Malo 1951, 31) of ten days each, called *anahulu* (PE, 22). Each "day" (or "night") of the month has a name, so that there are thirty named days in one month.

According to Malo (1951, 31–33), the days of the lunar month are as follows:

1. Hilo ⎫
2. Hoaka ⎬ *kapu-Kū*
3. Ku-kāhi ⎭
4. Ku-lua
5. Ku-kolu
6. Ku-pau
7. 'Ole-ku-kāhi
8. 'Ole-ku-lua
9. 'Ole-ku-kolu
10. 'Ole-pau (or 'Ole-ku-pau)
11. Huna
12. Mōhalu ⎫ *kapu-hua*
13. Hua ⎬
14. Akua
15. Hoku
16. Māhea-lani
17. Ku-lua
18. Lā'au-Ku-kāhi
19. Lā'au-Ku-lua
20. Lā'au-pau

21. 'Ole-ku-kāhi
22. 'Ole-ku-lua
23. 'Ole-pau   } *kapu-kāloa*
24. Kāloa-ku-kāhi }
25. Kāloa-ku-lua
26. Kāloa-pau
27. Kāne   } *kapu-Kāne*
28. Lono   }
29. Mauli
30. Muku

There is some question how this set of thirty named days applies to the lunar month, which lasts approximately twenty-nine and a half days. The major sources (Malo, *Mooolelo Hawaii* of 1838, S. M. Kamakau, and Kepelino) are silent on the subject, but a statement by Zepelinokalokuokamaile suggests a solution. According to him, if the new moon (Hilo) appears on the evening of the thirtieth day (Muku), the day lasts only for the diurnal period in which the planet is invisible (Muku means "cut short"). In other words, the day lasts only about twelve hours instead of twenty-four.

It follows that (1) in this case the rule that calls for the name of the day to correspond with that of the following night is violated; (2) the new month begins twenty-nine and a half days after the beginning of the preceding month.

At dawn after the Hilo night the usual rule, which calls for the day to be given the name of the following night, is again in force (Emory, n.d.). Consequently the second day of the month (Hoaka) begins only half a day after the beginning of the month. Or, to put it differently, the first "day" of the month in fact shrinks to a night (Hilo). When this happens, the last day of the month, Muku, lasts twenty-four hours. Hence this month, like its predecessor, lasts twenty-nine and a half days. The following month will again last twenty-nine and a half days because the duration of Muku will be limited to the diurnal part.

It seems to me, then, that if Zepelinokalokuokamaile is right, *every* Hawaiian month must last twenty-nine and a half days.[1] A month in which the last "day" is reduced to the diurnal period alternates with a month in which the first "day" is reduced to the nocturnal period. This is an elegant way of making the thirty names of "days" in the civil month correspond to the lunar month.

Yet this explanation seems to contradict the statements of missionaries Dibble (1909, 90) and Richards (1973, 30–31; cf. Wilkes 1845, 4:43, and N. Emerson in Malo 1951, 35, n. 5), according to whom a month of thirty days regularly alternates with a month of twenty-nine days.[2] It is possible, however, that they came to this conclusion because they did not understand that for the Hawaiians a "day" can last about half of a twenty-four-hour period. Note also that Fornander's informants (1916–20, 6:120, n. 2) deny the existence of a system in which months of different lengths alternate. Fornander, however, falsely deduces from this that the thirty-day month has a sidereal or solar basis and not a lunar one (1878–80, 1:120, n. 1; cf. Daggett in Kalakaua 1888, 159). This opinion seems difficult to defend, since at least some of the names of the days refer to phases of the moon (cf. Malo 1951, 31–32; Kepelino 1932, 80–83).

At any rate, the ritual monthly calendar is undoubtedly lunar. In each month are four periods, called *kapu pule*, that men must spend in the temples. The first *kapu pule* is called *kapu-Kū*. It begins on the first night of the lunar month and ends at dawn of the fourth day; thus it lasts two days and three nights. The second is called *kapu-hua*. It begins the night of the twelfth day and ends at dawn of the fourteenth. The third is called *kapu-kāloa*. It begins the night of the twenty-third day and ends at dawn of the twenty-fifth. The fourth is called *kapu-Kāne*. It begins at dusk of the twenty-seventh day and ends at dawn of the twenty-ninth. This is the calendar given by the *Mooolelo Hawaii* (1838, 38–39; Pogue 1858, 17–18), Malo (1951, 32–33), Kamakau (1976, 18), and Kepelino (1932, 98–112). Kepelino, however, adds the night of the fourteenth day to the *kapu-hua*.

For all sources except Kepelino, there are nine taboo nocturnal periods and five taboo diurnal periods in a month. This is confirmed by European voyagers (see, above all, Vancouver 1801, 5:25, 37–39, 56; Campbell 1967, 95, 127; Kotzebue 1821a, 1:331–32).[3] Alexander gives a different system without, however, indicating his sources: the *kapu-Kū* lasts from the third to the fifth; the *kapu-hua* from the thirteenth to the fourteenth; the *kapu-kāloa* (or, as he says, *kapu Kanaloa*) from the twenty-fourth to the twenty-fifth. On the *kapu-Kāne* Alexander is in agreement with the other sources (in Malo 1951, 153, n. 1).

Although the monthly ritual calendar follows the phases of the moon, the sidereal year is not unknown (see Richards 1973, 30, whose informant was Hoapili, Kamehameha's last astronomer; cf. Wilkes 1845, 4:41) and plays a role in determining the beginning of the year (Makahiki). At least this is according to 'Ī'ī, who writes that it was marked by the first rising of the Pleiades after sunset (1963, 72; cf. Alexander 1891, 50; Fornander 1916–20, 6:330).

One tradition (collected, it is true, by Mary Pukui—that is, in this century) states that in the Puna district (island of Hawai'i) there were four stone markers indicating the positions of the sun during the year: "Hawaiians in the vicinity say that these [markers—V. V.] were used to track the sun's limits north and south in order to mark the seasons in addition to use of seasonal migrations of the plover on their course north and south during the year" (Johnson and Mahelona 1975, 84). Thus it seems that the solar year was recognized as well.

In conclusion, the Hawaiians had two years: a lunar year of 354 days, comprising twelve months of twenty-nine and a half days, and a sidereal (and solar) year of 365 days. To make them correspond, an intercalation was necessary. According to Dibble (1909, 90) and Richards (1973, 30–31; cf. Wilkes 1845, 4:43; Freycinet 1978, 70; and Byron 1826, 11–12), a thirteenth month was periodically intercalated, but they do not tell us at what interval.[4] Alexander conjectures, without elaborating, however, that three lunar months were added in the course of eight years (in Malo 1951, 36, n. 6).

To verify this (or any other) hypothesis, one should have at hand a relatively long series of dates that would record year after year in the Gregorian calendar the performance of a single rite associated with the same month and day of the Hawaiian lunar calendar. But not many such dates exist. The study of the dates on which, according to some European observers, some of the annual Makahiki rites fell and those of festivals that over several years commemorated the anniversary of Kamehameha's death enables us to demonstrate the existence of intercalations but not to ascertain whether they were made according to a fixed formula.[5]

The most likely hypothesis, and the one that best accounts for the data, is that the intercalations were made ad hoc, when the difference between the first rising of the Pleiades after sunset and the phase of the lunar month theoretically associated with it was noticeable. In practice, a thirteenth month was probably intercalated between the last month (called Māhoe-Hope) of the season during which the temples were open and the first month (called 'Ikuwā) of the New Year's festival season.

The main Hawaiian sources do not mention the intercalary month, however. This might be explained by the fact that they were compiled at a time when the traditional system had been displaced by the Gregorian system introduced by the missionaries. Moreover, even traditionally, only some specialists had knowledge of it (cf. Kepelino 1932, 84).

It is also likely that different systems of intercalation were used on different islands of the archipelago. This perhaps helps explain the considerable differences in their calendars. Although the names of the months were identical everywhere (except on Kaua'i, where three names not found elsewhere were used—cf. Makemson 1941, 97–98), on each island they corresponded to different periods of the year (cf. Malo 1951, 33–36; Kepelino 1932, 80–113; Bryan 1965, 251–56; Makemson 1941, 288; Fornander 1916–20, 6:330–32; Handy 1972, 33–36). Also, the sources are sometimes in considerable disagreement. Thus, for example, according to Malo (1951, 30) the month of Welehu should have corresponded to our November, but according to Kamakau (1976, 13–14) it corresponded to a period between our months of March and April! In my exposition of the rites I will follow the calendar given by Malo, which was the one used in the western part of the island of Hawai'i, because the main descriptions of the ritual cycle refer to this area.

The year was divided not only into months, but also into seasons, which are part of the annual ritual cycle to be discussed later in detail. As I have just mentioned, there was a season of eight months when the temples were open and one could make human sacrifices and wage war. During the rest of the year (beginning in the month of 'Ikuwā) the rites for the New Year (Makahiki) took place, which forbade, at least theoretically, war and human sacrifice. However, this opposition between the Makahiki season and the temple ritual season is less clear-cut than is generally thought, and it could happen, moreover, that wars continued during the period of the year officially reserved for the New Year's festival (cf. Valeri 1982b, 24).

Let it also be recalled that the word *makahiki* has several referents: the whole year as a temporal unit (Malo MS, 146; Bryan 1965, 252, 253);[6] the period of the New Year's festival sensu lato, which comprises four months (Malo 1951, 141); and the New Year's festival sensu stricto, which lasts twenty-three days (Malo 1951, 145). Additionally, any rite annually repeated on a fixed date is considered a "Makahiki taboo." Thus the annual rites that make it possible to fish for *aku* (bonito or skipjack, *Katsuwonus pelamys*) and *'ōpelu* (mackerel scad, *Decapterus pinnulatus*) and that take place during the months of Kā'elo and Hinaia-'ele'ele (or Ka'aōna), respectively, are both considered "Makahiki rites" (cf. Malo 1951, 209), that is, annual rites.

As Vancouver writes, the taboo placed alternately on fishing for *aku* (from the month of Hinaia-'ele'ele to the month of Kā'elo) and *'ōpelu* (during the other months) was "an additional means of dividing their time, or, perhaps, properly speaking, their seasons" (1801, 5:31; cf. Malo 1951, 208–10; K. Kamakau 1919–20, 30–34; Titcomb 1972, 42–44).

Divisions of the year based on astronomical and especially climatic factors also exist. The most important of these is the opposition between the dry season (*kau*), lasting six months, which begins when the Pleiades set at dawn, and a wet period (*ho'oilo*), which occupies the other six months of the year and begins when the Pleiades rise at sunset (Malo 1951, 30; Kepelino 1932, 84, 96; Handy 1972, 33–36). The New Year's festival falls during the wet period.

Below is a list of the months and seasons based on Malo (MS, 39 ff.; 1951, 30–33, 141).

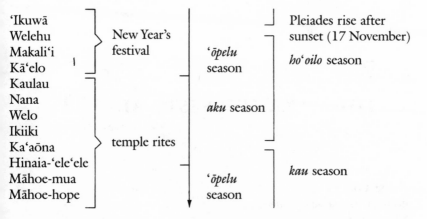

Since the lunar year is not in synchrony with the sidereal year it is clear that the Hawaiian months fall in different Gregorian months from one year to the next. It is therefore meaningless to attempt to give exact equivalents to the names of the Hawaiian months, as our sources do.

7
THE MAKAHIKI FESTIVAL

A hiki a ola,
no nei make ia oe e Lono.
Salvation comes
from this death by you, o Lono
Fornander 1878–80, 1:93–94

Cet homme appartenait-il à la double énigme du désordre et de l'ordre?
Etait-il concentrique à l'infraction et à la répression?
Hugo 1951, 882

The Makahiki Festival

The ritual cycle of the Makahiki (New Year's festival) begins in the month of ʻIkuwā, the last month of the dry season (*kau*), and continues during the first three months of the wet season (*hoʻoilo*): Welehu, Makaliʻi, and Kāʻelo.

The *Kapu-Kū* of ʻIkuwā

The first rite of the cycle is performed at the beginning of the month of ʻIkuwā (*kapu-Kū*).[1] On the evening of Hilo, the king places a rag (*welu*) before the *luakini*. This object represents the old year and thus signals that it is reaching its end (K. Kamakau 1919–20, 35; Malo MS, 146).

Then what appears to be the shortened *luakini* temple service, performed each month during the Kū period, takes place. Since we will study the more developed form of this service below, it is superfluous to treat the shortened one here. It is clear in any event that its performance in this context constitutes a kind of farewell to the gods, to whom a last sacrifice (including, notably, pigs, coconuts, and bananas) is consecrated.

The *Kuapola* Rite and the Rising of the Pleiades

The second rite of the Makahiki cycle is called *kapu kuapola*, according to ʻĪʻī, who furnished the most detailed description of it (1963, 72). In his

200

account, the date of the rite is determined by the first rising of the Pleiades (Huhui or Makali'i) after sunset. He claims that this always happens during the month of 'Ikuwā, which he identifies with October in the Gregorian calendar.

The rite lasts from the sunset until late at night. The king and his priests gather at the *kuahu* altar in the *luakini* temple and await the appearance of the Pleiades. When they become visible, a priest rises and "calls" each month (*malama*, "moon") by name with this formula: "O [name of the month], sacred will be (*e la'a*) your feeding (*hānai*), your nocturnal feeding (*hānai pō*), your diurnal feeding (*hānai ao*), until the rising (*hiki*) of the Uliuli star, until the rising of the Melemele star." This rite is named *hānai* "feeding."[2] Before the name of each month is uttered some coconuts are broken. This action is called *wāhi ka niu o kuapola*, "break the *kuapola* nuts." When the *kuapola* rite is concluded, the *kuahu* altar of the *luakini* temple is closed.

Almost certainly the coconuts employed in this rite are green. This is suggested by the fact that the water of young coconuts, signifying life, is used in a variety of rituals of purification and renewal (cf. Pukui in Handy 1972, 174). For instance, before sacrificing, the king purifies his hands with the water of a green coconut (Brigham, n.d.; Emerson in HEN, 1:530). This water is also used to wash the images of the gods before ritually decorating and anointing them (cf. Kamakau 1964, 136), that is, transforming them into receptacles of the gods.

The formula reported by 'I'ī seems to imply that the breaking of the ritual coconuts lasts until the Uliuli and Melemele stars have risen that night. Unfortunately, Uliuli has not been identified (PE, 340), but Melemele is probably the name for Orion's belt (Johnson and Mahelona 1975, 17), which rises about two hours after the Pleiades. Must we deduce, then, that the rite of the coconuts lasts as long as the interval between the rising of the Pleiades and that of Orion?

The association of the Pleiades (Makali'i) with Uliuli is confirmed by the following lines of a chant, published in the newspaper *Ka Hae Hawaii* and translated by Johnson and Mahelona (1975, 41):

With Uliuli and Polapola
the Pleiades [Makali'i] are victorious.

Here the "victory" is a metaphor for the rising of these stars. These lines also offer an interesting clue to the meaning of the term, *kapu kuapola*. In fact, *kuapola* could be formed by the word *kua*, an abbreviation of *akua*, "god" (cf. PE, 155), and *Pola*, which designates the star also called Polapola (PE, 312). *Kapu kuapola* would thus mean the "rite of the god [of the star] Pola." Since, as the two lines cited above demonstrate, the rising of the star Pola occurs in conjunction with that of the Pleiades, the fact that the rite greeting the appearance of the latter is called *kapu kuapola* becomes understandable. It is true that the star Pola is not mentioned in the prayer given by ʻĪʻī; however, this star is always implicitly paired with Melemele (PE, 312), which is mentioned in the prayer.

K. Kamakau (1919–20, 39) describes the *kuapola* rite somewhat differently than ʻĪʻī. According to him, on the night of Mōhalu (the first night of the *kapu-hua*) of the month of ʻIkuwā, the king and priests enter the *luakini* temple, inside which are found two men. The high priest approaches the latter, takes two coconuts, and prays with these words: "O Lono [of] wide expanse (Lononuiākea), here are the coconuts; give life to your care-taker (*kahu*) and to the land (*ʻāina*) and to the men (*kanaka*)." After consecrating this sacrifice (called *kaumaha* and also *mōhai*) and throwing the coconuts to the two men, he sits down and prays together with them. Then the two men rise, sing a chant (*kāhea*)[3] aloud, and "feed" (*hānai*) the stars and the moon.

It is likely that the two officiants mentioned by K. Kamakau chant the prayer cited by ʻĪʻī, since it refers to the "feeding" of the moons of the year and associated stars (cf. note 2). The king and his priests leave the temple at the conclusion of this rite. Then the people ratify the success of the rite by saying, "The king's coconut is good; there is life for the land (*ola no ka ʻāina*)." At dawn the king, the priest, and one other man return to the *luakini* to repeat the same rite. That evening the taboo is lifted and the temple is closed (K. Kamakau 1919–20, 39).

Malo refers to this rite as well. Both he and K. Kamakau also mention that it is repeated exactly twenty-nine days later, during the *kapu-hua* of the month of Welehu. For Malo, the first time "the king's coconuts" are broken (*nahā*) (MS, 146), the second time "the coconuts of the commoners (*maka ʻāinana*) and of all the *aliʻi* [the King excepted]" are broken (ibid., 147). For K. Kamakau, instead, "the coconuts of the priest and the *kanaka* [clients and servants of the aliʻi]" (p. 39) are broken (*wāhi*) in the second occurrence of the rite.

Thus, while for ʻĪʻī the *kuapola* rite takes place only once, on a movable date but always during the month of ʻIkuwā, for Malo and K. Kamakau it occurs twice, on fixed dates and during two consecutive months. Both versions pose some problems.

The thesis put forth by ʻĪʻī is doubly unacceptable. First, given that the twelve-month lunar year lags behind the sidereal year and that the probable system of intercalation involves interpolating one month every two or three years, it is impossible for the rising of the Pleiades always to take place during the month of ʻIkuwā. Second, by establishing a fixed equation between the month of ʻIkuwā and October, ʻĪʻī contradicts an astronomical fact. It is easy to calculate that toward the end of the eighteenth century the Pleiades became visible after nightfall on about 17 November and not in October (cf. Handy 1972, 330; Makemson 1941, 75).

The system described by K. Kamakau and Malo does not encounter the same difficulties because these authors place the two *kuapola* rites on fixed dates in the lunar calendar and do not state that either one is associated with the rising of the Pleiades. However, the absence of any reference to these stars in their version is astonishing—although in another chapter of his book Malo seems to imply that the Pleiades rise at sunset during the month of Welehu (1951, 30).

In sum, 'Ī'ī declares that the Pleiades appear during the month of 'Ikuwā, but Malo states that they appear during the month of Welehu. Both Malo and K. Kamakau describe two identical rites performed during the *kapu-hua* in two successive months. These rites are not said to have a connection with the Pleiades; nevertheless, they seem to resemble the rite that 'Ī'ī associates with the first appearance of this constellation after sunset.

I think that some of the contradictions among these accounts can be overcome if we adopt the following hypothesis. Let us suppose that, since the discrepancy between the sidereal and lunar years is compensated for by the periodic intercalation of a month, the first appearance of the Pleiades in the evening shifts, depending on the year, between the months of 'Ikuwā and Welehu.[4] For example, if, during a given year the Pleiades appear on the seventeenth day of 'Ikuwā, two years later they will appear on the ninth day of Welehu, since the lunar year is approximately eleven days shorter than the sidereal year. Let us then suppose that in the third year a month of thirty days is interpolated between 'Ikuwā and the preceding month, Māhoe-hope (since the latter is at the end of the *kapu pule* season). That year the Pleiades will appear on the nineteenth day of 'Ikuwā. Naturally, interpolations cannot be made only at two-year intervals; there must also now and then be an interpolation after three years. Even more probable are ad hoc interpolations. Nevertheless, the doubling of the *kuapola* rite could be interpreted as an indication that the first appearance of the Pleiades actually falls in either 'Ikuwā or Welehu, depending on the year, and that the rite may be performed at fixed times during the *kapu hua* of these two months in order to measure to what extent the lunar (ritual) year lags behind the sidereal year.

In any event, we will see that a paradigmatic relationship exists between the return of the Pleiades, the return of the god Lono, the return of the southwest winds, and the renewing of nature that marks the beginning of the new year. Ideally, these events should coincide from a calendrical point of view and together mark the beginning of the year.

The Procession of the Makahiki God

According to Malo and K. Kamakau, after the rite of the coconuts the riches (*waiwai*) destined for the king are gathered in each district. This "tribute" (*'auhau*), as Malo calls it (MS, 147, 36.14–15),[5] which consists of bark cloths (*kapa*), skirts (*pā'ū*), loincloths (*malo*), fish, dogs, "and many other things" (1951, 143; K. Kamakau 1919–20, 39), is gathered (*halihali*) by the overseers (*konohiki*) of each district between the eighteenth (according to Malo—the nineteenth, according to K. Kamakau) and the twentieth days of Welehu. In addition to the share destined for the king, each *konohiki* gathers a part (*waiwai maloko*) for his immediate superior, the lord of the district (Malo 1951, 143). During this collection, the gods of each land (*akua 'āina*) cannot remain upright but are placed in a horizontal position, doubtless as a sign of homage to the king, or rather, to his gods.

On the twentieth night of Welehu, all the riches are put together in front of the king's feather god (K. Kamakau 1919–20, 39). This night is extremely taboo; no fire may burn, and absolute silence must reign. The priests pray and then go to sleep.

On the following morning the king, his priest, and his principal favorite (*kanaka punahele nui*), who holds the drum, arrive at the place where the offerings are displayed. Then the king sacrifices a pig to his god. This sacrifice is called *kānaenae*, after the prayer chanted in accompaniment. According to Emerson (1965, 16), this prayer is a eulogy (cf. PE, 118). After it has been uttered, pigs are cooked (*mo'a*) and eaten (K. Kamakau 1919–20, 39). Malo, in contrast, denies that pigs are sacrificed and eaten during this period and maintains that only dog meat is eaten (MS, 147).[6]

According to K. Kamakau, after the meal the priest divides the pile (*pu'u*) of accumulated goods into portions. Then he asks the king, "How did your prayer (*pule*) go?" The king answers him, "Well; there was no rain or noise; it was accomplished in the best conditions." After which he puts an end to the taboos (*ho'onoa*) of this rite.

The redistribution of the goods follows. First, the king's gods receive their portion: one share is given (*kaumaha*) to them in person, but the rest is given to their *kahu*, "keepers" (Malo MS, 147; K. Kamakau 1919–20, 39). Then, in order, are attributed the part of the king's priest, that of the queen, that of the favorites (*punahele*), that of the clients ('*aialo*, "eating in the presence [of the King—V. V.]"—PE, 9), that of the remaining ali'i, and, finally, that of the warriors (*pū'ali*) (Malo MS, 147). Every individual of each category receives according to the number of his followers (Malo MS, 148). Nothing at all is given to the *maka'āinana*, the commoners who produce the goods (ibid.).

During these same days food is prepared for the upcoming festival, which constitutes the Makahiki ritual proper. In addition to the usual foods, which are accumulated in great quantity, sweetened foods or foods mixed with coconut cream are prepared (Malo MS, 147; K. Kamakau 1919–20, 41).

On the evening of the twenty-first day, the "feather gods" are carried in procession, and the following evening the same is done with the "wooden gods" (*akua lā'au*; also called *akua kā'ai*). After the second procession, the priests pray the whole night, and on the morning of the twenty-third day an image of the Makahiki god (*akua Makahiki* or *akua loa*, "long god," or Lonomakua, "Lono the parent," "Lono who feeds"—Malo MS, 148, 149; K. Kamakau 1919–20, 41), is assembled and decorated.

The "Makahiki god" is formed of a pole of *kauila* wood (Fornander 1916–20, 6:205) whose length varies from three and a half meters (Malo MS 147) to five and half meters (Fornander 1916–20, 6:204; cf. Ii 1963, 70) and whose circumference is about twenty-five centimeters. Notches are cut on the pole, and at the top is carved the image of the god (Malo MS, 48). In the sole surviving *akua Makahiki*, only the god's head is carved at the top (cf. Ii 1963, 70; MH, July 1822, 207). A crosspiece (*ke'a*) is attached to the pole, and to it are tied pieces of *pala* (*Marattia douglasii*),[7] feather wreaths, skins of *ka'upu* birds (albatross), and pieces of bark cloth (Malo MS, 48). The description Malo gives of the image of Lonomakua is corroborated by one of Webber's drawings (1779), the descriptions of several voyagers (King 1967, 627; Samwell 1967, 1173; Colnett, n.d., 175ʳ) and other Hawaiian authors (Fornander 1916–20, 6:204, 205; Kamakau 1961, 52–53; Ii 1963, 72), but it includes an element perhaps introduced at the time of Kamehameha: a square cloth that hangs from the crosspiece and, according to Sahlins (1979, 319–20), imitates the sails of Cook's ships.[8]

The fabrication of this image is called *ku-i-kepa'a* ("halt"—PE, 161). N. Emerson explains this name in the following manner:

The application of the word to this use is due to the fact that in going after the tree from which to make the *akua loa*, when the procession, at the head of which was the high priest, bearing a feather-idol, came to where the tree was growing, the priest halted, and, planting the staff that bore the idol in the ground, gave the order *kuikepaa*, and the whole company came to a stand-still. During the felling of the tree and the carving of it to make the idol, the feather-god was always present, the staff that supported it being planted in the ground. [in Malo 1951, 154]

The principal Makahiki god is called *akua loa*, "long god," because he makes a complete tour of the kingdom. But an *akua poko*, "short god," also exists, whose tour is limited to the district to which he belongs. A third god, *akua pā'ani*, "god of games," accompanies the *akua loa* and presides over the games performed in honor of the god (Malo MS, 149). According to 'Ii (1963, 70), it is made like the *akua loa*.[9]

On the evening of the twenty-third day, after the god is decorated, everyone gets dressed in his best. Nobles and commoners chant aloud prayers called *kauwō* (K. Kamakau 1919–20, 41; cf. PE, 129). Pigs are cooked in the oven for the men and dogs for the women. Then the celebration begins. Everywhere cries of people drunk on 'awa can be heard, as well as blasphemous, reviling, and cursing songs (kūamuamu). Everyone enjoys himself. Halfway through the night, nobles and commoners together go to bathe in the ocean.[10] The Makahiki gods are placed in the sand on the beach, and everywhere fires are lighted. This bathing, called hi'uwai, lasts until dawn (K. Kamakau 1919–20, 41; Malo MS, 149).

This night, particularly the bathing period, is the occasion for a sexual orgy and verbal obscenities. As Kepelino writes,

The effect of holding his hi'uwai at night was that the crowd were [sic] excited as if with rum by the beauty of the ornaments, the splendor of the whale-tooth pendants, bracelets of sea-shells, feather wreaths and the fragrance of different tapa garments; one person was attracted to another and the result was by no means good. [1932, 96, cf. 193–95]

At dawn of the twenty-fourth day all the people leave the sea, which, from that moment, just like any water, belongs to the god Lono (see below) and is forbidden to man.

For four days one only has to eat well and have a good time; working and even cooking are forbidden (Fornander 1916–20, 6:204). This period is the kapu Makahiki sensu stricto. K. Kamakau lists all the prohibitions in force during this time:

And the deity [Lono Makua—V. V.] had decreed his law that man was prohibited not [sic] to kill; war·was prohibited and no [sic] fighting,[11] the ocean was prohibited, not a canoe was to sail; the kapa block was prohibited and no cloth was to be beaten; the drum was prohibited to be beaten; the horn was prohibited to be blown; the land was prohibited to be loosened ["e kapu ka aina, aole e hemo," "the land is taboo, without exception"]; the heaven was sacred [kapu] to Lono, the thunder was sacred to Lono; the earth was sacred to Lono; life was sacred to Lono; the hills were sacred to Lono; the mountains were sacred to Lono; the ocean was sacred to Lono; the raging surf was sacred to Lono; the family ["ohana"] was sacred to Lono; the sailing canoe was sacred to Lono, Thus the deity enumerated his laws, which the chiefs and the priests and all the people duly observed. [p. 40]

Moreover, human sacrifices, sacrifices of pigs, bananas, or coconuts—that is, those consecrated in the temples in the so-called haipule rites—are forbidden (Malo 1951, 141; MS, 145–46; Kamakau 1964, 19). This is the time for "games," "play," and "jokes"—all designated by the word pā'ani—for all but the king, the priests, and the kahu akua (Malo MS, 146; cf. Kepelino 1932, 94), who should not take part in them.

On the twenty-fourth of Welehu, the akua loa and the akua poko begin their circuit. The circuit of the first god lasts twenty-three days, as long as the Makahiki festival proper; that of the second god lasts four days, as long as the so-called kapu Makahiki. The akua loa travels clockwise, keeping the interior on its right; the *akua poko* travels in the opposite direction, with the sea at its right.[12] When it reaches the boundary of the district it returns. As the *akua loa* travels, all the land to the left of the road (i.e., the land under cultivation) is taboo; if someone enters it he is condemned to pay a pig but is not put to death (Malo MS, 149–50; K. Kamakau 1919–20, 41).

During the four days of the *kapu Makahiki*, the high priest is secluded in a consecrated place (*'iu*);[13] he is blindfolded so that he does not see the people violating the normal taboos of which he is the custodian. Also, he is forbidden to eat fresh food during the *kapu Makahiki* (K. Kamakau 1919–20, 41), probably because it would not be consecrated, since the temples are closed.

Before beginning its circuit (K. Kamakau 1919–20, 42; Ii 1963, 75), the *akua loa* is brought to the king, who, according to K. Kamakau, greets it with the customary ritual tears and displays his love (*aloha*) to it. Then he cries to it, in unison with all those in the house, "May you be feared, o Lono!" (*"e weli ia oe"*).[14] Those who carry the god then ask, "Is it [the greeting] for me perhaps?" (*"na'u paha?"*). The king and his company reply, "Here is the king's love for you, O Lono." Follows the answer, "Here is Lono's love for you, O heavenly one [king]." Then the god enters the king's house and the god's priests utter prayers, which are taken up by the king's priests. The king places a *niho palaoa*—the whale-tooth necklace that is a symbol of royalty (cf. PE, 245)—about the god's neck and feeds the man bearing Lono's image with his hands. This man is in fact "the mouth of the god" (K. Kamakau 1919–20, 41). He eats some pork, some *uhau* (this is probably a sacrificial preparation of taro), and some *kūlolo* ("pudding made of baked or steamed taro and coconut cream"—PE, 166) and drinks some *'awa*.[15] This rite is called *hānaipū*.[16]

After being fed by the king, Lonomakua is fed by all the principal ali'i. Then the king holds a boxing match (*mokomoko*),[17] which is attended by the image of a small goddess of play, who "pleases" (*ho'oolu'olu*) the people and makes them very happy (*hoihoi*).[18] Men as well as women wear holiday garments[19] and box or fight (cf. Whitman 1979:55–56). After the *hānaipū* and the *'aha mokomoko* ("boxing assembly") rites, the god begins the circuit of the land.

This account of the *hānaipū* rite comes from K. Kamakau (1919–20, 41–43). Malo's is slightly different. According to him, in response to the welcome from the king's priest, Lono's priest and his followers say, "*Nauane!*" ("Coming along!"). This exchange is repeated a second time. Then the priest inside the king's *hale mua* invites Lono to enter (*"Hele mai a komo, hele mai a komo,"* "Come in this way and enter!").

After the god is fed, he is taken out of the *hale mua* so that a woman of the *nī'aupi'o* rank may offer him a *malo*.[20] This rite is called *ka'i-'oloa*, after the name of the white cloth (*'oloa*) that constitutes the *malo* and is fastened at the top of the image of the *akua loa* (Fornander 1916–20, 6:205; cf. PE, 109).

The *hānaipū* rite performed in the king's *hale mua* is identical to the one held at the eating houses of the other ali'i,[21] but only the king can place a *niho palaoa* around the god's neck (Malo MS, 152–53).

'Ī'ī adds some important details to the accounts of K. Kamakau and Malo. After his entry into the *hale mua*, the *akua loa* is anointed with an unguent made from chewed coconut. When the woman of *nī'aupi'o* rank gives him the *malo* (and sometimes also a pig), she says to him, "This is for your annointing [*sic*], o Lono, Hearken to our plea." If she has no child, she prays to the god to give her one (1963, 73–75).

Thus, like a boy being initiated, the god is introduced into the *hale mua*, where he is fed with male foods and receives his loincloth. In addition, he is given an insignia of royal power (the *lei niho palaoa*) and is consecrated by being anointed (cf. Kamakau 1964:136).[22] Once consecrated, the image can begin its tour of the kingdom.

When the god approaches the altar that marks the boundary of the *ahupua'a*,[23] a man precedes him bearing two stakes made of *kauila* or *māmane* wood, which are called *ālia* (Malo MS, 151; cf. PE, 18, and Thrum in Fornander 1916–20, 4:282, n. 3).[24] He thrusts them into the ground in front of the god, and it is in the taboo space separating them that the *konohiki* must stack the *ho'okupu* from the *ahupua'a* he manages. These *ho'okupu* consist of precious feathers, pigs, bark cloths, hard pounded taro (*pa'i 'ai*), and chickens (Malo MS, 150; K. Kamakau 1919–20, 43).[25] According to S. M. Kamakau, if the present is not judged adequate, the *kahu* of the god "would complain, and would not furl up the god nor twist up the emblems and lay him down. The attendants kept the god upright and ordered the *ahupua'a* to be plundered. Only when the keepers were satisfied with the tribute given did they stop this plundering (*ho'opunipuni*) [in the name of] the god" (1964, 21). But if the present is judged sufficient, the priest accompanying the god steps forward and utters the *hainaki* prayer to free the land from the taboo:

Your "bodies" (*kino*), O Lono who are in heaven,
[Are] a long cloud, a short cloud
A cloud that guards,[26] a cloud that peers (*hālō*)
A cloud in cumulus form (*ho'o'ōpua*) in the sky
That comes from [the star] Uliuli, from [the star] Melemele
From [the star] Polapola, from [the star?] Haehae
From [the star] 'Oma'o that shivers with cold (*kū'ululū*)
From the land ('*āina*) where Lono is born
Lono goes up to the very zenith ('*oi ho'oku'i aku 'o Lono*)[27]
The silent star in the heaven (*ka hōkū e miha i ka lani*)[28]

He rises high the great wooden god (*akua lāʻau*)
Lono
.... [29]

Arise, put on your *malo* and enter into action [in the game or sport]
[Malo MS, 151]

At this point the people respond (*hoʻoho*) to the priest, "Enter into action!" The priest chants again, "Lono!" ("*hea hou ke kahuna o Lono*"),[30] and the people answer him, "The wooden god." The priest intones again, "Is raging." The people answer, "Raging, O Lono" (Malo MS, 151).

It is probably following this prayer that the priest daubs the *ahu* altar with red ocher (*ʻalaea*) to signal that the *ahupuaʻa* is "free" (*noa*) (Lyons 1875a, 1 : 103).

The image of the god is then turned face downward and moved to the border of the next *ahupuaʻa*.[31] To "inspire the people to box" (Ii 1963, 75), the *akua pāʻani* is erected where the *akua loa* had stood. For four days, other sports and dances (*hula*) are also performed (cf. Kepelino 1977, 65). In the boxing matches two parties stand face to face, insulting and mocking each other. On one side are the boxers who follow the *akua Makahiki* during their tour; on the other are the champions of each *ahupuaʻa* (Ii 1963, 75–76; Malo MS, 153). Sometimes veritable battles are fought with stones; people are injured and even killed (Ii 1963, 76; Malo MS, 153; Kamakau 1964, 20; MH, September 1821, 279; Stewart 1839, 244).[32]

On Kāne's day (the twenty-seventh of the month) the *akua poko* arrives at the boundary of the district ("*ka palena o ka moku*") and returns to the *luakini* temple without demanding other *hoʻokupu*. It does not follow the road, as on the trip out, but goes through the wilderness (*nāhelehele*) on the mountainside (*uka*). People come to join the god and gather quantities of *pala* ferns. With this they decorate the *akua poko*. It is likely that these plants indicate the end of the taboo that has "bound" the gardens and irrigated fields and made them inaccessible (Malo MS, 154; K. Kamakau 1919–20, 43; Ii 1963, 76).

In the meantime the *akua loa* and the *akua pāʻani* continue their journey.

Before continuing the description of the ritual, I must note that, unlike the *hoʻokupu* offered between the eighteenth and the twentieth days of Welehu, which are consecrated to the king's "feather god" and redistributed among the nobles and their clients, the *hoʻokupu* given to the Makahiki gods (*akua loa, akua poko*) are for the most part eaten by the crowd that follows them during the procession. This fact, stated by S. M. Kamakau (1964, 21), is confirmed by an eyewitness, ʻĪʻī: "Many people followed the procession on its tour over the land, among them the boxers,

210 The Sacrifice of the Hawaiian King

and all partook of the foods that were contributed by the people of each place" (1963, 76).[33]

As a matter of fact, 'Ī'ī does not even mention that there is a *ho'okupu* for the king's "feather god" before the images of the Makahiki gods are assembled. From his description it emerges instead that the decoration of these gods takes place the very night of the *kuapola* rite—most likely in the *luakini* where they are kept and after the Pleiades have been sighted. I deduce this from 'Ī'ī's statement that the *hi'uwai* rite is performed immediately after the *kuapola* rite and that at dawn the "Makahiki gods" are brought to the beach where the *hi'uwai* has begun during the night (Ii 1963, 72). This implies that the images are assembled during the bathing. Then, according to 'Ī'ī, the very evening following the *hi'uwai*, after the boxing matches and the erotic and scatalogical songs, the Makahiki gods begin their tour of the land (1963, 75).

Lū'au and *Kalahu'a* Rites

According to Malo, on the night of the twenty-seventh (the night of Kāne), when the *akua poko* returns, the keepers (*kahu*) of the god Kāne prepare packages of *lū'au* ("young taro tops"—PE, 197; cf. Fornander 1916–20, 5:684), roast them, and hang (*kau*)[34] them on the walls of their houses, after which their gardens are freed (*noa*) and they can take the food that grows there.

On the twenty-eighth (night of Lono), the keepers of the god Lono perform the same rite and their gardens are freed. On the twenty-ninth (the night of Mauli), it is the turn of the keepers of the god Kanaloa to perform this rite.

During the same days, the king and ali'i perform other rites, which involve Kū as the god of fishing. On the evening of the twenty-seventh they light a great bonfire, called "Puea's fire." According to Malo, Puea is a divine image, but we have no knowledge at all of this god (cf. Fornander 1916–20, 6:155). This fire is lighted to guide the canoes; however, no canoe may put to sea before dawn of the twenty-eighth, and then only if it has not rained the preceding night, because the absence of rain is a sign that the god is favorable (Malo MS, 154).

According to K. Kamakau, when the *maka'ainana* learn that the Puea rite has been successful, they are very happy about it and exclaim, "We are saved; the night [of the rite] of food (*'ai*) was good, the night was generous to us."[35] Then on the morning of the twenty-eighth (the day of Lono) they wash to purify themselves (1919–20, 43).[36]

According to Malo, when the canoe sent to catch the first fish of the year returns, all male ali'i eat of the catch. Perhaps because the rite marks the renewal of contact with the god Kū, who presides over fishing, it is on this day (the twenty-eighth) that the blindfold covering the eyes of the high priest is removed (Malo MS, 154–55). On the twenty-ninth, *pala* is gathered in the mountains. That night the Puea fire is lighted again. The following morning the fishing canoe goes out to sea once more. This rite is repeated until the eleventh day of the month of Makali'i, when the king's wife, and then all the other women, eat fish for the first time in a ceremony called *kalahu'a*.[37]

K. Kamakau describes the *kalahu'a* rite in this way. On the second day of the month of Makali'i a short rite is performed in the *luakini* temple. The following day the king goes to fish for the *'ahi* fish.[38] Other people go in their canoes as well. The first to return from fishing is a priest called Hua; he is required to remove the eye from a fish, most likely to consecrate it to the god as a firstfruit of fishing.

The *Kāli'i* and *Pua'a he'a* Rites

From the twelfth to the sixteenth day of Makali'i it is taboo to fish and to swim in the sea. On the sixteenth, the *akua loa* returns from its circuit of the island. According to Malo, it is brought into the *luakini* temple immediately (cf. Malo MS, 156); according to K. Kamakau it remains outside with the other Makahiki deities (1919–20, 45).

In the evening, after bathing in the ocean for the first time in four days, the king, accompanied by his men, goes in his canoe to meet the god. When he lands, a large number of men armed with spears bar his way to keep him from reaching the god. According to Malo and K. Kamakau, no sooner has the king jumped on land than one of the men surrounding the god runs toward him, two spears in hand. He throws the first at the king, but it is warded off by the latter's champion (an expert in spear dodging). Then the armed man approaches the king and touches him with the second spear. A sham battle between the king's and the god's parties follows.

Eyewitnesses to this rite, called *kāli'i*, declare, however, that King Kamehameha at least did not have anyone at his side and that he asked that spears be thrown at him with the greatest possible force (cf. Barnard 1829, 230). Campbell writes, "He is obliged to stand till three spears are darted at him; he must catch the first with his hand, and with it ward off the other two. This is not a mere formality. The spear is thrown with the utmost force, and should the King lose his life, there is no help for it" (1967, 129; cf. Vancouver 1801, 3:254; Corney 1896, 101; Iselin, n.d., 81; Péron 1824, 162; Ross 1904, 71–72; Portlock 1789, 188–89; Ii 1963, 54–55, 66).

The *kāli'i* rite is performed not only during the New Year's festival, but each time a king or a high-ranking ali'i ceremonially disembarks from a canoe. Certain mythical episodes show that the *kāli'i* is a test; if the king is successful, his rule is legitimate.[39] For instance, when 'Umi, the usurper and conqueror par excellence, divides the island of Hawai'i among his men, his high priest puts him to the test of the *kāliʻi* to determine the length of his reign. He orders a warrior to throw a spear at ʻUmi. ʻUmi dodges and catches it. Then the priest tells him,

By warding off the spear away from you so successfully, so shall trouble be warded off from your kingdom until death overtakes you. Just as you caught the spear and held it at the end, so shall your kingdom fall to your son [*"keiki"*], your grandson [*"moopuna"*], your issue [*"pua"*], your offspring [*"mamo"*], until the very last of your blood. [Fornander 1916–20, 4:208]

Another example concerns Kawelo, the mythical aliʻi of Kauaʻi. When he disembarks at Oʻahu, seven warriors greet him with a barrage of spears that the hero dodges with ease. Then he asks his brother to hurl two spears at him with force. The point of the second brushes his navel when he dodges it. Kawelo then chants that this is the sign of possession of the land (Elbert 1959, 50–53).

For N. Emerson, *kāliʻi* means "to act like a king" (in Malo 1951, 155). It may also mean "to make the king" (*kā-* is in fact a causative prefix), however, or even "to strike the king" ("to strike" is another gloss for *kā*) (cf. PE, 99).

After the mock battle, according to Malo, the king enters the temple to "see" (*ʻike*) the *akua loa* and the *akua poko* in the *hale wai ea* (MS, 44);[40] but according to K. Kamakau, it is the king himself who brings these images into the temple.

Then the king sacrifices a pig to Lono and says to him, "O Lononuiākea, here is your pig; it is for your feet, tired because you visited our land belonging to us both (*kāua*). And since you have returned, take care of me and of our land that belongs to us both" (K. Kamakau 1919–20, 45, my translation). The pig is placed on the *lele* altar in front of the crescent formed by the images of the gods. Then the king and his company leave the temple.

On the following day, the seventeenth (Ku-lua) of Makaliʻi, no canoe may go out to sea (K. Kamakau 1919–20, 45). That evening, a temporary hut (*hale kāmala*) is built of *lama* wood in front of the *hale wai ea*. Kahōāliʻi spends the night in the hut, which is therefore referred to as "the house-net of Kahōāliʻi" (*ka hale kōkō o Kahōāliʻi*). That evening a pig, called *puaʻa heʻa* ("blood-red pig," "sacrificial pig"—cf. PE, 58), is cooked in the oven (*kālua*) along with preparations of coconuts (*kūlolo*) (Malo MS 156–57). During the night "*kaihaanalu*" and "*oe*" prayers are intoned (K. Kamakau 1919–20, 45). At dawn, when the pig is done, a great number of people eat it and the other food; any leftovers are thrown away (Malo MS, 157).

Now, on the eighteenth day of Makaliʻi, the Makahiki gods are taken down, wrapped up, and stored in the *luakini*.[41] Then the men who have transported the divine images are fed, and the priests end the rite with a prayer.[42]

The Rite of the *Maoloha* Net

On the same day (the eighteenth) a net (*kōkō*) with a large mesh is made and filled with all kinds of food: taro, sweet potatoes, breadfruit, bananas, coconuts, pork. Then the priest rises to give a prayer. When he says the word, *hāpai*, "lift," four men lift up the net and shake it to make the food drop through the mesh. If the food remains in the net, the priest declares that there will be famine; if it falls, abundance will reign.

Then the "tribute canoe" (*wa'a 'auhau*—cf. PE, 347) is built, which is supposed to be the canoe in which Lono returns to Kahiki. At the same time, the "white canoe" (*ka wa'a kea*) is sailed.[43] Unfortunately, Malo (MS, 157–58) does not explain exactly what these canoes are and what rites are performed with them. K. Kamakau's text dealing with these rites is lost (see Fornander 1916–20, 6:44). Thus we are reduced to giving the floor to N. Emerson, who collected the following details on the subject of the *wa'a 'auhau*: "This was a wicker-work crate, or basket, made out of peeled *wauke* sticks. Having been filled with all kinds of food, it was lashed between the two *iako*, or cross-beams that belong to the outrigger of a canoe; and being taken out to sea, it was cast off and allowed to drift away. It was also called *ka waa o Lono*, Lono's canoe" (in Malo 1951, 156, n. 26).

Handy (1972, 370) speculates that the crossbeams to which the *wa'a 'auhau* is lashed belong to the "white canoe" and that it is the latter that is allowed to drift off. Whatever the case, this rite puts an end to the Makahiki taboos. Now it is permitted to fish, farm the land, and so forth (Malo MS, 158). In short, the festival is over.

Interpretation
General Remarks

Two questions immediately come to mind. Why do the Pleiades announce the beginning of the year? Why is Lono the god of the New Year?

The rising of the Pleiades at night occurs during the beginning of the wet season (*ho'oilo*), when the winds are blowing alternately from the south and the northwest, bringing storms, thunder, and above all, clouds bearing rain. The worst storms take place during 'Ikuwā, which Kepelino defines as "a month of dark rough seas, wind, thunder, lightning and unceasing rain" (1932, 94). During this time vegetation grows more vigorously because of the rain; moreover, this is the most favorable season for replanting sweet potatoes in the dry areas of the islands, particularly in the western part of the island of Hawai'i (Handy 1972, 330).

The connection between the rising of the Pleiades in the evening, the rain and noisy storms, and the rebirth of vegetation is thus a fact of experience. Moreover, after the winter solstice the sun returns toward the north and becomes progressively more powerful. Thus we can understand why the passage to the new year takes place in this season. All the phenomena characterizing this season—rain, dark, rounded clouds, thunder, noise, southerly winds, growth—are associated with Lono and considered his manifestations. Therefore the period around the new year, announced by the rising of the Pleiades after twilight, is put under the aegis of Lono.[44]

Since Lono's return occurs in the form of rain, this god is conceived of as heavenly, and it is thought that he unites with the land to fertilize it. Lono's reproductive role at this time of year explains why during the New Year's festival he is called Lonomakua, that is, "Lono the father" and "Lono the provider" (PE, 213). Lonomakua is also the name "of Pele's fire keeper as represented in the fire sticks, symbol of fertilization" (Beckwith 1940, 41). In fact, the production of fire, which is a masculine privilege, is considered a symbol of male penetration of the female (cf. Handy and Pukui 1972, 161). Thus we can ask ourselves as well if the long pole topped by a rounded head, which represents the god, is not a phallic symbol.

The association of two decorative elements attached to the image of Lonomakua perhaps evokes the god's reproductive work. The first of these is constituted by the *pala* fern, which, as a food eaten in time of famine, probably connotes the exhaustion of resources preceding the god's arrival (Malo 1951, 22; cf. Handy 1972, 347). The second element is constituted by the skins of migratory birds, *ka'upu*, which, since they come to Hawaii at the beginning of the Makahiki season to lay their eggs (cf. Sahlins, n.d., 20), represent the reawakening of life that occurs in this season. The black of their plumage (Malo 1951, 40) could moreover evoke the black clouds laden with fertilizing rain.[45] In short, ferns and *ka'upu* skins would form a pair symbolizing the transformation produced by divine fecundation.

The identification of Lonomakua with a heavenly god uniting with the feminine earth is confirmed by the origin myth of the Makahiki festival. In outline it is as follows.

Lono, who lives in heaven, sends two of his brothers down to earth to seek a wife for him. They travel from island to island until they find, in the valley of Waipi'o on the island of Hawai'i, the beautiful Kaikilani. Lono comes down from heaven by walking on a rainbow (a sign of rain) and marries Kaikilani. The couple lives in Kealakekua (where the image of Lonomakua is kept in Hikiau temple). All goes well until a man tries to seduce Kaikilani. Convinced that she is unfaithful, Lono beats her to death. But before she dies Kaikilani assures him of her innocence and love. Maddened with sorrow and remorse, Lono goes from district to district and island to island, defying every man he meets to fight him. Having finished his circuit, he builds a strange canoe (in triangular form—see Bingham 1848, 32; cf. Varigny 1874, 16), which the Hawaiians fill with provisions. Then he departs alone, promising to return one day, "not by canoe but on an island shaded by trees, covered ovei by coconuts, swarming with fowl and swine" (Beckwith 1940, 37).[46]

This final detail (Lono departing in a triangular canoe—a European ship) seems to reflect the identification made between Cook and Lono (cf. Sahlins 1979). Other aspects of the myth could probably be explained by this identification. Nevertheless, the story itself is traditional, as is proved by its corresponding closely both to the ritual it is intended to legitimize and to the Tahitian myth of the origin of the Arioi society (cf. Beckwith 1940, 37–38).[47]

Lono's myth provides the key to several aspects of the Makahiki ritual. But for the moment I will confine myself to offering it as a proof for the existence of a connection between Lono as god of the Makahiki and the fecundating sky. I add that this relation enables us to understand better why the beginning of the year and that of the cosmogonic process are identified, as is evinced by the fact that both take place at the time the Pleiades rise in the evening (see *Kumulipo*, line 5). Clearly this identification results because the marriage of heaven and earth takes place, albeit in different forms, both at the beginning of the year and at the beginning of the cosmos.

By identifying the beginning of the year with the beginning of the world, Hawaiian ideology proves once more and in an extreme form that it is by bringing the empirical world back to its transcendental matrixes, represented by the gods, that it can be reproduced and made to live. The year will be good only if it has had its beginning in the divine, if it has been brought back to it. Thus, year after year it will be necessary to repeat the original cosmogonic process.

But the divine matrix to which the empirical world is brought is all the more powerful the more it is generalized, the more aspects of the real it encompasses and unifies in itself. This is why the beginning of all beginnings, in the *Kumulipo*, coincides with the most undifferentiated state of the divine. This undifferentiation is conceived of as powerful not because it is opposed to difference, but because it characterizes a being that contains within itself *in potentia* all differences, all acts, and thus realizes a sort of *coincidentia oppositorum*.

On a concrete, ritual level, the divine is never manifested in the absolute generality that it has at the outset of the cosmogony. Nevertheless, at certain times personal deities are capable of assuming this generalized aspect, which permits them to represent all of the divine in a relatively concrete form.[48] This is what happens with Kū in the *luakini* temple rites and with Lono in the Makahiki rites, as is indicated by the fact that in this context

Lono's taboos include all domains of reality and not only those that are attributed to him ordinarily (see K. Kamakau 1919–20, 40; supra).

An inevitable consequence of this return to the divine origin, to the "sources" (*kumu*), of this return of Lono that is in fact a return *to* Lono, is the divinization of the nature reproduced by the god. Indeed, that Lonomakua is conceived of as the father or producer of cultivated plants and the main domestic animal (the pig) means that these species are his "bodies," his "children," and belong to him wholly. The god's return, the reproduction of the productive origins, thus result in recreating a nature where—to use the words of the *Kumulipo*—"the god enters, man does not enter." This paradox must be overcome by the sacrifice of the firstfruits, without which the return to the sources would only make human life impossible. Thus Lono is called back, only to be immediately chased away. This is precisely why the rite at the heart of the Makahiki, the simple center of gravity of all its complex manifestations, is the firstfruits sacrifice, which appears then as the veritable founding institution of human life.

Let us now turn from these general remarks to the concrete analysis of the stages of the ritual.

The Reproduction of Time

The *kuapola* rite is the first stage of the process that engenders the year. The rite lays out the temporal framework that will then be filled out with concrete forms of life during the empirical year. Indeed, the twelve moons of the year and the stars associated with each are reproduced by it.

The symbolism of the rite is rather transparent. The green coconuts consecrated to Lono (in K. Kamakau's version) or directly to the stars and moon (for 'Ī'ī) symbolize the renewal and rebirth of these celestial bodies. It is also possible that the rite has some mimetic component (for instance, does the throwing of the coconuts imitate the movement of the stars?) that constitutes an anticipation of the desired result.

The act of breaking the coconuts is also significant. It permits the pure and nourishing liquid contained therein to spill out and perhaps also represents both the destruction of the old year[49] and the birth of the new. It is a kind of amniotic fluid that is thus spilled, a prelude to the birth that is enacted.

The Festival and Lonomakua's Triumph

We have seen that 'Ī'ī situates the assembling of the Makahiki gods (*akua loa, akua poko, akua pā'ani,* who all seem to represent Lono in different forms or stages) and the ritual bathing (*hi'uwai*) immediately after the *kuapola* rite. He thus describes a sequence that translates a logical relationship in terms of temporal contiguity. This has the effect of making the logic of the rite emerge more clearly. Therefore I will leave aside for the moment the differences existing on this point between the version given by 'Ī'ī and those given by Malo and K. Kamakau and proceed directly to the interpretation of the *hiʻuwai* rite.

There is a striking parallelism between the *hiʻuwai* rite and the rite of assembling and decorating the *akua loa* and other Makahiki gods. Men adorn themselves, the gods are adorned; men go to the beach, the gods are brought there as well. Since this parallelism concerns all other features of the two rites, it is perhaps legitimate to conclude that the union of men and women in the sexual orgy that takes place during the *hiʻuwai* rite corresponds to the union of the god Lono with the earth. In other words, men mimic and accompany the god's fecundating work and, reciprocally, the orgy is a means and already a result of this work. As always, then, the god brings about the human actions that it embodies and, reciprocally, is made by them. Moreover, since the orgy takes place on the beach, it can be said that the *hiʻuwai* rite completes the "marriage of heaven and earth" by the marriage—which is often associated with it in Hawaiian thought—of sea and land. Human and divine work conjoined thereby unite the fundamental categorical pairs (heaven/earth; sea/land) to reproduce the cosmos.

Naturally, the *hiʻuwai* is also a rite of passage. The seawater is supposed to "purify" the bathers of all ritual impurities contracted during the year just ended (Beckwith 1932, 194). Renewed at the same time as the god Lono, men can thus return to society or, more exactly, reproduce it by feasting, of which the beginning is marked by the *hiʻuwai*.

During the four days that follow the night of the *hiʻuwai* rite, the feasting reigns supreme; it is forbidden to work (and thus to go to the gardens or out fishing), to cook, and so forth. Scatalogical or obscene songs are improvised that reveal sins and faults and provoke laughter, which is a form of castigation (Ii 1963, 72–73). Thus people "purify" one another through play instead of purifying themselves, as normally happens, through sacrifice.

Undoubtedly this is also the time when hundreds (Vancouver 1801, 5:128–29), or even thousands (Stewart 1839, 95), of people participate in dances[50] that enact mythological and historical episodes (Ellis 1917, 59, 74, 78–80; Beechey 1831, 2:105–6; Stewart 1839, 145). These dances often have an erotic character,[51] especially since it is permitted, and even prescribed, to go on from words to deeds: the dancers, whatever their sex,[52] cannot refuse the sexual advances of the spectators they have aroused (cf. Pukui [1942] in Barrère, Pukui, and Kelly 1980, 78). Moreover, the aim of the ornaments, chants, and music, as well as of the elegant gestures of the dance and the allusive stories they mime is to provoke sexual excitement through aesthetic pleasure (cf. Kepelino 1932, 96).[53] But aesthetic pleasure does not need to be transformed into erotic acts in order to produce love among those who participate in the festival; all are drunk with beauty, finding pleasure in being together. Moreover, these marvelously coordinated dances provide the experience of a social action which seems to exist effortlessly and pleasurably at the junction between musical and corporal rhythms.[54] It is by realizing a perfect fellowship among men, by making them capable of giving each other pleasure, that the dance reconstitutes sociability, a necessary condition for the reproduction of society (cf. Valeri 1979a).

Laughter obtains the same results by similar means.[55] It has always been recognized that laughter reproduces sociability by creating a bond among those who laugh at the expense of the object of their laughter. But another fact has received less attention than it merits: to laugh at someone is to identify with him, for laughter is not possible without empathy, as Freud (1905), for example, has shown. Thus, laughter presupposes a recognition of a common humanity. Consequently, it implies that the roles of the one who laughs and the object of his laughter may be reversed. And doubtless they are during the Makahiki festivals, for everyone has his faults and the fine mockers who compose the satirical chants run a high risk of paying the price in satires directed against themselves. But they will laugh at them anyway, just as they laugh at their victims. It is precisely the genuine acceptance of this reciprocity that makes the collective feast possible.

Since it efficaciously reconstitutes the social, the festival appears as productive, generative. Moreover, by reconstituting the social it also reconstitutes the productivity of social labor and therefore the productivity of the natural species (especially vegetable) that depend on human labor. The belief that Lono as the god of feasting fertilizes the gardens is thereby reinforced by experience.

Note that the generative power of feasting, and more especially of the dance, justifies their use in other contexts. In particular, the dance is necessary to help develop the fetus of an ali'i and to ease his birth. It is also said that the dance neutralizes the attacks of sorcerers against the fetus or young infant (K. Kamakau 1919–20, 2–4; cf. Vancouver 1801, 5:128–30; cf. Malo 1951, 231; Kamakau 1961, 388; Stewart 1839:260–61). Dance is conceived of as productive of the lives of the ali'i and as a neutralizer of all that threatens them, because the life of an ali'i cannot be separated from the vast, well-organized social group that recognizes itself in him. Dance, by manifesting the enthusiastic support of this group and at the same time presenting it as a highly organized and socialized entity, contributes to affirming the reality of the ali'i's mana. This is why it is believed that by dancing people help engender their ali'i. Moreover, dancing probably involves sexual orgies. By reproducing itself, the group thus reproduces its representative, in the person of a new ali'i. This manifestation of the identity between ali'i and society is enough to neutralize the sorcerers who deny the ali'i's legitimacy or try to destroy it. At any rate, the opposition between the dance—the collective and public act par excellence—and sorcery—the most individualist and private of acts—is total. To the extent that all of society dances, it thus resists the sorcerers' disaggregating power, that is, the action of individualist forces. Hence those who do not take part in the dance are censured (K. Kamakau 1919–20, 24) and probably risk being suspected of practicing sorcery against the royal heir.[56]

Just as dance engenders the infant ali'i, it can be supposed that during the Makahiki it also engenders the god Lonomakua. It seems in fact that beginning with the *hi'uwai* rite, dances, games, laughter, all develop the god by developing the sociability whose manifestation he is.

In the space of a day Lonomakua is born, develops, and is initiated during the *hānaipū* rite, which marks his entry into maturity. I interpret the *hānaipū* as an initiation rite because the god, like any young boy, is introduced for the first time into the *mua* house, given "masculine" foods (pork, coconuts, *'awa*) to eat and, most important, the loincloth (in the *ka'i'-oloa* rite). Thus he becomes an adult capable of procreating, as is indicated by the fact that the *nī'aupi'o* woman asks him for a child.

The engendering of Lonomakua, like that of any god, is thus represented as the growth of a human; but while the engendering of other gods, particularly Kūnuiākea in the *luakini* rites, requires violent sacrifices, the engendering of Lonomakua is made possible essentially through feasting, dancing, sport, laughter, and so forth. This is why the enthronement of Lonomakua, who is engendered by feasting, includes the dethronement of the king and his gods, who are engendered by violent sacrifice. Sovereign feasting takes the place of the sovereign sacrifier, the sociability of play substitutes for the social order that derives from authority and force. The king himself cedes his place to Lonomakua by ceding to him one of the principal insignia of his dignity: the *lei niho palaoa* (necklace with a whale-tooth pendant). An indication of this dethronement is also given by the fact that the king and the *nī'aupi'o ali'i* are obliged to remain secluded in their houses after the initiation and installation of the god (Ii 1963, 75). This is because they cannot show themselves where the god reigns without making their loss of status obvious. The festival of Lonomakua, being the expression of pure and simple sociability, of a bond that is immediately realized through the pleasure of play, entails hierarchical undifferentiation. A choice thus presents itself to the ali'i—either not to participate in the festival or to take part, but as simple individuals, "human beings" among other human beings.

According to Malo, the high priest (according to 'Ī'ī, the *nī'aupi'o ali'i*) follows the first course, at least for a while.[57] But the high-ranking nobles apparently take part in the celebration, since they were seen by European voyagers attending the dances.

Thus, by becoming visible, by indiscriminately making love,[58] by mixing with people of lower rank, by risking being the victims of laughter (which destroys the taboos),[59] the ali'i become polluted, lose their sanctity. This is confirmed by the fact that immediately after the end of the Makahiki festival they are required to purify themselves with a complicated rite (Malo; see below, p. 228). A symbolic dethronement, the festival can even turn into regicide; Bell notes that Kamehameha, fearing assassination, takes part in the festival surrounded by a bodyguard of twenty-four warriors (1930, 126).[60]

Nevertheless, one cannot assimilate the Makahiki festival, where subversion is usually only the symbolic correlate of a state of society ordered by the principle of play and feasting, with the radical subversion and violent anarchy that follows the demise of the king or a person of royal rank. This death removes the foundation of the system of social rules. All taboos thus are violated, until the dead king's successor manages to reestablish order and perform rites of purification in a temple especially reconstructed or restored and in which the bones of his predecessor are placed (*hale poki*— cf. Malo 1951, 106).

Here is a description of the disorders produced by the death of the king:

On such an occasion, every restraint was cast off, and all were in the habit of following the impulse of any and every wild passion that might seize them. Rights of person or of property were no longer regarded; and he who had the greatest muscular powers committed whatever depradation he chose, and injured anyone he thought proper. Even the chiefs lost their ordinary preeminence, and could exert no influence of restraint on the excesses of their subjects. It was the time of redressing private wrongs, by committing violence on the property and person of an enemy; and every thing that anyone possessed was liable to be taken from him. Their grief was expressed by the most shocking personal outrages, not only by tearing off their clothes entirely, but by knocking out their eyes and teeth with clubs and stones, and pulling out their hair, and by burning and cutting their flesh; while drunkenness, riot, and every species of debauchery, continued to be indulged in for days after the death of the deceased. [Stewart 1839, 165–66]

Coming from a missionary, this testimony could be considered suspect were it not confirmed by numerous sources, including eyewitnesses (cf. Marin 1973, 230; Kamakau 1961 222, 266–67; Laanui 1930, 93; Bell 1929–30, 2:90; Campbell 1967, 101; Ellis 1842, 177–81).

It must also be noted that during the mourning period, hierarchical and sexual taboos not only are suspended, they are deliberately violated in an atmosphere of incredible violence that has nothing "ritual" (in the popular sense of the term) about it. Not only are others not respected, but even the integrity of one's own person may be violated through cruel self-mutilations (see the text cited above and Hunnewell 1895, 13–14; Bell 1929–30, 1:15; Manby 1929, 15; Cleveland 1843, 234; Samwell 1967, 1181; Ellis

1842, 176). These customs testify that every individual's integrity and even his existence are believed to be inseparable from the king's integrity and existence and are therefore threatened by his death.

What happens at a king's death offers a complete contrast with the customs observed during the *kapu Makahiki*, which excludes all violence. If during this festival gender and hierarchical distinctions diminish and may even lose their meaning, they are never completely abolished. For example, men and women continue to respect alimentary taboos and eat separately. In contrast, in the period of social disaggregation following the king's death, women eat taboo foods and even enter the temples (Marin 1973, 230; Kamakau 1961, 222). Similarly, one can contrast the amorous behavior during the *hi'uwai*, where beauty attracts and unites, and joy and laughter reign, with the "universal prostitution" (Campbell 1967, 101) that reigns during the entire period of mourning. During the latter, common men and high-ranking women unite in a kind of fury to violate all differences of rank (cf. Marin 1973, 230; Bell 1929–30, 2:90).[61]

The contrast between license at feasting and license at mourning is easy to understand. In one case society is truly breaking down, for the king is dead; in the other the king is fictitiously deposed or, more precisely, voluntarily cedes his sovereignty to the god of the festival—that is, to society as the expression of a spontaneous order. In the disorders following the king's death, all authority disappears; in the festival there is a carnival king (Lonomakua), but a king nonetheless. Thus the festival does not negate the social order but substitutes for the normal order founded on the king's sacrificial violence an order that springs from the pure pleasure of being in society, of love and good fellowship (cf. Valeri 1979a, 1981b, 232–34; Turner 1969).

Nevertheless, precisely because the ideology of the festival proclaims the uselessness of the regular king, at least implicitly it entails a ritual revolt. The deposing of the king is moreover made obvious by the fact that the *ho'okupu* offered to Lonomakua by the people do not go to the king and nobility (except, if 'Ī'ī is to be believed, for some precious objects), but are immediately appropriated by the undifferentiated mob that follows the god on his circuit and are eaten during the festival itself. Thus the offerings feeding the god of the feast feed the feast by feeding the feasters.

I have noted that according to 'Ī'ī the firstfruits are consecrated only to Lonomakua. This seems logical, since Lono is the generative god, situated at the beginning of the reproductive process of the year. Malo and K. Kamakau, however, place a *ho'okupu* given exclusively to the king between the *kuapola* rite and the assembling of the *akua loa*. Thus, it seems that for them the king's claim on the firstfruits precedes that of Lonomakua and is therefore superior to it. This, however, has the effect of giving a more subversive aspect to the god's successive triumph over the king.

It must be noted, yet, that the terms used by Malo and K. Kamakau to designate the *ho'okupu* given to the king distinguish it from the one given to Lonomakua. Malo, in fact, calls it the king's *'auhau*, "tribute," and *waiwai*, "riches," "portion" (K. Kamakau uses this last expression only). The people do not "sacrifice" to the king, then, as they sacrifice to Lono; they pay him a tribute and it is the king himself who consecrates this tribute to his "feather god" (K. Kamakau 1919–20, 39), that is, to Kūkā'ilimoku or some equivalent god.

The use of the term *'auhau*, and the fact that Kūkā'ilimoku obtains a place that is not his own (because this is Lono's festival), impels one to ask if this first *ho'okupu* rite, which 'Ī'ī does not mention—as if he were conscious that it is not truly a part of the festival—is not an innovation made by Kamehameha. We know in fact that Kamehameha introduced changes in the traditional festival, on the one hand, by making room for his own gods (particularly the sorcery gods and Kūkā'ilimoku—cf. Kamakau 1964, 19–20; 1961, 180), and on the other hand, by prescribing a tribute payable during this festival (Kamakau 1964, 19–20). Here perhaps we are witnessing a conflict between political and cosmological motivations: the development of royal authority under Kamehameha imposes the preeminence both of the king's tribute over the firstfruits sacrifice and of the god of force (Kūkā'ilimoku) over the god of the festival (Lonomakua).

Firstfruits Sacrifices

Having reached maturity, the plenitude of his being, and having been "installed" by the king himself, Lonomakua begins his triumphal circuit of the land. This tour has the goal of manifesting that the earth and its products belong to the god that has produced them and also of separating, by means of the firstfruits sacrifice, the producer-god from his products and consequently of dedivinizing the latter and making them accessible to humans.

Accordingly, a rite divided into two contrasting parts takes place in each *ahupua'a*. In the first part, the god arrives triumphantly and is treated with respect; his right over the land and its products is recognized, which makes both of them taboo. Whoever violates this taboo is symbolically sacrificed to the god, since he must offer him a pig as a substitute for himself. Moreover, the god can always plunder the *ahupua'a* to manifest his rights. This first part of the rite thus enacts the saying of the *Kumulipo*, "the god enters, man does not enter."

But as soon as the god receives the firstfruits, there is a complete reversal. The image of the god is turned toward the rear and—at least for a while—is placed in a horizontal position. Lono is thus "beaten" and "overthrown," perhaps even symbolically killed. According to 'Ī'ī, the image is turned toward the rear so Lono may look at his lost wife (1963, 72). In the origin myth of the Makahiki, this woman is the earthly Kaikilani, but in the rite she is certainly the land, to which Lono is united but from which he is immediately separated by men. The driving away of the god is also represented, it seems to me, by the boxing match that takes place between the god's followers and the inhabitants of the *ahupua'a*. Clearly the latter are supposed to win, since finally the god's boxers withdraw to join him in the next *ahupua'a*.

It is probable that these boxing matches, which sometimes become true battles fought with stones, are accompanied by verbal jousting. In fact the latter is associated with Lonoikamakahiki, the humanized but legendary equivalent of the Makahiki god. Like the god, this king makes the tour of the archipelago, challenging the chiefs of each land in verbal and athletic contests. At stake is the possession of the lands: Lonoikamakahiki wins them all (Fornander 1916–20, 4:247ff., 290, 300, etc.). On this point, however, the rite inverts the myth, since in the first, unlike the second, it is the inhabitants of each district who defeat Lono. The proof—he withdraws and does not retain possession of the land and its products.

The neutralization and distancing of the god is accomplished in reality in two stages, which correspond to a doubling of the god. In the first stage, the firstfruits sacrifice has the effect of driving away the *akua loa*; his place is then taken by the *akua pā'ani*, the god of play and games. Then boxing and other jousts constituting the second stage of the distancing process take place. When they end the *akua pā'ani* withdraws in turn to rejoin the *akua loa*. Thus it seems that the firstfruits sacrifice transforms the god from the state indexed by the *akua loa* to that indexed by the *akua pā'ani*, from being the god of the firstfruits sacrifice to being the god of play and games.

In the end, men make fun of the god in a double way. First they give him the part for the whole (the firstfruits sacrifice); then they beat him at games. We probably will not be very far from the truth if we suppose that they are even laughing at him. In fact, the defeated one is always mocked, and laughter is a powerful way to abolish the taboo, as we have seen. At any rate, the festival implies that everyone makes fun of everyone else and a fortiori of those in a position of authority. Does not Malo tell us that, during the *kapu Makahiki*, "blasphemies" against the gods are proffered (MS, 149)?

In short, the god, initially threatening enough to be offered sacrifices, is transformed by these sacrifices into a "god of play" (and even perhaps a god that is all in play), who is then completely neutralized in verbal and athletic jousts and probably even by laughter. We see that, like any ritual, the *kapu Makahiki* neutralizes the dangerous aspects of the god. But, moreover, it presupposes that Lonomakua is rather inoffensive at the outset, since he is born of the feasting and thus is already very close to humanity.

Basically, in this god man is less alienated from himself than he is in the others. This is why the sacrifices offered to Lonomakua are less serious, if one may say so, than those offered to the other gods. Here no human victims are involved; moreover, what is offered to the god is completely reappropriated by men (the crowd that follows the god), and no part of it is destroyed or left on the altar to rot. Here the sacrificial alienation has much more of a sham character than in the temple ritual; like the "service alimentaire [du dieu] dans les religions de l'Antiquité" (Loisy 1920, 67–68), the sacrifices of the Makahiki are a half-conscious comedy.

Lono's transformation from a state where he is connoted by a certain violence (for he has just asserted his rights over what he produces) to a nonviolent one (characterized by purely athletic or verbal contests) is clearly expressed by the *hainaki* prayer that consecrates the firstfruits to the god and, in an even clearer fashion, by the origin myth of the Makahiki. Moreover, the myth and the *hainaki* prayer are perfectly analogous. I would even consider this analogy the best proof of the myth's traditional character, which has sometimes been doubted.

In the prayer Lono is first invoked as a heavenly god associated with the stars and especially with the clouds bearing fertilizing rain. Then the "rage" that drives Lono to box with the champions of the *ahupua'a* is alluded to. This is a skeletal rendering of the myth of Lono and Kaikilani. The myth begins with Lono's descent from heaven to unite with a woman who seems to represent the land. Like the land he makes fertile each year, this woman belongs to him. But men are ready to steal her from him, just as they are ready to take the land and its fruits away from him. Lono reacts by killing his wife, thereby taking her away from the man who wanted to steal her. In one version of the myth this murder is assimilated to a true sacrifice, for the god leaves Kaikilani's corpse in a temple—probably Hikiau, since the couple lives at Kealakekua (Bingham 1848, 32). But Lono repents. He feels pain and remorse for killing a human being and therefore becomes closer to humanity. In a parallel manner, his destructive violence is transformed into the game of boxing, that is, into a regulated and fictive violence. Once his tour of the islands is finished, he departs for Kahiki (that is, the land of the gods), promising to return to Hawaii bringing abundance. Thus he clearly reveals his nature as a fertility god, but also the fact that he can be compatible with men only after he has been transformed by play and driven away from the land.

By enacting Lonomakua's transformation into the laughter-provoking god of play, the Makahiki festival seems to suggest that the ridiculous god is the alter ego of the serious one, the duped and impotent god the other side of the terrible, powerful one (cf. Valeri 1981a). The Hawaiians' curious attitude regarding Lonomakua—half-serious, half-bantering—is not an isolated phenomenon. In 1779 King noted the contrast between the reverent attitude the priests had in front of the image of Kūnuiākea in Hikiau temple and the disrespectful way they treated the images surrounding it (1967, 505). Other voyagers noted that the same gods that were treated with respect in some contexts were mocked or treated disrespectfully in others (von Chamisso 1864, 4:139–40; Choris 1822, 123).[62] And while in the Makahiki festival Lono is a god of the carnival, who is offered mock sacrifices (almost nothing goes directly to him), driven away, 'and laughed at, in the temple he is treated seriously and given real sacrifices.

After the sacrifice of the raw firstfruits to Lonomakua as fertility god, cooked firstfruits are sacrificed to three major gods (Kāne, Kanaloa, and Lono in his "serious" form) by their keepers. These firstfruits consist of young taro tops (lū'au) and thus of what has grown since the beginning of the year. In short, unlike the firstfruits offered to the Makahiki god, which are firstfruits only in the sense that they are picked at the beginning of the year, those offered in the lū'au rite are true firstfruits, the first manifestations of Lonomakua's reproductive power, mediated by the god who presides directly over the lands of a given category of people.

Here the opposition between raw and cooked marks—as it does in the fishing rites (see chap. 4)—two successive stages in the process of reappropriation of nature and therefore of reproduction of society. Indeed, by eating the cooked firstfruits of his worshipers each major god begins to be reproduced relative to the social categories he encompasses.

The King's Return

With the fishing rites, Kū returns to the scene. Associated with the sea and the ali'i, implicitly he is the antagonist of Lonomakua and the people, both of whom are associated with the land. This implicit antagonism becomes explicit when Lonomakua's image returns at the end of his circuit to the spot in front of the luakini temple where it is stored. Then the king, after purifying himself in the ocean, climbs into a canoe with his warriors and goes to meet the god. There is no doubt, although the sources do not explicitly mention it, that he is accompanied by his feather-covered war god (Kūkā'ilimoku, on the island of Hawai'i), since this image always accompanies the king in his ceremonial travels by canoe, especially when, as in this case, he is in war dress (see Samwell 1967, 1228; King 1967, 512; Rickman 1966, 303). Being associated with Kū, and thus with war and violence, the king readies himself to confront Lonomakua, who represents the spontaneous social bond produced by the festival.

As Frazer (1963, 372–73) had already seen, the kāli'i rite first entails the king's "execution," symbolized by the spear that touches him. It is precisely by "dying" at the hands of the people and the god Lonomakua that the king obtains the land. This is because death neutralizes his "wildness" and makes possible his transformation and incorporation into the community that has been newly re-formed in the festival. At this stage it is the king who is encompassed by society. But this is only the prelude to a reversal: the transformed king in turn encompasses the undifferentiated festive community and Lonomakua who symbolizes it, in order to give it a hierarchical form. This reversal implies that Lonomakua is killed in turn, which is what happens immediately after the king's symbolic execution. In fact, conquered after a sham battle between the king's warriors and Lonomakua's defenders, the "Makahiki gods" are brought into the king's temple and dismantled for storage.

The appropriation of the god by the king and his faction takes a sacrificial form, of course. After capturing Lono, the king hastens to sacrifice to him a pig, which is placed on the altar. The following day, the "blood-red pig" (*pua'a he'a*), that is, the men's share of the same sacrifice, is cooked. This pig is eaten in a collective meal in which the king's followers take part. This meal has the air of a true communion; its sacramental nature is further underscored by the prohibition against eating the leftovers in a different context. Indeed, the sacred meat that is the index of the community it reproduces cannot be eaten in private. This suggests that, by eating a pig metonymically associated (in time and space) with the pig attributed to Lono, the king and his followers absorb and take possession of the elementary social bond, the sociability that Lono represents at this stage.[63] They thus encompass, through Lono, the people and the land worked by the people.

Lonomakua's Departure

The short period of his reign over, Lonomakua, carnival king, must again depart. Nevertheless, he leaves behind him, incorporated in the real king, the sociability he has created. Yet this feeling will not survive the festival except as transformed into hierarchy. The pure festival cannot last. It belongs, together with Lonomakua who represents it, to the land of Utopia, where the god must now return.

But first a divinatory rite is performed to establish whether the festival has been successful. This is the rite of the Maoloha net. This rite is modeled on the myth of Makali'i, which exists in several versions summarized by Beckwith (1940, 433–34). Overall, the myth tells that Makali'i, a mythical ali'i of divine status, gathers all the food he produces in a net and hangs it from the sky. The hero, who is his antagonist, takes the form of a rat, climbs up to the net and gnaws at the center, thereby making all the plants fall to earth, where they proliferate.

The *maoloha* rite thus repeats the initial exploit that enabled men to steal food from the gods and combines in one figure the multiple threads of the ritual—if we may be permitted to take as a metaphor the net that is the principal instrument of this conclusive rite and that seems to have been put at the end of the festival as its emblematic summary.

It is also possible that the myth of Makali'i reflects a correlation perceived between an astronomical and a ritual process. Makali'i is another name for the Pleiades. Thus his hanging the food plants in the sky might reflect the connection between the progressive ascent of the Pleiades night after night during the Makahiki festival and the progressive inaccessibility of the gardens, which return to the god's possession during the same period. Moreover, this is also the season when new crops, developing because of the increased rain, are not yet ready for harvest. In contrast, the seasonal culmination of the Pleiades and the beginning of their decline approximately mark the end of the Makahiki festival and therefore the beginning of the period in which man fully reappropriates his gardens and the new crops reach maturity. Hence the "fall" of the Pleiades is translated on the mythical level into the "fall" of the food plants from the sky. The *maoloha* rite, which seems to take place at about the time of the culmination of the Pleiades, probably mimes this "fall" at the same time as it commemorates the founding myth that guarantees it.

Transitional Rites between the Makahiki Festival and the *Luakini* Temple Ritual

According to Malo (MS, 158), on the very day the New Year's festival ends, the gathering of the wood necessary for the construction of a new *heiau* of the *kūkoa'e* type begins. From the twentieth until the twenty-fifth day of the month of Makali'i, the rites of the *kaloakāmakamaka*[64] taboo are performed (ibid.); we are not told anything about their content.[65]

On the twenty-sixth day the king performs a purification rite (*ho'oma-'ema'e*). He consecrates five booths in succession. In order, they are called *hale pu'upu'uone* ("divination house"—cf. PE, 332);[66] *oeoe* ("whistling [house]"); *hale pōhue* ("house covered with *pōhue* vine"); *pālima* ("divided by five"); *kūkoa'e a hūwai* [*hāwai*].[67] The fifth booth probably coincides with the *kūkoa'e*, "temple," that Malo mentions earlier. The word *hūwai*, connected to the term *kūkoa'e*, is likely a slip of the pen on Malo's part. In fact, he calls this same house a *hale hāwai* in another chapter of his book (37.23; MS, 165). *Hāwai* means "to purify with water" (PE, 58), a sense that agrees with the function of the *kūkoa'e*. The latter, according to Pukui and Elbert (PE, 163), is indeed a temple for purification rites and is where one prays to obtain food.

On the twenty-seventh day the *kūkoa'e* is made taboo and apparently the king and the high priest remain enclosed there for an *anahulu* (period of ten days) (cf. N. Emerson in Malo 1951, 156).

These rites rid the king of the impurities (*haumia*) he has acquired by abandoning himself to pleasure (*le'ale'a*) during the Makahiki festival. They are necessary so he can recommence ordinary worship and thus eat pork, which cannot be consumed unless it has first been consecrated to the gods in the temple.

At the beginning of the *kapu-hua* of the month of Kā'elo, a small *ho'okupu*, called the "*kuapola* mound" ("*ka puu o kuapola*") is made. Since this rite has the same name as the one in which purifications with coconut water are made at the rising of the Pleiades, it is possible that it marks the king's purification. This interpretation can probably be confirmed by a detail given by Corney, according to whom the king breaks a coconut after the *kāli'i* rite (1896, 101).

In any event, at the end of the *kapu-hua* (according to Malo MS, 159) the king, the high priest, and the man who beats the sacrificial drum perform the rite that permits them to eat pork once again.

During the same taboo period, Kahōāli'i removes the eye from an *aku* fish and from a human victim and eats them. From this moment, and for the next six months, one can freely fish for *aku*, but fishing for the *'opelu* is now prohibited.

At the end of these rites, notes Malo (ibid.), the ritual cycle concerning the passage from the old to the new year is completed, and with the new moon begins the "New Year" ("*ka makahiki hou*"), that is, in this context, the period marked by the four monthly taboos (*kapu pule*), during which the *haipule* rites (temple rites) are performed.

An account of the rites performed during the *kapu-hua* to recommence the consumption of pork is furnished by Vancouver, who attended them in 1794. This unique testimony must be given in its entirety:

A very strict *taboo* was on this day, Wednesday the 12th [February], to be enforced all over the island, and required that the respective chiefs should retire to their own estates, for the purpose of rigidly observing the attendant solemnities; which were to continue two nights and one day. In the event of the omens proving favorable, the chiefs would be permitted to eat of such pork as they might think proper to consecrate on this occasion; and high *poory* [*pule*], that is, grand prayers would be performed; but should the omens be otherwise, the rites were instantly to be suspended.

I had frequently expressed to *Tamaahmaah* [Kamehameha] a desire of being present on some of these occasions; and he now informed me, that he had obtained for me the consent of the priests, provided I would, during the continuance of the interdiction, attend to all the restrictions which religion demanded.

Having readily promised to comply with this condition, I was with some degree of formality visited by several of the principals of their religious order, one of whom was distinguished by the appellation of *Eakooa, no Tamaahmaah* [*ke akua no Kamehameha*];[68] meaning the god of *Tamaahmaah*. This priest had been one of our frequent attendants, notwithstanding which, he was, on this occasion, detected in stealing a knife; for which offence he was immediately dismissed from our party, and excluded from the precincts of our encampment.

The restraints imposed consisted chiefly in four particulars; first, a total seclusion from the company of women; secondly, partaking of no food but such as was previously consecrated; thirdly, being confined to the land, and not being afloat or wet with sea water; and fourthly, not receiving, or even touching, the most trivial article from any one, who had not attended the ceremonies at the morai [*heiau*, "temple"].

These restrictions were considered necessary to be observed by the whole of our party resident on the shore; and about sun-set we attended the summons of the king at the morai, who was there officiating as high priest, attended by some of the principal residents of their religious orders, chanting an invocation to the setting sun. This was the commencement of these sacred rites; but as I propose to treat this subject more fully on a future occasion,[69] I shall for the present postpone the detail of my observations, and briefly state, that their prayers seemed to have some regularity and form, and they did not omit to pray for the welfare of his Britannic Majesty, and our safe and happy return to our native country. A certain degree of order was perceptible throughout these ceremonies, accompanied by many superstitious and mysterious formalities; amongst which, a very principal one was performed about the dawn of day. At this time the most profound silence was required of every creature within hearing of this sacred place. The king then repeated a prayer in a low tone of voice with the greatest solemnity, and in the middle of it took up a live pig tied by the legs, and with one effort dashed it to death against the ground; an operation which must be performed without the smallest interruption or cry from the victim, or without the prevailing silence being broken by any noise whatsoever, though of the most trivial kind. This part of the service is supposed to announce their being on terms of friendship with the gods, on which the further ceremonies were carried into execution.[70] A number of hogs, plantations, and cocoa-nuts, were then consecrated for the principal chiefs and priests; the more common productions, such as fish, turtle, fowls, dogs, and the several esculent roots, that compose their food during the intervals between these more sacred *taboo's*, were not now served up, but for the first time since our arrival, they fared sumptuously on those more delicious articles.[71] The intermediate day, Thursday the 13th, and the second night, were passed in prayer, during which we found no difficulty in complying with the prescribed regulations; and soon after the sun rose on Friday the 14th, we were absolved from any further attention to their sacred injunctions.

Most of our Indian friends returned to our party the following day, Saturday the 15th; and as we all now fed alike on consecrated pork, they were enabled to be infinitely more sociable. [1801, 5:36–39]

The rites described by Vancouver lasted from the evening of 12 February to dawn of 15 February. On 12 February 1794 the moon was at its eleventh day. The rite was thus performed during the *kapu-hua*, exactly as Malo tells us, but, it seems, a month later than on his schedule. This was probably because Vancouver's arrival on 8 January (the sixth day of the moon) interrupted the progression of the Makahiki rites. On this date

Kamehameha was in Hilo (the eastern part of the island of Hawai'i) with all the nobility, and was probably getting ready to conclude the purification rites in the *kūkoa'e* and the rites to begin eating pork and the *aku* fish. This is indirectly confirmed by what Bell learned on 8 January: "A kind of Festival that is held annually at this Island about the Months of October and November was lately over" (December 1929, 81). Thus we have proof that in that year the Makahiki festivals had begun in October, but contrary to Bell's statement, the ritual cycle had not yet ended at the beginning of January. In fact, Vancouver tells us that in early January having asked Kamehameha to follow him to Kealakekua, in the west of the island, the king

Avowed that he could not accompany us, as the *taboo*, appertaining to the festival of the new year demanded his continuance for a certain period, within the limits of the district in which these ceremonies had commenced. The time of interdiction was not yet expired, and it was not possible he could absent himself without the particular sanction of the priests. [1801, 5:8]

However, Vancouver eventually persuaded Kamehameha to accompany him as far as Kealakekua on board the *Discovery*. This must have produced an interruption in the performance of the rites. It is thus likely that they had to be taken up again and concluded during the following month. Indeed, it was a traditional custom to repeat a rite that had been interrupted (Malo 1951, 160).

But there is another difference between the accounts of Vancouver and those of his companions, on the one hand, and the ritual schedule given by Malo on the other. Malo writes that the *kapu aku* is performed during the *kapu-hua* period at the same time as the rite for recommencing the consumption of pork. According to Vancouver, in contrast, the two rites are performed at different times, and the first of them lasts ten days. In fact, in 1794 the *kapu aku* began, according to Vancouver, on 1 February and according to Menzies, on 2 February, that is, the very day of the appearance of the new moon. It ended ten days later everywhere on the island of Hawai'i except the Kona district, where Kamehameha had it end earlier[72] to permit the resumption of trade between English and Hawaiians (Vancouver 1801, 5:30–31). According to the same authors, in 1793 the *kapu aku* took place from the evening of 4 February to dawn of 15 February (Vancouver 1801, 3:183; Menzies 1920, 53, 57; cf. Puget, n.d., Journal, 13 February; 15 February 1793; Bell 1929–30, 1:61–62; Manby 1929, 39), that is, from the twenty-second day of the lunar month until the third day of the following lunar month.

It seems then that in the eighteenth century the annual rites for desacralizing the *aku* fish lasted for an *anahulu*. If Malo states, then, that they lasted only as long as the *kapu-hua* period, we can surmise that toward the end of his reign Kamehameha reduced their length and even fused them with the rites for resuming the consumption of pork. The same thing seems to have happened to the *kapu 'ōpelu* fishing ritual that forms a pair with the *kapu aku*. K. Kamakau, who being older than Malo witnessed the *kapu 'ōpelu* done in the old style, gives it the length of an *anahulu*,[73] but for Malo it is a brief affair, lasting a night and a day (1951, 209–10, 152).

Whatever the case, here are the few details that can be gleaned concerning the rite for inaugurating *aku* fishing. John Young, who regularly attended these rites, described them to Manby in these terms:

The present Taboo Bower [*kapu pule*] is an Invocation to the God that presides over fish: it is annually observed at this season of the year, as a notion prevails, was this ceremony neglected, the finny tribe would immediately quit the shores of Owhyhee [Hawaii]. While this religious interdiction remains in force it is rigidly attended to and Death is the consequence should any one disobey the mandate of the high Priest. [Manby 1929, 39]

As we have seen, Malo writes that a man is immolated (*pepehi*) at the same time as an *aku* fish (doubtless the first one caught; this is a firstfruits sacrifice). The occurrence of human sacrifice on this occasion is confirmed by three sources. A man was sacrificed during the *kapu aku* of 1793, as Bell, whose informant was John Young, attests:

During these Taboos no Canoes whatever (except some particular Fishing Canoes of the King's) can stir from the Beach. . . . So wonderfully strict, and so religiously tenacious are the Priests in the exaction of these Taboos, that a breach in the observance of them is punished with death—and a poor man had yesterday met this melancholy fate, for going clandestinely on the Water to Catch fish (not being of the privileg'd fishermen) at the request of his wife for her supper. [1929–30, 1:62]

Menzies's journal, dated 24 February 1793, also mentions this event:

Close to the foot of the Morai [Hikiau] some of the natives pointed out to us the grave of a Man that had been put to death about a fortnight before [thus during the *kapu aku*] on account of breaking the taboo, which was simply thus. The bay had been tabooed some days on account of a large shoal of Fish that appeared on the Coast, at which time this unfortunate Man was seen going across the entrance of it in a small canoe, he was immediately pursued, and when brought on shore, they first broke the bones of his arms and legs,[74] and afterwards put an end to his miserable existence by stabbing his body with their Pahonas [*pāhoa*, "daggers"]. [Menzies, n.d.; cf. 1920, 72–73]

Two observations are in order. (1) The legs and arms of certain sacrificial victims were indeed broken (see below, p. 336). (2) In theory, the victim of a human sacrifice is always a "transgressor," or "mischievous" man (*kolohe*), but it is always possible to find a "transgressor" when a human sacrifice is necessary. In my opinion, this is precisely what happened in the case mentioned by Bell and Menzies.

A third witness proves, I believe, that if no transgressors can be found a victim can be obtained in other ways. Marin mentions in his journal, in the entry dated 18 December 1809, that Kahōāliʻi (whom he calls "the king's god") captures men and animals to put them to death, and he adds that it "is the custom after the new year" (1973, 199). Now, on 19 December 1809 the moon was at its twelfth day; that is to say, this rite, like the one described by Malo, takes place during the *kapu-hua*. As usual it is difficult to establish whether the corresponding Hawaiian month was Makaliʻi or Kāʻelo, but if the rite described by Marin does not correspond to the *kapu aku*, it is hard to see what other rite it could correspond to, since human sacrifice is prohibited before it.

We have seen that the rites for the *ʻōpelu* are symmetrical with those for the *aku*; together they define a seasonal system. Malo says that both of them are "Makahiki rites," that is, performed yearly—not part of the Makahiki festival. We possess two very different descriptions of the rite for desacralizing the *ʻōpelu* fish. Malo's account reduces this rite to a *pule huikala*, that is, to a "purification" or "absolution" rite. His description of the *pule huikala* performed during the *kapu ʻōpelu* closely matches that of the *pule huikala* performed to purify the family of a dead person at the end of funerary rites (cf. Malo 1951, 97–99). It is possible, then, that the fishermen are supposed to undergo a symbolic death, which would be in agreement with the usual logic of the firstfruit sacrifices for fish, as we have seen.

After spending the night in the temple, the fishermen go out to fish. Then a sacrifice is made, which likely includes the consecration of the first fish caught. Afterward fishing for *ʻōpelu* becomes *noa*, "free," to everyone, but the *aku* fish is sacred once again and cannot be caught for six months.

K. Kamakau describes the *kapu ʻōpelu* as a much more complicated ritual, whose structure and main components are close or even identical to those of the *kapu luakini* (1919–20, 30–35).

The rites just mentioned or described do not call for an extended commentary. It is clear, in fact, that the king's purification rites mark the passage from the Makahiki festival to the ordinary sacrificial cult in the *luakini* temple. It is also clear that while the descriptions of the fishing rites are rather fragmentary, especially in the case of the *kapu aku*, we are in a measure to conclude that in their most developed form (attested, for example, by K. Kamakau) they differ from the other *luakini* temple rites only in that they considerably develop the ritual fishing which, as we will see, is an important component of the ritual inauguration of any *luakini*. The close connection between these two fishing rituals and the *luakini* temple ritual is also confirmed by the fact that, according to a myth, they were all instituted at the same time (Kamakau 1866, 1867a; Emerson 1893, 9). Since I am going to give a detailed analysis of the most developed form of the *luakini* temple ritual, it seems unnecessary to discuss the fishing rites here, especially the *kapu 'ōpelu* as described by K. Kamakau. As for the overall meaning of the firstfruits sacrifices of fishing, it has been discussed at length in chapter 2.

Before turning to the *luakini* temple ritual, let me recapitulate at a somewhat abstract level the meaning of the New Year festival as a whole. Its basic features are personified by the god Lonomakua, who presides over play, fertility, and a social situation characterized by equality. The most important of these attributes is play, from which the other two depend. Being an activity that has its end in itself, play is not differentiated by a variety of ends and results, as is the activity of work. Hence it furnishes a concrete approximation to the most general attribute of humans: creative activity as such. Furthermore, this generic property apperceived in play finds its objective correlative in the renewed creativity of nature during the season of the festival. By sacrificing firstfruits to Lonomakua, then, Hawaiians pay homage to the most influential attribute of their species as reflected in nature itself.

Play and work are correlated with two opposite social situations. The social situation in which play dominates is characterized by equality, since the only criterion for the evaluation of the agents is the generic activity they all share when they play. In contrast, the social situation in which work dominates is characterized by hierarchy, because it implies the differential evaluation of activities and agents on the basis of their contrasting aims and results.

The experience of a generic creativity shared by all—and the sociability that goes with it—is an essential presupposition of Hawaiian society. This is why the ritual year always begins with the festival. But society can fully exist and endure only after generic creativity has been turned into a system of specific and complementary activities, after the sociability of play (*pa'ani*) has become the hierarchy of work (*hana*). This transformation is effected by the king, first by the intermediary rites just described, then by his inaugurating the *luakini* temple and with it the sacrificial part of the year. Let us turn, then, to this inauguration ritual.

8

The *Luakini* Temple Ritual

Quel étrange mystère dans le sacrifice humain! Pourquoi faut-il que le plus grand crime et la plus grande gloire soient de verser le sang de l'homme?
  Chateaubriand 1967–68, 1:74

The aborigines say that the intent of *karwadi* is to make the young men "understand."
  Stanner 1963, 3

The king's purification rites are performed at the end of the month of Makali'i; those that permit the resumption of eating pork and *aku* fish take place during the month of Kā'elo. The following month, Kaulua, is the first in which the king can build (*kūkulu*—Malo 35.18) or, more often, restore (*ho'āla hou*) a *luakini* temple. But the two months after that, Nana and Welo, are also appropriate to this task (Malo MS, 159, 167; Ii 1963, 122; Andrews 1865, 155; Remy 1862, 74). I call all these rites taken together the "inauguration ritual of the *luakini* temple" or simply "the ritual of the *luakini*". In Hawaiian it is called *kapu luakini, kapu heiau*, and, sometimes, as we have seen, *kapu loulu*, although the precise referent of this last term is not clear (Fornander 1916–20, 4:79, 185, 341, 357, 409). Ideally, the rite is performed every year.

Preliminaries

First the king asks his priest (*kahuna pule*) if it is necessary to build a new temple or if it is enough to renovate an existing one (*luakini kahiko*), and in the latter case which parts must be restored. If the priest decides that a simple renovation is sufficient, the *huikala* rite is performed to make the temple *noa* so that the workers may enter it. If on the other hand it is necessary to construct a new temple, the *kahuna kuhikuhipu'one* is asked to draw up the plan and to choose a suitable site (Malo MS, 162). Most often the chosen site is covered with the ruins of an older temple and even

234

though the king passes for having constructed it from scratch, in fact he only restores a temple built by one of his predecessors. The difference between "construction" and "reconstruction" is often more ideological than real: "Tradition often assigns the first erection of a Heiau to a chief, when in reality he only rebuilt or repaired an ancient one on the same site" (Fornander 1878–80, 2:102; cf. Thrum 1908b, 60).

After the architect-geomancer has chosen the site and drawn up the appropriate plan, the king divides the work among his clients (*'aialo*, "[those—V. V.] eating [in the] presence"—PE, 9; that is, his commensals) (Malo MS, 163). In principle it is the nobles and their clients who build the temple. Nevertheless, "if the task were extremely laborious, then it became 'public work' (*hana aupuni*) and the people (*maka'ainana*) helped" (Kamakau 1976, 135). Women, however, are excluded from this work (Kamakau 1961, 154), obviously, because they are impure.

The construction of some temples can involve thousands of people (Fornander 1878–80, 2:36), who must be fed and whose work must be organized.[1] Thus the erection of the temple by itself enables one to measure the extent of the king's influence and ability and whether he has the support of his subordinates. Sometimes, as on the occasion of the construction of Pu'ukoholā temple by Kamehameha, this demonstration of force and success is enough to discourage an adversary and is the equivalent of a battle won. It can thus be said that kings fight by building temples and not only with arms (cf. Kamakau 1961, 85, 173, 135; Kaawa 1865b; Fornander 1878–80, 2:41–42; 1916–20, 4:408–9, 410; Thrum 1909, 44, 46–47; 1917, 52–53).

However, the attempt to build a temple can meet with failure and provoke the opposite of what is sought—for example, a rebellion. Thus the construction of the Wailehua temple by King Kamehamehanui of Maui (in the first half of the eighteenth century) provoked the people to revolt; they would not tolerate the hard work of carrying the building stones (Thrum 1909, 45; Kamakau 1961, 73).

Once the stones of the temple are in place it is time to raise the tower and then erect the secondary images. If we can judge by Malo's text, this phase of the construction does not seem to be accompanied by rituals (MS, 165). In contrast, the construction of the image of the main god (Haku 'ōhi'a) and that of the sacred houses is an integral part of the ritual for consecrating the *luakini* as the sources describe it.

The *Luakini* Temple and Its Furnishings

It is impossible to follow the description of the inaugural ritual of the *luakini* temple without a familiarity with the structure of the latter, as well as its furnishings—which calls for a rather lengthy discussion.

The extraordinary structural variety of the temples makes it hard to generalize concerning their plans and dimensions. An idea of the range of their dimensions can be given by saying that on Oʻahu the smallest temple is 12 by 15 meters; the largest measures 174 by 52 meters (McAllister 1933, 9; cf. Thrum 1907c, 51). On Kauaʻi, the average size of twelve temples enclosed by stone walls is 50 by 31 meters (Bennett 1931, 34). It is often impossible to determine the category to which a temple belongs by using archaeological data exclusively (Bennett 1931, 47–48), but it appears certain that most of the large *heiau* are *luakini*. For example, twenty-five of the thirty-two most important temples on Oʻahu seem to be *luakini* (cf. Thrum 1907b, 44–48).

Two components of the *luakini* temple can be distinguished: the fixed infrastructure, comprising courts or stone platforms, and the wooden superstructure, often modified according to the rites and their purposes.

Stone Infrastructures

The plans of the fixed structures are extraordinarily diverse: "In all the heiaus visited on the two islands of Oahu and Kauai, there are no two alike in plan. Some indicate such individuality even in their ruins as to make one hunger for their history" (Thrum 1907c, 50). This leads McAllister (1933, 9) to conclude that any classification of temples, at least on Oʻahu, is impossible.

Bennett (1930, 1931), however, tried to distinguish five types of "great heiaus" (evidently not all of them *luakini*) on Kauaʻi:

1. Temples comprising one or more open platforms (*paepae, kahua*).
2. Temples made up of a walled enclosure (cf. Kamakau 1976, 135).
3. Terraced *heiau*: "The terraced heiau is a series of platforms or enclosures on a slope that requires terracing to keep the platforms level" (Bennett 1931, 34). The number of terraces ranges from two to four.
4. Round temples (cf. Thrum 1907b, 42, 45)
5. Unclassified temples.

Each type is divided into subtypes (Bennett 1931, 32–35; cf. Thrum 1907c, 50–51).

The following additional components or annexes of the temples are worth mentioning:

1. A ledge on the walls of some temples—on Kauaʻi and Oʻahu—where those admitted to the rites were seated (Thrum 1907b, 40, 1907c, 52, 66).[2]
2. Large stones at some distance from the temple. On these stones the victims were put to death before being brought into the temple (Thrum 1907b, 37; 1908b, 56).
3. Polynesian ovens found outside the temple (HEN, 1:266) or even within the enclosure (Kamakau 1961, 116, 167), used to cook the corpses of certain victims to hasten their putrefaction and thereby clean the bones.
4. *Lua*, "pits," [3] where the remains of the victims were thrown (N. Emer-

son in Malo 1951, 178) and from which the name *luakini* appears to be derived. *Luakini*, according to Emerson (in Malo 1951, 178), in fact means "four hundred thousand pits" and thus evokes innumerable sacrifices. According to Malo (1951, 162) the *lua* is found inside the *'anu'u* tower, but this is not always confirmed by archaeological research (cf. Bennett 1931, 44), since pits are found even outside the temples.[4]

5. Tombs. These are sometimes found within the enclosure of the *luakini*. Nobles are buried here, but especially the priests who officiate in the temple.[5] Sometimes their *moepu'u*, "companions in sleep [death]"— that is, clients who are sacrificed during their masters' funerals (cf. Cook 1967, 270–71; Cook and King 1784, 2:202; Ellis 1842, 359–60; Anonymous 1924, 130; Kamakau 1964, 34)—are also buried there.

6. The *papahola*, "level pavement." According to Malo (1951, 161) this lies outside the temple enclosure, on the *'ākau* ("right" or "north") side. At the end of the *papahola* crossed sticks (*pe'a*—Malo MS, 164; Anonymous 1924, 129) mark the external limits of the *heiau*. The *kauila nui* rite takes place on this pavement (see below, p. 281), which is perhaps also the place where the victors share their loot, since *papahola* signifies "division of spoils among the victors" (PE, 292). Probably the majority of the audience stands on the *papahola* when the rites inside the temple are in progress (Ladd, Crozier, and Apple 1973, 33). A special functionary, the *papahola* priest, keeps them silent (see Malo MS, 164).

7. *Hale o Papa*, or "heiau of the female deities" (Kamakau 1961, 179), where the noblewomen (of the *pi'o* or *nī'aupi'o* ranks—Kamakau 1976, 129) stay during some rites of the *luakini* temple (see below). The hale o Papa lies on the *hema* ("left" or "south") side of the temple and on a special "platform" (according to Kamakau 1961, 325).

Wooden Superstructures and Images

We are well informed as to the furnishings of the most sacred part of the temple, that is, of the innermost court or the highest terrace, but our information about the rest is very vague. Judging by the descriptions of the rites, however, these courts, terraces, or platforms are occupied by houses where the priests and nobles reside and eat during the taboo periods, and where the portable gods of lower rank and other paraphernalia are stored (cf. McAllister 1933, 13).

The most important wooden superstructures of the temple are the following:

The *Paehumu*

The fence separating the temple or its inner precincts from the exterior is called *pā* (cf. Malo 37.15) or *paehumu* (Kepelino 1932, 59, cf. 137). The *paehumu* may be only an invisible barrier (McAllister 1933, 14),[6] but most

238 The Sacrifice of the Hawaiian King

often it is a fence of planks and poles on which images have been carved (Kamakau 1961, 202–3). Kamakau makes the doubtful claim that these images are male on the 'ākau, "right," side and female on the hema, "left," side (1976, 136) of the temple. He also maintains that the images of the paehumu fence are not regarded as sacred (1961, 203), but on this point opinions vary (King 1967, 516; Rickman 1966, 301; Remy 1862, 67–68; Fornander 1878–80, 2:186–87; Bishop 1916, 25–26; Stokes 1931; Thrum 1927; Sahlins 1979, 333–34). Often the heads of human victims are fixed on top of the poles that are part of the paehumu (Clerke 1967, 597; Samwell 1967, 1159, 1221; Ellis 1782, 2:180; Menzies 1920, 57; Boelen 1835–36, 3:44–45, 57). There were twenty skulls in Hikiau temple in 1779 (Samwell 1967, 1159).

Near the entrance made in the paehumu are two crossed pūlo'ulo'u poles, which defend the way to the sacred place (Anonymous 1924, 129). Sometimes their place is taken by statues (Ii 1963, 35). One of these, if we are to believe Kamakau (1961, 93), bears the banner that is a signal of a taboo; it is called Kūkalepa, "Kū [with] the banner." Banners or flags (lepa) that signal a taboo may be placed all around the temple (cf. PE, 187; Brigham, n.d., 97).

The Tower

The tower ('anu'u or, according to Malo, lananu'u mamao) is found at one end of the sanctum sanctorum. It is the first superstructure to be erected in the temple (Kamakau 1976, 135; Malo 1951, 162; cf. Emory 1929, 92). All the statues and houses are oriented relative to it.

According to Emerson (in Malo 1951, 176) the tower has three floors, of which the third is the most sacred: only the king and the high priests have access to it. Brigham (n.d., 145) rightly criticizes Emerson on this score and points out that no eyewitness ever mentioned the alleged floors. Consider, for example, Cook's excellent description:

The Pyramid which they call [Henananoo][7] was erected at one end, it was 4 feet square at the base and about [20][7] feet high, the four sides was [sic] built of small sticks and branches, in an open manner and the inside of the pyramid was hollow or open from bottom to top. Some part of it was, or had been covered with a very thin light grey cloth, which seemed to be consecrated to Religious and ceremonious purposes. [1967, 270; cf. Cook and King 1784, 2:200]

Ellis (1842, 97) gives another good description of the 'anu'u tower and its functions, probably based on information obtained from K. Kamakau. It confirms the one Brigham obtained from an old Moloka'i priest, according to whom the tower is a kind of tube reaching to heaven, through which the god speaks to the high priest (Brigham, n.d., 145). It is perhaps also used as an observatory for noting the positions of the stars and other heavenly signs of divine will.

A second tower (*ōpū*) can be placed on the side opposite the *'anu'u* tower (Ii 1963, 56; Kamakau 1976, 130). Nevertheless, this second tower must have been rather rare, since it did not occur in any of the *luakini* described by early European visitors.

The height of the towers can be considerable; Cook estimates that one of the towers he saw at Waimea was at least fifteen meters high. Not without reason does Bell compare the *'anu'u* of Hikiau (which he estimates to be from eighteen to twenty-one meters high) to a steeple (1929–30, 1:78; cf. Manby 1929, 44).

Houses

There are four houses in the sanctum sanctorum of the temple: *hale mana*, *hale pahu*, *hale wai ea*, and *hale umu*.[8] Their orientation and the wood used to build them indicates the nature of the temple; constructing them, moreover, is part of the temple's inauguration ritual (Kamakau 1976, 138).

The *hale mana* or *hale mua* or *hale malu* ("shaded house" = "under the shadow of the taboo"—Kamakau 1961, 155; PE, 215) is the most important and largest house of the temple. It symbolizes the whole temple by synecdoche; thus the expressions *luakini* and *mana* (an abbreviation of *hale mana*—cf. Malo 27.19–20) are sometimes interchangeable (cf. Kepelino 1932, 60). Here small images and cult paraphernalia are kept, as well as the feather gods (Kamakau 1961, 155; Brigham, n.d., 140)[9] when they are brought into the temple to take part in the rites. It may also contain tombs (Cook 1967, 271; Anonymous 1924, 130), probably of nobles and priests.

The latter live in this house during some rites (see below, p. 281; Freycinet 1978, 74; cf. Brigham, n.d., 142). According to Cook, the mana house in a temple at Waimea on Kaua'i was twelve meters long and three and a half meters in both height and width. It narrowed toward the ends, which gave it a form similar to that of the temple to which it belonged (Cook 1967, 504; Cook and King 1784, 2:201).[10] It was erected at some distance from the tower and faced it (Cook 1967, 270–71). In Hikiau temple this house was found on a lower level than the tower platform and faced the entrance to the temple (Samwell 1967, 1177).[11]

Another important house is the *hale pahu*, "drum house."[12] It is between the mana house and the *lele* altar, which is situated in front of the tower (King 1967, 506; Samwell 1967, 1177; Ellis 1782, 2:181–82; cf. Malo 1951, 162; Ii 1963, 35). The "gods' drums," which are hollowed from the trunk of a coconut palm (cf. Beaglehole 1967, 597, n. 4; Brigham, n.d., 141) and covered with sharkskin (Fornander 1878–80, 2:62–63), are kept in this house (Ii 1963, 33–35; Malo 1951, 162).[13] They are used to call the people to the temple, to send messages, to call for changes of posture during the rites (to raise or lower one's arms, etc.), to accompany prayers, and so forth (Kamakau 1976, 138; Brigham, n.d., 141). They also consecrate human sacrifices. Only the king has the right to use them or order their use, for only he may consecrate human sacrifices.[14] If the king cannot be present at the sacrifice and consecrate it himself, his drums will act in his stead; this implies that their sound has the same value as his voice (cf. Ii 1963, 35).

According to Kamakau, "The *hale pahu*, drum house, was the house where the kahunas did their work; in it were the large and small *pahu* drums to give pleasure [to the gods], and there the god keepers, *ka poʻe paʻa akua*, recited formal prayers, *kuili*, all night long, and called to the gods to the constant beating of the drums, from evening until the bright light of morning" (1976, 138).[15] Thus it seems that if the temple drums call men to the temple, it is because they signal that they are calling the gods, that the gods are present in the temple to be worshiped.

The *hale wai ea* is the smallest of the temple houses,[16] but it is "essential to the rites of the priest" (Fornander 1916–20, 6:18). According to Malo, it is in this house that "the *ʻaha* [cord] is pulled" (*"e kai ai ka ahaʼ*— MS, 164). The meaning of this expression will be considered below. *Wai ea* means, literally, "water of life."[17] Materially, it is seawater used in lustrations (PE, 350; Bennett 1931, 43). The house, then, takes its name from the holy water kept inside it, in a bowl made from a human skull.[18]

The *hale umu*, "house of the oven," is where the temple fires are lighted (*"e hoa [hōʻā] ai ke ahi o ka heiau"*—Malo MS, 164). Kamakau describes it as a shedlike structure where "the pigs were baked[19] for the 'burnt offerings' and 'sin offerings' (*mohai kuni, mohai hala*), and where the consecrated work was performed for the offerings on the *kuahu* altar of the god" (1976, 138).

Journals from the Cook expedition do not mention either the *hale umu* or the *hale wai ea*.

The relative positions of the houses, according to ʻIʻi and Malo, respectively, may be gathered from figures 4 and 5.

Altars

By "altar" I mean any place where sacrificial offerings are put for the god. The most simple altar is the pavement or level terrace (*kīpapa*) found before certain images and groups of images (Malo MS, 164; Kamakau 1961, 325). The tower itself may be used as an altar, since offerings are placed within it (Hiroa 1957, 522; cf. Brigham, n.d., 257).

The words most often used to designate the altar are *lele*[20] and *kuahu*. Overall, the sources suggest that *kuahu* is usually a pile of stones or a stone platform on which the image of the god is found (cf. Kepelino 1932, 21; Kamakau 1961, 238; cf. Ellis 1782, 4:116), while the *lele* is an elevated wooden structure that takes different forms (cf. Hiroa 1957, 522–25);

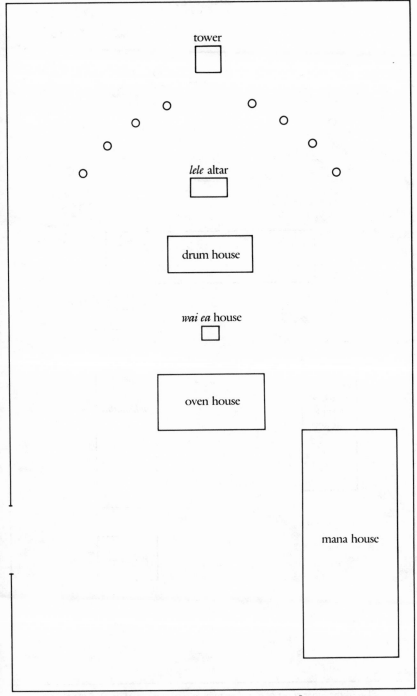

tower

lele altar

drum house

wai ea house

oven house

mana house

Fig. 4.   Plan of the inner court of a *luakini* temple according to ʻĪʻī (1963, 33–35).

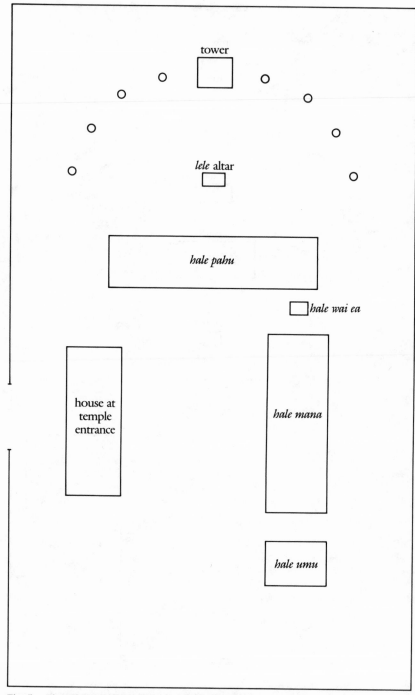

tower

lele altar

hale pahu

hale wai ea

house at temple entrance

hale mana

hale umu

Fig. 5. Plan of the inner court of a *luakini* temple according to Malo (MS, 164). This is a tentative reconstruction, since Malo's text is not completely clear.

usually it is a scaffold, but sometimes it is a simple pole on which offerings are hung (cf. Zimmermann 1930, 89; McAllister 1933, 14). Yet in some cases *kuahu* simply refers to a secondary altar, even if it is materially identical to a *lele*. Thus 'Ī'ī applies the term *kuahu* to the secondary altar found next to the entrance of 'Ahu'ena temple at Kailua (1963, 123). Acccording to the drawing that Choris made of this temple (reproduced in Barrère 1975, 7) this altar is a wooden scaffold. The *lele*, situated before the main image, which is at the foot of the tower, is the main altar. It is usually tall, so that the offering laid upon it may be seen from a distance (HEN, 1:203).[21]

Images

The images of the gods are the most important "objects of worship" (*mea ho'omanamana*—cf. HEN, 1:n. 69). Indeed, they are the receptacles for the gods[22] and at the same time an important instrument for their transformation. As such they are the focal point of the visual symbolism of the ritual.[23] A complete understanding of their meanings therefore is not possible if they are isolated from ritual action. However, it is useful as a preliminary to provide some pertinent data in order to constitute a frame of reference for the interpretation of their role in ritual.

Let us begin with their classification. First, a distinction can be made between fixed images, erected in the temple as a permanent fixture, and mobile images, which can be transported from one temple to another and follow their owners on any ritual journey. Fixed images can be divided in turn into major and minor images, while mobile images are made either of wood (*akua lā'au*) or of wicker covered with precious feathers (*akua hulu manu*).

Fixed Images

Major fixed images are located in the most sacred precinct of the temple. They are erected in front of the tower and are laid out either in a semicircle or in two parallel rows.[24] The main altar (*lele*) is inside the area they delimit. Moreover, these images can be erected on a stone *kuahu* in the shape of a horseshoe (*unu*), which as we have seen is itself considered an altar (cf. Samwell 1967, 1177).[25]

According to Malo and 'Ī'ī, the main image (which is identical in appearance to the other major images) is just in front of the tower. At any rate, this layout was adopted at Hikiau. The principal image may be called Haku 'ōhi'a ("Lord of the *'ohi'a* tree"), Kūka'ōhi'alaka ("Kū the *'ōhi'a* tree"—Samwell 1967, 1159, 1177), Kūnuiākea ("Kū of wide expanse"— King 1967, 621, cf. 516, 506), or Akua nuinui ("supreme god"—Choris 1822, 12). It may be smaller than the images surrounding it. According to King, the figure at Hikiau was less than a meter high, while the adjacent images were about two meters tall (1967, 505).

Some six major images have survived; all date from the beginning of the nineteenth century. The two largest are 2.66 meters high;[26] the smallest is a little over 1 meter tall. Apparently, all of these images come from Kona (island of Hawaiʻi) and are characterized by the following features:

1. The knees are bent, the body is massive and tensed, as if ready for action.

2. The mouth is immense and full of teeth and is open as if to devour (offerings are often placed in the god's mouth); the tongue is massive, and sometimes the tip protrudes slightly. Seen in profile, the mouth resembles a fishhook.

3. A wig ending in two long tails is carved on the image's head. These wigs correspond to the ones sometimes worn by people of very high rank, particularly priests (cf. Cox and Davenport 1974, 39; Ii 1963, 11): "Some of the men had a kind of wig made of human hair twisted together into a number of long tails, each a finger thick that hung down as low as the breach" (Cook 1967, 280–81; cf. Hiroa 1957, 562, 271). This headdress is most likely identical to the one that Malo calls nīheu (1951, 163).

4. The outer corners of the eyes are elongated and merge into the tails of the wigs.

According to Samwell (1967, 1177), the four images nearest the Haku ʻōhiʻa are called kāʻai, the rest, makaīwa.[27] But according to King (1967, 506; cf. Ellis 1782, 2:181), all the images forming a semicircle in front of the tower are called kāʻai. The most general meaning of the word kāʻai is "wrapped." It is therefore probable that these images are so called because they are wrapped in white cloth when they are consecrated (see below, p. 309; cf. Hiroa 1957, 466, and the drawing of ʻAhuʻena temple made by Choris 1822, pl. 5).

In the temple that Cook visited at Waimea (Kauaʻi) the main image was very different from the ones just described. In fact, it consisted of a very long pole, slightly curved toward the top. Halfway up the pole was carved a small image of the god (Kanaloa, apparently—cf. Cook and King 1784, 3:551). Below it the pole was notched; above the image it flattened and broadened out and on one side had a sawtoothed form (Cook and King 1784, atlas, pl. 33).

Our only document on the images in Hikiau temple in 1779 is a rough drawing by the surgeon Ellis. Yet it is enough to indicate that these images were also quite different from the ones dating from the early nineteenth century, as documented by surviving specimens and the drawings of Choris, Arago, and the missionary Ellis. In the images dating from 1779, the body seems less plastic than in those of the nineteenth century; the head is topped not by the representation of a wig but instead by a very tall ornament, a kind of headdress or miter, that recalls the upper part of the Waimea image. However, the difference in meaning between the wig and the miter is not great, as we shall see. Furthermore, at least one icono-graphic document dating from the nineteenth century (the sketch of the Hale o Keawe temple in Ellis 1825) testifies that images of the Kona type could have miters instead of wigs. Undoubtedly, the availability of iron tools after Cook's visit to the archipelago was a major factor in the stylistic differences between the images of 1779 and those of the nineteenth cen-tury or the end of the eighteenth.

Minor fixed images are placed throughout the temple.[28] Some are carved on poles, others are in the round, still others are carved on slabs.[29] A cer-tain number of the latter can be seen in Webber's drawing of the Waimea temple. Many minor images have headdresses or miters identical to those of the major images and the portable wooden images, which will be exam-ined below. In some images the miter is flat (cf. Hiroa 1957, 493–94, 526), but in most it is three dimensional.

For the most part the temple images are masculine, but goddesses (*akua wahine*) can also be found. Female images occupy spatially inferior posi-tions, however: outside the *paehumu* (Ii 1963, 56) or perhaps on the "left" side (Kamakau 1976, 136) of the temple. It is difficult to believe Kamakau when he writes that in the *luakini* temple the images on the left of the altar were feminine while those on the right were masculine (1961, 325). In fact, this is not confirmed by any other source or by the iconography. It is true that Cook saw goddesses in the *hale mana* of the temple in Waimea; this is perhaps explained by the fact that the temple was consecrated to Kanaloa, many of whose attributes have a feminine connotation (see chap. 1).

Choris made a drawing of the image of a goddess whom he calls "Hare o Papa" (Hale o Papa). It is obviously one of the portraits of Papa pre-served in the *hale o Papa* ("house of Papa"), the feminine annex of the *luakini* temple. Another image said to be a portrait of Papa is reproduced by Brigham (1898, 16, pl. 8). It represents a kneeling woman with a large vulva and with human teeth in her mouth. Cox and Davenport (1974, 163) think it is a "sorcery image," but the kneeling position suggests she is in labor; thus, chances are that the statue represents Papa/Haumea in her role as the patroness of childbirth (cf. Beckwith 1940, 283–85). It is pre-cisely in her generative role that she figures in the *hale o Papa* rites that conclude the inauguration ritual for the *luakini* (see below, p. 327).

Mobile Images

Wooden "portable" images (Cox and Davenport 1974, 38) are generally small and carved at the top of short handles[30] or on top of poles. In the first case they are held in the hand; in the second they are carried by bracing the poles against a belt.[31] The pole is often notched; thus a cord or strap of cloth can be rolled around it, and the ends may be tied around the bearer's waist. According to N. Emerson, it is precisely this technique of carrying them that causes these images to be named *akua kā'ai*. Indeed, according to him this expression means "god with a belt" (in Malo 1951, 80). We have seen, however, that this name is much more generally applied than Emerson thinks because it also refers to fixed images.[32]

Portable wooden images are adorned with banners and precious feathers (Malo 1951, 167–68). Carried into battle, in procession, and in rites, they are used as coats of arms for their owners and rallying points for their men (cf. PE, 16; Malo 1951, 135). These images display either a helmet, sometimes reduced to a simple crescent (*mahiole*) or "cock's comb," or a head ornament identical to the one sometimes found at the top of the major images and, like it, resembling a miter. Moreover, they often have a mouth that, again like that of the major images, resembles a fishhook when seen in profile. Sometimes the crescent-shaped head is in one piece with a hooklike mouth (cf., for example, items A17 and A23 in Cox and Davenport 1974).

Wicker images covered with feathers (*akua hulu manu*, "feather gods") consist of an anthropomorphic head made of feather-covered wicker, which is placed on a wooden body wrapped with cloth (cf. Ellis 1842, 89; Kamakau 1961, 179) or is affixed to the top of a pole, like a *kā'ai* god.[33] They may also wear feather cloaks, just like nobles in battle or on ritual occasions (Rickman 1966, 303–4; King 1967, 512; Samwell 1967, 1228).

The wicker is made from the split aerial rootlets of the '*ie'ie* plant (*Freycinetia arborea*—Plischke 1929, 5; Hiroa 1957, 505). Attached to this are red feathers from the '*i'iwi* bird (*Vestiaria coccinea*) and yellow feathers from the *ō'ō* bird (*Acrulocercus nobilis*). Dog's or shark's teeth are secured in the mouth (Hiroa 1957, 508, 512; Ellis 1825, 86; 1842, 166, 158; Byron 1826, 200; Bloxam 1925, 76; Dampier 1971, 67, 70; Kamakau 1976, 136; Feher 1969, 103, 109).[34]

The feathers decorating the *akua hulu manu*, like those covering the helmets (*mahiole*) and cloaks ('*ahu'ula*) of the ali'i, come from offerings (*ho'okupu*) (cf. Cook and King 1784, 3:16–17; Ellis 1782, 91; Ledyard 1963, 111; Ingraham 1918, 6, n.d., 82; Rickman 1966, 303; King 1967, 499, 512; Campbell 1967, 139; Corney 1896, 111; Byron 1826, 8; Judd 1880, 23; Kuykendall 1938, 6–7; Hiroa 1957, 215–31, 231–48). They are "riches," "valuables" (cf. Kamakau 1961, 109), and their number measures an *akua*'s influence, his power to attract and subordinate men. The more completely an *akua* is covered, wrapped with feathers, the more mana he has (cf. Brigham 1899, 52, 54).

The king's *akua hulu manu* are housed in the *hale mana* of a *luakini* temple that is either the main temple or a temple especially destined to hold them. The temples built for keeping the feather god Kūkā'ilimoku are called *hale o Kā'ili*, "house of [Kū]kā'ili[moku]") (Ii 1963, 58; Ellis 1842, 118–19; Fornander 1916–20, 6:156, n. 83, 156–58, 22).

Like the *akua kā'ai*, the *akua hulu manu* are mobile images that follow
the king and nobles everywhere they go to wage war, to meet their peers
in ceremony (Samwell 1967, 1228; King 1967, 512; Rickman 1966,
303–4), or to perform rituals. This explains why the images "were never
left continuously in one heiau" (Kamakau 1961, 202).

Three feather gods are well known: Kūkeolo'ewa (Ellis 1842, 92–93;
HEN, 1:388), Kūho'one'enu'u (Westervelt 1915b, 27), and Kūkā'ilimoku. The first is the war god of the kings of Maui, the second that of the
kings of O'ahu, and the third that of the kings of the island of Hawai'i.

The first two have the same origin myth (Westervelt 1915b, 23–27);
no myth is known concerning the origin of Kūkā'ilimoku. According to
Kamakau (1866, 1867a, taken up by Emerson 1893, 7), Kūkā'ilimoku was
brought from Kahiki to Hawai'i by the priest Pā'ao, who is supposed to
have introduced human sacrifice. But the traditions followed by Fornander
(1878–80, 2:37; cf. Emerson 1893, 8, n. 12) do not include this god
among those worshiped by Pā'ao. According to Fornander, Kūkā'ilimoku
appears for the first time in the story of King Līloa and his son 'Umi,
who lived nine generations before Kamehameha (1916–20, 4:188–89;
Kamakau 1961, 9, 179, 209; Brigham 1899, 31–38; Plischke 1929).
In any event, these three gods are manifestations of Kū as a war and sorcery god. This is why they enable their owners to conquer lands and
defend them. They are *akua 'imi aupuni*, "gods who seized govern-
ments" (Kamakau 1961, 179, 166). The name Kūkā'ilimoku ("Kū island
snatcher") is telling in this respect.[35]

This god's "warlike" aspect is well known (Kamakau 1961, 173; Ellis
1842, 158). He follows the army, and before the battle, which he attends
surrounded by his priests (Ellis 1842, 148), he is carried in procession
around the camp (ibid., 158; Byron 1826, 153; Fornander 1878–80,
2:236). If some of the feathers on the crest of his helmet—or those of
his equivalents on Maui and O'ahu—stand up, they announce victory
(Fornander 1878–80, 2:236; Kamakau 1961, 148).[36] His war whoops
and grimaces (in reality, those of his priest, who is possessed by him—cf.
Ellis 1842, 158–59; Manby 1929, 42, 44) terrify the enemy (Beckwith
1940, 28).

Less known, but no less important, especially if there is no open war, is
Kūkā'ilimoku's (as well as Kūkeolo'ewa's and Kūho'one'enu'u's) connection with the sorcery the king practices against his enemies at home and
abroad. Beckwith goes so far as to state that "all the images of war gods
named under the Ku group are in fact sorcery gods" (1940, 110).

Sometimes Kūkā'ilimoku takes on the aspect of a comet or a swiftly
moving will-o'-the-wisp; he then leaves his temple and flies over inhabited
places (Ellis 1842, 113). He shares this trait with the Kālaipāhoa sorcery
gods, who appear in the form of a comet or lightning, and indeed, with all
gods used by sorcerers (cf. Kamakau 1964, 137; Westervelt 1915a, 114).

Furthermore, Kūkā'ilimoku "might fly from its stand to the head or shoulder or some part of the person it fancied, and this was a sign that the request had been favourably received" (Kamakau 1961, 211). During certain rites, he sometimes indicates those guilty of treason or transgression by inclining toward them. Individuals so designated are immediately sacrificed to him (Kamakau 1976, 140).

Iconological Observations

It is not my purpose here to make a full study of the symbolism of the images, which in any case raises immense problems. But some observations are needed to understand their ritual role. First of all, let us note that very few images can be associated with any certainty with individual gods. We know that in 1779, and probably after this date as well, the main image of Hikiau represented the god Kūnuiākea (King 1967, 621). Again at Hikiau, the two images in front of the *hale o mana* apparently represented Lono, since Cook was worshiped between them as a manifestation of this god (cf. Sahlins 1981; Valeri 1982b).[37] Likewise, the two images before the *hale o Lono* adjacent to Hikiau represented Lono. We also know that at least one and probably several extant feather images represent Kūkā'ilimoku (Hiroa 1957, 504; Brigham 1899, 37–39). Indeed, the properties attributed to the *akua hulu manu* make one think that they always represent warrior and sorcery gods and are therefore mostly connected with Kū. However, it cannot be proved that in all cases they are representations of aspects of this god. Finally, the six major wooden statues from Kona mentioned above are said to be representations of the main god of *luakini* temples. This would make them images of Kū.

We can ask ourselves if, on the basis of these relatively sure or likely identifications, it is not possible to associate certain iconological aspects with certain gods; this would permit us to identify the gods represented by the images for which we lack positive information. But it is easy to discover that no fixed relations between iconological motifs and gods can be established on this basis.[38] On the contrary, it seems that the same motifs are associated with different gods.

Let us consider, for example, the images in Hikiau and those from the nearby *hale o Lono*. The two images of Lono found in front of the latter are represented clearly by Webber. His drawing permits us to observe that the facial shape of these images is rather close to that of the *akua loa* (also a representation of Lono) figuring in the Makahiki festival (reproduced in Cox and Davenport 1974, 91). Thus we are tempted to associate this facial form consistently with Lono. But let us turn to the drawing that the surgeon Ellis made in 1779 of the major images in Hikiau, of which the principal one represents Kūnuiākea. Here we find the same face, or at least the very same mouth shape, that characterizes the images of Lono mentioned above. Moreover, the image of Lono in the *hale o Lono* and the major images in Hikiau in 1779 have the same headdress, a kind of tall tiara. As for the later images from Kona, which also represent Kū, the shape of their mouths is identical to that of Lono and the Hikiau images in 1779. The only difference is that the lower lip of the Kona images protrudes more clearly, so that the mouth, when seen in profile, evokes a fishhook or perhaps the whale-tooth pendant of the *lei niho palaoa* (Cox 1967) which, however, is also worn by Lono as god of the Makahiki.

What about the *akua hulu manu*, which usually seem to represent forms of Kū? At least two have the same flattened mouth as Lono (Hiroa 1957, 511). All have the same nose as the images from Kona; most are topped with a helmet (*mahiole*) similar to that worn by the major Kona-style images in the temple of Keikipu'ipu'i (see drawing by Arago, reproduced in Freycinet 1978, 75); some have a wig of human hair, like the main temple images from Kona.[39] Last, all the feather images have toothy mouths—again, like the main temple images.[40] Moreover, we find all these motifs, either associated or separately, in the portable wooden images as well. These, it seems, represent *'aumakua* gods or lower manifestations of the main deities. It thus appears that at least the motifs considered above cannot be proved to be associated with any particular god. On the other hand, it is possible and even likely that different *combinations* of these identical motifs index different classes of gods. But there is no sure way to prove this concerning the images that are positively known to represent a given god.

What appears possible, instead, is to establish the meanings common to all images—or at least the wooden ones. More precisely, it is possible to show that certain iconological motifs are paradigmatically equivalent to others found *in the same spatial position* in other images.

The structural analysis of the iconological motifs presupposes, then, that they all have the same spatial organization in common. This is easy to show. All images seem to be spatially divided into two parts: the upper part, which means the headdress, and the lower part, which includes all that is below the headdress. The second part in turn is usually divided in two: the higher part consists of the anthropomorphic body of the image; the lower is constituted by a base or handle or pole. The intermediary section between the headdress and the lower part of the image is usually of considerable importance. It includes the head, or rather the face, of the image, but it can incorporate certain features of the adjacent sections.

Naturally, the relative dimensions of each of these parts vary considerably from one image to another. As we have seen, the portable images often greatly develop the base, for obvious functional reasons, while the temple images develop the anthropomorphic section at the expense of the base and, especially in the later Kona style, of the headdress. However, the main image in the temple visited by Cook at Waimea had a very elongated base (it is in fact a pole) and a very high headdress; thus it closely resembled certain portable images. It must also be mentioned that some of the extant specimens—especially of temple images—are mutilated at the base or sometimes even in the headdress; they thus fail to display all their original structural components.

With these observations in mind, let us proceed to the analysis. Three basic types of headdress exist. The first consists of a *mahiole* (helmet with a crescent) or simply a crescent put on top of the head of the god. The meanings of this motif are well known: it is a representation of the rainbow and at the same time has a bellicose connotation, for it juts out threateningly. As a representation of the rainbow, by which the gods descend from heaven to earth (cf. Beckwith 1940, 37; Emerson 1915, 152), the crescent forms, in combination with the anthropomorphic lower part of the image, a spatial equivalent of the ritual process that makes the god present. Indeed, the statue represents both the rainbow on which the god descends and the human form into which he descends to manifest himself. The image, which is consecrated, made into a "true god" (*akua maoli*) in the ritual process, thus summarizes this process in a single synchronic visual experience.

The crescent is also a symbol of aggressiveness because it is part of an image that represents a particular human type—that of the warrior. In fact, the image is a portrait of the defiant warrior ali'i, often completed by a protruding tongue, a gesture of defiance toward the enemy (cf. Cox and Davenport 1974, catalog K24; Handy and Pukui 1972, 190). The aggressive connotations of the crescent explain why it is often transformed into a cock's comb: the fighting cock is a metaphor of the warrior, as we have seen.

The second type of headdress is constituted by a high, tiered miter similar to the one that topped the main images in Hikiau in 1779 and the images of Lono in the adjacent *hale o Lono*. Each tier of the miter usually consists of crescent-shaped components placed at right angles to one another. The number of tiers varies from three to eleven, but nine and five are the most frequent. It is possible that the importance of the god is measured by (among other things) the number of tiers, but we have no way of proving this.

In this case as well, the headdress seems to represent the gods' point of passage from transcendence to immanence, but here it is constituted not by a single rainbow, but by a plurality of superimposed heavens, each represented by a tier. In other words, I am suggesting that there is a correspondence between these tiered structures and the tiered structure of the heavens through which the gods must pass to reach the earth in Hawaiian cosmology (cf. Beckwith 1919, 299).

Each tier, however, is constituted by inverted crescents. This may evoke the crescent of the first type of headdress, at least in its aggressive connotation. Such a connection seems to be supported by a text that describes a god (Lonoka'eho) whose eight "foreheads" strike his enemies. It is difficult not to recognize in these foreheads the superimposed clusters of crescents found in the image type we are discussing (cf. Cox and Davenport 1974, 39).[41] Thus this type condenses the symbol of the heavens and that of the "striking foreheads" that evoke the god's power over his enemies. The greater the number of heavens through which the god must descend, the higher he is and the greater his power; the greater his power, the more numerous his "striking foreheads." In other words, this second type of image is probably a more emphatic realization of the ideas conveyed by the first, simpler type.

The tiered headdress evokes both in form and signification the *'anu'u* tower, also a means by which the gods are made to descend from heaven to earth. In this respect the tower, which is usually behind the main image (for instance, at Hikiau), can be viewed as the magnified double of that image's headdress. Both contribute to making the god descend into a statue in which he appears in human form, by representing the "ladder" he must take to descend.

Another association is justified, although it is less apparent: that between the tiered headdress and the offerings piled in layers on top of altars of the *lele* type. The similarity of the tiered headdress to the offerings displayed on top of sacrificial poles (cf. Zimmerman 1930, 89; Whitman 1979, 24) is even more striking. First, note that this similarity seems to be explicitly underlined by an image in which the tiered headdress represents a sacrificial pig bound on top of a sacrificial pole (Cox and Davenport 1974, catalog K48). Then consider Webber's drawing of the *hale o Lono* adjacent to Hikiau: next to the image of Lono are two sacrificial poles decorated with plants placed in a way that very much recalls the god's tiered miter. Moreover, these decorations are on top of a gourd that is in a position identical to that of Lono's head in the adjacent image. It is known that Lono is often represented by a gourd in which are placed the offerings destined for him. Thus there is a relation between Lono's mouth (where the offerings that the god is supposed to devour are placed) and Lono's gourd (where certain offerings are placed) on the one hand, and between the god's miter and the bunch of vegetable offerings on the other (Cook and King 1784, Atlas, pl. 60; drawing by Ellis reproduced in Ii 1963, 60; cf. as well Hiroa 1957, 523). It seems possible to conclude that the god's image is an equivalent of the offering pole, an equivalence that is also indicated by the practice of fastening the offering to the image (cf. drawing by Arago in Freycinet 1978, 75).

Let us now consider the third major type of headdress. This includes the representation of a wig that, as we know, characterizes the six extant speci-

mens of major images from Kona. This type of headdress is also documented by Arago's drawing of the statues in Keikipu'ipu'i temple and by
Choris's and Arago's drawings of the main image in 'Ahu'ena temple (reproduced in Barrère 1975, 7, 19, 30; Freycinet 1978, 75)

Like the crescent headdress, the wig has an aggressive component, as we
shall see. For one thing, it forms a prominent forehead that reminds one of
Lonoka'eho's "striking foreheads" and of the points of the crescents that
are their equivalents on certain images. Like the tiered headdress, the wig
may evoke an offering. For instance, the knobs carved on the wig of one of
the principal images from Kona (Cox and Davenport 1974, catalogue T5)
represent the heads of sacrificial pigs, while its forehead forms, in conjunction with the nose, a complete pig (ibid., p. 39, cf. image K3). Thus the
passage from the upper to the lower part of the image evokes the effect of
the sacrifice: the passage from the offering to the god, that is, *the apperception of the human species in the natural species* that makes up the offering.

But whether the headdress represents the offering or the rainbow on
which the god walks or the heavens that are his ladder, it always evokes the
transition from a state in which he is not visible in human form to a state in
which he is. The lower, anthropomorphic part of the image must therefore
be seen as the result of a transformation of the god. From this point of view
the image is an equivalent of and a memorial to the ritual process that consecrates it and makes it, as the Hawaiians say, *maoli*, "true." This will be
demonstrated in full in the analysis of the temple ritual.

Something must now be said of the transitional part that connects the
headdress and the anthropomorphic part of the image. This section is invariably constituted by the eyes and mouth—in sum, by the face. It is my
contention that this area marks the transition between the two states of the
anthropomorphic god—the transcendent and the immanent, the potential
and the actual—because it includes the two principal organs of the sacrificial transformation. That the mouth is such an organ should be evident
by now, after all I have said about the importance of the metaphor of devouring in sacrifice. But the mouth cannot be separated from the eyes,
which are so to speak its intellectual counterpart in the work of transformation, since they embody consciousness. This will be demonstrated in
full at a later stage of the analysis. For the moment, let me say that in Hawaiian thought the eye always marks a transition or transformation.[42]
Moreover, it is associated in this context both with the stars, that is, with
what is most divine,[43] and with sight and intelligence,[44] which are what is
most human. The organ that enables man to grasp the divine is thus translated "objectively" into the ultimate expression of what it grasps, the gods.
The correspondence between the eye and the star seems thus to offer a
kind of transcendental guarantee of man's potential for understanding and
dominating the divine, and conversely, of the possibility of translating—
through knowledge—the god into concrete human actions and states.

The idea of this correspondence is rendered in the image by the blending of the eyes into the headdress, either in its vertical form or as a wig. In the first case, the eyes often merge into one of the tiers of the miter, and thus with the heavenly elements that constitute it (crescents, rainbows, etc.); in the second case they blend with the plaits of the wig and thus form crescents with them as well. The transitional (and therefore transformative) function of the face is made particularly evident in those images in which headdress and mouth blend to form a single crescent (see, for example, Cox and Davenport 1974, catalog A17, A23; and Ellis's and Dampier's sketches of Hale o Keawe). Here, in effect, the crescent on the top of the head continues downward to form a mouth. Thus the face is reduced to its meaning: the god descending on the rainbow devours the offerings and therefore encompasses the human, identifies with it, *becomes a face*.

In the context of the transformation represented by the images, it is important to correctly interpret the rather singular posture generally taken by the representation of the anthropomorphic body of these deities: knees bent, arms slightly stretched forward, back rigid, and so forth. Cox and Davenport believe that this posture "expresses potential action," and more specifically they identify it with the posture "taken by wrestlers and boxers preliminary to a match" (1974, 45). The first proposition is incontestable; the body of the image certainly represents the transformation of the god into a potentiality of human action. But for this very reason it is less certain that the god's posture necessarily represents a fighting position. Kaeppler (n.d.) has recently advanced the hypothesis that the god is represented as dancing. To support it, she points out that the recitation of prayers for the consecration of the *luakini* temple images is accompanied by dancing. The image would thus represent the dance that consecrates it. Within certain limits, Kaeppler's hypothesis seems well founded. Moreover, the hypothesis that the god's transformation is completed in dance— that is, in an action in which the individual coincides with the typical and the collective—is made to suit me (see the discussion above of dance in ritual).

Location and Orientation

A text by S. M. Kamakau shows that there is a relation between the nature and purpose of the temple and its site: "There were many kinds of sites, *kahua*, on which to build heiaus, and they were pointed out by those who knew their locations, the *po'e kuhikuhi pu'uone*. There were sites for heiaus for the increase of the population (*heiau ho'oulu kanaka*), for the health of the nation (*heiau ho'ola lahui*), for peace (*ka maluhia*) or for distant voyaging (*ka holo 'ana kahiki*)" (1976, 134).

It also seems that the relative "purity" or "impurity" of places is taken into account. In one story a priest has it made known to the king that his temple is built in "a place where to excrete" and suggests that he move it (HEN, 1:217–22). New temples are often built on the sites of old ones that have proved successful (Malo 1951, 161; Kamakau 1976, 132).

It is probable that the chosen site has an affinity with the god and is thus appropriate for his habitation. War temples are often built next to battle-fields. This is attested, for example, by the numerous *heiau* of Nu'uanu valley on O'ahu (Kamakau 1961, 291) and by Pu'ukoholā temple at Kawaihae, on the island of Hawai'i (Fornander 1916–20, 4:324–27; 1878–80, 2:121–22).[45]

As a general rule, *luakini* are not built in the middle of inhabited places (Thrum 1906, 118), but they are nevertheless found near royal residences.[46] They also tend to be placed on elevated spots, so they are easily visible (Bennett 1931, 35; Emory 1924, 61; Hiroa 1957, 516).

The only data we have on the orientation of the temples deal with the relation between the front and the position of the tower. Moreover, they are contradictory. According to Malo, if the front (*ke alo*) of the *luakini* faces (*huli*) west (*komohana*) or east (*hikina*), the *'anu'u* tower is found at the *'ākau* end of the temple; if it faces *'ākau* or *hema*, the tower is found to the east (*hikina*) (Malo MS, 163). Kamakau, on the other hand, writes that the *'anu'u* tower is found on the *'akau* side of the temple (1976, 135–36). To interpret these statements, one should keep in mind that the words *'ākau* and *hema* can have either absolute or relative referents. In the first case, *'ākau* means "north" and *hema* "south"; in the second, *'ākau* means "right" and *hema* "left."

In fact, Hawaiians use two systems of orientation. One is based on an east/west axis (*hikina/komphana*); the other uses an axis founded on the land/sea (*uka/kai*) opposition. In the first system the observer is always supposed to face west; his right (*'ākau*) coincides with the north, his left (*hema*), with the south. If, in contrast, the land/sea axis is used, the referents of *'ākau* and *hema* change depending on the position of the observer (Malo 1951, 9–10).

It seems that Malo, at least, uses an absolute orientation system, since all the cases he considers in his description of the temples' orientation imply that *'ākau* refers to north and *hema* to south. On the other hand, it is possible that for Kamakau *'ākau* means "right" here as it does at other points of his description of the temples. But he does not tell us whether "right" and "left" refer to the standpoint of an observer facing the entrance of the temple from the outside or from the inside. The second alternative is the more probable, as is shown by comparing the description 'Ī'ī gives of Hale o Keawe temple in Hōnaunau with a plan of the same temple drawn by A. Bloxam. 'Ī'ī says that inside the temple house the kings' bones are placed on the right side (1963, 139). Bloxam's plan shows that they are on the right as seen from the standpoint of someone inside the house facing the door. If what is true of this house may be generalized to include any enclosed space, it must be supposed that the "right" and the "left" sides that Kamakau speaks of are established with respect to an observer facing the entry door from inside the temple.

Are Malo's and Kamakau's statements (insofar as they differ) verified by the data? Archaeologists deny it (Bennett 1931, 35; McAllister 1933, 9), but let us consider the few temples for which we have relatively precise descriptions. The Hikiau and Hale o Keawe temples confirm Kamakau's as well as Malo's statements. At Hikiau the entrance is on the north side and the tower on the east side.[47] If we admit that the entrance of the temple opens onto its front,[48] we can affirm that the 'anu'u tower is on the right relative to someone *leaving* the temple precincts (as Kamakau would have it). The same is the case in the Hale o Keawe temple in Hōnaunau.

According to Freycinet, the sacred houses inside the Keikipu'ipu'i temple (at Kailua, Kona district, island of Hawai'i) are found to the right of the entrance. We have just established that the Hawaiian system to determine the right and left sides of an enclosed space is the inverse of the European system, which determines them with respect to an observer standing outside the entrance. The sketch Arago made of this temple shows that the tower was on the side opposite the houses, thus to the "left" according to the European system. It can be deduced that from a Hawaiian standpoint the tower at Keikipu'ipu'i was on the "right" and the houses on the "left," as Kamakau would have it (cf. Freycinet 1978, 74; Arago 1822, 2:114–15; 1844, 63; see as well Vancouver 1801, 5:103; Boelen 1835–36, 3:44).

In contrast, 'Ahu'ena temple in Kailua contradicts both Kamakau's and Malo's schemes. The entrance is found on the north side, but the 'anu'u tower is on the west. In Waha'ula temple (Puna district, island of Hawai'i), the entrance is on the south side, but the tower is on the west, which contradicts Malo's scheme but confirms Kamakau's (cf. Thrum 1908b, 50).

Pu'ukoholā (Kohala district), the most important of the *luakini* built in 1792 by Kamehameha certainly disproves Malo, for this temple faces west, but its tower is found to the south (cf. Brigham, n.d., 140). It could confirm Kamakau's scheme. Close to Pu'ukoholā is a much older temple, Mo'okini, that is in conformity with Malo's scheme as well as Kamakau's. In fact, the entrance and the front of this temple are on the west, and it is likely that the tower was situated at the north side, where the sacrificial pit can still be found, since this pit was usually near the tower, according to Malo (cf. Thrum 1908b, 59).[49]

That at Pu'ukoholā the tower and the main altar are found to the south has a plausible explanation. This southerly orientation was probably used because Keōua, whose sacrifice was the goal Kamehameha sought when he built the temple, lived in Ka'ū, which lies to the south. This suggests that the altar upon which Keōua was to be sacrificed (and thus the tower, which must be adjacent to the main altar) was pointed toward him. Can we suppose that in any *luakini* inaugurated during a time of war the tower and the altar for the human sacrifice are oriented in the enemy's direction?

The temples of Kona that are known to us and the Pu'ukoholā temple, taken together, suggest a broader principle, however. In all these temples the main image and the tower are on the side toward the mountains, that is, the direction from which both the god and the enemy (cf. Kamakau 1961, 14, 17, 18) are supposed to come.

Huikala Rites
The Consultation with the Priests of the Principal Rites

According to K. Kamakau (1919–20, 9), the king, after choosing the date for tabooing the *luakini*, consults with the priests who preside over the different rites. In order they are:

1. the priest of the order of Kū (*mo'o Kū*) (most likely, the *kahuna nui*);
2. the priest of the order of Lono (*mo'o Lono*);
3. the priest of the *helehonua* rite; [50]
4. the priest of the *kū'alaea* rite;
5. the priest of the Haku 'ōhi'a rite;
6. the priest of the *kāpapaulua* rite; [51]
7. the priest of the *hono* rite;
8. the *kāhala'alaea* [52] and the *hale o Papa* priests.

The function of each of these priests will emerge as I describe the rites they perform.

Huikala of Ali'i and Kahuna

The inauguration ritual of the temple is preceded by a time of purification (*huikala*) that begins when the moon is waning and, more precisely, on the night of Lā'au-Ku-kāhi (eighteenth night of the moon) of the month preceding the one in which the inauguration takes place. The ali'i and kahuna build for themselves, in succession, five booths: *hale pu'uone*, *hale pōhue*, *hale oeoe*, *hale pālima*, and *hale hāwai*. [53] They are consecrated and then made *noa* one after the other. This purification rite (*huikala*) enables the ali'i and kahuna to enter the temple.

Huikala of the Land
Malo MS, 165

After the purification of the ali'i and priests, the entire land is made *noa*, "free," by another *huikala* rite, which takes place from the twenty-fourth to the twenty-ninth day of the lunar month. The rite is as follows. On the twenty-fourth day, Kāloa-ku-kāhi, the main road (*ala nui*) surrounding the kingdom (*moku*) on the side toward the mountains (*mauka*) is cleared. A stone altar (*ahu pōhaku*) is erected where the road reaches the boundary of each *ahupua'a*. On this altar is placed a pig's head carved from *kukui* wood (*Aleurites moluccana*), with some *pa'i 'ai* ("hard, pounded but undiluted taro"—PE, 278; cf. Ellis 1842, 325). This carving is called *pua'a kukui* ("*kukui* pig"). Then all return home, and the road is left empty.

The *'alaea* priest, accompanied by a man carrying a calabash full of water mixed with ochre (*ipu wai 'alaea*) and a man with his hair done in the "*Nīheu*" style impersonating the god[54] [Kahōāli'i], then make the tour of the *moku* on the road. They stop at each *ahupua'a* in front of the altar. The priest says a prayer and smears the *pua'a kukui* with ocher. After eating some taro with his companions, the priest declares the *ahupua'a* "free" (*noa*).

The tour of all the *ahupua'a* is made between the twenty-sixth day and the twenty-ninth day.

K. Kamakau 1919–20, 9–11

When the day approaches on which the *luakini* is to be tabooed the king orders the *kāhala'alaea* priest to begin his rite and to inform him whether it is successful. This priest prepares himself and prays throughout the night of Kāne (the twenty-seventh). When the morning of Lono (the twenty-eighth) comes, he has readied a gourd containing red ocherous earth dissolved in water (cf. Wilkes 1845, 4:506). On the following day (the twenty-ninth), the king and a crowd of people come to hear the words of the priest. While he prays, the king approaches the *akua 'alaea*, "ochre god." This image lies next to the gourd and is covered with a thin white cloth. Then a man, his head covered with "the wig [made] of the hair of people of old" ("*ka papale o ka lauoho o ka poe kahiko*"), gets up and shakes spears before the eyes of the audience, who remain seated. He makes them wince but does not pierce their eyes. He looks at them threateningly and terrifies them by saying, "Be careful, be careful, or you will be struck by the owl's spear."

After this rite the king orders the "tribute collector" (*luna 'auhau*) to announce the arrival of his god (that is, the *akua 'alaea*) to the *konohiki* (caretakers) of the different *ahupua'a*. They must clear the road and prepare the tribute (*ho'okupu*); otherwise they will be dismissed.

During its tour of the land, the *akua 'alea* is preceded and followed by four flags (*lepa*). A herald goes before it to clear the way of men, pigs, and dogs. All fires must be extinguished. The gods stop before each *pua'a kukui*, which the priest marks (*kākau*) with red ocher, at the same time offering a prayer. Then the people of each land (*'āina*) in successive order bring their *ho'okupu*: pigs, food, feathers, and cloths.

On the evening of the twenty-ninth day (Mauli), the king and a priest perform the *lupa haʻalele* rite, which unfortunately is not described.[55]

Wilkes 1845, 4:506

"On the 29th, the priest, leaning on a spear, repeats prayers and begs lands."

Huikala of the Audience and the Temple
Malo MS, 166

On the evening of the thirtieth day, all those who will take part in the temple ritual assemble to be purified. A priest dips a bunch of *pala* in a bowl and sprinkles everyone with it after pronouncing a prayer.[56] After this rite, everyone returns home.

K. Kamakau 1919–20, 11

On the thirtieth, the priest makes the temple taboo by sprinkling it with tabooed water (*wai kapu*). After this rite it is forbidden to eat pork until evening. Priests and aliʻi in great numbers pray and chant the praises (*hiʻilani*) of the "wooden gods" (*akua lāʻau*) and the "feather gods" (*akua hulu manu*). After the prayers the king offers a pig in sacrifice, saying:

O Kūnuiākea, Lononuiākea, Kānenuiākea, Kanaloanuiākea, O all of my gods, come absolutely all of you, here is the pig, a live pig, so that I may receive life from you, O gods (*eia ka puaʻa la, he puaʻa ola e ola aʻu iā ʻoukou e ke akua*); here is your pig, your banana and your coconut; come save (*hoʻola mai*) the nobles and all the men; O all my gods, pay heed (*e hoʻolohe mai ʻoe*) to my words here to you; seek out the sinner (*kanaka hewa*), curse [or "sacrifice"] (*mōlia*) him, kill him (*e make ia*); preserve (*e malama ʻoe*) the just man (*pono*)[57] and do him good; have compassion (*aloha*) for my land (*ʻāina*) and take care (*mālama*) of the "people that attend the land" (*maka ʻāinana* "commoners"—PE, 207).

In this manner the king worships the gods (*hoʻomana ʻku i ke akua*). Then at nightfall, the nobles and priests with their feather gods congregate and lay down to sleep.

Wilkes 1845, 4:506

"On the 30th, palm-leaves are spread on the roof of the house in the heiau."[58]

Interpretation

The rite that *huikala*s the officiators is literally a rite of passage; aliʻi and kahuna must pass from one booth to another to represent the successive stages of their separation with respect to the ordinary world. This rite is identical to the one performed after the conclusion of the Makahiki festival in order to resume the consumption of pork, and therefore sacrificial contact with the divine. Its performance is motivated in both contexts by the necessity for separating the pure people (ali'i, kahuna), who enter into sacrificial contact with the gods, from the impure (women, commoners). This separation has been particularly blurred during the Makahiki festival; but even after it has been reinstated it is threatened in everyday life. Hence, whenever an important *luakini* ritual is to be performed, the high-ranking nobles must go through the rite of the booths again in order to be purified anew.

Apparently the purification rites preceding the entry into a new or renovated temple take five and a half "days" (from the night of the eighteenth to dawn of the twenty-fourth). It is likely, then, that a different booth is built each day to mark the stages of the purification. Probably the booths are erected within the temple enclosure but not in the sanctum sanctorum, which one may enter only at a later stage.

Immediately after the rite to *huikala* the officiants of the luakini ritual, the rite to *huikala* the land is performed. Although the first *huikala* can be translated "to purify," the second cannot. On the contrary, it seems that "to pollute" would be a more appropriate rendering, since the land is made accessible to human use (*noa*) by being desacralized and losing its divine purity. The contrast between the two cases shows that the more general signification of *huikala* is "to bring about a passage from a state that requires ritual action (*kapu*) to a state that requires no ritual action (*noa*)." It also shows that these two states are purely relative. Thus the purification of ali'i and priests makes them *noa* in that, having fulfilled the ritual prescriptions (*kapu*), they cease to be obligated to perform them. On the other hand, their new state involves other ritual prescriptions (*kapu*) for them and makes them *kapu* (objects of ritual behavior) for other people, those who are less pure. In other words, the state of *noa* is never absolute, but only relative to a given *kapu*; and the verb *huikala* refers to the lifting of that particular *kapu* and the creation of a state of *noa* relative to it.

Moreover, both what is marked *kapu* and what is marked *noa* can be pure or impure and are so only relatively. Thus, when the priests and nobles become *noa* relative to the *kapu* of purification, they are so because they are purer than they were before the performance of the rite. But when the land becomes *noa* relative to the *kapu* that bound it, it becomes *noa* because it becomes less pure, less divine—or not divine at all.

On the other hand, the two *huikala* rites are not simply opposed; they are also complementary. The land is made *noa* by a displacement of its sanctity onto a part (the offering) that substitutes for the whole; it can be polluted only on condition that its purity be symbolically preserved. But the identity of this part with the whole is fully realized only when the offering is consecrated in the temple to the god that represents the totality; thus, being eaten by him, the offering becomes him. This explains why only at the end of the temple ritual do the land and its products become fully accessible, while for the duration of the ritual productive activities are forbidden. Thus consecration that fully justifies the desacralization of the land requires a category of pure men who can approach the god and manipulate the offerings. This category, precisely, is renewed by the purification rite of the aliʻi and priests. Hence the two *huikala* complement each other.

Returning to the details of the offerings given at the level of the *ahupuaʻa*, we must note a difference between the accounts of Malo and K. Kamakau. According to Malo, these offerings are received both by a "man impersonating the god" and by the *ʻalaea* priest. K. Kamakau writes instead that the tour of the kingdom is made only by the *ʻalaea* priest together with his god, the *akua ʻalaea*. At the same time, he says that this god is consecrated in a rite in which a man wearing a wig (*pāpale*) threatens to blind the audience with the owl god's spear. This man closely corresponds to the "man impersonating the god" mentioned by Malo. Indeed, the "wig" of the first is not very different from the "hair in the style of Nīheu" of the second, since according to Malo this hairstyle consists of "sewn hair" (*ʻlauoho . . . / kui ia*), that is, of switches (*ʻākī*).[59] Moreover, the threatening gaze of the person described by K. Kamakau recalls the "large and searching" eyes of Nīheu (Emerson 1915, 114, n. 16), the hero who gives his name to the hairstyle of Malo's "man impersonating the god."

The latter characterization is equivalent to that of Kahōāliʻi, who is called "a god who is a true man" (*"Hookahi akua kanaka maoli"*—K. Kamakau 1919–20, 10; Kamakau 1964, 54) and the "king's god" (Vancouver 1801, 5 : 37; Kamakau 1961, 180).[60] Kahōāliʻi has the privilege of scooping out the eyes of his human victims and eating them. This is reminiscent of the fact that the man described by K. Kamakau has the right to threaten to pierce the eyes of the audience. Thus it seems likely that both Malo and K. Kamakau are referring to the same person and that this person is Kahōāliʻi. In sum, the two sources imply that Kahōāliʻi and the *akua ʻalaea* are associated in the rite for collecting the *hoʻokupu*.[61]

Two problems thus arise. Is it possible to establish the identity of these two gods more precisely? Why are they associated in this rite?

First, let us discuss the identity of Kahōāliʻi. This name is in reality a title signifying "royal companion" (PE, 385; Emerson 1915, 203) or "the peer of the king" (N. Emerson in Malo 1951, 157)[62] or even "the king's double, alter ego." We know, moreover, that he is a close relative of the king, which makes him particularly apt to function as his double. For example, the Kahōāliʻi of King Kalaniʻōpuʻu and King Kamehameha was an agnatic half-brother of Kalaniʻōpuʻu (Barrère in Kamakau 1976, 146). Kahōāliʻi is thus both the human incarnation of a king's god and the king's double. In short, he is a "divine double" of the king. But which aspect of the king's divinity, and more specifically which of the king's gods, does he incarnate?

S. M. Kamakau conjectures that "Kahoʻaliʻi of Kamehameha had been

Plate 1. Interior of a *luakini* temple, Kaua'i. The tower, the *lele* altar, and the pole-shaped main image are clearly recognizable. Drawing by John Webber, from Cook and King 1784, atlas.

Plate 2. Interior of the *hale mana* in a *luakini* temple, Kaua'i. Drawing by John Webber, from Cook and King 1784, atlas.

eⱭ View of a Morai at O'whyhee.
Published Decʳ 14. 1781. by G. Robinson.

Plate 3. Main images in Hikiau temple, Kealakekua, island of Hawai'i, as they were in 1779. From Ellis 1782, 2:181.

Plate 4. Offering being presented to Captain Cook in front of the *hale o Lono* adjacent to Hikiau temple. Note mitered images of Lono. From Cook and King 1784, atlas.

Plate 5. Execution of a human victim. Drawing by Jacques Arago, 1819, from Arago 1822.

Plate 6. Feather god. From Cook and King 1784, atlas.

.A MAN of the SANDWICH ISLANDS, with his HELMET.

Plate 7. An ali'i in cape and helmet. Drawing by John Webber, from Cook and King 1784, atlas.

Plate 9. Main temple image, representing Kū (Kona style). Detail of the face, showing the pig-shaped nose.

Plate 8. *Akua ka'ai* image with headdress.

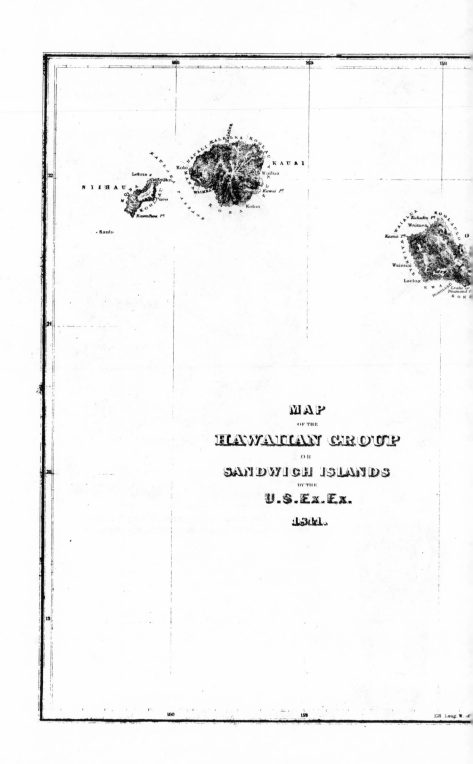

MAP
OF THE
HAWAIIAN GROUP
OR
SANDWICH ISLANDS
BY THE
U.S.Ex.Ex.
1841.

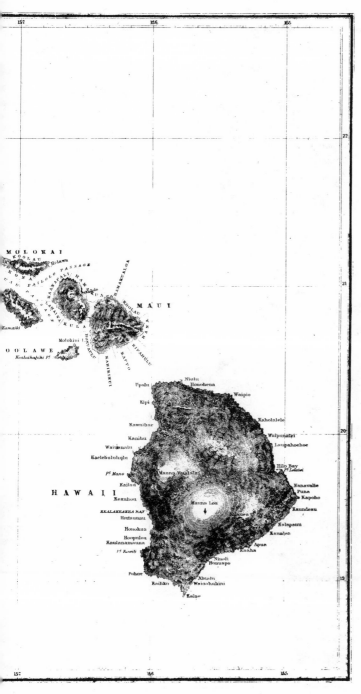

Plate 10. Map of
the Hawaiian
archipelago.
From Wilkes 1845.

Plate 11. Image of god or ancestral king from the royal mausoleum *hale o Keawe*. Field Museum of Natural History, Chicago.

made a god, perhaps because the spirit of an ancient god by the name of Kaho'ali'i possessed him (*noho pu ana*)" (1964, 20, cf. 54). Elsewhere he states that this god is a form of Kāne (ibid., 28), doubtless because, being associated with thunder, he is ipso facto associated with Kānehekili (or Kahekili), a form of Kāne as thunder god (ibid., 70). But in another text Kamakau places Kahōāli'i in the family of the volcanic deities, thereby associating him with Kamohoali'i ("the royal selected one"—PE, 387), with whom some identify him (cf. Beckwith 1940, 130; Handy 1972, 592).[63]

My impression is that S. M. Kamakau's rather contradictory hypotheses are not based on traditional lore and are his own rationalizations of the divine status of the man Kahōāli'i. But Kahōāli'i is clearly a human title, and it is not certain that a transcendent god bearing this title existed traditionally. Instead of mechanically postulating a transcendent double of Kahōāli'i, it is better to try to reconstitute the identity of the god or of the aspect of the divine that this man impersonates on the basis of the properties attributed to him and especially of the roles he plays in ritual. Let me begin with his ritual roles.

We have seen that in the annual rite for *aku* fishing Kahōāli'i eats the victims' eyes, that is, the firstfruits of fishing and the "first portion" of the human victims who expiate man's appropriation of fish. The *aku* is associated with Kū and even with Kūkā'ilimoku (Emerson 1892, 7–9). Since Kahōāli'i eats the firstfruits destined for this god, it must be inferred that he is impersonating him. In the *luakini* temple ritual Kahōāli'i also appears, as we will see, as a fisherman of both fish and men, whose eyes he devours, again on behalf of Kū, to whom these victims are offered.

In the *kauila nui* rite the relation of Kahōāli'i to Kū's violent aspect stands out sharply. As we will see, he precedes the feather images that represent this god in his "conquering," warlike forms; going in front of them, he represents them all.

That Kahōāli'i seems to be regularly associated with Kū, at least in the *aku* and *luakini* rituals, prompts us to suppose that he represents this god in the *ho'okupu* rite as well.[64] This hypothesis is again reinforced by the correspondences between the headdress worn by Kahōāli'i, the one carved on top of the temple images in the Kona style, and that of certain feather images, which consists of wigs or false hair quite similar to Kahōāli'i's (Ellis 1842, 89; cf. Cox and Davenport 1974, 39).

In sum, in all his ritual roles Kahōāli'i seems to represent the wild, violent, and therefore unregulated aspect of Kū's power (or perhaps of the divine power in general). This is confirmed by his behavior and privileges, which put him in a presocial, almost prehuman state. In fact, he is allowed to violate the rules upon which Hawaiian society is founded by eating with the women (Kamakau 1961, 180), by possessing them without restraint,[65] and by going around completely nude, his genitals exposed (K. Kamakau 1919–20, 11). Moreover, he is selected from among people who have strange birthmarks evoking anomalous and terrifying actions: "If a child born to some descendant of Kahoʻaliʻi has the hand streaked with black and a black ring around one eye, he will be a man who 'scoops out eyeballs,' a *puʻukoamakaiʻa*" (Kamakau 1964, 70; cf. N. Emerson in Malo 1951, 155).

By connecting Kahōāliʻi with a dimension of the divine power represented by Kū in the *luakini* ritual, I do not intend to rule out the hypothesis that the man-god also corresponds to a transcendent god named Kahōāliʻi, as S. M. Kamakau would have it. However, if this god exists, he is nothing other than the personification of a group of properties that belong in the first place to Kū and to a lesser extent to Kāne, as a thunder god (Kamakau 1964, 70; Beckwith 1940, 61).[66]

Let us now turn our attention to the *ʻalaea* god. It is likely that he is a particular form of Lono, for his priest, the *kahuna kuhi ʻalaea*, "priest who marks with ocher," belongs to the order of Lono (Malo MS, 172, 37.63). Moreover, the god's ocher and his image are consecrated during the twenty-eighth day of the lunar month, which belongs to Lono.

Why are Kahōāliʻi and the *akua ʻalaea* associated in the rite to collect the *hoʻokupu* offerings? Because, it seems to me, by being associated they are able to represent the transformation of the divine that is brought about by the consecration of the firstfruits. Kahōāliʻi impersonates the devouring aspect of the divine; by feeding him the firstfruits, he is neutralized. Thus he can be succeeded by the *akua ʻalaea*, who "frees" the land. The relation of succession here symbolizes a transformation. In one sense Kahōāliʻi/Kū becomes the *akua-ʻalaea*/Lono. This hypothesis is confirmed by the extreme frequency throughout the ritual of the Kū → Lono transformation, as we will see. The form it takes in this context constitutes its first rough outline and prefiguration; its full realization will have to wait until the end of the inauguration rite of the *luakini* temple.

In the end, the difference between Malo's and Kamakau's accounts amounts to this. In Malo the transformation Kahōāliʻi → *akua ʻalaea* is repeated in each *ahupuaʻa*, since the two gods take part in the procession around the entire kingdom. In K. Kamakau, the transformation takes place once and for all at the moment of consecrating the *akua ʻalaea*, and thus the ocher used to free the *ahupuaʻa*. I infer this from the fact that Kahōāliʻi plays a most important role in this consecration but is not said to take part in the circuit of the land.

Rites for Appropriating the Haku ʻōhiʻa
Rite for Incorporating the Audience into the Temple
Malo MS, 167

The temple is made taboo on the day of Hilo. The king, the nobles, and their followers enter the *luakini*, where they are seated in rows and ordered to keep silent. A priest holding a branch of *'ie'ie* (*Freycinetia arborea*) recites the *lupalupa* prayer.[67] When he utters the words "*E ku kaikaina hiki [i]a*" ("arise younger brothers, receive . . ."), the audience replies "*Ola*" (". . . life!").[68] Then the priest says "*Ia*,"[69] and the audience replies "*Ola, ola, o Kū*" ("life, life, O Kū"). All must then sleep in the temple. No one may leave it to spend the night with his wife. This taboo is sanctioned by death.

K. Kamakau 1919–20, 11

On the morning of the first day of the month (Hilo), priests have the crowd sit in eight rows (*lālani*), and they line up the feather gods, which are "forty" or "twice forty" in number. One god is impersonated by a man; it is Kahōāli'i. He stands in front of the other gods and is completely naked; he is not ashamed to be seen with his penis dangling (*ule lewalewa*).

A priest, standing, holds a white loincloth (*malo ke'oke'o*) and a branch of *'ie'ie* (*Freycinetia arborea*), a vine with a scarlet inflorescence (Neal 1929, 19) used to weave the wicker part of the feather gods. Over this branch the priest says some words (*kalokalo*),[70] thereby sacrificing it (*kaumaha*) to the gods:

The loincloth, the loincloth, the *'ie'ie*; the lightning (*ka uila*); this is the *'ie'ie*. O Kū, O Lono, O Kanaloa, give life (*e ola*) to your caretaker—and give moreover life to all the nobles and all the men (*i na kanaka a pau loa*).

Processional Rite
K. Kamakau 1919–20, 11–13

When the *'ie'ie* rite is over, the priests (approximately forty of them) rise, praying and praising "the god" aloud. Then the *akua hulu manu* are carried in procession by their keepers, who turn in a circle before the audience. They thus exalt the gods.

Then the *'alaea* priest enjoins the audience to remain still and pay attention to his prayer, and to stand up and sit down each time he tells them, that is, eight times. He takes a bunch of coconuts and waves it (*ho'āli*) before "the god" [the king's feather god?] and utters the following words: "O Kū, O Lono, O Kāne, O Kanaloa, here is a bunch of coconuts, give life to your caretaker."[71] Then he seizes his staff (*lā'au*) and stands, praying aloud. The people and the nobles listen to him attentively to discover any error in his prayer.

After praying, the priest repeats eight times to the people, "My younger brothers (*e ku'u kaikaina*),[72] receive life." Each time he rises and sits down the audience shouts loudly. Then the priest turns to the king and asks him, "O heavenly one (*e ka lani*), how was the prayer?" If the prayer was faulty (*hewa*), the king tells him so, but if it was completely satisfactory (*pono*), he approves it and then the priest asks him for land.[73]

After this rite, everyone returns home praising (*ho'ole'a*) the *akua hulu manu* and all the "minor" gods (*akua li'ili'i*).

Malo MS, 167

Malo only alludes to this rite, which he calls *kauila huluhulu*. According to him it takes place on the second day of the month (the morning of Hoaka) and not, as K. Kamakau states, on the first. During this rite people are seated in rows (probably corresponding to ranks).

Wilkes 1845, 4:506

On the first day of the moon, people are placed in eight rows in the temple. Prayers are said, and pigs and "fruit" are sacrificed.

The Consecration of Adzes (*Malu ko'i*)
Malo MS, 167

On the evening of the second day, the *kahuna Haku 'ōhi'a* ("priest of Lord 'Ōhi'a") [74] consecrates the adzes (*ko'i*) [75] used to cut down the trees for making the images of the gods. Three fowls are baked in the oven (*kālua*). One is intended for the priest, another for the king, and the third for the god.

K. Kamakau 1919–20, 13

On the evening of the first day, the king, the priest, and the ali'i, accompanied by all the portable gods, prostrate themselves, offering prayers in the *luakini*. This rite is called *malu ko'i* (cf. Ii 1963, 42).[76] They prostrate themselves until dark night, desiring a rainfall during the night. When it rains they praise the gods.[77]

Wilkes 1845, 4:506

On the first day of the moon, the Haku 'ōhi'a priest [78] asks the king for an offering of three fowls to bake at night; one is for the king, another for the priest, the third for the god.

The Fetching of the Haku 'ōhi'a Tree
Malo MS, 167–68

On the morning of Ku-kāhi (the third of the month), the king, ali'i, priests, and people depart for the mountain carrying sacrificial offerings (*mōhai*): pigs, bananas, coconuts, a "red fish" (*i'a 'ula*),[79] and a man who has broken a taboo (*kanaka lawehala*). The cortege goes up to the '*ōhi'a* tree selected for carving the image of the god. This tree must be perfect, without any hollows (*pūhā*). The man who is to cut it down and the *kahuna Haku 'ōhi'a* (who is also the priest of the *malu ko'i* rite) approach the tree from two opposite sides. The audience remains silent and keeps its distance while the priest, adze in hand, pronounces the '*aha mauha'alelea* prayer. At his side the king seizes a pig and awaits the end of the prayer to utter "'āmama" ("ended," "offered in sacrifice"—cf. PE, 21) and then to kill it by dashing it to the ground.

Then the priest asks the king, "How was our *'aha* belonging to us both?" If the audience has made no noise and has not interrupted the prayer, the king answers, "The *'aha* was excellent (*ua maika'i ka 'aha*)." Then the priest declares, "Tomorrow your adversary (*hoa paio*) will die; the *'aha* for your god was successful; on the death of your adversary, (his) land will be yours, and this business (*mea*) will be completed." Then the priest cuts (*'oki*) a chip from the tree and immediately afterward cuts off (*'oki*) the transgressor's head. Afterward the tree is cut down.

While the pigs are cooking in the oven (*kālua na pua'a*), the image of the god is carved in the tree trunk. The pork is eaten by the king and all those who take part in the rite. Only the priest of the Haku 'ōhi'a does not partake of this meal, for he begins a fast of six days. The remains of the pig are buried with the body of the sacrificed man ("*ke kanaka i pepehi ia*") at the foot of the tree that has just been felled. The human victim is called "the *mauha'alelea* man."

After the sacrifice they go to take *pala* fern and fruits and flowers of the *'ōhi'a-'ai* (*Eugenia malaccensis*). Then the image is escorted on its progression toward the coast. If someone is encountered on the god's path, he is killed. There is shouting and chanting of the words

"*E kuamu, e kuamu; mu,*
E kua wa e kua wa Wa,
Aiau e lanakila, Uo."

When they arrive at the temple, they put the image on the *papahola* platform and cover it with *'ie'ie* vines.

Commentary

The text of the chant above is almost identical in the accounts of K. Kamakau, Wilkes, and 'Ī'ī. However, 'Ī'ī gives the third line in a slightly different form from that of Malo, "*Wa i ka ua lanakila uwa. Uwa!*" M. K. Pukui translates it as "Shout aloud of victory! Shout!" S. M. Kamakau transcribes the same line as "*Wawa i ka lanakila uwa! Uwa!*" (the meaning is unchanged) and adds to this another line, "*Wawa i ke 'auhe'e, he'e he'e*" ("shout to those who are routed, flee, flee!").

M. K. Pukui translates the first two lines of the text given above as follows: "O silent ones, silent ones, hold your silence! / O loud voiced ones, loud voiced ones, shout aloud!" (Ii 1963, 39; Kamakau 1976, 138). Her translation seems to be inspired by a note by N. Emerson:

Kua-mu, Kua-wa and Kua-wao were gods of the woodlands. It was Kua-mu who felled a tree in silence. Kua-wa did it with noise and shouting. Kua-wao, not mentioned in this prayer, felled a tree anywhere and everywhere and as he pleased. The tumultuous and joyous rout down the mountain was a farewell to the woodland deities. [in Malo 1951, 181; see also Malo 1951, 83]

However, the chant may refer to the god Kū, and in this case the first two lines should be translated, "O Kū of silence (Kū-a-mū), Kū of silence. Silence. / O Kū of noise (Kū-a-wā), Kū of shouting, shouting." The god would thus be associated with two opposing terms, the silence of death and defeat and the noise of life, of victory. The chant, like the procession, would represent the god's transition from death to a new life,[80] and this transition would be equated with a victory.

This interpretation is supported by a version of this chant, published in Fornander (1916–20, 6:53),[81] where the name of Kū is clearly identifiable as part of "Kuamu":

Ku-e-kuamu-mu.
Ku-e-kuawa-wa,
Kuawa-wa lanakila.

K. Kamakau 1919–20, 13–15

On the morning of the second day of the month, the nobility, their men, and the priests gather before the feather gods to pray. Then they take them "to the mountain toward the lord-*'ōhi'a*-tree, the god" (*"i uka i ka haku ohia o ke akua ia"*). The king's stewards (*'a'īpu'upu'u*) bring some ten pigs for the gods, the people, and the king. When they approach the *'ōhi'a-lehua* forest up in the mountains, the priest declares that the tree that is found in front (*mamua*) of the others[82] is the god: "This is the god that desires the pig, for he is ahead of the others."[83]

The king approves the choice and orders the priests to offer prayers to the tree. Then he approaches it with a pig and a man and he prays. He consecrates the pig and the man to the tree with the following sacrificial chant (*kānaenae*):

E Kūka'ōhi'alaka[84] *eia ko pua'a a me ko niu,*
O Kūka'ōhi'alaka here is your pig and your coconut,
E ola ia'u, e ola iā na 'lii a me na kanaka a pau loa
Make me alive, make the nobles live and all men.

Then the priest arises and waves (*ho'āli*) the sacrificial adze (*ke ko'i kaumaha*) at the god and touches the tree trunk with it. He sits down and prays aloud while a man chops down the tree. Then the man that the king must offer as a "gift" (*makana*) to the god is put to death (*'oki*, lit., "cut").

The king has the ten pigs cooked in the oven (*kālua*), and finally he offers (*kaumaha*) the human victim to the god.[85] This man is "forsaken," "left" (*ha'alelea*) "in the weeds (*i ka nāhelehele*)."[86] When the pigs are cooked, they are eaten. After the meal a procession forms, in which the *akua 'ōhi'a*, completely wrapped *(wahī)* in weeds *(nāhelehele)* precedes the *akua hulu manu*, and the latter precede the men. All go down the mountain praising *(hi'ilani)* the god in a loud voice. A priest shouts, "*E Kuamu e Kuamu*," and all answer, "*Mu e kuawa, e kuawa, wa, e ku wau, a lanakila no*" (see commentary above for translation).

Until they reach the temple entrance no fire may be lighted. When they arrive at the seaward side of the temple, they pray to the *akua 'ōhi'a*. Then the feather gods, the nobility, and the people go back to their places. Meanwhile, those who attend to the *akua hulu manu* sing their praises and beat the drums loudly. In the evening a priest feeds *(hānai)* the *akua ōhi'a* with broiled *(pūlehu)* bananas and utters a short prayer.

Wilkes 1845, 4:506

The account in this text is very close to that of Malo and K. Kamakau. However, it gives an additional detail. The priest prays to obtain land at the moment that the tree is cut; the direction the tree falls indicates where one can go to conquer land and rob and kill its inhabitants.[87]

Interpretation

We have seen that the *huikala* rites preceding the inauguration of the *luakini* temple have the purpose of separating the profane from the sacred. The latter is constituted both by the sacred part of the population (ali'i and kahuna: the sacrificers) and by the sacred part of the land (the firstfruits that constitute, at least in part, the offering in the sacrificial rites of the temple). In order that these two "sacred parts" together produce efficacious sacrifices, two conditions must be fulfilled: first, they must be integrated into the sacred space of the temple; second, the god himself must be brought into the temple.

The first condition is fulfilled, at least as far as the sacrificers are concerned, on the first day of the lunar month by a rite that consists of the solemn entrance of the king, the nobility, and their followers accompanied by their portable gods into the *luakini* temple. The three main sources (K. Kamakau, Malo, Wilkes) agree in reporting that this entrance rite is marked by a purificatory prayer called *lupalupa*, during which the officiant consecrates a branch of *'ie'ie* by praying over it and, apparently, by wrapping it with a white bark cloth. According to Kepelino (1932, 18–19), the *lupalupa* prayer is accompanied by aspersions. Thus, it may be speculated that the priest takes the *'ie'ie* branch from the cloth with which it has been consecrated and uses it as an aspergillum to "purify," that is, to give life to the congregation. The text of the prayer makes it clear that this life comes from Kū (with whom the three other major gods are, however, associated) and that the *'ie'ie* is the means of its transmission, both because this vine is one of Kū's natural bodies [88] and because, having been "sacrificed" (*ka-umaha*) to him, it has absorbed his mana.

Note that the '*ie'ie* plays a major role throughout the *luakini* temple ritual. Its shiny foliage is used to cover the sacrificial altars, particularly the *lele* (Emerson, "*pule ha'i*" [*sic*], in HEN, 1:525, 528), and to make the wreaths or garlands (*lei*) that decorate both the images of the gods (Kelsey in HEN, 1:745; Brigham 1906, 61) and the officiants, or even the audience (Handy and Pukui 1972, 114). In these roles it is associated with or replaced by some ferns, vines or *maile* or '*ilima*, flowers of the '*ōhi'a-lehua* or '*ōhi'a-'ai* (*Eugenia malaccensis*), or pandanus (*hala*). The use of these plants is justified first of all by their scent. As Handy and Pukui write,

These were an essential part of every ritual, bringing the life of the *wao akua* (hinterland of the gods) into the house [or the temple—V. V.], and making it delightful for gods and guardian spirits, as for the people there. The people were all wearing leis or flowers, or *maile* vine interwoven with fragrant fern. [1972, 114]

According to Kamakau, these "fragrant things" (1964, 12) are even burned in sacrificial fires and used in some rites to attract a soul back into the body it has left (ibid., 53). [89]

Thus we can suppose that the perfume of these plants has a role complementary to that of the aroma of food offerings; both attract the gods into the temple and images. At the same time they are attractive to men: in this way they make possible the conjunction of men and gods. This dual power of fragrant plants makes them functionally similar to other ritual instruments—drums, prayers, chants, dances, and even offerings—that are supposed to attract both men and gods, and in the case of offerings to represent them both.

Note also that, like music, speech, or color, perfume has the property, precious from a ritual standpoint, of evoking immateriality in materiality, abstraction and generality in the concrete and the individual (cf. Lewis 1980, 69). Moreover, everything that affects the sense of smell provides impressions that are completely different from those of sight and hearing, since smell is both the least "realistic" sense and the one that gives the most indefinite impressions. Thus it is the most apt to furnish experiences that are capable of multiple interpretations and may at the same time verify the most imaginary representations.

In my opinion, the synesthetic aspects of ritual have been overemphasized at the expense of those in which the impressions of different senses are contrasted in order to justify representations that contradict the ordinary experience of reality. Thus, if visual experiences deny the validity of the judgment "the gods are there," olfactory experiences can confirm it. The gods can thus exist in experience thanks to a contrast between "absence from sight" and "presence in smell." The contrast is, moreover, peculiarly apt to realize the purpose of ritual, which is to make the gods exist both *far* from men and *close* to them, to make them both absent and present, to fill one domain with their presence in order to empty out another.

We find this contrasting of sight (the most "realistic" of senses) and smell (the most "unrealistic")—or else a similar contrasting of sight and hearing—at several points throughout the ritual. The first kind of contrast is created in the *lupalupa* rite examined here by wrapping a bunch of *'ie'ie* with a cloth. Ostensibly this wrapping has the purpose of consecrating the plant, but the consecration is nothing but the actualization of the relation of the plant to the god. It is thus equivalent to making the god's presence in the plant manifest to the mind, and therefore effective on it. However, this presence cannot find support in experience unless the visual component of the latter has been removed, for sight provides indexes that contradict the statement that the god is present. But when the visual experience of the plant is suppressed, its olfactory presence can become a perceptible equivalent of the god's invisible presence. Hence the god will become fully present in the branch only when the latter is wrapped up, that is, "consecrated." Thus we see that "consecration" in fact coincides with the creation of an experience that suggests the god's presence in a natural object.

After Kū has been made present in his generic form in the *'ie'ie*, he is made present in all his particular forms during the *kauila huluhulu* rite. Indeed, this rite consists of a procession of the *akua hulu manu*, that is, of the forms of Kū related to individual nobles and their factions.

Kū's differentiation thus reproduces that of the society: the generically purifying, because life-giving, divine mana becomes the multitude of *particular* manas that give life to particular social groups. This spiritual process is manifested by a material fact. Since the wickerwork that constitutes the *akua hulu manu* is woven with parts of the *'ie'ie* plant, Kū's passage from an undifferentiated to a differentiated state is manifested by his passage from a material embodiment that is natural, and more precisely phytomorphic (the *'ie'ie* branch), to another embodiment that is cultural and, moreover, anthropomorphic (the *akua hulu manu*).

It also seems that in this rite the *akua hulu manu* are covered with fresh feathers. At least this seems to be indicated by the name of the rite, *kauila huluhulu*, which means "*kauila* wood covered with feathers." Here *kauila* is perhaps a metonymy for the feather gods, which are supported by a handle or pole made from *kauila* wood.[90] A further association could be made with lightning (*ka uila*), that is, a manifestation of the divine power in its luminous but violent (as befits the *akua hulu manu*) form. Moreover, this would again link the *akua hulu manu* with the *'ie'ie* branch in the *lupalupa* ritual, since the prayer that consecrates it states that the *'ie'ie* is equivalent to the lightning (cf. above, p. 263). Indeed, "to the Hawaiians the forking *ieie* was similar to lightning" (Neal 1929, 19).

Let us return, however, to the use of fresh feathers to cover the *akua hulu manu*. This has the function of reviving the images, of making them "real," that is, really imbued with the divine presence. But probably the feathers thus employed come from the *ho'okupu* offering preceding the temple ritual; hence the revivification of the *akua hulu manu* is made possible by the complete actualization of an offering. Moreover, these feathers went first to the king and his god as representatives of Kū in his general form. Now the king redistributes them among his nobles so that they may revivify the particular forms of the god associated with them. Hence the "downward" movement of the feathers from king to nobles parallels the "downward" movement of Kū from his generic to his specific forms.

Now let us turn to the second condition of the efficacy of the temple ritual: the god Kū in his fixed and all-encompassing form must be brought into the temple. This form, as we have seen, is represented not by the feather gods, not even those of the king, but by a wooden image that stays permanently in the temple. This image is made not of just any wood, but of the *'ohi'a-lehua* (*Metrosideros macropus, M. collina*), a large tree (it can reach a height of thirty meters) whose red wood is very hard and resistant (Beckwith 1940, 16). These properties make it an ideal material for carving, but they are also the most generic attributes of the god Kū, who encompasses all that is vertical, strong, and red. Even in its natural state, the *'ohi'a-lehua* thus evokes the god that will be carved from it (the tree itself is called *"akua"*—see above, K. Kamakau). The carving of a human image from it, and its successive transformation in the temple, where it will be "born" and "reach maturity" as a "real god" (*akua maoli*), is thus the *objectivation of the process of apperception of the human species in a natural species that evokes certain properties of humanness to the highest degree*. These properties evoked by the *'ohi'a-lehua* are those of the human male, who, as we have seen (chap. 4), stands for the entire human species because he is its superior form.

Hence the end of the ritual consists in transferring these properties from the natural to the human realm. This is attained by transforming the god-tree into a god-image, that is, by actualizing its implicit humanness.

By making visible the concept of the human species that is the society's reference value, the transformed god reconstitutes society and therefore symbolizes it as well. The ritual thus appears as the "taming" of a god who at first is extraneous to society, then becomes its foundation. Since this "taming" coincides with the passage from a particular to a universal and from something natural to something human, it is also the symbolic form that stimulates an analogous passage in each individual who participates in the ritual.

In other words, each subject first finds a correlate of his own pure individuality and presocial or antisocial state in the individual tree. But at the end of the transformation each finds in the anthropomorphic image of the god the correlate of the apperception of his own species in himself. It is this apperception, inchoate as it may be, that makes him a social being—that is, somebody who recognizes a common human element, realized in diverse but complementary forms, in all other subjects.

As I have shown elsewhere (Valeri 1982b), the *luakini* temple ritual is also the process whereby individual desire becomes collective desire, whereby the disruptive and disordered play of individual interests is ideally transformed into a cohesive collective interest. This process of transformation is particularly necessary whenever conquest and war, bringing forth the play of individual interests and ambitions, create social disorder. Hence the *luakini* temple ritual is also conceived as the process whereby the winner is transformed into a fully legitimate king. In other words, it is the process whereby the leader of the strongest faction is recognized as everyone's leader (cf. Valeri 1982b, 1984). The process by which the king moves from being a disordered, "wild" individual to being an ordered, "cultural" representative of the collectivity and of the concept of ideal humanness on which it is founded thus parallels both the transformation of the god himself and the transformation of the consciousness of every individual who takes part in the ritual. The latter, then, shows us in action the mediating role of the king, who manifests the divine by acting as the man par excellence, that is, by representing for everyone a process of consciousness that takes place in everyone and that he must induce in everyone by acting thus.

The god's passage from an individual to a collective status is also a passage from the impure to the pure. As an individual or not fully collective force the god is incomplete—and therefore impure. To become complete, pure, he needs to represent all men, to be recognized by them as their species. "Wild" force is therefore a movement toward encompassment, the achievement of which makes the god complete and therefore "tame," immobile. This transformation is represented by a change in name. In his "wild" state the god is called by the name of the tree, Haku 'ōhi'a; in his "tame" state he is referred to as Kūnuiākea, the all-encompassing form of Kū, or, if we are to believe Malo, as Mō'ī, that is, "supreme." Thus, by letting themselves be conquered by the god as a wild force (cf. the Haku 'ōhi'a's violent descent from the mountain), men tame him and make him a cultural force that guarantees the integrity, the invincibility, of their society.

It was necessary for me to anticipate the global meaning of the transformation of the Haku 'ōhi'a at this point, because otherwise the rites I have to analyze in this section would make no sense. Indeed, they all emphasize the need for "taming" the god, for transforming him, and at the same time for bringing out his essential humanity, which is still hidden in the tree. It should therefore be clear that the transformation of the Haku 'ōhi'a in the *kapu luakini* is analogous to the transformation of the offering in sacrifice. Indeed, the former transformation is made possible by a great number of sacrificial transformations: it is their cumulative effect. With this in mind let us return to the Haku 'ōhi'a as he presents himself in his natural state.

It must be noted that the *'ohi'a-lehua* evokes the god's mana not only by its intrinsic properties but also because it forms a group with the *'ie'ie* and birds with precious plumage. The *Freycinetia arborea* (*'ie'ie*) often twines about the *'ōhi'a-lehua* trees (Brigham 1906, 60). The nectar of the trees' flowers attracts large numbers of birds—*'i'iwi* (*Vestiaria coccinea*), *apapane* (*Himatione sanguinea*), and *'ō'ō* (*Acrulocercus nobilis*)—whose red or yellow feathers are used to cover the *akua hulu manu* and the cloaks and helmets of the gods and nobles. Moreover, the *mamo* bird (*Drepanis pacifica*) which furnishes the most precious yellow feathers, is captured by luring it with fruits of the *'ie'ie* (Emerson 1895, 109), whose red flowers also prove attractive to the red-feathered birds listed above.

During the flowering of the *Metrosideros collina*, its crown is literally "alive with hordes of crimson *apapane* and scarlet *iiwi*, while, continually crossing from the top of one tree to another, the *oo* could be seen on the wing sometimes six or eight at a time" (Perkins in Munro 1960, 69). The *'ōhi'a-lehua* thus seems to realize in nature that which characterizes mana in the eyes of the Hawaiians: the capacity to give life to other beings by encompassing, attracting, and totalizing them. Moreover, the relationship between tree and birds involves a mutuality, a mirroring that recalls the relationship between mana and *ho'omana*: red flowers attract red birds (cf. Emerson 1895; Malo 1951, 20), the tree gives life to the birds that feed on the nectar of its flowers, but, reciprocally, the birds make the tree "alive," as Perkins says so well.[91]

This natural complex of relationships is perpetuated in a transformed state at the cultural level. The tree, immobile and attractive, appears as the complete, encompassing element. Thus it is transformed into the image of Kūnuiākea, "Kū of wide expanse," the supreme form of Kū. The *'ie'ie* and birds appear as inferior forms; that they are attracted by the tree, that they depend on it, their very mobility—all betray their incompleteness. Thus they are transformed (or rather, some of their parts are transformed) into feather-covered images that represent Kūkā'ilimoku and other "mobile" and "incomplete" forms of Kū.

It follows, as we will see, that the mobile and immobile images of Kū index the two stages of his transformation. The first is characterized by a power that makes possible the passage from desire to plenitude, that is, from movement to immobility; the second is characterized by the final state of perfection marked by immobility and the encompassing of totality.

The fact that the Haku 'ōhi'a is inseparable from the birds that furnish the feathers of the *akua hulu manu* perhaps explains why the inauguration ritual of the *luakini* temple is performed at the beginning of one of the three months (from March to May, approximately, depending on the location) when the *'ōhi'a-lehua* trees flower on the lower slopes of the mountains (Emerson 1895, 104; cf. Sahlins, n.d.), that is, where the Haku 'ōhi'a is fetched, according to Malo and K. Kamakau. The same fact perhaps explains why the season in which the *luakini* temples are open extends approximately from March to October, that is, during the period when the tree blooms at different altitudes (cf. Emerson 1895, 104), making it possible to continually capture the birds and therefore to obtain the fresh feathers needed for the ritual.

Last, it must be noted that the *'ōhi'a-lehua* is an adequate symbol for Kū and for divine mana in general not only because of its metaphorical values but also because of its metonymic association with the inland forest regions called *wao akua*, "hinterland of the gods" (Handy and Pukui 1972, 114; PE, 353), or *wao lani*, "mountain area believed occupied by gods" (PE, 353). These regions are called "divine" because in the abundance of their vegetation and other life forms they manifest the productivity of the divine mana and also because they are opposed to the cultivated *wao kanaka*, "hinterland of man" (cf. Malo 1951, 17), as gods are opposed to men.

The forest hinterland and mountain region are thus the domain to which the gods can be driven off[92] or, inversely, from which they can be recalled to fertilize the land or for any other purpose for which their power is needed.

Like the appropriation of any object considered divine, the appropriation of the *'ōhi'a-lehua* tree for carving the image of Kūnuiākea is shrouded in euphemisms. In a sense it is denied that this appropriation is the result of human initiative and need. The god's approbation is sought (it is manifested on the evening of the *malu ko'i* rite by rain or a clear night). Special adzes are used that, according to S. M. Kamakau (1976, 137), belong to Kahōāli'i and through him to the gods, if not to Kū himself.[93] Thus the god lets himself be killed with the adzes that he himself has given. It is claimed that the chosen tree designates itself, since it stands out from the other trees; moreover, it is said that it "desires the pig"—that it wishes to be felled to eat with men and consequently become part of society.

In addition, insofar as the responsibility for killing the divine tree is recognized, it is shifted from one officiant to the other. Thus the king, who is the one who really wants the tree, lets a priest act in his stead; but the priest in turn merely touches the tree with the ritual adze and lets a woodman do the actual felling. On the other hand, it is possible that by symbolically taking on the responsibility of "killing" the tree the priest relieves the woodman of any guilt. More likely, the ambiguity as to who is responsible is deliberate: the god must be made as confused on this matter as we are. Perhaps the necessity for confusing the god also explains why he must be attacked from two sides, as the priest and the woodcutter come to the tree from opposite directions and in a sense "corner" it.

In any event, the final responsibility falls on the sacrificial victims, whose lives pay for the god's life. Hence the symmetry that the rite establishes between the tree's death and that of the victim: having cut a chip from the trunk (or touched it), the priest must cut off the human victim's head; then the latter's body must be buried at the foot of the fallen tree to take its place (cf. Ii 1963, 42). This symmetry relates the ritual felling of the Haku 'ōhi'a to the other great rites of appropriation (particularly, the annual fishing rites). Moreover, if S. M. Kamakau is to be believed, here, as in the firstfruits sacrifices, a part that stands for the whole is restituted. In fact, he reports that the top of the tree is cut off ritually, and it seems likely that he is implying that this equivalent of the "head" is left behind in the divine forest (1976, 137).

According to Malo, the anthropomorphic image of the god is carved immediately after the tree is cut down and its bark removed. K. Kamakau does not explicitly say so, but as he does not describe at a later point the carving of the tree, it seems sensible to suppose that he does not differ from Malo on this point. Moreover, K. Kamakau writes that the akua 'ōhi'a (as he calls it) is carefully wrapped during the trip from the mountain to the temple. Now, it is hard to understand why the log should be made invisible if the image of the god had not already been carved from it.

Yet 'Ī'ī and S. M. Kamakau contradict Malo. 'Ī'ī (1963, 42) states that the trunk is simply stripped of its bark; Kamakau (1976, 136) maintains that not even the bark is stripped; indeed, it should not be scraped. These differences are less significant than might be imagined. In fact, although Malo claims that the divine tree is carved immediately, he also says that the anthropomorphic image of Kū must remain invisible and is therefore wrapped in weeds, which signal the god's still "wild" state. Thus all sources agree that the god becomes visible in human form only inside the temple.

But whether the god-tree is immediately given human form or is simply reduced to the state of a log, he has become closer to man following the appropriation rite. This closeness is increased by the sacrificial meal that, according to Malo, takes place once the carving of his image is completed. It is indeed likely that this meal entails a more or less direct relationship of commensality between man and god—all the more so because what remains of the meal is buried at the foot of the tree.

Then the return procession is formed. The Haku 'ōhi'a, covered with weeds, probably fragrant ones, precedes the feather gods, which precede the men. The latter carry scented flowers and ferns.[94]

The god's penetration into the land inhabited by men is represented as a violent conquest. People encountered on the god's path are killed; men cry victory and shout. Moreover, according to the text published by Wilkes, by the direction of its fall the Haku 'ōhi'a tree indicates what land the king will conquer. S. M. Kamakau reports something similar: by cutting the tree, the rival's government is "cut down" and made to fall (*"e oki i ke aupuni e hina ai"*—1870b).

The god's wild power enables the king and his men symbolically to re-conquer the land and the commoners who inhabit it. From this standpoint the *ho'okupu* that precede the arrival of the Haku 'ōhi'a appear as a pre-paratory and almost prophylactic measure; the "firstfruits" are separated from the land that has produced them, so that a part that allows the ran-soming of the whole may be offered. In other words, the conquest of the land by the god and his adepts (the king and the nobility) is limited to the further appropriation of the firstfruits already appropriated by another manifestation of the sovereign god and king (the couple Kahōāli'i and *akua 'alaea*). Accordingly, the god is immediately brought in front of the temple, where the offerings gathered earlier in the *ahupua'a* will be eaten by him and the ali'i.

Kū's "return" in the Haku 'ōhi'a rite can be likened to his "return" in the *kāli'i* rite. In the latter, Kū, the king, and the nobility symbolically re-conquer the land and the people by arriving from the ocean; in the Haku 'ōhi'a rite, they reconquer them by arriving from the forest. Ocean and forest are indeed the two complementary divine realms. On both occasions Kū makes off with the yield of the *ho'okupu* ritual. Following the *kāli'i* he appropriates the Makahiki gods as *products* of the people's *ho'okupu* (more-over, he takes the more precious objects received by the gods). Following the Haku 'ōhi'a rite, he gets the *ho'okupu* themselves, the "firstfruits" that will constitute the substance of the temple sacrifices.

In sum, the *luakini* ritual can be considered as a development of the *kāli'i* rite, as an elaborate enactment of ideas already sketched out in this rite. Conversely, the *kāli'i* rite can be considered as a preface to the *luakini* rite.

By appropriating the divine *lehua* tree, the king becomes assimilated to it. Thus he is rightly called "*lehua* of the land."[95] The use of this metaphor implies that he is assimilated to a warrior as powerful and as violent as the Haku 'ōhi'a himself. Indeed, the *'ōhi'a-lehua* tree and its flowers are fre-quent metaphors for warriors. Kamakau writes, "Like the fiery petals of the lehua blossoms of Pi'iholo were the soldiers of Ka-hekili" (1961, 87). In the line, "O great Kauai, island [filled] with *lehua*," *lehua* refers to war-riors (Fornander 1916–20, 4:28; cf. 5:698). Of course the *lehua* tree is an apt metaphor for the warrior because its properties connote virile strength and also because, being covered with red flowers and red birds, it recalls a warrior wearing a red feather cloak.

The redness of the *lehua*'s flowers, and probably that of its wood as well, is associated with bloodshed. Thus, the expression "*E waimaka o Lehua,*" "Lehua shed her tears," refers to menstruation (Kamakau 1961, 3), and *lehua* is the name of the bloody corpse of the "first victim of war" (ibid., 9). As the last two referents remind us, spilled blood is impure. The association of the god and ali'i with the *lehua* and, more generally, with the color red as it connotes blood thus suggests that, insofar as they are connected with war, violence, and conquest they are tainted with impurity. This confirms what I said earlier about the inherent impurity of the god as a particular and therefore incomplete power. The neutralization of this impurity, of this lack, is effected by the offerings as substitutes for the land and people that the god must "devour," encompass, in order to be complete. Thus the double value of the offerings, which are both distinct from what they symbolize and their effective equivalents, ensures that the destructive power of the god (and king) can be transformed by men into a guarantee of human life.

The king's relationship to the Haku 'ōhi'a and the "divine forest" it evokes is illustrated by several myths that in addition constitute an equivalent on the narrative level of the transformation that the king and his divine double undergo on a ritual level. Let us consider, for example, the myth of Palila, who, like other heroes of Hawaiian mythology, is a metaphor for the ali'i (cf. Elbert 1956–57, 69:100).

Palila's birth is impure but extraordinary. His mother gives birth to an abortion in the form of a cord, which is thrown on a refuse heap. But Palila's grandmother, doubtless a goddess because she has divine powers and lives in a temple in the mountains, saves him and gives him a human form. Then she leads him into another temple in the heart of the forest, where he is trained in the martial arts by what seem to be war gods (Fornander 1916–20, 5:136–37). Palila's god is Kū, and like Kū, Palila can transform himself into the *'ōhi'a-lehua*, which is his *kino*, "body" (ibid., 141, 148). Thus he is interchangeable with the god he worships.

Palila's father is a king who, having waged war with another king, is on the verge of defeat. Palila learns of this and comes to his aid. He descends from the mountain, destroying everything and everyone in his path. His father and the army are terrified, but Palila's violence is neutralized by his mother, who shows him her genitals and thereby makes him laugh. Having laughed, Palila becomes inoffensive; his mother completes his taming by incising his penis and giving him a loincloth to wear (Fornander (1916–20, 5:140–41). Thanks to these events, Palila's father becomes king of the entire island of Kaua'i.

Having spent ten days in the temple of 'Ālanapō, Palila goes off in search of adventure. On the island of O'ahu, he kills a half-human, half-shark monster that terrorizes the island. In recompense the king gives him his two daughters in marriage, but he stipulates that Palila will be allowed to consummate the marriage only after being transformed into a completely human being. To this purpose he is led into a *luakini* temple, where his penis is incised in the proper way (apparently his mother had failed in properly performing this operation, which should be done only by men). Then he is united with the king's daughters. After other peripeteias, Palila becomes king of Hilo on the island of Hawai'i (Fornander 1916–20, 5 : 136–53, 372–75).

The homology between this myth and the *kapu luakini* is immediately apparent. At birth Palila, who is both god and ali'i, is monstrous and therefore nonhuman and impure. Raised in the forest by warlike gods, he is identified with the '*ōhi'a-lehua*, which is at once his body and that of his god, Kū. His descent from the mountain to inhabited land is disastrous in its violence, yet it permits the destruction of his father's enemy and makes his father the sole king of the island of Kaua'i. However, this is possible only following the hero's humanization, first through laughter and then by initiation, which includes the incision of the penis and the donning of the loincloth.

This humanization is repeated a second time in the temple on O'ahu. This second phase of Palila's transformation is identical to the one performed on the Haku 'ōhi'a inside the *luakini* temple. As we will see, the god's humanization in the temple is concluded by the girding of the loincloth of '*oloa* on his image and the symbolic fertilization of the noble women that marks the transformation of his destructive power into a creative one. The first phase of Palila's humanization—the one that takes place outside the temple—seems to correspond to the humanization undergone by the Haku 'ōhi'a when a human image is carved into it. Moreover, the first incision on Palila's penis perhaps corresponds to the felling of the tree in the Haku 'ōhi'a rite; in both cases the symbolic death eventually enables the wild being to be reborn as a fully human one.

In the myth of 'Umi, the paradigmatic ali'i, we find a schema similar to the one underlying both the myth of Palila and the *kapu luakini*. After inaugurating a *luakini* temple, King Līloa wanders in the forest, where he finds a beautiful woman. He makes love to her, although she is menstruating. The king thus transgresses a taboo normally sanctioned by death. However, according to Hawaiian belief, a woman whose blood still flows can be made pregnant. Hence Līloa makes the woman conceive. 'Umi, the child born of this affair, does not know his father and lives with his mother. However, when he discovers his own true identity he goes to the court and secretly enters his father's lodging, hoping to be recognized by him. Initially, Līloa refuses to recognize him as his son and condemns him to death, but later he changes his mind. He then has him brought into the temple, has his umbilical cord symbolically cut, and has him undergo other rites, following which he is "reborn" as a noble (Fornander 1916–20, 4:182–84; cf. Kamakau 1961, 7).

Thus, like Palila's, 'Umi's career begins with an impure but extraordinary birth.[96] His powers are manifested at first in the form of disordered, "mischievous" behavior (he is called kolohe or kalohe, "mischievous," "lawless"—Fornander 1916–20, 4:181). He goes off in quest of higher status and succeeds in making himself recognized by his father the king. But like Palila's power, like that of the Haku 'ōhi'a, the "conquering" and desiring power of 'Umi (who succeeds in imposing himself by disturbing the established social order) must be transformed. After a symbolic death (the death sentence that is not enacted), 'Umi is reborn in the temple and thereby completely humanized. Indeed, by becoming an aristocrat, he now comes closer to incarnating the human species (cf. ibid., 186–205; Kamakau 1961, 9–14).

The rest of the story repeats 'Umi's transformation on a political level. At Līloa's death the kingship (or its supreme expression) goes to his legitimate son, Hākau; 'Umi receives the god of war and conquest, Kūkā'ilimoku. Opposed by Hākau, 'Umi takes refuge in the mountain, where he attracts many partisans and trains them in the arts of war. When Hākau commands his priests to seek the Haku 'ōhi'a (Kamakau 1961, 14) to inaugurate the temple in order to secure his military successes against 'Umi, the latter descends from the mountain with his partisans, surrounds Hākau, and kills him. Apparently 'Umi finishes the temple ritual begun by Hākau, because after killing the latter he performs the kāpapaulua rite that, as we will see, allows the god to reach his full develpment. Then he proceeds to divide the conquered lands among his followers (Fornander 1916–20, 4:205).[97]

In this second part the myth fully corresponds to the rite, as it narrates the conqueror's transformation in the kapu luakini. In addition, the myth identifies the conqueror with the Haku 'ōhi'a, since 'Umi descends from the mountain in the god's place. More exactly, the raid of the Haku 'ōhi'a should have represented the reconquest of the land by Hākau, whose power was threatened by 'Umi; but Hākau, deceived by treacherous priests, does not personally go to the mountain to seek the god, and the latter thus returns in the form of his adversary. The myth thereby highlights the ambiguity of the first phase of the ritual. The raid of the Haku 'ōhi'a can represent the raid of the reigning king, but also that of a usurper, since it is characterized by military violence. In other words, the king's symbolic reproduction of his conquest of the land can unleash a process whereby a stronger man may take his place. Like Hākau, the reigning king can be transformed from a sacrifier into a victim. This transformation is described by another myth, according to which an unpopular king is killed by plotters who make the Haku 'ōhi'a tree fall on him (Cheever 1851, 43–44). In sum, the victorious Haku 'ōhi'a can represent the king but also his enemy.

The rite of conquest is thus also a rite to exorcise the enemy's conquest, which is produced in fiction so that it will not take place in reality. But, as the myth of 'Umi and Hākau teaches us, if this real conquest takes place, the rest of the ritual is already set up to transform the conquering enemy into a legitimate king. In the end this is possible because even the "legitimate" king is only a violent conqueror before he is transformed in the temple. One violence equals another; the king and his adversary form a pair of absolutely identical terms, as we have seen. Only the death of one decides who becomes the "legitimate" king. Legitimacy is therefore recognized in the course of the rite that follows military victory.

To conclude, let me mention that the equivalence between the victim sacrificed in the forest, the *'ōhi'a-lehua* tree, and the king is connoted by their common association with the word *nāhele*, "wilderness." It can be said of any king, as it is said of Kūali'i, that he is born in the *nāhele*.[98] The texts describing the Haku 'ōhi'a situate the latter in a region also called *nāhele* (see above, p. 266). The victim who is "left in the *nāhele*" is a transgressor or a *kauwā*, since, according to Malo (1951, 71), the *kauwā* are people of the wilderness, *nāhelehele*. We can conclude that by leaving the victim behind in the wilderness, god and king leave behind their most disordered, wild aspect; this enables them to enter, though in a still-violent form, human society.

The *'Aha Helehonua* Rite
Description
Malo MS, 169–70

On the evening of the third day of the month, the foundations (*kahua*) of the mana house are measured and its orientation is determined. In the rear part a post called *nanahua*[99] is thrust into the ground; it faces the entrance and marks the spot where the *lua mua* image [representing a god] will be placed. Another post, called *ka pouomanu*,[100] is erected to mark the emplacement between the *makaīwa*[101] images where the Haku 'ōhi'a will be erected.[102]

When night has fallen, the four corners of the future mana house are marked with as many stakes. Then the king and the *helehonua* priest perform the *'aha helehonua* rite.[103] The priest stands next to the *pou hiō*, "bent corner post" (PE, 316), of the mana house and utters his prayer. Next to him is the king, who holds a sacrificial pig. When the prayer is ended, the priest grasps the end of the cord (*ka piko o ka 'aha*); he then gives it a turn around each stake, running in a circle from one to another. When he has thus connected the four stakes with the cord, he returns to his starting point, where the king, after pronouncing the *'āmama* formula, kills the pig by dashing it against the ground (*honua*).

Then follows the dialogue that concludes any *'aha* rite. The priest asks the king, "Has our *'aha* succeeded?" If no noise and no voice have been heard during the rite, the king answers that the *'aha* has been successful. Thereupon the priest declares that the government (*aupuni*) is firmly established (*pa'a*), since the *'aha helehonua* has been successful.

K. Kamakau 1919–20, 15

K. Kamakau does not describe the *'aha helehonua* rite directly, but he undoubtedly alludes to it in his obscure account of the ritual activities at the beginning of the third night of the month. During this night, the king sends two chickens [104] to two priests, one of whom is in charge of the *lama* leaves; the other is the *kahuna helehonua*. [105] The king also has it announced that the people must be still, keep silent, and not light any fires during the entire night. The name of the priest suggests that the rite he performs with his colleague is the *'aha helehonua*. It also appears that it is done without the king, since on the morning after the *kahuna helehonua* goes to the king to announce the success of the rite. The priest assures him that the night has been favorable (*mahalo*), for it has been clear and cloudless, and that the god gives him riches (*waiwai*). He concludes with these words, "When you are rich, take care (*mālama*) of me."

Wilkes 1845, 4:506

The priests each take a fowl, the chief two, and two are given to the god Kaili: these are eaten by them, the god's by his keeper, after which they went to sleep. If it rained during the night, it was considered a good omen.

This text describes a rite that, like the one related by K. Kamakau, includes gifts of chickens but that bears no relation to the *'aha helehonua* as narrated by Malo.

Interpretation

The purpose of the rites of the third night is to prepare within the temple the emplacements for the gods, especially the Haku 'ōhi'a. The *'aha helehonua* itself is the ritualized form of a practice that is included in the construction of any house, as is shown by this passage from Malo's *Mooolelo*:

The corner posts are set up and made fast. Then a rope is stretched from post to post, a rope at the top, a rope at the bottom, so each post is put in line with all the others. [Brigham's translation, 1908, 76–77; cf. Apple 1971, 110, 125]

In short, this *'aha* consists of ritually aligning the corner posts of the house. [106] But it also has a symbolic aspect, revealed by its name, which means "cord binding the land" (Hiroa 1957, 520). This seems to indicate that the running priest's tying the cord to the four corner posts symbolizes the encompassing of the land by god and king. [107]

The construction of the mana house, in which certain divine images will be preserved, therefore allows control of the land through control of divine mana. The house thus has a function and signification homologous to that of the Haku 'ōhi'a. Their correspondence will be emphasized by the rites that will follow the *'aha helehonua*, but it is already indicated by the fact that the *pouomanu* post indicating the emplacement of the Haku 'ōhi'a is erected at the same time as the *nanahua* post of the *hale o mana*.[108]

The circular movement that characterizes the *'aha helehonua* cannot be separated from the linear movement of the Haku 'ōhi'a descending from the mountain. The passage from one movement to the other marks a transformation of the god. The first movement connotes the god's violent penetration into the land and thus the destructive aspect of his mana; the second, on the other hand, connotes a protective encompassing. To surround something doubtless means to take it, to make it prisoner, but it also means to protect it and make it live.[109] Moreover, the circular movement combines contact and separation. By "gravitating" around the land the god is both connected to and separate from it; both present and absent, as he must be to make human life possible. The alternation between circular and linear movements has a great operative importance in the entire *luakini* ritual. In this respect, note that the passage from rectilinear to circular movement in the sequence "entrance of the Haku 'ōhi'a into the land → *'aha helehonua*" is preceded by an inverse passage. In fact, the expedition to the mountain to fetch the divine tree (violent rectilinear movement) is preceded by the *kauila huluhulu* rite that involves a circular procession. The latter seems, moreover, to be a sort of recapitulation of the "king's god's" circuit of the land in the *ho'okupu* rites.

In sum, we have the following sequence of movements: circular → rectilinear 1 → rectilinear 2 → circular. The two intermediate movements are equally violent, but the first symbolizes man's violence against the god and the second, the god's violence against man. Even on a spatial level, then, we find the symbolic symmetry between god and man that characterizes every rite of appropriation of the divine.

The *Kauila Nui* Rite
Description
Malo MS, 170–72

On the fourth day of the month (Ku-lua), the commoners go en masse to the temple bringing the materials to build the sacred houses. The house frames are completed, but they will not be thatched until after the *kauila nui* rite, which takes place the same day.

During the *kauila nui* the king and his entourage stay at a distance from the temple, in a spot called *kālewa*.[110] The officiating priest and most of the audience are seated by rank on the *papahola* platform.[111] Then the keepers (*kahu*) of the *kā'ai* gods belonging to the king and nobles enter. Each keeper sits in front of his god.[112] When all are ready, the high priest steps forward. He wears a large white loincloth and holds a bunch of *pala* in his hand. A man carrying a human skull full of seawater accompanies him. The audience is silenced, and when the priest utters the words "Grasp! Grasp!" ("*Ahopu* [*a hopu*] *ahopu*") the keepers of the *kā'ai* gods stand and, well aligned, hold the images in front of them. Kahōāli'i stands before them nude, with his penis "dangling" (*lewalewa*). The priest then says a very obscure prayer that, according to N. Emerson (in Malo 1951, 182), metaphorically likens Kahōāli'i's penis to a spear (*ihe*).

Kahōāli'i then begins to run a circular course, and the *kā'ai* gods follow him in order. When the priest says, "*A mio i ke lani o mamalu*,"[113] Kahōāli'i turns left, still followed by the *akua kā'ai*, and at one point a man holding a staff[114] joins him and they all return together to their starting point. When the praying priest comes to a passage whose meaning is unclear,[115] the bearers of the *kā'ai* gods stop and stand in ranks before the priests and the assembly. The man with a staff takes his place between them.

Of this man the high priest asks twice, "Who does the land belong to?" ("*No wai honua? No wai honua?*") There follows a passage that in the manuscript is garbled by several corrections and additions. As a consequence it is very difficult to understand. Emerson bemoans its ungrammatical character and conjectures that it means:

"The earth belongs to Ku," answered the priest, "a priest has ratified the transaction" (*hana mai a mana ke kahuna*). Then the *kahuna* again asked the question of this man, who was himself a *kahuna*, and he answered, "To Ku belong the small pieces of land" (*no Ku ka hai makaokao*). [in Malo 151, 168]

Emerson's translation of the first sentence seems dubious. The text actually begins with the sentence, "*Alaila, hai mai ua kanaka la*," which means "Then the aforementioned man replies." Following this is the expression "*iku*," which Emerson considers an answer to the high priest's question and therefore translates as "[the earth belongs] to Ku." If this were the case, one would rather expect to find "*No Ku*." My reading of the following sentence is different from Emerson's: "*No hano mai amama[?] ke kahuna*." But I am unable to find a plausible meaning for it. Perhaps it refers to the priest's '*āmama*, that is, "putting an end to a rite"—"ratifying it," as Emerson would have it.

The rest of Emerson's translation is acceptable until we reach the sentence "*No Ku ka hai makaokao*." This means, I believe, "To Kū belongs the high (*māka'oka'o*) sacrifice." Can we suppose that the "high sacrifice" is the land itself, or rather its sacrificial substitute? If so, Emerson's translation, although inaccurate, would give an idea of the general thrust of the dialogue reported by Malo.

After this dialogue, one of the two priests[116] recites a long prayer called *kai-o-pō-keo* ("seawater of the bleached skull"—cf. PE, 109).[117] When they have finished they sit down. Then a priest of the order of Lono, the *kahuna kuhiʻalaea* ("priest who smears with ocher"), holding a staff with a white cloth (*ʻoloa*) tied to it, recites a very long prayer called *kai-o-Kauakahi*.[118] At the end of this prayer, the usual dialogue takes place:

Priest: "O younger brothers, arise to receive" ("*E kū kaikaina e hiki [i]ā*")

Congregation: "Life" (*Ola*).

Priest: "*Iā*."

Congregation: "Life, life, O Kū."

With this prayer the rite is over.

Then all go home to eat. After the meal they return to the temple to thatch (*ako*) the roofs. Some men climb on the houses to place the *ʻaho*, "thatch purlins and rafters" (PE, 7), to which the *ako*, "thatch," is attached.[119] The work is regulated by the praying of a priest.[120] After thatching the houses, the commoners bring gifts (*hoʻokupu*) of pigs, coconuts, bananas, red fish (*iʻa ʻula*), *ʻoloa* cloths to be tied like loincloths around the images of the gods, and *kōpili* cloths[121] to be used to cover the tower and mana house during the rites of the following days.

K. Kamakau 1919–20, 15–17

The king commands that the temple houses be thatched. When this work is ended, he has everyone come with the feather gods.[122] The priests seat the people, arranging them in double rows of eight. The gods are also put up in rows. The high priest, wearing a wide white loincloth (*malo keʻokeʻo nui*), rises and, waving (*hoʻāli*) a bunch of *ʻieʻie*, offers it (*kaumaha*) first to the gods Kūnuiākea, Lononuiākea, Kānenuiākea, Kanaloanuiākea, and Kūkaʻōhiʻalaka and then to his own *ʻaumakua*.

Afterward the priests rise, praying and praising the feather gods. Many prayers are said on that day. It is a glorious (*hanohano*) day for the high priest and all the other priests. At the proper time, the attendants lift the *akua hulu manu* and stand first at the inland side (*mauka*). After a while the priest orders them to move to the seaward side, then he enjoins them to turn in a circle and to be careful to run properly, lest they be put to death. They finish the circuit on the seaward side, where they stand in rows.

Then the priest recites the *pōkeo* prayer. When he has finished, the people bearing the *akua hulu manu* return to the inland side and sit down. At this point the *ʻalaea* priest rises and puts a *hala* wreath[123] around the king's neck and another around the god's[124] and still another around his own.

After silencing the audience, he turns to the king and says, "Listen to my prayer on your behalf; if an aliʻi shouts (*walaʻau*),[125] he is a traitor to the land; if it is a common man (*kanaka*) who shouts, let him die for your god." He grasps his staff and prays for a long time. Then he commands the congregation to rise and tells them, "O younger brothers, receive the life that I administer to you" (*e ku'u kaikaina hiki [i]ā ola ia'u*). He has them rise and sit down eight times. Then he bids them to sit still and make no noise and announces to the king that the rite has been successful.

Everyone then goes inside the temple for the rite of the placing of the *'au'au* ridgepoles ("*e hele ana lakou e kau i na auau*"),[126] which is directed by the "priest of the *luakini*" ("*kahuna no ka luakini*").[127]

Wilkes 1845, 4:506–7

The description given in this text is very close to that of K. Kamakau, but according to it, after the gods are carried in procession [*kauila nui* rite], "the priest and king exchange their wreaths of okea [*'ohi'a*] flowers, at which time the people made sixteen exclamations; the people then eat, and finish the house afterwards, which is done with much ceremony."

Ii 1963, 41–42

The priest who has accompanied the men into the mountain has them sit in rows, "as though on canoes." Between rows he places *lama* trees in the ground. Then he smites some *hala* clusters. As they break up, pieces fly among the sitting men. Seeing them dodge the flying pieces, the audience laughs. This is for play (*hana pā'ani*); therefore one can laugh with impunity.

Then the procession of the *akua hulu manu* moves forward, preceded in order by a herald[128] who carries a staff called *kapuō*[129] and by Kahōāli'i.[130] The last image in the procession is called *akua hulu pānauea* ("slow feather god") because it moves slowly. The procession itself is better described in 'Ī'ī's own words (see also fig. 6):

> According to the rules of this rite of the procession of gods, the *kapuo* stick bearer, who was directly in front of the line at the center of the kahunas

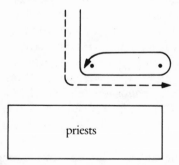

Fig. 6.   Route of the gods in the *kauila nui* rite according to 'Ī'ī. The solid arrow shows the route of the *kapuō* stick bearer, Kahōāli'i, and the feather gods; the broken arrow shows the route of the *akua pānauea*.

standing there, made a left turn and marched to their [the priests'—V. V.] right. The line of gods followed and turned where he had until the last one [except for the *akua panauea*] reached the spot from which the *kapuo* stick bearer had started. Then he turned again and came back to the left, as the rest remained standing. Again they each turned at the same spot and returned, finishing the procession. On their return, Kahoalii hurried to catch up with the *kapuo* stick bearer and the *akua panauea* on the latter's left. The *akua panauea*, because of his slowness, had just reached the spot from which to turn left the first time. Having reached this spot, the *kapuo* stick bearer and Kahoalii stopped. Each of those following behind drew up to his proper place. Then they all turned left again. The *akua panauea* moved slowly in front of them and returned to his place at the end of the line. His slowness was prescribed, for that was the nature of this god, perhaps. [1963, 41]

As the gods stand thus in a row before the priests, the priests question the herald bearing the *kapuō* staff: "The great news is told of what?" The herald answers, "The great news is borne of such-and-such, a canoe hauled for so-and-so." The canoes referred to are those of the high-ranking ali'i and probably include their men, who sit "in the *kauila* ceremony as though on canoes" (Ii 1963, 41). The rite is concluded by the priest uttering the usual formula, "*E ku kaikaina hiki a ola*," and the audience shouting (probably "*ola*," "life") in response.

Interpretation

According to 'Ī'ī, the *kauila nui* begins when a priest smites some *hala* clusters and the men who sit "as though on canoes"[131] try to duck the flying pieces. At this the audience laughs. Then the procession of the feather gods takes place. When the gods stop, their guide, "the bearer of the *kapuō* stick," is asked about the "great news," and he answers by saying that the "great news" is borne about the various chiefly canoes. It seems certain that the chiefly canoes referred to are represented by the men sitting as though "on" canoes and that these men must be their crews. Moreover, the "great news" is news of victory and therefore news of the conquest of the land by the king and his nobles. Indeed, in 'Ī'ī's account the dialogue about "the great news" is in the same structural position as the dialogue about Kū's conquest of the land in Malo's account (as interpreted by Emerson). The two therefore seem to be paradigmatically related.

'Ī'ī's account, then, correlates the procession of the feather gods with the conquest of the land by the chiefly canoes. It thus makes apparent the homology between the *kauila nui* and *kāli'i* rites. Recall that the *kāli'i* stages the king's and his warriors' "return" from the sea and that in all likelihood they are accompanied by Kūkā'ilimoku and other feather gods. When they land, they are attacked and the king is symbolically put to death, which allows him to take possession of the land again.

The chiefly "canoes" at the beginning of the *kauila nui* rite, then, correspond to the chiefly canoes of the *kāli'i* rite. Moreover, it is easy to demonstrate that the rite of the *hala* clusters is homologous to the mock attack and killing of the king and his men. Indeed, the *hala* plant has negative connotations owing to the meanings of its name: "sin, error, offense, to sin," and "to miss, to die" (PE, 47). Therefore, wearing a *hala* wreath is considered unlucky (NK, 1:71). It is likely, then, that the flying pieces of *hala* directed against the men sitting as if in canoes are supposed to "kill" them; this is precisely why they attempt to duck them, provoking the laughter of the beholders. This laughter itself "kills," in the sense that it destroys the mana of those laughed at and removes their taboos (cf. Valeri 1981a, 19; Propp 1975, 43, 81). But, as the myth of Palila demonstrates, laughter "kills" only to "humanize" its victims. In other words, laughter here is a mild equivalent of the process whereby the invading nobles and gods are "killed" in their wild state in order to be incorporated in the society and therefore made closer to humanity.

If the "canoe aspect" of the *kauila rite* directly relates to the "killing" and "humanization" of the ali'i, its processional aspect relates to the "killing" and "humanization" of their gods: Kahōāli'i and the *akua hulu manu*. Although the three sources at our disposal vary on some details, they all make it clear that there is a significant change in the gods' movement during the procession.

K. Kamakau's account seems to recapitulate the gods' descent from the mountains and to connect it with a "bending" of their rectilinear thrust now taking place, but which was already anticipated, if my interpretation is correct, in the *'aha helehonua*. Thus according to him the procession moves from the inland side to the seaward side, where it assumes a circular motion.

K. Kamakau does not tell us whether the gods turn clockwise or counterclockwise, but both Malo and 'Ī'ī make it clear that, as a result of human intervention (the high priest's words in Malo, the *kapuō* stick bearer's[132] joining the procession in 'Ī'ī), the gods turn sharply to the left at one point. In Malo this "turn to the left" seems to correspond to a change in the gods' course from clockwise to counterclockwise (he mentions no linear movement); in 'Ī'ī's account it marks the passage from a rectilinear movement (probably from the inland side to the seaward side, as in K. Kamakau) to a circular movement. Now this turn to the left clearly connotes the "killing" of the gods and a change in their relation to the land and the humans. This is suggested by the fact that the opposition of right and left correlates with that of life and death,[133] and also that of male and female, and therefore of erect (like the Haku 'ōhi'a before it is felled) and prostrate (like the selfsame god after it has been "killed"), of higher and lower,[134] and so forth (Kamakau 1976, 64, 136; Malo 1951, 100; Beckwith 1919, 346; Pukui 1942, 359; Handy and Pukui 1972, 129, 88).

Moreover, there is a precise homology between the inversion of the gods' movement from clockwise to counterclockwise, according to Malo, and the opposite movements of the *akua loa* and the *akua poko* during the Makahiki festival. If we consider these two images as two forms of Lono (Sahlins 1981, 19), it is possible to say that the *akua loa*'s circuit to the right (clockwise) indexes Lono's conquest of the land,[135] while the *akua poko*'s "return to the left" (counterclockwise) indexes the fact that Lono is neutralized by the offerings and symbolically killed (cf. Sahlins 1981, 19).

We may suppose, then, that in Malo's account the clockwise movement of the gods corresponds to their rectilinear movement in the other two accounts, in that they all index the conquest of the land by the divine powers, while the counterclockwise movement signifies, in his account as well as in ʻĪʻī's and perhaps K. Kamakau's, the domestication of the divine powers.

Perhaps the fact that a "killing" of the gods takes place in the *kauila nui* rite explains why the noble owners of these gods do not directly participate but stay at a distance. Moreover, high-ranking nobles always avoid situations where there is laughter, since laughing puts an end to taboos. Be that as it may, the gods' keepers undoubtedly substitute for the nobles who own them. This is also demonstrated by the fact that if a keeper makes a mistake during the procession and is put to death, his place must be taken by the noble he represents (Malo 1951, 167).

In ʻĪʻī's account the process of "taming" the gods is also represented, it seems to me, by the opposition existing between the "wild" Kahōāliʻi, who runs in front of the feather gods guiding them in their wild course, and the "tame" *akua pānauea* who, being very slow, arrives last. Interestingly, this god appears on the scene at the exact moment and spot where Kahōāliʻi concludes his counterclockwise circuit. This seems to indicate that the *akua pānauea* is the result of Kahōāliʻi's transformation, represented by his turn to the left—that is, his symbolic death. After this "death" the *akua pānauea* slowly moves between the group of gods and the group of men (the priests); this perhaps symbolizes the mediation between divine and human obtained by the transformation of the divine.

A further aspect of this transformation must be mentioned. Although a priest of Kū (in fact, the high priest) officiates during the *kauila nui* procession, at the end, when the fruits of the transformation it indexes are collected in the form of life that is imparted to the audience, the officiant is a priest of Lono: the *kahuna kuhiʻalaea*. We find that the priest (or any other representative) of Kū and the priest of Lono intervene in the same order in other rites: for instance, in the *hoʻokupu* rite that precedes the *kapu luakini*.[136] More important, we shall see that while Kū's entry into the temple is effected by a rite in which the officiant is a priest of Kū, his "birth" and "maturity" are brought about by a rite in which a priest of Lono officiates. Moreover, as I have already noted (chap. 6), the entire ritual cycle is based on the passage from the Kū pole to the Lono pole (cf. Valeri 1982b).

Thus the initial manifestation of the divine power and the priests of Kū seem to be paradigmatically related, and the same paradigmatic relation seems to exist between the *final* transformed state of the divine and the priest of Lono. In its most extreme form, the "initial" (i.e., dangerous) state of the divine is named Kū, while the most "final" state is best represented by Lono. But this extreme opposition is realized, as we have seen, only when we consider the most encompassing level of the ritual cycle; at lower levels it becomes apparent that each god has a wild, untransformed aspect and a tame, transformed one. Thus the transformations occurring in the *kauila nui* rite, like those in the rites inside the *luakini* temple, concern Kū alone. It is significant, however, that a priest of Lono officiates in the final stage of the transformation of Kū. This anticipates that the transformed Kū will eventually, once the *luakini* ritual is over, become Lono outside the temple. It is therefore evident that a category of divine power exists that is more encompassing than the individual gods. From its point of view *the individual gods are particularizations associated with certain stages of the process of transformation of the divine as it occurs at different levels of the ritual cycle.* They are the stages of this process frozen into personalities, the discontinuous points in which the continuous process is analyzed.

I mentioned above that a *hala* wreath connotes death or, more exactly, transformation through death. We may surmise, then, that by putting a *hala* wreath around the neck of the god, the king, and himself (K. Kamakau), the *'alaea* priest recapitulates the transformation of the gods that has just taken place and associates the king and his god with it. Thus the king and god "die" in one form in order to assume a superior one. In Wilkes's version, king and priest exchange *'ōhi'a-lehua* wreaths. Presumably in this way the king and the Haku 'ōhi'a are associated with the transformation brought about by the *'alaea* priest. But this version, by revealing that *hala* and *lehua* can be used in the same context, confirms that the *lehua* tree and the god that it embodies still connote pollution.

Rites for Incorporating the God into the Temple
'Aha Hulahula Rite
Malo MS, 173

On the evening of Ku-lua (the fourth), after the *kauila nui* rite and the thatching of the houses, the Haku 'ōhi'a is taken into the temple and erected at the emplacement of the post named *pouomanu*, between the tower and the *lele* altar. The Haku 'ōhi'a, like all the other images, is still naked, his "penis dangling" ("*kulewalewa ka laau*"). A priest "performs the *'aha* rite" (*"kai i ka aha"*), called *poupouana*, to erect the image of the god. A man guilty of a transgression (*kanaka lawehala*) is dispatched (*"pepehi ia"*), and his corpse is thrust into the hole where the base of the god's image is to stand. This man is sacrificed (*mōhai*) in order to "soften" (*'olu'olu*) the god.[137] Then the ali'i and priests return home.

Before the beginning of the king's *'aha hulahula*, everyone—commoner or noble—prays to his gods that there be no rain, wind, thunder, lightning, or heavy surf and that no fire be lighted and no noise, from either man or beast, be heard: without this the *'aha* will not be perfect.[138] When the night sky becomes clear, the king and the priest go in front of the *hale wai ea*. The king holds a pig; the priest utters the *'aha hulahula* prayer. If when he has finished the silence is complete, the king kills the pig by dashing it against the ground and then offers (*kaumaha*) it to the god with this prayer, "O Kū, O Lono, O Kāne, O Kanaloa,[139] here is the pig; give me life, take care (*mālama*) of the kingdom (*aupuni*); *'āmama*, it is free (*noa*), [the taboo] has flown away (*lele wale aku la*)."

Then twice the priest asks the king if the *'aha* has been successful and the king answers him that it is "perfect" (*maika'i*). After which they move toward the congregation and the king asks them if the *'aha* has been successful.[140] They answer that it was perfect and that they have heard no noise. Then they shout several times, "The *'aha* flies away [is ended] (*lele wale ka 'aha e*)." The news is passed to the commoners outside the temple; they are very happy that the king's *'aha* is a success and think that the kingdom will enjoy peace in the coming years.

K. Kamakau 1919–20, 17–19

In the evening the king and high priest, with the feather gods, pray before the temple while the people say in a deep voice (*ho'oko'iko'i*) that the temple rite has failed (*hā'ule*) that evening. And they go back to their houses.

Then the king gives fowls to all the *akua hulu manu* and all the priests; these fowls will be used to worship (*ho'omana*) the gods during the night. That night everyone's mood is "affable" (*'olu'olu*, "cool"). But if a ritual fault (*hewa*) happens to be committed, they are not happy and are greatly afraid of the god. If on the other hand the "work" (*hana*)[141] of the king and priest is good, they are safe (*palekana*). It is a fearful night (*maka'u loa*). On that night the agricultural food (*'ai*) of the king, the nobles, and all the men is "pulled" (or "extracted," *ka'i*).

When night falls there is a "feeling of awe," "an oppressive quiet" (*ano ano*). There is no sound, no fire burning, no pig squealing, dog barking, or child crying. Everyone holds his breath (*pili no ka hanu*). This is the night of the *'aha hulahula*, which distinguishes[142] sin (*hewa*) from correct behavior (*pono*), death from life. Late in the night they awake and go to the outside of the temple. Not a word is exchanged. All wait for early dawn. When it comes the king and high priest prepare themselves for the rite, while most of the people "worship" (*ho'omana*) the voice[143] of the rats, chickens, birds, dogs, and pigs, which are their deities ['*aumakua*]. They tell them, "Make your mana great, O gods (*e i nui ka mana o oukou e na akua*), in the king's '*aha* (*i ka aha a ke alii*), where your house post will stand (*i kahi e ku ai kou pou hale*)."[144]

When dawn approaches the priest takes the god,[145] some *lama* leaves, and an '*oloa* cloth; the king takes the sacrificial drum and a pig. The two men enter the temple alone. The priest bundles some *lama* leaves, which he wraps with the '*oloa*, and exhorts the king to pay attention to anything that might adversely affect the rite.

If a cloud bank keeps them from seeing the stars, they pray and the stars become visible again. When the priest sees that all goes well in the heavens, he exhorts the king to listen "for the squeak of the mouse, the song of the bird, and the crowing of the rooster," and he gets up to say the '*aha hulahula* in a conversational tone (*kalokalo*). Then he sits down, praying. As soon as he has finished, he turns to the king. When the king meets the priest's eyes, he dashes the pig against the ground (*hahau*), saying, "*E Kū iā hulahula*,[146] here is your pig to obtain life from you, and here is your good house (*hale maika'i*),[147] a gift (*makana*) of mine to you; give life to my land ('*āina*), and to the ali'i, and to all men; curse the rebel who steals land (*mōlia*[148] *i ke kipi i kā'ili 'āina*), the hard warrior (*koa kani*) who perhaps in his heart (*na'au*)[149] desires to rout me (*e he'e ia'u*), let the end of the cord (*ka piko o ka 'aha*) of us both (*kāua*) entangle him (*kāhihi*)."[150]

This prayer finished, the priest brings the '*aha* cord to hide it in the *hale wai ea*. After "slapping" (*ho'opa'i*) the '*aha*, he turns his face to the king and asks him, "How is our [of us both] '*aha*?" "Successful" is the answer. He also asks him if he has heard any bad omens—for example, the song of a bird, the crowing of a cock, or the barking of a dog—and if anything is wrong. To each question the king answers no, and the priest then says to him: "Your '*aha* is a success, you are saved, as well as your land, the ali'i, and all men."

Then they leave the temple and in a low voice ask the people what they have heard, and the people answer in a whisper that nothing wrong was heard outside. Then the priest addresses the king by calling him "*E ka lani e*" ("heavenly") and says to him, "Here is what I have to say to you; your prayer is good, the night (*pō*) thanks you and the god says you shall have life." Then they gather outside the temple, chanting aloud the formula "*Lele wale ka 'aha e*" ("the '*aha* flies away," it is ended). Shouts resound everywhere that word of the success has reached. This pleases the king and everyone else.

Wilkes 1845, 4:507

In the evening the high-priest arrived with three fowls; one for the god, another for the king, and a third for himself. If rain fell during the night, they would conquer their enemies.

On the fourth day, before it was light, the "Aha" and "Kaili"[151] prayers were said, at which time the priest brands the land that they are to conquer. After this, the chief brings a hog, holding his snout,[152] when the king again prays the idol; the chief, repeating his "Amama" (invocation), killed the hog. The priest cautiously asks the chief if he heard any noise, or voice of a mouse, dog or bird: if none, it was a good omen. Then the chief and priest advance towards the people, the former wearing a feather cloak, while the latter was naked, who demanded of the people if they heard any noise; and being answered in the negative, the priest then said the god had declared they should eat of the fruit of the land of their enemies. At night nine hogs are offered.

Kuwā and *Kuili* Rites
Malo MS, 174–75

On the morning of the fifth (Ku-kolu) the high priest, who performed (*ka'i*) the *'aha hulahula*, and who is the chief priest of the *luakini*, joins the priest of the Haku 'ōhi'a in a fast. They eat only the nectar of banana flowers. They both fast (*ho'okē'ai*), the high priest in view of the upcoming *'aha* and the other priest "so that the Haku 'ōhi'a turns into a real god" (*"no ka hakuohia i lilo ia kua maoli"*). On the same day a sacrifice is offered (*"hai ka haina"*).[153] Four pigs are cooked in the oven (*kālua*): one is put on the *lele* altar (*"o kekahi puaa, e kau ia maluna o ka lele"*); another is given to the priest; the third is given to the god's keeper, and the fourth to the king and his men. The king's pig is called "the pig of the pebble" (*"ka puaa o ka iliili"*).

On the same day two[154] men carry four bundles of white *'oloa* cloth (*"makuu oloa keokeo eha paha"*), which they fasten "with the mana cord" (*"me ka aha mana"*) to the ridgepole of the mana house. Then the priests below pray, while two men on the roof of the house make gestures with their hands as if in a dance (*hula*). This *'aha* is called *ho'opi'i na 'aha limalima*, an expression that means, according to Pukui and Elbert (PE, 190), the assembly (*'aha*) that gestures with its hands (*limalima*) rises (*ho'opi'i*). Indeed, they write, "The priest gestured with his hands" (ibid.).

In contrast, Emerson believes the name refers to the hanging of cords (*'aha*), called *limalima*, over the ridgepole. According to his informants the *'aha limalima* "was a decorative, netlike arrangement of cords, fringed with tassels (*limalima*) (in Malo 1951, 184). He also gives the following prayer, which he says is called *pule kuwā*; I reproduce it here, since it is of great interest:

E Kū i ka lani
O Kū who is in heaven
Ke ʻaha o makuʻu hālala [or, *ke ʻaha ʻo makuʻu hālala*]
The cord of the big bundle [the cord bundled in a big bundle]
E Kū i kaupaku o Hanalei
O Kū on the ridgepole of Hanalei [155]
Makuʻu ʻoloa
ʻ*Oloa* bundle
E pū, e hīkiʻi, e paʻa iā ʻoloa
Coil, bind, make fast by means of the ʻ*oloa*
ʻ*O ʻoloa hulihia ka mana*
The ʻ*oloa* [by which] the mana is entangled
He mana pūkī no ka ʻaha ʻoloa
A mana is curbed because of the ʻ*oloa* cord
E mana i ke akua
Let it be mana by the god
E ʻoki i ka piko o mana
Cut the umbilical cord of mana [= the mana house]
Ua mana, mana ka ʻaha limalima
The *limalima* cord has become potent, potent
I ka hale o ke akua o Kāne
In the house of the god Kāne
ʻ*Okia ka piko!*
The umbilical cord be cut!
A noa! Ua noa
And then it is free! It is already free.
    [My translation]

This is undoubtedly the text of the prayer uttered in the ʻ*aha limalima* rite, since we find in it some expressions used by Malo in his description of this rite: for example, "*makuʻu ʻoloa*," "*hīkiʻi*," "*paʻa*." Moreover, it is obvious that the prayer contains orders to those on the roof of the mana house who tie ʻ*oloa* parcels to the ridgepole (see line 6).

The last lines of the prayer refer to the *pule kuwā* rite proper, during which the bunch of grass that hangs from the door and is called *piko* ("navel") is trimmed. This rite, which according to Malo is performed immediately after the ʻ*aha limalima*, makes possible the entrance of the officiants into the house. Then the Kahuanuʻunohoniʻoniʻo image is put in the place of the *nanahua* post, which is found in the back part of the house just opposite the door.

At night the priests gather in the mana house and uninterruptedly repeat in unison prayers appropriately called *kuili*, "to repeat." The priests are divided into two groups, seated on the two sides of the mana house. Each group receives four hundred pigs cooked in the oven (*kālua*). Their

men also participate in the meal. The *kuili* prayers continue without interruption until the evening of 'Ole-ku-kāhi (the seventh day of the month).
The distributions of pigs continue as well. During the daylight period
of the sixth the priests receive four hundred pigs; in the evening, two hundred and forty; on the following day, eight hundred.[156] Each amount is
divided into two equal parts, one for each group of priests. This meat
is intended for the priests exclusively; ali'i may not eat of it.

K. Kamakau 1919–20, 19–23

On the morning of the fourth day, three prayers are recited outside the
temple: the *waipā*, the *kuwā*, and the *kuwi*.[157] Then all the ali'i, the portable
gods, and the priests enter the temple and sit in front of the inner court.
The high priest gets up, and "he waves the *'aha*" ("*a hoali ae la i ka aha*")[158]
while reciting a very sacred prayer called *koli'i*.[159]

This prayer over, they go outside the temple and give (*ha'awi*) a pig to
every *akua hulu manu* and one to each of the principal priests (*kahuna
wāwae*). Then the king orders his stewards to cook ten large pigs in the
oven (*kālua*), and he goes back inside the temple with his entourage to
clothe the images of the gods (*ki'i*) with strips of *kōpili* cloth and to recite
solemn prayers. These prayers ended, the priest waves (*ho'āli*) his hand and
sits down, and all pray once more in unison. Fires are lighted outside the
temple and by the commoners in the back country, and after a new prayer
the king offers (*mōhai*) a broiled (*pūlehu*) pig. It is indeed prescribed to
offer a broiled pig and not one cooked in the oven (*kālua*). After this sacrifice, the congregation returns home.

When the pigs intended for the *akua hulu manu* are cooked, the keepers
of these gods sing their praises (*hi'ilani*). After the ten or twenty pigs reserved for the king have been cooked they are brought into the temple,
where a single priest offers a short prayer over them. Then the king's portion (*waiwai*) and those of the other ali'i are brought outside and apparently eaten by them.

In the evening, the king orders his servants to cook forty pigs in the
oven for the *kuili* rite. After sunset, some priests recite the "*kaulahale*"
prayer. When night has fallen, torches are lit in the temple and temple
houses, where the ali'i, priests, and portable gods are assembled. They pray
ceaselessly through the whole night. The prayers are recited in such a loud
voice that the priests seem to be arguing. They also gesture with their
hands as though dancing and praise the gods by clapping their hands.

After this the pigs are brought into the temple and a priest ties them.[160]
At dawn the prayers stop and all return home. Then the king again orders
his attendants to cook forty pigs in the oven. At noon all the ali'i, priests,
and gods enter the temple to pray (*pule*), worship (*ho'omana*), and praise
(*ho'ole'a*). When they are finished they leave the temple. In the afternoon
they go back inside to recite the *kulawā*,[161] the *kūpapa'a*, and the *kūaīwa*

prayers. At sunset they go before the *kuahu* platform[162] to say the *kūlewa-lewa* prayer.

Then the king orders one of his priests to go look for the *akua 'ōhi'a* and to bring it inside the temple. When the god arrives the king orders that a man (*kanaka*)[163] and a pig be brought so that they may be sacrificed to the god. The man is led before the king, who has a prayer said. The priest gets up and waves a "piercing instrument" (*'ō*).[164] Then he sits down to pray with the king. The man is killed (*pepehia*), and the king offers (*mōhai*) him with the pig. When they have finished, the sun sets and they go home.

Wilkes 1845, 4:507

The fifth day opens with a prayer. The king or chief gives forty hogs for each end of the temple.[165] In the evening, the idol they had hewn out of the tree was brought down to the temple, and placed in front of the steps of the heiau. A large hole was then dug, and a man sacrificed and placed in it; on this the idol is put, and the earth thrown around it: the multitude now retire. The priest now demanded of the king three fowls—one for the god, another for the king, and the third for himself. The god's is devoured by his keeper, while the king and priest feast on theirs, when they all go to sleep, under the impression that some omen will occur. If rain, with thunder and lightning, ensue, the omen is very favourable.

This description is close to that of K. Kamakau and completes it in certain particulars.

Interpretation: Basic Symbols

Two basic symbols are used in the rites just described: binding with a cord, and wrapping with bark cloth. Moreover, the *hale mana* is second only to the Haku 'ōhia as a focus of ritual action. Let us consider, then, the symbolism of binding and wrapping as well as the symbolism of the mana house.

Binding

Almost all the rites taking place in the temple, as well as the sacrifice performed in the forest before the Haku 'ōhi'a (see above, p. 265), are called *'aha*. The word *'aha* designates any cord braided from coconut husk (coir) or from human hair or intestines (Andrews 1865, 35; Stokes 1906, 147, n. 47; PE, 5; Malo 1951, 78).[166] It has, moreover, two other meanings: (1) a group of persons gathered or associated for a given purpose; (2) sacrificial rites accompanied by prayers (cf. Andrews 1865, 35; PE, 5).

These two meanings result from the metaphorical sense of the cord. The cord "binds," "connects," "links." People who gather are connected by their purpose; thus the word that is usually translated "feast" (*'aha 'aina*) literally means "a company for eating" (Andrews 1865, 36). As for the application of the word *'aha* to the temple rites described above, Andrews explains it in this manner: "The name originated in the fact that cocoanut fibre . . . is very strong when braided into strings; so this prayer, with its rigid kapus, was supposed to be very efficacious in holding the kingdom together in times of danger" (1865, 35).[167] Pukui and Elbert, on their part, write that the temple *'aha* was "A prayer or service whose efficacy depended on recitation under taboo and without interruption. The priest was said to carry a cord (*'aha*)" (PE, 5).

The descriptions of the *luakini* temple ritual show that cords are actually used by the officiants in most *'aha* rites. Thus, in the *'aha helehonua* the priest uses a cord to bind the posts marking the corners of the mana house. The expression *'aha helehonua* designates both the cord and the rite in which it is used (cf. PE, 5; Malo MS, 169). A cord is also used in the *'aha hulahula* rite by the priest, who is said to "slap" it and to hide it in the *hale wai ea* at the end of the rite.[168] Probably he holds it while the king says the sacrificial prayer, since the latter ends with these words: "Let the end of the cord (*ka piko o ka 'aha*) belonging to us both [the king and the god] entangle [the enemy]." That the expression *ka piko o ka 'aha* refers to a real cord is confirmed by the fact that in Malo's description of the *'aha helehonua* this same expression explicitly refers to the end of the cord with which the four posts of the house are connected.

According to Malo, the *'aha hulahula* is followed by the *'aha limalima.* It is not certain that the expression *'aha limalima* refers to a true cord, but it is clear that in this rite a cord called *'aha mana* is used to tie bark-cloth bundles to the ridgepole of the mana house. A cord is also mentioned in the description that K. Kamakau gives of the *koli'i* prayer: while the high priest recites it, he waves a cord (*'aha*).

In view of these facts, it does not seem unreasonable to assume that the expression used to refer to the performance of an *'aha* rite, namely *ka'i ka aha,*[169] does not simply mean "to lead the *'aha,*" but also means to manipulate a cord in various ways. Specifically, the expression seems to refer to the fact that the priest carries a cord (cf. PE, 5) or does something ritually important with it. Dorothy Barrère (personal communication) suggests that *ka'i* "refers to the measured step of the kahuna as he carries the *'aha* cord in these rites (as well as the name of the rites)." This certainly applies to several *'aha* rites. *Ka'i* also means "to pull," and I wonder if in certain cases this meaning is not present. For instance, that the *'aha hulahula* is said by K. Kamakau to "pull" (*ka'i*) the food of the king, the nobles, and their clients (which means to procure them land; see Wilkes) suggests that *ka'i ka 'aha hulahula* may mean "to pull the *hulahula* cord." In other words, by (metaphorically) "pulling" the cord, the king "pulls" the land and therefore the food. This is only a hypothesis, though.

I believe that the cords used in the *'aha* rites are identical to the so-called *'aha kapu* or *'aha 'ula* ("sacred sennit cords")[170] that are—among other things—representations of the king's genealogical relationship with the god (Stokes 1932). One indication that they are the same thing is given by the very name of the culminating ʻaha rite, namely, the ʻaha hoʻowilimoʻo. As Stokes has noted, hoʻowilimoʻo probably means "to twist [as the strands that make up the ʻaha cord—V. V.] the genealogy [moʻo or moʻo kūʻauhau—V. V.]" (1932, 19) connecting king and god. Thus the ʻaha hoʻowilimoʻo seems to involve the reproduction, real or metaphoric, of a cord that represents the king's genealogy, exactly like the ʻaha kapu. Hence the conclusion that the sacred cord (or cords) used in the ʻaha rites and the ʻaha kapu are identical seems obvious. Alternatively, it is possible to suppose that the "metaphoric cords"—the ʻaha rites—renew the material cords—the ʻaha kapu carried by the aliʻi outside the temple.

These sacred cords [171] are used by the king as symbols of his mana (PE, 6), and as such they are put on the masts of his canoes (Kamakau 1961, 43) or at the entrance of his house (ibid., 7). It is said that the ʻaha kapu cord protects the king's (or the high chief's) house from trespassers and people of inadequate rank. When such people try to enter, they are killed by the cord. If, on the contrary, people related to the king or of high rank approach, the cord falls and lets them enter (PE, 6; article in Ka Leo o ka Lahui, trans. M. Pukui in HEN, 1:1679–80; Fornander 1916–20, 4:553).

This account seems to me to be the mythological transposition of the ceremony that takes place in the hale naua. Recall (cf. chap. 5) that people admitted to this house must prove their genealogical connection with the king and are given a specific status with respect to him (Malo 1951, 191–92; Fornander 1878–80, 2:63–64). It seems likely, therefore, that the king's ʻaha kapu, which represents his genealogy, is hung at the entrance of the hale naua and that the magical way this cord is supposed to admit or reject people who claim kinship with the king reflects their inclusion in or exclusion from his genealogy. This hypothesis is reinforced by the fact that S. M. Kamakau gives a "nonmagical" account of the way the ʻaha kapu protects the king's house: if a foreign chief wants to be admitted, he must recite his own genealogy; then the guards will let him step over the ʻaha kapu and enter. If he is unable to give his genealogy and prove his connection with the master of the house, the guards will keep the ʻaha kapu raised and not let him in (1961, 55).

I have just said that the sacred cord (ʻaha kapu) represents the king's relationship—genealogical or otherwise—with the gods. But as the ceremony in the hale naua, or simply the customs referred to by Kamakau, demonstrates, the ʻaha kapu is also the genealogy that binds together all other genealogies, since it is their reference point and the locus of their legitimacy or their truth. Hence, the king's "cord" (ʻaha) is in fact also the "association" or "congregation" (ʻaha) of nobles. The cord becomes the community; the link that connects the king with the god becomes the so-cial bond itself. It seems likely, then, that if a '*aha kapu* hangs in front of the *hale naua*, it is one of the cords used in the temple ritual.

In sum, we may say that three relationships coincide in the cord: that between the king and the god, that between the king and his followers, and that among the followers. Moreover, these relationships are hierarchized in that the reproduction of the superior one is the condition of possibility for the reproduction of the inferior. Thus the reproduction of the relationship between king and god in the temple makes it possible to reproduce the relationship between king and nobles; and the latter relationship makes it possible to reproduce the relationships between nobles, since they must all pass through the king's genealogy. At the same time, however, the temple ritual clearly shows that there is a dialectical aspect to the hierarchical rela-tionship between the three components of the "sacred cord," that is, of the social bond itself. Indeed, from the very beginning of the ritual the repro-duction of the king's relationship with the god presupposes the reproduc-tion of his relationship with his "men" and is not simply its presupposi-tion. And of course the king's relationship with his "men" also presupposes that a certain recognized bond exists between these men. But the dialec-tical relationship between the three components is put in the background and a hierarchical representation is preferred because the three elements are not equal from the standpoint of their symbolic value; the bond between king and god is capable of symbolizing the other two bonds but not vice versa. This is because the god, and the king immediately after him, embod-ies the concepts that are the presupposition of all social relations.

At any rate, it is clear that the power of the '*aha kapu* derives from the fact that in it the three fundamental relationships—between king and god, between king and men, and between men—coincide.

Note also that the coincidence of the three relationships through the cord makes the latter the means of a kind of transcendental deduction by which the god, who represents the idea of the human species, is translated into the ideal social system (that is, the system of partial but complemen-tary realizations of the species by social actors), and the latter is then trans-lated into concrete social relationship. Insofar as the king controls this de-duction, embodies the ideal species in society, and reproduces the ideal of the species in the society, he is represented as a "binding cord." Thus King Kūali'i, to take one famous representative of kingship, is called "*Ku ka hele a maua*," "Kū our bond," "Kū who binds us" (Fornander 1916–20, 4: 401). Of another king, Kihapi'ilani, it is said, "*Ka maawe lau huna ia o ke 'lii*," "the chief is like a hidden strand" (Fornander 1916–20, 4: 240–41). Indeed, one is reminded of Goethe's "red thread." Another king, Kekau-like, bears the title Kalaniku'ihonoikamoku, "the king who sews the is-land" (Kamakau 1961, 83). Moreover, as we shall see, the equivalence between the royal mana and the "cords that bind the kingdom" is represented in the most direct form [172] in the course of the *luakini* ritual itself.

Let us also recall that several heroes who represent the sacred ali'i in mythical form are born in the shape of a cord and revert to this shape to accomplish their exploits. Among these the most famous are Kaulu (one of the forms that Maui takes in Hawaii) and Kana (Fornander 1916–20, 4:522–23, 436–37). It is in the shape of a cord "with four strands" (Emerson in Malo 1951, 227, 228)—also a fishing line—that Kana manifests his divine powers by connecting in successive feats the mountain with the coast (Fornander 1916–20, 1:436), the islands of the Hawaiian archipelago (Fornander 1878–80, 2:33), and this archipelago with Kahiki and thus with the gods (Emerson in Malo 1951, 227, 228; Fornander 1878–80, 2:30–33; 1916–20, 4:436–49; 5:518–21; 6:489–91; Rice 1923, 93–102). These myths emphasize that the king's mana is the power to bind, to unify things that are separate, and in the first place, to "sew" the islands together.

The fact that the '*aha kapu* represent the king as the embodiment of the social bond receives striking confirmation in the parallelism that exists—at his death—between the dissolution of this bond (see above, p. 220) and the undoing of his sacred cords (PE, 6). The strands obtained from the undoing of the cords are woven into caskets in which the bones of the king are enshrined (Hiroa 1957, 575–77). Thus the cords that connected the king to living men now separate him from them. It is also interesting that the custom implies that the cords are not inherited. This seems to indicate two things: (1) The social bond created by each king is contingent on him and must be entirely recreated by his successor. This confirms indeed our preceding analysis of the "political system." (2) The cords of the new king must be made anew: presumably their fabrication is ritualized. Hence it is likely that they are made in the temple during the '*aha* rites. Be that as it may, there is no doubt that by braiding his sacred cords the king braids social relationships or, to put it differently, binds men with his cords. The idea that the king is a "binder" or "weaver" is reflected in the literal meaning of the title, *haku*, which is given to him when he is viewed not simply as noble (ali'i), but specifically as "lord" and "ruler." Indeed, the latter two meanings of *haku* derive from another one: "to weave" and, by extension, "to put in order," "to compose a chant" (PE, 47).[173]

Andrews thinks that "the specific and perhaps original idea of *haku* was to sort out feathers of different qualities and colors, and arrange them in the ancient war cloaks, *kahilis* or wreaths for the chief. It was a work requiring art and skill. A secondary idea was to regulate, to reduce to order; to compose, to put words in order, and is used like the Greek *poieo*" (1875, 27).

In truth, in Hawaii the political function coincides with the poetic function. The way in which the chants (*mele*) are composed shows concretely how, by "weaving" them, the *haku* weaves relations among men: "A chief would select his most able warriors and his principal men, and propose the subject of the *mele* and appoint each one to furnish what we would call a line of verse and the others to act as critics or correctors, and so on till the whole was finished" (Andrews 1875, 35). When the *mele* (chant) is finished, it is "fastened in the memory" (*pa'a na'au*) of all those who have taken part in its composition (cf. Kamakau 1961, 241). Thus the poem, a collective work, becomes a bond that, bound in the memory of all, binds them all. The text is the texture of society. The creation of the chant is the creation of society through the chant. In the same vein, by "weaving" the *'aha* (ritual cord) the king "weaves" his men. Moreover, the ritual "weaving," just like the "weaving of the chants," is also an intellectual weaving, since social relations are reconstituted by the reproduction of the ideas that are their correlate and justification.[174]

The cord evokes not only a static bond, but also the idea of transformation, since it can be used both to tie and to untie. This transformative aspect is made evident in string games,[175] which are used to represent mythical transformations or even to produce ritual ones. The latter are illustrated by the following medical rite.

After praying, the medical priest makes a chain with a string. With this chain he connects the patient's navel and head. Then he pulls the two ends of the chain, which comes undone, and the string is straight. Then another chain, this one stretched across the chest, is loosened and pulled apart in the same way. Each operation is repeated five times. According to Dickey "the loosing of the chain probably was a symbol of the loosing of the patient from his sickness" (1928, 144). Then the priest makes a knot that is placed at each transition point between the different parts of the body and undone by pulling the end of the string. If the knot does not untie or does so only with difficulty, the patient is still supposed to be entangled in his sickness.

We see, then, that knots and chains are made in such a manner that they can be undone in a single movement. The goal is to produce a bodily transformation with the transformation of a string figure that is its equivalent.

Let us turn to an example of the use of a string game to illustrate a mythical transformation. It concerns a string figure called the "net of Makali'i," which is made in such a fashion that when the string at its center is cut the figure immediately comes undone. The chant that accompanies the production of this figure narrates the myth of Makali'i, who, as we have seen, gathered up all the vegetable foods in a net and hung it from heaven. A man-rat gnawed the central knot of the net and easily undid it, making its contents fall to earth (Emerson 1924, 10–11; HEN, 2:114; Kepelino 1932, 78–79; Fornander 1916–20, 4:122–25, 160–65,

168–71; 6:272). The string game reproduces the mythical net and illustrates its sudden collapse. It also corresponds to the *maoloha* net used to commemorate the same event at the end of the Makahiki festival.[176]

Thus we see that in myth as in ritual the cord, the unvarying element of two opposing states (tied and untied), permits the representation of the passage from one to the other. In the myth of Makali'i, the cord in its tied state represents the inaccessibility of divine nature; its untying represents the process whereby this nature becomes accessible, is desacralized. In the medical rite, the tied cord represents the patient's entanglement in sickness (and probably in the sin that causes it); its untying represents his disentanglement and therefore healing.

In conclusion, it is certain that cords are used in several, if not all, 'aha rites. At any rate, these rites are conceived of as metaphorical cords binding the members of a congregation (also called 'aha) by binding them, through the king, to the god. Their use also marks ritual transformations.

Wrapping

In the course of the temple ritual several objects regarded as manifestations of the gods, such as plants and statues, are consecrated by being wrapped in bark cloths.[177] I have already said that "consecration" is in fact the full actualization of an already presupposed relation of the object with the god. Why does wrapping have this effect? In the first place, this happens by convention; wrapping is the collectively accepted sign of the god's presence. But the relation of this sign to the belief in the god's invisible presence is not purely arbitrary (in the Saussurean sense). Indeed, the act of *removing* the object from sight, of making it invisible, favors the implantation of the belief in the god's invisible presence because it creates the experience of a passage from a concrete reality to an invisible one, from a thing of perception to a thing of the mind, and therefore from an individual object to a general concept. In other words, wrapping has become a sign of consecration because it reproduces the process by which the mind reaches the idea of the god.

Neither the pure postulation of the invisible presence of the god nor the visual representation of the god in an object would alone be effective in implanting this belief; only a process that combines the two can have this effect. In other words, first the visible sign of the god must be presented in experience to make him real; then this sign must disappear, in whole or in part, from experience to make him *truly* a god. It is because of this process that the god is more than a concept, more than a signified; he is the reified signified, the signified that has taken on the reality of the signifier at the same time that it is distinguished from it. Indeed, it can be identical to its signifier only when the latter is made invisible. Thus, throughout the ritual the visual evocation of the god (for instance, in images) is combined with, or alternates with, the removal of his material manifestation from sight. In the end, as we shall see, the whole movement of the ritual consists of increasingly soliciting sight, increasingly making the god visible, in order better to establish his radical invisibility.

As we have seen (chap. 5), what is valid for the natural or artificial manifestations of the gods is no less valid for their human manifestations, that is, the high-ranking ali'i, who come fully to embody the divine only by passing from the visible to the invisible and vice versa. This passage is often made possible by wrapping and unwrapping with bark cloth, feather mantles, and so on (see again chap. 5).

There is more to wrapping than sacralization, though. What is wrapped is also bound, constrained. Wrapping can thus represent man's control of the divine, his taming of it at the very moment it becomes divine in full, "true." It is significant that the embodiment of the divine in its wildest form, that is, Kahōāli'i, goes about naked; analogously, the temple images are naked until by being wrapped they are both controlled and made "true."

The idea that wrapping involves control is also illustrated by the custom followed by noble women on certain ceremonial occasions, when they roll themselves up in skirts (*pā'ū*) made of ten layers of cloth, each thirty meters long (Kooijman 1972, 166–67; cf. Brigham 1911, 186; cf. Ellis 1782, 2:87–88; Samwell 1967, 1180, 1160; Manby 1929, 42; Bell 1929–30, 2:120, 125; Townsend 1921, 8; Ross 1904, 70; Stewart 1839, 145; Ellis 1842, 111; Bishop 1916, 14). Here, for example, is a description of the ceremonial wrapping of Kamāmalu, Liholiho's favorite wife:

The favorite queen presented herself to her husband, according to etiquette, wrapped around with a piece of native cloth so long and broad that she was almost hidden under the folds, like a caterpillar beneath its web. To array herself in this unwieldy robe, the cloth had been spread out on the ground, when, beginning at one end, she threw her body across it, and rolled over and over, from side to side, till she had wound the whole about her. After she had shown herself thus appareled in "the presence," her majesty lay down again upon the floor, and unrolled the cloth, by reversing the process of clothing; she then gathered it up and presented the bundle to the king. [Tyerman and Bennett 1832, 2:64]

The meaning of this rite is clear enough. By giving the cloth to her husband, Kamāmalu signals that only he is empowered to possess her. Through the cloth, Liholiho controls his wife and the divine rank of the children she can engender. He makes her taboo for others and free for himself.[178] The rite itself (rolling up and unrolling) evokes the transformative function of the cloth, which, like the cord, permits both sacralization and desacralization, for it can connect two opposite states.

Furthermore, the wrapped woman is an immobilized woman;[179] she thus represents a wild potentiality that has been tamed and made productive by her husband. From this point of view the relationship between the king and his wife is analogous to the relationship between the king and the Haku 'ōhi'a. The latter, like the wife, is unstable and dangerous in a "free" state but becomes productive when it is bound, wrapped, encompassed in the temple. We shall have to return to this connection between the transformation of the god and that of the wife.

The House

With the images of the gods, the temple houses—the *hale mana* in particular—are the most important and meaningful ritual objects. Moreover, the construction of the *hala mana* proceeds in parallel with that of the Haku 'ōhi'a, as will be shown in detail. It seems to me that the *hala mana* is the archetypal house,[180] which embodies in the most perfect form the meanings that are embodied in lesser degrees by every house in the society.[181] All symbolic significations of the house derive from a basic equation, that between house and man.

This equation is made apparent by the ritual of inauguration of the house, which is identical for every house from the *hale mana* down to the humblest habitation of a commoner. This rite consists of trimming the tuft of thatch (called *piko*, "navel cord") hanging above the door. Cutting it, the officiant says, "I am cutting the navel cord of the house" (Kamakau 1976, 106; cf. Malo 1951, 124–25; Brigham 1908, 103; Ladd, Crozier, and Apple 1973, 40, fig. 28; Handy 1972, 292–93). Thus the house is born like a human being, and its structure confirms its equivalence to men.

The different parts of the house are placed in correspondence to the different parts of the human body (cf. Kamakau 1976, 102; Fornander 1916–20, 5:403); for instance, its four corners correspond to the "four corners of the body" (the shoulders and thigh bones—cf. NK, 1:189). Another example: the ridgepole of a chief's house is equated with his crest of hair or helmet (*mahiole*), and its height is said to vary with his rank (Kamakau in Apple 1971, 3). This indicates that the house is also a diagrammatic representation of social categories and relations. In particular it represents the fundamental social opposition, that of the sexes. This is indicated, for example, by the names of the ends of the rafters and posts: "the *oa* or rafters equalled in number the front and back posts, and the lower ends were cut all alike into a heel and fork, the latter called *kohe* [vagina] as it was to fit the *ule* [penis] of the posts" (Brigham 1908, 93).

On the other hand, the front rafters seem to be assimilated to the husband, while the back rafters appear to be equated with the wife. This at least is what it seems possible to infer from the following rule. If, when the rafters are being fitted over the ridgepole, a back rafter must be discarded because it does not mesh properly with a front one, it is believed that the owner's wife will be quarrelsome (Apple 1971, 147).

We can also suppose that the roof, which at least in the mana house is connected with Kū, is masculine, while the lower part of the house is feminine. A similar opposition must exist between the posts, which being erect (*kū*) must be masculine, and the floor, which being horizontal must be feminine. We also know that the head of the family, the ali'i, or the priest is equated with house posts (cf. Apple 1971, 29; Handy and Pukui 1972, 174; Kamakau 1961, 135). This implies that the house as a whole is assimilated to a social group. A commoner's house is equated only with his family, but the house of a chief is equated with the social group he rules. There are indeed indications that different parts of the king's house symbolize different districts of his realm, since each is built by a different *ahupua'a* and thus embodies its work (cf. Ellis 1842, 321; Brigham 1908, 87).

Given these equations, one can easily understand why a house built according to the rules preserving the proper symbolic relations between its parts promotes the life of those who live in it;[182] inversely, a disordered house produces disorder and illness in its inhabitants or in the society over which its owner rules (cf. S. M. Kamakau cited by Hiroa 1957, 76; Haleole in Fornander 1916–20, 6:76–82; Apple 1971, 22–23).

It appears, in short, that, exactly like the image of the god, the house embodies the human species in its perfect state and that, insofar as it represents the human species, it produces what it represents in those whom it contains. This explains precisely why the ritual development of the Haku 'ōhi'a is parallel to the ritual development of the house. Both embody in different forms the human species. But while the image represents the species only in the form of the perfect individual, the house represents it as it is realized in social relations. Indeed, as we have seen, the symbolism of the house is more sociomorphic than anthropomorphic. I would say, then, that the human species, manifested as an individual in the divine image, is transformed by the mana house into a matrix of society. Hence it is inside the mana house that the highest levels of social relations are reproduced— those represented and sustained by the ali'i and their priestly representatives. Moreover, there is a dialectical relation between the development of the two main terms of the ritual process. Each increase in the mana of the image translates into an increase in the mana of the house and the latter into an increase in the mana of the king and nobility contained in the house. But reciprocally, each increase in the mana of the social group reverberates on the mana of the house, which reverberates on the mana of the image. Thus, as usual, the power of the god and the power of his worshipers reinforce each other; but it is interesting that the process is mediated by the house as the embodiment of society.

Interpretation: The Ritual Sequence

Let us now consider this symbolism as it is displayed in the syntagmatic order of the ritual. First of all, it is necessary to note that the parallelism between the construction of the mana house and the transformation of the

Haku ʻōhiʻa exists even before the *hulahula* rite. The felling of the Haku ʻōhiʻa tree is followed by the felling of the trees that furnish the wood for constructing the mana house and other temple houses. Further, the delimitation of the emplacement of the mana house in the *ʻaha helehonua* rite is followed by marking with a *pouomanu* post the site where the Haku ʻōhiʻa will be erected.

According to some sources, the name *pouomanu* is also given to one of the posts of the mana house, to which a human victim is attached while awaiting sacrifice (Elbert 1959, 205; PE, 316, 317; Thrum 1907a, 223; cf. Apple 1971, 95, 144, 278; Brigham 1908, 92; Anonymous 1914, 197). It seems, then, that a correspondence is established between the post of the mana house and the post marking the emplacement of the Haku ʻōhiʻa; in addition, both these posts are sacrificial.

After the correlative erection of the house frame and the *pouomanu* post that marks the emplacement of the Haku ʻōhiʻa, two other correlative rites occur: according to Malo, Kū's transformation in the *kauila nui* rite is followed by the thatching of the roofs of the houses; according to K. Kamakau, the inverse happens, although the ridge of the house is completed only after the *kauila nui*.

Let us now examine the ritual sequence that concerns us here. Since there are important differences, at least on first inspection, between Malo's and K. Kamakau's accounts, I will consider them separately.

According to Malo, the Haku ʻōhiʻa is brought into the temple on the evening of the fourth day, after the houses have been thatched. The divine image, freed of the wrapping of ferns and vines that had covered it, is made visible. Furthermore, it takes the place of the man sacrificed at the post. This man thus prefigures the god—or, more exactly, the god, who represents man in his ideal, "pure" state, derives from the transformation of a victim that represents man in his disordered and impure state. The sacrifice of the victim, then, represents all the sacrificers' transcendence of their own disorder, a transcendence that gives them the experience of the god as ideal humanness and therefore "creates" the god.

The next rite, the *ʻaha hulahula*, has the purpose of transferring via a sacred cord a part of the mana that the preceding sacrifice has constituted in the Haku ʻōhiʻa. This cord, full of mana, is materially preserved in the *hale wai ea* but is metaphorically used first to bind the high priest and the king, then to bind them to all the people, and then to bind all the people together through them. It will be noted that the success of the *ʻaha hulahula* rite is determined by its *collective recognition*, which extends even to commoners. *It is all of society that decides whether the king has succeeded in creating the bond that constitutes it* and that is embodied in the *ʻaha*. Any sound, any external interference is enough to offer a pretext for invalidating it. Thus, ideally, the rite cannot continue unless the relations among all members of society are "perfect in the king" or, to put it more realistically, unless the relations of force are such that the king manages to prevail. Even in the latter case, however, the rite represents the king's mana as dependent on the recognition of the community.

The need in the ritual to solicit the consensus of the community reveals that the latter is not automatically obtained and does not exist in a permanent way; it must be constantly demanded and reproduced. Like the ancient Indic kingship (see Heesterman 1957, 1978), Hawaiian kingship must periodically reproduce itself through a ritual that is a kind of gigantic ordeal; an installation whose effects would last indefinitely is unknown. The king must constantly respond to an open or implicit challenge and renew his power by successfully meeting it. This, as we have seen, is in the nature of "political relations." Hence, all the 'aha prayers evoke the defeat of enemies, rebels, opponents, and even those who simply plan the king's downfall.

Let us also note that in the 'aha hulahula, as well as in all other 'aha rites, the consensus is manifested by two opposing forms of unanimity. Before the success of the 'aha, unanimity is indexed by silence, which manifests the universal recognition of the king's right to speak to the god on behalf of all his men. But as soon as his prayer has been successful, all shout and boisterously manifest their joy. Thus the king's word becomes a collective shout, that is, the manifestation of the vital and victorious society that his word has brought to be.

To continue with Malo's account, the morning after the night when the 'ala hulahula is performed the high priest, who officiated in it, rejoins the priest of the Haku 'ōhi'a in the fast that the latter had begun the moment the tree was felled. This fast has the stated purpose of helping to transform the Haku 'ōhi'a into a "true god" (*akua maoli*). Thus it is natural that the officiant of the rite constituting the second stage of this transformation joins the officiant of the first stage. But why is the fast of these two priests supposed to promote the transformation?

A probable answer can be found in the following detail: the fast is not total; the two priests eat the nectar of banana flowers. Since this nectar is used as baby food (Handy 1972, 166), the two priests thus assume the status of infants. But we have seen that the priests represent their gods; consequently, the priest of the Haku 'ōhi'a and the high priest (who belongs to the order of Kū) represent Kū as a baby. The purpose of the rite is then clear; it brings about the growth of a god who, having just barely entered the men's temple, is like a small infant, still on the threshold of the human world into which he must be integrated. This "baby" is in fact not yet truly born, since the rite of the god's birth will take place later. But we must not take the metaphors of the rite too literally; this birth will not be the god's first (since each sacrifice uses the birth/death metaphor), but only his final and definitive "birth"—a little like that of 'Umi in the temple where his father sends him to "be born" a second time.

In the meantime a sacrifice is made. Four pigs are cooked, each intended for one of the actors in this sacred representation: the god, the high priest, the keeper of the god, and the king and his men. As usual, they "eat together separately"; the sacrifice is both unifying and articulating. Thus one can say that in this rite the god eats, for the first time since he has been integrated into the temple, with the ali'i and priests.

This sacrificial meal connects the erection of the Haku 'ōhi'a with its complement, the completion of the mana house. The latter takes place, according to Malo, when the four packets of 'oloa cloth are tied to the ridgepole. In light of what has been said on the subject of wrapping, we can understand that these bundles are supposed to transfer into the house the divine mana in its "tamed," controlled state. Furthermore, these bundles are tied to the ridgepole with a "mana cord." Having received the god's mana, the house can come to life (kuwā rite). Its "umbilical cord" is cut, and this in turn contributes to making it possible to cut the "umbilical cord" of the Haku 'ōhi'a—again, a parallel between the production of the house and that of the god (see p. 309).

Note as well that the incorporation of divine mana in the house provokes a dance: on the ridgepole according to Malo, inside the house (during the kuili rite) according to K. Kamakau. This dance can be compared with the dance that is represented by the image of the god according to A. Kaeppler's hypothesis. This makes evident the correspondence between ideal man (the god) and concrete men, as well as the mediating role of the house, which I mentioned above. Moreover, the kuili rites make it apparent that by concretely enacting the divine model men demonstrate its power and therefore make it more powerful. As a consequence, the singing, dancing, and commensal eating by the priests—activities that are the strongest realizations of the ordering power of the divine—contribute to the further development of the Haku 'ōhi'a and prepare his final and definitive rebirth.

Now let us turn to the problem raised by the differences between Malo's and K. Kamakau's versions of the ritual. K. Kamakau differs from Malo on two principal points. (1) According to him, the 'aha hulahula is not preceded by the Haku 'ōhi'a's entrance into the temple. On the contrary, it seems that the king and the high priest introduce the king's principal feather god. As for the Haku 'ōhi'a, he is introduced after the kuili rite has been completed. (2) He does not mention the existence of the ho'opi'i na 'aha limalima rite, and he relates the kuwā rite to the inauguration of the temple and not to that of the mana house.

Concerning the first point, K. Kamakau is not contradicting the basic scheme presented by Malo, he is only dividing Kū's integration into the temple into two stages and using a different image in each stage. The feather god appears in the first stage because it represents Kū in his wild, conquering, and warlike aspect, while the wooden image represents the final stage of Kū's transformation, in which Kū, having conquered all the land and all the men, is at rest and becomes a stabilizing and life-giving force (cf. Valeri 1982b).

Thus, while in Malo's account Kū's transformation is represented by successive changes in the status of the Haku 'ōhi'a/mana house pair, in K. Kamakau's this same transformation is enacted by the sequence formed by the feather image and the wooden image. Both authors, however, are in agreement in giving the *kuili* rite an important role in Kū's transformation.

Here is a synoptic table of Malo's and K. Kamakau's versions of this ritual sequence:

Malo	K. Kamakau
1. *'aha hulahula*: the Haku 'ōhi'a is introduced into the temple	1. *'aha hulahula*: the feather god is introduced into the temple
2. *pule kuwā*: concerns the mana house	2. *pule kuwā*: concerns the temple (see n. 157)
3. *kuili* rites: continuation of inauguration rites of the mana house	3. *kuili* rites: inauguration rites of the mana house
	4. the Haku 'ōhi'a is introduced into the temple

In the matter of scheduling, both Malo and K. Kamakau, as well as the anonymous author published by Wilkes, state that the Haku 'ōhi'a is introduced into the temple on the evening of the fourth day of the moon. The "redoubling" of Kū's entrance rite in K. Kamakau's account thus provisionally puts an end to the delay of one day that this author's ritual schedule had until this time with respect to that of Malo. It thus seems that K. Kamakau's schedule was one day in advance of Malo's in order to accommodate this duplication.

As for the lack of any mention of the *ho'opi'i na 'aha limalima* rite by K. Kamakau, all I can say for the moment is that since K. Kamakau has fused some aspects of this rite with another one, which is performed at the *'anu'u* tower, we must wait until this second rite is encountered before we can discern the reason he is at variance with Malo on this point.

Concerning the description of the individual rites included in this section of the ritual, neither K. Kamakau nor the text published by Wilkes brings, broadly speaking, any element to contradict Malo's description. Let me emphasize, however, certain details of the *'aha hulahula* rite as they emerge from K. Kamakau's account. According to him this rite is preceded by a state of general "affability" among all classes of society. The term used to designate this state is *'olu'olu*, the very word Malo uses to describe the effect the sacrifice has upon the god. This highlights the correspondence between the state of the god and that of society; thus K. Kamakau's text makes it clearer that the god's "affability" is the result of the "affability" reigning in society rather than the reverse, since the latter precedes the former.

K. Kamakau also reports that the 'aha hulahula rite is preceded by the priest's wrapping of lama leaves in a cloth. We will see that the same operation occurs before the 'aha ho'owilimo'o, which is a double of the 'aha hulahula. How should this rite be explained?

"Lama" means "light." This plant is supposed to "enlighten" and at the same time purify and thus heal (cf. PE, 177; Neal 1929, 674; Handy 1972, 44). It is therefore probable that by wrapping the lama leaves one is consecrating them to the god to make him "luminous," that is, one is summoning the god to manifest himself as both an intellectual and a lustral light.[183] Of course the intellectual acceptance of the god is what makes him a purifying and generative force. The more clearly the god manifests himself in men's thought, the more ordering, and therefore life giving, is the power he has over them.

The text given by Wilkes prompts another reflection. It reports that during the 'aha hulahula rite the king is covered with a cloak of precious feathers whereas the high priest is completely nude. According to another source, however, they are both nude when they sacrifice (Fornander 1916–20, 5:325). The rule that enjoins both participants in this sacrifice (or the priest only, in that he is a representative of the king) to undress in the god's presence carries to the extreme the principle that the inferior must uncover himself before the superior; like prostration, it marks a total abandonment of the self to the sacred person and is a sign of impotence relative to him. Moreover, by disrobing, one leaves the human realm and enters the divine. Consequently, to disrobe has the same meaning as to die (cf. Baudrillard 1976, 108). This equation is proved, for example, by the fact that one undresses during funeral rites, in which those who survive the deceased symbolically die with him. For the same reason one must undress when entering a tomb or the mausoleum of an ali'i (Campbell 1967, 101; Byron 1826, 134).

Note that the nudity of the high priest and eventually that of the king corresponds to that of the human victim (Ellis 1842, 152; Brigham, n.d., 257; Ii 1963, 14–15). This constitutes another indication of the interchangeability of victim, sacrificer, and sacrifier. The latter two "die" with the first when he dies for them.

Rites for the Final Transformation of the God
Description
Malo MS, 175–77

On the evening of the seventh day ('Ole-ku-kāhi), when the kuili rites are over, the king and the high priest "perform" (ka'i) the 'aha ho'owilimo'o. If this rite is successful, it is a very good omen for the *luakini*, and the priest asks the king for land as a gift and says to him, "O heavenly one (*e ka lani*), we two have asked the god to maintain the government (*aupuni*) in order and life for you and for the people; and we have seen that he has consented; the *'aha* is already perfect; after which if you succeed in killing your enemy, it will be because your family god is perfect."[184]

During the night, the priest who catches the *ulua* fish goes out to sea with several fishermen and they try to catch the *ulua* with lines,[185] using squid for bait. If they do not succeed in catching a fish, they come back to shore and go from house to house, trying with some lie to make the inhabitants come out. If someone does come out, they kill him. They thrust a hook in his mouth and carry him to the temple. However, if there are many people in a house, the residents defend themselves against the priests' attack.[186]

The next morning they gird the Haku 'ōhi'a with a long belt of braided coconut leaves, which is called his "umbilical cord that comes from his mother." Then the king takes a pig and the priest recites this prayer: "This is the bamboo[187] for the umbilical cord of the mysterious (*aīwaīwa*) heavenly one [the god]; this is the splitting of the bamboo for the umbilical cord of the mysterious god; this is the cutting (*moku*) of the umbilical cord of the mysterious god; this is the severing of the navel cord of the mysterious god." Then he cuts the "umbilical cord" made of coconut leaves and, wiping it with a rag, prays thus: "Sop the blood, sop the bright (*aka*) wreath;[188] to animate (*hālapa*)[189] your wooden god."

Then the king ends the rite by consecrating the pig to the god (*"amama ke alii me ka puaa"*). During the same day (the eighth of the month) the so-called great sacrifice (*"ka haina nui"*) takes place. The pigs for this sacrifice are given by the ali'i and their men (*kanaka*). The important ali'i (*ali'i nui*), with many men (*"a nui ko lakou mau kanaka"*), give ten hogs; ali'i of less importance, with few men, give less. As for the "men" (*kanaka*), they give according to their means. When all the pigs are put to cook in the ovens, the king and all the priests go and gird the loins of the Haku 'ōhi'a with a loincloth. All the priests recite the "prayer of the loincloth" (*pule malo*): "Put on the loincloths; spread the news (*e lono!*),[190] declare war, tell it clearly (*ha'i le'a*), spread the report! (*ha'ilono e*),"[191] and they gird the loins first of the principal god, who now receives the title "*mō'ī*" ("sovereign"),[192] then of the other gods, to whom they give titles corresponding to their positions (*wahi*).

When the pigs are cooked (*mo'a*), the priests are given one of the forequarters of each animal. This part is called *hainaki*. In addition they are given some *pa'i 'ai* taro. The rest goes to the ali'i and their entourage.

After the meal, the king offers his gods a great sacrifice, which consists of four hundred pigs, four hundred bananas, four hundred coconuts, four hundred red fish (*i'a 'ula*), four hundred *'oloa* cloths, and some human victims. First they burn the pigs' bristles and remove the viscera, then all the offerings are placed on the pebbles (*ili'ili*) beneath the *lele* altar. The priests offer a prayer to the images (*akua ki'i*); then the offerings are put on the *lele* altar.[193] After that, the *kāpapaulua* priest goes into the tower holding the *ulua*[194] and recites an *'aha*. When he has finished he asks the king, "How is the *'aha* of us both?" And the king answers him that the *'aha* is perfect; upon which the priest continues, "Perfect, indeed; the fishing line did not break, the hook did not break (*ka'i*—cf. Andrews 1865, 231), your government is already firmly established (*pa'a*)."

Then the *ulua* is laid (*kau*) on the altar and sacrificed (*mōhai*). This day is called "day of the great transparent cloth" (*lā kōpili nui*) because after the sacrifice the tower is decorated with white transparent cloth called *kōpili*.

K. Kamakau 1919–20, 23–25

After the rite for erecting the *akua 'ōhi'a*, and when night has fallen, the *ulua* priest (*kahuna ulua*) goes out to sea and tries to catch the *ulua* fish with a line. If the bait is eaten up by the fish he becomes very anxious, but if the bait remains it is good; if, however, the hook breaks, it is a sign that his prayer and the rite have gone wrong. He therefore prays earnestly before returning to shore.

In the meantime another priest—this one in the temple—offers a prayer called *maua*.[195] After midnight the king makes his entrance into the temple, and they pray earnestly before the *kuahu* altar.[196] No fire may burn during this very taboo night. First the high priest says the prayers, "*piikuma*" and "*leiau*."[197] Then the king and the priest of the order of Lono (*kahuna mo'o Lono*) perform the *'aha ho'owilimo'o*. They remain silent and immobile for a while until the priest, having wrapped a bunch of *lama* leaves with an *'oloa* cloth, stands up and begins to say the *'aha* prayer in a conversational tone (*kalokalo*). Then, still praying, he sits down.

When he has finished he turns his gaze to the king, who, seeing his look, smites the pig and sacrifices it (*mōhai*) to the god, saying: "O Kū by *ho'owilimo'o* (*e Kū iā ho'owilimo'o*); here is your pig, the pig that permits me to obtain life from you; watch over me; curse the rebel (*a mōlia i ke kipi*) who seizes the land (*i kā'ili 'āina*); sacrifice him in the house of bones (*a mōlia i ka hale iwi*);[198] let him die (*e make ia*)."

When the king has finished the sacrifice, the priest asks him, "How is the *'aha* of us both?" The king answers, 'It is excellent. Did you hear anything wrong (*hewa*)?" "No." Then "the priest slaps the cord[199] ("*hoopai ae la ke kahuna i ka aha*") and makes a small rite of desacralization ("*a hoonoa uuku ae la*")," after which they quietly go back to the congregation. They ask the congregation if they have heard anything, and the answer is negative.

This same night the *ulua* priest, the priest of the *maua* rite, the high priest, and the priest of Lono gather together and pray much. At dawn of the sixth day, the priest[200] waves his hands (*ho'āli*) and stands up to say (*kalokalo*) the *koli'i* prayer. He then sits down, still praying. When this ends the congregation raise their hands at the tower, from which two men chant in a loud voice (*kāhea*) toward the audience, and while the priests below chant prayers (*pule*) the two men above dance.[201] This rite is called *maki'i lohelohe*.

Then the king comes out of the temple to give (*hā'awi*) some pork to the feather gods, to the priests, to the ali'i and all the people of distinction ("*kanaka maka hanohano*"), and to the *pū'ali*.[202] Each receives a share according to his rank. The crowd of "very little" people (*kanaka li'ili'i loa*) also receives their share, after that of the king has been cooked. Moreover, about two hundred hogs are allotted to the temple's "wooden gods."

Then the priests and ali'i go back inside the temple, where they utter the *kōpili nui* prayer before the "wooden gods" (*akua lā'au*).[203] Then the high priest rises and offers a prayer (*kalokalo*) to the '*aulima* stick[204] and sits down again. All then pray before the images while a great number of fires are lighted to broil (*pūlehu*) the two hundred sacrificial pigs.[205] The broiled pigs are then brought into the temple and placed (*waiho*) before the "wooden gods" with a great number of unripe bananas (*mai'a maka*), coconuts, and two or three transgressors (*kanaka lawehala*).

This done, the *ulua* priest comes to the temple to announce to the king the success of his rite. No one can pass by outside on pain of death; and during the priest's progress, solemnity prevails outside and no one can walk about. The priest comes praying and holding a baited hook in his hand. This is the same hook he had used to fish for the *ulua*. Upon his arrival in the temple, the other priests, frightened, flee into the *hale pahu*. When the *ulua* priest has ended his prayer, he addresses the king thus: "O heavenly one, listen to this speech of the god; I went out to sea last night, my hook did not break, my bait was not eaten, your prayer was excellent, the traitor will not have life from you; our[206] ali'i will not have life from you." After which he returns to his place.

Then the congregation begins to pray again before the images (*ka po'e ki'i*), and the king offers in sacrifice (*mōhai*) the pigs and the human corpses placed (*waiho*) before the gods, as well as the coconuts and bananas. After which they return to their houses. When the pigs for the feather gods are cooked, the gods' praises are sung. After that, the pigs of the king, of the ali'i, of the warriors, and of the people of distinction are all cooked. These pigs are then brought into the temple where a priest performs the *hainaki* rite over them.[207] Then the king's share (*waiwai*) is returned to him; he gives it (*ha'awi*) to the needy as their portion.

In the evening[208] the ali'i, the priests, and all the portable gods return to the temple to pray. The king offers pigs, bananas, coconuts, and the corpse of a man in sacrifice (*mōhai*).

Wilkes 1845, 4:507–8

Before dawn of the sixth day the feather god Kāʻili is brought to the Haku ʻōhiʻa, where the king kills a hog "with a single blow." The officiating priest "strikes a few blows on the drum" to indicate that the rite [209] has been completed. Then all the priests gather in the temple, where they pray in chorus until daylight, when the king gives the ʻāmama. On the day that now begins (the sixth of the month) the king gives a hog to each god, "frequently to the number of forty." In addition, he gives two pigs to each priest. Two pigs, coconuts, and bananas are placed before the Haku ʻōhiʻa, "where they are left to putrefy."

Then the king and the priest retire to the hale pahu [210] to pray. At nightfall, a priest goes to catch the ulua fish; if he is not successful, he hooks in the mouth a man who has broken a taboo, kills him, and drags him in this manner to the altar. [211] If a man was sacrificed, "the king took hold of one of the feet of both the hog and man, and thus presented them to the god, saying, 'Here is my offering to you; let me live; let me have the country I desire to conquer.' Then they all retire and feast."

Interpretation

At the beginning of this sequence we find two closely related rites: the ʻaha hoʻowilimoʻo and the kāpapaulua (ulua fishing). K. Kamakau is the only author who describes the first rite in any detail. From his account it appears that the ʻaha hoʻowilimoʻo is practically indistinguishable from the ʻaha hulahula. Like the latter, it is preceded by the wrapping of the lama leaves. Here as well it is a matter of producing an "enlightenment" that is the preliminary condition for the success of the rite.

The two ʻaha differ not in structure or content but in their officiants: in the ʻaha hulahula the officiant is a priest of the order of Kū; in the ʻaha hoʻowilimoʻo he is a priest of the order of Lono, even though the rite is addressed to Kū (that is, to the Haku ʻōhiʻa). Considered in light of my interpretation of the kauila nui rite, the presence of a priest of Lono in a rite concerning Kū is not surprising. I believe in fact that we can establish a correspondence between the ʻaha hulahula and the beginning of the kauila nui rite, on the one hand, and between the conclusion of this rite and the ʻaha hoʻowilimoʻo, on the other.

We have seen that during most of the kauila nui Kū manifests himself in all his wild violence, but toward the end of the rite he is brought under control. The priest of Kū officiates as long as the wild Kū must be tamed; this indicates that he is closer to the "wilder" aspect of the divine. On the other hand, that the priest of Lono officiates at the end indicates that he is closer to the "tamed" pole of the divine. Analogously, it is a priest of Kū who in the ʻaha hulahula makes possible the contact with Kū in a still relatively wild form, while it is a priest of Lono who mediates between the sacrifier and Kū in the *'aha ho'owilimo'o*, which takes place a little before the god's birth in a completely human form. This seems to indicate that the transformation of Kū requires the mediation of Lono, that is, of the god who represents—among other things—the "kingless society." We thus understand why the king leads Lono into his temple at the end of the New Year's festivals: he needs him to operate the transformation of Kū and thus his own transformation into a legitimate king. The transformation of Kū in the *'aha ho'owilimo'o* rite thus coincides with the full integration of the king and aristocracy into society. Note also that in K. Kamakau's version the transition from *'aha hulahula* to *'aha ho'owilimo'o* involves the transition from the use of Kū's feather image (which connotes mobility and "wildness") to the use of his wooden image (which connotes stability and "tameness"). In Wilkes's account, the passage from one form of the god to the other is represented visually in the *'aha ho'owilimo'o* rite, when the "king's feather god" (i.e., Kūkā'ilimoku) is brought before the Haku 'ōhi'a. Thus we are shown the turning of Kūkā'ilimoku ("Kū island snatcher"), the god who makes the process of encompassing the land possible, into Kūnuiākea ("Kū of wide expanse"), the immobile god who represents the permanence of the encompassment and thus the completion, the transcendence of Kūkā'ilimoku.

This transformation of Kūkā'ilimoku into Kūnuiākea is effected not only by bringing their images into contact, but also by the mediation of a sacrificial pig. The mode of the pig's death indicates that it is a piglet, since otherwise it could hardly be lifted by one person and dashed against the ground. It thus seems that by incorporating a very young victim in Kū, the god's rebirth in a new form (Kūnuiākea) is brought about.

But to return to Malo's and K. Kamakau's accounts, it is clear from their descriptions that the god's taming also entails the taming of the king's adversary. This is just what the priest of the *ho'owilimo'o* rite implies by saying to the king that since "the god is perfect," that is, perfectly tamed and thus favorable, his rival will be vanquished and therefore "tamed."

The king's killing and appropriation of his adversary are then represented by the *ulua* fishing. Since this fish is very vigorous and thus difficult to catch, it is a perfect metaphor for the recalcitrant adversary. The successful catch of this fish can thus appear as a "victory." The identification of the *ulua* fish with the adversary [212] is confirmed a posteriori by the way the rite is performed in the case where the adversary has already been captured and killed. In fact, it is feigned that he is a fish: "The ruler came forth, and grasped the line from which hung the famous hook called Manaiakalani, and hooked it into the mouth of the dead victim—a chief defeated in war, or some other victim perhaps (Kamakau 1976, 142; cf. also Wilkes, above).

Moreover, the *ulua* fishing expedition is a thinly disguised "manhunt"; everyone knows that the fishermen are trying to capture human victims, for the latter are much more adequate representations of the adversary than the *ulua* fish (cf. also Ii 1963, 43). Indeed, it seems to me that Malo's account of the fishing makes it clear that first a substitute for a human victim, that is, an *ulua* fish, is sought; but if the substitute is not caught, the priest must resign himself to catching a human victim. This is in perfect agreement with the principle that animal sacrifice is a tentative substitute, so to speak, for human sacrifice.

We have seen that every ali'i embodies the land over which he reigns. Consequently, by appropriating enemy ali'i the king appropriates their lands. It follows that "fishing" for the *ulua*, which represents the adversaries, is equivalent to fishing for land. We find confirmation of this equivalence in the chant of Kuali'i (Fornander 1916–20, 4:370–71, lines 1–19; 1878–80, 2:385), but especially in one of the origin myths of the islands of the Hawaiian archipelago. According to this myth, one day Maui (or Kanaloa—see Fornander 1878–80, 2:18) took an *ulua* with a hook. Drawing in his line to bring in the fish, he made the islands emerge. This process of emergence would have continued until all the islands were linked together in one single mass had Maui's brothers not violated the taboo of looking behind them. This made the fishing line break (Westervelt 1910, 18–19; cf. 123–24). In another version, it is the hook that breaks (Remy 1862, 85). Now this mythical hook is supposed to be identical to the Manaiākalani hook used in the ritual fishing for the *ulua* (Fornander 1916–20, 4:370, 547) and in hooking the victim's mouth when he is being led into the temple.

Thus the myth confirms that fishing for the *ulua* is also fishing for land. It contains a component, moreover, that accounts for the necessity of repeating the mythical event on the ritual level: the brothers who break the taboo and thereby ruin Maui's unifying work prefigure the king's enemy brothers who prevent him from realizing the political unification of the kingdom and who must therefore be sacrificed.

The relation between the *ho'owilimo'o* and *kāpapaulua* rites is represented in a slightly different form by Malo and by K. Kamakau. According to the first author, the *kāpapaulua* rite follows the *ho'owilimo'o* rite and completes its work. According to the second author, in contrast, fishing for the *ulua* takes place before the *ho'owilimo'o* rite, but the announcement of the successful fishing is made after this rite is performed. Furthermore, K. Kamakau situates a "fishing for men" later in the ritual sequence.

Fishing, which represents the neutralization of any enemy, any force not encompassed by the god, permits the god to attain perfection. This is why for Malo the morning after the *ulua* fishing the god "is born" as a man, as the ideal man made possible by an ordered society. This birth rite and the rite for putting the loincloth on the god that follows it are identical to those performed for any male child to transform him fully into a social being. The transformation of the god into the perfect type of the human male is thus completed. Therefore the true human nature of the god becomes fully apparent, and this is why it is said that the Haku 'ōhi'a has become an *akua maoli*, a "true god."

In sum, the ritual of the *luakini* consists in developing diachronically the transformation that the divine image already represents synchronically in its structure (see above, p. 252). The image is at once the potentiality of the ritual action and the result of this action. More exactly, diachronic action, by activating the synchronic schema, makes it "true" by realizing it in the social and intellectual relations "woven" by the rite. Thus at the end of the rite the divine image, which had been the anticipation of the human action that produces its truth, turns into the summary, the trace of this action. Standing as a memorial to it, the divine image will continue to feed it and to find in it the source of its truth: *verum ipsum factum*.

It should be noted that Malo is the only author who describes the rite of the god's birth; K. Kamakau, 'Ī'ī, and S. M. Kamakau put the *maki'i lohelohe*, which Malo does not present, in its place. Before trying to explain this divergence we must cite the most detailed account of the *maki'i lohelohe*, which is furnished by 'Ī'ī (1963, 38) as well as by S. M. Kamakau, who follows him very closely (cf. Kamakau 1976, 143–44, and below).

Two men, each carrying two coconut leaves plaited with coconut fibers, enter the space enclosed by the *'anu'u* tower. The first prays at the right front corner of the tower, holding in his right hand one of the plaited objects. The prayer says:

Thus goes the *'aha*
The *'aha* for Kū, for Lono, for Kāne and Kanaloa.
Curse (*mōlia*) the rebel who takes the land
Who holds out his hand to seize
Let him be cursed by you.[213]

Then he ties the plait to the corner of the far side, and his companion ties another one to the left corner. The first man repeats his prayer and ties a second plait to the back corner of the tower, again on the right side. He is imitated by the other, who attaches the fourth plait to the left back corner.

After this they stand up (*kukū*) on the tower, and when the drum rolls below and voices chant, they move as if to dance. Here are the words of the chant:

O Maki'i, Maki'i lohelohe
It is dark on the mountain
It is dark on the Ocean
There is a sign on the sea, on the vast sea;

High are the stars; low is the moon;
O '*ōhiki* crab,[214] '*ōhiki* crab, come ashore.[215]

According to S. M. Kamakau, the four plaits represent the *ali'i nī'aupi'o* as the "'binding cords' of the chiefdom (*kaula helehonua o ke aupuni*)" (1976, 143). Since there are four plaits, it is likely that each is made to correspond to one of the four major gods, following a hierarchical order of precedence determined by the opposition of front and back and right and left.

It seems, then, that if one can connect the *nī'aupi'o* with the gods by tying them to the tower, the latter is equivalent to the divine image. Moreover, the cords that symbolically surround the divine tower (since they are tied to its four corners) seem to be equivalent to the "umbilical cord," which includes a belt tied around the god's waist. Also, while the plaits attached to the tower reproduce the *ali'i nī'aupi'o* (who include the king), the "navel cord" attached to the divine image reproduces the king.

Given these equivalences, we can assert that the "umbilical cord" is a "cord that binds the kingdom" and, reciprocally, that the four "cords that bind the kingdom" are "umbilical cords." Moreover, the *piko*, "umbilical cord," is also identical to the "cord that binds the kingdom" in that both represent the genealogical relations centered on the king-god that give form to the society. Let me explain.

According to Hawaiian theory each individual has three *piko*. These are, in addition to the umbilical cord or navel proper, "the crown of the head (located by the whorl of hair or 'cowlick')," and the genitals (NK, 1, 183). The first *piko* unites the individual to all his consanguineous kin; the second unites him with his divinized ancestors, who may enter him by the head; the third unites him with his descendants (cf. NK, 1:183) and, it seems to me, his affines. It is probable that the "umbilical cord" of the divine image represents not one but all three *piko*, and therefore all social relationships, which converge in the king's god. But as such, it is also identical to the "cords that bind the kingdom." The "umbilical cord" that makes the god be born, that gives him life, thus symbolizes society itself and the continuity of its life. It also symbolizes the king as the "cord" that mediates between god and men and ensures the conversion of the life of the one in the life of the others. This is why the reproduction of the god, the reproduction of society, and that of the king all coincide in the same ritual.

It will have been noted that for K. Kamakau, 'Ī'ī, and S. M. Kamakau the *maki'i lohelohe* rite not only takes the place of the birth rite of the divine image, it also takes on the principal features of the '*aha limalima* rite. In fact, one cannot help relating the four plaits attached to the corners of the tower with the "four bundles" attached to the ridgepole of the mana house during the *limalima* rite. Moreover, both in this rite and in the *maki'i lohelohe* rite, the two persons who attach either the plaits or the parcels "dance" by making gestures with their hands while the priests chant below.

In sum, two rites distinguished by Malo are fused by the other sources into a single one, centered on the tower, which therefore assumes the significations of both the mana house and the divine image. On the other hand, that image and house find their point of coincidence in the tower confirms that they are paradigmatically equivalent—a fact already suggested by the analysis of the Malo text alone.

In conclusion, the comparison of the different versions of the rite reveals new aspects of its meaning and confirms the cogency of our previous interpretations. It also shows that Malo's, K. Kamakau's, 'Ī'ī's, and S. M. Kamakau's descriptions presuppose the same sense relationships, thus the same "grammar"; this is why it seems likely to me that their texts differ because they reflect alternative practices rather than because one of them reflects the "true" form of the ritual while the others do not.

The equivalence of the *maki'i lohelohe* rite in K. Kamakau's account and of the image's birth rite in Malo's account appears to be truly paradigmatic because the two rites occur in the same syntagmatic position. Indeed, not only are they preceded by the *'aha ho'owilimo'o* and the *'kāpapaulua* rite, they are also followed by the same rite, which Malo calls *ka haina nui*, "the great sacrifice."

There are, however, some surface differences in the two accounts of this "great sacrifice" and of the rites that accompany it. In Malo, the pigs are first given by all participants in quantities varying with their rank. Then, while the pigs cook in the ovens, the king and the priests go and girdle the loins of the Haku 'ōhi'a and the other images. When the pigs are cooked, the first portion of each is given to the gods through their priest. This *hainaki* portion makes the rest accessible for human consumption.[216] Then a new offering is consecrated to the gods, which is capped by the *ulua* fish after the *kāpapaulua* priest has brought it into the temple. No share of this sacrifice is given to the humans. K. Kamakau's account is somewhat more complicated and moreover rather obscure in that it is difficult to distinguish the stages of consecration of the same offerings from the sacrifice of different offerings at different stages. But a reasonable rendering of his account is as follows.

First the offerings are divided among the different categories of gods and people. Then the girdling of the images with loincloths of *kōpili* takes place. After the preparation of the sacrificial fire, the gods' shares of the offerings that have already been apportioned and some human victims are broiled and placed before the images. At this point the *ulua* priest enters the temple. After this priest's rite is performed, the king consecrates the offerings previously placed in front of the gods and presumably the *ulua* as well.

Only after the consecration of the gods' shares are the men's shares cooked. When they are done, the *hainaki* part is first given, then the rest is distributed.

The sequence is concluded by a new sacrifice to the gods which, as in Malo's account, is not shared by men.

In sum, Malo's and Kelou Kamakau's accounts have the same basic structure:

1. *kāpapaulua* and *'aha ho'owilimo'o*;
2. girdling of the image with a navel cord (Malo) or "girdling" of the tower in the *maki'i lohelohe* rite (K. Kamakau, completed by 'Ī'ī);
3. *ka haina nui* ("the great sacrifice"), which involves girdling the images with *kōpili* loincloths;
4. offering that is entirely left to the gods.

The two accounts differ in that K. Kamakau distinguishes a greater number of stages in the "great sacrifice" and in that they connect differently the bringing of the *ulua* fish into the temple with the rest of the ritual sequence.

Note also that according to Malo the final sacrifice is followed by decoration with *kōpili* cloth of the tower.

Given the substantial agreement of our two main sources, how can we interpret the meaning of the "great sacrifice"? Clearly, this sacrifice is the end stage of a series of sacrifices that mark the final transformation of the Haku 'ōhi'a and of the other gods. Therefore it coincides with the girdling of these images' loins, that is, with the rite that signifies that the gods have become adult, complete men.

At the same time, the "great sacrifice" is a "hierarchical communion" that makes it possible to reproduce society as a hierarchy of approximations to what the gods stand for. This hierarchy is represented and effected by the order in which the sacrificial shares are received and by their value (both quantitative and qualitative).

But as a communion this rite makes men and gods too close. This is probably why it is followed by a sacrifice that is *entirely* abandoned to the gods and that can therefore represent their separation from men. This sacrifice, moreover, includes the *ulua* (fish or human adversary or both of them) and thus marks the final neutralization of any hostile or transgressive force resisting the god—that is, the king—that is, the society.

The triumph of Kū and all other gods encompassed by him is now complete.

The Rite of Kahōāli'i and the *Hono* Rite
Description
Malo MS, 177–78

On the evening of the eighth day, the priests and other people, with the movable gods and with Kahōāli'i, go inland to fetch branches of *koa*

(*Acacia koa*). They return noisily, as they do when they bring in the Haku 'ōhi'a. With the *koa* branches they build a hut, and that evening the *hui o Papa* rite[217] begins. At the same time they begin to cook in the oven a pig called *pua'a he'a* ("blood-red pig").[218]

On the morning of 'Ole-ku-kolu (the ninth) they gather in great numbers to eat the *pua'a he'a*. The remains of the meal are thrown away, for they cannot be kept for another time. On this occasion Kahōāli'i eats the eye of a man who has been offered in sacrifice on the *lele* altar and the eye of a pig.[219] Then the *lukamaea*[220] rite is performed, and the priests, the ali'i, and their men, bringing the *akua kā'ai* with them, go bathe in the sea.[221] Coming back, they bring pieces of coral (*ko'a*) that they heap (*ho'āhu*) before the temple.[222] Back at the temple, after putting the pigs to cook in the oven (*kālua*), they sit down in rows before the *hale pahu*. This "work" (*hana*) is called *hono*.[223]

When everyone is in his place the priest in charge of this ritual comes forward and, while standing, utters the *hono* prayer. As he comes to the words "*o ka hoaka o ka lima aia iluna*," "the palms of the hands are turned upward," everyone holds up his hands and remains seated, motionless and silent. Whoever stirs is put to death. By the end of this long prayer the pigs have finished cooking; they are eaten, and all go to sleep.

K. Kamakau 1919–20, 25–27

After the sacrifice mentioned at the end of the preceding section, the congregation leaves the *luakini* and goes to the *hale o Papa* to pray. That very evening they begin to perform the *hui o Papa* rite. This ended, they return to their places. When it is dark again they return to the *luakini* to recite the *weweke*[224] prayer before the *kuahu*. At the same time the priests, in company of "one of the king's gods" (*ko ke ali'i akua ho'okāhi*),[225] go among the houses[226] attempting by deceit to entice people to come out. But the people know that the priests' true intention is to kill them, and they avoid going out. This night is consecrated to Kahōāli'i, and the prayer uttered by the deceiving priest is called *lālākoa*.[227]

At dawn,[228] the king goes to the *hale o Papa* to lead the *'aha* of the *hale o Papa* in the company of the priest who knows its rules (*loina*). At the end of the rite, this priest addresses the king: "Listen to my words." "Yes," answers the king. "Your prayer is already perfect, your god has considered you favorably (*a 'ua nānā mai no akua iā 'oe*)," adds the priest.

Then the king returns to his house, and when it is daylight he returns to the *luakini* temple to offer a short prayer to the god. After praying, he sacrifices some pigs, bananas, coconuts, and human corpses (*kanaka make*) to the god.[229] This rite is called *holua*.[230] Afterward the king's feather god is carried to the beach, and everyone prostrates himself as he passes. Then the king returns to the *hale o Papa* to pray, and all the people and the ali'i go there to be "blessed" (lit., "prayed on") by the priest of Papa in order to be allowed to bathe in the sea. The goddess [Papa] "mitigates" (*ho'onā*) the taboo of the *luakini*, and thanks to that, the filth (*ka maea*) of the men who have taken part in the rites can be eliminated by bathing. Yet the bathing does not completely free them from the temple taboos.

After bathing they return inside the *luakini*, where the priest of the *hono* rite makes them sit down in eight rows before the *kuahu* and the images of the gods (*po'e ki'i*)[231] and orders them to be quiet, not to move, to align their knees and keep their backs down so as to make the congregation (*anaina*) of the god excellent (*maika'i*). Then the priest gets up and, praying, stirs (*ho'ēhu*) a *lama* branch before the congregation, whom he orders to raise the palms of their hands. All obey and avoid making any other movements, so as not to be put to death.

When the priest has finished reciting the prayer of the *hono* rite, he declares to the king that the prayer has been successful and that thanks to the *hono* he will retain his land. After the priest lifts the taboo (*ho'onoa*), all leave the temple for the sharing of the pigs, bananas, and coconuts. The "men" (*kanaka*)[232] and the priest of the *hono* rite are the ones who receive these prestations.

Wilkes 1845, 4:508

After the feasting that concludes the "great sacrifice,"

A chief, called the "Turtle,"[233] then came forward, and prayed with uplifted hands. If any one offended by making a noise, he was instantly killed. The women afterwards brought their tax of tapa, which is put into the fifth house[234] in the heiau.

On the seventh day, they all bathed; after which they were all clothed in new maros [*malo*, loincloths] from the tapas [*kapa*, "bark cloth"]; they then sat down in rows, placing themselves in various attitudes, with the hands raised up or placed on their shoulders, and each was obliged to remain in the same attitude until the ceremony of prayer was concluded. Afterwards, eighty hogs were distributed among the people.

'Ī'ī (1869f; 1963, 43–44) and S. M. Kamakau (1870c; 1976, 142)

According to 'Ī'ī, those who have participated in the rites of the temple go to bathe in the ocean to cleanse themselves of the grease and odor of the pigs that they have eaten in the temple. Meanwhile, three or four pigs are cooked for the *hono* rite.

Back in the temple, the people sit down "like the row of images that stands before the tower from one side to the other" ("*elike me ka lalani kii e ku ana mamua o ka anuu mai o ao*"). More exactly, the men sit one behind the other, and each row begins at one of the images, which thus serves as the head of the row. S. M. Kamakau (1976, 142) specifies that these rows are like canoes and that they reach the *lele* altar, on which they apparently converge. The men forming them are turned toward the king and the high priest, who stand before the door of the mana house, which faces the *lele* altar. The kahunas are seated below this altar. This arrangement can be represented by the diagram in figure 7.

According to ʻĪʻī, "The men sat crosslegged. . . . Both elbows rested on the upper part of the thighs, the left wrist under the right one" (1963, 44). When the order is given to raise their hands, some raise both hands but most raise only the right arm and "rested the left one on the right knee, assuming as humble a posture as [they] saw fit" (ibid.). They hold their heads down and all remain thus while the priest recites a long prayer. If a man becomes tired he can lower his arm, but raising one's head means death.

According to S. M. Kamakau, the people are seated on their buttocks, the left leg crossed over the right and the left hand crossed over the right. When the priest cries, "Hands up!" they all raise their right hands and point them "to the place of the god in the heavens" (1976, 142). At the

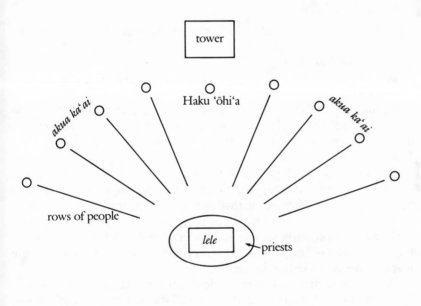

Fig. 7.   Seating arrangement in the *hono* rite according to ʻĪʻī.

same time they pray in unison and are careful not to move; otherwise they are put to death. They pray thus for a long time, until the burnt offering is brought forth. This offering consists of a human victim ("a captured chief") and two pigs that are broiled (*'ōlani*) over a fire with him. This human sacrifice is not mentioned by the other sources, however. Its mention by S. M. Kamakau is explained by the fact that he places this rite before the one where the king consecrates his enemies to the god and has the rites of the tower (*maki'i lohelohe*) performed. In addition, S. M. Kamakau identifies the *hono* rite with the *kauila nui* rite. More exactly, he writes that *hono* is the name of the "taboo" of the *kauila nui* rite. The meaning of this statement is not clear. Kamakau adds that Kāne has a preponderant role in this rite, since the *hono* taboo in its developed form is called *Kānehonokapa'a*, "Kāne who unites the people." He also writes that the *luakini* is decorated during this rite with the branches of trees and weeds (*nāhelehele*).

Interpretation

This sequence of the ritual includes three rites, performed one after the other:

1. a rite of Kahoāli'i;
2. some rites of the *hale o Papa*, followed by bathing in the sea;
3. the *hono* rite.

For the rite of Kahoāli'i I shall rely on Malo's account, for K. Kamakau only makes an oblique allusion to it. Note also that K. Kamakau conflates it with the rite in which—according to Malo—the *kāpapaulua* priest "fishes" for men by deceit.

In Malo's account, the rite Kahoāli'i performs here is identical to the rite he performs in the month of Makali'i, after the conclusion of the Makahiki festival. The only difference is that there he spends the night in a hut of *lama* branches, while here he sleeps in a hut of *koa* branches. Actually, Malo does not explicitly say that Kahoāli'i spends the night in the *koa* hut, but the identity of the two rites in every other respect leads us to suppose that they are also identical in this respect.

We have seen that the habitation determines the state of the inhabitant. It is therefore likely that by making Kahoāli'i stay in a hut of *koa*, the properties associated with this tree are transmitted to him. Now the properties of the *koa* are similar to those of the *'ōhi'a-lehua*. Along with the latter, the *koa* is the largest Hawaiian tree. The wood of both is reddish (Neal 1929, 129). Height and redness are two qualities associated with Kū, as we have seen; therefore it is likely that the *koa*, like the *'ōhi'a-lehua*, is one of Kū's bodies. This is indirectly confirmed by the following two lines of a chant:

Ku ke koa, ku ka oʻa
Ku ka lehua, ku ke alii

The *koa* stands, the *oʻa* stands,
The *lehua* stands, the king stands
   [Fornander 1916–20, 4:401, lines 210–11]

Of the three trees to which the king is compared in these lines, two are directly connected with Kū. We already know this for the *lehua*; as for the *oʻa*, it is nothing other than the *kauila* tree (*Colubrina oppositifolia*—PE, 253, 125), whose wood is used to make spears (an attribute of Kū) and the carrying poles for the feather gods, which in the main represent Kū. Hence Kū's association with this tree appears clear. It seems likely, therefore, that Kū is associated with the *koa* as well. A proof of the *koa*'s association with Kū is given by its very name. *Koa* means "brave, bold, fearless, valiant," and "warrior"—signifieds that are indeed evoked by this high, straight, and hard-wooded tree. The *koa* further indexes the warrior in that it is principally used to build the large war canoes. Now these canoes, as well as the warrior and all his attributes, belong to Kū's domain.

The *koa*, in sum, indexes Kū in his "fearless," "bold" aspect. We must therefore infer that building a hut of *koa* emphasizes the presence of these aspects of Kū in the temple; moreover, it is likely that by sleeping in the hut Kahōāliʻi becomes imbued with the properties of Kū that the *koa* conveys, and in fact he embodies the god himself for a specific purpose. This can only be the devouring of the human eye, a feat that evidently is supposed to require a certain fearlessness.

We have seen that the eye stands for the entire victim: by eating the victim's eye as Kū's representative, Kahōāliʻi makes the god's devouring of the entire victim partially visible. The metonymic equivalence of part and whole thus becomes the metaphoric equivalence of the visible and invisible sacrificial process, of the symbol and the symbolized. In other words, Kahōāliʻi's act is visible enough to suggest the reality of the god's devouring and of the victim's transformation into the god, but it is also partial enough to reconfirm that the whole process, and therefore the divine, is fundamentally beyond representation, invisible. Thus, paradoxically, the apparently extreme humanization of the god in the person of Kahōāliʻi makes the god's distance from the concretely human emerge all the more clearly.

Moreover, the eye is not simply the part that is equivalent to the whole, it is also, and more important, the organ of vision. Thus, since the victim is a substitute for the sacrifiers, the god's devouring his eye clearly signifies that the god's existence is ultimately based on his feeding on the negation of the sacrifiers' empirical vision with regard to him. Indeed, the god's truth is the truth of a concept. As we have seen, the transcendence, hence the invisibility, of the god depends in the first place on his conceptual nature.

At the same time, the idea of this god has been formed in the minds of the congregation with the help of a *visible* image. Thus the visible symbol must turn into an invisible reality; only in this way does the image become an *akua maoli* enshrining the idea of a true god. As we saw when we studied the rite in which a bunch of '*ie'ie* is consecrated by wrapping it, the transition from knowledge of the visible (which is particular and limited) to knowledge of the invisible (which is general and unlimited) can be obtained only by negating man's empirical vision, by blocking it with regard to an initially visible manifestation of the god.[235]

The gouging out of the eye of a victim that represents all the sacrifiers is the strongest form of this blocking; moreover, the devouring of this eye by the god's visible representative represents the passage from empirical to intellectual vision. The Hawaiians believe that the *'uhane*, the soul that represents the "principle of consciousness"—(Fischer 1965, 247), has its preferred seat in the socket of the eye, where it can "look through the eyes" (Bastian 1888, 118), and that in dreams or at death it comes out through the lacrimal duct (*lua 'uhane*, "soul pit") (ibid.; Achelis 1895, 44; Beckwith 1932, 114; 1940, 144; Handy and Pukui 1972, 146; PE, 197, 336; NK, 1:124). By eating the victim's eye, then, the god feeds on human consciousness, or rather on its transformation. And indeed the god exists as a result of the transformation of man's consciousness, which moves from empirical vision to intellectual vision, from the particularity of percept to the universality of concept.

This transformation may be represented as a transformation of the eyes of the victim into the eyes of the god, that is to say, as the passage from an inferior to a superior state of *'ike*, "vision," "knowledge." The following facts seem to indicate that this transformation is indeed believed to occur. The first is that the moon and sun, which like the other stars are believed to be divine eyes,[236] are fed with the eyes of human sacrifices whenever their existence is threatened by an eclipse (Lehmann 1930, 225). The second is that in several chants or sacrificial prayers the eyes of the gods are said to become animated and restless when the sacrificial offering is given to them (see, for instance, Fornander 1916–20, 4:607; 1878–80, 1:75, 93–94; Kepelino 1932, 36–37). This explains why the major temple images are referred to as *makaīwa*, "mysterious eyes" (Samwell 1967, 1177; Malo 1951, 169).

There seems to be a connection, then, between the revivification of the god by means of the offering and the revivification of his eyes, hence, of the "divine knowledge." Is it too audacious to suppose that this connection becomes even more direct when the offering is the eye? Note, at any rate, that the eye is considered the paradigmatic share of the god in sacrifice.

Observe also that the searching, all-seeing eyes of the gods seem to be the objectified form of moral consciousness: once the subject has become aware of the principles and norms dictated to his species, he cannot escape his awareness of them: therefore he always feels under the scrutiny of the god's penetrating gaze.[237]

I have pointed out that the negation of sight brings about a higher vision, that the devoured eye becomes a divine eye, the subject of a superior knowledge accessible to man. The rite of Kahōāli'i also represents the acquisition of that knowledge through the transformed eye. It will be recalled that Kahōāli'i not only is a human incarnation of Kū but is also, by the same token, the king's double, as witnessed by his being called the "royal companion." Thus he is both the representative of the god, who by eating the victim's material eye transforms it into a spiritual eye, and the representative of the king, who eats this transformed eye and therefore obtains the superior vision it embodies. In other words, the eating of the victim's eye by Kahōāli'i is supposed to transfer to the king the superior vision embodied in that eye. Although this last proposition is speculative, it is confirmed by the fact that a similar Tahitian eye-gouging rite is supposed to give the king a powerful vision (Henry 1968, 202).

Moreover, according to Malo Kahōāli'i's devouring of the victim's eye on behalf of the king occurs in the context of a sacramental meal in which the participants in the *kapu luakini* eat a pig. Since Kahōāli'i participates in both the divine and the human meals, he connects the two and thus makes his commensals indirectly participate in the divine knowledge that he has himself absorbed by eating the eye.

In sum, Kahōāli'i connects the transcendent god, his supreme immanent token (the king), and the inferior tokens who are the other ali'i. Thus this god-made-man, who fully manifests the humanness of the god, is able to reconstitute the social hierarchy by connecting it with its ultimate transcendent formulation, the man-made-divine.

It is because it makes more evident what was already apparent in the "great sacrifice" that the rite of Kahōāli'i is performed. But as I have suggested above, there is a more important reason for its performance: the invisible reality of the gods must be reaffirmed at the end of a process that has made the gods present through visual images. In this respect, Kahōāli'i's rite synthesizes the two contradictory movements respectively expressed by the "great sacrifice" and the next sacrifice. As we have seen, the "great sacrifice," which occurs when the images (and therefore the visual manifestations of the gods) are complete, makes the gods too close to men and to their senses. Accordingly, there is a risk that the gods' transcendence will be lost from sight. This is why the next sacrifice, which is entirely left to the gods and thus marks their separation from men, begins moving the ritual process in a direction contrary to the one it has moved in until then: it starts making the gods distant again, transcendent again.

This new movement accelerates with Kahōāli'i's rite and, as we shall see, with the *hono* rite; moreover, it is the counterpart of a process whereby the men are progressively desacralized in order to return to the profane world outside the temple. In sum, Kahōāli'i's rite has a pivotal role in the passage to this new stage of the temple ritual, a stage in which the gods are made transcendent again and the men immanent again.

Let us turn our attention, then, to the rite of the *hale o Papa*, which makes the men progressively less *kapu*.

As a matter of fact, both Malo's and K. Kamakau's accounts show that a first rite in the *hale o Papa* is made before the rite of Kahōāli'i. However, the most important rite, the one that allows the purifying bath to be taken, occurs after the rite of the "royal companion."

Why must the male congregation be separated from the temple with the help of the goddesses sheltered in the *hale o Papa*? The answer to the question is rather obvious. As it was necessary for men to separate from impure women in order to establish contact with the pure male gods, now, in order to reenter the profane world, it is necessary for them to be relatively polluted by contact with the feminine principle embodied by the goddesses.

In other words, the rites of the *hale o Papa* that begin at this moment are the reversal of the rites of purification that are the prelude to the men's entrance into the temple. There men and women were dramatically separated; here they are dramatically rejoined. The value of the women thus changes with the context: negative at the beginning of the rite, it is positive at the end, since it makes it possible for men to return to the real world of life after having entered the dubious world of eternal life that is in fact a world of sacrificial death.[238] This return to the women, and hence to the profane world, takes place in several steps, however. The rites in the *hale o Papa* mentioned here are a beginning that is followed by a return to the temple to perform the *hono* rite.

On the whole, all the accounts of the *hono* are similar and complete each other. This rite is characterized by a rigorous spatial distribution and bodily control among the participants. They are seated in eight rows, according to K. Kamakau, or in lines stretching like canoes from each image of the *kuahu* to the *lele* altar, according to 'Ī'ī and S. M. Kamakau. All versions thus indicate that the participants, the sacrifiers, are ordered by the gods. Eight is certainly seen as a multiple of four, that is, of the number that indexes the divine. Hence, by sitting in eight rows men display the divine in social form, that is, the fact that they are ordered by the gods. This is made even more evident by 'Ī'ī's and S. M. Kamakau's accounts, since in them the gods are like pilots steering the "canoes" formed by the men.

There is no doubt, then, that the *hono* rite depicts the final transfer of the divine form into the social relations. But the complete achievement of this transfer also justifies the separation of gods and men that will occur hereafter.

Thus, as I have said, the gods become less visible, more transcendent at this point. This increased transcendence also justifies the increased authority of those who remain in close contact with the gods, that is, the king and the high priest. That now the gods are an invisible presence guiding men's actions in society and that king and high priest are the gods' privileged interpreters because they are the only ones who can continue looking at them is made perfectly clear by 'Ī'ī's and S. M. Kamakau's versions of the *hono* rite. According to them, all those who participate in the rite turn their backs to the images of the gods; they do not look at them but face the victims on the *lele* altar. I interpret this arrangement as a dramatic representation of the idea that the "real gods" just produced by the ritual must now become invisible in order to invisibly guide men's action and their vision of the empirical world. Men can experience the invisible gods only through the visible victims who are the representations of men as they transcend empirical reality through death. Only the king and high priest face the gods and are therefore allowed to see them. But even these two look at the gods through the *lele* altar piled up with victims.[239]

In absolute silence and immobility all contemplate society's form and listen to the words of the priest, the king's mouthpiece. They do not *see* the gods but are *told* by those who see them what they will, and therefore why the social hierarchy must be. Thus in the end it is made clear that society rests on a transcendent truth, but that this truth in turn rests on a human authority who speaks about it in words and ritual images. Or, to put it more clearly, the thinking of the ideas that found society presupposes this selfsame society. Thus the rite demonstrating that social structure is based on ideology also demonstrates that the reproduction of ideology is based on social structure and particularly on its main feature, the differential authority, that is, power to speak and comment upon symbols. Ideology, then, gives certain men the power to control its social reproduction and to some extent to control its very content. It thus demonstrates its own dependence on the social form it generates.

The Final *Hale o Papa* Rites
Description
Malo MS, 178–79

On the morning of the day of 'Ole-pau (the tenth), the king's female relatives[240] come forward "pulling" (or "walking processionally with") a long loincloth (*e ka'i malo lō'ihi*) that is their sacrifice (*mōhai*) for the divine image (*akua ki'i*).[241] All the men[242] gather at the *hale o Papa* to mix (*hui pū*) with the women. The king[243] carries one end of the loincloth into the temple (*heiau*),[244] while the other end is held by the noble women (*na li'i wahine*). In the meantime the priest recites the *ka'i-'oloa*[245] ("to pull (or "walking processionally with") the *'oloa* bark cloth") prayer. Then the audi-

328   The Sacrifice of the Hawaiian King

ence sits down in rows and the officiating priest comes forward. When he comes to the words *'eli'eli* ("deep"), the entire audience answers "*noa*" ("freedom"). Then the priest exclaims, "*ia e*," and all answer him in chorus, "total freedom" (*"noa honua"*). Upon which the "work of the *luakini*"²⁴⁶ is rendered completely *noa* (*noa loa*) (i.e., the requirements of the *kapu luakini* are fully met).

On the twelfth day begins a rite called *ho'omāhanahana* ("to warm"— PE, 202), which lasts three days. Unfortunately, we have no details concerning this rite. What Malo tells us (MS, 160, 179) shows that it is a "purification" rite (*huikala*—Malo MS, 160). It entails a sacrifice, if we are to believe S. M. Kamakau (1976, 85).²⁴⁷

K. Kamakau 1919–20, 27–31

When night has fallen, the priest of Papa recites the *kuili* and the *koli'i maomao* prayers²⁴⁸ in the *hale o Papa*. The king is not with him but joins him the next morning to hear his verdict, which is as follows: "The night of your goddess (*akua wahine*) was excellent; the women with guilty mouths (*waha hewa*)²⁴⁹ will not have life from you; they will be killed by your goddess." Then all the people, the ali'i, and the priests go before the priest of the house of Papa, who will free (*ho'onoa*) both them and the *luakini* temple.

The king orders his overseer to give about forty dogs and chickens to the goddess. When these animals are gathered, the priest waves a piercing instrument (*'ō*);²⁵⁰ then he sits down. At this point the king orders the priest of the *hale o Papa*, "Go seek my wife's cloth (*malo*) and the pig that is her gift (*makana*) for the goddess."

The priest, chanting a prayer, brings in the king's wife, and during his progress he holds the pig in one hand and in the other the front end of the cloth, of which the queen, who wears a white (*ke'oke'o*) skirt (*pā'ū*), holds the back end. When they come before the goddess, the priest ends his chant, and the queen, on whom all eyes are fixed, sacrifices (*mōhai*) the cloth and the pig to the goddess, saying: "Here is your cloth and your pig, my husband and myself will have life by you, O goddess; and give us a male child, to fetch *pala* for you (*i ki'i pala nou*), O goddess; if not, a daughter who will beat *'oloa* cloth for you; O goddess, it is already free (*noa*)."

Then the "seers," "prophets" (*po'e kāula*) come in great numbers to worship (*ho'omana*) their goddesses.²⁵¹ They sacrifice (*mōhai*) riches to them: pigs, chickens, cloths, and other things, saying, "Here are pigs, here are chickens, here are cloths, our gifts (*makana*) to you; give life to your descendants; let us be efficacious (*e mana*) before you; make the ali'i treat us well when we are in their presence, and see to it that we are granted forgiveness (*kala*) when we ask for it."

When they have gone, the priest of the *hale o Papa* gets up, waves the fire stick (*'aulima*), then sits down and prays to the goddesses. The fires are lighted to broil (*pūlehu*) the dogs and chickens, which, when they are cooked, are gathered before the goddesses and sacrificed (*mōhai*) by the king. After which the priest of the *hale o Papa* shouts before the people, "*'Eli 'eli.*" And the people answer, "*Kapu.*" The dialogue continues, "*'Eli, 'eli.*" "*Noa.*" "*Ia e.*" "*Noa honua.*"[252] The temple is then completely *noa*, and those who have taken part in the rite can unite with their wives and mix with the common people.

Having worshiped the king's gods in the *luakini*, the ali'i return to their houses to worship (*ho'omana*) their own gods. This is a sequel to the king's temple service. The duration of each ali'i's worship is different: some "taboo" their temple for two days, others for three; still others for four or five. Only the taboo of the king's temple lasts eight and sometimes ten days.

Wilkes 1845, 4:508

After the *hono* ritual, the *'aha* and *kuili*[253] prayers are repeated, and then the king's favorite wife comes with a pig and a "fine mat," which she offers in sacrifice while requesting "that she might live and be preserved by the king."

On the eighth day, the whole ceremony was finished, all the taboos removed, and a general council of the chiefs held, as to the mode of carrying on the war, when they went to conquer the land they had sacrificed and prayed for. After the wars were ended, heiaus for peace and the prosperity of the kingdom were built, to insure fertility and plenty to the land.

Ii 1963, 44–45

'Ī'ī, whose account of the *hale o Papa* rite is close to those of K. Kamakau and Malo, specifies that two or three images of goddesses are kept in the house. The goddesses are Kalamainu'u (also called Kihawahine), Haumea, and Walinu'u. These images are brought before the audience, and here pigs and dogs are sacrificed. Then each high-ranking woman offers them a suckling pig and cloth of the *ninikea* type, which is white and thin.

After the sacrificial animals are cooked, they are eaten by the congregation. After this the king stands up and gives the *'āmama* to indicate that the rite is concluded. Then the priest of the *hale o Papa* admonishes the congregation with these words:

Let the dishonored one (*waia*)
    be silent
Be silent
Let the one who eats without respecting the taboos [*'ai ku*; *'aiā*—cf. PE, 8, 9]
    be silent.

Let the transgressor (*lawehala*) be silent
Be silent.

The audience repeats each line of this speech in unison as soon as the priest has recited it. The remains of the meal and the offerings are placed on the *lele* altar of the *hale o Papa* with bananas of the *pōpō'ulu* or *iho-lena* varieties, which are the only ones appropriate for goddesses and women.

Thus the rites of the *luakini* temple end. After some two or three days a new taboo period begins,[254] which is called *kapu ho'omāhanahana* and lasts two nights and one day. Pigs are sacrificed, but in a small number. Then the *luakini* temple is closed.

Interpretation

The *hale o Papa* rite described in this section of our sources terminates the process of relative "desacralization" of the male congregation by bringing them closer to the women and their goddesses. Moreover, as the preceding rite had socially reproduced the society of men by reproducing the god who is their model and reference point, the *hale o Papa* rite reproduces the society of women with reference to the goddesses. This is made particularly clear by K. Kamakau, according to whom the rite sanctions the main taboo that differentiates women from men. As the priest declares, "They will not live, the women with the guilty mouth [= who eat forbidden food]; your goddess will make them die." 'Ī'ī puts a similar speech in the priest's mouth. Thus, only after women have been reproduced as a separate category can men effectively reunite with them without fear of completely losing the mana acquired in the temple.

This conjunction, moreover, will make it possible to reproduce concrete individuals (children) after the abstract reproduction of the ideal individual (the god, who embodies the species) has been accomplished. In other words, the "pure," that is, nonsexual, reproduction of the species as a concept is the sine qua non for the "impure" (sexual) reproduction of the species incarnated in concrete individuals, in new children. From this point of view, that the reproduction of the god is represented as the engendering of a child acquires its full signification: it is in fact the symbolic anticipation of a multiplicity of concrete processes of generation that take place after the ritual is finished.

Before concrete men and women can unite to produce children, however, the fertility of women must be symbolically reproduced by connecting women as a category to the goddess that embodies their fertility—Papa/Haumea. In the rite that ensures this reproduction the queen, or more generally the high-ranking women, probably represents all other women. Thus it is likely that by sacrificing to the goddess and by being connected to her through a long cloth, the chiefly women obtain fertility not only for themselves, but also for all women. However, it must be remembered that fertility is actualized only by men; thus each woman must relate to men of her rank to fully obtain the mana that makes her pregnant. It is precisely in this way that the ideal reproduction of the species by men translates into its empirical reproduction by women, as noted in chapter 4.

Moreover, the fertilizing conjunction of men and women is paralleled by the equally fertilizing conjunction of men and land, which is female and is in fact personified by Papa—like the women themselves. By establishing a connection with Papa and all she represents, then, men pass from a pole in which their main referent is Kū to a pole in which their main referent is Lono, the god of human and agricultural fertility. I have already noted (parts 2 and 3) that this transition from Kū to Lono occurs after the end of the *luakini* ritual (and eventually after the war that follows it—the text published by Wilkes reminds us of that).

It remains to be explained, however, why in the rites of the *hale o Papa* Haumea/Papa is associated with two other goddesses (Ii 1963, 44): Kalamainu'u (or Kihawahine) and Walinu'u. Some myths concerning these goddesses will help us in the task. According to a version published by 'Ī'ī (1869g, h), a man, Puna'aikoa'e, first marries Walinu'u on O'ahu and then he moves to Moloka'i, where he marries Kalamainu'u; when the latter reveals herself to be a dragon (*mo'o*), he escapes and returns to O'ahu. There, however, he is sacrificed by the king's men and his body laid on top of a breadfruit tree. His first wife, Walinu'u, learns that her husband has died, and to join him she enters the breadfruit tree. In another version she succeeds this way in resuscitating her husband (Beckwith 1940, 282). In a version published by Westervelt (1915b, 28–36), the husband and his "good" wife are given the names of the spouses who form the typical human couple: Wākea and Papa. Also, the tree that the wife has entered is cut down and transformed into the wooden image of Kāmeha'ikana (goddess of childbirth). This is another name for Haumea (PE, 386, 117), which in turn is another name for Papa, as we have seen; this equation is further demonstrated by another version of this myth, also given by Westervelt (1915a, 160–62), in which the "good" wife is called Haumea.

It seems, thus, that Walinu'u = Kāmeha'ikana = Haumea = Papa. This demonstrates that Walinu'u is a special form of Haumea. In this form she has a positive value for her husband; she "saves" him, or simply loves him. In contrast, Kalamainu'u represents the wife as sorceress, as polluting and destructive (cf. Kamakau 1964, 82). Let me mention that there is a parallelism between this myth and the *luakini* temple ritual, in that both depict an inversion of women's value for men. In the myth, at one point the good wife is replaced by a bad and polluting one. Hence Puna'aikoa'e must separate himself from her. But during this separation he is sacrificed, after which his "good" wife finds him and, in one version, saves him. Analogously, at the beginning of the *luakini* temple ritual men must separate from women because the latter are polluting and make it impossible for their male companions to achieve life by entering into contact with the gods. This contact implies sacrifice, however—the sacrifier's symbolic death that can always turn into the real thing.[255] At this point women become positive for men; their love recalls them from the dangerous realm of sacrifice and brings them back to the profane world, which involves a measure of pollution but is real life.

Thus the myth clarifies the connection of the three goddesses (who in fact are two, since Walinu'u is a form of Haumea)[256] with the rite in which, by virtue of a transformation that men bring about in their own status, the value of women is correlatively transformed from negative to positive, from one in which they connote death to one in which they connote life.

I maintain, then, that by showing the people the images of the goddess in the *hale o Papa* rite (cf. K. Kamakau) the priest makes visible and recapitulates the transformation of the value of women. At the same time he reminds the audience that the transformation is entailed by the transformation of men, which in turn is obtained by the action that transforms a "wild" and dangerous god into a "tame" and life-giving one.

The Ritual Syntagma according to 'Ī'ī and S. M. Kamakau

The texts of Malo and K. Kamakau form the most complete, sure, and consistent source on the rites for inaugurating the *luakini*. Overall, they correspond to and complete each other, despite differences in detail, the most important of which we have seen. Another of these differences must now be mentioned. For K. Kamakau (as well as the author of the text given by Wilkes), the length of the ritual of inauguration sensu stricto is eight days, but it can be prolonged up to ten days. For Malo, in contrast, it is ten (an *anahulu* period) and sometimes fourteen days (1951, 160). Consequently, K. Kamakau and the unknown author of Wilkes's text distribute over a shorter period the rites that for Malo are spread out over an *anahulu*. Malo's schema is closer to the ideal model, for in principle the ideal length of a ritual period is ten days.

More radical are the differences between the sources concerning the syntagmatic order of the rites. If Malo, K. Kamakau, and Wilkes's text are rather close in this respect, as we have seen, the texts of 'Ī'ī and S. M. Kamakau differ from them as well as from each other. Let us then take their views into account.

It should be said at the outset that 'Ī'ī is somewhat confusing for he narrates the rites in a different order from the one in which he says they are performed. As if to complicate matters further, 'Ī'ī's translator and editor have somewhat altered the original order of the exposé and made cuts. I shall therefore refer to the original text (in *Ka Nupepa Kuokoa*, 1869d, e, f, g, i).

'Ī'ī begins his account with the description of an actual ritual event (which, however, he did not witness): the consecration of Liholiho as the successor and associate of Kamehameha in the *luakini* of Papa'ena'ena on O'ahu (cf. Valeri 1982b). First he explains the political context that led Kamehameha to prefer Liholiho to his older sons Kīna'u and Lunalilo and the immediate occasion for the rite, which is the sickness of Queen Keōpūolani (Liholiho's mother) and of Kamehameha himself. The year is thus 1803 or 1804, since 'Ī'ī writes that the rite was performed before the death of Ke'eaumoku.

To show that he has chosen Liholiho as his successor, Kamehameha charges him to consecrate a human sacrifice. This sacrifice takes place the very day on which the *kauila nui* rite is performed (Ii 1963, 35) and the day after the *'aha* had been performed (*ka'i*) with success (ibid.). It is followed by the *maki'i lohelohe* rite, which is followed in turn by the great sacrificial meal.

Since in K. Kamakau's account the *maki'i lohelohe* is preceded by the *'aha ho'owilimo'o*, it is tempting to say that the sacrificial rite performed by Liholiho was an *'aha ho'owilimo'o*. Thus 'Ī'ī's account, like that of K. Kamakau, would imply the sequence: *'aha ho'owilimo'o* → *maki'i lohelohe* → sacrificial meal.

Yet this hypothesis contradicts 'Ī'ī's claim that the *kauila nui* was performed on the same day as Liholiho's sacrifice and that an unspecified *'aha* had taken place the preceding day. Since this *'aha* preceded the *kauila nui*, it could only have been an *'aha helehonua*. Hence Liholiho's rite should be identified with the *'aha hulahula* rite and not with the *'aha ho'owilimo'o*. This would presuppose, however, that 'Ī'ī implicitly follows Malo's and K. Kamakau's sequence. But this is not the case, since in his description of the ideal ritual sequence—which comes after his account of the ritual event of 1803/4—'Ī'ī places the *'aha hulahula* before, not after, the *kauila nui*. Based on this we should identify the unspecified *'aha* with the *'aha hulahula*, all the more because 'Ī'ī nowhere mentions the *'aha helehonua*. Thus the *'aha* performed by Liholiho following the *kauila nui* would indeed be the *'aha ho'owilimo'o*.

In sum, we have to postulate the following sequence:

1. *'aha hulahula*
2. *kauila nui*
3. *'aha ho'owilimo'o*
4. *maki'i lohelohe*
5. sacrificial meal

If, however, we take into account the whole of the ritual sequence proposed by 'Ī'ī in the articles in which he describes the *ideal form* of the temple ritual, we must conclude either that he contradicts himself or else that the actual ritual event he first describes followed a simplified or even different scheme than the ideal one. In fact, 'Ī'ī claims that the latter is as follows:

1. *'aha hulahula*
2. expedition to the mountain to procure the wood for building the temple houses
3. *kauila nui*
4. expedition to the mountain to procure the Haku 'ōhi'a
5. night dedicated to *kuili* prayers
6. *kāpapaulua* rite
7. *'aha ho'owilimo'o*
8. *hono* rite
9. *hale o Papa* rite

To explain the divergences between these two schemes, the most probable hypothesis seems to be the following. It is clear from the description of the events of 1803/4 that the temple houses already in place were not rebuilt. Thus we can suppose that the divine images were not renewed either. Consequently the rites in the mountain (to obtain the wood for the Haku 'ōhi'a) did not take place, and the fishing and *kuili* rites, which have the purpose of bringing the Haku 'ōhi'a to "maturity," did not take place, either. 'Ī'ī's first account would thus give us the example of a temple reconsecration without a renovation of its superstructure.

Having thus explained the divergences between 'Ī'ī's two accounts, let us turn to the divergences between his ideal scheme and the one given by Malo, K. Kamakau, and, in part, by Wilkes's text. The following table enables us to compare the two versions:

'Ī'ī	Malo/K. Kamakau
1. *'aha hulahula*	1. *kauila huluhulu*
2. expedition to obtain wood	2. expedition to obtain the Haku 'ōhi'a
3. *kauila nui*	3. *kauila nui*
4. expedition to obtain the Haku 'ōhi'a	4. *'aha hulahula*
5. *kuili*	5. *kuili*
6. *kāpapaulua*	6. *kāpapaulua*
7. *'aha ho'owilimo'o*	7. *'aha ho'owilimo'o*
8. *hono*	8. *hono*
9. *hale o Papa* rite	9. *hale o Papa* rite

It appears from this comparison that the two groups of sources differ only on the first part of the sequence. These differences are less considerable than they appear at first sight. In fact, it cannot be denied that a homology exists between the *kauila huluhulu*, in which the feather gods, which must go to the mountain to meet the Haku 'ōhi'a, are revived and the *'aha hulahula*, in which, at least according to K. Kamakau, the principal feather god is revived. An obvious homology also exists between the expedition to procure the lumber for the temple houses and the one to obtain the Haku 'ōhi'a:[257] thus we are not surprised to see one take the place of the other. Ultimately we note that the differences between the versions are systematic, since they amount to this: one version fuses the *'aha hulahula* and the *kauila huluhulu* rites but differentiates between the appropriation of lumber and of the Haku 'ōhi'a, while the other differentiates between the *'aha hulahula* and the *kauila huluhulu* but fuses the two appropriations into one.

It will be noted that the placing of the *'aha hulahula* at the beginning of the ritual syntagma is found not only in 'Ī'ī, but also in K. Kamakau's version of the *kapu 'ōpelu* (Fornander 1916–20, 6:31–35), which in turn is only a variant of the *kapu luakini*. This confirms that 'Ī'ī's version is not due to an error on his part but instead reflects a possibility inherent in the system. This possibility does not at all contradict the fundamental "grammatical" relationships presupposed by the ritual of the *luakini* temple. On the contrary, it makes the opposition of feather god and Haku 'ōhi'a all the more clear, as well as the necessity to make Kū pass from the first to the second form. In addition, it emphasizes the feather god's dominant role in the first part of the ritual.

This shows once again that the different versions of the rite, like those of a myth, do not reveal new paradigmatic relations but simply confirm the same relations that can be discovered by analyzing any single version in depth. Still, the different versions recorded must have their raison d'être on the pragmatic level: the choice of one rather than another is no doubt significant and is a function of the context. Unfortunately, we have very little information concerning the relation between the ritual choices and extra-ritual contexts. I refer readers to an essay where I have tried to analyze the little we know on the subject (Valeri 1982b).

Let us now consider the version given by S. M. Kamakau. His articles (published in *Ke Au Okoa*, 1870a, b, c, d) are based on disparate information, given by old men on O'ahu and especially by his *kupuna kāne* (grandfather or great-uncle) "Kuikealaikauaokalani," who, according to D. Barrère, was a priest on O'ahu or Kaua'i (in Kamakau, 1976, 146). His description thus may reflect certain practices current on O'ahu and Kaua'i. This is perhaps confirmed by his associating Kāne with the *hono* rite; we have seen, in fact, that this god was probably supreme on Kaua'i. Kamakau also borrowed information from the articles by 'Ī'ī published the year before his own, especially concerning the fetching of the Haku 'ōhi'a and the *maki'i lohelohe* rite.

Without going into unnecessary detail, we can thus summarize the ritual syntagma related by S. M. Kamakau:

1. rites to fetch the Haku 'ōhi'a (like 'Ī'ī, he calls these rites *malu ko'i*)

2. house building and *kuili* rites
3. so-called *'aha ka'i* rite
4. *hono* (also called *kauila nui* by him)

Clearly, S. M. Kamakau simplifies the ritual syntagma even more than 'Ī'ī does. This is not only because he ignores several rites described in the other sources, but also because he fuses rites that are formally or functionally analogous. Thus he reduces all the *'aha* rites to a single one, which he calls *'aha ka'i* and which greatly resembles the *'aha hulahula* as K. Kamakau describes it. Similarly, he unites under one heading (*hono*) the *kauila nui*, the *'aha ho'owilimo'o*, and the *hono* rites.

This process of reduction could be the result of a paradigmatic analysis by S. M. Kamakau or of a selective process in the memory of his informants;[258] but it could also correspond to legitimate collapsings made when it is desirable to shorten the length of the *kapu heiau*. My overall impression, however, is that S. M. Kamakau's text is heteroclitic. Although he gives interesting details on individual rites, his account of their syntagmatic order cannot be trusted.

The Treatment of Human Victims

The ritual texts we have used so far do not say much about the way human victims are prepared for sacrifice, immolated, and so forth. Information on these subjects can however be assembled from a variety of sources. On the basis of this information, it is possible to distinguish four stages in the treatment of human victims: (a) preparation for sacrifice; (b) immolation; (c) treatment of the body; (d) final destination of the body.

Preparation for Sacrifice

As soon as the victim is captured, he is *immobilized* and *set apart*—a sign of his consecration. Thus, his hands and feet are bound (Vancouver 1801, 3:353; Stewart 1839, 237; Ross 1904, 65) and he is relegated to a house, generally within the temple enclosure (Ii 1963, 23; Tyerman and Bennett 1832, 2:49; Fornander 1916–20, 4:589). Sometimes his arms and legs are broken (Menzies, n.d.; Tyerman and Bennett 1832, 2:49), his hair is cut (Vancouver 1801, 3:353; Kamakau 1961, 192), and one or both of his eyes are torn out (Meares 1916, 22; Vancouver 1801, 5:2; Freycinet 1978, 89; Arago 1822, 2:225; Campbell 1967, 123; Tyerman and Bennett 1832, 2:49, 59; Kamakau 1961, 60; Ii 1963, 101; Fernander 1916–20, 4:342–43; 5:212; 1878–80, 2:123).[259]

It also seems that the victim's penis may be partially mutilated as part of his preparation for sacrifice. Thus, when Keōua prepares himself as a victim before submitting to Kamehameha, he cuts off "the end of his penis (*'ōmu'o*), an act which believers in sorcery call 'the death of Uli' and which was a certain sign that he knew he was about to die" (Kamakau 1961, 156). This last statement would make no sense if the victim's penis were not customarily mutilated.[260]

Last, it must be mentioned that the victim is stripped naked or, as 'Ī'ī puts it, "his eggs [testicles] were exposed to view" (1963, 15). Again, sexual humiliation is involved here, but also the anticipation of death, which is often symbolized by undressing (cf. Baudrillard 1976, 108). All these practices indicate that the victim has ceased to belong to the human world and that in several respects he is considered already dead.

Immolation

The victims do not have to be alive when they reach the moment of sacrifice proper. As the texts examined above show, sacrifice is defined in Hawaii by the consecration of the victim to the god rather than by the actual execution, which does not have the crucial role it has in other sacrificial systems such as those described by Hubert and Mauss (1899). Thus, as we have seen, the human victims offered in the "great sacrifice" are usually already dead when they arrive at the temple. More generally, any enemy fallen on the battlefield (Kamakau 1976, 134; Ellis 1842, 151) or transgressor put to death by the executioner (*ilāmuku* or *mū*—cf. Fornander 1916–20, 4:147; Hiroa 1957, 462 ff.; Kamakau 1964, 12; Kepelino 1932, 146–47) can later be offered to the gods in the temple.

Actually, several sources say that the victims must be immolated *outside* the temple, because blood, which is polluting, must not be spilled inside it. Only after having been washed of any trace of blood can their bodies be brought to the temple to be "sacrificed," that is, offered up on the altar (Fornander 1916–20, 4:215; Ellis 1842, 151–52; Kalakaua 1888, 145, 264; Thrum 1907b, 37; Plischke 1929, 29; Schoch 1954, 17; Brigham, n.d., 256–57), since the gods "despise" anything bloody (Kamakau 1961, 3).[261] This rule appears to be contradicted, however, in K. Kamakau's account of the sacrifice of the human victim whose body is put in the hole where the base of the Haku 'ōhi'a is thrust. In fact, he writes that the man is dispatched with a club inside the temple, near the Haku 'ōhi'a. Malo is less specific, since he does not say that the victim is killed in the temple. It seems to me, however, that the taboo of spilling blood in the temple is enforced only after the god has been completely transformed from a violent, wild power into a peaceful and tamed one. In other words, when the god is erected in the temple he is still bloodthirsty; thus the victim sacrificed to him is dispatched in a bloody way. In contrast, when the process of the god's transformation has been completed, the victim must be offered bloodlessly and entire, without any trace of violence. Only at this moment can it be said that "the slaughtering for sacrifices is not slaughtering" (Bühler 1969, 175).

In a sense, even a denial of the victim's death occurs. The enemy or transgressor killed outside the temple is washed and purified; then he is introduced into the temple to be consecrated to the god and therefore to become the god and be reborn in him. Thus the slain enemy is transformed into his slayer's god, and his slayer's fratricidal guilt is denied or expiated in sacrifice.

This interpretation is fully confirmed by the fact that the human sacrifice preceding the one made for the erection of the Haku ʻōhiʻa in the temple is even bloodier. Indeed, the man who is sacrificed in the forest before the ʻōhiʻa tree is decapitated,[262] which implies a large effusion of blood. Hence the existence of a gradual progression from a bloody to a "bloodless" sacrifice, which parallels the god's progression from wild to tamed, is confirmed.

Treatment of the Bodies

The victims that have been killed at the spot where they were captured are brought near the temple,[263] washed if necessary (Ellis 1842, 151–52), and then introduced into the sanctum sanctorum of the temple. There they are generally placed on the sacrificial fire to singe their skin and hair; and it is thus, "scorched" (Ii 1963, 35) or "toasted" (Kamakau 1964, 105), that they are placed on the altar[264] (Kamakau 1976, 130; Tyerman and Bennett 1832, 2:49, etc.), where they are sprinkled with water to be purified (Kamakau 1961, 324).

It is also reported that sometimes fallen enemies are baked in the oven (Fornander 1916–20, 4:602; Kamakau 1961, 78; HEN, 1:266). I find it unlikely that these baked bodies are then offered in sacrifice,[265] since the god's share is usually "broiled" (K. Kamakau) or burned (S. M. Kamakau) rather than baked. On the other hand, it can happen, as in the case of Keōua in 1792 (cf. HEN, 1:266),[266] that the bodies first placed on the lele altar are taken down after a few days and cooked in the oven in order to separate the flesh from the bones more quickly. Normally, however, the victims are left to rot on the altar (Pogue 1858, 32).

Final Destination of the Body

Once placed on the altar, the body is henceforth part of the divine realm and cannot be reintroduced into the profane world. Thus crosses made with two sticks bound together are thrown among the offerings (Samwell 1967, 1177) to signal the taboo and keep potential polluters at a distance.[267] Guardians are also left in the temple to keep the victim's relatives or any of the king's enemies from stealing the body (Ii 1963, 51).

When the victim's flesh, which is entirely appropriated by the gods,[268] is loosened from the bones, the latter are taken down from the altar. The skull is often put on a paehumu pole: as the most important part of the body it stays in the temple with the gods (cf. PE, 10; Pogue 1858, 32; Samwell 1967, 1209; Lisiansky 1814, 121–22).[269] Sometimes, however, the head is cut off immediately after the end of the rites (Lisiansky 1814, 122)[270] or even on the battlefield (Fornander 1878–80, 2:90).[271] In some cases the head or skull goes, in whole or in part, to one of the aliʻi—especially, it seems, to the one who has killed the man or taken him prisoner (cf. Manby 1929, 43). This is another indication of the equivalence of high-ranking aliʻi and gods.[272]

More often, however, it is the teeth (and jaw) that are awarded to one of the aliʻi, generally the king. They are attached to his loincloths and feather cloaks or to his vessels (spittoons, bowls, etc.), sacrificial drums, or sacred conch shells (Fornander 1878–80, 2:72; Ii 1963, 28; Brigham 1918, 35; Lisiansky 1814, 113; Campbell 1967, 155; Turnbull 1813, 229; Choris 1822, 2). But it is especially the long bones that go to the king; they often constitute the handles of his *kahili* (Clerke 1967, 577; Portlock 1789, 88; Vancouver 1801, 3:369–70; Lisiansky 1814, 122).[273]

The destination of the different parts of Cook's body gives us an example of the hierarchical attribution of the victim (Samwell 1967, 1215). The head was given to Kekuhaupiʻo, who was the son-in-law of the high priest Holoaʻe (cf. Fornander 1878–80, 2:150; cf. 192, n. 1).[274] Thus we can suppose that through him the head was given to the god or to his representative, the *kahuna nui*. The hair went to Kamehameha.[275] The bones of the legs and arms and the lower jaw (with teeth) went to King Kalaniʻōpuʻu. The flesh was "burnt."[276]

If there are several human victims, the one of the highest rank is attributed to the aliʻi of the highest rank[277] and so on down the line with victims of lower rank.

This leads us to ask why the durable remains of the victim are appropriated by the aliʻi as relics. Having been in contact with the gods, they are imbued with their power. At the same time, they are a visible memorial of the king's victory and, as we have seen (chap. 5), of his possession of the land of the vanquished. Thus, by concluding his adversary's sacrifice and preserving a memento of it, the king concludes the process of encompassing the land.

CONCLUSION

Il y a moins de force dans une innovation artificielle que dans un répétition destinée à suggérer une vérité neuve.
Proust 1954, 1 : 894

Als Denkender bin ich mit allen Anderen verbunden, ja vielmehr geeint; ja man kann sagen: "Als Denkender bin ich alle Menschen."
Feuerbach 1910, 4 : 306

Il n'y a de progrès pour le sujet que par l'intégration où il parvient de sa position dans l'universel.
Lacan 1966, 226

The study of the *kapu luakini* has demonstrated that the reproduction of Hawaiian society requires the reproduction of the concept of man on which this society is based. The concept is embodied by the totality of the gods that appear in the ritual, but especially by the so-called Haku ʻōhiʻa, which summarizes them all and is the most encompassing ritual symbol created by the Hawaiians. Thus the ritual reproduction of this image has, or should have, the effect of reproducing the concept that the image represents.

Can the reproduction of this concept in the minds of those who participate in the ritual be considered simply as the illocutionary effect (in Austin's and Searle's sense) of a communicative act? To put it differently: Is there a purely conventional relation between the signs employed in ritual and the concepts it produces, so that the production of the signs would automatically produce the concepts? All this amounts to asking whether ritual meaning is analogous to linguistic meaning. Let us consider, then, a widely accepted account of linguistic meaning, that of Searle, and see if it can be transferred to ritual.

Searle writes: "To say that a speaker S meant something by X is to say that S intended the utterance of X to produce some effect in a hearer H by means of the recognition of this intention" (Searle 1969, 43). This summarizes Grice's view, to which, however, Searle adds a fundamental point: the effect is possible only if speaker and hearer share a grammar, that is, the rules that allow them to generate the same sentences and that therefore provide "a conventional means of achieving the intention to produce a certain illocutionary effect in the hearer," that is, the effect we call "understanding."

In a more structuralist language, we may say that the speaker and the hearer must share the same *langue*, that is, the same system of paradigmatic and syntagmatic associations. This implies that the hearer's recognition of the speaker's intention is in fact his recognition of a choice between the possible combinations and substitutions of signs allowed by the *langue*.

The first thing we must establish is: Do we find in ritual an equivalent of the "speaker" in linguistic communication? It is obvious that such an equivalent cannot be the performer of the ritual, because he is not free—except in a very limited sense—to change anything in the ritual text. The only real choices open to him concern the act of performance itself: when and where to perform the rite; whether or not to perform it; with whom, and so forth. These choices manifest intentions that are themselves understandable only in terms of conventions associated with the acts of performance.

The real "speaker" of ritual must therefore be its author, that is, the one who has made the original "choices" and produced the "sentences" that constitute the ritual text. But is it a fact that the existence of this author is postulated by the participants in ritual?

It is notable that in many cultures rituals are given an author, divine or human. In Hawaii Kamakau at least claims that the *kapu luakini* was instituted by a priest, Pā'ao, who was also responsible for the present form of kingship (Kamakau 1866, 1867a). But whether a hypothetical author is associated with a ritual matters little, since it can be maintained that, insofar as the "hearer" attempts to identify a meaning in a rite, he presupposes ipso facto an intention and therefore an "author" responsible for it. If he did not presuppose him, he would make no distinction between "natural" and "nonnatural" meaning, that is, between inference and communication proper.

The fact that the attribution of meaning presupposes the recognition of an implicit intention, however, should be no reason for overlooking the profound differences that exist between a communicative situation in which the author is only an implicit postulate and one in which he is a real, acting person. If we contrast, for instance, the case I would call "dialogic communication" with the case of ritual, we see that in the former it does not simply happen that the hearer attempts to identify the intention of the speaker; it also happens that the speaker attempts to establish whether he has been understood and adjusts his speech accordingly. Moreover, the hearer can himself turn into a speaker and ask for clarification. The reciprocity that characterizes dialogic communication therefore fosters unambiguous communication (cf. Valeri 1981b, 223). But as soon as we have a written or a frozen oral text (as in ritual), the author becomes detached from what he states, and there is no way for him to establish whether his intentions have been correctly identified or for the hearer to ask questions to establish whether he has correctly identified the author's intentions. Inevitably, the "hearer's part"—or the "beholder's part"—and therefore the imputed rather than the actual intentions of the author come to the foreground. More than communication by an author with his "hearer," we have here a projection of the hearer's own understanding onto the frozen word or image, although this projection is usually not recognized but is viewed as the intention(s) of an implicit author.

We may speak in this case of communication, but then it is a communication of the hearer (or the community of the hearers) with himself (or itself) through the text. The speaker and the hearer objectively become indistinguishable.

We must now establish a second fact: Is the relation between the concrete ritual text and the rules—the "grammar" that, as we have seen, they presuppose—analogous to the relation between *parole* and *langue* in linguistic communication?

As is well known, a *langue* allows for the production of an indefinite number of choices and therefore of sentences. In theory, the "grammar" of ritual creates the possibility of generating an indefinite number of ritual sentences. However, in practice ritual texts cannot be freely produced, nor can the form of the existing ones be changed, although they allow for some alternatives, as we have seen. In other words, a potentiality exists but is not actualized or only partially actualized. There seem to be two reasons (among others) for this. First, the text becomes identified with the authority it reproduces and must therefore be as unchangeable as that authority. Those who "speak" the text impersonate its explicit (priestly, kingly, etc.) authors or its implicit one (the community), and by virtue of speaking it they acquire the authority of those authors. At the same time the fact that they have few or no choices on how to speak, that they must follow an established text, implies that those who impersonate authority are themselves controlled by the superior authority of the text. Moreover, as we have seen, the audience is the guardian of this superior authority, because it has the right to judge the performance and to invalidate it. If ritual had no fixed text, if it were not law, then authority could not be acquired or denied by virtue of the performance of ritual.

The second main reason has to do with the ambiguity of ritual communication. This ambiguity implies that the text can accommodate an indefinite number of interpretations; thus, to communicate new meanings it is not necessary to generate new sentences, but it is sufficient to rely on the context or to give more emphasis to elements already present in the text. Moreover, as we have seen, ambiguity makes it possible for a variety of meanings to be projected quite spontaneously by the audience. Thus it is possible for differences in meaning to coexist, both synchronically and dia-chronically, with an unchanging text. Synchronically, ritual can combine the claim of unanimity with actual dissent or, less dramatically, basic agreement and differences of viewpoint—that is the hierarchical unity that is its principal aim. Diachronically, ritual can accommodate historical change at the same time that it denies it by using an unchanging text.

In sum, it seems that the unchangeability of ritual is structurally related, for a variety of reasons, to its ambiguity. The result of all this, however, is that the distinction between *langue* and *parole* becomes blurred in ritual, not only because there is no free production of *paroles*, but also because a frozen *parole* takes some of the normative character of the *langue* and some of its functions in the creation of shared understanding.

To round off this brief comparison of linguistic meaning and ritual meaning, I must say a few words about the "grammar" of ritual. This grammar involves paradigmatic and syntagmatic associations just as *langue* does; but these associations function according to rather different rules in ritual and in language. Language tends to distinguish each concept along the temporal dimension: thus the choice of one element of a paradigm in a given context excludes the presence of all other elements in the same context. These other elements can therefore appear only in later occurrences of the same context, according to the same law of exclusion. In contrast, in ritual the choice of one element of a paradigm does not rule out the use of other elements in the same context. One can say that these are not really paradigms, but it seems to me more accurate to say that they share with the paradigms of language one trait (they have a common feature, opposed to another feature characterizing another paradigm) but not, or rather not necessarily or not always, another trait (mutual exclusion of the paradigmatic elements in the same context). This is related to the fact that ritual does not differentiate as many contexts as language, and therefore that it stresses the equivalence of signs more than their difference. Here lies, precisely, the reason for the ambiguity of ritual, but also for its poetic properties that after all, if we follow Jakobson, result from the projection of the paradigmatic axis over the syntagmatic one.

The comparison of linguistic and ritual communication has revealed such important differences of degree between them that they must be considered qualitative differences as well. While ritual can be said to communicate, it communicates with a grammar too poor to establish meaning unambiguously. And since it is impossible to pair unambiguously and regularly the occurrence of a ritual sign X with the occurrence of an effect

Y (understanding of the concept signified by X), it becomes difficult to view that effect as purely illocutionary. Indeed, it seems that communication is only part of the process whereby ritual attempts to create the effect of understanding. Ritual does not simply communicate the concepts that must be understood—it also creates artificial situations in which those concepts are likely to emerge or reemerge by pre-predicative or even predicative inference. Of course those situations are created by virtue of communicative acts; but the effect of these acts is to produce further thoughts that are not conventionally related to them in the same way a linguistic sign is related to its meaning. My point is that ritual communicates in order to produce typical experiences from which typical results are likely to emerge, but that this connection between experience and result is regular yet not conventional. In other words, understanding in this case can be described more as a perlocutionary than as an illocutionary effect of the messages; or better, illocutionary and perlocutionary, communicative and inferential effects combine to produce understanding.

The main reason ritual produces knowledge by creating "model" experiences, and not simply by communicating concepts by conventional means, seems to be as follows. As has been recognized ever since Durkheim (1912, 552) and Radcliffe-Brown (1922), ritual reproduces society by reproducing dispositions that are at the same time bodily, emotional, and mental. To obtain this effect, the subject must be stimulated not simply to decode messages from other peoples' gestures, words, emotions, and so forth, but also to learn how to reproduce them. He must therefore acquire the "practical" (in Bourdieu's [1980] sense) knowledge that makes it possible for him to act, feel, speak, and think in the prescribed way. Thus ritual must resemble a drill, as Bergson (1959, 1146) perceptively remarked. Put another way, ritual does not simply send messages, it creates situations in which the codes underlying those messages—which are not themselves objects of messages—can be inferred and mastered in "simulated' situations. Ritual is in an important sense made quite evident by the *kapu luakini*, programmed learning through activities that involve the apperception of codes, principles, concepts, and their reproduction in practice, in action.

Moreover, the "understanding" that ritual creates is an understanding of the premises of the cultural system. But these are fundamentally implicit and unformulated: the only clear knowledge that exists about them is that they can be "felt"—and felt to have an effect on action and mental dispositions—in certain experiential situations. These are precisely the situation created by ritual. These ritual situations, in turn, regularize and emphasize certain elements of diffuse, everyday experience that are associated with the "practical" or "inchoate" apperception of the presuppositions of the cultural system as reflected in the acting subject.

Thus, as we have seen, sacrificial rituals select among the natural objects of everyday experience those that mirror more clearly aspects of human subjectivity and of its cultural presuppositions. Ultimately, then, the reason ritual does not simply communicate is that it attempts to promote awareness of basic notions whose knowledge is inchoate or that, to be believed, must be discovered through experience.

Because of the inchoate nature of these notions, their signs, when they exist, can only be the signs of all the experiences in which their presence is felt and in which they are learned. Those signs, then, can truly become signs only after those experiences and the inchoate inferences that they allow have occurred. This is precisely what happens with the Haku 'ōhi'a, which is the sign of the most fundamental of those concepts, the one that provides the basis for the unity in difference, for the hierarchical structure of society. As we have seen, the Haku 'ōhi'a is supposed to become a "real god," that is, to *actually* signify the corresponding concept, only after most of the ritual has been performed. This is so, of course, because of a conventional representation: the metamorphosis of the Haku 'ōhi'a represents the passage of thought from the consciousness of a natural object over which it works to the consciousness of the properties of that work, that is, of human subjectivity in the object. But this representation can be understood because it is the representation of what happens in an experience of which it is only a part: the collective appropriation of a *'ōhi'a-lehua* tree. This appropriation furnishes all the participants in the ritual with the only experience they can have of society manifesting itself as unity and multiplicity, that is, of the unity of the species realized as a coordinated complex of social actors. The communicative process therefore accompanies an experiential process that it presupposes and requires in order to be fully communicative—to be fully understood. In this rite the production of the signifier requires a work that makes it possible to obtain its signified in full.

My point, in sum, is that the necessity that the Haku 'ōhi'a be produced is what fundamentally guarantees that it can be understood as a sign.

This view of ritual as creation of awareness through "model experiences," which consist in appropriating objects that are implicitly symbolic of the presuppositions of action but are fully made symbolic by their *actual* programmed appropriation, explains that those presuppositions are conceived as objects, that is, as gods, not as properties of the collectively constituted subject.

Indeed, the subject is made to experience those properties as something that various natural objects have in common. These common human properties mirrored by the objects when men interact with them are rendered evident by giving the objects a human form, as in the case of the *'ōhi'a* tree, or by metonymically connecting them with an anthropomorphic image, as in most sacrifices. But the human form remains an external object. The dialectical circle in which the subject unconsciously reflects himself in the

The Sacrifice of the Hawaiian King

objects, then apperceives himself in them, is not completed. The subject becomes aware of his properties in the object, but not of their subjective nature. In other words, he only half-recognizes himself in them: he conceives them as an external, human active being that underlies the natural objects—as a god.

In sum, the ritual apperception of the principles of action is necessarily correlated with their objectification and therefore with a theology rather than an anthropology. I have attempted to supply that missing anthropology.

You will have noticed, I hope, certain similarities between my approach to the explanation of deities and sacrifice and that of Evans-Pritchard (1956) and especially that of Lienhardt (1961). These similarities are due to direct influence but also, and more important, to the fact that we have all been inspired by those theories that view sacrifice as a representation (or "symbolic action"), efficacious because it acts upon objectified mental processes. In my review of theories of sacrifice I left out Evans-Pritchard and Lienhardt because I considered other authors (particularly Loisy) holding the theory of "efficacious representation," but also because a general theory of sacrifice remains implicit—if it exists at all—in *Nuer Religion*, while the relatively explicit theory of Lienhardt, I felt, could be better discussed after my own argument had been given in full. Let us turn, then, to a discussion of the similarities and differences that exist between Lienhardt's approach and mine.

Lienhardt's idea, as is well known, is that divinities are "representations" or "images" or "schemes" of experience. He does not explain how the passage from experience to image is effected, or why the images are reified and personified, although he points out that reification is connected with the absence of a theory of mind (as mediating between the subject and the world) in Dinka thought (Lienhardt 1961, 149).

But that he has an implicit empiricist model of the passage from experience to concept cannot be doubted. According to him, concepts "reflect" experiences that, in turn, "reflect" ecological and social conditions that preexist them and are quite independent from them (cf. p. 170). Lienhardt writes, for example, that "clanship . . . does not proceed from the existence of the clan-divinity. The presence of the clan-divinity proceeds from the fact of clanship" (p. 167, cf. 247). Hence the clan-divinity would reflect the experience of a clan that preexists it and that, we must assume, functions wholly without it.

This reflectionist approach, it seems to me, contradicts Lienhardt's insight that the divinities make it possible to *interpret* the experience from which they are derived. Indeed, if they make interpretation possible, they cannot be considered simple images or reflections of experience: they must add something to it—be concepts and not just images.

Lienhardt's empiricist model of the relation between representation and experience, if taken rigorously, would only justify the claim that the representation, being more regular and stable than the experience from which it derives, simply reinforces and regulates that experience. This is in fact the view often taken by Lienhardt, especially when he considers the relation between divinity and corresponding experience. However, in other cases, particularly when he considers the relation between ritual and experience, he goes beyond that view. This is indicated by his claim that ritual, by dramatizing a problematic experience, makes it possible to symbolize its resolution and therefore favors its real resolution insofar as it depends on the moral relations of the agents. This implies that representation brings about a state of affairs and is not simply its mere reinforcement or regulation.

My own view is that deities and other representations used in sacrifice have the role of concepts that allow participants to classify and interpret impressions. Without these preexisting concepts (that they are reified does not matter), there would not be an experience in the first place. Concepts therefore have a constitutive role relative to experience and are not simply derived from it. Experience, in sum, is an *act* of the subject that involves a synthesis of concept and percept. Analogously, the concept of an action is not simply derivative of a preexisting behavior; the action is the synthesis by a subject of a concept and a behavior. Hence the action presupposes, by definition, some form of apperception of the concept that constitutes it. Again, the concept of an acting subject—individual or collective—is not the simple reflection of a subject's experience of itself; on the contrary, the concept of the subject is the condition of that experience. In this book, I have tried to demonstrate that rituals, and more particularly sacrifices, are reflective experiences in which the constitutive concepts of action are apperceived. Moreover, sacrifice encourages the subject's awareness that his experience and his actions depend on those concepts, that is, on "the gods." Here lies the real difference between Lienhardt's model of sacrifice and my own. For Lienhardt, sacrifice controls and possibly resolves a problematic situation by manipulating the symbols of the mental components of that situation. I agree with this view, but I maintain that that aspect of sacrifice presupposes another one, in which the active (i.e., human) components of the situation are reactivated and reconstituted in a situation (problematic or not) by bringing about the apperception of their constitutive concepts. It is by apperceiving himself and his powers that the subject—individual or collective—can act efficaciously in any situation represented in ritual. In truth it is apparent from Lienhardt's descriptions that Dinka sacrifices aim at creating a situation in which the group, by acting in a coordinated manner, becomes aware of itself and therefore of its capacity to act, and thus can effectively act to resolve the problem that motivates the ritual.

That the apperception of the concepts of the subject and of his actions as parts of a social context are the essence of every sacrifice, because they are the first condition of its efficacy, is at any rate made evident by Hawaiian sacrifices. These, as we have seen, are predominantly representations of the god's devouring of the offering—that is, as I see it, symbols of the process by which the subject and his actions are subsumed under their constitutive concepts.

Saying this is not denying that experience may transform its constitutive concepts. On the contrary, as we have seen, the very way ritual encourages awareness of those concepts also ensures that they are modified, although it does not make it possible to become aware of their modification (cf. Valeri 1981b).

Finally I shall say a few words on the relation between the material and the ritual reproduction of society. As we have already seen in chapter 5, Hawaiian society is very much based on war as a means of conquest and of internal control. A successful war makes available resources that allow the king to maintain the support of a large number of nobles and clients and to acquire more. At the same time, as a show of force, it discourages potential rebels (cf. Valeri 1982b, 1984).

The institution of human sacrifice—and in fact the *kapu luakini* as a whole—is able to translate the successful war into renewed internal cohesion, not simply because it is terrifying, but because it connects the acquisition of land as source of life with the introjection by the members of the society of its image and of its principles of order.

Human sacrifice is able to effect this because the vanquished chiefs who are sacrificed are symbols both of their conquered land and of the sacrifiers in their disordered state. The incorporation of these victims into the god, then, represents the coincidence of the acquisition of the land with the reproduction of society by its renewed apperception. The god is therefore the synthesis of the land acquired and the people ordered. As a result of this synthesis, the conquerors' relationship with the land is transformed: from destructive and disordered, it becomes productive and ordered (cf. Valeri 1982b). The sacrifier's work—once his sacrifice is ended—will fertilize the land and the women: life will be empirically reproduced after having been reproduced symbolically, by anticipation, in the *kapu luakini*.

It must be stressed, moreover, that the relationship between war and sacrifice is reciprocal: a war of conquest motivates the sacrificial employment of its victims, but the necessity of reproducing internal order by sacrifice may motivate a war of conquest to procure victims. Thus, whatever the initial motivation at a given moment, the system ensures that the material and the conceptual conditions for the reproduction of society are always given together and mediated.

How could it be otherwise?

NOTES

Introduction

1. Some of these were furnished to me by Marshall Sahlins, whom I most warmly thank. Copies of the most important journals are found in the libraries and archives in Honolulu, where I was able to consult them.

2. See also Gould 1928; Extract 1930; Clerke 1930; Manwaring 1931, 130–42, which are partial editions of unpublished journals or contain excerpts from them. The Journal of George Gilbert (1982) has just been published.

3. Davis died on Oʻahu in 1810 (Kotzebue 1821a, 3:258) and Young in 1835 (Freycinet 1978, 102, n. 23).

4. Alexander Ross, who met Young in 1811, wrote that "from his long residence among the natives, he has imbibed so much of their habits and peculiarities, that he is now more Indian than white man" (1904, 59).

5. See also Howay 1930, 1930–34, 1932, 1933, 1936, 1937.

6. Von Chamisso's voyage inspired a strange novella by another Berliner, E. T. A. Hoffmann (see Moore 1978).

7. Arago was guilty of an even more discreditable fabrication in the chapter on Hawaii in his book *Comme on dîne partout* (1842).

8. On the abolition of the taboos, see Webb 1965; Levin 1968; Davenport 1969; Sahlins 1981.

9. On the history of the mission see Evelith 1829; Anderson 1865.

10. An excellent journal by a male missionary is that of Loomis (1937).

11. See also the modifications he made—out of Christian prudishness—in the myth of Wākea and Papa (see below, p. 375).

12. Malo also compiled a life of Kamehameha, which unfortunately has been lost.

13. Several of these works, especially those dealing with myth, were translated by Thrum (1907a, 1923) and Westervelt (1910, 1915a, b, 1916, 1923). Two collections of chants were published by N. Emerson (1915, 1965 [1909]). On these translations, see Leib and Day 1979, 14–24.

Chapter 1

1. The original Hawaiian text and an English translation have been published by Beckwith (1951). Queen Liliʻuokalani published the first complete translation in 1897 (reprinted 1978). Bastian (1881) had already made important excerpts known to the public. In my discussion, reference to the lines of the *Kumulipo* implies reference to the Hawaiian text, as printed in Beckwith (1951).

2. This is what Liliʻuokalani affirms, but Beckwith denies that we have proof

of it (1951, 181). However, she recognizes that "Every birth of a *niaupi'o* [high-ranking ali'i—V. V.] child was in fact regarded as a repetition of the first human birth" (ibid.).

3. Cf. the canonical expression *mai ka pō mai*, "out of the unseen" [out of the "night"] (Handy and Pukui 1972, 131), which refers to anything of divine origin or "supernatural" (cf. N. Emerson in Malo 1951, 241).

4. See line 1917 of the *Kumulipo*: "Wakea as Ki'i [image] slept with Hina-ka-we'o-a" (Beckwith 1951, 127).

5. Cf. the term Kahiko, "ancient," which, like Kahiki, was "the term that vaguely described place and era of the beginning of the race" (NK, 2:294) but more often referred to an ancestor, sometimes the first Hawaiian (Malo 1951, 4), sometimes the father of Wākea, who was the apical ancestor of all Hawaiians (ibid., 238–39).

6. We have seen that the *Kumulipo* divides the animal realm into five major categories: corals and mollusks, fish, winged animals (of which there are two sub-classes, insects and birds), and mammals. In grouping natural species under a deity, Hawaiians disregard these taxonomic categories as well as other ones, which can be found in Pukui and Elbert's *Hawaiian Dictionary* (PE).

7. In fishponds (cf. Titcomb and Pukui 1972, 59–60, 64–66) or in irrigated taro fields (*lo'i*; Kamakau 1976, 34; Wilkes 1978, 484).

8. See the enumeration of the *kino lau* of Kamapua'a in Kahiolo (1978, 95–97).

9. Warriors are compared to "spotted pigs that bared their teeth" (Kamakau 1961, 86). The pig evokes virility because of its unbounded sexual activity and because it is identified with clouds, whose rain is assimilated with ejaculation (*"Mehe ao pua'a la, ke aloha e kau nei*, like a cloud [literally, "pig-cloud"—V. V.] resting on the mountain is the love alighting here"—PE, 317).

10. There is also a base five system (*lima*) used in some contexts (NK, 2:53).

11. "Divine attributes are represented here as many different gods (*akoua*)" (Freycinet 1978, 70; cf. Lévi-Strauss 1971, 602–3).

12. "There was·a great diversity as to cult among those who worshipped idols in Hawaii nei, for the reason that one man had one god and another an entirely different god. The gods of the *ali'i* also differed from one another" (Malo 1951, 81). "Each chief has his particular god" (Freycinet 1978, 71). "A single deity may appear under different titles according to the particular aspect under which he or she is worshiped by a given family branch" (Beckwith 1951, 145).

13. For example, different dynasties own different war gods, which are all differently named particularizations of Kū (Pakele 1864; Beckwith 1951, 145).

14. This theory resembles the one formulated by Dumézil to account for the proliferation of *dii minores* in Roman religion. According to him they are probably the *familia* of a "great god" (1970, 37–38).

15. With regard to numbers, I have found only one association between Kū and the number five (cf. Beckwith 1940, 81), which is perhaps due to Kū's connection with fishing, since to count fish a numerical system based on five is used (NK, 2:53).

16. It goes without saying that it is necessary to make a considerable effort to distinguish original traditions from later manipulations of them influenced by the Bible (cf. Barrère 1969). Failing this, the confusion would be almost complete.

17. Any manifestation of the divine is in fact ambivalent. For example, dreams (NK, 2:176), sharks (NK, 2:178), and rainbows. The last are connected with ali'i as principles of life but also announce death (cf. NK, 2:179, 279; Fornander 1916–20, 6:100).

18. Just as Hina is the wife of Kū, Haumea, who seems to be an "encompassed" form of Hina, is the wife of Kūwahailo, an "encompassed" form of Kū. Haumea and Papa are almost always equated (see Beckwith 1940, 223; Kamakau 1964, 28, and below).

19. The ambivalence is inherent in Kapo herself, not only in the pair she forms with Laka: "the Hawaiian goddess Kapo seems to have lived a double life whose aims were at cross purposes with one another—now an angel of grace and beauty, now a demon of darkness and lust" (Emerson 1965, 25).

20. According to Isaac Kihe, the shark is the best 'aumakua next to the owl (HEN, 1:569–70; cf. Beckwith 1940, 128).

21. "E kela mea make loa he pueo" (Fornander 1916–20, 4:590–91): "that thing, an owl, eminently connected to death."

22. Some masculine mo'o exist (Beckwith 1940, 127).

23. As the shark 'aumakua grant sea fish, mo'o 'aumakua grant freshwater fish (Kamakau 1964, 82).

24. According to Isaac Kihe, moreover, real lizards are also 'aumakua (HEN, 1:566).

25. "All four species [of geckos] occurring in the Hawaiian Islands are . . . found in houses" (Stejneger 1899, 787).

26. The existence of analogical or metonymic relations among certain natural manifestations of an 'aumakua and some diseases is noted in at least one other case. For obvious reasons, the 'aumakua of Pele's family (volcanic phenomena) are associated with diseases of the eye (Emerson 1892, 7).

27. Note that in Hawaiian usage the manifestations of the 'aumakua are themselves called 'aumakua, just as statues or other embodiments of akua are called akua (see K. Kamakau, 1919–20, passim). Hence the species considered here are referred to in the texts used below as 'aumakua.

28. According to Handy (1968, 53–56) only certain "families" have "totems," and he concludes, "We do not know that such relationship was general" (ibid., 54). This is not the impression one receives going through the Hawaiian texts, particularly those of S. M. Kamakau (1964). Above all, it is arbitrary to limit the use of "totems" to "families" (it is unclear what Handy means by this term, moreover), since individuals may also acquire "totems."

29. "They were never known as deceased human identities, such as 'Kimo who lived six generations ago,' but they were given 'aumākua names and identities, and even locations and specific kino lau (changed forms or bodies) of mineral, plant or animal life" (NK, 2:294).

30. "At every meal during the lifetime of the kahu [the one who "feeds"], [the 'unihipili] must be invited to partake of the food" (Emerson 1892, 4).

31. The same is true of the akua lele, which is a variety of the same species as the 'unihipili (see NK, 1:26).

32. The classic formulation of the contradictory conception of the being of the gods has been given, of course, by Hegel and Feuerbach (cf. Taylor 1975, 197–213; Wartofsky 1977, 309). Its antecedents are already in many theories of religion of the Enlightenment (cf. Manuel 1959).

33. Besides the anomalous phenomena already considered, the following anomalous phenomena connected with the divine may be mentioned. Monstrous humans (Kekoa 1865) and animals are both considered so divine that they are consecrated to the gods, that is to say, "returned" to them. Thus all deformed fish caught in a fishpond are "returned" to the mo'o deity that presides over the fishpond (Kamakau 1964, 84). As we shall see in chapter 4, the anomalous species of the sea are often treated as extremely divine and not appropriated.

Anomalous events such as a clap of thunder when it is not raining, an eclipse, the scent of a flower when no flower is present, the sudden appearance of an animal in an unexpected context, inexplicable bruises or marks on the skin, mysterious sickness, and so forth, are also considered divine manifestations (NK, 1:156–57, 54, 58; 2:270, 244; Kamakau 1964, 87–88). Indeed, they are often treated as omens (hōʻailona) and are said to be ʻeʻepa, "inexplicable, remarkable, strange, unexpected" (NK, 1:11, 120, 122, 193, 195; 2:243–44, 268; Kepelino 1977, 51; Kamakau 1964, 70–71, 82, 83; 85, 86; MH, June 1823, 183).

The sources do not connect each of these with specific categories of gods: it seems that most may be manifestations of any god.

34. This view is clearly expressed by Horton (1970, 146–47) in his famous reformulation of the intellectualist theory of religion. It is also present in Godelier's Marxist approach: "l'homme, spontanément, se représente le monde, la causalité des niveaux invisibles de la nature et de la société analogiquement à sa propre expérience d'être conscient, doué de volonté et agissant intentionnellement sur les autres et sur lui-même" (Godelier 1973, 339–40).

Chapter 2

1. We can consider as a variant of the marriage ceremony the sacrifice of a small pig, which is eaten by the families of a man and woman who thereby enter into an "adoptive platonic marital relationship" (Handy and Pukui 1972, 54–55).

2. According to Kamakau, these rites are neglected if the cultivated lands are naturally fertile (1976, 25). Not everyone is religious, at least where gardening is concerned (ibid., 31).

3. According to some, hewa refers only to ritual faults or to the infraction of a vow (see J. S. Emerson in HEN, 1:584). The contrary of hana hewa, "guilty action," is hana pono, "moral action" (NK, 2:54, 56).

4. A propitiatory sacrifice makes the deity maliu, "look upon [the sacrifier] with favor" (PE, 215), while an expiatory sacrifice "cools" or "softens" (ʻoluʻolu) the deity (see, for example, HEN, 1:704–7; Malo 38.12; Kahiolo 1978, 175). This distinction is not absolute, however; in some cases the word ʻoluʻolu indicates the effect produced by a propitiatory sacrifice (see, for example, Malo 24.3: "E oluolu mai ai ke akua i ke keiki").

5. Guilt is explicitly considered a condition for the effectiveness of a curse (ʻānai). If the person struck by the curse does not accept it as a sanction because he feels innocent, the curse falls upon the one who pronounced it (NK, 1:31, 82, 88, 155).

6. Sacrifices made to induce the deities to manifest themselves through mediums (haka) (Handy and Pukui 1972, 133–36; Green and Beckwith 1926, 204–8) can be likened to divinatory sacrifices, for in both cases contact is sought with the deity to obtain information. Only the method differs.

7. In fact, even the first portion of a wild food appropriated by man is sacrificed to the deity that produced it (for an example, see Ellis 1842, 234–36).

8. According to Kamakau, in addition to the firstfruits of the harvest, the first leaves growing from the top of the young taro plant are consecrated to the god at the appropriate time (1976, 34–35).

9. The consecration of a newborn aliʻi is made according to a ritual identical to the one used in the consecration of a sacrificial victim. The infant's umbilical cord is cut in the temple while a drum is beaten, as if during a human sacrifice. Then the baby "was wrapped snugly in tapa [as we shall see, to wrap is to conse-

crate—V. V.] and taken by the king to the *kuapala* offering stand and presented to the gods" (Kamakau 1964, 27; cf. Malo 1951, 136–37). We have seen that according to Kamakau the firstborn of all animals are consecrated to the gods (1961, 190–91; cf. Kamakau 1964, 63), although this could be a case of an *interpretatio biblica* of the Hawaiian ritual.

10. The sacrifice of the first object made—of the "masterpiece," as it was called by the craftsmen of medieval Europe—"consecrated not only that first thing, but all of the same type that would be made by that person" (Handy and Pukui 1972, 102).

11. At least one king, Māʻilikukāhi, is known for having claimed for himself not only the firstfruits of agricultural harvests but also the firstborn of his subjects. These consecrated children lived at the royal court (Fornander 1878–80, 2:89).

12. For example, the first catch of the *kala* fish is given to the "lord of the land," who then consecrates half or two-thirds of it to the god (Kamakau 1976, 84, 85). As Kamakau writes, "The first portion was given to the gods, then to the ruling chief's household. The gods were the first to be considered by chiefs and people" (1961, 190).

13. In an early work, Handy (1927) denied that Polynesians sacrificed the god's own manifestations to him. However, he recognized that natural species, including those making up the offering, were seen as "children" or "descendants" of the gods (p. 190). This metaphor of the relations between species and deities does not seem very different to me from the one that makes the species the bodies of the deities. Later Handy seems to have changed his opinion, since the works he has written in collaboration with Kawena Pukui claim that one offers the deities some of their bodies (cf. 1972; Handy 1972, 1968, passim).

14. Apparently the dog, which is most often viewed as the "body" of Kū in mythology (see, for example, the mythical dog Kūʻilioloa "Ku long dog"), is also sacrificed to Kū. We have some proof of the existence of these sacrifices. The missionary Ellis learned that when the image of Kūkāʻilimoku was brought into the temple of Puʻukoholā, "vast offerings of fruit, hogs and dogs, were presented" (1842, 98). In 1793 Bell saw carcasses of dogs among the offerings found in Hikiau temple at Kealakekua, which was consecrated to Kū (1929–30, 78–79; cf. Manby 1929, 44). This confirms the information Lisiansky received in 1804 from a priest who said dogs were sacrificed at Hikiau. It is true that John Young, a European who was well informed regarding local customs, later assured Lisiansky that the priest had lied to him (Lisiansky 1814, 120, 122). However, a few years later Whitman saw dogs on the altar of the principal temple in Honolulu, which was dedicated to Kūkāʻilimoku (Whitman 1979, 25; Valeri 1982b). According to one of Beckwith's informants, dogs began to be used as sacrificial victims in the *luakini* temples only at the beginning of the reign of King Kalaniʻōpuʻu, that is, in the second half of the eighteenth century (1951, 90). But this information, recorded a century and a half after the time to which it refers, is questionable. The dog is not consecrated to Kū exclusively. Perhaps different varieties of dog correspond to different deities (see, for example, note 16).

The *moano* fish, one of the marine forms corresponding to the pig (which explains why it is considered a *puaʻa kai*, "sea pig"), is another sacrificial species that has a close relation to Kū and is probably considered one of his "bodies." In fact, this fish is associated with the *ʻōhiʻa-lehua* tree, which is a manifestation of this god: "Hawaiians believed that this fish ate *lehua* blossoms, which are a deep red, and derived their colour from the flowers. Sometimes this fish was referred to as *moano-nui-ka-lehua* (great *moano* of the *lehua*)" (Titcomb and Pukui 1972, 110).

See also the expression *moano ka lehua* (Fornander 1916–20, 6:293), in which the word *moano* functions as a verb meaning "to become red." The sentence as a whole is to be translated "the *lehua* flowers turn red."

15. The red rooster, considered a manifestation of the pair Kāne/Kanaloa (Titcomb 1948, 152), appears mostly in sacrifices consecrated to these gods (see Beckwith 1940, 32).

16. According to other sources, it is the hairless dog that corresponds to the *moʻo* (cf. Sterling and Summers 1962, 242–43).

17. This is also the case with the *kūmū* fish, which is considered a *puaʻa kai*, "sea pig" (Titcomb and Pukui 1972, 92; Handy and Pukui 1972, 50). This fish is an offering generically appropriate for all gods because of its red color, which connotes "sacredness" in general (PE, 339), and because of its name. *Kūmū* is associated with *kumu*, which means "foundation," "basis," "beginning," "origin," "source," "model," and so on. These concepts are connected with all deities (cf. HEN, 1:165).

18. A symbol sometimes used is a special form of plaited cordyline leaves on which the offering may be placed. Each kind of plait corresponds to a different deity (Handy and Pukui 1972, 133; NK, 1:191).

19. A good example is furnished by the varieties of *ʻawa* (kava). The *hiwa* variety may be sacrificed to all deities because its name means "black," which is a divine color. The *papa* variety is sacrificed to goddesses because it bears the name of Papa, who is the type of most goddesses (cf. Beckwith 1940, 94).

20. Below are some examples of the masculine connotations of the principal sacrificial species: (a) The banana is a phallic symbol, as indicated, for example, by the expression *Eia mai ka maiʻa*, "Here is the banana," which designates "the exposed genitals" as represented by an insulting gesture (NK, 2:223). (b) Coconuts are associated with testicles (cf. Kamakau 1961, 120; Handy 1972, 168–69; cf. Neal 1929, 51–52). (c) The pig also has phallic connotations. The "pig's snout" (*ka nuku o ka puaʻa*) is a metaphorical expression referring to the penis (Kamakau 1976, 33). Kamapuaʻa, the porcine god, is an intensely masculine character, in a boundless, unruly fashion and to such a degree that in a sense he plays the role of a bestial double of the human male (cf., for example, Kahiolo 1978, 124; Emerson 1892, 14). The pig is also a metaphor for the warrior, the supreme expression of virility. Probably it is given this value because of its aggressiveness. See chapter 1, note 9. (d) In mythology, the dog is also represented as a warrior (cf. Beckwith 1940, 347f.) and therefore has male connotations. (e) The rooster is another symbol of manhood in its warriorlike aspect. In a famous chant, the war between the chiefs of different districts of Hawaiʻi is compared to a cockfight: "Hawaii is a cockpit; the trained cocks fight on the ground. The chief fights,—the dark red cock awake at night for battle" (Andrews 1875, 72). (f) The *ulua* fish is also a metaphor for the warrior, because of its prodigious strength and predatory habits (cf. Goodson 1973, 70; Titcomb and Pukui 1972, 152–56).

21. For example, the person being initiated into sorcery must sacrifice a black sow (Kamakau 1964, 120). See also the expiatory sacrifice offered to an *ʻaumakua*, probably feminine: in addition to a black sow, it includes bananas of the *pōpō-ʻulu* and *iho-lena* varieties, which are reserved for goddesses (Kamakau 1964, 97).

22. "All through the Pacific there is a close relationship between men and pigs" (Brigham 1908, 57).

23. Sometimes women give them the breast as if they were children (Handy 1972, 253).

24. One myth tells that the swineherd Pūmaiʻa felt such an affection for his favorite pig that "he had vowed he would never part from [it]. This hog was to be kept until the death of Pumaia when it was to be killed" (Fornander 1916–20, 4 : 470). But the emissaries of King Kūaliʻi tried to make away with the pig to sacrifice it in a temple. Pūmaiʻa killed all of them except one, who went back to tell the king what had happened. The same thing was repeated three times. Finally Kūaliʻi obtained from his god the capture of Pūmaiʻa, who was sacrificed in the temple. His body was thrown into the sacrificial pit with the bodies of the men he had killed. In this myth the identity between man and pig is confirmed by the inversion of its ordinary effects. It is not the pig that is sacrificed in place of his master, but the master in place of the pig.

We have many documents revealing the close relationship between a master and his favorite pig. For example, the pig may take the master's name. Thus the favorite pig belonging to Queen Kaʻahumanu is called Kaʻahumanu and is treated with the same deference displayed toward its mistress (Mathison 1825, 106, cf. 365, 373; see also Stewart 1839, 105).

25. Note also that in Hawaii cockfights are an aristocratic pastime, a representation on the level of a game of the rivalry between nobles. A man is identified with his fighting cock; if the cock is beaten and killed, its owner is humiliated, insulted, and sometimes, when he has wagered his life, lands, or sacred objects, even killed or degraded (Malo 1951, 230–31).

26. The equivalence of the animal victim and man is indirectly confirmed by the use of animal metaphors to refer to human victims: puaʻa wāwae loa, "long-legged pig" (PE, 353); puaʻa hinu, "greasy pig" (PE, 318); ulua, "fish" (PE, 341), and, generically, iʻa, "fish" (J. S. Emerson in HEN, 1 : 525) or iʻa wāwae loa, "long-legged fish" (Emerson 1892, 21).

27. Teeth, hair, blood, or eyes can be sacrificed to redeem the whole body in case of sickness or misfortune, in funeral rites (in order to avoid dying with the dead), war rites, and those that take place in the luakini temple (Ellis 1842, 159; Tyerman and Bennett 1831, 2 : 27; Kotzebue 1821a, 1 : 342; Kamakau 1961, 149; Kamakau 1964, 14; Iselin, n.d., 66; cf. as well Schoch 1954, 17, n. 31).

The equivalence between the sacrificed hair and the sacrifier is perfectly expressed in the following prayer: "Here is a part of my body, my hair. May it be as a token of me in the spirit world" (NK, 1 : 184, taken from Pukui 1942, cf. also 137). The tooth sacrificed is probably a substitute for the whole person, since to dream of losing a tooth means death (see NK, 2 : 181). Tattoos and burns inflicted on the body during funeral rites can also be considered equivalents of self-sacrifice (Byron 1826, 136).

28. "Le seul sacrifice authentique serait le suicide" (Lévi 1898, 133).

29. In fact, funeral rites are the only rites of passage for which human sacrifices are explicitly required (Menzies 1920, 172; Marin 1973, 199; Kotzebue 1821a, 1 : 342; von Chamisso in Kotzebue 1821a, 3 : 248; Kamakau 1964, 8, 34, 39). However, the consecration of human sacrifices during state temple rituals may be related to an aliʻi's transition from one status to another (see part 3).

30. Bingham 1848, 55; Stewart 1839, 226–27; Gough 1973, 195; Barrot 1839, 425; Kuykendall 1938, 63; Ii 1963, 33; Malo 1951, 189; Schoch 1954, 17.

31. Westervelt 1915b, 190–91.

32. Ibid.

33. Malo 1951, 159–60; K. Kamakau, 1919–20, 8–30; Ii 1963, 35–45; Kamakau 1976, 130–31, 136–45; Kalakaua 1888, 265; Thrum 1908b, 58, 61).

34. Cf. Ellis 1842, 150–51, 119, 98; Freycinet 1978, 71–72; Gough 1973, 195; Barrot 1839, 425.

35. See below, parts 2 and 3.

36. "Troubles and afflictions which befall the nation require that the ruling chief himself offer the propitiatory sacrifice" (Kamakau 1961, 185).

37. "Les citoyens croyant d'être massacrés dans les guerres désiraient vivement un chef qui les rendît victorieux" (Remy 1862, 157).

38. Malo 1951, 56, 165, 169–70, 188–89; Laanui 1930; Freycinet 1978, 72; Alexander 1891, 51. We cannot deduce from this, with Lisiansky, that human sacrifice can be assimilated with capital punishment and that therefore it is "more a political than a religious institution" (1814, 120). In fact capital punishment can exist along with sacrifice; guilty women are put to death but are not sacrificed (Kamakau 1961, 154). And sacrifices are not made only when it is necessary to punish transgressors; on the contrary, transgressions are often artificially provoked when a sacrifice is necessary. "Tarboos were instituted, such as it were next to impossible to observe, and the first offender, was seized and dragged to the morair [temple] for sacrifice" (Whitman 1979, 25; cf. as well the 'aha 'awa ko'o rite, during which the participants had to remain immobile until one of their number moved and was therefore sacrificed, in Kamakau 1976, 134). Sometimes a manhunt was organized or someone was captured by a ruse or treachery (Whitman 1979, 25; Paumakua in HEN, 1:2805).

When von Chamisso writes, "they sacrifice culprits to their gods, as we sacrifice them in Europe to justice" (in Kotzebue 1821a, 3:248), he shows more perspicacity than Lisiansky, because instead of considering Hawaiian sacrifice a form of penal justice, he considers European penal justice a form of sacrifice. On the difference between capital punishment and human sacrifice, see Gernet 1968a,b.

39. Kamakau 1964, 9–10, 12.

40. For other examples of verbal motivations for the choice of certain components of the offering, see NK, 1:3, 48.

41. See the last verse of the prayer given by N. Emerson in his notes to Malo's text (1951, 111).

42. In fact, the state of the offering determines the state of the deity. Thus, if one feeds excrement to a deity, it becomes polluted and can then be used to pollute one's enemies (Pukui in Kamakau 1964, 91, note 6).

43. See, for example, J. S. Emerson in HEN, 1:588 (prayer to a shark 'aumakua); J. S. Emerson in HEN, 1:526 (second prayer for a human sacrifice).

44. See J. S. Emerson 1892, 3, 20–21, 22–23; HEN, 1:572; N. Emerson in Malo 1951, 157, 158, 179, 180, 183; Kamakau 1976, 107, 143; Pogue 1858, 21, and sacrificial prayers from the rites of the royal temple given by K. Kamakau and studied below.

45. "Eia ka 'ai, eia ka i'a" (Kamakau 1976, 30), "Here is vegetable food, here is flesh food [literally, 'fish']."

46. "E molia e alana ia 'oe," "Set apart is an offering to you" (Kamakau 1976, 27, 28); see also Ii 1963, 37.

47. "Thoughts had to be put into words before they took effect, either as sorcery spell ('anā 'anā) or human-to-human curse ('ānai)" (NK, 1:25).

48. "Eia ka ai, e ke Akua," "Here is the food (sacrifice), O god" (Fornander 1878–80, 1:92; cf. Kamakau 1964, 51; Handy and Pukui 1972, 97, after Malo 1951, 88–89; Handy and Pukui 1972, 140; NK, 2:122, cf. 139; Fornander 1916–20, 4:60, 63).

49. Fornander 1916–20, 5:339; Handy 1972, 169, 620; J. S. Emerson in HEN, 1:526; Kamakau 1964, 64, 125.

50. Fornander 1916–20, 4:606–7, 5:329; Kahiolo 1978, 37.

51. According to one myth, the god's tongue comes down from heaven to devour the offerings (Fornander 1916–20, 4:219–20; cf. Kamakau 1961, 14). This motif betrays a biblical influence, but the representation of the devouring tongue in statues of the gods is traditional.

52. "The starving god can only whisper softly, / Hunger! Famine! / Dead for lack of food, but there is indeed food" (Kahiolo 1978, 82; cf. Emerson 1892, 24).

53. Cf. Emerson 1965, 23; NK, 2:20, 1:115. Sometimes the transmission of the god's invisible essence is indicated by waving (hō'ali) the offering, which is then eaten by the sacrifiers (Kamakau 1964, 60, 77; Ii 1963, 38). This essence is often materialized, however, in the smoke or smell of the cooked victims (cf. Kamakau 1964, 70, 77; Emerson 1915, 88; Fornander 1878–80, 2:239, n. 1; Kamakau 1961, 150). The stench of rotting victims probably has the same symbolic value (cf. Bell 1929–30, 78–79; Manby 1929, 43). Note also that the smoke rising from the offerings is supposed to be identical to the shadow of the god to which they are offered (Pukui, Elbert, and Mookini 1974, 218; Westervelt 1915a, 5). Indeed the essence of the offering is called aka, "shadow" (PE, 11; NK, 1:10). The sacrificial smoke, then, represents the victim's incorporation into the god and even its transformation into the god. The scent of aromatic plants used in rituals probably represents the same transformation (see Kamakau 1964, 12, 53; Handy and Pukui 1972, 114; Choris 1822, 14; Marin 1973, 312 [cf. PE, 203]; HEN, 1:745; cf. Lewis 1980, 69).

54. See the formula, "O ke aka ka 'oukou e ke akua, 'o ka 'i'o ka mākou," "Yours is the essence, O god; ours the material part" (NK, 1:10). Also, "The sacrifices and offerings were eaten by the people (kanaka), with repentance for their wrongdoing, and that would cause the god to look upon them with favour (ho'omaliu 'ia mai)" (Kamakau 1964, 60); "They should all eat together of the sacrifices and the offerings" (Kamakau 1964, 58).

55. When the offering consists of animals, this "first portion" is often the head or part of the head, notably an eye or ear or the brain (see, for example, PE, 10; Malo 1951, 87–89; Emerson 1965, 26, 34; Kahiolo 1978, 93; Kamakau 1976, 30). These parts are the seat of the soul or the points from which it leaves the body (NK, 1:109; Achelis 1895, 44). Thus, when they are given to the god, it is the life of the whole animal that is being given to him. Like smoke, they also represent the transformation of the victim from the empirical to the divine realm, since as points of transition they symbolize transition. After being incorporated by the god, these parts are very often eaten by the principal sacrifier (Ellis 1842, 346; HEN, 1:704; NK, 1:151; Malo 1951, 87), who thereby absorbs the deity's mana.

56. For similar reasons it would be false to consider the so-called 'aha 'aina ("meal gathering"—PE, 5) rites different in nature from the sacrificial rites made in the temples. Like the latter, the 'aha 'aina are sacramental meals in which the deities receive the essence, or the "first portion," of the food (cf. NK, 1:1–2). The use of the expression 'aha 'aina seems, however, to indicate that these sacrifices are made at the domestic level or outside the temples proper (cf. Handy and Pukui 1972, passim).

57. Kauhane perfectly expresses the principle of this unity in separation when he writes, on the subject of the kauila rite that forms part of the luakini temple ritual: "The kauila is the kapu of the god, therefore, pigs are put in the oven, and when baked, portions are placed on the altar, with coconuts, bananas, red fish, and the human (sacrifice). The remaining portion of the pigs and other things, that is food for the people" (Kauhane 1865).

58. The idea that men and god eat the same food is explicitly stated in a sacrificial prayer, a few lines of which are as follows: Here is the food, the leafed 'awa, / A root of the dark 'awa, a kea sugar cane, / Some iholena bananas, some aheahea, / I am calling to you to partake of food with me (trans. by Pukui in Handy and Pukui 1972, 139–40). On the commensality between men and deities, see also NK, 1:1, 5; 2:137. As Pukui writes, "The god or gods were not offered their portion and then mentally retired to their shelves. A sense of their presence remained throughout the eating. The gap between man and god was indeed narrowed" (NK, 1:1).

59. The cremation of animal victims is practiced in certain sorcery rites, not as a prestigious form but, it seems, because it represents the destruction of enemies that is the intent of these rites (see Malo 1951, 102; Ellis 1842, 294).

60. See, however, the expression mōhai kuni, "burnt offering," in the text given by Fornander 1916–20, 4:219. Perhaps this text reflects biblical influence.

61. In 1779 Cook and his companions noted that in the luakini temple of Hikiau the pig placed on the main altar was "barbicued" (Law, n.d., 18 January 1779), that is, pūlehu.

62. Most sacrifices made outside the main temples and in domestic surroundings include cooking the offering in an oven (kālua). This becomes clear if one reads the original Hawaiian texts of the works by Malo and Kamakau; it is also confirmed by the accounts found in Handy and Pukui (1972). In these sacrifices, the deities invoked are close to men because for the most part they are 'aumakua, that is, relatives with whom they maintain a relationship of commensality. Like men, then, these ancestral deities eat foods that are kālua. Lono is frequently invoked in these sacrifices, since of all the major gods he is the closest to men (cf., for example, the pule ipu rite in Malo 1951, 87–90).

63. Kamakau (1964, 13) distinguishes the different types of mōhai by means of suffixed words.

64. Uku ("retribution," "reparation," "redemption") is another term from the vocabulary of exchange used in sacrificial prayers (Kamakau 1964, 97, 13; cf. Fornander 1916–20, 4:485). This term is sometimes treated as the equivalent of three technical terms referring to sacrifice: mōhai, 'ālana, and kānaenae (see Emerson 1965, 33, 44–45).

65. In Hawaii, as everywhere else, the gift signifies first of all the relation between the giver and the recipient. Accepting the gift thus entails recognizing the relationship. For example, a woman succeeds in being recognized as the "daughter" of the ali'i Keali'imaika'i by sending him cloths by a messenger who presents them with the words "Your daughter sends her respects." Keali'imaika'i accepts the gift but comments that the woman is not his daughter. One of his companions, however, reminds him that indeed she is his daughter, since he has just accepted her gift! (Ii 1869k).

But the gift is meaningful not only as gift. Its efficacy also depends on the meaning conveyed by the objects constituting it. As we have seen, this aspect is essential in sacrifice; it actually becomes dominant with respect to its aspect as a "gift" pure and simple. Also, more than the ordinary gift, the sacrificial gift is a gift of oneself (on this point see Gusdorf 1948, 18). One is led to think of the famous Brahmanic saying: "Sacrifice is man. The sacrifice is man, for it is man who offers it; and each time it is offered the sacrifice has the size of the man. Thus the sacrifice is the man" (Çat. 1, 3, 2, 1, trans. by Lévi 1898, 77).

66. An interpretation strongly influenced by Frazer (1890).

67. Which was later rejected by Durkheim (1912, 490–91).

68. Some of these authors use an economic metaphor to describe the process of sacrificial circulation. They note that both in sacrifice and in the economic process the result of circulation is growth, a "profit." The idea that sacrifice produces growth exists in Hawaii, as can be observed, for example, in the name given the first man fallen on the battlefield and consecrated to the god Kū: *ulukoko*, "increasing blood" (Ellis 1842, 159). This name is used because the consecration of the victim it designates makes more enemies fall and results in a kind of "growth" of the enemy blood spilled.

On the notion of sacrifice as a process of exchange that involves a "return" or a "countergift," see an episode of the myth of 'Aukelenuiaiku in Fornander 1916–20, 4:62. Sometimes the "return" is conceived of as the god's own return to the altar, whereby he gives his mana to the sacrifier. See, for example, the following prayer:

O ke akua i ke kuahu nei la, e!
God of this altar here
E ho'i, e ho'i a noho i kou kuahu.
Return, return and reside at your altar!
Hoo-ulu ia!
Bring it good luck!
Emerson 1965, 42–43, cf. 20–21; and Kamakau 1964, 60]

69. Which he has the merit of developing and clarifying (see also van Baal 1975a).

70. In part, Gusdorf develops ideas implicit in Hubert and Mauss (cf. Mauss 1968–69, 1:305) and worked out by authors such as Will (1925, 1:110–11).

71. Note that this view seems to be incorporated in the term for "sacrifice" in certain languages: for instance, the German *Opfer*, which derives from *operari* (Burkert 1972, 9–10).

72. Surprisingly, Hocart never mentions Loisy. Even more surprising is that the similarity between the theory of ritual of these two authors has gone unnoticed, even by meticulous writers such as Needham (1970).

73. Girard's theory is in some respects anticipated by de Maistre (1884a).

74. Besides all the facts already mentioned, see the prayers given by J. S. Emerson (1892, 17–20) and Kamakau (1976, 26ff.) and the origin myths of the breadfruit tree (Handy and Pukui 1972, 33) and coconut palm (Pukui 1933, 179–85). These plants are transformations of Kū. Myths recounting the origins of two of the most important fish, the *'o'opu* (*Eleutheris fusca*) and the mackerel, present these species as derived from the dismembered bodies of certain gods (Fornander 1916–20, 5:514; Green 1926, 99).

75. See, for instance, the following texts:

When one deflowered the woods of their fronds of '*ie-'ie* and fern or tore the trailing length of *maile*—albeit in honor of Laka herself—the body of the goddess [who manifests herself in these species] was being despoiled, and the despoiling must be done with all grace and etiquette. [Emerson 1965, 16]

the Hawaiians would ask forgiveness for taking from nature's bounty. The bird-catcher would speak to Kū in his manifestation as god of *hulu* (feathers): "Oh Kū-*huluhulu*, forgive me for catching this bird and taking his feathers—they are needed for a *kihei* [mantle] for my chief [named]. [NK, 2:134]

Before you picked a plant, you would pray and say, "Please forgive me for taking this plant. I need it to cure grandmother who is sick." Or, if it was necessary to walk on volcanic land, "Forgive me, *Pele*, for walking on your domain." [NK, 2:246]

Even to make a hole in the earth it is necessary to ask forgiveness from the deity that inhabits the place (NK, 2:122). To this day these beliefs and practices survive among the Hawaiians (NK, 2:138).

Other practices that are motivated by the belief in the divinity of nature and attest to it regard the process of acquisition. For example, the main food plants (taro, bananas, etc.) cannot be cultivated by women, who are impure. The men who plant them must strip naked (Kamakau 1976, 33, 38; NK, 2:50), a sign of humility when one is in contact with the divine. Other phases of cultivation require men to dress in their ceremonial ornaments, as if for a rite, and for ali'i of the highest rank to be present (Kamakau 1976, 24, 34).

76. The principle that in sacrifice, as Granet says, "donner la partie, c'est donner le tout" (1929, 227; cf. Granet 1926, 2:501) is well attested in Hawaii, where expressions such as "to possess the head of a fish" (or of a pig, dog, etc.)— that is, to possess the first portion, the one given to the god—mean "possession of the whole" (Fornander 1916–20, 5:274n. 5).

Elsewhere in Polynesia we find that the Maori, for example, free the first fish caught (Taylor 1870, 200), thereby symbolically denying their appropriation of the whole catch.

That in many cultures firstfruits are conceived not as gifts to the gods (How could they be, since one would give the gods what one had just taken from them?) but as symbolic restitution has long been recognized (cf. Frazer 1911–15, 8:204–73; Loisy 1920, 45; Gusdorf 1948, 75; Meuli 1975; Lot-Falk 1953; Vorbichler 1956, 198; Harva 1959, 291–307, 317–72; Lanternari 1959, 280–408; Burkert 1972, 20–31; 1979, 54, 59).

77. See also the version collected by Stokes, "Report to T. Brigham," 21 December 1919, 52–56, MS GR 1, box 9.47, Bishop Museum Library.

78. In this context 'ai means "food in general."

79. Details on the way this sacrifice is set up are given by Manu in Thrum 1907a, 226–28.

80. Cf. Fornander 1916–20, 6:323.

81. Cf. Ovid, Fasti 2.685ff., and the commentary by Frazer, ed., 1966, 394–95.

Chapter 3

1. Thus the ali'i carefully conceal their wounds instead of displaying them, as warriors are wont to do in other cultures (Ii 1963, 101).

2. I infer their impurity from the fact that a virgin is usually deflowered by her grandmother before marriage, so that her husband will not "be offended by blood from a woman's private parts" (NK, 2:79).

3. For instance, flies, which alight on excrement, give rise to a veritable horror (cf. Stewart 1839, 121).

4. "[They] were people set apart from the rest and treated like filthy beasts. They could not associate with other men" (Kepelino 1932, 142; cf. Kamakau 1964, 8).

5. Thus the kauwā were assimilated to the soles of the feet (Remy 1859, 19).

6. Indeed, several statements show that there is a correspondence between the purity or impurity of the ritual performer and the purity or impurity of his deities. Thus Kamakau writes that the kahunas "who did not keep their bodies clean and did not obey the laws of the land as well as those of the akua were likely to be led wrongly by their "angel watchmen" (anela kia'i), and their work would

be made erroneous. Evil spirits (*'uhane 'ino*) would aid them, and their work would be wrong" (Kamakau 1964, 95–96).

7. That sorcery involves impurity is demonstrated by several facts, some of which have already been mentioned. Thus, sorcerers must manipulate parts of corpses or aborted fetuses from which they "make" gods such as the *'unihipili* (cf. chap. 1 and Malo 1951, 105). Both royal sorcery and other forms of sorcery involve the use of "bait" (*maunu*), that is, exuviae from the body of the intended victim. These probably attract the god and direct him against the victim. But such exuviae are impure; therefore both sorcerer and god must be made impure by them (on the impurity of the sorcerer who uses "bait," see Kamakau 1964, 37).

Finally Kamakau writes: "The work (*'oihana*) of learning the magical prayers, the *pule 'ana'ana*, was a laborious undertaking, filthy and deadly and dangerous (*po'oko'i*); one that required the eating of disgusting and poisonous foods [probably used as offerings—V. V.]" (Kamakau 1964, 120).

8. The impurity of these forms of the gods is confirmed by the fact that Malo connects the so-called Kālaipāhoa gods (among whom one finds the sorcery forms of Kāne; cf. Valeri 1982b, 26, 28), with the *'unihipili*, who are most impure (Malo 1951, 82).

9. For instance, among the main gods, Kū marries his sister Hina (Fornander 1916–20, 4:192; 5:266; cf. NK, 2:86); Kāne, his sister La'ila'i (*Kumulipo*, line 702).

10. In some respects Dumont's relational view of purity in India recalls Vernant's earlier statement about the pure and the impure in ancient Greece (Vernant 1980, 125–28). At the same time, the Greek case is somewhat closer to the Hawaiian one, in that the Greek gods could be polluted (ibid., 112).

Jean Smith (1974) has demonstrated that Maori gods are polluted by humans, indeed that they have to be. This Polynesian case indirectly confirms my claim that Hawaiian gods may be made impure by human actions.

11. Dumont's own contrast with what he believes to be the "Polynesian" system is quite wrong, because, following Steiner, he thinks that Polynesians make no distinction between pure and impure: "the sacred is left undifferentiated in its opposition to the profane," he writes (1959, 29). But nothing could be further from the truth, as already noted by Jean Smith (1974, 93): the ambivalence of the sacred should not be confused with the undifferentiation of its polar opposites.

12. High-ranking ali'i must also be preserved from the pollution of death (cf. Malo 1951, 96–104; Kamakau 1964, 35). Note also that for a high-ranking woman the loss of virginity involves a loss of purity and mana (cf. Beckwith 1919, 510–12; Fornander 1916–20, 4:545; 5:188).

13. That hierarchy manifests itself on the syntagmatic axis is what should be expected. Jakobson has noted that any linguistic disorder involving the axis of combination "damages the capacity for maintaining the hierarchy of linguistic units" (1971, 254).

14. In this respect *la'a* is reminiscent of the biblical notion of "contagious holiness," which "is conceived of as being virtually tangible, a physical entity, the existence and activity of which can be sensorially perceived. Any person or object coming into contact with the altar (Exod. 29:37) becomes 'holy,' that is, contracts holiness and, like the tabernacle appurtenances themselves, becomes consecrated. At the opposite extreme there is a tangible, contagious defilement" (Haran 1978, 176).

15. The history of the interpretation of mana remains to be written. Brief surveys of the earlier interpretations of this notion can be found in Lehmann (1922) and Firth (1967).

16. I thank professor Keesing for sending me a copy of his paper, which I found very helpful and which prompted me to reorganize somewhat the original version of this section.

17. "Efficacious" is a meaning often given to mana by lexicographers (cf. Tregear 1891, 203; Williams 1971, 172). The idea that in central Polynesia the primary meaning of mana is efficacy is also found in Williamson (1937, 110; cf. also Capell 1938, 95).

Hubert and Mauss had already noted that mana is "l'éfficacité véritable des choses, qui corrobore leur action mécanique sans l'annihiler" (Hubert and Mauss 1978, 104).

18. In some contexts, therefore, the notion of mana can be compared to that of "honor" or even "baraka" (cf. Blake Palmer 1946; Pitt-Rivers 1974). Mauss himself compared mana to "honor." Pitt-Rivers (1974, 6) sees in this a "startling insight." In reality, mana was often translated as "honor" well before Mauss (see, for example, Tregear 1891, 203).

19. "Make no kekahi kanaka i mea e mana ai ua kii ohia la," "A man was put to death (sacrificed) to make the 'ōhi'a image [which represents the god Kū] mana" (Mooolelo Hawaii 1838, 76; Pogue 1858, 32).

20. "E Kihanuilulumoku / ko makou akua mana," "O Kihanuilulumoku / Our god of mana" (Fornander 1916–20, 5:413); "Lono-a, ke akua mana," "Lono, the god of mana" (prayer noted by N. Emerson in Malo 1951, 178); "Ke akua mana," "the god of mana" (ibid., 180); "Kane ke akua mana," "Kane the god of mana" (ibid., 184). "O Ku ka inoa o ko Palila akua, he akua mana a me ka ikaika loa," "Ku is the name of the god of Palila, a god which has mana and much strength" (Fornander 1916–20, 5:149–51; cf. as well Malo 1951, 117; Kamakau 1961, 180).

21. Malo 38.24; 35.2; Fornander 1916–20, 5:367. Cf. also the prayer given by N. Emerson (in Malo 1951, 185), where the expression "mana i ka lani," "mana in the sky," probably refers both to the god in the sky and to the king, one of whose titles is lani.

22. The kahuna heal diseases and work hana mana, "works of mana," "miracles," by means of mana obtained from the gods (Kamakau 1961, 211; Malo 1951, 103). This is why they are called kanaka mana, "men endowed with mana" (Fornander 1916–20, 4:265, cf. 293, 295, 297). Mana is a component of the name of some priests; for example, Laeanuikaumanamana is the name of the high priest of Kings Kihanui and Līloa (Fornander 1878–80, 2:114).

23. Some examples are "He pule mana ko me[a]," "a powerful prayer has such a one" (Ellis 1842, 295); "'oihana mana," "rites or prayers which have and produce mana" (Ii 1869d); "the mana of prayers and the help of the god saved him" (Kamakau 1961, 23).

24. Thus, the 'ōhi'a image (ki'i 'ōhi'a), which represents the god Kū in the rites of the luakini temple, is made mana (Pogue 1858, 32). The term mana is also the predicate of natural objects that are considered the manifestations of a god. For example, Kamakau mentions the existence of a rock called Kūmanamana ("Kū who has great mana") or Pōhakumanamana ("rock which has great mana") (Kamakau 1961, 222; cf. NK, 2:123).

25. For example, the 'aha mana, or ritual cord, mentioned by Malo 37.87. We will see the role it plays in the rites of the luakini temple.

26. One should also mention the "works of mana," or "miracles" (hana mana), that the priests are able to perform because of their relation to the gods. The following text illustrates the relationship established between the mana of the gods, the mana of priests, and hana mana:

He mau kanaka haipule hoi, a ua oleloia
They [two priests] were also religious men, and it was said of them
he mau kanaka mana laua
that they were men gifted with mana
a he hiki ia laua ke hana i na hana mana
and that they were able to perform works of mana
he nui ma ka inoa o ko Keawenuiaumi akua
numerous in the name of the god of Keawenui the son of 'Umi
a me ko laua akua hoi
and of their own god as well.
[Fornander 1916–20, 4:265]

27. See the *pule kuwā* prayer, reported by Emerson in Malo 1951, 184, and translated by me in chapter 8. This text uses the substantive, stative, and intransitive forms of mana to refer to the same event.

28. Note that it can be nominalized, as in the expression "*he hoomananui ana ko ka luakini*," "numerous rites of the *luakini*" (Malo MS, 178–79).

29. *Kaumaha*, as a sacrificial rite, belongs to the class of actions called *ho'omana*.

30. For examples see note 20 and the already-quoted expression "*o ka mana o na ali'i maluna o ka 'aina*," "the mana of the ali'i over the land" (Kamakau 1961, 229). Examples in which gods are the possessors include: "*ka mana o ke akua*," "the mana of the god" (Fornander 1916–20, 5:147); "*ka mana o ka pua'a*," "the mana of Kamapua'a" (Kahiolo 1978, 25); "*ka mana o Kane a me Kanaloa*," "the mana of Kane and Kanaloa" (Fornander 1916–20, 5:197); "*ka mana o ka Wahine*," "the woman's [here, the goddess Laka] mana" (Emerson 1965, 17, line 23).

Chapter 4

1. The second criterion implies that a dimension of Hawaiian hierarchy involves a "scale of forms" type of classification, in which the variable "is identical with the generic essence itself" (Collingwood 1933, 60).

2. The chiefess Kalaniakua also "was . . . allowed to climb about the tabu heiaus of the tabu gods, so high was her tabu" (Kamakau 1961, 260). Nevertheless, tradition does not say that she was permitted to consecrate sacrifices in the state temples.

3. "*Ua laa ia mau mea a pau na ke akua; nolaila, aole pono ka wahine e ai*" (Kepelino 1932, 65). Beckwith, Kepelino's editor, translates this passage as, "all these things were dedicated to God, hence women could not eat them" (p. 64). For my part, I would give the word *la'a* a more "substantialist" meaning (see chap. 3): these species are sacred because they partake of the divine substance (see also Kamakau 1961, 222–23).

4. On the king's right to reserve turtles and whales washed upon the shores of his realm for himself, see Kamakau 1961, 129; Malo 1951, 189; and the chant *Haui ka lani*, in Fornander 1916–20, 6:375, line 107. On his right to consecrate man-eating sharks (*niuhi*), see Fornander 1878–80, 2:271. European sailors noted that kings received with pleasure these sharks as presents (Dixon 1789, 101) and considered them "an inestimable treasure" (Portlock 1789, 180).

5. The whale is a metaphor for the warrior (cf. Kamakau 1961, 80), that is, a violent and uncontrollable power.

6. Since Kāne is closely associated with Kanaloa and sometimes indiscernible from him, the *hīhīmanu* and the cetaceans—like all great ocean fish, moreover—are sometimes assimilated with Kāne (see Fornander 1916–20, 6:363).

7. The whale is considered the sign of a rather threatening god-produced event: its appearance announces a storm (Green and Beckwith 1928, 15). As for the porpoise, it is closely linked with the shark (Titcomb and Pukui 1972, 113), a dangerous fish used to sanction human transgressions, as we have already seen.

8. Even before the official abolition of the taboo system in 1819, women of the common people began, in the last part of King Kamehameha's reign, to cook, garden, and even fish! (Kamakau 1961, 238–39). It seems that this modification of the traditional rules came about because the men were obliged to work for the king to provide him with sandalwood to sell.

9. According to Bennett (1930, 60), women could prepare poi only on the island of Kaua'i.

10. The *Mooolelo Hawaii* assures us, in fact, that the woman cannot eat her share until after her husband has finished his (*"a ma ka mua ke kane e ai ai a pau ia, alaila ka ka wahine e ai ai"*—Pogue 1858, 24).

11. But the desacralizing role of the women's fire is itself attenuated because this fire is tended by a male cook.

12. Any violation of this separation produces troubles in the functioning of at least one of the terms that must remain separate. For example, if a woman eats taboo foods, her reproductive processes are negatively affected. A European voyager learned thus that Kamehameha "had lately a Child born with only one hand caused as THEY SAY by his Queen eating some Fish that was Tabooed, and to appease the Deity, it is resolved for six Moons that the King and all his Subjects shall not wear any Cloth over their boddies except the Marro Tho' the Taboo allows them to carry their Tappas or Cloak in their hands, and this is Strictly observed, even by Tom Himmy Haw [Kamehameha], himself" (Bishop 1967, 144).

13. "The custom of the country is to have a separate house for each purpose" (Rose de Freycinet in Basset 1962, 150). This explains the high number of houses observed by European travelers. For instance, in 1812 in Honolulu, there were 740 houses for 2,025 inhabitants (Ross 1904, 61), that is, 2.7 inhabitants per house. If we admit that each *kauhale* was composed of five houses, we have a total of 13.5 inhabitants per domestic group. This urban average must be higher than the rural one.

The abolition of the taboo system brought with it the abolition of most specialized houses. Thus, in Honolulu in 1822, only 550 houses were found for a population that was twice as large as that of 1812 (4,000 inhabitants—MH, October 1823, 315). Moreover, 50 of these houses were not inhabited at all. In another town, Lāhainā (on the island of Maui), there were 400 houses for 2,500 residents in 1824 (MH, February 1825, 39–45).

14. Boys were admitted into the *hale mua* at the age of five or six (Malo 1951, 27–28; Handy and Pukui 1972, 9; Handy 1972, 302).

15. Iselin (n.d., 76), Lisiansky (1814, 127), and Malo (1951, 29) all state that men are admitted to the *hale 'aina*, but they are contradicted by the 1838 and 1858 *Mooolelo* and by accounts of eighteenth-century voyagers. It must again be recalled that because of the modifications of Hawaiian society in the early nineteenth century, some customs ceased to be strictly enforced, especially among the common people. On the prohibition against women's entering the men's house on pain of death, see also Campbell 1967, 131; Corney 1896, 100; Patterson 1817, 68–69.

16. According to some travelers, menstruating women had to leave inhabited places and hide in the mountain forest, where they stayed for three days when they had their periods and ten days when they delivered (Campbell 1967, 137; Iselin, n.d., 71; Patterson 1817, 69; Hussey 1958, 35; Shaler 1935, 93). During these

times of impurity, men and women could not meet, look at one another, or speak, on pain of death (Hussey 1958, 35; Iselin, n.d., 71; Shaler 1935, 93; Kamakau 1961, 3).

17. "The nobility here are not permitted to borrow, or to take any fire from one of the commonality; but must provide it themselves, or obtain it from their equals" (Lisiansky 1814, 127). As a general rule, fires are hierarchized. Consequently, what is cooked on one fire must remain separate from what is cooked on another (cf. Kotzebue 1821a, 1:310: "Not only the pork, but all the dishes were taboo, because they had been dressed over the same fire"). This separation involves pipes as well: "The multiplicity of tarboos, renders it necessary for almost every person to have a pipe of their own, as it would be derogatory to any one to have their pipe used by a person of inferior grade, and some of them are tarbooed to use no pipe but their own, and no fire but what is generated purposely for them, and to suffer no other person whatever to use either their pipe or their fire" (Whitman 1979, 20).

18. "The King, queens and principal chiefs remained with us all day, and had their dinner sent on board to them, not being allowed to eat ship provisions" (Corney 1896, 36). The priest of the Hikiau temple, Iselin recounts, "will partake of nothing cooked at our fire, even to light his pipe, a candle or coal will not do, but he would only use the fire struck with flint and steel" (n.d., 71).

19. "We understand that Kamehameha was to be put under a taboo in the evening which was to continue for ten days, in consequence of his having eaten with us, who profaned ourselves by eating with women" (Menzies 1920, 98–99).

20. Cf. Menzies 1920, 78–79; Whitman 1979, 79.

21. This is because, "the higher a person's rank is, the more sacred are the duties he has to perform" (Kotzebue 1821a, 1:332).

22. The purity of the food eaten by the ali'i must be preserved even when the food is still raw. If raw food has been polluted by contact with the impure parts of an inferior's body, it is taboo for an ali'i (Fornander 1916–20, 4:188) and will not be cooked for him.

23. One remark concerning the order in which the cups are served. Here as elsewhere the fundamental principle is that the most honorable part is given to the highest-ranking person. However, while for other foods this part is the first one, in the 'awa rite it is the last. Why this irregularity? Titcomb, after an attentive examination of the sources, arrives at the following conclusion: "It is likely that the last cup, being the most potent because it contained the residue of 'awa, was the one carrying the greatest honour and would go to the highest chief, who would therefore have to wait for his cup. The chief second in rank would receive the first cup and others would take their turn according to their rank" (1948, 130). This conclusion seems indirectly confirmed by two texts, in which the "intoxicating portion" (ka 'ona o ka 'awa), which is also the last, of a cup of 'awa goes to the eldest brother in one case (Fornander 1916–20, 5:365), to the divine sisters in the other (ibid., 311). To receive the most potent cup means to become the most intoxicated and therefore the closest of all to the gods, for drunkenness is the experience of self-transcendence. Thus there is no violation here of the fundamental principle presiding over the division of food: through food, the highest-ranking man is the closest to the god, whether he eats the first portion or the most efficacious one, as in the case of 'awa. Note, however, that even in the 'awa rite the order of succession corresponds to the order of rank for everyone except the ali'i of the highest rank; moreover, several cases are also reported in which the highest-ranking person is served first, not last (Titcomb 1948, 130–31; Beckwith 1940, 94).

24. The prayer uttered (and sometimes chanted, see King's text cited above,

p. 125) by the priest before the ali'i drinks his cup of 'awa is called lelea (Ii 1963, 58–59). It makes the essence of the 'awa fly away (lele) to the gods (PE, 186).

25. During a good part of the remaining months the temples are closed. Consequently, sacrifices of pigs do not take place and it is forbidden to eat the flesh of this animal, as well as all foods used sacrificially.

26. Kepelino explicitly says that the priests' food is constituted by "na mea i mohaia na ke Akua," "the things sacrificed [mohaia] to the god" (1932, 23). Since alimentary prescriptions concerning priests do not generally seem to be different from those imposed on ali'i, Kepelino's remark applies to the ali'i as well. (See, for example, the description of the meal of the priests given above; King observes that the meal of the ali'i follows the same rules.)

Patterson's comment about the ali'i's consumption of 'awa, that they "partake of the liquor as in a sacrament" (1817, 67), can be extended to their entire meal, of which 'awa forms only the beginning. ("If other things were given, 'awa came first"—Kauea [1867] in Titcomb 1948, 139.)

27. Emerson translates: "He [the ali'i—V. V.] was then permitted to eat of pork that had been baked in an oven outside of the heiau—but not of that which had been put to death by strangulation, in the manner ordinarily practiced, and then baked in an oven outside the heiau without religious rites" (Malo 1951, 138). Here is the text and a word-for-word translation:

Ai oia i ka puaa i kaluaia ma ka heiau,
He eats the pig cooked in the oven in the temple,
Aole no e ai i ka puaa umi wale,
He does not eat the strangled pig
A ka lua wale, aole ma ka heiau, me ka pule ia
And cooked in the oven not in the temple, with the prayer
    [Malo 35.18]

We see that Emerson makes an error (Malo does not say that the ali'i can eat pork cooked outside the temple, but precisely the opposite) and adds a sentence that does not come in the text ("in the manner ordinarily practiced"). It follows that the meaning of Malo's sentence is altered; he establishes an opposition not between an "extraordinary" way of eating pork and an "ordinary" one, but between the way appropriate for an ali'i and an inappropriate, or even forbidden, way.

28. An eyewitness even states that the consumption of "marked" species can take place exclusively in the temples of the community: "After entering the sacred enclosures [temples], no person can eat of any of these kinds of articles [sacrificial species], except they have been previously consecrated in the Morai or temple" (Shaler 1935, 92).

29. These occasions are above all rites to initiate boys into the hale mua, and also incision rites, or even some healing rites.

30. Since the consumption of pork is an exclusively ritual act, it naturally ensues that people of high rank, whose lives are penetrated with ritual, are primarily those who eat pork. This state of affairs moves one European observer to state, "The Hogs are to the Natives of very little value, as their religion prohibits their eating of Pork, but in very sparing quantities" (Bell 1929–30, 1:63). (This incidentally explains why the Hawaiians were in a position to provide fabulous quantities of pork to European ships. Instead of giving pigs to the gods they began to sell them to the sailors. Before that time came, however, they sacrificed pigs to Europeans as to their gods—cf. Sahlins 1979, 1981).

Bananas and coconuts are also eaten primarily by ali'i and priests. Bananas "were sometimes restricted to the chiefs and priests for consumption at ceremonial fests" (Handy 1972, 165). As for coconuts, their consumption by commoners must not have been frequent, since it seems that the ali'i had the monopoly on coconut palms (cf. Ii 1963, 113). This is indicated, I believe, by the fact that a coconut tree can be felled only by a very high-ranking ali'i (Kamakau 1961, 120) and that ali'i are reported to provide coconuts to commoners in exchange for *olonā* fibers or other products (ibid., 306, 308).

It is above all '*awa* (*Piper methysticum*), rare in Hawaii, that is reserved for the ali'i when they communicate with the gods. The first European observers are quite positive on this point and on the prohibition against women's drinking it (Cook and King 1784, 2:127; Dixon 1789, 102–3, 252–53; Quimper 1937, 6; cf. Ellis 1842, 381). In an article published in 1873, a Hawaiian writes, "When the whites first came to this archipelago, and in the years following, *awa* was not much drunk by the people for it was unobtainable. Only the chiefs, the *kahunas*, and members of the royal household had *awa* to drink. *Awa* was not much planted in those days but later when many of the ancient *kapus* were abolished, the common people began to drink it" (in Titcomb 1948, 137). However, Titcomb thinks it possible to conclude that commoners and women consumed '*awa*: "It is possible to assume that '*awa* was used by both chiefs and commoners, but what the commoners were denied was the right to indulge to the point of dissipation" (ibid., 138). But the facts Titcomb uses to support this hypothesis are sparse and all date from the nineteenth century.

According to Handy (1972, 193), only some varieties of '*awa* were sacred and reserved for the nobles. This is also Beckwith's opinion: "Only the most common variety could be used by the commoner; the rarer kinds were reserved for the chiefs. For the gods and on ceremonial occasions the moi (royal), hiwa (black) and papa (recumbent) were used, the papa from which the moi was often an offshoot, being especially offered to female deities" (1940, 94). It is indeed likely that '*awa* of inferior varieties was used by commoners in their rites (cf. Malo 1951, 89 and Kamakau 1976, 133).

31. Besides the ali'i, "the Priests only enter the morair [temples—V. V.], and the common people have nothing to do in matters of [state—V. V.] religion" (Whitman 1979, 23).

32. The connection between the ali'i's meal and those of his subordinates is often indicated by the ali'i's distribution of the less prized parts of his food to those of his dependents who are present.

33. Kekuaokalani, Liholiho's cousin who took up arms to fend off the transgressors and restore the taboo system, accused the Regent (Ka'ahumanu, Kamehameha's widow) and her brothers of having "poussé le roi au manger libre ['*ai noa*] et à l'abolition de leurs *kapu* de chefs" (*Mooolelo*, trans. Remy 1862, 141).

Chapter 5

1. The term *kahuna* can denote any expert or artisan with technical knowledge (see Kamakau 1961, 176–77).

2. Hale'ole writes that the occupation ('*oihana*) of the priests is knowledge ('*ike*) (Fornander 1916–20, 6:57). On priests as experts in different rituals, see Malo 1951, 59, 97, 189, 197; Fornander 1916–20, 6:9.

3. "The priest office in Hawaii nei is an office whereby man had connected himself with God" (Kaulia in HEN, 1:156, cf. Kamakau 1964, 95). "Each division priest had a god" (Fornander 1916–20, 6:70).

4. "Le respect que ces sauvages ont pour leurs prêtres, va presque jusqu'à l'adoration: ils regardent leurs personnes comme sacrées" (Franchère 1820, 57).

5. This is an important condition of the efficacy of sacrifice in many religious systems (cf. Loisy 1920, 33–34, 77).

6. This is why knowledge is not sufficient in itself; it is essential that it be possessed by someone who is in relation to the god over which the knowledge has its effects: "If priestly calling was being taught by some one without a god, then knowledge of the priesthood could not be imparted by such a one" (Fornander 1916–20, 6:70). On the idea that the efficacy of the rite also depends on the divine mana inherent in the kahuna, see Malo 1951, 103; Kamakau 1964, 95.

7. "A person into whom a god entered was regarded as a god during the time of possession" (Beckwith 1940, 106).

8. Thus the kahu, guardian and bearer of a god's image, is identified with this god (N. Emerson in Malo 1951, 80, n. 1; cf. Ii 1963, 75).

9. The equivalence of victim and sacrificer is sometimes indicated by the name or title given to the sacrificer. Thus, the sons and heirs of one high priest are named after his sacrificial victims: Kapua'aolomea, "the striped hog," and Kapua'ahiwa, "the sacred black pig" (Fornander 1916–20, 5:322, n. 25). The title of the sacrificer of a hula company, po'o pua'a, "pig's head," also indicates the equivalence of sacrificer and victim, since this sacrificer gives the head of the sacrificial pig to the dance deities (Emerson 1965, 26).

10. It will also be remarked that, as some natural species are supposed to be the bodies of a certain god because they evoke his characteristics, some persons are viewed as the god's body for the same reason. For example, "a brown-haired woman (ehu) belongs to the Pele family and may be Pele herself or one of her spirit followers in human form" (Beckwith 1940, 136). Such individuals are inevitably destined for the priesthood or related functions. At times the priest is metaphorically assimilated to a part of the god's body, for example one of his eyes (cf. Ellis 1842, 266).

11. They must even avoid mentioning impure things or hearing them mentioned (Ii 1869c).

12. Except, apparently, in cases of mourning (Campbell 1967, 101; Marin 1973, 230; Ellis 1842, 175; Arning 1931, 10, pl. 2; portrait of Kamehameha by Tikhanov in Golovnin 1979) or war (cf. Cook and King 1784, 3:134). But those who take part in funerals or warfare are automatically polluted. Thus, either the sacred persons avoid participating in either event or else they lose their purity, at least temporarily. Another possibility is that by their presence they put an end to battle (cf. Ii 1963, 52; Kamakau 1961, 88).

13. A priest's life is not all ease, then. As the saying emphasizes, "The paths of the priests are narrow and can never be reached by crawling" (Fornander 1916–20, 4:444). On the ascetic ideal of the priests, see Arago 1822, 179.

14. For the taboo on the kahuna's garments, see Kepelino 1932, 19, 22–23.

15. According to Elbert and Pukui (1979, 82) the word kahuna derives from kahu plus the nonproductive nominalizing suffix -na, which in this context means "person."

16. Note that the reduplication of kahu, kahukahu, means "offer sacrifices to the gods" (see Andrews 1865, 246; Tregear 1891, 444; PE, 106).

17. "Kahunas were sought in the chiefly family which had the right of the kahuna from their parents as ancestors" (Kepelino 1932, 60).

18. Kepelino's statement (1932, 140) that priests belong to the ali'i class is valid for the kahuna pule, but it is extremely doubtful that it applies to the other

categories. Likewise, when Malo states that priests are used by ali'i and not by commoners, he is probably referring to the *kahuna pule* only (1951, 81–82).

19. The priests' inferiority to the ali'i is even indicated by the natural signs that are supposed to announce their respective presence. While a priest is announced by a single rainbow, a high-ranking ali'i is announced by two rainbows (Fornander 1916–20, 4:238). In short, one ali'i equals two priests.

20. What Fornander writes with respect to Tahitian priests is also true of Hawaiian priests. They are "delegates of the presiding chief for religious purposes" (1878–80, 1:109). Thus in a Hawaiian legend we read, "Counselors and priests are retained and cared for to be used by the chiefs" (Fornander 1916–20, 4:264).

The custom of delegating some taboo services to inferiors or younger siblings is of broad application in Hawaii. Here is a rather striking example. To make it possible for sacred ali'i to participate in the construction of Pu'ukoholā temple, Kamehameha ordered his younger brother Keali'imaika'i to take on temporarily all the taboos of the ali'i. This had the effect of making all high-ranking nobles free of any taboo and therefore able to work (Kamakau 1961, 154–55). As usual, the part can substitute for the whole.

21. Kamakau calls the order of Kū the "order of Holoa'e" and that of Lono the "order of Kuali'i" (1964, 7). Holoa'e was the chaplain serving Kamehameha during the first part of his reign (ibid.; cf. Valeri 1982b).

22. Moreover, priests could earn their living through nonpriestly activities as well (Shaler 1935, 92). In the sources we find numerous references to priests who are also warriors (Kamakau 1961, 163; Thrum 1909, 47; Shaler 1935, 81, 92).

23. The title of *kahuna nui* can, however, be also attributed to a priest who masters all branches of knowledge (according to Haleole in Fornander 1916–20, 6:71).

24. Some high priests belonged, moreover, to the order of Lono. For example, Ka'oleiokū, King 'Umi's *kahuna nui*, "descended from the priestly line of Lono" (Kamakau 1961, 12).

25. Without the cooperation of the *kahuna nui*, the king risks losing the gods' support and thus his legitimacy (cf. Fornander 1878–80, 2:222, 146; Fornander 1916–20, 5:320; Anonymous 1924, 127–28, 132; Kamakau 1961, 129). Even after the abolition of the taboo system, the last high priest maintained "encore beaucoup de considération parmi ses concitoyens," and the most important nobles regularly gave him gifts (Duhaut-Cilly 1834–35, 2:311).

26. Not only does the king offer the principal sacrifices, but he is familiar with all branches of the ritual (Kepelino 1932, 62–63). Whitman goes so far as to say that the king is also a high priest (1979, 85; cf. MH, July 1820, 335).

27. Kamakau describes the areas of competence of these two classes in this way: "Another ancient art was that of the diviners who revealed hidden things about the land, called "Pointers-out-of-sandhills" (*Kuhikuhi pu'uone*) and "Class of changes on the earth" (*Papahulihonua*). They were able to find things hidden away from the eyes of men; they could locate water in places where water had not been found. They knew the land boundaries from Hawaii to Kauai; the running of the affairs of government, how to handle people, the location and building of houses" (1961, 242).

28. The last five classes in the list belong to the *kilokilo*, "diviner," category (Hale'ole in Fornander 1916–20, 6:75, 83–87; Malo 1951, 112). *Kilokilo* also select the best sites for building a house and lay out its plans and orientation (Hale'ole in Fornander 1916–20, 6:59–65, 77–83).

29. For more details, see Kamakau 1964, 99–128; Malo 1951, 107–9, 245; Ii 1963, 46–48; Hale'ole in Fornander 1916–20, 6:87–91.

30. Sorcery (*kuni*) is a branch of '*anā'anā* (Kamakau 1964, 122; Malo 1951, 100–103); the art called *ho'opi'opi'o* is similar to '*anā'anā*, according to Hale'ole (Fornander 1916–20, 6:74). The *kahuna hui* class was apparently connected with royal sorcery (Malo 1951, 105; cf. Valeri 1982b, on the *hui* temples).

31. They are often called "remnant eaters (*aihamu*)" (Hale'ole in Fornander 1916–20, 6:74), a name that clearly indicates their "residual" and "marginal" nature. It also means "murdering *kahuna*" (Kamakau 1961, 121), for these "residual" persons are destructive, as is any residue with respect to the system that produces it.

32. It is by repressing his desires that a sorcerer paradoxically succeeds in satisfying them. As Kamakau penetratingly observes, the true sorcerer was the "one who suppressed [I would translate "repressed"] his lusts" (1961, 214). But in this manner he again encounters his desires in the form of the deities that secretly satisfy them (ibid.; 1964, 120). The "true sorcerer," then, is externally the complete opposite of what he is internally and what he does not admit to be: "The true kahuna of this class was a person who lived quietly, was lowly, unassuming, humble of heart, not a gad-about, not a seeker of companions [n.b.], not a pleasure seeker, a proud talker, or covetous" (Kamakau 1961, 214).

33. Rebellions against kings can be fomented by *kāula*, who foretell their downfall following the loss of their divine "mandate" (see, for example, Fornander 1878–80, 1:99).

34. "What indeed is the chief doing in front [of his group]? He is standing to inquire of the gods" (*Haui ka lani* chant, lines 619–20, in Fornander 1916–20, 6:403–4).

35. "To the pious one, to the chief, belongs the island; / To the resident under Ku, the chief greatly loved by Lono; / A precious one to the forty thousand gods" (*Haui i ka lani*, lines 153–55, in Fornander 1916–20, 6:378).

36. The term *mō'ī*, "majesty," "king," was applied to the Hawaiian king only after 1842 and as a result of foreign influence, as Stokes has shown (1932, 2). The terms traditionally used to designate the king are as follows: *ali'i 'ai moku* ("noble who eats the island or district"), *ali'i nui* ("great noble," "supreme noble"), *ali'i nui 'aimoku, ali'i 'ai aupuni* ("noble who eats the kingdom"), or simply *ali'i* ("noble"). Sometimes, and especially as a form of address, the title *Lani* "heaven" is used (Stokes 1932, 11).

But none of these terms are reserved exclusively for the king, except perhaps *ali'i 'ai moku* (cf. von Chamisso in Kotzebue 1821a, 3:245–46 [informant, John Young]; Stokes 1932, 11–12). At any rate, the term most frequently used in the Hawaiian texts is the most unmarked, ali'i. Only the context permits one to determine if the term refers simply to a member of the nobility or to the king.

37. Following Dickey, without, however, naming him, the translators of the Kamapua'a chant (Kahiolo 1978) have decided to render *akua* by "ghosts." Thus they translate, "The chiefs of Kona are ghosts." Rather than admitting that the ali'i are considered "gods," they prefer to believe that they are considered as "ghosts," which seems absurd. At any rate this translation only displaces the problem, for "ghosts" are obviously put in the same class as gods, since they bear the same name (*akua*). Thus, the equation ali'i = *akua* still holds.

38. "*Na 'li'i wela kua*," "the great chiefs of divine descent" (Ii 1963, 152).

39. This is why I preferred not to use them in the discussion above.

40. The most notable of these animals are the shark (Fornander 1916–20, 6:393–94, lines 388–91; Pukui and Korn 1973, 4–5), the stingray, the frigate bird (Pukui and Korn 1973, 4–5), the '*io* bird, the '*a'o* bird, the *moano* fish, the

wild pig (Fornander 1916–20, 6:380, 381 lines 191, 192–94, 199, 204), and the *ulua* fish (Fornander 1916–20, 5:266).

41. He is the "vital breath" (*ka hā*) of the land (Fornander 1916–20, 6:405, line 646) or its soul (*'uhane*) (Fornander 1916–20, 6:370, lines 28–29).

42. Thus, in the *Haui ka lani* chant Kamehameha is called Kohala, after the district over which he reigns (Fornander 1916–20, 6:391, line 359); Puna is the name given to the ali'i ruling the district of Puna (line 47, p. 371; see also Beckwith 1940, 403, 413).

43. Thus the sacrifice of the rulers of Ka'ū and Puna transforms these lands into "putrefied meats" because the corpses of their kings have rotted; by dragging their corpses to the sacrificial altar (cf. Kamakau 1976, 142), Kamehameha "drags" the districts over which they reigned, that is, he appropriates them (Fornander 1916–20, 6:375, line 116; 377, lines 138–40, 143–44; 378, line 149; 395, line 429; cf. ibid., 4:215, 5:46).

44. The rainbow is called *he 'ehu wāwae no ka lani*, "a trace of the high chief's steps" (PE, 36). It always hovers above an ali'i of royal rank (Fornander 1916–20, 4:134, 168, 188, 218, 238, 244, 532, 546; Beckwith 1919, 334, 348, 398, 494, 540, 570, 578; Kamakau 1961, 11, 24, etc.).

45. The king is identified with the sun (see Pukui and Korn 1973, 18; cf. Ii 1963, 73). Stars are named after the ali'i (Beckwith 1951, 122). Ali'i are sometimes identified with clouds (Kepelino 1977, 60; Fornander 1916–20, 6:404, line 630); thus the imminent arrival of royal visitors can be deduced from the appearance of clouds having peculiar shapes (Fornander 1916–20, 5:166; Beckwith 1919, 394, 514).

46. We have seen that *akua* refers to the full moon, which is perfectly circular.

47. The king is called *o ka papa o ka lewa*, "the foundation of heaven" (Fornander 1916–20, 4:284).

48. The missionaries, naturally, thought otherwise: "Eating, drinking, sleeping, bathing, gambling &c. consume most of the time of the king and chiefs" (MH, April 1821, 118; cf. Stewart 1839, 108). On the other hand, no one ever accused the missionaries of wasting their time washing.

49. For example, Kūkā'ilimoku (Ii 1963, 95) and Kūnuiākea (Cook and King 1784, 3:7) have the *kapu moe*; these state gods thus have the same rank as ali'i of the *pi'o* rank.

50. The nurse of an ali'i of divine rank must completely disrobe before giving him the breast (Kepelino 1932, 126; NK, 2:29).

51. See, for example, the farewell to the people of Hawaii improvised by Queen Kamāmalu at the time of her departure for London (Kuykendall 1938, 77–78). According to Hawaiian ideology, poetry makes invisible realities manifest; this is why composers of chants are called "seekers of unseen things" (Kamakau 1961, 132).

52. "The body of the King is sacred" (Kamakau 1961, 335). The most sacred part of his body is the head, where, according to Pukui (NK, 1:189), ancestral deities (*'aumakua*) are supposed on occasion to reside. (Regarding taboos concerning the head of the ali'i, see Cox 1831, 53; Corney 1896, 47; Ruschenberger 1970, 2:333; Patterson 1817, 69; Iselin, n.d., 71).

53. Or to pollute the sacred places in which their mana is incorporated (cf. Fornander 1878–80, 2:243; Kamakau 1961, 160).

54. That the divine members of the royal lineage are conceived of as the foundation of the social body is indicated, among other things, by the vigor with

which the Hawaiians try to avenge their degradation at the hands of the enemy. Thus, war between the districts of Hilo and Kona is provoked by the desacralization of an ali'i of Hilo by the ali'i of Kona (Kamakau 1961, 62). When King Lonoikamakahiki beats his wife and cousin and commits the enormity of hitting her on the head, his people rebel against him (Fornander 1916–20, 4:272–74).

55. The king is called *ka lani makua*, "the father king" (Fornander 1916–20, 6:372, line 55). When Kamehameha becomes king of the island of Hawai'i, the poet chants, "*Noho hookahi makua i luna o ka moku*," "One only parent now rules over the land" (Fornander 1916–20, 6:372, line 56).

56. The king has the right to have sexual relations with any woman of common rank (NK, 2:91). Generally he is welcomed by these women; it is even an honor to consecrate virgins to him so that he may deflower and fecundate them (cf. Kekoa 1865). Moreover, the inferior always offers his women to a superior, even when the latter is a missionary (Ruggles, in the *Boston Recorder*, 21 April 1821).

57. "Thou art satisfied with food, thou common man / To be satisfied with land is for the chief" (Fornander 1916–20, 6:386, lines 276–77; cf. Beckwith 1919, 310, n. 1; Fornander 1916–20, 6:400, lines 540–46).

58. For example, the mythical shark Manokalanipō engenders the shark Kawelo, who engenders the king of the same name (Beckwith 1940, 439, 447; Malo 1951, 170). Sharks are represented in myths as ali'i, and one never tires of telling their stories and adventures (Beckwith 1940, 138).

59. These birds are the owl and the frigate bird (Malo 1951, 38, 40). Added to their feathers are those of migratory birds, which, by uniting opposite terms, evoke the ali'i as a totalizing force. These birds are the *nēnē* (goose), which unites mountain and shore by its seasonal migrations (Malo 1951, 40), and the *koa'e*, "tropic bird," which Malo classes with those which "dwell in the mountains by night, but during the day fly out to sea to fish for food" (1951, 40).

60. An episode of the myth of Lonoikamakahiki demonstrates that the *kāhili* is considered equivalent to the land (Fornander 1916–20, 4:280).

61. Hence their immense value (cf. Kamakau 1961, 109). Giving Vancouver a cape adorned with feathers to take to the king of England, Kamehameha assured him that it was "the most valuable thing in the island of Owhyhee [Hawaii]" (Vancouver 1801, 3:263; cf. Menzies 1920, 68).

62. Malo seems to imply that the king controls the partition of land on down into the lower echelons (1951, 192), but he is contradicted by the other sources. Perhaps he describes conditions occurring at the time of Kamehameha.

63. An obvious dissimilarity with the European feudal system, however, is the absence of serfdom (see Shaler 1935, 95; Townsend 1921, 17).

64. Children do not inherit from their father, and they can obtain land only if they manage to replace him in the relationship of allegiance. The latter is thus a personal connection, not transmitted by filiation (cf. Campbell 1967, 98, 122; von Chamisso in Kotzebue 1821a, 3:245–46; Tyerman and Bennett 1832, 2:17; Malo 1951, 60–61; Richards 1973, 21–24; Wilkes 1845, 4:33; Lydgate 1925, 58–60; Kuykendall 1938, 52, 269–70). The rather rare cases of perpetual tenure are limited to powerful lines of nobles or priests who have succeeded in establishing their independence vis-à-vis the sovereign (cf. Kamakau 1961, 219; Fornander 1878–80, 2:103; Lyons 1875a, 3:119; Kalakaua 1888, 290).

65. The quantity of land available is always greater than the labor necessary to cultivate it fully (cf. Handy 1940; Handy 1972, 280).

66. Each parcel has its own name (Lyons 1875a, 1:104), and its bounda-

ries are exactly settled and marked (Iselin, n.d., 67; Shaler 1935, 86, 95; Ellis 1842, 349).

67. These include both the firstfruits proper and the firstfruits harvested on a conventional calendrical date, especially the New Year (see part 3).

68. The use of the term *kanaka* to designate the clients, and more generally, the subordinates (with or without land) of a lord (*haku*) is amply documented by K. Kamakau's description of the *luakini* temple rituals. A term (*iwikuamoʻo*) referring more specifically to servants who are related by blood to their masters also exists (Kamakau 1961, 8).

69. Malo does not explicitly state that all who can trace a genealogical relationship to the king are noble, but this is implied by the association of commoner status with a lack of genealogies and aliʻi status with their possession.

70. "Commoners" mistranslates the word *koneke*, which must refer here to low-ranking clients of the king. Indeed, how could commoners be admitted to the *hale naua* when they were not allowed to preserve their genealogies and did not know the names of their ancestors?

71. "If they are not contented with their present Chiefs, they are allowed to change masters as often as they please" (Dampier 1971, 47; Corney 1896, 105).

72. "The work for the strong is to establish themselves upon the land" (Kamakau 1961, 73).

73. "Should the king die, war would follow, they said" (Ii 1963, 45).

74. According to ʻIʻi, these decisions were made collectively by the nobility after the death of Kalaniʻōpuʻu, who left no instructions (1963, 13). Accounts from Cook's expedition confirm, however, that even before Kalaniʻōpuʻu's death, Kamehameha was in second place for the succession (cf. King 1967, 616). At any rate, the approval of the high-ranking aliʻi was necessary to whomever took the succession.

75. "Keoua knew that he was to die, and those who were with him" (Kamakau 1961, 156).

76. Only his brother Kaʻoleiokū is saved, because he is also the son of Kamehameha by Kāne(i)kapolei, who was Kalaniʻōpuʻu's wife and mother of Keōua (Ii 1963, 7; Kamakau 1961, 208, 311).

77. As several details indicate (for example, his position as chief of Kamehameha's personal guard—cf. Ii 1963, 139), Kekuaōkalani is opposed to Liholiho as a warrior-prince to a priest-prince (cf. Valeri 1982b).

78. In January 1819, shortly before Kamehameha's death, Roquefeuil learned that "on s'attendait à une révolution à la mort de T. [Kamehameha]" (1843, 2:342n).

79. Note in passing another reason for choosing victims to substitute for the sacrifier (king) from among his relatives: there is a good chance that they even resemble the king physically and thus provide particularly adequate "images" of his person. An episode illustrates this. When the rebel chief ʻImakakoloa "was brought [into the temple] to be sacrificed an old *kahu* of his who pitied him shouted out to the chiefs, 'that is not I (makakoloa) the chief, that is I his servant; I can point out to you [the chief! So a young *kahu*, a relative who resembled him, was sacrificed in his place" (Kamakau 1961, 109n).

80. The identity *kauwā* = transgressor is clearly indicated by the descriptions of the sacrificial rite made when the Haku ʻōhiʻa god is fetched (part 3). The man sacrificed on this occasion is a transgressor, but K. Kamakau (p. 13) also writes that he is one abandoned "in the weeds" (*i ka nāhelehele*) (i.e., forsaken).

Now, this epithet is also used to designate the *kauwā*; in fact, they are called the "people of the weeds (*nahelehele*) [*nāhelehele*]" (Malo 1951, 71).

81. The "family" (*'ohana*) of a transgressor is collectively responsible for his transgression (cf. Ii 1963, 23). Consequently, the family members are also killed or take on the status of *kauwā* if they are temporarily spared. The descendants of people who have become *kauwā* are also *kauwā*. Lineages are thereby formed that depend on ali'i (Malo 1951, 68) and from which ali'i can always draw victims for their sacrifices. The companions of an ali'i that according to custom should be sacrificed on his death but who are spared also become *kauwā* (Kamakau 1964, 34). Nevertheless they are spared only in view of future sacrifices, for it is precisely from among the *kauwā* that the victims of funeral sacrifices are chosen (von Chamisso in Kotzebue 1821a, 3:247).

82. We have seen (chap. 3) that no taboo exists between equals (cf. Kamakau 1964, 4).

83. Numerous facts prove that the transgressor is polluted by his transgression. For example, most diseases (which constitute an impurity, as a diminution of the plenitude of being that they effect) are supposed to be sent by the deities to punish transgressions (Kamakau 1964, 95). Moreover, since those who carefully respect taboos are considered pure (ibid.), it must be supposed that those who do not respect them are considered impure (see also Kamakau 1964, 37). Last, transgressions are often eliminated by aspersions or purifying baths (see, for example, Kamakau 1964, 113–14); this obviously implies that the transgressor is in a state of impurity. As for the pollution induced in the person whose taboos have been transgressed, to prove its existence it should be enough to recall that any taboo surrounding a pure sacred being has as its aim to protect his purity; thus it necessarily follows that a transgression of the taboos of this being entails his pollution and that such a pollution can be eliminated only by reconstituting the difference between the pure and the impure that has been abolished by the transgression. The impurity striking the *kauwā* is sufficient by itself to show that transgressors and "transgressed" are equally polluted. In fact, some *kauwā* are transgressors, as we have seen, but others—as defeated and fallen ali'i—can be considered "transgressed."

84. Sometimes the "mothers."

85. "The King always looked with jealousy on any chief who had a wife of as high birth as his own. For this reason mainly, if there were several women of the same or nearly equal high rank, the king felt it important to secure them all as his wives, in order that there might be no possibility for competition on the ground of rank after his death, at least that there might be no danger of the crown going out of his family. On this account and not on account of affection, Kamehameha I had five wives at the same time. For the same reason Kings often married their own sisters" (Richards 1973, 20).

86. See also the myth of Keānini'ulaokalani, which narrates the voyages of two grandparents throughout the whole archipelago in search of a girl identical to their grandson. Only such a girl, indeed, is worthy of becoming his wife (Anonymous 1914; cf. Kamakau 1961, 58–59).

87. There is, however, a logical and factual connection between the idea of royalty and that of twinship. The perfection innate in royalty implies that any plurality manifested within it is a plurality of identical beings. In fact, by definition, two or several perfect beings cannot be different without some of them being imperfect, since their perfection consists in fully instantiating the same type. This explains why some crucial ancestors of royal dynasties are twins: for instance, the two

perfect ancestors, born of incest, who are at the origin of the *kapu moe* (prostration taboo for the high-ranking ali'i) (Fornander 1878–80, 2:293; Kamakau 1961, 223; Beckwith 1940, 410–411). Likewise, the three apical ancestors of the royal dynasties of Kaua'i and O'ahu, the sons of La'amaikahiki, can be likened to triplets, even though their mothers are different, because they are born on the same day and have equally perfect rank (Fornander 1878–80, 2:55). It will also be noted that if in some versions the apical ancestors of the dynasties of Hawai'i and Maui are hierarchized as the youngest or eldest, in others they are considered twins (Fornander 1878–80, 2:26–27).

For cases of twins in royal families, see Beaglehole 1967, 616; Kamakau 1961, 119–20, 86, 310; Ii 1963, 69. The notion of twinship is so highly valorized that it is sometimes extended, for unknown reasons (physical resemblance? the simultaneous birth of two children of the same father from two different mothers?) to half-brothers (Kamakau 1961, 310).

88. "Women in those days were especially devoted to their brothers, and brothers to their sisters" (Kamakau 1961, 315; Fornander 1916–20, 4:608).

89. The genealogy reproduced in figure 2 is based on information contained in the sources above, as well as in Kamakau (1961) and Fornander (1878–80, vol. 2, passim). For a more detailed summary of the genealogy of the ali'i of Kaua'i, see Earle 1978, 176 (based on information given to Earle by D. Barrère).

90. "Kamehameha . . . declared a law that any man who slept with Kaahumanu should be put to death, and this not because he was jealous of her, but because he feared lest some man win her affections and rebel against his government; for a great many of the chiefs were her blood relations" (Kamakau 1961, 189).

91. Cf. Choris: "Deux de ses fils devinrent amoureux de Kahoumanou; il en fut instruit et résolut de les punir; il les étrangla de ses propres mains sur une place publique, en présence du peuple" (1822, 4).

92. As he later sacrificed his enemy "brothers" from O'ahu (Kamakau 1961, 188; Fornander 1878–80, 2:260).

93. Neither Tinker's nor Remy's translation brings out this detail.

94. According to Pukui and Korn (1973, 26), Hāloa probably means "long breath" and "is based on the form *hā*, referring to breath expelled to impart *mana*, 'magical power,' as when a priest would exclaim 'Hā!'" (ibid.). This explanation seems artificial to me. Pukui and Elbert's dictionary accepts the classical translation "long stalk" (p. 51).

95. Malo (1951, 44) tries to deny Wākea's incest. He pretends in fact that Ho'okukalani is in reality the daughter of Komoawa, the priest of Wākea (ibid., 240). It is obvious that this denial is due to the influence of his missionary teachers and loathing of traditional sexual mores (cf. N. Emerson in Malo 1951, ix; Wilkes 1845, 4:6). Wākea's incest is confirmed, moreover, by Kepelino (1932, 66) and by a text composed during the second half of the nineteenth century (Beckwith 1932, 192; see also Thrum 1923, 238; Pukui and Korn 1973, 26; Beckwith 1940, 280). See also the following lines from the *Kumulipo*:

Papa lived with Wakea
Born was the woman Ha'alolo (= Ho'ohokukalani)
Born was jealousy, anger
Papa was deceived by Wakea.
  [Beckwith 1951, 124]

96. The *Kumulipo* attributes these incarnations to Haumea (lines 1764–90), but according to Malo, Papa and Haumea are the same person: "Wakea had a wife

named Haumea, who was the same as Papa" (1951, 5; cf. Barrère 1961, 425; 1969, 45; Beckwith 1940, 280).

Chapter 6

1. The data gathered by Stokes are preserved in his papers, deposited at the Library of the Bishop Museum in Honolulu, where I was able to consult them. On the basis of these notes, Stokes also compiled a long report (dated 21 December 1919, SC Stokes, n.d., GR 1, box 9.47), which was used by Brigham in his deservedly unpublished work on Hawaiian religion (n.d.).

2. "I found that about half of the Hawaiians say '*haiau*'" (McAllister 1933, 8).

3. "The reference made by Mr. Malo in this book to the *mua* as a place to which the *kahuna*, or any one desiring to consult his *aumakua*, or to receive warning or council from heaven in a dream, would go to spend the night, those references I say, are so numerous that there seems to be no doubt that the *mua* and the *heiau* were integrally one" (N. Emerson in Malo 1951, 133).

4. And on the edges of the settlements, according to Stokes (MS Report 1919).

5. This is why they are also called *heiau ho'oūlu i'a*, "temples to make the fish grow" (Stokes 1919; PE, 60).

6. The *ko'a*, like any temple, is also a "house" (cf. Kamakau 1961, 201), since it is inhabited by the fish gods. It is constructed "close to the seacoast where schools of fish come" (ibid.).

7. Kāneko'a is probably another name for Kānemakua, which Kamakau (1961, 201) puts on the list of fishing gods, but who is found there, I believe, as a god of fish that are raised rather than caught.

8. There are also altars, called '*aoa*, where sacrifices are made for fishponds. These sacrifices consist of a black pig "once or twice a year," raw taro, fish raised in a fishpond ('*ama'ama*) and, moreover, *kohekohe*, a grass that grows in the taro fields (Ii 1963, 26). They are apparently made to Kāne (the god that presides over fishponds, as we have seen), for they are performed on Kāne's day (ibid.).

9. An article published in *Ka Hoku o Hawaii* defines the *unu* as "the place of the offering of the chief" (22 February 1912). In the legend of Kawelo, *unu* designates the temple where the king offers human sacrifices (Fornander 1916–20, 5:67, 69). The term *unu* is a frequent toponym, an index of the ancient presence of temples (cf. Stokes *Report* 1919, 227).

10. Barrère, in the note where she discusses the *heiau* of the *unu* and *waihau* types, writes, "In *Ka Po'e Kahiko*, Kamakau (1964) applied the term *waihau* to the *heiaus* for the *mo'o*, or female deities, who were guardians of fish ponds, and for the *akua mo'o*, the major gods of the female chiefs" (in Kamakau 1976, 145, n. 7). This is true of one passage (where the *mo'o* are also associated with the *ko'a* type; Kamakau 1964, 85–86), but not of others in the same book (cf. Kamakau 1964, 59, 86, 89)—and notably the one (p. 59) where he writes that the gods Kamehameha, Lononuiākea, and Kūnuiākea were worshiped in *waihau* temples just as much as in *unu*, *luakini*, and *loulu* temples.

11. Andrews (1865, 504) gives both definitions, but Pukui and Elbert give only the second one (PE, 350). It is not sure, then, that this name can evoke "round temples."

12. 'I'ī states that 'Ahu'ena temple (which is *not* a temple consecrated to Lono) belongs to the *hale o Lono* type (1963, 123; cf. Valeri 1982b). According to

the iconography, 'Ahu'ena includes a half-circle of images and an altar. This probably identifies it as a *hale o Lono* of the *unu* type. Does this indicate that in this particular context 'Ī'ī uses the term *hale o Lono* as a synonym for *unu*?

13. Malo calls the rain temple *ewe'ai* (1951, 189).

14. Only the twenty-eighth night is consecrated to Lono; the period itself and the night of the twenty-seventh are consecrated to Kāne.

15. But elsewhere, mentioning the *hale o Lono* at the same time as the *māpele*, Malo says that they are both *heiau ho'oūlulu 'ai* (1951, 176). It is true that the latter category is extremely large and may include, as we will see, temples that do not have as their permanent or unique function the securing of abundant harvests.

16. According to Andrews (1865, 386), *māpele* is the name of the tree whose wood is used to build a temple to Lono. Since Malo (1951, 189) says that the *māpele* was made of *lama* wood, it must be supposed that *māpele* is another name for *lama*. But *māpele* is the name given on Kaua'i to the species *Cyrtandra cyaneoides* (Barrère in Kamakau 1976, 153).

17. According to Stokes (1919), agricultural temples are situated between the fields and inhabited zones.

18. Since he describes *loulu* rites taking place in the temple of Papa'ena'ena in Lē'ahi (O'ahu), which is a *luakini*.

19. Note also that, according to Malo, the king can build a *luakini* to increase food (*ho'oūluulu 'ai*), that is, the fertility of the fields (1951, 152, 160–61; cf. Malo MS, 145, 162).

20. It can even be considered a *heiau ho'oūluulu 'ai*. For example, Waha'ula, a temple of the Puna district (island of Hawai'i) that the myths declare to be the first *luakini* built in the archipelago and consequently the most sacred, is also, according to some traditions, a *ho'oūluulu 'ai* temple (HEN, 1:262). Likewise, Pākini *heiau* in the Ka'ū district (island of Hawai'i), where the rebel chief 'Imakakoloa was sacrificed, is known both as a *heiau* where human sacrifices are made and as a *heiau ho'oūluulu 'ai* (Handy 1972, 387, 580–82; Pukui, Elbert, and Mookini 1974, 175; cf. Fornander 1878–80, 2:202).

21. Also, we know of at least one case in which houses of '*ōhi'a-lehua* wood were erected to perform rituals for an apotropeic and curative purpose (Kamakau 1961, 210).

22. On page 188 of N. Emerson's translation of Malo's text, *kūkoa'e* is defined as "a temple to propitiate heaven for food." This is just an interpolation made by Emerson (cf. Malo MS, 180).

23. This runs counter to those who, like Beckwith (1940, 46), claim that worship of Kāne excludes human sacrifice. This idea is actually due to Kepelino who, influenced by Christian theories of religious "degeneration," deluded himself into believing that in Hawaii an ancient cult, without idols and human sacrifice, had preceded the cult of Kū.

24. Note, for example, that the *luakini* temple visited by Cook on Waimea (Kaua'i) was consecrated to Kanaloa (Anderson in Cook and King 1784, 3:549), while to my knowledge no trace exists of a single *luakini* consecrated to Kanaloa on the island of Hawai'i.

25. The Kālaipāhoa (sorcery gods) were forms of Kāne, as their personal names indicate (Kāneikaulana'ula, Kānemanaiāpai'ea, etc.), or were subordinated to Kāne gods (see HEN, 1:197, cf. 199–201; Fornander 1916–20, 4:287; Beckwith 1940, 109; Valeri 1982b).

26. See Valeri 1982b for a discussion of this question.

27. For example, Hikiau temple was linked with the *ahupua'a* of Kealakekua

(Restarick 1928, 7; cf. Stokes, n.d., GR 1, box 5, n. 4). In the Hālawa valley (island of Molokaʻi) archaeologists have uncovered thirteen structures that the natives call *heiau* and that Kirch (1975, 178) believes to be *mua*, men's houses. We have seen that the two terms are interchangeable. Each of the *heiau* corresponded in Kirch's view to a territory and social group inhabiting it: "Their rather uniform distribution throughout the residential zone of the taluvial slopes would thus fit a pattern of an equal number of localized, corporate social groups, each sharing a men's house with its incorporated shrine. That these sites are indeed associated with named local land divisions is suggestive of such an interpretation" (ibid.). It seems to me that this interpretation is confirmed by two excellent ancient sources. In fact, according to Campbell (1967, 131), there is one *mua* house for six or seven "families," and Franchère (1820, 57) writes that "chaque village a un ou plusieurs *morai* [*heiau*]."

28. On the relation between the king's fishing rites and those of his subjects, see Malo 1951, 209–10; Manby 1929, 39; Bell 1929–30, 1:62; Menzies 1920, 72–73; K. Kamakau, 1919–20, 30–35.

Introduction to Part 3

1. Note that neither Emory and Buck nor their informant reached this conclusion.

2. According to Kukāhi, on the other hand, two successive months (Kāʻelo and Kaulua) are thirty days in length; two other successive months (Hinaia-ʻeleʻele and Māhoe-mua) are twenty-nine days long (J. L. Kukahi, letter in *Ka Makaainana*, 22 April 1895).

3. On the *kapu pule* and their relation to the phases of the moon, see also Corney 1896, 101; Campbell 1967, 95, 127–28; Bell 1929–30, 1:77; Manby 1929, 18; Menzies 1920, 94–95; Shaler 1935, 93; Kotzebue 1821a, 1:331–32; Hunnewell 1895, 15; Townsend 1921, 14–15; Colnett, n.d., 176ff.; Choris 1822, 11–12.

4. The list of months that Gaimard, a naturalist on the Freycinet expedition, received from the Spaniard Marin gives two names for this thirteenth month. One of them ("Onagño") is impossible to identify, as it has been so deformed by the combined effects of a Spanish mouth and a French ear. The other ("Kaono") probably corresponds to Kaʻaōna, the month that on Oʻahu, where the list was compiled, was considered the equivalent of April. Marin's entire list of months is dubious in any event (Freycinet 1978, 70).

5. For example, the dates of the festivals commemorating the death of Kamehameha, who died on 8 May 1819 (the fourteenth day of the moon—Kamakau 1961, 212), are

8 November 1819 (Marin 1973, 234): twenty-first day of the moon
26 April 1820 (Marin 1973, 239: MH, May 1821, 133; Thurston 1882, 40): thirteenth day of the moon
24 August 1820 (Marin 1973, 242): fifteenth day of the moon
16 May 1821 (Hunnewell, n.d.; Marin 1973, 250): fourteenth day of the moon
13 August 1821 (it should in fact have been performed 12 August but was postponed) (MH, August 1822, 249): fourteenth day of the moon
24 April 1823 (MH, July 1824, 208): fourteenth day of the moon
(there was also a parade on 10 May 1823—MH, August 1824, 246–47)

This list shows that during a four-year period the anniversary clearly fell on the same day of the lunar month. Moreover, since 25 April 1823 is said to be the fourth anniversary of Kamehameha's death, we must suppose that in this period one month was intercalated, as otherwise the anniversary would have fallen forty-four instead of thirteen days before 8 May. The first anniversary of the death of Keōpūolani was celebrated on 6 September 1824. She died on 16 September 1823. This confirms that anniversaries were calculated according to the lunar calendar and were readjusted to the solar year through more or less periodic intercalations (Stewart, MH, February 1826, 37; 1839, 240).

6. Contrary to what some think (Stokes 1932, 23–24), the Hawaiians used the year as a unit of measurement; cf. Townsend (1921, 15): "They speak of time by so many *marhahitas* [*makahiki*]."

Chapter 7

1. Only K. Kamakau (1919–20, 35–39) describes the rite in detail. Malo mentions only its beginning. 'Ī'ī describes a similar rite but places it in the Kū period of the month of Hili-na-ehu (1963, 72). According to him, this month corresponds to August. But in a calendar from Moloka'i Hili-na-ehu is said to correspond to October (Malo 1951, 33). S. M. Kamakau's calendar has it correspond to January–February (1964, 22). In most other calendars the month does not even appear. In any event, as we have seen, any fixed correspondences established between Hawaiian lunar months and months in the Gregorian calendar is necessarily misleading.

2. There appears to be a parallel between this ritual engendering of the moons and associated stars, on the one hand, and a "genealogy" of months published by Johnson and Mahelona (1975, 40–44), on the other. In the latter, each moon, beginning with 'Ikuwā, is paired with a star that is considered its wife. Together this moon and star engender the next lunar month. Secondary stars are added to the twelve principal calendrical stars.

3. According to PE, 104, *kāhea* means, among other things, a "recital of the first lines of a stanza by the dancer as a cue to the chanter." Thus it is possible that the two men dance, with coconuts in hand, and chant in alternation with the priest. Moreover, there is a similar rite (to be described below, p. 315) in which dancers chant antiphonally with the priests. In this rite the dance enables the relationship with the god to be renewed or shows that it has been renewed. The same may be true of the *kuapola* rite.

4. This oscillation would explain why according to some sources the year ends with 'Ikuwā, while for others it ends with Welehu (see Fornander 1878–80, 1:123; 1916–20, 6:203; Kepelino 1932, 97; Remy 1862, 75; Lisiansky 1814, 119). The oscillation is confirmed by the European accounts, which show that the same rites of the Makahiki festivals fall on different dates of the Gregorian calendar in consecutive years. See, for instance, the journal by Marin (1973, 199, 202, 203, 204, 214, 217, 220–21, 227, 234, etc.).

5. Contrary to Malo, K. Kamakau does not use the verb *ho'okupu* to designate these prestations.

6. A European voyager's account (1788) corroborates Malo's statement: "The other chiefs sat at some distance during the dinner, and then made their meal on roasted dogs, taro-roots and potatoes; as at this season of the year even the

chiefs are forbidden to eat hogs and fowls, from the king down to the lowest Eree [ali'i]" (Meares 1916, 15).

7. Pieces of *'iwa'iwa* (maidenhair fern *Adiantum* spp. or *Asplenium adiantum nigrum*), according to 'Ī'ī (1963, 72).

8. Malo writes, however, "Captain Cook was named Lono after this god because of the resemblance the sails of his ship bore to the *tapa* of the gods" (1951, 145).

9. For a description of the *akua pā'ani* observed by the English in 1779, see King 1967, 627; Samwell 1967, 1173. Other Makahiki gods took part in the procession. Kamehameha added many gods that were not traditionally paraded, particularly some sorcery gods (Kamakau 1964, 20; Kepelino 1977, 62).

Another documented innovation was the incorporation of Cook's bones in an image that was perhaps carried in procession with the other Makahiki gods (cf. Sahlins 1979). According to Mathison, "This image, during the procession, was immediately preceded by a person bearing in his hand a spear, to which was prefixed an instrument containing twenty lashes, each a yard in length, woven with the same sort of feathers that are used in the manufacture of cloaks and idols. He brandished it before the image, as it were to clear the way; and any person who had the misfortune to be touched by it, was summarily put to death as guilty of violating the taboo regulation" (1825, 432). If the latter statement were true, doubts could be raised about whether Cook's bones were actually carried in procession with the other Makahiki gods, because human sacrifices to these gods were strictly forbidden (K. Kamakau, 1919–20, 41).

10. It is only on this occasion that the commoners can see the most sacred ali'i, "untouched by males, untouched by females," who are invisible throughout the rest of the year (Kepelino 1977, 62).

11. Cf. Townsend 1921, 15.

12. In K. Kamakau (1919–20, 41), the inland side stands to the seaward side as the right to the left. According to Kepelino (1977, 62–63) the *akua loa* receives gifts of *malo* (loincloths) while the *akua poko* receives *pā'ū* (skirts). The first god has a masculine connotation, then, and the second a feminine one.

13. Such is the meaning of the expression "*ka iu*" (Malo MS, 150; K. Kamakau 1919–20, 41), which is not, as N. Emerson writes (in Malo 1951, 145), "a place in Waimea, where was a famous shrine." According to K. Kamakau (1919–20, 43) and 'Ī'ī (1963, 75), the king himself is relegated to the *ka 'iu*, or else he is obliged to close his eyes each time he goes out (K. Kamakau 1919–20, 41). 'Ī'ī claims that those who are isolated are the *ali'i nī'aupi'o* who feed the *akua loa* in the *hanaipū* rite (1963, 75). (See below.)

14. N. Emerson claims that this form of greeting is "of earlier usage" than *aloha* (in Malo 1951, 154). Be that as it may, its use emphasizes the difference in rank between the speaker and the addressee.

15. He also receives coconut and bananas (Malo MS, 157). According to 'Ī'ī (1963, 75), the food offered to the god "consisted of a cup of *'awa* and banana or sugar cane to remove its bitterness, and some *'a'aho*, a pudding made of coconut and *pia* [arrowroot] starch thickened by heating with hot stones. This food was laid on ti leaves to be eaten after the other foods. Then a side of well-cooked pork was given him with some poi." The rite naturally takes place in the king's *hale mua* (ibid.).

16. Detail confirmed by 'Ī'ī (1869j): "*Nolaila ua kapaia ia, 'he hanai pu.'*"

17. 'Ī'ī claims that the boxing matches are held before and during the *hanaipū* rite (1963, 73).

18. K. Kamakau's text calls this goddess Makawahine. It is possible, however, that the editors misread the original or that there was a slip of the pen on K. Kamakau's part and that the name of this goddess is in fact Mokowahine, "female boxer." Indeed, according to Whitman women have their own goddess of boxing (*moko, mokomoko*), since women and men are forbidden to box together (1979, 56).

19. "They display considerable taste in the arrangement of their dress and finery during the great festival of the Mucahita [Makahiki], when all in animation, life and gaiety, especially at the Hura Hura or dances where they vie with each other in richness of dress, display of ornaments, and gaiety of colors" (Whitman 1979, 18–20).

20. Which is approximately five and a half meters long (Fornander 1916–20, 6 : 204).

21. According to 'Ī'ī (1963, 75), only ali'i of the *nī'aupi'o* rank can perform this rite.

22. Because anointment divinizes, it taboos. One can, for example, anoint a house to taboo it (Hunnewell, n.d., 6 February 1818; 1895, 14). The rites for anointing described by K. Kamakau and 'Ī'ī correspond to those performed in 1779 on Cook, who was considered an incarnation of Lono. He was smeared with the grease of a sacrificial pig in the *luakini* Hikiau, and in the adjacent *hale o Lono* he was anointed with coconut oil (Samwell 1967, 1159, 1162).

As this event shows, it is possible to anoint with both animal and vegetable fat. The latter is used especially during the *kapu Makahiki*, when animal sacrifice is forbidden, but during the rest of the year the images and temples are made sacred by the grease of human and animal victims: "There were many heiaus made famous because of the shine of the grease (*hinu*) of burnt offerings from Hawaii to Kauai; they were offered by the hundreds and thousands (*he lau, he kini, he lehu*). The soil became fertile and saturated with slime from the grease of the heavenly chiefs and from the burnt offerings. It is impossible to count the hundreds and thousands of years of sacrificing" (Kamakau 1976, 145). Like other peoples, the Hawaiians probably associated fat or grease with life. This explains why to give life to the image of a god they smear it with grease.

23. As we have seen, the *ahupua'a* is the basic territorial unit associated with the altar (*ahu*) found at its boundary (Lyons 1875a, 1 : 103).

24. According to one text (HEN, 1 : 260), Ālia is a "god of war" to which Kamehameha sacrificed his rival, Keahiawela. It is likely, however, that this text confuses Ālia with "Kakalia," another name for Kahōāli'i (Kepelino 1977, 50).

25. The list given by S. M. Kamakau is much longer: "Pigs, dogs, fowl, poi, tapa cloth, dress tapas (*'a'ahu*), *'oloa* tapa, *pa'u* (skirts), malos, shoulder capes (*'ahu*), mats, *ninikea* tapa, *olona* fishnets, fishlines, feathers of the *mamo* and the *'o'o* birds, finely designed mats (*'ahu pawehe*), pearls, ivory, iron (*meki*), adzes, and whatever other property had been gathered by the *konohiki*, or land agent, of the *ahupua'a*" (1964, 21). Kamakau, however, describes these *ho'okupu* as they were at the time of Kamehameha, who increasingly transformed them into tribute.

26. Malo's original text says "*he ao kiai [kia'i]*," not "*he ao kiei*" as in the printed text (1951, 146).

27. Up to this line, the prayer given by Malo seems identical to a prayer given, unfortunately only in translation, by Fornander (1916–20, 6 : 510). In the Fornander version the rest of the text refers to a sacrifice.

28. The conjectural reading of the last two lines was proposed to me by John Charlot, whom I gratefully thank. According to him we can also interpret *e miha* in

the second line in this manner: "who makes quiet, peaceful" (personal communication, 1980).

29. Then come two lines that are difficult to interpret, and of which N. Emerson gives an unacceptable translation. Note that immediately after the last line I translate comes the expression "*kuikui* [*ku'iku'i*] *papa*," which designates the prayer that ends the Makahiki (K. Kamakau 1919–20, 45; see note 42).

30. N. Emerson mistranslates this sentence (Malo 1951, 147).

31. According to 'Ī'ī, "the attendants of the gods [of the Makahiki] carried them facing backward when they traveled. Therefore it was said that the eyes of Lono remained upon the activities of the people when the gods left the presence of the chiefs for the circuit of the land" (1963, 75). But elsewhere 'Ī'ī writes that "the front of these long poles faced backward when carried, so that the 'wife' could be seen." This refers to the origin myth of the rite, to which I will return.

32. Although S. M. Kamakau is a very unreliable source on the Makahiki rites, I must mention his ideas on the order in which the gods pass through the *ahupua'a*. According to him, the *akua pā'ani* comes first; when the boxing matches and such are over, then comes the *akua kāpala 'alaea*, "a god painted (*pena 'ia*) red with '*alaea* earth. On one side he was kapu, and on one side, free" (1964, 20; cf. Kepelino 1977, 63). Then comes the *akua loa* and, finally, the *akua poko* with the goddesses (Kamakau 1964, 20). This sequence seems improbable to me. For example, it is the *akua kāpala 'alaea* that through its priest smears the altars with ocher to make them *noa*. Now, how can the god free the land if the *akua loa* has yet to arrive and receive the *ho'okupu*? On the other hand, it is indeed probable that the *akua poko* and the goddesses follow the *akua loa*, as S. M. Kamakau claims.

Note also that S. M. Kamakau differs from all the other sources in placing the *hi'uwai* rite after and not before the circuit of the Makahiki god (1964, 21). Here again I cannot accept this modification, which makes the rite lose its meaning.

33. The original Hawaiian text (Ii 1869j) fully bears out this important detail.

34. *Kau* also means "to sacrifice" (PE, 124).

35. Malo writes that if the Puea rite succeeds, that is, if it does not rain, "the land lives" ("*ola ka aina*") (MS, 154).

36. Because of a lacuna in K. Kamakau's manuscript we no longer have his description of the rites performed from the morning of the twenty-eighth to the evening of the first day of the month of Makali'i (see Fornander 1916–20, 6:42).

37. "Removal of taboo on fruits of land and sea" (PE, 112).

38. The word '*ahi* designates different species of tuna, and especially the species *Neothunnus macropterus* (albacore) (Titcomb and Pukui 1972, 58–59; PE, 7).

39. A great king is, by definition, skilled in the art of dodging spears (see, for example, Fornander 1916–20, 4:268).

40. The *hale wai ea* is, as we will see, a house inside the *luakini* temple and not a "unique" *luakini* temple, as N. Emerson maintains. He is completely mistaken on this point (in Malo 1951, 155, n. 23).

41. At least at the beginning of the nineteenth century the "Makahiki gods" on O'ahu were kept in the *luakini* temple, Lē'ahi (Ii 1963, 70; cf. Marin 1973, 202–3, according to whom the Akua Makahiki leaves from Waikīkī, where Lē'ahi temple is found); on Hawai'i they were kept in the *luakini* Hikiau (Ii 1963, 115). Each of these *luakini* was the principal one for the island at that time. An ancient chant testifies that formerly on the island of Hawai'i the Makahiki ended at the *luakini* temple Waha'ula—at that time the principal one on the island. This implies that the *akua loa* was kept there (*Haui ka lani* chant, lines 603–4 in Fornander 1916–20, 6:403).

42. According to K. Kamakau, the prayer to end this rite is called *ku'iku'i-papa* 1919–20, 45).

43. According to N. Emerson this is a canoe of unpainted wood (Malo 1951, 151).

44. The connection between Lono and the Pleiades is also revealed in a comparison of two prayers whose texts were given above. In the *kuapola* prayer, the Pleiades are associated with the stars Uliuli and Melemele; these same stars are associated with Lono in the *hainaki* prayer.

45. The color black itself connotes fertility (Malo 1951, 189).

46. This myth is given with slight variations by H. Lyman in Beckwith 1940, 36–37; Byron 1826, 20–21; Boelen 1835–36, 3:157; Kotzebue 1830a, 2:88–89; Bingham 1848, 32; Varigny 1874, 16).

47. Since the story told by this myth is also attributed to a king named Lonoikamakahiki (Lono at the Makahiki) (Kamakau 1961, 47–48), Beckwith speculates that the story of this king and that of the Makahiki god were confused because of the identify of their names (1940, 39). This interpretation, derived from Kamakau himself (1961, 61), does not explain anything. There is nothing accidental about the so-called confusion of the two stories, since the historicization of divine legends is extremely common in Hawaii. Lonoikamakahiki the king represents the translation of Lonoikamakahiki the god onto the level of royalty.

48. Thus, Kū, Kāne, or Lono takes the place of Pō, the undifferentiated divine principle, in certain cosmogonic chants that exist aside from the *Kumulipo* (Fornander 1878–80, 1:72–75, 92–95; 1916–20, 6:363–65).

49. Breaking a receptacle full of water can in fact symbolize death (Kepelino 1932, 120). More generally, it symbolizes a transition. Thus, when a cure using 'awa is ended the cup (made from a coconut shell) used to drink it is broken. This symbolizes the passage from the state of sickness to the state of health (Titcomb 1948, 157, 116, 121; Kamakau 1976, 43).

50. But dancing goes on during the whole Makahiki period (see Beaglehole 1967, 285–87, 1157, 1221–22; Menzies 1920, 168–69; Bell 1929–30, 2:124–25; Vancouver 1801, 5:75; Campbell 1967, 146–47).

51. Both Cook and Vancouver found these dances obscene (Beaglehole 1967, 1221–22; Vancouver 1801, 5:75; see as well texts cited by Barrère 1980, 48 and passim).

52. Both men and women dance (Barrère 1980, 13–14).

53. "Hula belongs to pleasure . . ." (editorial in *Ka Nupepa Kuokoa*. 7 July 1866, cited by Barrère 1980, 46, cf. also p. 47).

54. The coordination of gestures is accompanied by that of the voices (Vancouver 1801, 5:128–30; Bingham 1848, 125; Bloxam 1925, 60; Beechey 1831, 2:105–7; Ruggles 1913, 235; MH 1823, 558–59; Barrère, Pukui, and Kelly 1980, 21 and passim).

55. Moreover, comical themes pervade the danced chants of the Makahiki period, as D. Onaona testifies: "Chants are composed with thoughts of love making or ridiculing" (in *Ka Nupepa Kuokoa*, 21 October 1871, cited by Barrère 1980, 47). See also this observation, "When I arrived at the place where dancers danced, I saw many others there laughing till the tears ran" (D. W. Golia in *Ka Nupepa Kuokoa*, 31 March 1866, cited by Barrère, Pukui, and Kelly 1980, 45). The dance of the marionettes (*hula ki'i*)—probably developed under European influence—produced "shouts of laughter and great commotion" (art. in *Ka Nupepa Kuokoa* 4 December 1886, cited by Barrère, Pukui, and Kelly 1980, 55). These texts refer to the dances as they still occurred in the 1860s, 1870s, and 1880s, but the comic character they mention was probably even more developed in traditional times.

56. One also dances each time a rite of passage puts the king's mana to test, or when death puts an end to his mana (cf. Beaglehole 1967, 622; see also the dances done during the commemorative feasts for King Kamehameha mentioned by Marin 1973 [May 1821, May 1822, March 1823]). In short, one dances to resist the risks of social disaggregation involved in any threat to or decrease of the powers of royalty.

57. According to Malo the guardians of the gods, *kahu akua*, do the same.

58. It seems that even the female ali'i must, against all customary rules, accede to the sexual advances of their inferiors, not only because these women take part in the festival but also because they dance for the people (Barrot 1978, 55; Barrère, Pukui, and Kelly 1980, passim) and must thus obey the laws of the dance (for example, let themselves be kissed by any spectator, etc.). It may be that this somewhat enigmatic and perhaps specious text refers to what happens during the Makahiki festival: "once a Year for 6 Days the women indiscriminately, married or single . . . Kings' wives & all, are obliged to go to the Mountains and there remain during the Taboo, during which time any women is free for any Man that choose[s] to go to her; and She dare not brake the Taboo at the expense of her life" (Hussey 1958, 35). At any rate, women of high rank are obliged to have sexual intercourse indiscriminately during the orgies that follow the death of an important ali'i (see below).

59. For example, "It was a law with Palila [a mythical hero] that whenever he laughed the *kapu* would end; people could then stand up, speak, or run about" (Fornander 1916–20, 5:140). On the antagonism between laughter and taboo, see Valeri 1981a; Propp 1975.

60. European voyagers noted with astonishment the scant respect given the king and other ali'i during the festival (see, for example, King 1967, 627).

61. Only these "hypogamous" sexual relations are transgressive, for, as we have seen, hypergamous relations are licit and frequent.

62. This ambivalent attitude is found elsewhere in Polynesia: for example, in the Marquesas (Dening 1980, 19–20).

63. The mana of the god that is appropriated comes very close, then, to the "fellowship" Johansen speaks of in the context of the Maori.

64. And not *kalokāmakamaka*, as N. Emerson in his translation and Pukui and Elbert in their dictionary (PE, 115) erroneously write.

65. Perhaps there is a relation between the name of these rites and the *kapu* of *kāloa* (= Kanaloa) that they encompass.

66. It has the shape of a cone, according to N. Emerson (in Malo 1951, 178).

67. Pukui and Elbert, without naming their source, define *kūkoaʻe a hāwai* as a "ceremonial blessing of a stream so that water may continue flowing" (PE, 163).

68. He was doubtless Kahōāliʻi, whom Marin calls "the king's god" (1973, 199). Kamakau writes, "One of his [Kamehameha's] gods was a real man; Kaho'ali'i was his name" (1961, 180); "the man-god (*akua kanaka maoli*) Kaho'ali'i of Kamehameha had been made a god, perhaps because the spirit of an ancient god by the name of Kaho'ali'i possessed him (*noho pu ana*)" (1964, 20). We know the name of the bearer of the Kahōāliʻi title in Vancouver's time: Kalaninuikaleleau. He was the agnatic half-brother of King Kalani'ōpu'u (cf. unpublished documents cited by D. Barrère in Kamakau 1976, 146).

69. Unfortunately, Vancouver does not describe these rites anywhere else.

70. Obviously, this rite is the *'aha hulahula*. See below, p. 279.

71. This probably corresponds to the "great sacrifice" cum collective meal that is performed during the temple ritual. See below for its most developed form, p. 309.

72. According to Vancouver, it ended on the fifth; but Menzies reports that on the fourth already it was not "as strict as the day before" (1920, 174).

73. More exactly, he describes a ritual that lasts three nights but declares that the taboo placed on fishing on the occasion of this rite lasts for nine days. The observations of two voyagers confirm that the *kapu 'ōpelu* lasted for an *anahulu*. In 1796 Broughton noted a taboo period that lasted from 2 July to 10 July. In terms of the lunar calendar this period extended from the twenty-sixth day of the moon to the fourth day of the following moon (Broughton 1804, 68). Two years later, on 14 August 1789, Schocklesby, a European resident, informed Townsend that a taboo of ten days was in force (from about the sixth to the fifteenth): "There was one of the annual tabous on, which was a prohibition from going on the water for ten days" (Townsend 1921, 5–6). The period in question ran from the twenty-third of one lunar month to the third of the following moon.

In contrast, at a later period (1818) we are told of a fishing ritual lasting only one day (Hunnewell 1895, 15) and taking place on the eleventh day of the moon (12 August 1818), that is, during the *kapu* period of *Hua*. Both the monthly *kapu* period and the duration of this rite are identical to those of the rite for the *aku* as recorded by Malo. This seems to confirm that the twin rituals had undergone parallel reductions in length by Kamehameha.

74. "This operation was called '*lua*'" (note by W. F. Wilson in Menzies 1920, 73).

Chapter 8

1. Fornander has this to say about a very old man's description of the construction of Pu'ukoholā temple in 1792: "His description of the thousands of people encamped on the neighboring hillsides, and taking their turns at the work, of their organization and feeding, their time of work and relaxation, the number of chiefs that attended, and who, as the old man said, caused the ground to tremble beneath their feet; and the number of human victims that were required and duly offered for this or that portion of the building—this description was extremely interesting and impressive" (1878–80, 2:328, n. 1).

2. Commoners, who could not go into the temple, could sometimes watch the rites from afar; thus, in a valley on Kaua'i, they stood on the tops of the hills surrounding Hauloa temple (Thrum 1907c, 63).

3. Also called *lua iwi*, "bone pits" (Thrum 1908b, 53), and *lua pa'ū*, "damp pit" (PE, 197; Kepelino 1932, 60; Fornander 1916–20, 4:140, n. 1; HEN, 1:266), or *ka lua mihi'ole*, "the place of no repentance" (HEN, 1:1677–78).

4. In Pu'ukoholā, one of the two pits inside the temple was on the side of the principal altar (*lele*), and the other was close to the sacred house, called the *hale mana* (HEN, 1:266). In Waha'ula the *lua iwi* was nothing but the beach near the temple where the remains of the sacrifices were thrown, undoubtedly because, like fire, the sea is purifying (Thrum 1908b, 53). In Mo'okini temple at Kohala (island of Hawai'i) a pit is found east of the main entrance (Fornander 1878–80, 2:36).

5. This is only logical, since these priests are "consecrated" or "devoted" (*ho'ola'a*) to their temple and should therefore remain there even after their death.

6. According to Campbell (1967, 127), four pillars found at some distance from the buildings mark the limits of the sacred space. Any temple, moreover, has a sacred barrier, marked or not, extending well beyond the *paehumu*; it encompasses the area that women (unless they are of very high rank) cannot penetrate. Corney (1896, 101) estimates that they must remain some thirty-six meters from the temple buildings.

7. Added by Captain King.

8. These houses "sont *tabu* pour tout le monde et celui qui oserait en violer la sainteté serait puni d'une manière cruelle" (Arago 1822, 2:182).

9. According to Campbell (1967, 127), "In the inside of the principal house there is a screen or curtain of white cloth, hung across one end, within which the image of Etooah [*akua*] is placed. When sacrifices are offered, the priests and chiefs enter occasionally within this space, going in at one side and out at the other."

There were four wooden gods in the *hale mana* at Hikiau (Ellis 1782, 2:181). According to Kamakau (1976, 138) the principal image (which he, like Malo, calls *mōʻī*) is kept in the mana house. But according to all the other sources this image is found in front of the *ʻanuʻu* tower.

10. Hikiau also had the form of an "oblong square" (Samwell 1967, 1177).

11. Malo (1951, 162) mentions another house at the temple's entrance. King (1967, 505) mentions two houses close to the entrance of Hikiau: one of them is the *hale mana*; another seems to be a guardhouse through which one entered the temple (cf. Samwell 1967, 1177). Yet these accounts are not completely clear, and several interpretations of them are possible.

12. King (1967, 506), Samwell (1967, 1177), and Ellis (1782, 2:181–82) all mention its existence, but only Samwell reports the name, "*hara-pahoo*" (*hale pahu*). According to ʻĪʻī (1869d) the *hale pahu* opens like a veranda on the altar side.

13. Probably together with the "god's conch shell" (cf. Brigham, n.d., 179).

14. To announce to his councillors that Kamehameha (still a child) gives him the right to make human sacrifices, Kalaniʻōpuʻu says, "He is telling me to beat the drum and offer the human sacrifice" (Ii 1963, 6). According to Choris the sacrificial drum "est orné d'un grand nombre de dents, sur-tout de celles des victimes humaines qui ont été immolées aux dieux" (1822, 12).

15. Hiroa (1957, 520–21) does not believe the drums are beaten in the *hale pahu*; since in the official version of Cook's *Voyage*, published in 1784, it is said that the *hale pahu* is no larger than a "kennel," he thinks that there is no room in it to beat them. But the "kennel" found in the temple at Waimea is not called a *hale pahu* in Cook's original journal; it is probably a *hale wai ea*. (See note 16.)

16. It is "twice the length of the distance from fingertip to elbow in length, its height and breadth being half that measure" (Ii 1963, 35).

17. Hence Kamakau calls the *hale wai ea* "*ka hale i kamauliola*" "the house to revive life" (1976, 138).

18. A stone bowl from Kauaʻi now in the Bishop Museum is supposed to have contained *wai ea* (Brigham, n.d., 182). A human face is carved on the outer surface of this bowl (Bennett, 1931, pl. 10)—is it thus a representational equivalent of the skull normally used?

19. "Baked" corresponds to "*kalua*" in the Hawaiian text: "*e kalua ai na puaa mohaikuni*, etc." (S. M. Kamakau 1870b).

20. Cf. the expression *lele wale ka ʻaha*, "the *ʻaha* (sacrificial rite, prayer) has flown away (*lele*)" (Fornander 1916–20, 4:149). *Lele* also means "messenger" (cf. Ellis 1842, 153). The altar is indeed a "messenger" that allows men and gods to communicate.

21. The *lele* altar is thus defined in a text: "*Lele* altar, that is a high place on which they lay the victims" (HEN, 1:206). It is called "*lele kai*" in another text (Fornander 1916–20, 4:297). *Kai* indicates seawater or salt water used in ritual purification. Another text (Kaawa 1865a) opposes *lele* and *kuahu* on the basis of the offerings placed on each: bananas (cf. as well Kamakau 1976, 64), hogs, and men on the *lele*; *ʻawa* and coconuts on the *kuahu* altar. This classification is not confirmed by the accounts of sacrificial rites, however.

22. To such an extent that the word *ki'i*, "image," is used as a synonym for "god" and reciprocally, throughout Malo's and K. Kamakau's ritual texts.

23. As Jarves writes, "The features of their religion were embodied in these images" (1843:28).

24. Hikiau temple offers a good example of the first kind of arrangement, Keikipu'ipu'i, of the second.

25. I give here a list of temples for which the number of images is known:

1. Hikiau (in 1779)	Twelve images (King 1967, 505; Samwell 1967, 1177; Ellis 1782, 2:181)	
2. Hikiau (in 1804)	Fifteen images (Lisiansky 1814, 106)	
3. Keikipu'ipu'i	Twelve images (drawing by Arago in Freycinet 1978, pl. 87)	
4. Hale o Keawe	Twelve images (Ellis 1842, 165)	
5. 'Ahu'ena	Twelve images (according to Arago 1822, 2:112–13; but a smaller number of images appears in the drawing by Choris, which perhaps does not give all the details).	

26. One is found in the British Museum, the other in the Peabody Museum (T5 and T4 in the catalog of Cox and Davenport 1974).

27. *Makaīwa* means "mysterious eyes" (cf. Malo 1951, 169; PE, 209). This name refers to the fact that the eyes of these images are encrusted with mother-of-pearl (cf. Kamakau 1976, 136).

28. At Hikiau, just after entering the temple one came before two images situated in front of the *hale mana* (King 1967, 505; Samwell 1967, 1117). According to 'Ī'ī (1963, 35) there is a statue on each side of the *hale wai ea*. Kamakau (1961, 203) mentions an image that stands at the sacred drum and that is called Kūkalepe'oni'oni'o "Kū [with] the embroidered fringe." Other carved images can form the *paehumu* of the temple (Kamakau 1976, 136).

29. Refer to the catalog of Cox and Davenport (1974) for examples of these different types.

30. The smallest surviving images measure about thirty centimeters, including the handle (cf. for example Cox and Davenport 1974, 159).

31. On the stylistic and technical features of the portable images, refer also to Cox and Davenport 1974, 81–89.

32. It also refers to the woven caskets in which the bones of kings and sacred ali'i were enshrined (hence the name, *kā'ai*) (Kamakau 1961, 258; Ii 1963, 155; Beckwith 1951, 16). The surviving specimens look like dolls: they have head, ears, mouth, and eyes of mother-of-pearl (Hiroa 1957, 575). The caskets were covered with feathers and their mouths filled with dog's or shark's teeth (cf. Ellis 1842, 166; Dampier 1971, 67; Byron 1826, 200).

33. They themselves are sometimes called *akua kā'ai* as well (cf. Cox and Davenport 1974, 85).

34. According to Zimmermann (1781, 76), pig's teeth are placed in the mouths of some images. But no such teeth are found in the surviving *akua hulu manu*.

35. When Kamehameha approaches the island of O'ahu with his fleet he asks his god, "Say, Ku-ka'ili-moku, seize that island" (Kamakau 1961, 171).

36. These feathers are supposed to have a mythical origin; they were plucked by the hero 'Aukelenuiaiku from the head of the cannibal bird Halulu (Fornander 1916–20, 4:42, 64–67; Kamakau 1964, 141; 1961, 148, 179; Beckwith 1940, 91–92). In reality they are taken from the frigate bird (Beckwith 1951, 92).

37. Cf. King (Cook and King 1784, 3:13), who says that they are of the same kind as those in the *hale o Lono*.

38. A. Kaeppler (n.d.) has attempted to pair each iconological motif with a god. However, it would be easy to show that many of these motifs belong to quite different gods; moreover, Kaeppler's attempt is methodologically unsound because it is not based on a structural—that is, exhaustive—study of the properties of the gods and of the rituals in which their images are used. Unfortunately, I became acquainted with Kaeppler's interesting attempt when my own discussion of the images had already been completed, but I have used one of her conclusions below (see p. 253).

39. Some, like the image of Kūkeolo'ewa, combine wig and helmet (Ellis 1842, 89). This combination also exists in a portable wooden image (see item K24 in the catalog by Cox and Davenport 1974).

40. The extant *akua hulu manu* are reproduced in Hiroa 1957, 510–12; Brigham 1899, 31–39.

41. Incidentally, although the text mentions a god named after Lono, it does not establish that the tiered miter is associated only with this deity, since this miter is also found on other deities. Kūnuiākea in Hikiau in 1779, for instance, had one. See Barnes 1977.

42. The same is true in much of Austronesia. See Barnes 1977.

43. See, for example, the expression, *ka'ōnohi o ka lā*, "the pupil of the sun" (Ellis 1842, 145), which designates the sun. An indication of the association of eyes and stars is given by the fact that human eyes were sacrificed during eclipses (cf. Lehmann 1930, 225).

44. Hawaiian, like many other languages, makes "seeing" (*'ike*) the equivalent of "knowing" and "understanding" (PE, 90).

45. The first Pu'ukoholā temple dates back to the time of King Lonoikamakahiki, who had it built near the spot where he awaited the passage of a rebel army (Fornander 1916–20, 4:326).

46. For example, at the end of the eighteenth century, the royal residences at Kealakekua, Kailua (Vancouver 1801, 5:103) and Hōnaunau on the island of Hawai'i, and those at Waikīkī on O'ahu (Thrum 1926) and at Waimea on Kaua'i (Cook and King 1784, 2:200–203; Cook 1967:269–71; Bennett 1931, 104–8), were all adjacent to major state temples.

47. This fact, which is not clear in the journals of Cook's voyage, emerges from Lisiansky's account. This author says that the entrance of the temple is found on the same side as the residence of Kamehameha, which is near a "pond." The latter still lies on the north side of the temple. Bell (1929–30, 1:78) and Manby (1929, 43) confirm that the entrance to Hikiau opens on the same side as the royal residence.

48. However, this is not always true, and notably not for Pu'ukoholā temple.

49. Thrum (1908b, 61) also mentions that according to a report the *lele* "stood at the right hand of the entrance." If "right hand" in the Hawaiian sense is meant, the *lele* was near the tower at the northern side.

50. Wise wrongly translates this priest's name as "He who precedes the King" (K. Kamakau 1919–20, 8).

51. The form "*kakapaulua*" found in the text is obviously a slip of the pen. Wise renders this priest's name as "the priest of human sacrifice" (K. Kamakau 1919–20, 8). This translation is not specific enough, as we shall see.

52. According to Thrum (in Fornander 1916–20, 6:8, n. 14) he is a priest whose face is smeared with red ocher (*'alaea*). This is the priest who prepares the red ocher for lifting the taboo from the land.

53. This hut seems to be of the *hālau* type, that is, a "long house" (PE, 49; cf. N. Emerson in Malo 1951, 178), like the *hale mana* or even like the canoe sheds (cf. Hiroa 1957, 77–78; Ellis 1842, 320; Malo 1951, 122). As we have seen, the *hale hāwai* coincides with the *kūko'ae a hūwai* (or *hāwai*). According to Emerson (in Malo 1951, 178), the "priestesses of the order of Papa" (probably the women of very high rank) take part in the purification rites held in the *hale hāwai*. Perhaps this rite reunites the sexes to represent their subsequent separation more emphatically.

54. More exactly, Malo writes that it is "the god who is truly a man" (*"ke akua, ke kanaka maoli no"*). Only Kahōali'i corresponds to this definition. (See note 68, chap. 7.)

55. "*Lupa haalele iho la ka alii a me kahuna, he loina liilii na ke kahuna no ka luakini.*" Wise interprets this as "The king and the priest secretly buried the remains of certain things used in the service, a minor duty performed by the priest in the temple." And Thrum adds in a footnote that *lupa ha'alele* means "secret burial or disposal." I do not find this meaning in the dictionaries. On the contrary, *lupa* (or *lupalupa*) designates a purification rite (PE, 199; Andrews 1922, 389); *ha'alele* means "to leave behind, abandon, reject, remove, etc." (PE, 42). The expression, *ha'alelea*, "left behind," "abandoned," refers to the man sacrificed and buried at the foot of the *'ōhi'a-lehua* tree (see below). This is perhaps the basis for Wise's interpretation of the *lupa ha'alele* rite; however, nothing proves that the two rites have anything in common. The only thing that can be assumed with any degree of certainty is that the *lupa ha'alele* is, at least in part, a rite of expiation and purification.

56. The text of this prayer is published—with several errors in transcription—in Malo 1951, 163–64 (cf. the original text in Malo MS, 166). Emerson's translation is often erroneous. The prayer is similar to the prayers of purification used in other contexts (cf. Malo 1951, 98).

57. Literally, *pono* means "in perfect order" (PE, 314).

58. Thrum's statement (1910, 54, n. 2) that "the loulu was a kapu period embracing several ceremonies which preceded the kauila, or decoration day ceremonies of the temple," could be supported by the sentence above—if the palm fronds mentioned there belong to the *loulu* palm. The source of Thrum's statement is probably Kamakau (cf. 1964, 59).

59. N. Emerson confirms that this headpiece can include switches (in Malo 1951, 179).

60. Remy undoubtedly refers to Kahōali'i when he writes, "Quelquefois les rois étaient accompagnés par un homme issu des dieux. Cet heureux mortel avait seul le droit de suivre *in naturalibus* son auguste maître et le peuple disait en parlant de lui qu'il était un dieu: *he akua ia*" (1859, 19–20).

61. Strictly speaking, Malo mentions only the *kahuna 'alaea*; but surely this priest is inconceivable without the god who gives power to the ocher.

62. Fornander (1916–20, 6:266) relates a tradition according to which the title *kahōāli'i* designates all high-ranking ali'i; they were purported to descend from Kāne and to be "anointed" with "water from Kane's coconut." In my opinion this "tradition" was invented by Kepelino, who believed in the existence of an original bloodless (and Christianlike) cult of Kāne.

63. Kahōali'i is interchangeable with Kamohoali'i in several myths (see, for example, Fornander 1916–20, 4:92).

64. K. Kamakau calls Kahōāli'i's spear "the spear of the owl." By implication he assimilates him to the owl. Moreover, as we have seen, Kahōāli'i is assimilated to Nīheu, whose eyes are described as "large and searching" (Emerson 1915, 114) like those of an owl. But the owl is the bird of Kūkauakāhi, who is a form of Kū

(Kamakau 1964, 87, 88). Hence once again we find that Kahōāliʻi is connected with Kū.

65. See the article in *Ka Loea Kalaiaina*, 13 May 1899 (ms. trans. by M. K. Pukui, communicated by Marshall Sahlins). This article implicitly identifies Kamohoaliʻi and Kahōāliʻi, since it affirms that the latter lives in the Kīlauea volcano—it is Kamohoaliʻi who is usually said to live there.

66. Note also that a character named "Kahoalei"—identified by Beckwith (1940, 50–51) with Kahōāliʻi—appears in one myth as a god of the underworld who captures the sun and the stars, thereby preventing men from seeing. This story is perhaps the mythical amplification of Kahōāliʻi's role as blinder (Rice 1923, 102–3; cf. Fornander 1916–20, 4:86; Ellis 1842, 393–94; N. Emerson in Malo 1951, 155).

67. It is, as we have seen, a purification prayer (PE, 199).

68. Emerson's translation ("Stand up and hold aloft the spears"—Malo 1951, 164) is erroneous. I follow Pukui's translation (in Ii 1963, 42). The expression *hiki a ola* (= *hiki iā ola*) follows an impersonal construction for which there is no English equivalent; accordingly, I translate it in different ways depending on the context. But the sense is always the same: the success of the rite "saves," ensures life (*ola*). Wise translates this expression in this context by "we are saved" (K. Kamakau, n.d., 32).

69. This "*ia*" must be read as "*iā*" and is a repetition of the particle *iā* of the preceding sentence. Emerson's conjecture that it is the name of some deity is evidently groundless (see Malo 1951, 180, n. 19).

70. *Kalo* or *kalokalo*: "conventional prayer to the gods (informal appeal and not a memorized chant)" (PE, 115).

71. The text says *haku* ("master"); *kahu* ("keeper," "caretaker") should be read instead.

72. In this formula, *kuʻu* ("mine") replaces the usual *kū* ("get up") that one expects in this context. See also K. Kamakau 1919–20, 35.

73. This is probably why the king always finds something to criticize in the priest's prayer; at least this is what the text seems to imply.

74. The Haku ʻōhiʻa is both the name of the main temple image and that of the individual *ʻōhiʻa-lehua* tree (*Metrosideros macropus, M. collina*) from which it is carved. K. Kamakau calls it *akua ʻōhiʻa*, "ʻōhiʻa god."

75. Adzes are made of obsidian (cf. Samwell 1967, 1186).

76. *Malu koʻi* literally means "adze shadow." "Shadow" is a metaphor for "taboo," since the thing "shaded" is protected. Hence *malu koʻi* means "adze taboo" (PE, 216).

77. Rain is a sign of the divine presence, of the communication between heaven and earth. Thus it is also "an indication of approval of the services" (Thrum in Fornander 1916–20, 6:12, n. 20). However, according to Kamakau (1976, 136) and ʻĪʻī (1963, 42; cf. Thrum 1910, 59–60), it is not rain but a perfectly clear sky that is the sign of divine approbation. These are just two alternative ways of representing the communication of gods and men.

78. *Haku ʻōhiʻa* is transcribed by Wilkes as "*nukuokea*"; *ʻōhiʻa* is always given as "*okea*." These are misreadings or typographical errors.

79. Most likely a *kūmū* fish, as Emerson speculates (Malo 1951, 165). Recall that red (*ʻula*) is synonymous with "sacred."

80. *Kuamū* is also the name of a rain-laden mountain wind that blows through the forests of *ʻōhiʻa-lehua* trees (Emerson 1915, 166). Are the "Lord" *ʻōhiʻa* and his violent procession also assimilated to this wind blowing down the mountains?

81. I am not considering the entire chant because it is somewhat anomalous and most difficult to interpret.

82. "*O ka laau ohia i oioi mai ke ku ana mamua.*"

83. "*O ke akua no keia i ono mai i ka puaa ke oioi mai nei mamua.*"

84. "O Kū-of-the-'*ōhi'a-laka* [= *lehua*]-tree." The '*ōhi'a-lehua* is thus a manifestation of the god Kū. Laka is the name of a god worshiped by canoe builders (Malo 1951, 82). In this connection, note that the Haku 'ōhi'a ritual is similar to the canoe-building ritual.

85. It is clear that this human sacrifice is made in three steps. First, a chant (*kānaenae*) consecrates both the human victim and the other victims to the god; then, after the tree is cut down, the human victim is put to death (*make*); finally, before the beginning of the men's meal, the human victim is given to the god as his share of the meal (*kaumaha*). The pigs are the men's share. As usual, sacrifice combines a commensal relationship between men and gods with their hierarchical separation.

86. Note the association of *ha'alelea*, "forsaken," "rejected"—which refers to the victim who by transgressing has placed himself outside society—and *nāhelehele*, which is a reduplication of *nahele* "wilderness" (PE, 238). The transgressor's disorder corresponds to that of the weeds, of the wilderness.

87. Brief descriptions of the rite of the fetching of the Haku 'ōhi'a can be found in Tyermann and Bennett (1832, vol. 2), *Mooolelo Hawaii* (1838, 76–78; Remy 1862, 161) and Pogue (1858, 21–22, 32). See also Haleole 1863 (in Fornander 1916–20, 6:154) and Kamakau 1961, 1–2, 13–14.

88. See table 1. In addition, Kū and the '*ie'ie* have the same position in the set formula used to refer to them both: (a) "our Kū is born in the forest" ("*hanau ka maua Ku i ka nahele*"—Fornander 1916–20, 4:384); (b) "Born in the tangled ieie in the forest" ("*hanau ka ieie i ka nahele*"—Brigham 1906, 61).

89. The bark cloths offered to the gods and used to wrap their images are often perfumed with sandalwood oil (Choris 1822, 14; Marin 1973, 312, n. 45; PE, 203) and can therefore be put among the "fragrant things" offered to the gods.

90. It could also refer to images of *kauila* wood to which feathers are glued (cf. Fornander 1916–20, 4:200, 201, 202; PE, 125).

91. The close connection between the *lehua* and the birds it attracts is confirmed by the fact that the names of two species of these birds are given to two varieties of the tree: the *lehua-mamo* and the *lehua-'āpane* (or '*apapane*) (Handy 1972, 241–43; PE, 26, 184).

92. One myth, reported by Ellis (1842, 430), recounts that before man's arrival the islands of the archipelago were inhabited exclusively by the gods. Having sacrificed to them, men obtained permission to live there. Clearly what is implied is that sacrifice made the gods retreat inland, leaving the coastal zones to men.

93. At any rate, according to K. Kamakau, the adze used to symbolically chop down the tree is consecrated to the god before being used.

94. That is, flowers of the *Eugenia malaccensis* and *pala* ferns. The latter are used as components in the wreaths of *maile*, "as the fern brought out the fragrance of the *maile* and made a handsome lei" (Neal 1965, 6).

95. More exactly, he is called "*Lehua o kuu aina*" "*lehua* of my land" (Fornander 1916–20, 4:306; cf. Kamakau 1961, 310).

96. Liloa's engendering of 'Umi in the forest can be assimilated to the king's fetching of the Haku 'ōhi'a in the forest. It follows that from the beginning 'Umi occupies a position homologous to that of the Haku 'ōhi'a.

97. The various sources on the myth of 'Umi are listed in Beckwith 1940, 391.

98. "Our Kū [ali'i] is born in the wilderness" ("*Hanau ka maua Ku i ka nahele*"—Fornander 1916–20, 4:384, line 379).

99. *Nanahua* is also defined by PE, 241 as the "name of the two posts at the entrance of a temple to which the '*aha* (taboo cord) was fastened."

100. Literally, "the bird's pillar." *Manu* is not a proper name—as Emerson implies (Malo 1951, 166) by capitalizing it. It is *not* capitalized in Malo's Hawaiian text (cf. also PE, 317).

101. Emerson has Malo say that these are "images of Lono" (Malo 1951, 166). I find no trace of this statement in Malo's text.

102. Pukui and Elbert misread Malo when they state that according to this author the Haku 'ōhi'a is installed in the place of the *nanahua* post in the mana house (PE, 241, misquoting Malo 1951, 166).

103. "*Hele aku ke lii me ke kahuna, e kai i ka aha helehonua*" (Malo MS, 169).

104. These chickens, called *moa kauō* (*kauwō*), "subsistence chickens," are apparently used to feed the priests officiating at this rite (cf. Andrews 1865, 237)—at least if we have to believe Wise's translation and Thrum's footnote 23 to K. Kamakau 1919–20 (p. 14).

105. The text does not immediately identify the second priest, but it does so later on the same page of the Hawaiian text. His name is dropped from Wise's translation.

106. Moreover, one of the meanings of the word '*aha* is "to stretch the cord by which the first posts of a house were put down or set straight" (Andrews 1865, 36).

107. A circular movement seems always to indicate encompassment, possession. Thus, it is by making a circuit of the land that the king takes possession of it or renews his rule over it (see Fornander 1916–20, 4:214, 330; 1878–80, 2:122, 142). In myth, the circumnavigation of an island is often used to signify its conquest (cf., for example, Tyerman and Bennett 1832, 2:56; Fornander 1878–80, 2:25). Note also that Hawaiian kings used to make one or more ceremonial tours with their canoes around the ships (called *moku* "islands") of the first European navigators (Cook 1967 and King 1967, passim; Portlock 1789, 155–56; Vancouver 1801, 3:211–12; Manby 1929, 41), possibly to indicate that they controlled them.

108. Moreover, both the foundation of the mana house and the space in back of the *lele* altar where the Haku 'ōhi'a is erected are called *honua*, as is witnessed by this text: "These kahunas occupied a place in the heiau called 'honua' (earth) and that was the spot back of the lele or sacrificial altar to offer a human being" (HEN, 1:1677).

109. Thus the king's circuit of the land, if "successful" (*maika'i*), is supposed to produce peace and therefore life (Ii 1963, 139).

110. According to Brigham (n.d., 148) *kālewa* means "a separation," thus, a secluded spot in the temple area.

111. Where the Haku 'ōhi'a also lies, still wrapped with ferns and vines.

112. The '*kā'ai* gods on this occasion have a *lā'au pe'a*, that is, a crosspiece (Malo MS, 170) perhaps similar to that of the *akua loa* during the Makahiki festival.

113. Which Brigham (n.d., 148) translates as "Go gently, fly softly to the cloudy heaven."

114. Later, Malo says that this man is himself a priest.

115. The text of the passage is given incorrectly by Emerson (Malo 1951: 168). The correct text is as follows: "*Kuikui, kahiko, i ke lani au, / Wai la make o manalu*" (Malo MS, 171).

116. It is unclear which one: the high priest or the priest with the staff?

117. Malo's spelling is "*kaiopokeo*" (cf. as well Malo MS, 172, 62), not "*kaia-pokea*," as Emerson writes and Pukui and Elbert repeat (p. 107).

118. Emerson considers *kauakāhi* as a proper name. In this case it would refer to a form of Kū: Kūkauakāhi ("Kū the single battle"—cf. Kamakau 1964, 58). This form of Kū manifests itself in an owl (Kamakau 1964, 88).

119. For the parts of the house, see Apple 1971, 278, 160 (see also 181–88).

120. After the thatching is over, two operations still remain to finish the house: weaving a "bonnet" of thatch over the upper ridgepole (cf. Apple 1971, 188 ff.) and the symbolic cutting of a bunch of thatch above the entrance door. These operations are the object of another temple rite (see below, p. 292).

121. Emerson wrongly translates *kōpili* as "braided sugarcane." The *kōpili* and '*oloa* cloths are the finest, whitest, and most precious. *Kōpili* cloth is, moreover, transparent (cf. PE, 262, 154).

122. As the rest of the text makes clear, they remain outside the temple, probably on the *papahola* platform.

123. *Pandanus odoratissimus* (screw pine). The wreath is made with the orange sections of the fruits, which are found on the female trees (Neal 1929, 21).

124. It is not said who this god is. It is undoubtedly one of the king's gods, probably his principal *akua hulu manu*.

125. Thereby interfering with the king's rite.

126. Wise translates this expression as "they . . . went into the temple to purify themselves" (Fornander 1916–20, 6:16). This translation is surely false. The expression used by K. Kamakau ("*e kau i na auau*") is found in identical form in the text where Malo describes the placing of the '*au'au* ridgepoles. It is thus obvious that K. Kamakau alludes to the rite described by Malo without, however, describing it himself. The two texts complete and confirm each other.

127. Perhaps the high priest, whom Malo defines as "the head of the *luakini*" ("*ke poo o ka luakini*"—MS, 174).

128. He is the assistant of the high priest of the order of Kū.

129. The name of this staff indicates that the herald is the same one who precedes a god or sacred ali'i to announce his taboo with the cry "*kapuo*" (Kepelino 1932, 137–39). According to Kepelino (1932, 25), the *pule kapuwō* (var. of *kapuō*) is the order given to the congregation to prostrate themselves as the sacrifice is offered.

130. 'Ī'ī says that Kahōāli'i is nude except for a narrow white band covering his genitals. In this he differs from Malo, for whom Kahōāli'i goes about completely naked.

131. Note that in several rites performed inside the temple the audience sits as though in canoes. This explains why Kamakau refers to the audience with the expression *wa'a 'aha ka'i*, "canoe of the '*aha ka'i*" (1976, 141). '*Aha ka'i* is Kamakau's name for the most important rites that take place inside the *luakini*.

132. Note that he does not represent a god but is an assistant of the high priest (Ii 1963, 42).

133. On the association between the left hand and death, cf. also the way Cook's vessels were detabooed by the Hawaiians when for the first time they saw them approaching Kaua'i—like threatening gods moving in a straight line. An ali'i and a kahuna climbed on board the ship of these new gods and "stepped forward with the left fist clenched and, advancing before Captain Cook, stepped back a pace and bowed as they murmured a prayer; then, seizing his hands, they knelt down and the tabu was freed" (Kamakau 1961, 93). Such at least is the Hawaiian legend. What matters in this description is that the gods are desacralized and therefore

tamed with the left hand; moreover, the left fist probably evokes death, since it is believed that a blow inflicted by a left-handed person is always fatal (cf. Kamakau 1961, 85).

134. The equivalence of high and right, and low and left, is exemplified in the fact that the upper jaw is made to correspond to the right hand, while the lower jaw is connected with the left hand.

135. Like the circuit of the conquering gods, the circuit of the king who "eats the land" is clockwise: the land is always at his right (cf. Ii 1963, 137–39).

136. Moreover, in both cases the priest of Lono is specifically a *kahuna kuhi'alaea*.

137. It is difficult to render '*olu'olu* with a single English word. It is a reduplication of '*olu*, the fundamental meaning of which is "cool." The god must metaphorically be "cooled," "softened," "made pliant," "flexible," "kind": in a word, he must be tamed.

138. Perfect (*maika'i*) must be taken here in the sense of "completed."

139. Quite arbitrarily, Emerson's translation gives only the names of Kū, Kāne, and Lono, in this order.

140. When speaking to the priest, the king refers to the '*aha* as "the '*aha* of us both," using the inclusive dual pronominal form. When he addresses the congregation he speaks of "the '*aha* of us all," using the plural inclusive form. This indicates that the '*aha* does not belong to the king alone: by being recognized by the priest, it becomes the '*aha* of them both, and when it is recognized by the congregation it becomes its '*aha*. I shall consider the significance of this commonality shortly.

141. Naturally this is "ritual work." But in Hawaiian, no distinction is made between material and ritual work; both are called *hana*.

142. "Distinguishes" translates a very complex word, *hailona*, which means "to put to the test by divination," "to indicate the true value or meaning of something." Therefore there is an element of the ordeal in this rite. Andrews (1865, 133), who apparently considers *hailona* a contraction of *hō'ailona*, also gives it the value of the latter word: "a sign" (cf. PE, 10). It is a sign that permits one to differentiate, to decide. It is a differential element.

143. Apparently this means that they ask their '*aumakua* deities not to give forth any ominous sound through the animals in which they are incarnated in order not to spoil the king's '*aha*.

144. To understand this last line, we must recall that '*aha* also means "assembly." In this context '*aha* seems to designate the "society of the king," where the '*aumakua* gods will be admitted with their worshipers (and descendants).

145. K. Kamakau writes "the god" without specifying which one. It is certainly not the Haku 'ōhi'a, because K. Kamakau, contrary to Malo, places the Haku 'ōhi'a's entrance into the temple at a later stage of the ritual. Hence it is likely that "the god" referred to here is the king's main feather god, that is, Kūkā'ilimoku or some similar form of Kū.

146. *Hulahula* means "to dance," or "twitching," "fluttering." Here *ia* marks an agent, an instrument, a cause, a source (cf. Elbert and Pukui 1979, 133). Thus "*E Kū iā hulahula*" could mean "O Kū because of [caused by] the dancing [or the 'twitching']." If indeed *hulahula* means "dancing," then the sentence would confirm Kaeppler's hypothesis that the Haku 'ōhi'a is represented as dancing. It would confirm, moreover, that dancing, as the maximum expression of the social, is generated by the god and generates it in a mutual process.

147. Probably the *luakini* temple, which is the god's "house."

148. According to Pukui and Elbert, *mōlia* means "to set apart for the gods; to sacrifice or offer to the gods; to bless; to curse. *E mōlia mai e make*, curse so [he] shall die" (PE, 233).

149. The text has *nau*, but I propose the emendation "*naʻau*." Wise translates the whole sentence, "The tattler who would seek our defeat" (Fornander 1916–20, 6:18).

150. Wise translates, "Here is where the object of our service is directed," which is somewhat vague.

151. Obviously we must read *kuili*.

152. Probably to keep him from grunting.

153. N. Emerson's rendering of this sentence is unacceptable (cf. Malo 1951, 171, par. 86).

154. The text first has "some men," then "two men."

155. The name of a valley on Kauaʻi, literally, "the valley of the necklaces" (PE, 53; Pukui, Elbert, and Mookini 1974, 40–41; cf. Emerson 1915, 65). In a chant, the valley of Hanalei is compared to a house, "apparently because the rain-columns seem to draw together and enclose the valley within walls, while the dark foreshortened vault of heaven covers it as with a roof" (Emerson 1965, 155). The ridgepole of Hanalei is thus the sky itself; we can infer, then, that the roof of the mana house is assimilated here to the sky, Kū's home (cf. as well Fornander 1916–20, 5:57).

156. All in all, 1,800 pigs are given to the priests in the *kuili* rites. But Malo's account must not be taken too literally; perhaps many of the "pigs" consisted of "leaf pigs" or "sea pigs," that is, vegetable or marine food substituted for this animal. Moreover, the other sources give a much smaller number of pigs.

157. K. Kamakau does not give any details on these prayers, but note that the *kuwā* is said to be a prayer of inauguration (PE, 172; Malo 1951, 184) and that it corresponds by name to the one that, according to Malo, is recited for the inauguration of the mana house. The *kuwā* is uttered here in front of the temple and therefore seems to refer to its inauguration, not that of the mana house. The latter is only indirectly alluded to throughout K. Kamakau's text, perhaps because "The better known a fact, the less chance there is that it will be mentioned" (Hocart 1938, 99).

158. Wise translates "offered a prayer" (Fornander 1916–20, 6:20), but there is no doubt that *ʻaha* here means a cord that the high priest waves during his prayers (PE, 5).

159. *Koliʻi* means "to disappear" (PE, 150). Is this a purification prayer that makes sins "disappear"?

160. This seems to indicate that the pigs are alive; perhaps, then, K. Kamakau does not refer here to the pigs already cooked but to another herd, which is first brought inside the temple (= consecrated to the gods) and then (the morning after) cooked in the oven outside the temple (see below).

161. *Kula*, "source"; *wā*, "noise," "source of noise" (i.e., the prayer is noisy—see above p. 293).

162. Where the Haku ʻōhiʻa is going to be erected.

163. Literally, "The king commands a man for the god" ("*a kena ae la ke alii i kanaka na ke akua*").

164. Cf. PE, 253; Hiroa 1957, 12. Is this the instrument used to kill the man? According to Ellis (1842, 151), the victims sometimes are stabbed.

165. "Temple" here refers to the mana house, on each side of which sit the two teams of priests who receive the pigs.

166. According to Apple (1971, 75), "the generic Hawaiian name for cor-

dage was *'aha.*" However, cords not made of coir, hair, or intestines are called *aho* (Stokes 1906, 147, n. 47).

167. The word *'aha* can be used as a verb, too. Then it has a literal and a figurative meaning. Literally, it means "to stretch the cord by which the first parts of a house were put down or set straight; *e kii i ke kaula e aha ai,* fetch the rope to make straight with" (Andrews 1865, 36; cf. PE, 5; Brigham 1908, 117). Figuratively, *'aha* means "to direct the government," as in the expression, *"oia ka ana a me ka aha pololei no ke aupuni, aha,* that is, to measure and *direct straightly* the government" (Andrews 1865, 36).

168. Besides K. Kamakau's mention of this rite, see also Malo MS, 166.

169. Cf. also Fornander 1916–20, 4:330; Kamakau 1976, 139–40, 141; Kamakau 1961, 85; Kamakau and 'I'i, articles, passim; K. Kamakau 1919–20, 31.

170. On the latter name, see Fornander 1916–20, 4:552; HEN, 1: 1679–80.

171. Each has its own name (PE, 6).

172. Cf. also the epithets given, respectively, to Kalanimoku ("the cable that held fast the nation") and Ka'ahumanu ("the cable that held the ship of state") (Kamakau 1961, 277, 308; cf. Byron 1826, 100).

173. On the Hawaiian *haku mele,* "composer of chants," and his Polynesian equivalents, see Gizycki 1971, 169–74.

174. Remember that for the Hawaiians, as for all Polynesians, "to think" is "to bind," "to weave" (Koskinen 1968, 66–67).

175. As Dickey notes, "the Hawaiian is fond of motion and change in a string figure" (1928, 11).

176. Indeed the net of Makali'i is called "the net of Maoleha [Maoloha]" in one version of this myth (cf. Fornander 1916–20, 5:369; Beckwith 1940, 437).

177. There are innumerable examples of the consecration of idols, temple houses, and bones by wrapping them (see Ellis 1782, 2:180; Samwell 1967, 1216; Manby 1929, 43, 44; Campbell 1967, 149; Ross 1904, 70; Tyerman and Bennett 1832, 2:73, 74, 55; Ellis 1842, 15, 139; Kamakau 1961, 285). According to Emerson (1965, 20, 23), a simple log of *lama* wood is transformed into Laka, the protective goddess of the *hula,* when it is wrapped with an *'oloa* cloth dyed yellow with curcuma.

178. The ceremony reported by Tyerman and Bennett has some similarity to the marriage rite, which consists "in the bridegroom's casting a piece of tapa or native cloth over the bride, in the presence of her parents or relations" (Ellis 1842, 435; cf. Mathison 1825, 474; Kamakau 1961, 62). Covering someone with a cloth is a sign of his appropriation (see also Samwell 1967, 1165).

179. Cf. this description of Kīna'u, one of Kamehameha's daughters: she was "wrapped in such quantities of native cloth, as not to be able to move a step without assistance: having a supporter on each side and a number of attendants preceding and following her, bearing the ends of her drapery" (Stewart 1839, 241–42).

180. Apple believes that the "houses of major temples were structurally similar to those occupied by high chiefs" (1971, 36, cf. 41). It is not certain that this is always true on a material level. In fact, in some temples the *hale mana* is similar to a *hālau* ("long house, as for canoes or hula instruction"—PE, 49), not to a regular house. But what Apple maintains is true in principle, and in any event there is a symbolic equivalence between the *hale mana,* which is the king's most "sacred" house, and the house where he ordinarily lives, which is less sacred.

181. In describing the symbolic principles that preside over the construction

of houses, our sources do not distinguish between different categories of habitation but speak of the "house" in general. I believe this is not so much because they describe the undifferentiated house in use after the abolition of the taboo system as because they emphasize the identity of the symbolic principles presiding over the construction of every house. Of course, the more important the house, the stricter the application of the principles. Probably in each household the *hale mua* realizes them more than the other houses, while the archetypal house is fully realized by the *hale mana*.

182. This is why it is called in prayer *hale ola*, "house of life" (Kamakau 1976, 106).

183. The lustral virtue of light is recognized in many cultures. The very word "lustral" is derived from Latin *lustrare*, which means both "to illuminate" and "to purify."

184. "Family god" is the translation of *akua ʻaoʻao*. It is clear that the god is treated here as an ancestral being; this seems to confirm Stokes's claim that the *ʻaha hoʻowilimoʻo* also has the aim of reestablishing a genealogical connection with the god.

185. Malo's text makes it clear that the fish is caught with a line and hook; however, the priest's work is called *kāpapaulua*, which literally means "to push the *ulua* into a net by striking the side of the canoe with a paddle" (PE, 122). For a description of the technique used for *ulua* fishing, see Fornander 1916–20, 6:188.

186. See also this text: "In the night of Muku, that being the last day of the month, the priests with their men went out ulua fishing. Upon arriving at the place where the canoes were kept, a tatu beat was sounded on the edge of the canoes. As the men came up one of them would be caught and killed and the great hook Manaiakalani was put into the dead body and it was taken to the temple. If no one came to the canoes, instructions were given that a great ball of seaweeds be gotten and the hook was placed in it" (Fornander 1916–20, 4:204). The hook Manaiakalani is the one Maui used when he fished the islands of the Hawaiian archipelago up from the bottom of the sea.

187. The bamboo referred to is the one that will be split to make the knife with which to cut the god's umbilical cord. Each line of the prayer publicly declares each of the priest's ritual acts.

188. This wreath is probably the god's belt, that is, his navel cord. Unlike Emerson (p. 173), I attach *aka* to the preceding word, *lei*. Moreover, I see no reason for translating, as he does, "*kupenu lei*" by "wear it as a wreath."

189. *Hālapa* is equivalent to *hoʻolapa*, which could also be translated "to form a clot of blood," since one of the meanings of *lapa* is "clot of blood" (PE, 179).

190. Here "*lono*" is a verb and not the name of the god Lono—as Emerson believes (Malo 1951, 173). Lono has nothing to do with this rite (M. K. Pukui is of the same opinion—cf. Handy 1972, 379).

191. There is a parallel between "*haʻilono*" and "*e lono*" in the preceding line. This confirms that "*e lono*" means "listen to the news."

192. *Mōʻī* is perhaps related to *ʻī*, "supreme" (PE, 231). According to Stokes (1932, 1–10), the word *mōʻī* is of recent origin and appears in print for the first time in 1832. Perhaps, however, only the habit of applying this title to the king is of recent origin.

193. Obviously, only part of the offering is put on the altar, which does not have room for four hundred pigs.

194. The *ulua* can be a fish or, as Malo explained above, a man treated like a fish.

195. *Maua* means "to receive without giving in return" (PE, 223).

196. Presumably, the platform where the Haku 'ōhi'a and the surrounding images are set up.

197. These are said to be *kalokalo*: "conversational prayer to the gods (informal appeal and not a memorized chant)" (PE, 115).

198. The *luakini* temple?

199. Of course this can also be interpreted as "puts an end to the *'aha* rite." But I believe that here again a sacred cord is involved.

200. The high priest?

201. The use of the word *kāhea* in the preceding line implies that the two dancers sing the first lines of a stanza as a cue to the priests below, who chant the rest to accompany the dance (cf. PE, 104). Since the dance takes place on the tower, it must consist mostly of gesticulations.

202. The *kanaka maka hanohano* seem to be people who are favored by some noble. The term *pū'ali* means, according to 'Ī'ī, "one who had no servant or servants. It applied to an adopted man or boy" (1963, 38). However, Pukui's and Elbert's dictionary glosses this term as "warrior" (PE, 319).

203. The name of this prayer indicates that it refers to the *kopili* loincloths that girdle the images of the gods. K. Kamakau has already placed a girdling of images after the *kuwā* rite. But he refers to those images by the term *ki'i*, whereas here he refers to *akua lā'au*, "wooden gods." The latter seem to be, in this context, the principal statues adjacent to the tower, including, perhaps, the Haku 'ōhi'a.

204. A stick that is rubbed on a piece of wood called *'aunaki* to produce fire (cf. Hiroa 1957, 17). The prayer consecrates the sacrificial fire.

205. Since the text says that the cooked pigs are brought inside the temple, we must infer that, although the sacred fire is started in the temple, the actual cooking of the pigs takes place outside, or at any rate outside the sanctum sanctorum.

206. The exclusive pronoun is used. The priest refers to the king's enemy as "our chief," because this enemy is represented by the *ulua* fish that he and his assistants have just caught. At least this seems to me to be the only plausible explanation of the use of that pronominal form.

207. *Hainaki* is also the name of the firstfruits given to Lonomakua during the New Year's festival. Here it refers to the first portion that, given to the gods, makes the rest accessible for human consumption. 'Ī'ī describes this *hainaki* rite as follows: "They [the pigs—V. V.] were bundled and laid on the pebbled area within the enclosure, which had images standing both inside and outside of it, where stood the kahuna in charge. After he had offered dedicatory prayer over the pigs, he took the right legs of the king's pigs and waved them for emphasis, as prescribed by the ritual, perhaps" (1963, 38). Then the meat is divided by the king and chiefs among themselves and their dependents. 'Ī'ī confirms K. Kamakau's statement that the king shows particular generosity by giving a share (not all) of his own pork to the "dispossessed ones" (ibid.).

208. This is still the sixth day.

209. Obviously the *'aha ho'owilimo'o*.

210. The text has "*nule-pahu*." "*Nule*" is obviously a misprint.

211. The text adds that if no transgressors were to be found, "a squirrel was substituted, and offered to the idol in like manner" (p. 508). Since there are no squirrels on Hawaii, another animal must be meant (squid or squirrel fish?).

212. The identification of the adversary with the *ulua* fish is illustrated by an event famous in the Hawaiian annals. Kamehameha wishes to be rid of his adversary Kaumuali'i, king of Kaua'i. An adviser suggests that he lure him into a trap by

inviting him to come to Oʻahu. When Kaumualiʻi has arrived by sea, Kamehameha must "lay in his hand a fishhook and a line [the very ones that are used in the *ulua* rite—V. V.], a symbol of the fish of the dark sea [= Kaumualiʻi—V. V.] which the king has brought hence. I say that Kaumualii shall not die in his own native haunt, but where he seizes the hook and line, there eventually his corpse shall be found" (Ii 1963, 81).

The symbolic equation between the caught fish and the sacrificed man (or the man killed in battle) is widely documented; see Emerson 1892, 20–21; Beckwith 1919, 323; Fornander 1878–80, 2:152; Kamakau 1961, 86, 87, 88, 161; Beckwith 1940, 66; Thrum 1916, 94–95; Kepelino 1932, 120). This equation is found throughout Polynesia (see, for example, Gill 1876, 291–93; Best 1925, 1059).

213. My translation.

214. *ʻŌhiki* means "to shell," "to pick out," "to clean out"—this is why this crab (probably the *Ocypode ceratophthalma*) is used as a sacrificial offering in purification rites, which "pick out" sin and "clean out" pollution (cf. Titcomb and Pukui 1972, 60).

215. My translation. In Pukui's translation the chant is followed by the sentence, "Figuratively, this means, 'Let which is unknown become known,'" which is not found in the original Hawaiian. I think that the coming ashore of the *ʻōhiki* crab, which represents purification (see note 214), is a metaphoric invocation of purification.

216. Cf. a similar rite, in which the consecration of a pig's right leg has the effect of "free[ing] the rest of the pigs for eating" (Kamakau 1976, 144).

217. "Papa's chorus." According to Pukui and Elbert, this is a purification prayer, chanted before dawn in the *hale o Papa* (PE, 82). Malo gives no details; Emerson's translation is erroneous.

218. According to Pukui and Elbert this expression designates a sacrificial pig and can also refer to a human victim (PE, 317). Here, however, it refers to a pig.

219. Of the *puaʻa heʻa*. Emerson writes "the eyes of the pig" (Malo 1951, 175), but Malo's text gives the singular form.

220. Andrews (1865, 353), quoting this passage, defines *lukamaea* as "a prayer used by females from the time of Papa." Is this one of the rites performed in the *hale o Papa*? *Luka* is the abbreviated form of *lukaluka*, which is a variation of *lupalupa*, "purification." *Maea* means "stinking, stench." Thus it is probable that *lukamaea* refers to the purifying bath that men take in the sea at the conclusion of the rites (see below) and to the prayer that precedes it and makes it possible—a prayer that is recited by the women in the *hale o Papa* (cf. K. Kamakau's text for evidence confirming this interpretation).

221. The *akua kaʻai* are thrust into the sand on the beach.

222. This is probably a way of counting the number of participants in the *kapu heiau* and perpetuating the memory of their number, according to the method inaugurated by ʻUmi at the time of the construction of ʻAhu a ʻUmi temple (see Baker 1917).

223. *Hono* means "to stitch, sew, mend, patch"; it also designates a "group of islands in a circle" (PE, 74).

224. Probably *wekeweke* should be used. This word is the reduplication of *weke*, which means "to separate, loosen, free." The name is also given to certain species of the Mullidae (surmullets or goatfish), which are popular offerings because of the meaning of their name (PE, 354). The rite to which K. Kamakau refers perhaps includes the offering of these fish and is therefore a rite of purification.

225. This is undoubtedly Kahōāliʻi, as the night of the rite is "consecrated" to him (cf. also Malo).

226. Outside the temple.

227. "Branch of *koa*." Another point in common with the rite of Kahōāliʻi, as described by Malo.

228. This is the dawn of the seventh day of the month.

229. Apparently those captured by Kahōāliʻi.

230. *Holua* is the passive/imperative of *holu*, "pliable" (PE, 73). (The sacrifice makes the god "pliable.")

231. These are obviously images found on the *kuahu* platform.

232. That is, the clients of the aliʻi.

233. This is a mistranslation due to a misreading: *honu* ("turtle") instead of *hono*.

234. Obviously the *hale o Papa*.

235. There are several other cases in the *luakini* ritual in which the god's presence is established by blocking the spectators' sight after first attracting it. This is made especially possible by wrapping the visible manifestations of the gods in cloth. Thus the truth of the gods' presence in the statues and the tower is established when they are partially covered with cloths (*kōpili*), which moreover are almost transparent and allow a glimpse at the same time that they hinder proper vision. The god's presence is thus established in the transitional area between the visible and the invisible.

In the rite of the "spear of Pueo," in which Kahōāliʻi seems to anticipate the final rite in which he gouges out human eyes, it is the blinking of the eyes, the rapid alternation between seeing and not seeing, that situates the perception of the god on the threshold of the invisible. Note also that the *ʻalaea* god consecrated by this rite is covered with a thin white cloth through which one can thus glimpse it. Therefore the rite combines an operation upon the object (the god) with an operation upon the subject (the spectator) in order to locate the truth of the god on the border between the visible and the invisible.

To these examples drawn from ritual can be added the mythical motif of the deity or hero who is bundled up with cloth; he is not visible, but his splendor can be perceived through the covering. Thus he is both visible and invisible (cf. Fornander 1916–20, 4 : 164, 520).

236. Thus one speaks of "the pupil of the sun" (*ka ʻōnohi o ka lā*) (Ellis 1842, 145). Another god is called "the great eye messenger" (Kamakanuiʻahaʻilono—Pukui, Elbert, and Mookini 1974, 122).

237. On the role of eyes in Hawaiian mythology, see Elbert 1951, 349; cf. also Beckwith 1940, 171; 1919, 511). On the gods as devourers of human eyes, see Fornander 1916–20, 4 : 583, 592–93. Even the eyes of animals are the gods' share (cf., for example, Thrum 1907a, 237).

238. Hence its ambivalence: it is both purifying, life giving—and polluting (as demonstrated by the fact that the congregation must purify itself in the sea—cf. Ii 1963, 43).

239. S. M. Kamakau describes the orientation of these victims thus: "*E momoe like ana ke poo i ka mana i ka anuu.*" Thrum (1910, 68) translates this as: "all were laid alike with the head toward the *mana* in the structure." Pukui translates it more correctly as "the heads [of the man and the pigs] lay in the same relation (*momoe like ana*) to the *ʻanuʻu* and to the *mana* house"—which is a bit vague. I think Kamakau means that the corpses are always placed along an ideal line that goes from the tower to the door of the mana house and that the heads can be oriented toward one or the other of these buildings, but always all in the same direction.

According to the information obtained by Lisiansky (1814, 121) from the high priest at Hikiau, the victims' feet are oriented toward the principal image; thus the heads are oriented toward the mana house. The principal victim is placed in the center of the *lele* altar. Secondary human victims are laid out at his sides, and the interstices are occupied by pigs or dogs. According to John Young, however, the victims are oriented with their heads toward the god (Lisiansky 1814, 121–22), and no dog is offered on the *lele* altar. It is probable that Lisiansky understood Young better than the high priest. I find this orientation meaningful, because the victims must constitute a substitute for and extension of the pair, king/high priest. Thus their heads must be oriented toward the god and their feet pointed toward this pair. At the same time they probably serve to transmit divine mana to the mana house, which ideally they unite with the god.

If there are many victims they are piled up to form a pyramid. According to Ellis's informants (1842, 152), the pigs are placed on the human corpses, at right angles to them. Pogue (1858, 32) claims that victims are always killed and placed on the altar two by two. Along with the horizontal relationship between god (= the image) and men, the stacked victims thus realize a vertical relationship as well (the god is also in heaven).

240. Who, ideally, are also his wives.

241. Other sources (K. Kamakau, 'Ī'ī) specify that it is the goddess (Papa). Nevertheless, Malo's text could be interpreted as describing the union, through the loincloth brought into the *luakini*, of the king's wives (who stay in the *hale o Papa*) and the god. In fact, not only does Malo not specify that the *akua ki'i* is the goddess, but he writes that the king carries an end of the loincloth offered by his wives (see below) inside the "heiau." In the context of the ritual we have studied, this term usually designates the *luakini* temple. Moreover, why would Malo use two different terms (*hale o Papa* and *heiau*) *in the same context* if both referred to the same thing?

242. Who have participated in the temple rites.

243. And not the priests, as in Emerson's translation (Malo 1951, 175).

244. Either the *luakini* temple or the *hale o Papa* is meant (see note 241).

245. PE, 109 interprets it as "*kai-'oloa*"—wrongly, in my view.

246. "*Ka hana o ka luakini.*" The word *hana* indicates the whole of the "material" and "ritual" work necessary to build and inaugurate the temple.

247. Malo mentions the *ho'omāhanahana* rite in another somewhat obscure passage (MS, 160), where he states that "if the '*aha* is not successful (*i loa'a 'a'ole ka 'aha*), it [the temple] is not made *noa* quickly ('*a'ole e noa wawe*)." In this case the *ho'omāhanahana* rite is performed in order to interrupt the state of taboo ("*e huikala ia nae keia pule a noa*"), and the temple is thus "redeemed" (*ku'ai*), that is, made "free."

It seems likely, then, that the *pule ho'omāhanahana* is a "purification" rite (*huikala*) that is performed to put an end to the *kapu luakini*, even when all the conditions for the success of the rite have not been fulfilled during the canonical period of ten days. In this case, the *noa* state created by the rite is only provisional: it is a pause that allows one to await a more favorable moment for completing the ritual properly.

248. *Koli'i*, "to disappear"; *maomao*, "calm, clear."

249. Not guilty of gossip, as Thrum writes (in Fornander 1916–20, 6:28, n. 30), but of breaking the food taboos ('*ai kapu*).

250. Presumably a dagger or spear used to symbolize the killing of the victims, if not actually to kill them.

251. Those who are mentioned by K. Kamakau are members of the family of

Pele and Pele herself. These goddesses are the most common in the mediumistic rites of *kāula*. The text makes it clear that these goddesses are ultimately controlled by the king and associated with the house of Papa.

252. K. Kamakau gives all these expressions in sequence without indicating that they form a dialogue. Malo, however, gives them in the form of a dialogue. Undoubtedly because of an error, the last two words of the dialogue (*"noa honua"*) have become *"noho mua"* in K. Kamakau's text as published.

253. The text has *kaili* by mistake.

254. The English translation makes 'Ī'ī say that these rites take place in the *hale o Papa* (1963, 45). As a matter of fact, 'Ī'ī does not explicitly write this. However, the editor evidently thought that the adverb *malaila* ("there") found in the title that 'Ī'ī gives to the section of his article in which he describes the *hoʻomāhanahana* rite refers to the *hale o Papa*. It is a reasonable conjecture, but should be given as such.

255. Recall that the death of victims is always conceived as the death of the sacrifiers through an *interposed person* (this is one of the reasons for the ambivalent treatment of the victims throughout the ritual; see below). But there is always a risk that the principle of substitution will not work and that the symbolic death of the sacrifier will turn into a real one. This risk is illustrated by the story of the consecration of a *luakini* temple at Waipiʻo (island of Hawaiʻi). After sacrificing his prisoners of war, King ʻUmi hears the voice of Kūwahahilo (a "devouring" aspect of Kū), who asks him for still more victims; thus, little by little ʻUmi and his high priest are obliged to sacrifice all the sacrifiers present in the temple (about eighty of them). The last victim is ʻUmi's favorite, and the king at first refuses to sacrifice him. This is because his sacrifice touches him more directly than all others; after the favorite, the only possible victim is the king himself! (Ellis 1842, 362–63).

256. Indeed, 'Ī'ī writes that often only two, Kalamainuʻu (= Kihawahine) and Haumea are sheltered in the *hale o Papa* (1963, 44; cf. Westervelt 1915b, 152).

257. The analogy between the two rites is further reinforced by the analogy existing between the Haku ʻōhiʻa and the mana house, which I have demonstrated at length.

258. The latter is not, however, arbitrary: different rites can fuse in memory because they have common properties from a formal and functional standpoint, and thus it becomes difficult to keep them differentiated in thought. From this standpoint it is possible that Kamakau's version reveals the truly essential and distinctive components of the ritual.

259. Sometimes the eye gouging takes an even crueler form, in order to humiliate the victim and make him suffer the maximum: thus, when he is captured by Kamalalawalu (king of Maui), Kanaloakuaʻana (sovereign of the western part of the island of Hawaiʻi) has his eyes gouged out and his sockets pierced with points; then he is killed and his eyes "are tattooed" (Fornander 1916–20, 4:342–43). According to one chant, the eyes of the victims are gouged out with the handle of a *kāhili*—the scepter, covered with feathers at the top, that is the symbol of an aliʻi of supreme rank (Fornander 1916–20, 4:583). The custom of urinating in the eyes of the adversary destined to be sacrificed is also documented (cf. Kamakau 1961, 91).

260. Note that the castration—real or symbolic—of the adversary is mentioned in war accounts (cf. Kamakau 1961, 81) or in myths where conflicts between adversaries are expressed in sexual terms (cf., for example, Fornander 1916–20, 5:47). An episode of the myth of Kaulu illustrates the idea that attacking the adversary's sexual parts is equivalent to defeating and killing him. Kaulu pinches

the mons pubis of the god Makaliʻi, telling him, "You are dead!" The god is obliged to give him precious information so as to be released (Fornander 1916–20, 4:528).

261. To avoid shedding blood, the victim is often strangled (von Chamisso in Kotzebue 1821a, 3:250; Lisiansky 1814, 121; Arago 1822, 2:161; Freycinet 1978, 89; Ellis 1842, 389; Brigham, n.d., 256; Richards 1973, 28).

262. Malo is the only source to mention execution by decapitation in this rite. One can doubt that it was an ancient practice; it is not easy to cut off a man's head with a stone adze. I believe that traditionally the head was cut off *after* the victim had been put to death by strangulation or a blow. After the introduction of metal axes decapitation became frequent as a punishment for men guilty of adultery with high-ranking women (Ellis 1842, 421; Kamakau 1961, 255) and for sorcerers (Kamakau 1964, 130, 137; see also Richards 1973, 28).

263. According to one of Brigham's informants the corpses of the warriors fallen in battle "were usually brought in canoes wrapped on banana leaves, or if the journey must be by land, then slung on a long *pololu kauila*, or spear, between two bearers" (Brigham, n.d., 256).

264. Pigs undergo the same treatment, as we have seen. In principle, all that belongs to the victim, including his house, is also burned (cf. Anonymous 1924, 129). If he is a transgressor, "though he alone was thought to have committed the misdeed, the whole family was held guilty" (Ii 1963, 23).

265. According to Westervelt (1915b, 190), the remains of men thus cooked are thrown into the sea. Cooking is "a method of showing indignity to dead chiefs" (cf. Beckwith 1940, 152).

266. And also in the case of Cook. According to the *Mooolelo Hawaii* of 1838, Cook was first offered in sacrifice by the king Kalaniʻōpuʻu ("*Alaila, hai iho la o Kalaniopuu ia Lono* [= Cook]"), then he was cooked in the oven to loosen the flesh from the bones, which were to be distributed among the principal aliʻi (Remy 1862, 34–35; Martin 1817, 2:66–69; Ellis 1842, 67; Tyerman and Bennett 1831, 2:15; cf. Burney in Manwaring 1931, 138; Zimmermann 1930, 95; Dampier 1971, 67; etc.).

267. "For the pollution of offerings made to the gods and of those things belonging to the king or to the chiefs, the penalty was death" (Kamakau 1961, 191).

268. The accusations of cannibalism sometimes made against the Hawaiians (cf., for example, Rickman 1966, 324; Tyerman and Bennett 1832, 2:49; Hogg 1958, 165–66) are groundless (cf. King 1967, 561; Extract, 380; Meares, 1916, 40; Campbell 1967, 150–51; Westervelt 1915b, 190). The only documented act of cannibalism is the consumption of the victim's eyes by Kahōāliʻi.

269. According to Samwell (1967, 1209) the skull can also be broken. Destruction is an irreversible means of assigning something to the gods: men can no longer use it.

270. Two or three days after the sacrifice, according to Samwell (1967, 1177); cf. as well Lisiansky (1814, 132).

271. The hands of fallen enemies are sometimes cut off (Kamakau 1961, 31), as are the ears and the little fingers (Fornander 1916–20, 4:430).

272. The long bones can also go to either the gods (Pogue 1858, 32) or the king (see below).

273. Some aliʻi supposedly have houses built for themselves out of the bones of their enemies or surround their ordinary houses with a palisade of bones (Kamakau 1961, 138–39; Burney 1819, 114–15). Hooks are also made from the victims' bones (Ellis 1782, 2:176; Clerke 1967, 577).

274. According to Kamakau (1961, 86), he was his grandson.

275. On the awarding of the victim's hair to high-ranking ali'i, see also Vancouver 1801, 3:353.

276. The bodies of Hergest and Gouch—members of Vancouver's expedition killed by the Hawaiians—were also cut into pieces and distributed among the different ali'i (Manby 1929, 36).

277. Thus, as a Hawaiian declares to Clerke, among the different sailors killed at Kealakekua in 1778, "Capt. Cook being the principal Man he of course became the property of King Terre'oboo [Kalani'ōpu'u], . . . the others were taken by various Arees [ali'i] who were now dispers'd in different parts of the Isle" (1967, 546–47; cf. King 1967, 566).

GLOSSARY

'Aha.   Cord; gathering, assembly; rite in which a cord is carried or involved.
'Aha 'aina.   "Meal gathering," sacrificial meal.
'Aha helehonua.   Rite for measuring the dimensions of the mana house.
'Aha ho'owilimo'o.   Rite connected with the inauguration of the main image in the *luakini* temple.
'Aha hulahula.   Rite connected with the erection of the main image in the *luakini* temple.
'Ahi.   Albacore.
Ahupua'a.   Land division usually extending from the uplands to the sea. It is usually taken care of by a *konohiki*.
'Ahu'ula.   Feather cloak of a god or an ali'i.
'Ai.   Food, particularly vegetable food; to eat; to rule.
'Aialo.   "Eating in the presence": clients of an ali'i.
'Ai kapu.   "To eat under taboo; to observe eating taboo" (PE, 9).
'Ai lolo.   Sacrificial rite usually concerning the beginning of an activity or an inauguration.
'Ai noa.   "To eat without the observance of taboos" (PE, 11).
'Āina.   Land.
Aku.   Skipjack.
Akua.   God, goddess, divine image, corpse.
Akua hulumanu.   Feather god images.
Akua kā'ai.   Images that are wrapped or carried with a belt.
Akua lā'au.   "Wooden god."
Akua loa.   Long god. An image of Lono in the Makahiki festival.
Akua pā'ani.   God of games. One of the images of the Makahiki festival.
Akua poko.   Short god. One of the images of the Makahiki festival.
Akua wahine.   Goddess.
'Alaea.   Red ocher.
'Ālana.   Offering.
Ali'i.   Noble, king, royal.
Aloha.   Love, compassion.
'Āmama.   It is effected.
'Ana 'āna.   "Black magic, evil sorcery" (PE, 22).
Anahulu.   Period of ten days.
'Anu'u.   Temple tower.
'Auhau.   Tribute.
'Aumakua.   Family or personal god, often an ancestor; sometimes connected with hereditary professions.

405

'*Awa.*   Kava.

'*E'epa.*   "Extraordinary, incomprehensible, peculiar" (PE, 35).

Hā'awi.   To give.

Hai.   Sacrifice; to sacrifice.

Haina.   Offering, sacrifice, victim.

Hainaki.   First portion of sacrifice or firstfruits given to a god, and prayer for their consecration.

Haipule.   "To hold prayers or service, as to consecrate a *heiau*" (PE, 46).

Haku.   Lord.

Haku 'ōhi'a.   "Lord '*ōhi'a.*" Name of the main image in the *luakini* temple.

Hale.   House.

Hale mana.   Mana house. The most sacred house in the *luakini* temple.

Hale naua (or *nauwā*).   House in which the nobility's genealogical connections with the king are checked.

Hale o Lono.   Temple of Lono.

Hale o Papa.   "House of Papa": small temple annexed to the *luakini*, in which the goddesses are worshiped.

Hale pahu.   Drum house; one of the temple houses.

Hale wai ea.   Small house in the *luakini* temple, connected with purification.

Hana.   Work, activity of any kind; ritual activity.

Hānaipū.   Rite in which the Makahiki god is fed.

Haumia.   "Uncleanliness, defilement; defiled, unclean, contaminated" (PE, 57).

Heana.   "Corpse, especially of one slain in battle; victim, human sacrifice" (PE, 59).

Heiau.   Temple.

Heiau po'okanaka.   Temple in which human sacrifices are consecrated.

Hewa.   Sin, transgression.

Hiapo.   Firstborn.

Hihia.   Entangled.

Hi'uwai.   Ritual bathing in the sea.

Hiwa.   Entirely black; desirable blackness characterizing offerings.

Ho'āli.   Ritual waving of an offering.

Hono.   Sacrificial rite at the end of the *kapu luakini.*

Ho'oilo.   Wet season.

Ho'okupu.   Offering, tribute to the king or the gods he sends around the land.

Ho'omana.   To worship; to empower.

Huikala.   To free from *kapu*; to purify.

Hula.   To dance.

I'a.   Fish, flesh food.

'*Ie 'ie.*   *Freycinetia arborea.*

Imu.   Underground oven.

Ipu.   Bottle gourd.

Kahiki.   Distant in time and space; the space where transcendent gods are situated.

Kāhili.   "Feather standard, symbolic of royalty" (PE, 105).

Kahu.   Keeper.

Kahuna.   Priest, ritual specialist.

Kahuna nui.   High priest.

Kākū'ai.   To sacrifice food to the gods or the ancestors; to treat the spirit of a dead relative as a god by sacrificing food to it—and therefore to deify it.

Kala.   To untie, to release.

Kāli'i.   Ritual hurling of spears at an ali'i when he lands from his canoe.

Kalokalo.   Conversational prayer to the gods—in contrast to a memorized chant.

Kālua.   To bake in an underground oven.
Kānaenae.   Sacrifice and accompanying prayer.
Kanaka.   Human being; subject or client of a chief; human sacrifice.
Kāne.   Male.
Kapa.   Bark cloth.
Kāpapaulua.   Ritual fishing for the *ulua* fish.
Kapu.   Taboo, marked off, forbidden, prescribed rite.
Kapu heiau.   Temple ritual.
Kapu-hua.   Monthly taboo period from the twelfth "night" to the end of the thirteenth.
Kapu-kāloa.   Monthly taboo period from the twenty-third "night" to the end of the twenty-fourth.
Kapu-kāne.   Monthly taboo period from the twenty-seventh "night" to the end of the twenty-eighth.
Kapu-kū.   Monthly taboo period from the first "night" to the third.
Kapu luakini.   Ritual of the *luakini* temple.
Kapu moe.   Prostration taboo.
Kapu noho.   Sitting taboo.
Kapu pule.   Prescribed prayer, prescribed ritual.
Kau.   Dry season.
Kaua.   War.
Kauhale.   Homestead.
Kauila.   Processional rite in which feather images are readorned and paraded.
Kāula.   Prophet, seer.
Kaumaha.   Sacrifice, particularly the share of the god before eating.
Kauwā.   Outcasts.
Kiʻi.   Image, usually of gods.
Kino.   Body, physical manifestation of a god.
Kino lau.   The multiple forms taken by a god.
Koa.   *Acacia koa*; warrior; brave.
Koʻa.   Shrine, usually for fishing.
Konohiki.   Steward, caretaker of land.
Kōpili.   Thin, transparent bark cloth.
Kuahu.   Variety of altar; platform for offerings.
Kuapola.   Ritual concerning stars in the initial period of the Makahiki festival.
Kuili.   Prayers recited in unison during the *kapu luakini.*
Kūkoaʻe.   Purification hut or temple.
Kuleana.   Domain, jurisdiction, right.
Kumu.   Foundation, model, source.
Kuni.   Type of black magic, sorcery.
Laʻa.   Holy or defiled; dedicated.
Lā.   Day.
Lama.   Ebony tree.
Lani.   Heaven; very high noble.
Lei niho palaoa.   Whale-tooth pendant.
Lele.   Type of altar (scaffold).
Loulu.   Fan palms, used for thatch in certain temple houses.
Luakini.   Large temple in which kings consecrate human sacrifices.
Makaʻāinana.   Those who attend the land, commoners.
Makahiki.   Year, New Year festival.
Makai.   On the sea side, in the direction of the sea.

Makana. Gift.
Maki'i lohelohe. Rite connected with the temple tower.
Maliu. To look upon with favor; effect of sacrifices on gods.
Malo. Male's loincloth.
Mana. Efficacy of divine origin; potency; potent.
Manō. Shark.
Maoli. True, genuine.
Mauka. Inland, upland.
Mele. Song, chant.
Mele inoa. Name chant.
Mele ma'i. Chant praising the genitals.
Mōhai. Sacrifice; to sacrifice.
Moku. District, island.
Mōlia. To set apart for the gods; to sacrifice.
Mo'o. Lizard, dragon; succession, genealogical line; tradition; priestly order.
Mo'olelo. Story, tradition, legend.
Mua. Before; oldest, senior; same as *hale mua*, men's eating house and home-stead shrine.
Naha. Category of high-ranking noble.
Nī'aupi'o. Category of high-ranking noble.
Niu. Coconut.
Noa. Without *kapu* or freed from it.
'Ohana. Family, kindred, kin group.
'Ōhia-lehua. A tree (*Metrosideros macropus, M. collina*) from which the main image in the *luakini* temple is carved.
Ola. Life.
'Oloa. White bark cloth.
'Olu'olu. Reduplication of *'olu*, cool, supple, kind.
'Ōpelu. Mackerel scad.
Paehumu. Enclosure about a temple or a noble's house.
Pala. A fern, *Marattia douglasii*.
Pā'ū. Skirt.
Pi'o. A category of high-ranking noble and the union from which such noble issues.
Pō. Night; the realm of the gods; the undifferentiated divine.
Poi. Taro puree.
Pono. Correct behavior; morality; moral.
Pua'a he'a. Blood-red pig; sacrificial pig.
Pule. Prayer.
Pūlehu. To broil.
Pūlo'ulo'u. Bark-cloth-covered ball on a stick: insignia of a high-ranking ali'i.
'Uhane. Soul.
Ulua. Jackfish.
'Unihipili. Spirit of a dead person kept in residue from his body; often used in sorcery.
Unu. Kind of temple or shrine and area in the *luakini* temple.
Waihau. Kind of temple.

REFERENCES

Abbagnano, Nicola
1961   *Dizionario di filosofia*. Torino: UTET.
Achelis, Thomas
1895   *Über Mythologie und Cultus von Hawaii*. Braunschweig: Vieweg und Sohn.
Alexander, William DeWitt
1891   *A brief history of the Hawaiian people*. Published by order of the Board of Education of the Hawaiian Kingdom. New York: American Book Company.
1896   On an autograph letter by Jean B. Rives. *Hawaiian Historical Society Fourth Annual Report*, 19–29.
Anderson, Rufus
1865   *The Hawaiian Islands: Their progress and condition under missionary labors*. 3d ed. Boston: Gould and Lincoln.
Andrews, Lorrin
1865   *A dictionary of the Hawaiian language*. Honolulu: H. M. Whitney.
1875   Remarks on Hawaiian poetry. *Islander* (Honolulu) 1:26–27, 30–31, 35–36.
1922   *A dictionary of the Hawaiian language*. Rev. Henry H. Parker. Honolulu: Board of Commissioners of Public Archives of the Territory of Hawaii.
Andrews, Lorrin, trans.
1875   Haui Ka Lani, by Keaulumoku. Ed. S. B. Dole. *Islander* (Honolulu) 1:31, 36, 42, 47, 55, 64, 72, 79–80, 89, 97, 104.
Anonymous
1837   Obituary of Don Francisco Paula de Marin. *Sandwich Islands Gazette* 4 November, 3.
1912   Article in *Ka Hoku o Hawaii*, 22 February.
1914   Keanini-ula-o-ka-lani: Oahu version of a popular Hawaiian legend. *Hawaiian Annual for 1914*, 186–201.
1924   Luahoomae, the avenged priest. *Hawaiian Annual for 1924*, 127–33.
1927   The gods of ancient time. *Hawaiian Annual for 1927*, 74–79.
Apple, Russel A.
1971   *Hawaiian thatched house: Use, construction, adaptation*. San Francisco: U.S. Department of the Interior, National Park Service, Office of History and Historic Architecture, Western Service Center.
Arago, Jacques
1822   *Promenade autour du monde pendant les années 1817, 1818, 1819, et 1820, sur les corvettes du Roi l'Uranie et la Physicienne*, 2 vols. Paris: Leblanc.

1842   *Comme on dîne partout.* Paris: Librairie Curieuse de Bohaire.
1844 [1840]   *Souvenirs d'un aveugle: Voyage autour du monde.* 2 vols. Paris: H. Lebrun.
Arning, Eduard
1931   *Ethnographische Notizen aus Hawaii, 1883–86.* Mitteilungen aus dem Museum für Völkerkunde in Hamburg vol. 16. Hamburg: Friedrichsen, de Gruyter.
Austin, John L.
1975   *How to do things with words.* 2d. ed. Cambridge: Harvard University Press.
Baal, J. van
1975a   De fenomenologie van offer en geschenk. *Nederlands Theologisch Tjidschrift* 29:1–19.
1975b   Offering, sacrifice and gift. *Numen* 23 (3):161–78.
Baker, Albert S.
1917   Ahua a umi . . . an ancient temple on the island of Hawaii. *Hawaiian Annual for 1917*, 62–70.
Baldwin, James M., ed.
1940   *Dictionary of philosophy and psychology.* 3 vols. New York: Peter Smith.
Barnard, Charles H.
1829   A narrative of the sufferings and adventures of ―― ―― in a voyage round the world, during the years 1812, 1813, 1814, 1815, and 1816. New York: Printed for the author by J. Lindon.
Barnes, Robert H.
1977   *Mata* in Austronesia. *Oceania* 47:300–319.
Barrère, Dorothy
1961   Cosmogonic genealogies of Hawaii. *Journal of the Polynesian Society* 70 (4):419–28.
1969   *The Kumuhonua legends: A study of late nineteenth century Hawaiian stories of creation and origins.* Pacific Anthropological Records no. 3. Honolulu: Bishop Museum Press.
1975   *Kamehameha in Kona: Two documentary studies.* Pacific Anthropological Records no. 23. Honolulu: Bishop Museum Press.
Barrère, Dorothy, M. K. Pukui, and Marion Kelly
1980   *Hula: Historical perspectives.* Pacific Anthropological Records no. 30. Honolulu: Bishop Museum Press.
Barrot, Theodore-Adolphe
1839   Les îles Sandwich. *Revue des Deux Mondes* 19:225–55, 418–42.
1978   *Unless haste is made.* Trans. Daniel Dole. Kailua: Press Pacifica.
Barth, Frederick
1975   *Ritual and knowledge among the Baktaman of New Guinea.* Oslo: Universitetsforlaget; New Haven: Yale University Press.
Bassett, Marnie (Masson)
1962   *Realms and islands: The world voyage of Rose de Freycinet in the corvette Uranie, 1817–1820, from her journal and letters and the reports of Louis de Saulces de Freycinet, capitaine de corvette.* London: Oxford University Press.
Bastian, Adolf
1881   *Die heilige Sage der Polynesier: Kosmogonie und Theogonie.* Leipzig: Brockhaus.
1888   *Allerei aus Volks- und Menschenkunde*, vol. 1. Berlin: E. S. Mittler und Sohn.

Bataille, Georges
    1955   Hegel, la mort et le sacrifice. *Deucalion* 5:21–43.
Baudrillard, Jean
    1976   *L'échange symbolique et la mort.* Paris: Gallimard.
Bayly, William
    1782   *The original astronomical observation, made in the course of a voyage to
    the Northern Pacific Ocean.* . . . London: Richardson, Elmsly, Mount & Page.
Beaglehole, John C., ed.
    1967   *The journals of Captain James Cook on his voyages of discovery. Vol. 3. The
    voyage of the Resolution and Discovery, 1776–1780.* Parts 1 and 2. Cambridge:
    Cambridge University Press, for the Hakluyt Society.
Beckwith, Martha W.
    1940   *Hawaiian mythology.* New Haven: Yale University Press.
    1951   *The Kumulipo: A Hawaiian creation chant.* Chicago: University of
    Chicago Press.
Beckwith, Martha W., ed. and trans.
    1919   The Hawaiian romance of Laieikawai (from the Hawaiian text of
    S. N. Haleole, 1863). *Bureau of American Ethnology, Thirty-third Annual Re-
    port, 1911–1912,* 285–666.
    1932   *Kepelino's traditions of Hawaii.* Honolulu: Bishop Museum Press.
Beechey, Frederick W.
    1831   *Narrative of a voyage to the Pacific . . . performed in His Majesty's ship
    Blossom . . . in the years 1825, 1826, 1827, 1828.* Published by authority
    of the lords commissioners of the Admiralty. London: H. Colburn and
    R. Bentley.
Bell, Edward
    1929–30   Log of the Chatham. *Honolulu Mercury* 1 (September):7–26;
    (October): 55–69; (November): 76–96; 2 (December):80–91; (Janu-
    ary): 119–29.
Bennett, Frederick D.
    1840   *Narrative of a whaling voyage around the globe from the year 1833 to
    1836* . . . 2 vols. London: R. Bentley.
Bennett, Wendell C.
    1930   Hawaiian heiaus. Ph.D. dissertation, University of Chicago.
    1931   *Archeology of Kauai.* Bernice Pauahi Bishop Museum Bulletin no. 80.
    Honolulu: Bishop Museum Press.
Benveniste, Emile
    1969   *Le vocabulaire des institutions indo-européennes.* 2 vols. Paris: Editions
    de Minuit.
Bergson, Henri
    1959   Les deux sources de la morale et de la religion. In *Oeuvres.* Paris:
    Presses Universitaires de France.
Bertholet, Alfred
    1942   *Der Sinn des kultischen Opfers.* Berlin: W. de Gruyter for Akademie
    der Wissenschaften.
Best, Elsdon
    1924   *The Maori.* 2 vols. Polynesian Society Memoir no. 5. Wellington:
    Polynesian Society.
    1925   *Tuhoe: The children of the mist.* Polynesian Society Memoir no. 6.
    New Plymouth, N.Z.: Avery and Son.
Biardeau, Madeleine, and Charles Malamoud

1976   *Le sacrifice dans l'Inde ancienne*. Bibliothèque de l'Ecole des Hautes Etudes, Section des Sciences Religieuses, vol. 79. Paris: Presses Universitaires de France.

Bingham, Hiram
1848   *A residence of twenty-one years in the Sandwich Islands; or, the civil, religious, and political history of those islands*. 2d ed. Hartford, Conn.: H. Huntington.

Bishop, Charles
1967   *The journals and letters of Captain Charles Bishop on the North-West Coast of America, in the Pacific and in New South Wales, 1739–1799*. Ed. Michael Roe. Cambridge: Cambridge University Press for the Hakluyt Society.

Bishop, Sereno
1916   Old memories of Kailua. *Friend* 58, 11 (1900) and 59, 4 (1901). Reprinted as *Reminiscences of old Hawaii*, Advertiser History Series no. 1. Honolulu: Hawaiian Gazette Company.

Black, John S., and George Chrystal
1912   *The life of William Robertson Smith*. London: A. and C. Black.

Blake Palmer, G.
1946   Mana—Some Christian and Moslem parallels. *Journal of the Polynesian Society* 55 : 263–75.

Bloch, Maurice
1974   Symbols, song, dance and features of articulation: Is religion an extreme form of traditional authority? *European Journal of Sociology* 15 : 55–81.

Bloxam, Andrew
1925   *Diary of Andrew Bloxam, naturalist of the "Blonde" on her trip from England to the Hawaiian Islands, 1824–25*. Bernice Pauahi Bishop Museum Special Publications no. 10. Honolulu: Bishop Museum.

Bloxam, Rowland
1924   Visit of H.M.S. Blonde to Hawaii in 1825, as described by Rev. R. Bloxam, chaplain in a letter to his uncle. *Hawaiian Annual for 1924*, 66–82.

Boelen, Jacobus
1835–36   *Reize naar de Oost -en Westkust van Zuid-Amerika, en, van daar, naar de Sandwichs -en Philippijnsche eilanden, China enz, gedaan, in de jaaren 1826, 1827, 1828 en 1829*. Amsterdam: Ten Brink and De Vries.

Boit, John, Jr.
1920   Remarks on the ship Columbia's voyage from Boston (on a voyage round the globe). *Massachusetts Historical Society Proceedings* 53 : 217–75.

Bourdieu, Pierre
1980   *Le sens pratique*. Paris: Editions du Seuil.

Bradley, Harold W.
1942   *The American frontier in Hawaii: The pioneers, 1789–1843*. Stanford: Stanford University Press.

Brigham, William Tufts
n.d.   The ancient worship of the Hawaiian Islanders with references to that of other Polynesians. Manuscript, Bernice Pauahi Bishop Museum Library, Honolulu, Special Collections.
1898   Report of a journey around the world undertaken to examine various ethnological collections. *Occasional Papers of the Bernice Pauahi Bishop Museum* 1(1) : 1–72.
1899   Hawaiian feather work. *Memoirs of the Bernice Pauahi Bishop Museum* 1(1) : 1–86.

1906   Mat and basket weaving of the ancient Hawaiians. *Memoirs of the Bernice Pauahi Bishop Museum* 2(1) : 1–105.
1908   The ancient Hawaiian house. *Memoirs of the Bernice Pauahi Bishop Museum* 2(3) : 185–378.
1911   Ka hana kapa: The making of bark cloth in Hawaii. *Memoirs of the Bernice Pauahi Bishop Museum* 3 : 1–273.
1918   Additional notes on Hawaiian feather work, second supplement. *Memoirs of the Bernice Pauahi Bishop Museum* 7(1) : 1–64.

Broughton, William R.
1804   *A voyage of discovery to the North Pacific Ocean . . . performed in His Majesty's sloop Providence . . . in the years 1795, 1796, 1797, 1798.* London: Cadell-Davies.

Bryan, E. H., Jr.
1965   Astronomy and the calendar. In *Ancient Hawaiian civilization*, rev. ed., 251–56. Rutland, Vt., and Tokyo: Charles E. Tuttle.

Bühler, Georg, ed. and trans.
1969   *The laws of Manu.* Reprint ed. New York: Dover.

Burkert, Walter
1972   *Homo necans: Interpretationen altgriechischer Opferriten und Mythen.* Religionsgeschichtliche Versuche und Vorarbeiten vol. 32. Berlin and New York: De Gruyter.
1979   *Structure and history in Greek mythology and ritual.* Berkeley: University of California Press.

Burney, Captain James
1819   *A chronological history of north-eastern voyages of discovery, and of the early eastern navigation of the Russians.* London: Payne and Foss Murray.

Byron, George A.
1826   *Voyage of H.M.S. Blonde to the Sandwich Islands, in the years 1824–25.* London: Murray.

Campbell, Archibald
1816   A voyage round the world, from 1806 to 1812, in which . . . the Sandwich Islands were visited. . . . Edinburgh: Archibald Constable and Company.
1967   *A voyage round the world, from 1806 to 1812.* . . . Facsimile reproduction of the 3d American edition, 1822. Honolulu: University of Hawaii Press.

Canguilhem, Georges
1968   *Etudes d'histoire et de philosophie des sciences.* Paris: Vrin.

Capell, A.
1938   The word *mana*: A linguistic study. *Oceania* 9 : 89–96.

Chamisso de Boncourt, L. K. Adelbert von
1821   *Bemerkungen und Ansichten auf einer Entdeckungsreise unternommen in den Jahren 1815–1818, unter dem Befehl von Otto von Kotzebue.* Weimar: Hoffman.
1837   *Über die Hawaiische Sprache.* Leipzig: Weidmannischen Buchhandlung.
1864   *Chamissos Werke; Reise um die Welt mit der Romanzoffischen Entdeckungs-Expedition in den Jahren 1815–18 auf der Brigg Rurik, Capitan Otto v. Kotzebue*, vols. 3 and 4. Berlin: Deutsches Verlagshaus Bong.

Charlot, Jean
1958   *Choris and Kamehameha.* Honolulu: Bishop Museum Press.

Charlot, John

n.d.   Religio-political ideas in post-contact Hawaiian poetry. Typescript obtained from author.

Chateaubriand, François Auguste René
1967–68   *Mémoires d'outre-tombe*. 6 vols. Paris: J. de Bonnot.

Cheever, Henry T.
1851   *Life in the Sandwich Islands; or, The heart of the Pacific as it was and is.* New York: Barnes.

Chinen, Jon J.
1958   *The great Mahele: Hawaii's land division of 1848*. Honolulu: University of Hawaii Press.

Choris, Louis (Ludovik)
1822   *Voyage pittoresque autour du monde, avec des portraits de sauvages d'Amerique, d'Asie, d'Afrique, et des îles du Grand Océan; des paysages, des vues maritimes, et plusieurs objets d'histoire naturelle*. Paris: Firmin Didot.
1826   *Vues et paysages des regions equinoxiales, recueillis dans un voyage autour du monde, par Louis Choris, avec une introduction et un text explicatif.* Paris: Paul Renouard.

Clerke, James
1930   Extract from the Journal of Captain James Clerke. *Honolulu Mercury*, February, 254–66.
1967   Journal. In Beaglehole (1967).

Cleveland, Horace William Schaler, ed.
1886   *Voyages of a merchant navigator of the days that are past, compiled from journals and letters of the late Richard J. Cleveland*. New York: Harper and Brothers.

Cleveland, Richard J.
1843   *A narrative of voyages and commercial enterprises*. 2 vols. 2d ed. Cambridge, Mass.: John Owen.

Cochran, Doris M., and J. Goin Coleman
1970   *The new field book of reptiles and amphibians*. New York: Putnam.

Codrington, R. H.
1891   *The Melanesians: Studies in their anthropology and folk-lore*. Oxford: Clarendon.

Collingwood, R. G.
1933   *An essay on philosophical method*. Oxford: Clarendon Press.

Colnett, James
n.d.   The journal of Captain James Colnett aboard the Prince of Wales and Princess Royal from 16 October to 7 November 1788. London: Public Records Office, Admiralty 55, ser. 2, 146. Typescript in the Gregg H. Sinclair Library, Honolulu.
1798   *A voyage to the South Atlantic and round Cape Horn into the Pacific Ocean . . . undertaken and performed by Captain James Colnett of the Royal Navy, in the ship Rattle*. London: Printed for the author by W. Bennett.

Comte, Auguste
1877   *Cours de philosophie positive*, vol. 5. Paris: Baillère.

Conrad, Agnes C., ed.
1973   The letters and journal of Francisco de Paula Marin. In *Don Francisco de Paula Marin: A biography*, by Ross H. Gast. Honolulu: University Press of Hawaii for the Hawaiian Historical Society.

Cook, James
1967   Journal. In Beaglehole (1967).

Cook, James, and James King
  1784   *A voyage to the Pacific Ocean, undertaken by the command of His Majesty, for making discoveries in the Northern Hemisphere* . . . *under the direction of Captains Cook, Clerke, and Gore, in His Majesty's ships the Resolution and Discovery, in the years 1776, 1777, 1778, 1779 and 1780.* 3 vols. London: Nicol and Cadell.
Corney, Peter
  1896   *Voyages in the Northern Pacific from 1813 to 1818.* Honolulu: Thrum.
  1965   *Early voyages in the Northern Pacific, 1813–1818.* Fairfield, Wash.: Galleon Press.
Cox, J. Halley
  1967   The lei niho palaoa. In *Polynesian culture history—Essays in honor of K. P. Emory,* ed. Genevieve Highland et al., 411–24. Bernice Pauahi Bishop Museum Special Publications no. 56. Honolulu: Bishop Museum Press.
Cox, J. Halley, and William H. Davenport
  1974   *Hawaiian sculpture.* Honolulu: University Press of Hawaii.
Cox, Ross
  1831   *Adventures on the Columbia River including the narrative of a residence of six years on the western side of the Rocky Mountains, among various tribes of Indians hitherto unknown: Together with a journey across the American continent.* 2 vols. London: H. Colburn and R. Bentley.
Dampier, Robert
  1971   *To the Sandwich Islands on H.M.S. Blonde.* Ed. Pauline King Joerger. Honolulu: University Press of Hawaii.
Davenport, William H.
  1969   The "Hawaiian cultural revolution": Some political and economic considerations. *American Anthropologist* 71, 1 (February): 1–20.
Davis, Eleanor Harmon
  1979   *Abraham Fornander: A biography.* Honolulu: University Press of Hawaii.
Delano, Amasa
  1817   *A narrative of voyages and travels in the Northern and Southern Hemispheres; comprising three voyages round the world.* Boston: Printed by E. G. House for the author.
Dening, Greg
  1980   *Islands and beaches: Discourse on a silent land—Marquesas, 1776–1880.* Honolulu: University Press of Hawaii.
Dibble, Sheldon
  1839   *History and general views of the Sandwich Islands' mission.* New York: Taylor and Dadol.
  1843   *A history of the Sandwich Islands.* Lahainaluna: Missionary Seminary Press.
  1909   *A history of the Sandwich Islands.* Honolulu: T. G. Thrum.
Dickey, Lyle A.
  1917   Stories of Wailua, Kauai. *Hawaiian Historical Society, Twenty-fifth Annual Report,* 14–36.
  1928   *String figures from Hawaii, including some from New Hebrides and Gilbert Islands.* Bernice Pauahi Bishop Museum Bulletin no. 54. Honolulu: Bishop Museum Press.
Dixon, George
  1789   *A voyage round the world* . . . *performed in 1785, 1786, 1787 and 1788 in the "King George" and "Queen Charlotte."* London: George Goulding.

Dodge, Ernest S.
   1978   *Hawaiian and other Polynesian gourds.* Honolulu: Topgallant.
Douglas, Mary
   1966   *Purity and danger: An analysis of concepts of pollution and taboo.* London: Routledge and Kegan Paul.
   1975   Self evidence. In *Implicit meanings.* London: Routledge and Kegan Paul.
Duhaut-Cilly, Auguste Bernard
   1834–35   *Voyage autour du monde, principalement à la Californie et aux îles Sandwich, pendant les années 1826, 1827, 1828 et 1829.* 2 vols. Paris: A. Bertrand.
Dumézil, Georges
   1970   *Archaic Roman religion.* Trans. Philip Krapp. Chicago: University of Chicago Press.
Dumont, Louis
   1959   Pure and impure. *Contributions to Indian Sociology* 3:9–39.
   1966   *Homo hierarchicus: Essai sur le système des castes.* Paris: Gallimard.
Durkheim, Emile
   1912   *Les formes élémentaires de la vie religieuse: Le système totémique en Australie.* Paris: Alcan.
Earle, Timothy
   1978   *Economic and social organization of a complex chiefdom: The Halelea district, Kauaʻi, Hawaii.* Anthropological Papers no. 63. Ann Arbor: University of Michigan, Museum of Anthropology.
EH
   1971   *Hawaiian dictionary.* Part 2, English-Hawaiian. Compiled by Mary K. Pukui and Samuel H. Elbert. Honolulu: University Press of Hawaii.
Elbert, Samuel H.
   1951   Hawaiian literary style and culture. *American Anthropologist* 53: 345–54.
   1956–57   The chief in Hawaiian mythology. *Journal of American Folklore* 69:99–113, 341–55; 70:264–76, 306–22.
Elbert, Samuel H., ed.
   1959   *Selections from Fornander's Hawaiian antiquities and folk-lore.* Honolulu: University Press of Hawaii.
Elbert, Samuel H., and Mary Kawena Pukui
   1979   *Hawaiian grammar.* Honolulu: University Press of Hawaii.
Ellis, William [missionary]
   1825   *A journal of a tour around Hawaii, the largest of the Sandwich Islands.* Boston: Crocker and Brewster.
   1842 [1829]   *Polynesian researches during a residence of nearly eight years in the Society and Sandwich Islands.* Rev. ed. Vol. 4 of 4 vols. London: Fisher and Jackson.
   1917   *A narrative of a tour through Hawaii.* Reprint of London ed., 1827. Honolulu: Hawaiian Gazette.
Ellis, William [surgeon]
   1782   *Authentic narrative of a voyage performed by Captain Cook and Captain Clerke in His Majesty's ships "Resolution" and "Discovery"* . . . *1776–80.* 2 vols. London: Robinson.
Emerson, Joseph S.
   n.d.   Gods. In *Hawaiian ethnographical notes.* Emerson's collection, 1:

605–6. Honolulu: Bishop Museum Library Collection.
1892 The lesser Hawaiian gods. *Hawaiian Historical Society Papers* 2: 1–24.
1924 Hawaiian string games. Ed. M. W. Beckwith. *Vassar College Folklore Foundation Publication*, no. 5: 1–18.
Emerson, Nathaniel B.
1893 Long voyages of the ancient Hawaiians. *Hawaiian Historical Society Paper*, no. 5.
1895 Bird hunters of ancient Hawaii. *Hawaiian Annual for 1895*, 101–11.
1915 *Pele and Hiiaka: A myth from Hawaii*. Honolulu: Honolulu Star-Bulletin.
1965 [1909] *Unwritten literature of Hawaii: The sacred songs of the Hula, compiled and translated with notes and an account of the Hula*. Reprint ed. Rutland, Vt., and Tokyo: Charles E. Tuttle.
Emory, Kenneth
n.d. How the Hawaiians kept track of the time of the year. Typescript obtained from author.
1924 *The island of Lanai: A survey of native culture*. Bernice Pauahi Bishop Museum Bulletin no. 12. Honolulu: Bishop Museum Press.
1929 Ruins at Kee, Kauai, the court of Lohiau. *Hawaiian Annual for 1929*, 88–94.
1971 Preface of 1971 reprint of Malo (1951).
Evans-Pritchard, E. E.
1956 *Nuer religion*. London: Oxford University Press.
1965 *Theories of primitive religion*. Oxford: Clarendon Press.
Evelith, Ephraim
1831 *History of the Sandwich Islands: With an account of the American mission established there in 1820*. Philadelphia: American Sunday School Union.
Extract
1930 Extract from a pocket diary by one of the officers of H.M.S. "Resolution." *Honolulu Mercury*, March, 375–82.
Extracts
1804 Extracts from a journal kept on board ship Atahualpa, bound on a voyage from Boston to the N.W. Coast and Sandwich Islands. Collections of the Massachusetts Historical Society. 1st ser., 3: 242–45. Boston: Hall and Hiller.
Feher, Joseph, comp.
1969 *Hawaii: A pictorial history*. Bernice Pauahi Bishop Museum Special Publications no. 58. Honolulu: Bishop Museum Press.
Feuerbach, Ludwig
1910 Über die Vernunft. *Sämmtliche Werke*, ed. Wilhelm Bolin and Friedrich Jodl, vol. 4. Stuttgart: Frommans Verlag E. Hauff.
1956 *Das Wesen des Christentums*, vols. 1–2. Ed. Werner Schuffenhauer. Berlin: Akademie Verlag.
1970 Vorläufige Thesen zur Reformation der Philosophie. In *Kleinere Schriften*, vol. 2 (1839–46). Berlin: Akademie Verlag.
Firth, Raymond
1930–31 Totemism in Polynesia. *Oceania* 1: 291–321, 377–98.
1967 The analysis of mana: An empirical approach. *Journal of the Polynesian Society* 49 (1940): 485–510. Reprinted in *Tikopia ritual and belief*. Boston: Beacon Press.

Fischer, Hans
    1965   *Studien über Seelenvorstellungen in Ozeanien.* Munich: K. Renner
    Verlag.
Fleurieu, C. P. Claret
    1965   [1801] *A voyage round the world, performed during the years 1790, 1791,
    and 1792 by Etienne Marchand.* 2 vols. Reprint. New York: Da Capo Press.
Fontenelle, Bernard Le Bovier de
    1932   [1724] *De l'origine des fables.* Critical edition with introduction, notes,
    and commentary by J. R. Carré. Paris: Alcan.
Fornander, Abraham
    1878–80   *An account of the Polynesian race, its origin and migrations and the
    ancient history of the Hawaiian people to the times of Kamehameha I.* 3 vols.
    London: Trübner.
    1916–20   Fornander collection of Hawaiian antiquities and folk-lore.
    Ed. T. A. Thrum, trans. John Wise. *Memoirs of the Bernice Pauahi Bishop Mu-
    seum,* 4–6.
Foulquié, Paul, and Raymond Saint-Jean
    1969   *Dictionnaire de la langue philosophique.* Paris: Presses Universitaires de
    France.
Franchère, Gabriel
    1820   *Relation d'un voyage à la côte du nord-ouest de l'Amérique septentrionale
    dans les années 1810, 11, 12, 13 et 14.* Montreal: C. B. Pasteur.
Frazer, James G.
    1890   *The golden bough: A study in comparative religion.* 2 vols. London and
    New York: Macmillan.
    1911–15   *The golden bough: A study in magic and religion.* 3d ed. 12 vols.
    London: Macmillan.
    1922   *The belief among the Polynesians.* Vol. 2 of *The belief in immortality and
    the worship of the dead,* in 3 vols. London: Macmillan.
    1963   *The golden bough: A study in magic and religion.* Abridged ed. Lon-
    don: Macmillan.
Frazer, James George, ed. and trans.
    1966   *Ovid's "Fasti."* Cambridge: Harvard University Press; London:
    Heinemann.
Freud, Sigmund
    1905   *Der Witz und seine Beziehung zum Unbewussten.* Leipzig and Vienna:
    F. Deuticke.
Freycinet, Louis Claude Desoulses de
    1825–39   *Voyage autour du monde, . . . executé sur les corvettes de S.M. l'Ura-
    nie et la Physicienne, pendant les années 1817, 1819 et 1820 . . . historique.* 2
    vols. in 3. Paris: Pillet Aîné.
    1978   *Hawaii in 1819: A narrative account by Louis Claude de Soulses de
    Freycinet.* Trans. Ella L. Wiswell, ed. Marion Kelly. Pacific Anthropological
    Records no. 26. Honolulu: Bishop Museum Press.
Freycinet, Rose de Soulces de
    1927   *Journal de Madame Rose de Soulces de Freycinet d'après le manuscrit
    original accompagné de notes par Charles Duplomb.* Paris: Société d'Editions
    Géographiques.
Fullaway, David T., and Noel L. H. Krauss
    1945   *Common insects of Hawaii.* Honolulu: Tongg.

Gast, Ross H.
  1973   See Conrad (1973).
Gernet, Louis
  1968a   Quelques rapports entre la pénalité et la religion dans la Grèce ancienne. In *Anthropologie de la Grèce antique*, 288–301. Paris: F. Maspéro.
  1968b   Sur l'exécution capitale: A propos d'un ouvrage récent. In *Anthropologie de la Grèce antique*, 302–20. Paris: F. Maspéro.
Gilbert, George
  1926   *The death of Captain James Cook*. Pamphlet. Hawaiian Historical Society Reprints no. 5. Honolulu: Hawaiian Historical Society.
  1982   *Captain Cook's final voyage: The journal of midshipman George Gilbert*.
  Honolulu: University Press of Hawaii.
Gill, William W.
  1876   *Myths and songs from the South Pacific*. London: H. S. King.
Girard, René
  1972   *La violence et le sacré*. Paris: Bernard Grasset.
Gizycki, Renate von
  1971   *Haku Mele: Der Poet in Polynesien. Ein sozialanthropologischer Beitrag
  zur Rolle des Kunstlers*. Munich: K. Renner Verlag.
Godelier, Maurice
  1973   *Horizon, trajets marxistes en anthropologie*. Paris: Maspéro.
Golovnin, V. M.
  1979   *Around the world on the Kamchatka, 1817–1818*. Translated with an
  introduction and notes by Ella Lury Wiswell. Honolulu: University Press of
  Hawaii.
Gombrich, Ernest H.
  1970   *Aby Warburg: An intellectual biography*. London: Warburg Institute.
Goodson, Gar
  1973   *Fishes of Hawaii*. Palos Verdes Estates, Calif.: Marquest Colorguide
  Books.
Goody, Jack
  1966   Introduction to *Succession to high office*, ed. Jack Goody, 1–56. Cambridge: Cambridge University Press.
Gough, Barry M., ed.
  1973   *To the Pacific and Arctic with Beechey: The journal of Lieutenant George
  Peard of H.M.S. "Blossom," 1825–28*. Cambridge: Cambridge University
  Press for the Hakluyt Society.
Gould, Rupert T.
  1928   Bligh's notes on Cook's last voyage and some unpublished accounts
  of Cook's death. *Mariner's Mirror* 14 : 371–85.
Granet, Marcel
  1926   *Danses et légendes de la Chine ancienne*. 2 vols. Paris: Alcan.
  1929   *La civilisation chinoise: La vie publique et la vie privée*. Paris: Renaissance du Livre.
Green, Laura
  1926   *Folk-tales from Hawaii*. Poughkeepsie: Vassar College.
Green, Laura C., and Martha W. Beckwith
  1924   Hawaiian customs and beliefs relating to birth and infancy. *American
  Anthropologist* 26 : 230–46.
  1926   Hawaiian customs and beliefs relating to sickness and death. *Ameri-*

can Anthropologist 28 : 176–208.

1928   Hawaiian household customs. *American Anthropologist* 30 : 1–17.

Green, Laura C., and Mary K. Pukui, trans.

1929   *The legend of Kawelo.* Ed. Martha W. Beckwith. Poughkeepsie: Vassar College.

Griaule, Marcel

1940   Remarques sur le mécanisme du sacrifice Dogon. *Journal de la Société des Africanistes* 10 : 127–29.

Grice, H. P.

1957   Meaning. *Philosophical Review* 66 : 377–88.

Gusdorf, Georges

1948   *L'expérience humaine du sacrifice.* Paris: Presses Universitaires de France.

Handy, Edward S. C.

1927   *Polynesian religion.* Bernice Pauahi Bishop Museum Bulletin no. 34. Honolulu: Bishop Museum Press.

1940   *The Hawaiian planter, I: His plants, methods and areas of cultivation.* Bernice Pauahi Bishop Museum Bulletin no. 161. Honolulu: Bishop Museum Press.

1968   Traces of totemism in Polynesia. *Journal of the Polynesian Society* 77, 1 (March) : 43–56.

1972   *Native planters in old Hawaii: Their life, lore and environment.* Bernice Pauahi Bishop Museum Bulletin no. 233. Honolulu: Bishop Museum Press.

Handy, Edward S. C., and M. K. Pukui

1972 [1958]   *The Polynesian family system in Ka-'u, Hawai'i.* Rutland, Vt., and Tokyo: Charles E. Tuttle.

Handy, Edward S. C., Mary K. Pukui, and K. Livermore

1934   *Outline of Hawaiian physical therapeutics.* Bernice Pauahi Bishop Museum Bulletin no. 126. Honolulu: Bishop Museum Press.

Haran, Menahem

1978   *Temples and temple-service in ancient Israel: An inquiry into the character of cult phenomena and the historical setting of the Priestly School.* Oxford: Clarendon Press.

Harva, Uno

1959   *Les représentations religieuses des peuples altaïques.* Translated from German by Jean-Louis Perret. Paris: Gallimard.

Heesterman, Johannes C.

1957   *The ancient Indian royal consecration: The Rājasūya described according to the Yajus texts and annotated.* The Hague: Mouton.

1978   The conundrum of the king's authority. In *Kingship and authority in South Asia,* ed. J. F. Richards. Madison: University of Wisconsin Press.

Hegel, Georg Wilhelm Friederich

1952   *Phänomenologie des Geistes.* Ed. Johannes Hoffmeister. Hamburg: Felix Meiner.

1974   *Vorlesungen über die Philosophie der Religion.* Ed. G. Lasson. 2 vols. Hamburg: Felix Meiner.

HEN

Hawaiian ethnographical notes, vols. 1–3. Typescript, Bernice Pauahi Bishop Museum Library, Honolulu.

Henry, Teuira

1968   *Tahiti aux temps anciens.* Translated from English by Bertrand Jaunez. Paris: Musée de l'Homme.

Hertz, Robert
    1922   Le péché et l'expiation dans les religions primitives. *Revue de L'His-*
    toire des Religions 86:1–60.
Hiroa, Te Rangi [Sir Peter H. Buck]
    1957   *Arts and crafts of Hawaii.* Bernice Pauahi Bishop Museum Special
    Publications no. 45. Honolulu: Bishop Museum Press.
Hocart, Arthur M.
    1914   Mana. *Man* 14:97–101.
    1922   Mana again. *Man* 22:11–13.
    1927   *Kingship.* Oxford: Clarendon Press.
    1938   *Les castes.* Annales du Musée Guimet. Paris: Geuthner.
    1952   *The northern states of Fiji.* London: Royal Anthropological Institute.
    1970   *Kings and councillors: An essay in the comparative anatomy of human*
    society. Chicago: University of Chicago Press.
Hogbin, H. Ian
    1935–36   Mana. *Oceania* 6:241–74.
Hogg, Garry
    1958   *Cannibalism and human sacrifice.* London: R. Hale.
Holman, Lucie Ruggles
    1931   *Journal of Lucie Ruggles Holman.* Bernice Pauahi Bishop Museum
    Special Publications no. 17. Honolulu: Bishop Museum Press.
Horton, Robin
    1970   African traditional thought and Western science. In *Rationality*, ed.
    G. Bryan R. Wilson, pp. 131–71. Oxford: Blackwell.
Howay, Frederic William
    1930   Early relations with the Pacific Northwest. In *The Hawaiian Islands*,
    ed. Albert Pierce Taylor. Honolulu: Printshop Company.
    1930–34   A list of trading vessels in the maritime fur trade, 1795 . . . to
    1825. *Transactions of the Royal Society of Canada*, 3d ser., 2:24–28.
    1932a   Last days of the *Atahualpa*, alias *Bering*. In *Forty-first annual report*
    of the Hawaiian Historical Society for the year 1932. Honolulu: Hawaiian His-
    torical Society.
    1933   The ship *Eliza* at Hawaii in 1799. In *Forty-second annual report of the*
    Hawaiian Historical Society for the Year 1933, 103–13. Honolulu: Hawaiian
    Historical Society.
    1936   The *Caroline* and the *Hancock* at Hawaii in 1799. In *Forty-fifth an-*
    nual report of the Hawaiian Historical Society for the year 1936, 25–29. Hono-
    lulu: Hawaiian Historical Society.
    1937   The ship *Pearl* in Hawaii in 1805 and 1806. *Forty-sixth annual report*
    of the Hawaiian Historical Society for the year 1937, 27–38. Honolulu: Hawai-
    ian Historical Society.
Howay, Frederic William, ed.
    1938   *The voyage of the New Hazard to the Northwest Coast, Hawaii and*
    China, 1810–1813, by Stephen Reynolds. Salem: Peabody Museum.
    1941   *Voyages of the "Columbia" to the Northwest Coast, 1787–1790 and*
    1790–1793. Massachusetts Historical Society Collections no. 79. Boston:
    Massachusetts Historical Society.
Hubert, Henri, and Marcel Mauss
    1899   Essai sur la nature et la fonction du sacrifice. *L'Année Sociologique*
    2:29–139. Reprinted in Mauss (1968–69, 1:193–307).
    1929 [1909]   Introduction à l'analyse de quelques phénomènes religieux.
    Preface to *Mélanges d'histoire des religions.* Reprint. Paris: Alcan.

1978   Esquisse d'une théorie générale de la magie. Reprinted in *Sociologie et anthropologie*, by M. Mauss. Paris: Presses Universitaires de France.
Hugo, Victor
    1951   *Les misérables*. Edited and annotated by M. Allem. Paris: Gallimard.
Hume, David
    1826   The natural history of religion. In *The philosophical works of David Hume*. Edinburgh: Black and Tait.
Hunnewell, James
    n.d.   Journal 1817–1822. Manuscript. Hunnewell Collection, Baker Library, Harvard University.
    1895   Voyage in the Brig *Bordeaux Packet*, Boston to Honolulu, 1817. . . . *Hawaiian Historical Society Papers* 8 : 3–18.
Hussey, John Adam, ed.
    1958   *The voyage of the Raccoon: A "secret" journal of a visit to Oregon, California and Hawaii, 1813–1814*. San Francisco: Book Club of California.
Huysmans, Joris-Karl
    1961   *A rebours*. Paris: Fasquelle.
Ii, John Papa
    1841   John Ii's speech, delivered at Rev. H. Bingham's church on Thanksgiving Day, January 1, 1841. *Polynesian* 1 (5 May) : 186–87.
    1869a   Article in *Ka Nupepa Kuokoa*, 24 April.
    1869b   Article in *Ka Nupepa Kuokoa*, 8 May.
    1869c   Article in *Ka Nupepa Kuokoa*, 5 June.
    1869d   Article in *Ka Nupepa Kuokoa*, 14 August.
    1869e   Article in *Ka Nupepa Kuokoa*, 21 August.
    1869f   Article in *Ka Nupepa Kuokoa*, 28 August.
    1869g   Article in *Ka Nupepa Kuokoa*, 4 September.
    1869h   Article in *Ka Nupepa Kuokoa*, 11 September.
    1869i   Article in *Ka Nupepa Kuokoa*, 18 September.
    1869j   Article in *Ka Nupepa Kuokoa*, 2 October.
    1869k   Article in *Ka Nupepa Kuokoa*, 27 November.
    1963 [1959]   *Fragments of Hawaiian history*. Trans. Mary Pukui, ed. Dorothy Barrère. Honolulu: Bishop Museum Press.
Ingraham, Joseph
    n.d.   *Log of the brigantine Hope from Boston to the Northwest Coast of America and journal of events, 1790–1792*. Typewritten copy of original manuscript. Chicago: Newberry Library, Ayer Collection.
    1918   *The log of the brig "Hope," called the "Hope's trek among the Sandwich Islands."* Hawaiian Historical Society Reprints no. 3.
Iselin, Isaak
    n.d.   *Journal of a trading voyage around the world, 1805–1808*. New York: Press of McIlroy and Emmet.
Jakobson, Roman
    1971   *Word and language*. Vol. 2 of *Selected Writings*. The Hague and Paris: Mouton.
Jarves, James Jackson
    1843   *History of the Hawaiian or Sandwich Islands*. . . . Boston: Tappan and Bennet.
Jensen, Adolph E.
    1963   *Myth and cult among primitive peoples*. Trans. Marianna Tax Choldin and Wolfgang Weissleder. Chicago: University of Chicago Press.

Johansen, J. Prytz
1954   *The Maori and his religion in its non-ritualistic aspects.* Copenhagen: Munksgaard.
Johnson, Rubellite Kawena, and John Kaipo Mahelona
1975   *Nā inoa hōkū: A catalogue of Hawaiian and Pacific star names.* Honolulu: Topgallant.
Judd, Bernice
1974 [1929]   *Voyages to Hawaii before 1860.* Enlarged and edited by Helen Yonge Lind. Honolulu: University Press of Hawaii.
Judd, Laura Fish
1880   *Honolulu: Sketches of life, social, political and religious in the Hawaiian islands from 1828 to 1861.* New York: Randolph.
Judd, Walter F.
1975   *Palaces and forts of the Hawaiian kingdom: From thatch to American Florentine.* Palo Alto, Calif.: Pacific Books.
Kaaie, J. W. K.
1862   O na uhane mahope iho o ka make ana o ke kino. *Ka Hoku o Ka Pakipika* (newspaper), 8 May.
Kaawa, P. W.
1865a   Article in *Ka Nupepa Kuokoa,* 2 December.
1865b   Temples, sacrifice altars and their various offerings. *Ka Nupepa Kuokoa,* 25 May, 1865. Manuscript translation by T. Thrum, in the Bernice Pauahi Bishop Museum Library, Thrum Collection.
Kaeppler, Adrienne
n.d.   Genealogy and disrespect: A study of symbolism in Hawaiian images. Typescript obtained from author.
Kahiolo, G. W.
1978   *He moolelo no Kamapuaa: The story of Kamapuaa.* Trans. Esther T. Mookini and Erin C. Neizmen. Honolulu: Hawaiian Studies Program, University of Hawaii, Manoa.
Kaiwikonakona
n.d.   Letter from a Kahuna to the king, concerning illness (8 June 1889). *Hawaiian Ethnographical Notes* 1:250. Honolulu: Bishop Museum Library Collection.
Kalakaua, David
1888   *The legends and myths of Hawaii: The fables and folklore of a strange people.* Ed. R. M. Daggett. New York: Webster.
Kamakau, Kelou
1919–20   No na oihana kahuna kahiko. In Fornander collection of Hawaiian antiquities and folk-lore, ed. T. A. Thrum, trans. John Wise. *Memoirs of the Bernice Pauahi Bishop Museum* 6:2–45.
Kamakau, Samuel M.
1865   Article in *Ka Nupepa Kuokoa,* 12 August.
1866   Article in *Ka Nupepa Kuokoa,* 29 December.
1867a   Article in *Ka Nupepa Kuokoa,* 5 January.
1867b   Article in *Ka Nupepa Kuokoa,* 21 September.
1867c   Article in *Ka Nupepa Kuokoa,* 16 November.
1870a   Article in *Ke Au Okoa,* 17 February.
1870b   Article in *Ke Au Okoa,* 24 February.
1870c   Article in *Ke Au Okoa,* 3 March.
1870d   Article in *Ke Au Okoa,* 10 March.

424   References

1891   Instructions in ancient Hawaiian astronomy. *Hawaiian Annual for 1891*, 142–43.
1911   Ancient Hawaiian religious beliefs and ceremonies. *Hawaiian Annual for 1911*, 149–58.
1961   *The ruling chiefs of Hawaii*. Honolulu: Kamehameha Schools.
1964   *Ka poʻe kahiko: The people of old*. Bernice Pauahi Bishop Museum Special Publications no. 51. Honolulu: Bishop Museum Press.
1976   *The works of the people of old: Na hana a ka poʻe kahiko*. Trans. Mary Kawena Pukui, ed. Dorothy B. Barrère. Bernice Pauahi Bishop Museum Special Publication no. 61. Honolulu: Bishop Museum Press.
Kauhane
1865   The story of Ku, his character and his works. Translated from *Ka Nupepa Kuokoa* by T. G. Thrum (26 January 1865). Bishop Museum Library, Thrum Collection.
Kaula, S. E.
1865   On Hawaiian cannibalism. Translated from *Ka Nupepa Kuokoa* by T. G. Thrum (13 April 1865). Bishop Museum Library, Thrum Collection.
Keesing, Roger
n.d.   Rethinking mana. *Journal of Anthropological Research*. In press.
Kekoa
1865   Birth rites of Hawaiian children in ancient times. Translated from *Ka Nupepa Kuokoa* by T. G. Thrum. Bishop Museum Library, Thrum Collection.
Kelly, Marion
1967   Some problems with early descriptions of Hawaiian culture. In *Polynesian culture history: Essays in honor of Kenneth P. Emory*, ed. Genevieve A. Highland et al. Bernice Pauahi Bishop Museum Special Publication no. 56. Honolulu: Bishop Museum Press.
Kenn, Charles W., trans.
1978   *Moolelo of ancient Hawaii by the Reverend John F. Pogue*. Honolulu: Topgallant.
Kepelino, K.
1858   *Hooiliili Havaii: He mau hana, olelo, manao, e pili ana i to Hawaii nei*. Honolulu: Pai-palapala Katolika.
1932   *Kepelino's traditions of Hawaii*. Ed. Martha W. Beckwith. Honolulu: Bishop Museum Press.
1977   See Kirtley and Mookini (1977).
Kihe, Isaac
n.d.   Notes on "Aumakuas." J. S. Emerson's collection. Typescript in *Hawaiian Ethnographical Notes*, 1 : 566–72. Bishop Museum Library, Honolulu.
King, Lieutenant
1967   Journal. In Beaglehole (1967).
Kirch, Patrick Vinton
1975   Halawa Valley in Hawaiian prehistory: Discussion and conclusions. In *Prehistory and ecology in windward Hawaiian valley: Halawa Valley, Molokai*, ed. P. V. Kirch and M. Kelly, 167–84. Pacific Anthropological Records no. 24. Honolulu: Bishop Museum Press.
Kirtley, B. F., and E. T. Mookini, trans.
1977   Hooiliili Havaii. He mau hana, olelo, manao, e pili ana i to Hawaii nei, by K. Kepelino. *Hawaiian Journal of History* 11 : 39–68.
Kojève, Alexandre
1947   *Introduction à la lecture de Hegel*. Paris: Gallimard.

Kooijman, Simon
1972   *Tapa in Polynesia.* Bernice Pauahi Bishop Museum Bulletin no. 234. Honolulu: Bishop Museum Press.
Koskinen, Aarne A.
1967   *Linking of symbols: Polynesian patterns II.* Annales Societatis missiologicae Fennicae no. 12. Helsinki: Finnish Society for Missionary Research.
1968   *Kite: Polynesian insights into knowledge. Annals of the Finnish Society for Missiology and Ecumenics* 14 (Helsinki).
Kotzebue, Otto von
1821a   *A voyage of discovery into the South Sea . . . in the years 1815–1818.* 3 vols. London: Longman et al.
1821b   *Entdeckungs-Reise . . . in dem Jahren 1815, 1816, 1817 und 1818 . . . auf dem Schiffe Rurick.* . . . 3 vols. Weimar: Hoffman.
1830a   *A new voyage round the world, in the years 1823–1826.* 2 vols. London: Henry Colburn and Richard Bentley.
1830b   *Reise um die Welt in den Jahren 1823, 24, 25 und 26.* 2 vols. Weimar: Hoffman.
Krusenstern, Adam J. von
1813   *Voyage round the world, in the years 1803, 1804, 1805 and 1806 . . . on board the ships Nadesha and Neva.* 2 vols. Trans. R. B. Hoppner. London: John Murray.
Kukahi, J. L.
1895   Letter in *Ka Makaainana,* 22 April.
Kupahu
1865   Article in *Ka Nupepa Kuokoa,* 15 June. Trans. T. G. Thrum. Bishop Museum Library, Thrum Collection.
Kuykendall, Ralph S.
1938   *The Hawaiian kingdom,* vol. 1. Honolulu: University of Hawaii Press.
Laanui, Gideon
1930   Reminiscences of Gideon Laanui, reared in the train of Kamehameha I, 1800–1819. Translated from "Kumu Hawaii," March–April 1838. *Hawaiian Annual for 1930,* 86–93.
Lacan, Jacques
1966   *Ecrits.* Paris: Editions du Seuil.
1973   *Les quatre concepts fondamentaux de la psychanalyse.* Paris: Editions du Seuil.
Ladd, Edmund J., S. Neal Crozier, and Russel A. Apple
1973   *Makaha Valley Historical Project interim report no. 4,* March. Pacific Anthropological Records no. 19. Department of Anthropology. Honolulu: Bishop Museum Press.
Lagrange, Marie Joseph
1905   *Etudes sur les religions sémitiques.* 2d rev. ed. Paris: Victor Lecoffre.
Lalande, André
1960   *Vocabulaire technique et critique de la philosophie.* Paris: Presses Universitaires de France.
Langsdorff, G. H. von
1968 [1817]   *Voyages and travels in various parts of the world, 1803–1807.* 2 vols. London: Colburn. Reprint, Ridgewood, N.J.: Gregg Press.
Lanternari, Vittorio
1959   *La grande festa: Storia del capodanno nelle civiltà primitive.* Milan: Saggiatore.

Lapérouse, Jean François de Galaup
1970   *Voyage de Lapérouse autour du monde, pendant les années 1785, 1786, 1787 et 1788.* Paris: Cercle du Bibliophile.
Law, John
n.d.   Journal of Captain Cook's last voyage 1778–1779 by John Law. Addit. Ms. 37327 British Museum. Photostat in Archives of Hawaii, Captain Cook no. 96; typewritten copy in Bishop Museum Library.
Leach, Edmund R.
1964   Anthropological aspects of language: Animal categories and verbal abuse. In *New directions in the study of language*, ed. Eric H. Lennenberg, 23–63. Cambridge: MIT Press.
1966   Ritualization in men in relation to conceptual and social development. *Philosophical Transactions of the Royal Society of London*, ser. B, 261: 403–8.
1968   Ritual. In *International encyclopedia of the social sciences*, 13:520–26. New York: Macmillan.
Ledyard, John
1963 [1783]   *A journal of Captain Cook's last voyage to the Pacific Ocean . . . performed in the years 1776, 1777, 1778, and 1779.* Reprint, ed. J. K. Munford. Corvallis: Oregon State University Press.
Leeuw, Gerardus van der
1920–21   Die *do-ut-des*-Formel in der Opfertheorie. *Archiv für Religionswissenschaft* 20:241–53.
1938   *Religion in essence and manifestation: A study in phenomenology.* Trans. J. E. Turner. New York: Macmillan.
Lehmann, Friedrich
1922   *Mana, der Begriff des "ausserordentlich Wirkungsvollen" bei Südseevölkern.* Leipzig: Institut für Völkerkunde.
1930   *Die polynesischen Tabusitten, eine ethno-soziologische und religionswissenschaftliche Untersuchung.* Leipzig: Voigtländer.
Leib, Amos P., and A. Grove Day
1979   *Hawaiian legends in English: An annotated bibliography.* 2d ed. Honolulu: University Press of Hawaii.
Lévi, Sylvain
1898   *La doctrine du sacrifice dans les Brâhmanas.* Paris: E. Leroux.
Lévi-Strauss, Claude
1962a   *La pensée sauvage.* Paris: Plon.
1962b   *Le totémisme aujourd'hui.* Paris: Presses Universitaires de France.
1971   *L'homme nu.* Paris: Plon.
Levin, Stephanie Seto
1968   The overthrow of the Kapu system in Hawaii. *Journal of the Polynesian Society* 77, 4 (December): 402–30.
Lewis, G.
1980   *Day of shining red: An essay on understanding ritual.* Cambridge: Cambridge University Press.
Lienhardt, Godfrey
1961   *Divinity and experience: The religion of the Dinka.* Oxford: Clarendon Press.
Liliuokalani, Queen, trans.
1978 [1897]   *An account of the creation of the world according to Hawaiian tradition.* Photographic reprint. Kentfield, Calif.: Pueo Press.
Lisiansky, Urey

1814   *Voyage round the world, 1803–1806, in the ship "Neva."* London: Longmans.

Little, George
1843   *Life on the ocean; or, Twenty years at sea; being the personal adventures of the author.* Aberdeen: G. Clark and Son.

Lods, Adolphe
1921   Examen de quelques hypothèses modernes sur les origines du sacrifice. *Revue d'Histoire et de Philosophie Religieuses*, 483–506.
1935   *Les prophètes.* Paris: Renaissance du Livre.

Loisy, Alfred Firmin
1920   *Essai historique sur le sacrifice.* Paris: E. Nourry.

Loomis, Elisha
1937   *Copy of the journal of E. Loomis.* Mimeographed. Honolulu.

Lot-Falck, Eveline
1953   *Les rites de chasse chez les peuples sibériens.* Paris: Gallimard.

Luomala, Katharine
1960   The native dog in the Polynesian system of values. In *Culture in history: Essays in honor of Paul Radin.* New York: Columbia University Press.

Lydgate, J. M.
1925 [1904]   A sea island land system. *University of Toronto Monthly*, January 1904, reprinted in *Hawaiian Annual for 1925*, 57–64.

Lyons, Curtis J.
1875a   Land matters in Hawaii. *Islander* 1:103–4, 111, 118–19, 126–27, 135, 143, 150–51, 159, 168–69, 174–75, 182–83, 190–91, 206–7, 214–15, 222–23.

Lyons, Curtis J., ed.
1875b   A song for Kualii. *Islander* 1:202–3, 210–11, 217–18, 225–27, 230–33, 239–41.

Lyons, John
1977   *Semantics*, vol. 1. Cambridge: Cambridge University Press.

McAllister, J. Gilbert
1933   *Archaeology of Oahu.* Bernice Pauahi Bishop Museum Bulletin no. 104. Honolulu: Bishop Museum Press.

Macrae, James
1922   *With Lord Byron at the Sandwich Islands in 1825.* Honolulu: Wilson New Freedom Press.

Maistre, Joseph de
1884a   Eclaircissement sur les sacrifices. In *Oeuvres complètes*, vol. 5. Lyons: Vitte et Perrussel.
1884b   Les soirées de Saint-Pétersbourg. In *Oeuvres complètes*, vols. 4 and 5. Lyons: Vitte et Perrussel.

Makemson, Maud W.
1938   Hawaiian astronomical concepts I. *American Anthropologist* 40: 370–83.
1939   Hawaiian astronomical concepts II. *American Anthropologist* 41: 589–96.
1941   *Morning star rises: An account of Polynesian astronomy.* New Haven: Yale University Press.

Malo, David
n.d.   *Ka Mooolelo Hawaii.* Manuscript in the Bernice Pauahi Bishop Museum Library.

1951 [1903]   *Hawaiian antiquities (Mooolelo Hawaii)*. Trans. N. B. Emerson. 2d ed. Bernice Pauahi Bishop Museum Special Publication 2. Honolulu: Bishop Museum Press.

Manby, Thomas
1929   Journal of Vancouver's voyage to the Pacific Ocean, 1791–1793. *Honolulu Mercury* 1, 1 (June): 11–25; 1, 2 (July): 33–45; 1, 3 (August): 39–55.

Manu, Moke
1901   Kuula, the fish god of Hawaii. Trans. M. K. Nakuina. *Hawaiian Annual for 1901*, 114–24.
1928   Prophecy of Kekiopilo, translated from Moke Manu MS of about 1890. *Hawaiian Annual for 1928*, 87–91.

Manuel, Frank
1959   *The eighteenth century confronts the gods*. Cambridge: Harvard University Press.

Manwaring, G. E.
1931   *My friend the admiral: The life, letters and journals of Rear-Admiral James Burney, F.R.S.* London: Routledge and Son.

Marcuse, Adolph
1894   *Die hawaiischen Inseln*. Berlin: Friedländer.

Marett, R. R.
1936   *Tylor*. New York: Wiley.

Marillier, Léon
1897–98   La place du totémisme dans l'évolution religieuse. A propos d'un livre récent. *Revue de l'Histoire des Religions* 2 (1897): 208–53, 321–63; 3 (1898): 204–33, 345–404.

Marin, Francisco
1973   Journal. In *Don Francisco de Paula Marin*, by Ross H. Gast, ed. Agnes C. Conrad. Honolulu: University Press of Hawaii for the Hawaiian Historical Society.

Martin, John
1817   *An account of the natives of the Tongan Islands . . . arranged from the extensive communications of Mr. William Mariner*. 2 vols. London: John Murray.

Mathison, Gilbert F.
1825   *Narrative of a visit to Brazil, Chile, Peru, and the Sandwich Islands, 1821–1822*. London: Knight.

Mauss, Marcel
1909   La prière. Reprinted in Mauss (1968–69, 1: 357–477).
1968–69   *Oeuvres*. 3 vols. Paris: Editions de Minuit.
1978a [1926]   Effet physique chez l'individu de l'idée de mort suggérée par la collectivité. Reprinted in *Sociologie et Anthropologie*, 6th ed. Paris: Presses Universitaires de France.
1978b   Essai sur le Don. In *Sociologie et anthropologie*, 6th ed. Paris: Presses Universitaires de France.

Meares, John
1790   *Voyages in the years 1788 and 1789 from China to the Northwest Coast of America*. London: Logographic Press.
1916   Extracts from voyages made in the years 1788 and 1789 from China to the northwest coast of America. . . . *Hawaiian Historical Society Reprints*. Honolulu: Hawaiian Historical Society.

Menzies, Archibald
  n.d.   *Journal*. British Museum Addit. Ms. 32641.
  1920   *Hawaii nei 128 years ago*. Ed. W. F. Wilson. Honolulu: New Freedom Press.
Meuli, Karl
  1975   Griechische Opfergebräuche. In *Phyllobolia für Peter von der Mühll zum 60. Geburtstage*. Basel, 1946. Reprinted in Karl Meuli *Gesammelte Schriften*, vol. 2. Basel/Stuttgart: Schwabe.
Meyen, F. J. F.
  1834   *Reise um die Erde . . . auf Prinzess Louise Commandirt von Capitain W. Wendt in den Jahren 1830, 1831 und 1832*. 2 vols. Berlin: Sander.
Meyers, John
  1817   *The life, voyages and travels of Captain John Meyers, detailing his adventures during four voyages round the world*. London: Longman, Hurst, Rees.
MH
  n.d.   American Board of Commissioners for Foreign Missions. "Journal of the Missionaries." *Missionary Herald*.
Mooolelo Hawaii
  1838   Lahainaluna: Mea pai palapala no ke kula nui.
Moore, Anneliese W.
  1978   E. T. A. Hoffmann's *Haimatochare*, translation and commentary. *Hawaiian Journal of History* 12 : 1–27.
Mortimer, Lieutenant George
  1791   *Observations and remarks made during a voyage to the . . . Sandwich Islands: Owhynee . . . in the brig Mercury, commanded by Captain John Cox, Esq*. London: Printed for the author and sold by T. Cadell.
Munro, George C.
  1960   *Birds of Hawaii*. Honolulu: Tongg.
Nakuina, Emma M. B.
  1894   Ancient Hawaiian water rights. *Hawaiian Annual for 1894*, 79–84.
Neal, Marie Catherine
  1929   *In Honolulu gardens, with legends by Berta Metzger*. Bernice Pauahi Bishop Museum Special Publication no. 13. Honolulu: Bishop Museum Press.
  1965 [1948]   *In gardens of Hawaii*. Bernice Pauahi Bishop Museum Special Publication no. 40. Rev. ed. Honolulu: Bishop Museum Press.
Needham, Rodney
  1970   Introduction. In *Kings and councillors*, by A. M. Hocart. Chicago: University of Chicago Press.
Nicol, John
  1822   *The life and adventures of John Nicol, mariner*. Edinburgh: William Blackwood; London: T. Cadell.
Nietzsche, Friedrich
  1968   Zur Geneologie des Moral: Eine Streitschrift. In *Studienausgabe*, ed. Hans Heinz Holz. 4 vols. Frankfurt am Main: Fischer.
NK
  1972–79   *Nānā i ke kumu* (Look to the source), by Mary K. Pukui, E. W. Haertig, and Catherine A. Lee. 2 vols. Honolulu: Queen Liliuokalani Children's Center Publications.
Northwood, J. d'Arcy
  1940   *Familiar Hawaiian birds*. Honolulu: T. Nickerson.

Pakele, P. S.
    1864   Article in *Ka Nupepa Kuokoa*, 12 November.
Patterson, Samuel
    1817   *Narrative of the adventures and sufferings of Samuel Patterson, experienced in the Pacific Ocean, and many other parts of the world, with an account of the Feegee and Sandwich Islands.* Palmer, Mass.
Paulding, Hiram
    1831   *Journal of a cruise of the United States Schooner Dolphin . . . in pursuit of the mutineers of the whale ship Globe.* New York: G. and C. and H. Carvill.
PE
    1971   *Hawaiian dictionary.* Compiled by Mary K. Pukui and Samuel H. Elbert. Honolulu: University Press of Hawaii.
Péron, François
    1824   *Mémoires du Capitaine Péron, sur ses voyages . . . aux Îles Sandwich. . . .* 2 vols. Paris: Brissot-Thivars.
Pierce, Richard A.
    1965   *Russia's Hawaiian adventure, 1815–1817.* Berkeley: University of California Press.
Pitt-Rivers, Julian
    1974   *Mana,* an inaugural lecture. London: London School of Economics and Political Science.
Plischke, Hans
    1929   *Kukailimoku, ein Kriegsgott von Hawaii.* Abhandlungen der Gesellschaft der Wissenschaften zu Göttingen, Philologische-Historische Klasse, n.s., vol. 24. Berlin: Weidmann.
Pogue, John F.
    1858   *Ka mooolelo Hawaii.* Honolulu: Hale Paipalapala Aupuni.
Portlock, Nathaniel
    1789   *A voyage round the world 1785–1788 in the "King George" and "Queen Charlotte."* London: Stockdale and Goulding.
Principles adopted by the Board of Commissioners to quit land titles.
    1925   *Revised Laws of Hawaii,* 2:2120–2236. Honolulu: Honolulu Star Bulletin.
Propp, Vladimir
    1975   Il riso rituale nel folklore. In *Edipo alla luce del Folclore—Quattro studi di etnografia storico-strutturale.* Turin: Einaudi.
Proust, Marcel
    1954   *A la recherche du temps perdu.* 3 vols. Paris: Gallimard.
Puget, Lieutenant
    n.d.   *A log of the proceedings of His Majesty's armed tender Chatham . . . 1793–4.* London: Public Records Office Adm. 55/17.
Pukui, Mary K.
    1933   Hawaiian folktales. *Folklore Publications,* 3d ser., no. 13:127–85 (Poughkeepsie, Vassar College).
    1942   Hawaiian beliefs and customs during birth, infancy and childhood. *Bernice Pauahi Bishop Museum Occasional Papers* 16:357–81.
    1949   Songs (meles) of old Ka'u, Hawaii. *Journal of American Folklore,* 247–58.
Pukui, Mary K,; trans.
    1939   The canoe making profession of ancient times. *Hawaiian Historical Society Papers* 20:26–37.

Pukui, Mary K., Samuel H. Elbert, and E. T. Mookini
    1974   Place names of Hawaii. Honolulu: University of Hawaii Press.
    1975   The pocket Hawaiian dictionary. Honolulu: University of Hawaii Press.
Pukui, Mary K., and Alfons Korn, trans., eds.
    1973   The echo of our song: Chants and poems of the Hawaiians. Honolulu:
            University Press of Hawaii.
Quimper, Manuel
    1822   Islas de Sandwich. Madrid: E. Aguedo.
    1937   The Sandwich Islands: A brief description of this archipelago so named by
            its famous discoverer, Captain Cook. . . . Manuscript translation by Clark Lee.
            Honolulu: Bishop Museum Library.
Quoy, Jean René Constant, and P. Gaimard
    1824   Zoologie par MM. Quoy et Gaimard. . . . Vol. 3 of Voyage autour de
            monde . . . par M. Louis de Freycinet. Paris: Pillet Aîné.
Radcliffe-Brown, A. Reginald
    1922   The Andaman islanders. Cambridge: Cambridge University Press.
Rappaport, Roy A.
    1979   Ecology, meaning and religion. Richmond, Calif.: North Atlantic
            Books.
Remy, Jules M.
    1859   Récits d'un vieux sauvage pour servir à l'histoire ancienne de Havaii.
            Châlons-sur-Marne: Laurent.
Remy, Jules, ed.
    1862   Ka mooolelo Hawaii: Histoire de l'archipel havaiien. Text and transla-
            tion. Paris and Leipzig: Franck.
Restarick, Henry B.
    1928   Historic Kealakekua Bay. Hawaiian Historical Society Papers 15 : 5 – 20.
Rice, William H.
    1923   Hawaiian legends. Bernice Pauahi Bishop Museum Bulletin no. 3.
            Honolulu: Bishop Museum Press.
Richards, William
    1973   William Richards on Hawaiian culture and political conditions of the
            Islands in 1841. Ed. Marshall Sahlins and Dorothy Barrère. Hawaiian Jour-
            nal of History 7 : 18 – 40.
Rickman, John
    1966 [1781] Journal of Captain Cook's last voyage to the Pacific Ocean on Dis-
            covery, performed in the years 1776 – 1779. London. Reprinted by Readex
            Microprint.
Roquefeuil, Camille de
    1843   Voyage autour du monde. 2 vols. Paris: Béthune et Plon.
Ross, Alexander
    1849   Adventures of the first settlers on the Oregon or Columbia River. . . .
            London: Smith, Elder.
    1904   Adventures of the first settlers on the Oregon or Columbia River. . . .
            In Early western travels, 1748 – 1846, vol. 7. Ed. Reuben Gold Thwaites.
            Cleveland: Arthur M. Clark.
Rousseau, Jean-Jacques
    1782   Collection complète des oeuvres de J. J. Rousseau. 12 vols. Geneva.
Ruggles, Samuel
    1821   Mission to the Sandwich Islands: From the MS. Journal of Mr. and
            Mrs. Ruggles. Boston Recorder, 21 April.
    1913   Letter of Samuel Ruggles, dated 4 July 1820. Friend, October, 235.

Ruggles, Samuel, and Nancy Ruggles
    1924   From a missionary journal. *Atlantic Monthly* 36 (November):
    648–57.
Ruschenberger, W.
    1970   *Narrative of a voyage round the world.* Vols. 1–2. Reprint of the London ed., 1838. Folkestone and London: Dawson of Pall Mall.
Sahlins, Marshall
    n.d.   A synthesis of riches: Raw women, cooked men and the other "great things" of Fiji. Typescript obtained from author.
    1979   L'apothéose du Capitaine Cook. In *La fonction symbolique: Essais d'anthropologie.* Ed. Michel Izard and Pierre Smith. Paris: Gallimard.
    1981   *Historical metaphors and mythical realities: Structure in the early history of the Sandwich Islands kingdom.* Association for Social Anthropology in Oceania Special Publication no. 1. Ann Arbor: University of Michigan Press.
Samwell, David
    1786   *A narrative of the death of Captain James Cook.* . . . London: printed for G. G. J. and J. Robinson.
    1967.   *Journal.* In Beaglehole (1967).
Schoch, A.
    1954   *Rituelle menschentötungen in Polynesien.* Ulm: Privately printed.
Searle, John R.
    1969   *Speech acts—An essay in the philosophy of language.* Cambridge: Cambridge University Press.
Shaler, William
    1808   Journal of a voyage between China and the North-western Coast of America, made in 1804. In *American Register* . . . 3 : 137–75. Philadelphia: C. and A. Conrad.
    1935   *Journal of a voyage between China and the Northwestern Coast of America, made in 1804.* Introduction by Lindley Bynum. Claremont, Calif.: Saunders Studio Press.
Smith, Jean
    1974   *Tapu removal in Maori religion.* Polynesian Society Memoir no. 40. Wellington: Polynesian Society.
Smith, William Robertson
    1892   Sacrifice. In *Encyclopaedia Britannica*, 9th ed., 21 : 132–38. Chicago.
    1894   *Lectures on the religion of the Semites.* 2d ed. London: A. and C. Black.
Snyder, John W.
    1919   Notes on Hawaiian lizards. *Proceedings of the United States National Museum* 54 : 19–25.
Stanner, W. E. H.
    1963   *On aboriginal religion.* Oceania Monograph no. 11. Sydney: University of Sydney.
Steiner, Franz
    1967   *Taboo.* With a preface by E. E. Evans-Pritchard. Harmondsworth, Middlesex: Penguin.
Stejneger, L.
    1899   The land reptiles of the Hawaiian Islands. *Proceedings of the United States National Museum* 21 : 783–813.
Sterling, Elspeth P., and Catherine C. Summers
    1962   *The sites of Oahu.* Honolulu: Bishop Museum Press.

Stewart, Charles S.
    1830 [1828] *Private journal of a voyage to the Pacific Ocean, and residence at
    the Sandwich Islands in the years 1822, 1823, 1824, and 1825.* 2d ed. New
    York: J. P. Haven.
    1831 *A visit to the South Seas in the United States ship "Vincennes"* . . .
    1829–1830. 2 vols. New York: Haven.
    1839 *A residence in the Sandwich Islands.* 5th ed. New York: Weeks, Jordan.
Stokes, John F.
    n.d. Notes on Hawaiian temples. Manuscript in the Bernice Pauahi Bishop
    Museum Library.
    1906 Hawaiian nets and netting. *Memoirs of the Bernice Pauahi Bishop Mu-
    seum* 2 (1): 105–62.
    1919 Typescript report. In Notes on Hawaiian temples. Manuscript in the
    Bernice Pauahi Bishop Museum.
    1931 Origin of the condemnation of Captain Cook in Hawaii. *Hawaiian
    Historical Society Thirty-ninth Annual Report,* 68–104.
    1932 The Hawaiian king. *Hawaiian Historical Society Papers,* no. 19: 1–28.
Tambiah, Stanley J.
    1979 [1981] A performative approach to ritual. *Proceedings of the British
    Academy* 65: 113–69. London: Oxford University Press.
Tautain, Jules
    1921 Sur quelques textes relatifs à la signification du sacrifice chez les
    peuples de l'antiquité. *Revue de l'Histoire des Religions* 84: 109–19.
Taylor, Charles
    1975 *Hegel.* Cambridge: Cambridge University Press.
Taylor, Richard
    1870 [1855] *Te ika a Maui; or, New Zealand and its inhabitants: Origin,
    manners, customs, mythology, religion, rites, songs, proverbs, fables and language
    of the Maori.* 2d ed. London: Macintosh.
Thompson, R. J.
    1963 *Penitence and sacrifice in early Israel outside the Levitical law: An exami-
    nation of the fellowship theory of early Israelite sacrifice.* Leiden: Brill.
Thrum, Thomas G.
    1906 The heiau (temple) of Kupopolo and incidentally others. *Hawaiian
    Annual for 1906,* 117–22.
    1907a *Hawaiian folktales: A collection of native legends.* Chicago: McClurg.
    1907b Heiaus and heiau sites, throughout the Hawaiian Islands. *Hawai-
    ian Annual for 1907,* 36–48.
    1907c Tales from the temples, part I. *Hawaiian Annual for 1907,* 49–69.
    1908a Heiaus and heiau sites throughout the Hawaiian Islands: Island of
    Hawaii, part I. *Hawaiian Annual for 1908,* 38–47.
    1908b Tales from the temples, part II. *Hawaiian Annual for 1908,* 48–78.
    1909 Tales from the temples, part III. *Hawaiian Annual for 1909,* 44–54.
    1910 Heiaus: Their kinds, construction, ceremonies, etc. *Hawaiian An-
    nual for 1910,* 53–71.
    1916 Completing Oahu's heiau search. *Hawaiian Annual for 1916,* 87–91.
    1917 Maui's heiaus and sites revised. *Hawaiian Annual for 1917,* 52–61.
    1918 Brief sketch of the life and labors of S. M. Kamakau, Hawaiian histo-
    rian. *Hawaiian Historical Society Twenty-sixth Annual Report,* 40–61.
    1923 *More Hawaiian folk tales.* Chicago: McClurg.
    1926 Leahi heiau (temple): Papa-ena-ena. *Hawaiian Annual for 1926,*

109–14.
1927   The paehumu of heiaus non-sacred. *Hawaiian Historical Society Thirty-fifth Annual Report*, 56–57.
Thurston, Lucy Goodale
1882   *Life and times of Mrs. Lucy G. Thurston*. Ann Arbor: Andrews.
Tinker, Reuben, trans.
1839   Ka mooolelo Hawaii: Hawaiian history written by scholars at the High School. *Hawaiian Spectator* 2:58–77, 211–30, 334–40, 438–46.
Tinker, Spencer W.
1978   *Fishes of Hawaii: A handbook of the marine fishes of Hawaii and the central Pacific Ocean*. Honolulu: Hawaiian Service.
Titcomb, Margaret
1948   Kava in Hawaii. *Journal of the Polynesian Society* 57:105–71.
1969   *Dog and man in the ancient Pacific with special attention to Hawaii*. M. K. Pukui, collaborator. Bernice Pauahi Bishop Museum Special Publication no. 59. Honolulu: Bishop Museum Press.
Titcomb, Margaret, and M. K. Pukui
1972 [1952]   *Native use of fish in Hawaii*. 2d ed. Honolulu: University Press of Hawaii.
Townsend, Ebenezer
1888   Diary of Mr. Eb. Townsend Jr. ship "Neptune." *Papers of the New Haven Historical Society* 4:1–115.
1921 [1888]   *Extract from the diary of Ebenezer Townsend, Jr., supercargo of the sealing ship "Neptune" on her voyage to the South Pacific and Canton . . . arranged and indexed for the Hawaiian Historical Society by Bruce Cartwright. . . .* Hawaiian Historical Society Reprints no. 4. Honolulu: Hawaiian Historical Society.
Tregear, Edward
1891   *The Maori-Polynesian comparative dictionary*. Wellington: Lyon and Blair.
Tumarkin, Daniel D.
1979   A Russian view of Hawaii in 1804. *Pacific Studies* 2, 2 (Spring): 103–31.
Turnbull, John
1813 [1805]   *A voyage around the world, in the years 1800, 1801, 1802, 1803, and 1804*. 2d ed. London: A. Maxwell.
Turner, Victor
1969   *The ritual process: Structure and anti-structure*. Chicago: Aldine.
Tyerman, Daniel, and George Bennett
1831   *Journal of voyages and travels . . . in the South Sea Islands, China, India, &c., between the years 1821 and 1829*. 2 vols. London: F. Westley and A. H. Davis.
1832   *Journal of voyages and travels . . . in the South Sea Islands, China, India, &c., between the years 1821 and 1829*. From the 1st London edition, revised by an American editor. 3 vols. Boston: Crocker and Brewster/New York: J. Leavitt.
Tyler, Stephen
1978   *The said and the unsaid: Mind, meaning and culture*. New York: Academic Press.
Tylor, Edward Burnett
1889 [1871]   *Primitive culture*, vol. 2. 3d American ed. New York: Holt.

Valeri, Valerio
    1970   Struttura, trasformazione, "esaustività": Un'esposizione di alcuni concetti di Claude Lévi-Strauss. *Annali della Scuola Normale Superiore di Pisa*, Classe di lettere, Storia e Filosofia, ser. 2, 39 : 347–75.
    1972   Le fonctionnement du système des rangs à Hawaii. *Homme* 12 : 29–66.
    1976   Le brûlé et le cuit: Mythologie et organisation de la chefferie dans la société Hawaiienne ancienne. Thèse de doctorat de 3ème cycle. Ecole Pratique des Hautes Etudes, Paris.
    1979a   Festa. In *Enciclopedia* 6 : 87–99. Turin: Einaudi.
    1979b   Feticcio. In *Enciclopedia* 6 : 100–115. Turin: Einaudi.
    1980   Regalità. In *Enciclopedia* 11 : 742–71. Turin: Einaudi.
    1981a   Pouvoir des dieux, rire des hommes: Divertissement théorique sur un fait hawaiien. *Anthropologie et Société* 5(3) : 11–34.
    1981b   Rito. In *Enciclopedia* 12 : 209–43. Turin: Einaudi.
    1982a   Review of *Negara*, by Clifford Geertz. *Journal of Asian Studies* 41 (May) : 631–33.
    1982b   The transformation of a transformation: A structural essay on an aspect of Hawaiian history (1809–1819). *Social Analysis* 10 (May) : 3–41.
    1984   The conqueror becomes king: A political analysis of the Hawaiian legend of 'Umi. In *Transformations of Polynesian society*, ed. Antony Hooper and Judith Huntsman. Wellington: Polynesian Society.
Vancouver, George
    1801 [1798]   *A voyage of discovery to the north Pacific Ocean, and around the world . . . performed in the years 1790, 1791, 1792, 1793, 1794 and 1795.* New ed. 6 vols. London: J. Stockdale.
Varigny, C. de
    1874   *Quatorze ans aux Iles Sandwich.* Paris: Hachette.
Vernant, Jean-Pierre
    1980   The pure and the impure. In *Myth and society in ancient Greece*, trans. from French by Janet Lloyd. Sussex: Harvester Press; Atlantic Highlands, N.J.: Humanities Press.
Vico, Giambattista
    1959   *Opere.* Milano: Rizzoli.
Vorbichler, Anton
    1956   *Das Opfer auf den uns heute noch erreichbaren ältesten Stufen der Menschheitsgeschichte: Eine Begriffsstudie.* Mödling bei Wien: St.-Gabriel-Verlag.
Wartofsky, Marx
    1977   *Feuerbach.* Cambridge: Cambridge University Press.
Webb, M. C.
    1965   The abolition of the taboo system in Hawaii. *Journal of the Polynesian Society* 74 : 21–39.
Westervelt, W. D.
    1910   *Legends of Ma-ui, a demi-god of Polynesia and of his mother Hina.* Honolulu: Hawaiian Gazette Company.
    1915a   *Legends of gods and ghosts (Hawaiian mythology).* Boston: Ellis; London: Constable.
    1915b   *Legends of old Honolulu.* Boston: Ellis/London: Constable.
    1916   *Hawaiian legends of volcanoes (mythology).* Boston: Ellis/London: Constable.
    1923   *Hawaiian historical legends.* New York: Revell.

Whitman, John B.
    1979   An account of the Sandwich Islands. Ed. John Dominis Holt. Hono-
    lulu: Topgallant/Salem: Peabody Museum of Salem.
Wilken, Georg A.
    1891   Eine nieuwe theorie over den oorsprong der offers. De Gids. Re-
    printed in Verspreide Geschriften 4:153–95. Semarang, Soerabaja, The Hague:
    Van Dorp, 1912.
Wilkes, Charles
    1845   Narrative of the United States exploring expedition during the years
    1833–42. 5 vols. and atlas. Philadelphia: Lea and Blanchard.
    1978   Autobiography of Rear Admiral Charles Wilkes, U.S. Navy, 1798–1877.
    Washington, D.C.: Naval History Division, Department of the Navy.
Will, Robert
    1925   Le culte: Etude d'histoire et de philosophie religieuses. Vol. 1. Le caractère
    religieux du culte. Strasbourg: Librairie Istra.
Williams, Herbert William
    1971 [1844]   A dictionary of the Maori language. 7th ed. Wellington: Gov-
    ernment Printer.
Williamson, Robert W.
    1933   The religious and cosmic beliefs of central Polynesia. 2 vols. Cambridge:
    Cambridge University Press.
    1937   Religion and social organization in central Polynesia. Ed. Ralph Pid-
    dington. Cambridge: Cambridge University Press.
Wittfogel, Karl A.
    1981   Oriental despotism. 2d ed. New York: Vintage Books.
Yzendoorn, Reginald
    1909   The song of creation. Paradise of the Pacific 22 (January): 17–21.
    1927   History of the Catholic mission in the Hawaiian Islands. Honolulu: Ho-
    nolulu Star-Bulletin.
Zimmermann, Heinrich
    1781   Reise um die Welt, mit Captain Cook. Mannheim: C. F. Schwann.
    1930   Zimmermann's Captain Cook: An account of the third voyage of Captain
    Cook around the world, 1776–1780, by Henry Zimmermann. Trans. Elsa Mi-
    chaelis and Cecil French, ed. Frederick William Howay. Toronto: Ryerson
    Press.

INDEX

Agriculture, 21; and gods, 14; as male, 121; rites, 40, 43; temples, 177, 183. *See also* Firstfruits; Food

'Aha, 293; meaning, 294–95, 392n.106, 394n.144; possession of, 394n.140; prayers, 329; queried in rite, 265, 280, 289, 290, 309, 310. *See also* Cord

'Aha ho'owilimo'o rite: description, 308–9, 310, 312; interpretation, 313, 314, 317, 318

'Aha hulahula rite: correspondences, 312; description, 288–91; interpretation, 304–5; place in sequence, 306–8, 333–35, 336

'Aha limalima rite, 316–17

Āholehole fish: and gods, 16n.14, 45; as pig, 11

Ahupua'a: description, 155–56; in Makahiki circuit, 208, 209, 222–23, 224

Aku fish: as 'aumakua, 28; eating of eye, 228; and Kū, 261; and myth, 79; rites, 40, 79, 185, 198, 261; season, 199; timing of rites, 229–30, 232

Akua: defined, 31–36; and kanaka, 143. *See also* Gods; Images

Akua kā'ai. *See* Images

Akua loa. *See* Makahiki gods

Akua pā'ani. *See* Makahiki gods

Akua poko. *See* Makahiki gods

'Alae, 21, 22–23, 24

'Alaea, use in rite, 257, 388n.52

'Alaea god: in huikala, 257; identity of, 260, 262; wrapping of, 400n.235

'Alaea priest, 260, 262; in Haku 'ōhi'a rite, 263–65; in huikala, 256, 257, 260; in kauila nui, 283, 288

Ali'i: and clients, 160, 237; and dance, 218; duality of, 174; as gods, 143–45, 147, 301; mana of, 98; meal of, 126–27, 366n.27; in myth, 276, 277, 298; names of, 145; rites of passage, 4, 39; and sacrifice, 44, 49, 133, 134; separateness of,

170, 258–59, 267; term, 370n.36; violence of, 276. *See also* Hierarchy; King; Rank

Aloha, 99, 207, 380n.14

Altar: description, 240, 243; in hale mua, 174; in huikala, 257; and land, 155

'Ama'ama fish: in birth rites, 51; and gods, 16n.14, 45; symbolism, 11, 49, 50

Ancestors: as 'aumakua, 27, 28, 29, 30; and god, 397n.184; of Hawaiians, 350n.5; as 'unihipili, 30, 86. *See also* Genealogy

Ao, 4, 6

'Aumakua: images of, 249; position in pantheon, 14, 19–29, 34; and purity, 86; as sign, 32, 110, 351nn.26, 27; worship of, 45, 175, 290, 358n.62

Austin, John L., 73–74. *See also* Performativity

'Awa: drinking of, described, 125, 365n.23; in Makahiki, 206; and mana, 104; as masculine, 219; as offering, 59, 131, 178, 207, 365–66n.24, 366n.26, 367n.30; varieties, 354n.19

Baal, J. van, on sacrifice, 66

Banana: and gods, 15; as metaphor, 46, 354n.20; as offering, 45, 59, 283, 309, 311, 319, 366–67n.30; tabooed to women, 116

Bataille, Georges, 48

Bennett, Wendell C., on temples, 172, 236

Benveniste, Emile, on the sacred, 93–94

Bible: on holiness, 361n.14; influence of, xxvii, 350n.16; and theory of sacrifice, 64. *See also* Christianity

Bingham, Hiram, as source, xxiii

Biology, in theories of sacrifice, 70

Birds: and ali'i, 372n.59; as 'aumakua, 26–27, 28; and Kū, 12; in origin myth, 5; symbolism, 31, 214, 272. See also 'Alae; Feather gods; Feathers

437

Tapa. See *Kapa*
Taro, 121; and Lono, 10, 177; as offering,
52; origin myth, 80–81, 169–70; rites,
40, 123
Temples, 98, 99; archaeology of, 172, 236,
237, 254, 377–78 n.27; building of,
227, 253–54, 385 n.1; defined, 173; and
efficacy of rites, 267; typology, chaper 6
passim, 236–37; *unu*, 175–77; *waihau*,
176–77. See also *Hale mana*; *Hale mua*;
Hale o Lono; *Hale o Papa*; *Luakini*
temple; Tower, temple
Thrum, T. G., as source, 172
Tikopia, mana on, 96, 100–101
Tombs, 237, 239
Tower, temple (*'anu'u*), 235, 237, 240;
description, 238–39, 254, 255, 256;
in iconology, 251; in ritual, 283, 310,
315–16, 317
Tree: and image, 273–74; in symbolism,
272, 275. See also *Lama*
Tribute. See *Ho'okupu*
Tylor, Edward Burnett, on sacrifice, 62–63

Ulua fish: and human victim, 312, 313–
14, 355 n.26, 397 n.194, 398 nn.206,
212; and Kū, 45, 354 n.20
Ulua priest, 309, 310–11, 312
Ulua rite (*kāpapaulua*): description, 309–
12, 397 nn.185, 186; interpretation, 312,
313–14, 318; and myth, 278, 314
'Umi, 306, 363 n.26; myth of, 211–12,
247, 277–79, 402 n.255; as transgressor,
164
'Unihipili. See Ancestors

Vancouver, George, 228, 229; journals,
xviii, xx; and Kamehameha, 230
Victims, human: bodies of, 231, 236, 265,

308, 336–39, 403 nn.269, 271, 272,
273; and celebrants, 131, 132–33, 140,
373 n.79; consecration of, 337, 352 n.9;
mentioned, 355 n.26, 403 n.264; obtaining, 231, 248, 319, 374 n.81; placement
of, 279, 304, 400–401 n.239; symbolic
function, 274, 323, 327, 348; in theory
of sacrifice, 64–65, 67–68; as transgressors, 50, 69, 72, 163–64, 231, 279,
356 n.38, 391 n.86. See also Offerings;
Sacrifice, human; *Ulua* rite
Violence: and divinity, 261, 269, 281, 312;
Girard on, 67–70; and human sacrifice,
60–70, 273, 337–38; in Makahiki
myth, 224; in mourning king, 220–21;
royal, transformation of, 279, 348. See
also Gods; War
Visibility: and ali'i, 147–48, 219,
380 n.10; and divinity, 131, 252, 274,
323–24, 327, 350 n.3, 400 n.235; and
prostration taboo, 149–50; symbolism,
131, 252, 274, 323–24; symbols of,
152, 268–69, 300–301

Wākea and Papa, 80, 169–71, 331,
375 n.95. See also Pāpa
War, 44, 185; and feather gods, 225, 247;
and Kū, 11, 12, 15; and ritual, 40, 75,
271, 331; season for, 198; and society,
50, 160–61, 184, 348; and sorcery, 247;
temple for, 180, 183, 254, 256
Warrior, symbols of, 250, 275, 350 n.9,
354 n.20, 363 n.5
Whale tooth. See Insignia
Wilkes, Charles, expedition accounts, xxii
Wittfogel, Karl A., use of Kepelino, xxvi
Women. See Females

Young, John, 231